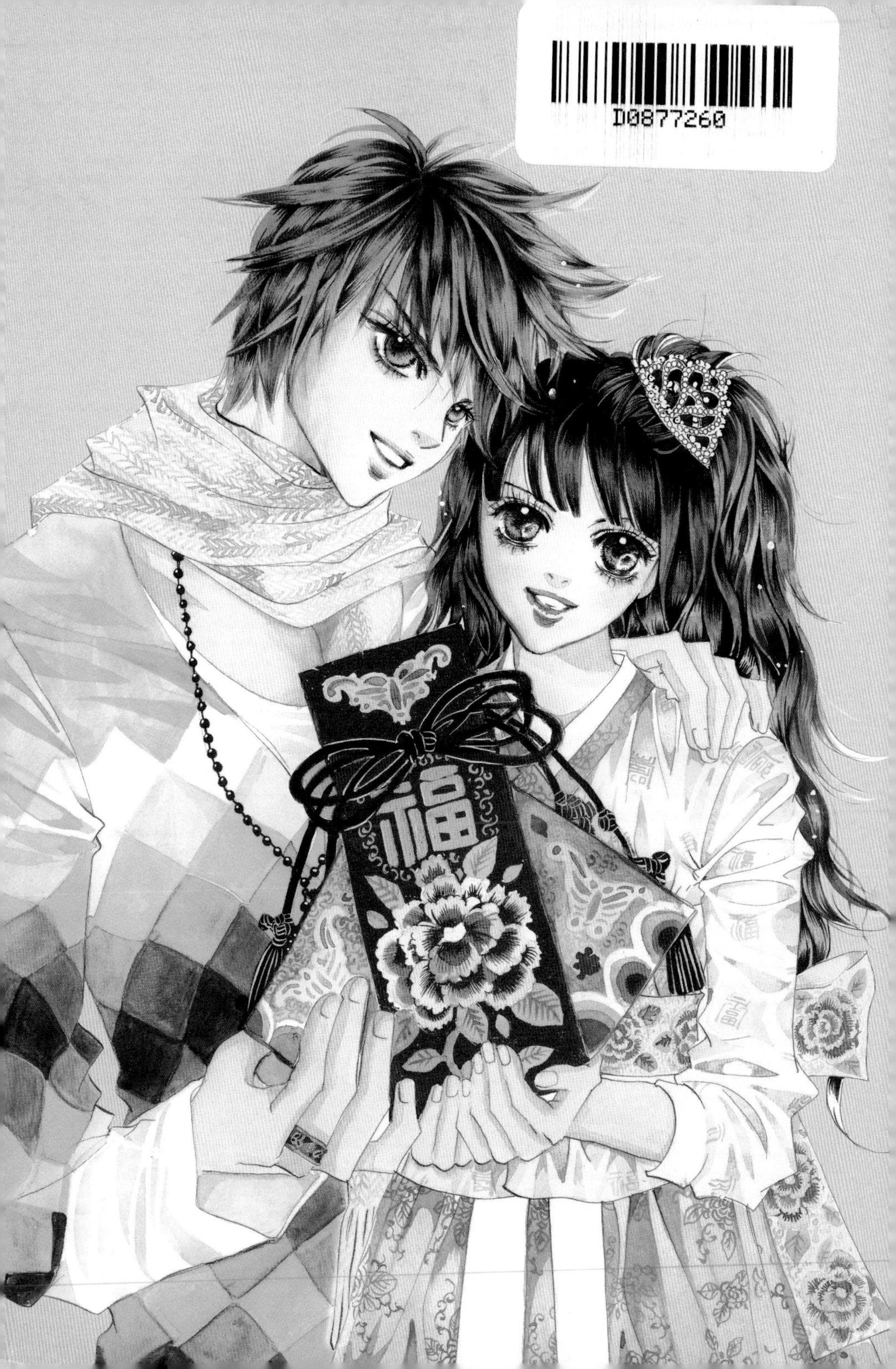
福

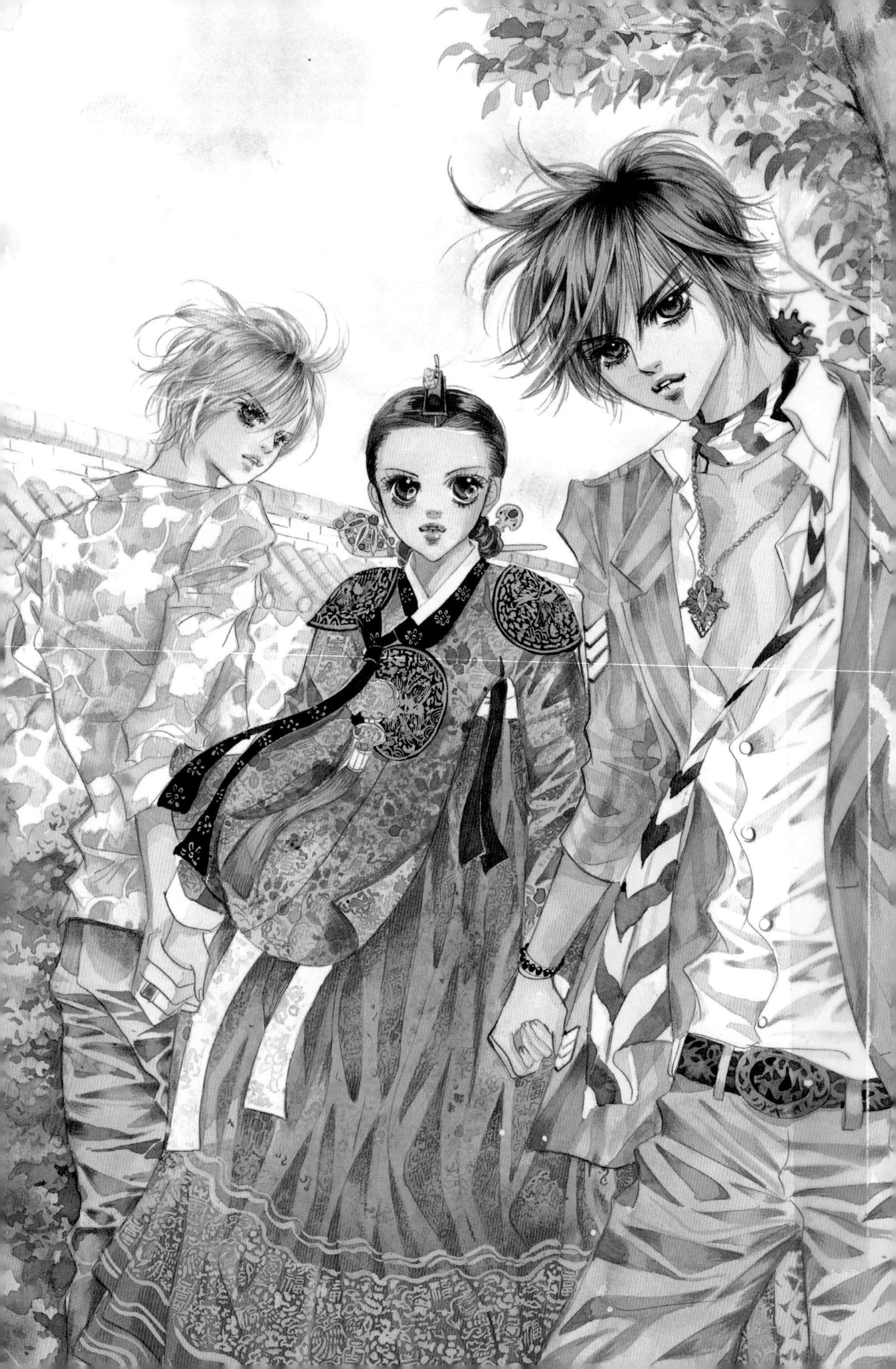

Goong
THE ROYAL PALACE

vol. 9

Park SoHee

Yen
Press

Words from the Creator

When I was a child, I once asked my grandma if there was a Korean king when she was young. My grandma smiled and answered me, "Yes, there was a king, but when I was a little girl, he passed away. Every little girl wore a black ribbon and cried her eyes out." She was probably talking about King Soon-Jong. I felt sad when I heard that.

King Soon-Jong was the last king in Korea, but he was a figurehead with no real power. His funeral procession was probably quite humble and the Royal Family following behind probably looked miserable. And people who were watching the funeral march must have felt hopeless. Even though I draw people who are excited about the royal family and their celebrations, the past should not be forgotten. Still, I am excited that I get to draw a happy royal family, and I hope everyone who reads this comic book feels happy too.

SoHee Park

Words from the Creator

When I first started working on **Goong**, my mission statement was, "The book has to be light and not serious at all. Just enjoy the work!" Only thing is, the story has to get serious now. I can't help it. That's the way the tale is heading, no matter how much I would like to recapture the mind-set of working for the pleasure of it all.

I would like to thank the editors who have helped me with publishing the book, the friends who are always by my side, Dong-Yun who connects anti-social me to the rest of the world, Burned Potato, cute Yun-Joo, and Young-Ran.

SoHee Park

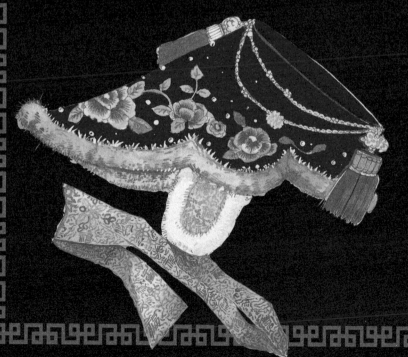

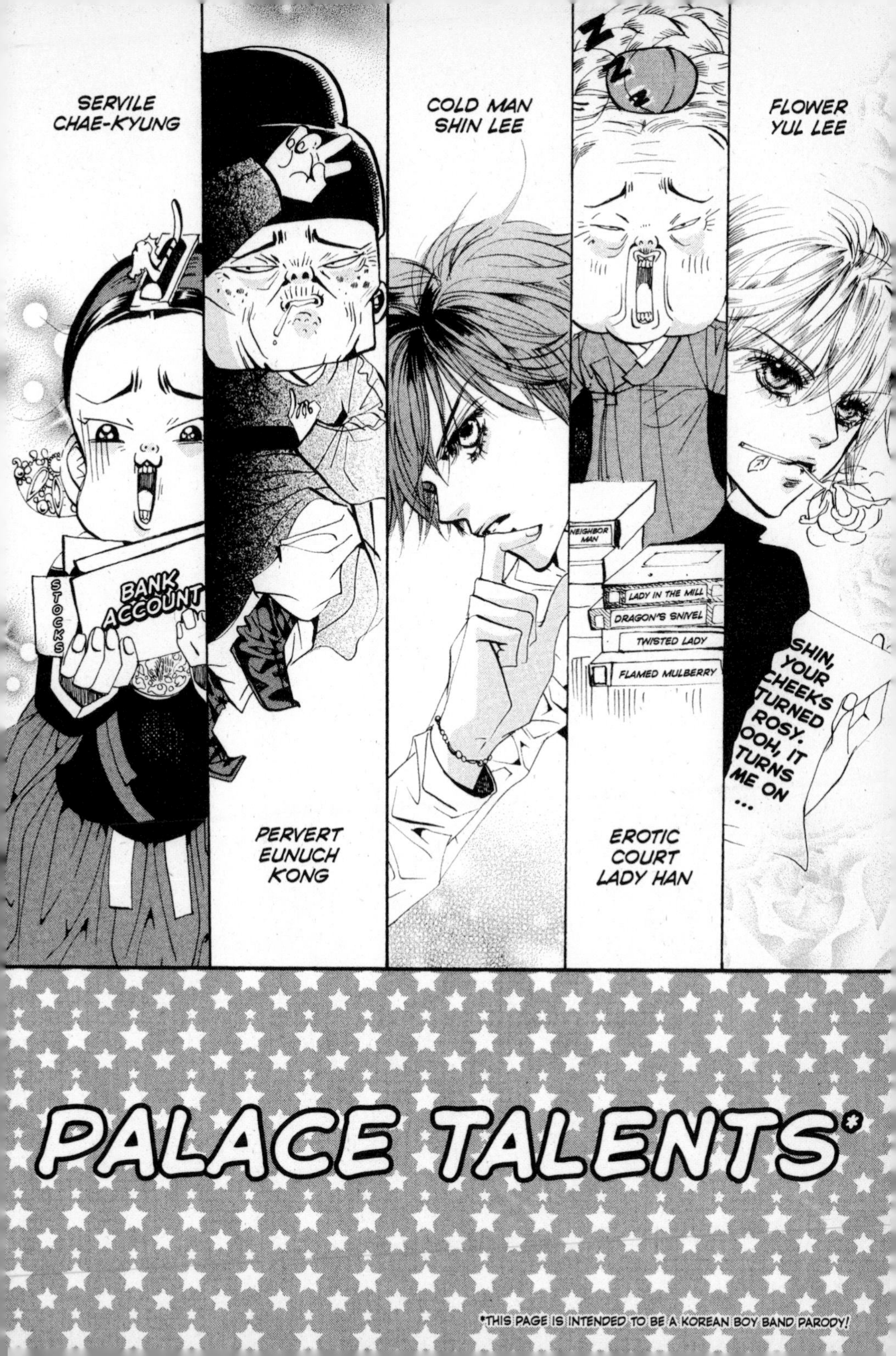
SERVILE CHAE-KYUNG
STOCKS
BANK ACCOUNT
PERVERT EUNUCH KONG
COLD MAN SHIN LEE
NEIGHBOR MAN
LADY IN THE MILL
DRAGON'S SNIVEL
TWISTED LADY
FLAMED MULBERRY
EROTIC COURT LADY HAN
FLOWER YUL LEE
SHIN, YOUR CHEEKS TURNED ROSY. OOH, IT TURNS ME ON ...

PALACE TALENTS*

*THIS PAGE IS INTENDED TO BE A KOREAN BOY BAND PARODY!

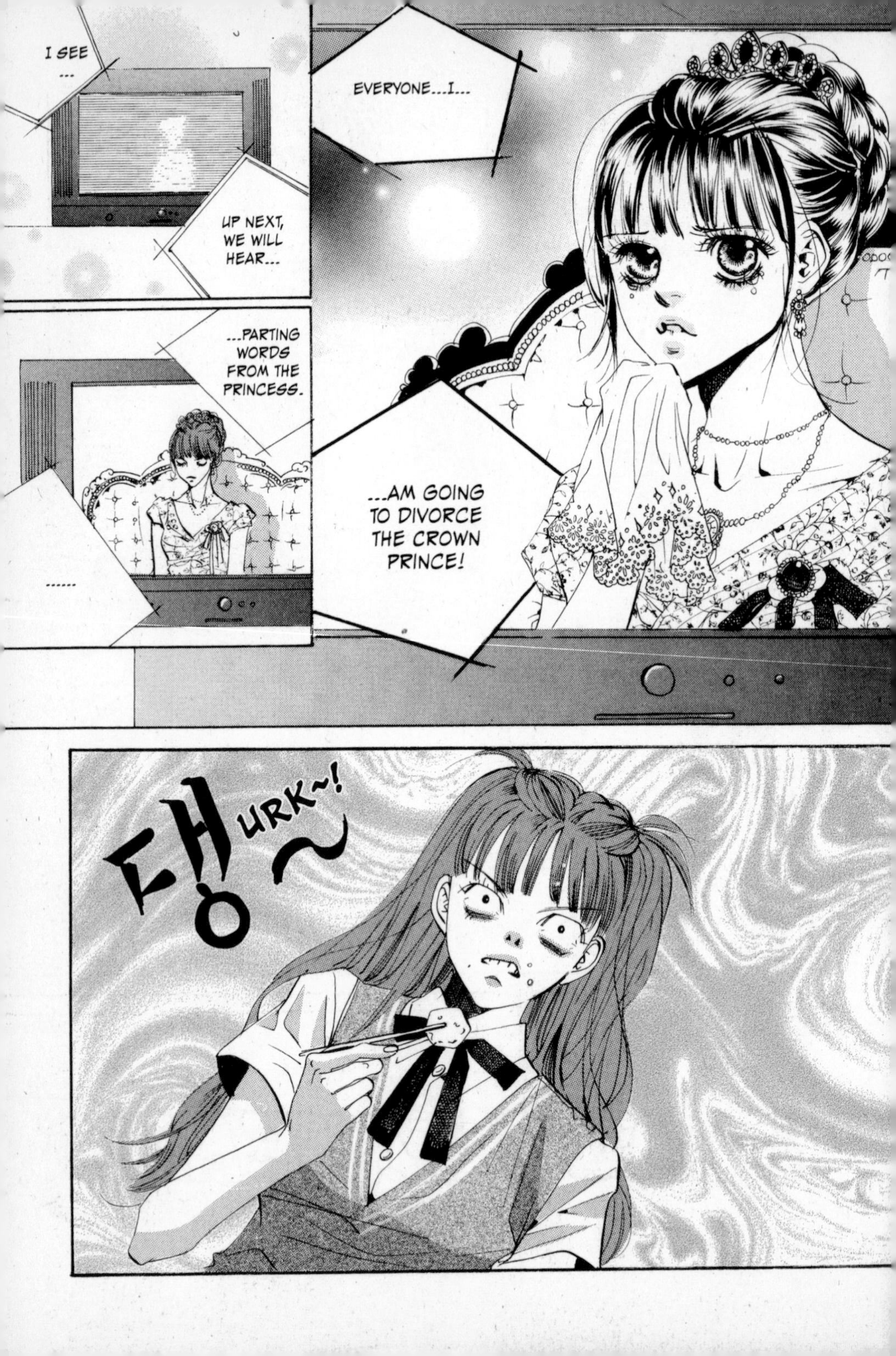
I SEE ...
UP NEXT, WE WILL HEAR...
...PARTING WORDS FROM THE PRINCESS.
......
EVERYONE...I...
...AM GOING TO DIVORCE THE CROWN PRINCE!
댕
URK~!

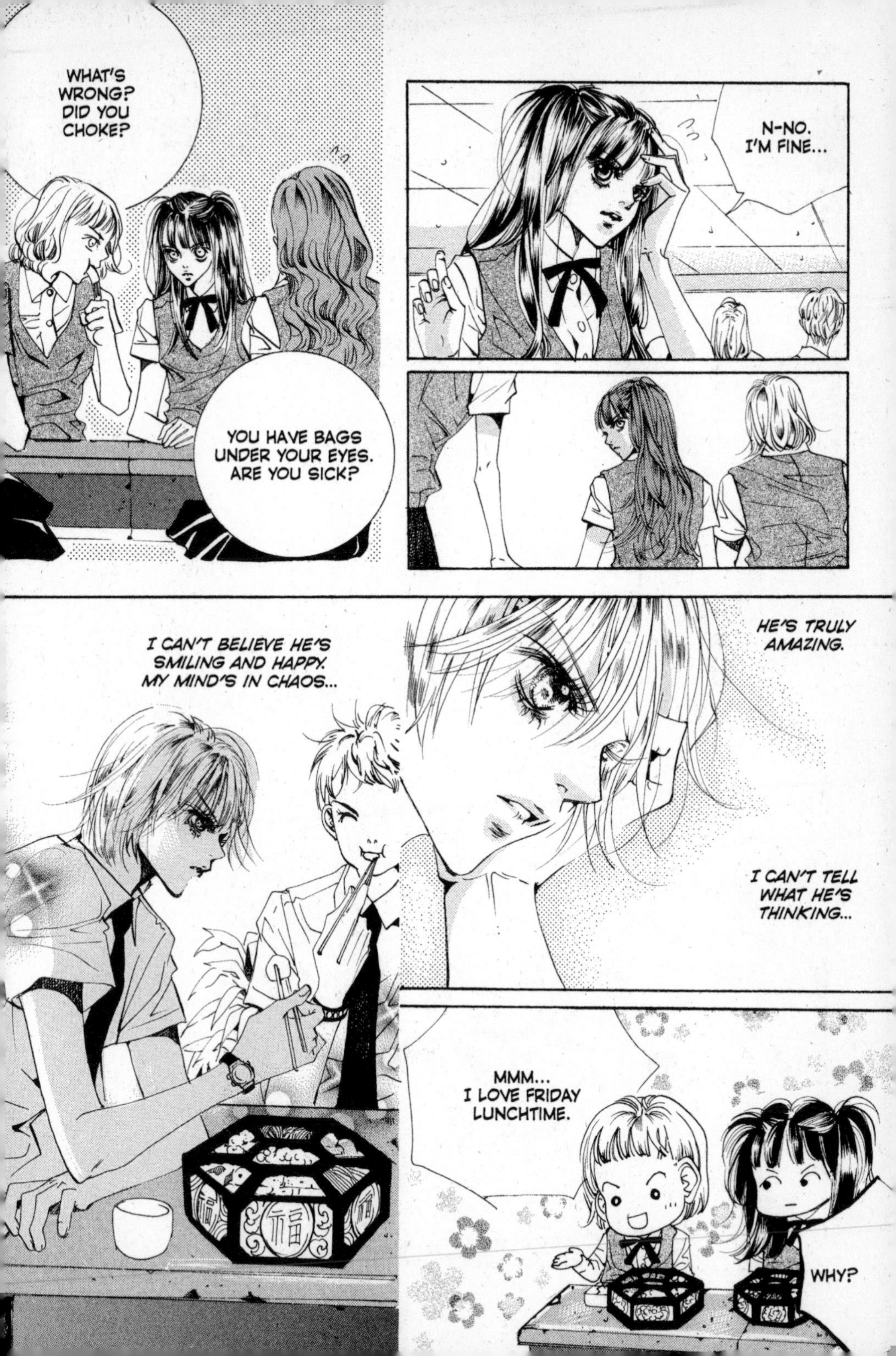
WHAT'S WRONG? DID YOU CHOKE?
YOU HAVE BAGS UNDER YOUR EYES. ARE YOU SICK?
N-NO. I'M FINE...
I CAN'T BELIEVE HE'S SMILING AND HAPPY. MY MIND'S IN CHAOS...
HE'S TRULY AMAZING.
I CAN'T TELL WHAT HE'S THINKING...
MMM... I LOVE FRIDAY LUNCHTIME.
WHY?

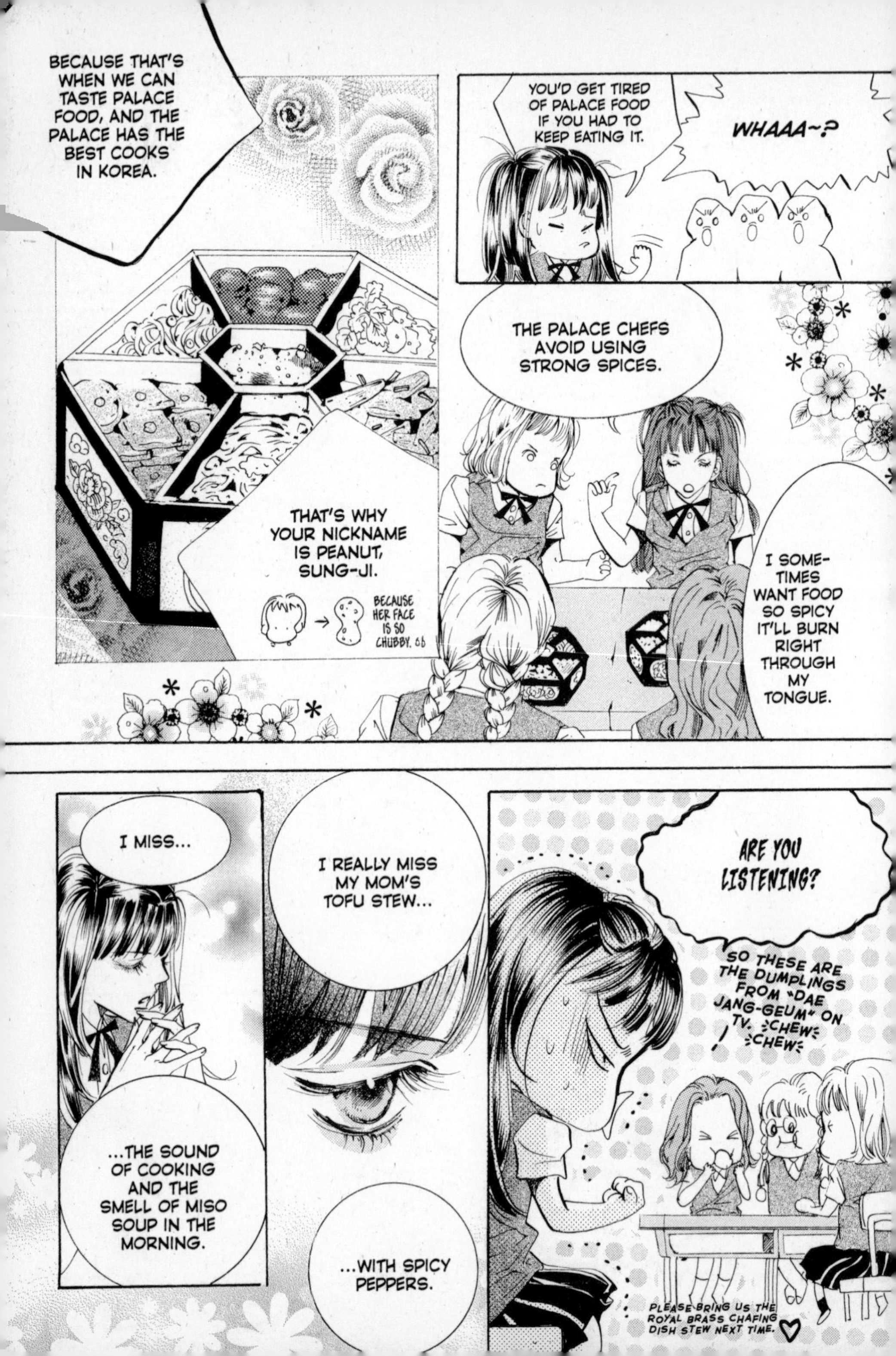

BECAUSE THAT'S WHEN WE CAN TASTE PALACE FOOD, AND THE PALACE HAS THE BEST COOKS IN KOREA.
THAT'S WHY YOUR NICKNAME IS PEANUT, SUNG-JI.
BECAUSE HER FACE IS SO CHUBBY.
YOU'D GET TIRED OF PALACE FOOD IF YOU HAD TO KEEP EATING IT.
WHAAA~?
THE PALACE CHEFS AVOID USING STRONG SPICES.
I SOMETIMES WANT FOOD SO SPICY IT'LL BURN RIGHT THROUGH MY TONGUE.
I MISS...
...THE SOUND OF COOKING AND THE SMELL OF MISO SOUP IN THE MORNING.
I REALLY MISS MY MOM'S TOFU STEW...
...WITH SPICY PEPPERS.
ARE YOU LISTENING?
SO THESE ARE THE DUMPLINGS FROM "DAE JANG-GEUM" ON TV. CHEW CHEW
PLEASE BRING US THE ROYAL BRASS CHAFING DISH STEW NEXT TIME.

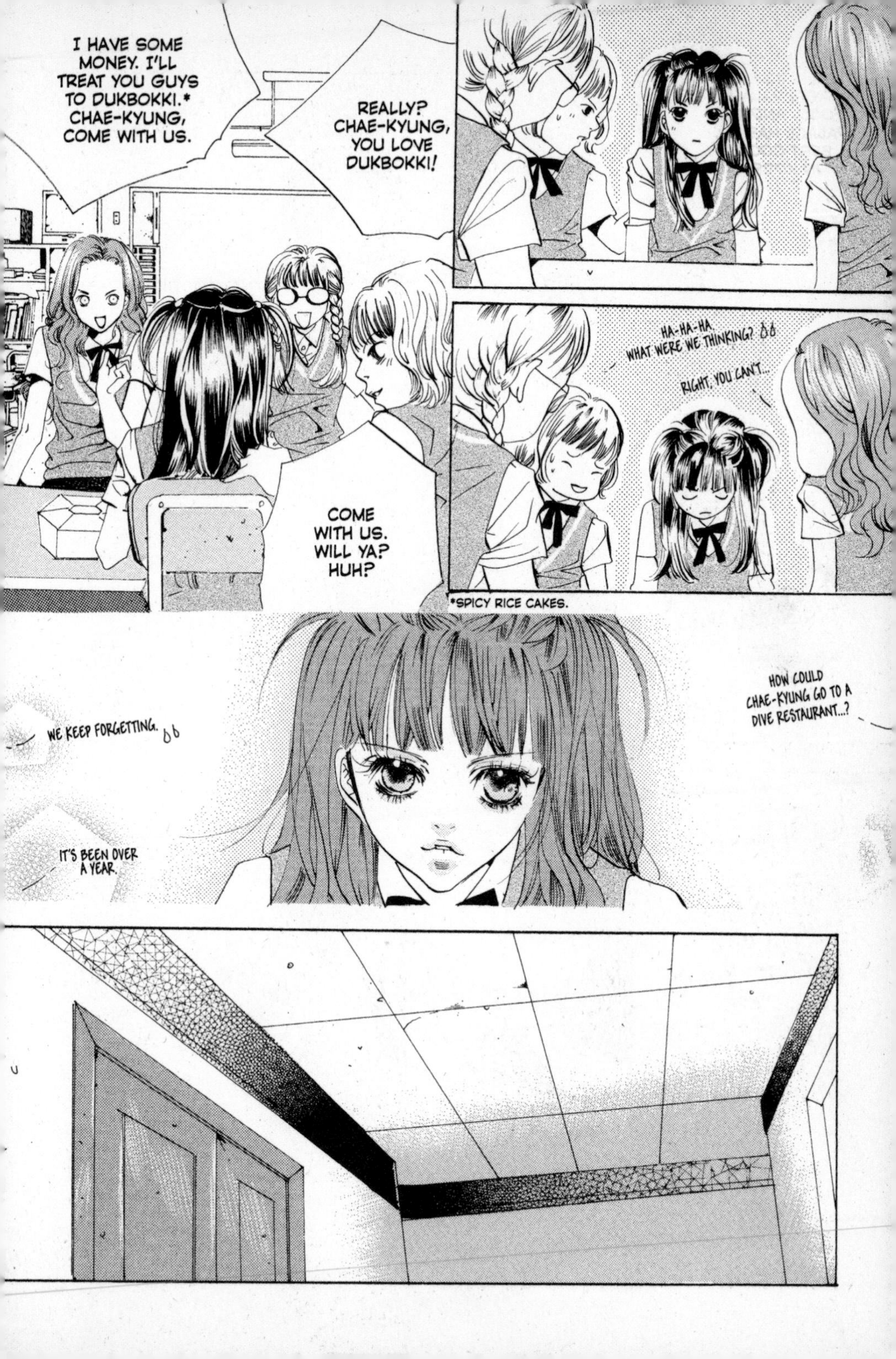
I HAVE SOME MONEY. I'LL TREAT YOU GUYS TO DUKBOKKI.* CHAE-KYUNG, COME WITH US.
REALLY? CHAE-KYUNG, YOU LOVE DUKBOKKI!
COME WITH US. WILL YA? HUH?
HA-HA-HA. WHAT WERE WE THINKING?
RIGHT, YOU CAN'T...
*SPICY RICE CAKES.
HOW COULD CHAE-KYUNG GO TO A DIVE RESTAURANT...?
WE KEEP FORGETTING.
IT'S BEEN OVER A YEAR.

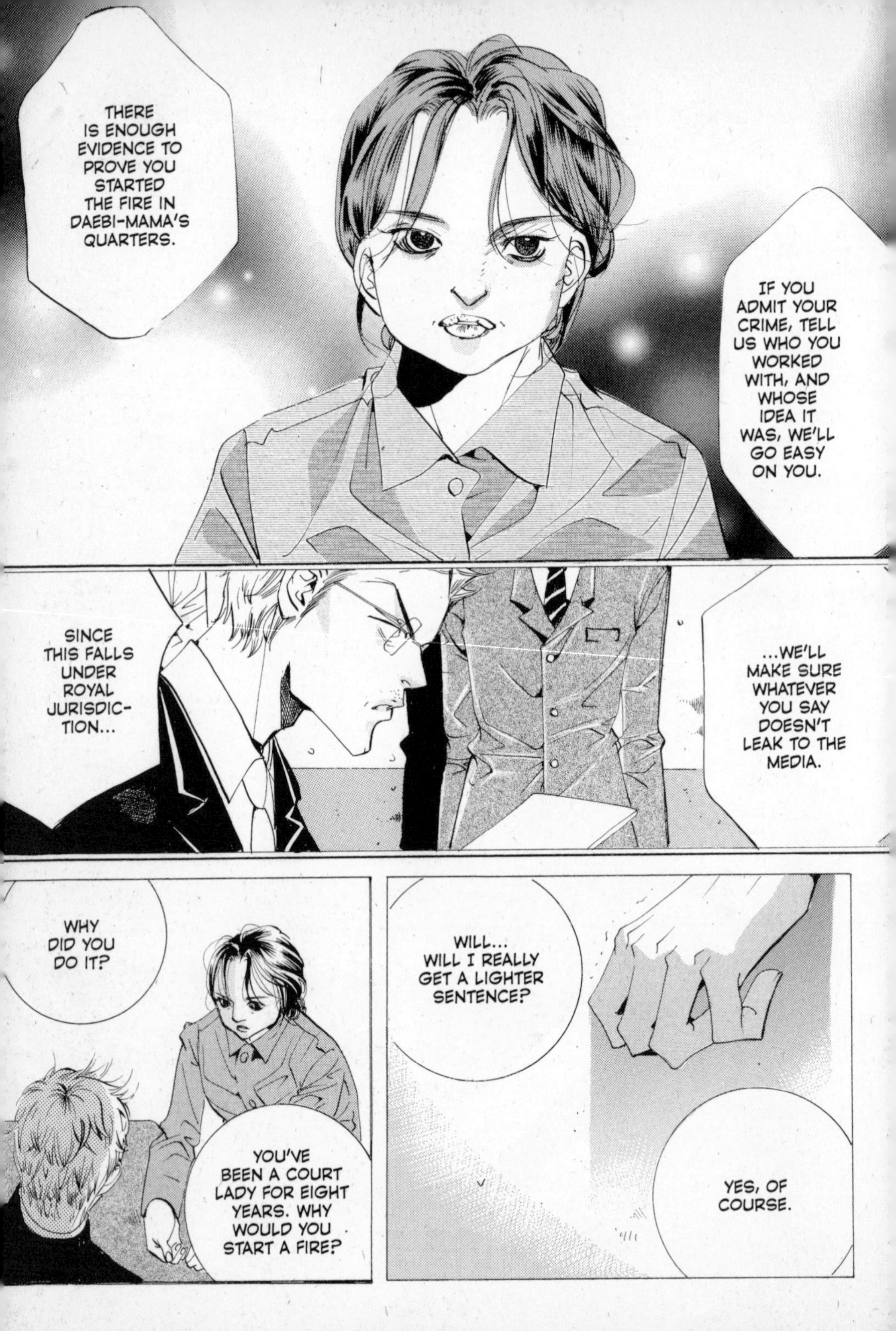
THERE IS ENOUGH EVIDENCE TO PROVE YOU STARTED THE FIRE IN DAEBI-MAMA'S QUARTERS.
IF YOU ADMIT YOUR CRIME, TELL US WHO YOU WORKED WITH, AND WHOSE IDEA IT WAS, WE'LL GO EASY ON YOU.
SINCE THIS FALLS UNDER ROYAL JURISDIC-TION...
...WE'LL MAKE SURE WHATEVER YOU SAY DOESN'T LEAK TO THE MEDIA.
WHY DID YOU DO IT?
YOU'VE BEEN A COURT LADY FOR EIGHT YEARS. WHY WOULD YOU START A FIRE?
WILL... WILL I REALLY GET A LIGHTER SENTENCE?
YES, OF COURSE.

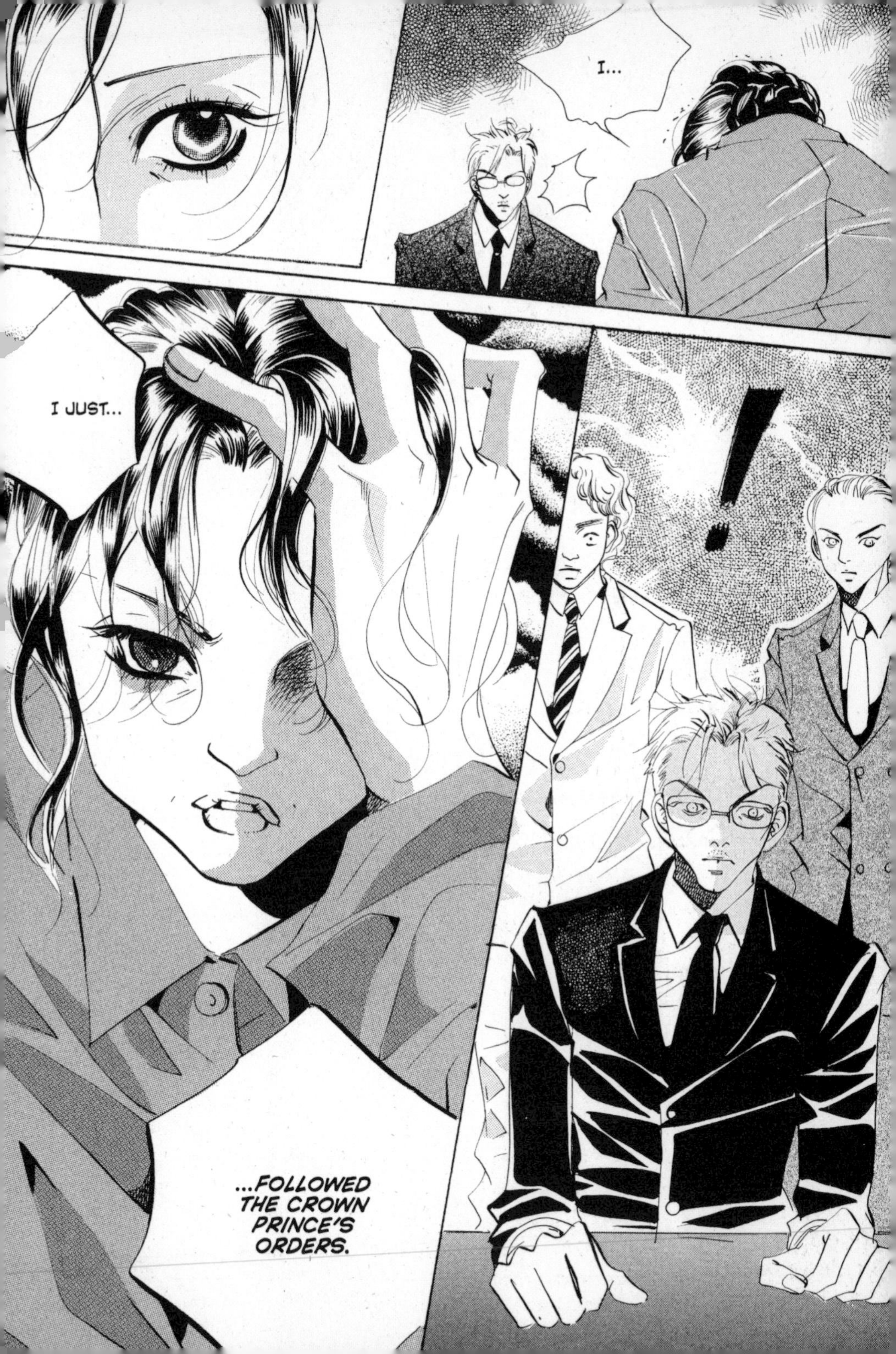
I...
I JUST...
!
...FOLLOWED THE CROWN PRINCE'S ORDERS.

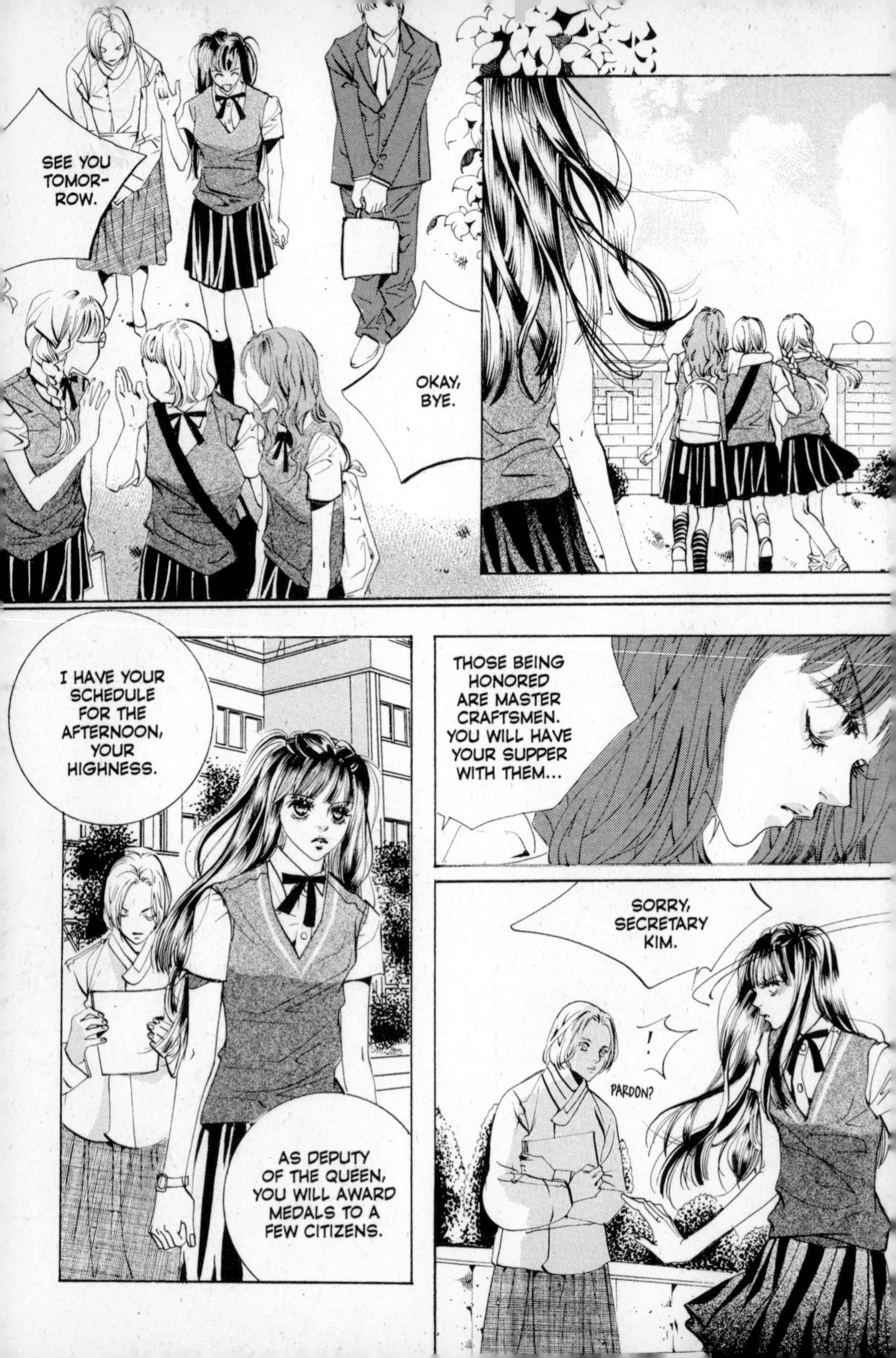
SEE YOU TOMOR-ROW.
OKAY, BYE.
I HAVE YOUR SCHEDULE FOR THE AFTERNOON, YOUR HIGHNESS.
AS DEPUTY OF THE QUEEN, YOU WILL AWARD MEDALS TO A FEW CITIZENS.
THOSE BEING HONORED ARE MASTER CRAFTSMEN. YOU WILL HAVE YOUR SUPPER WITH THEM...
SORRY, SECRETARY KIM.
!
PARDON?

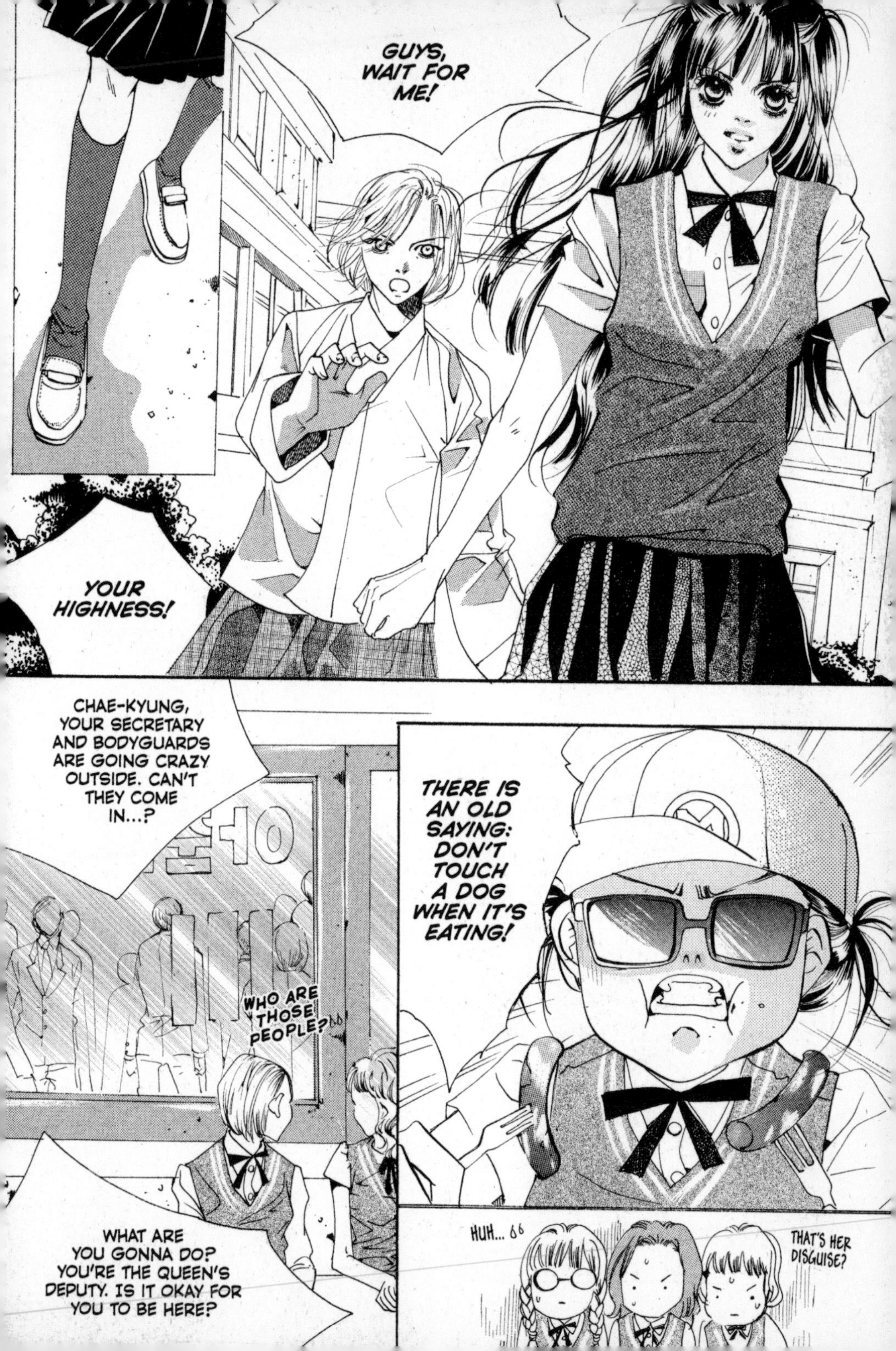
GUYS, WAIT FOR ME!
YOUR HIGHNESS!
CHAE-KYUNG, YOUR SECRETARY AND BODYGUARDS ARE GOING CRAZY OUTSIDE. CAN'T THEY COME IN...?
WHO ARE THOSE PEOPLE?
WHAT ARE YOU GONNA DO? YOU'RE THE QUEEN'S DEPUTY. IS IT OKAY FOR YOU TO BE HERE?
THERE IS AN OLD SAYING: DON'T TOUCH A DOG WHEN IT'S EATING!
HUH...
THAT'S HER DISGUISE?

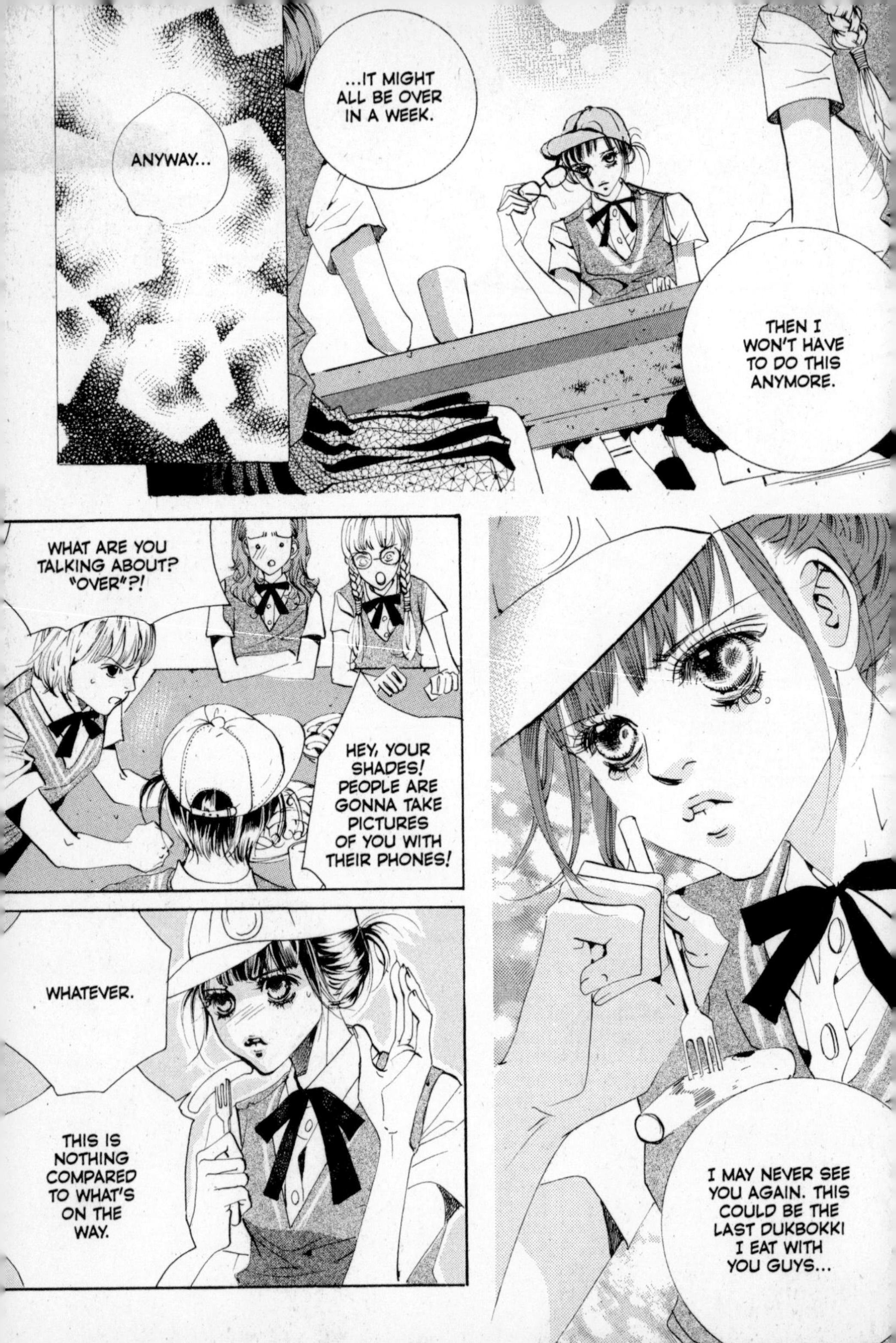
ANYWAY...
...IT MIGHT ALL BE OVER IN A WEEK.
THEN I WON'T HAVE TO DO THIS ANYMORE.
WHAT ARE YOU TALKING ABOUT? "OVER"?!
HEY, YOUR SHADES! PEOPLE ARE GONNA TAKE PICTURES OF YOU WITH THEIR PHONES!
WHATEVER.
THIS IS NOTHING COMPARED TO WHAT'S ON THE WAY.
I MAY NEVER SEE YOU AGAIN. THIS COULD BE THE LAST DUKBOKKI I EAT WITH YOU GUYS...

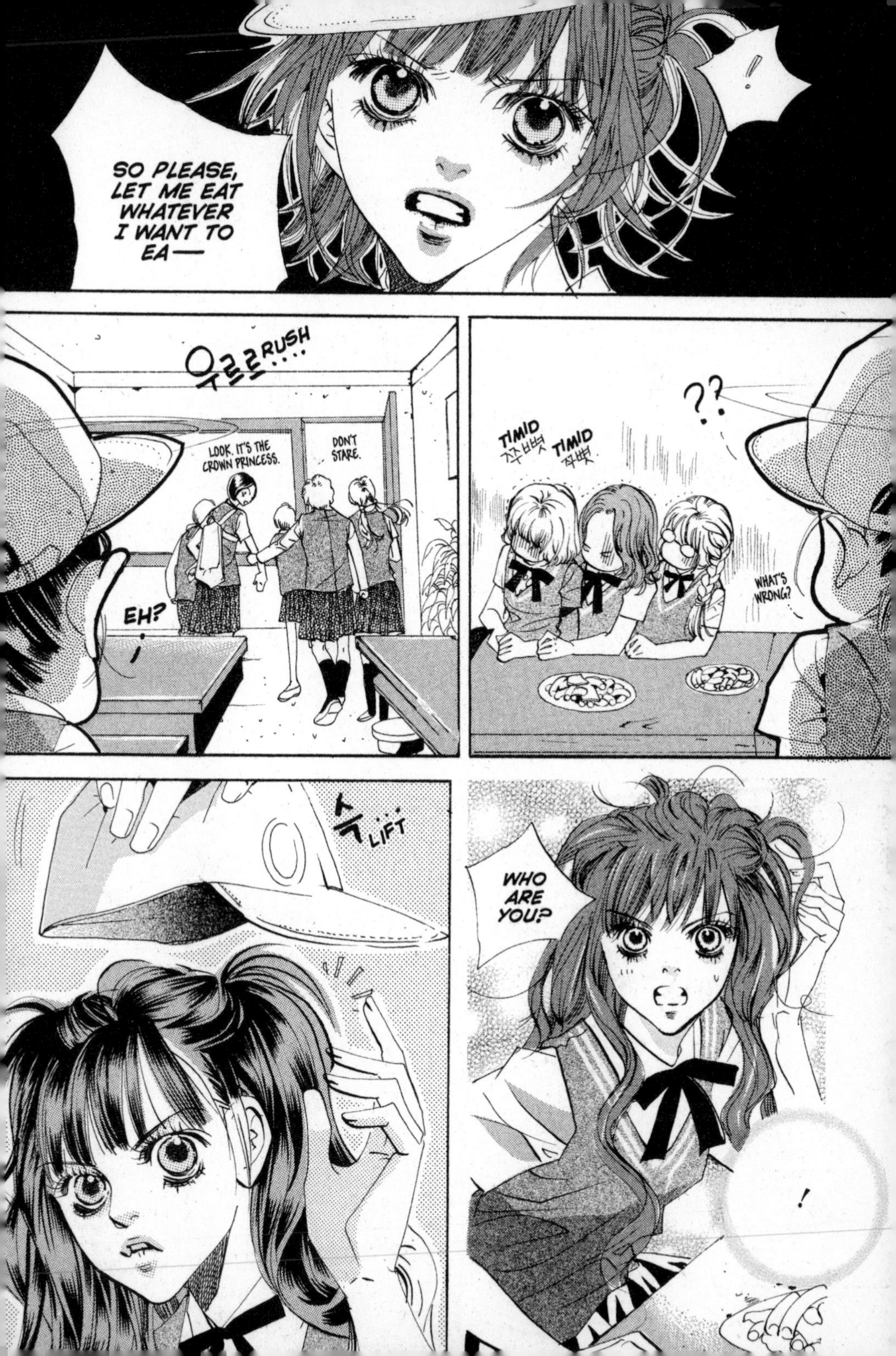
SO PLEASE, LET ME EAT WHATEVER I WANT TO EA—
!
우르르 RUSH....
LOOK. IT'S THE CROWN PRINCESS.
DON'T STARE.
EH?
TIMID 쭈뼛
TIMID 쭈뼛
??
WHAT'S WRONG?
슥 LIFT
WHO ARE YOU?
!

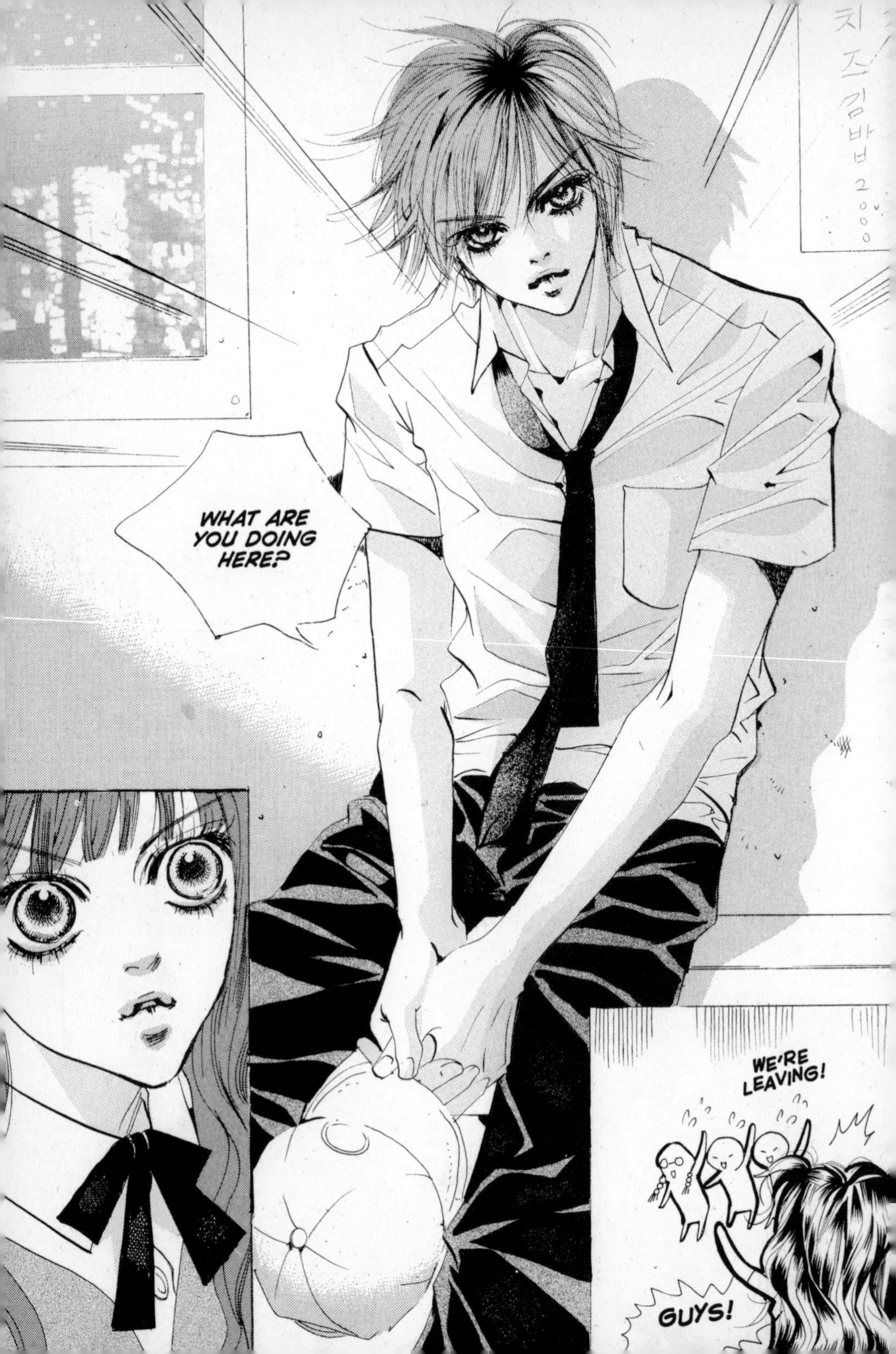
치즈김밥 2000
WHAT ARE YOU DOING HERE?
WE'RE LEAVING!
GUYS!

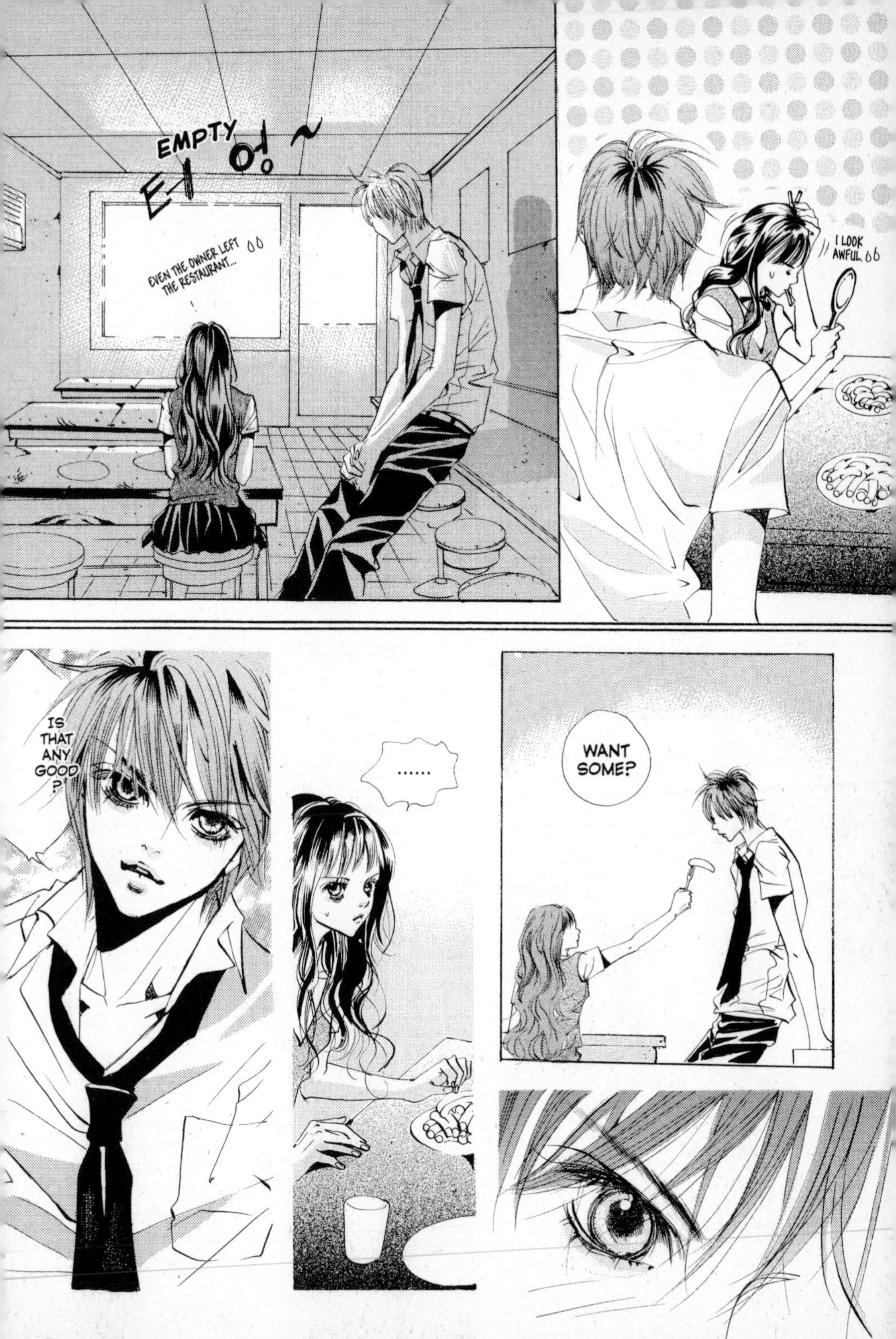
EMPTY
EVEN THE OWNER LEFT THE RESTAURANT...
I LOOK AWFUL.
IS THAT ANY GOOD?
......
WANT SOME?

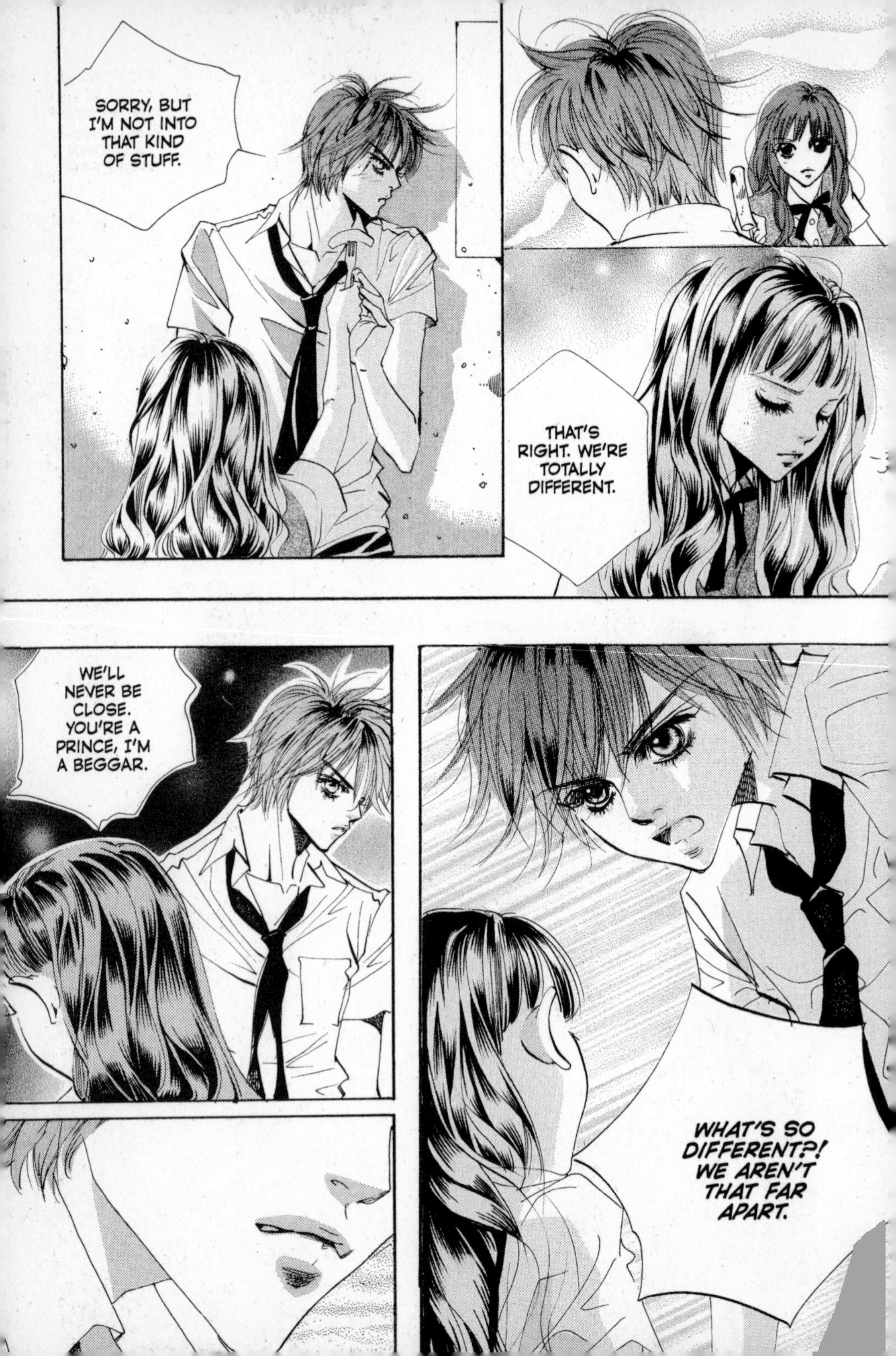
SORRY, BUT I'M NOT INTO THAT KIND OF STUFF.
THAT'S RIGHT. WE'RE TOTALLY DIFFERENT.
WE'LL NEVER BE CLOSE. YOU'RE A PRINCE, I'M A BEGGAR.
WHAT'S SO DIFFERENT?! WE AREN'T THAT FAR APART.

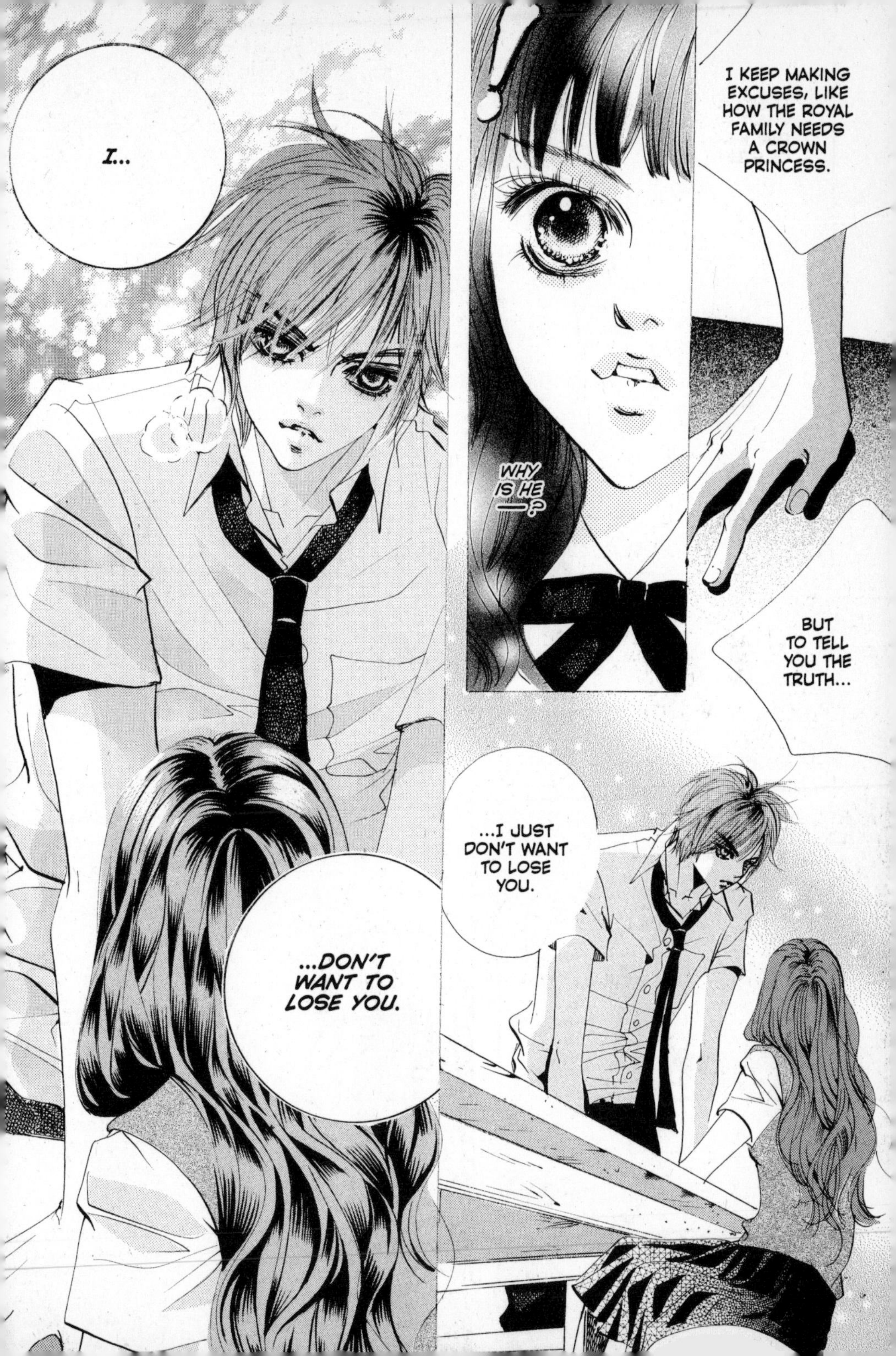
I...
...DON'T WANT TO LOSE YOU.
WHY IS HE —?
I KEEP MAKING EXCUSES, LIKE HOW THE ROYAL FAMILY NEEDS A CROWN PRINCESS.
BUT TO TELL YOU THE TRUTH...
...I JUST DON'T WANT TO LOSE YOU.

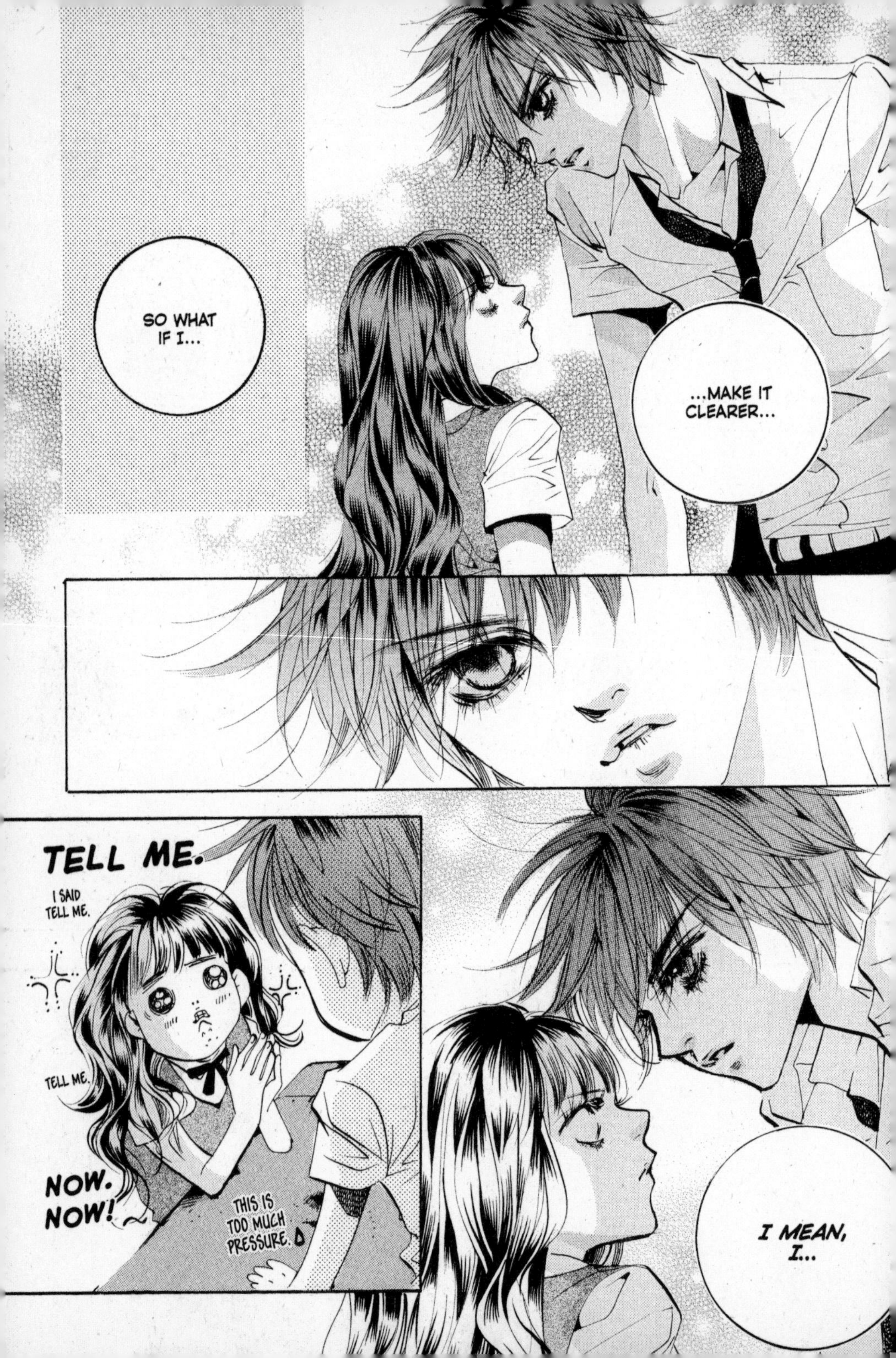
SO WHAT IF I...
...MAKE IT CLEARER...
TELL ME.
I SAID TELL ME.
TELL ME.
NOW. NOW!
THIS IS TOO MUCH PRESSURE.
I MEAN, I...

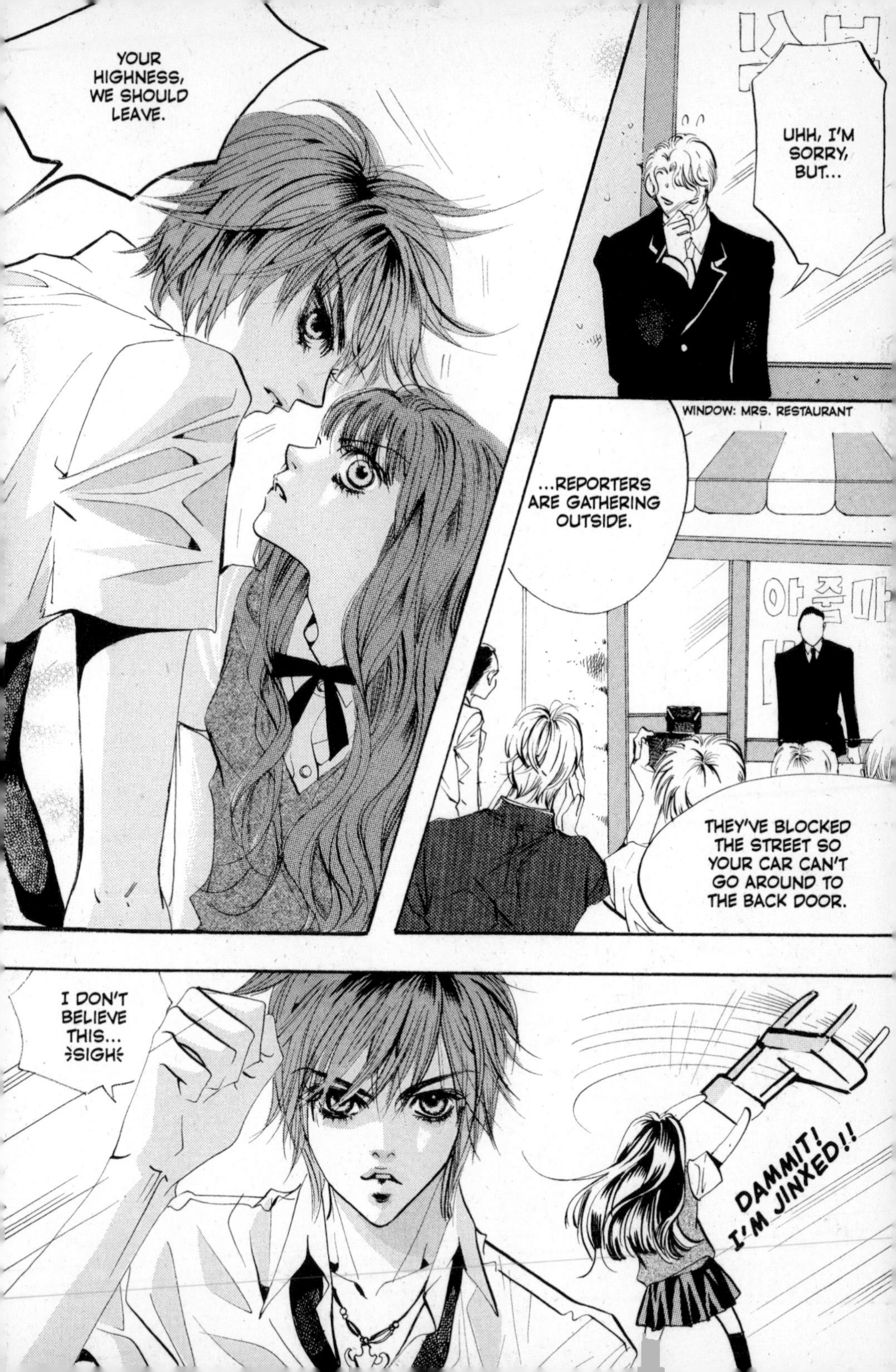
YOUR HIGHNESS, WE SHOULD LEAVE.
UHH, I'M SORRY, BUT...
WINDOW: MRS. RESTAURANT
...REPORTERS ARE GATHERING OUTSIDE.
아줌마
THEY'VE BLOCKED THE STREET SO YOUR CAR CAN'T GO AROUND TO THE BACK DOOR.
I DON'T BELIEVE THIS... ⋟SIGH⋞
DAMMIT! I'M JINXED!!

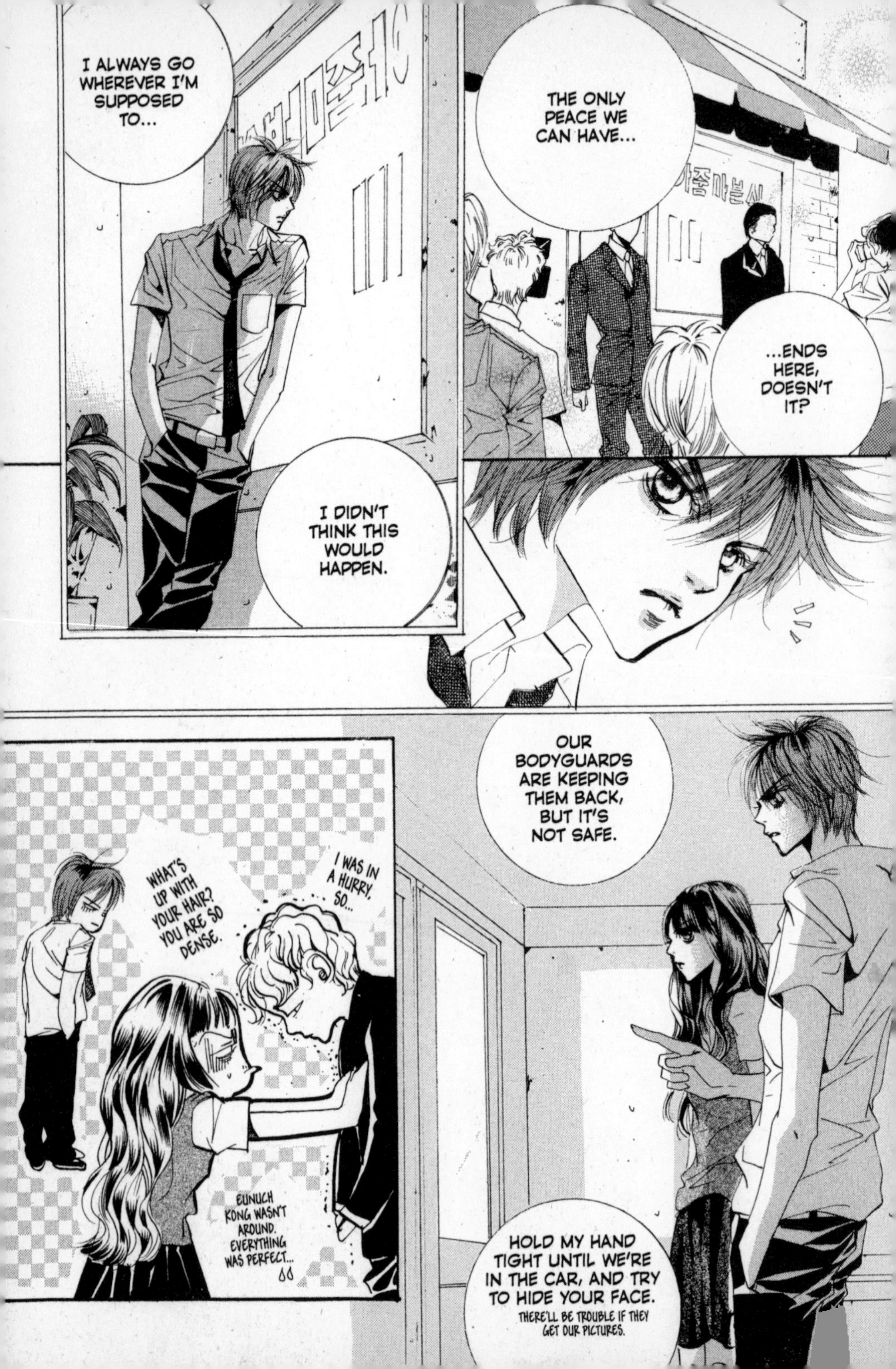
I ALWAYS GO WHEREVER I'M SUPPOSED TO...
I DIDN'T THINK THIS WOULD HAPPEN.
THE ONLY PEACE WE CAN HAVE...
...ENDS HERE, DOESN'T IT?
WHAT'S UP WITH YOUR HAIR? YOU ARE SO DENSE.
I WAS IN A HURRY, SO...
EUNUCH KONG WASN'T AROUND. EVERYTHING WAS PERFECT...
OUR BODYGUARDS ARE KEEPING THEM BACK, BUT IT'S NOT SAFE.
HOLD MY HAND TIGHT UNTIL WE'RE IN THE CAR, AND TRY TO HIDE YOUR FACE.
THERE'LL BE TROUBLE IF THEY GET OUR PICTURES.

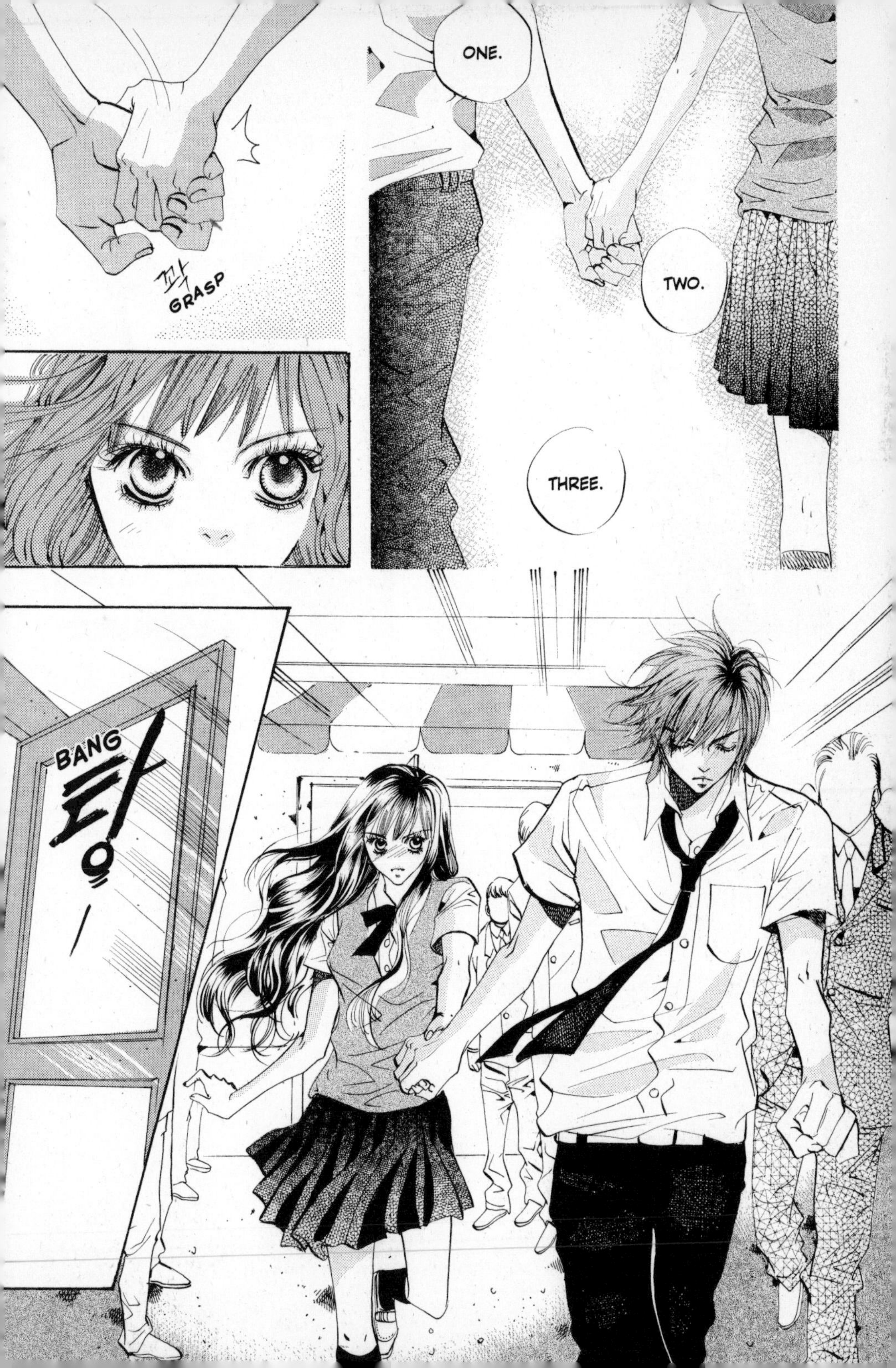
꽉
GRASP
ONE.
TWO.
THREE.
BANG
탕!

I DON'T WANT TO LOSE YOU.

SHIN...

AFTER THE INTERVIEW...

...WILL I BE ABLE TO SEE YOU AGAIN?

YOU...

...FINALLY STARTED OPENING UP TO ME...

WILL YOU WANT TO SEE ME AGAIN?

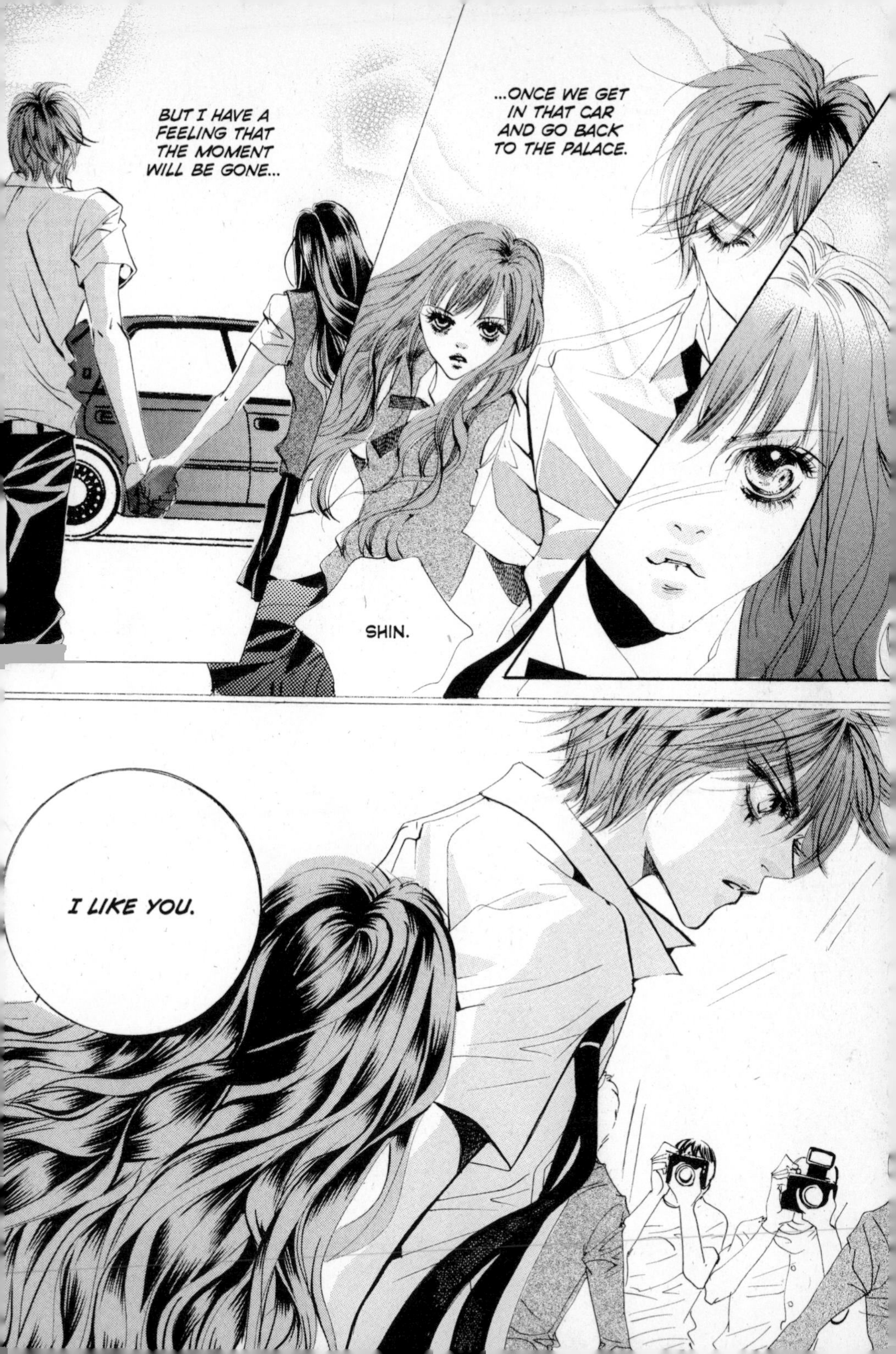
BUT I HAVE A FEELING THAT THE MOMENT WILL BE GONE...
...ONCE WE GET IN THAT CAR AND GO BACK TO THE PALACE.
SHIN.
I LIKE YOU.

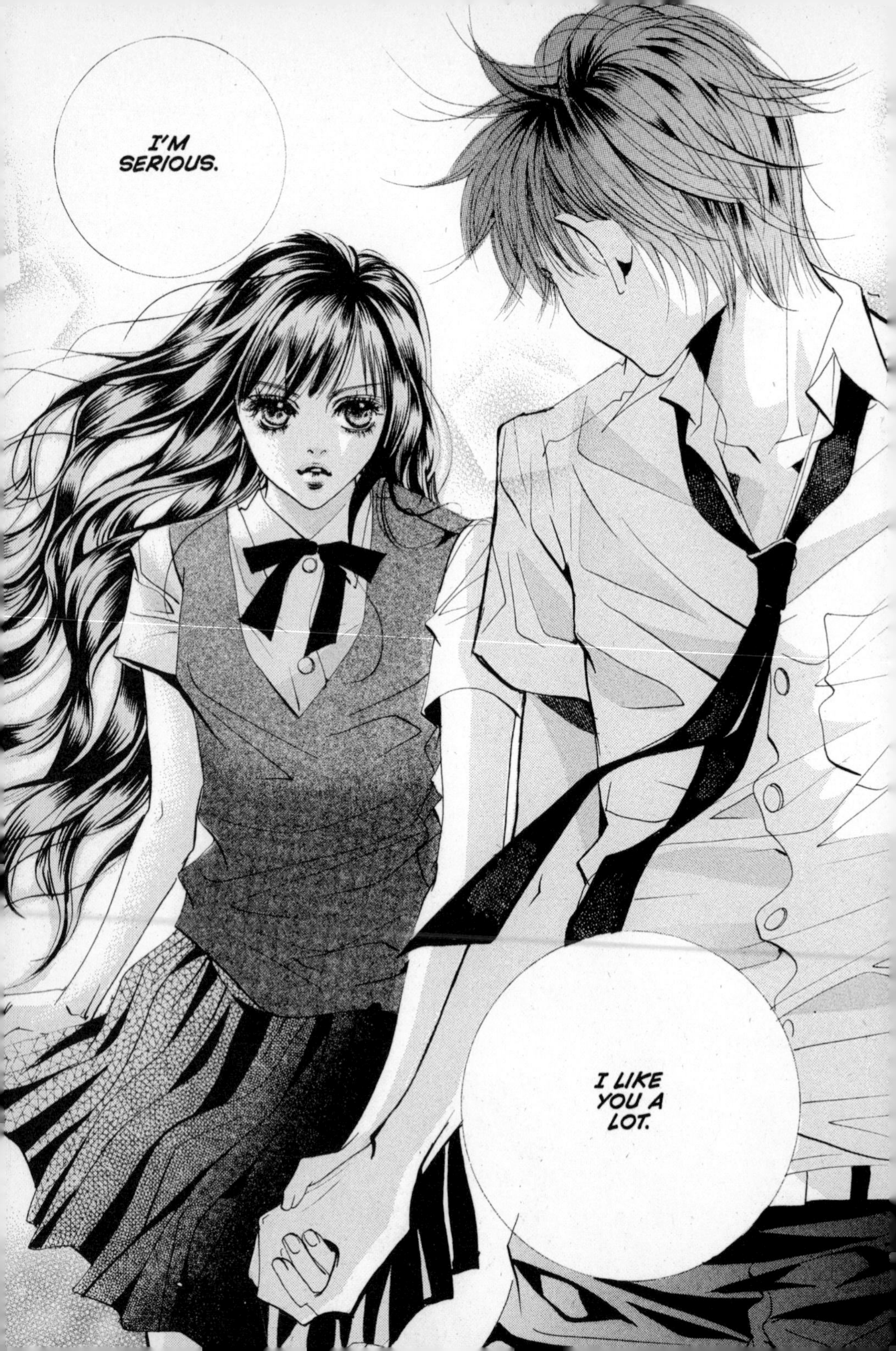
I'M SERIOUS.
I LIKE YOU A LOT.

THE ROYAL PALACE

Goong

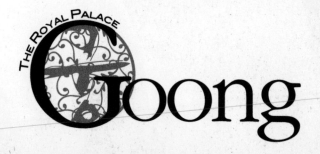

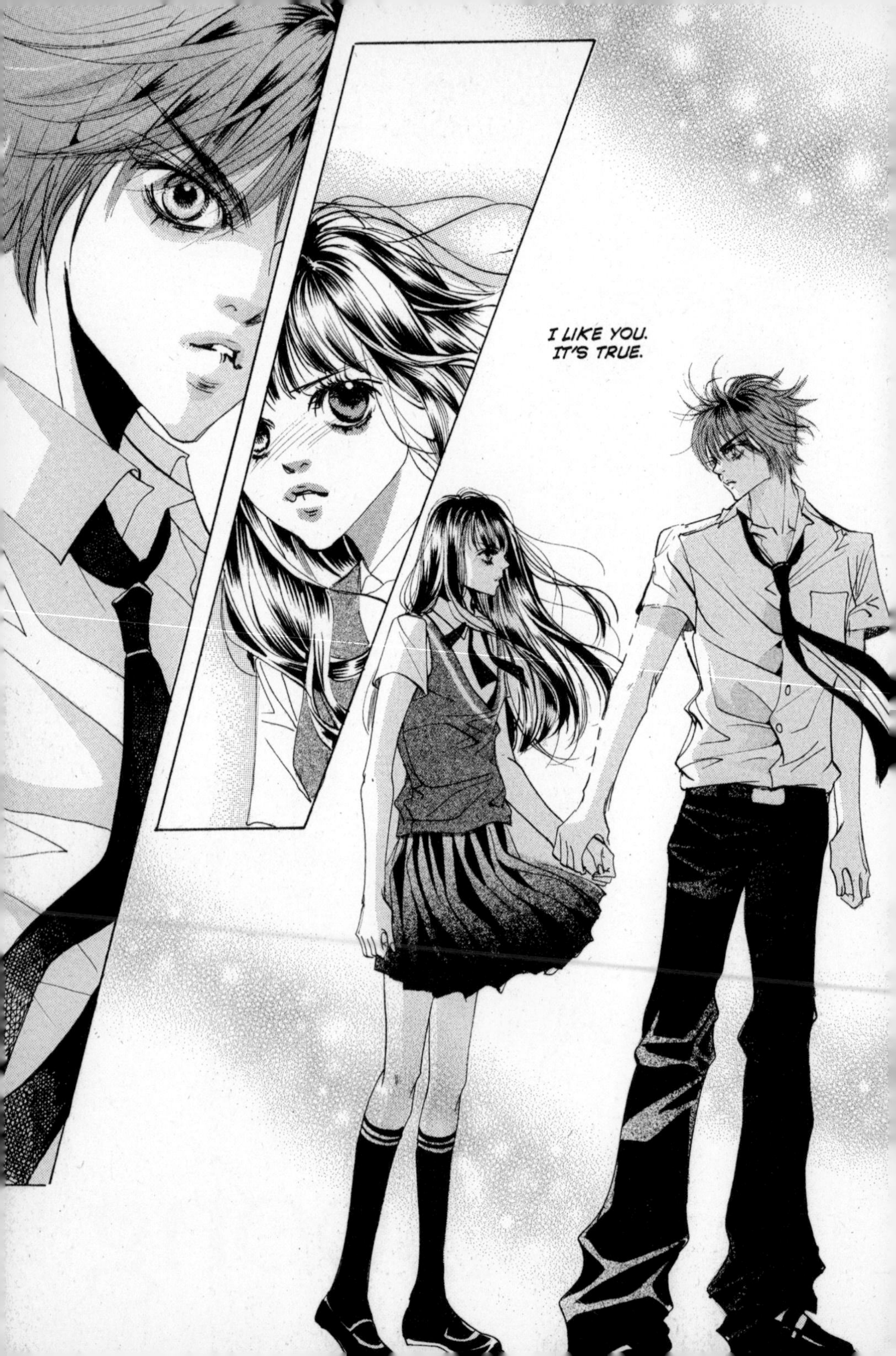
I LIKE YOU. IT'S TRUE.

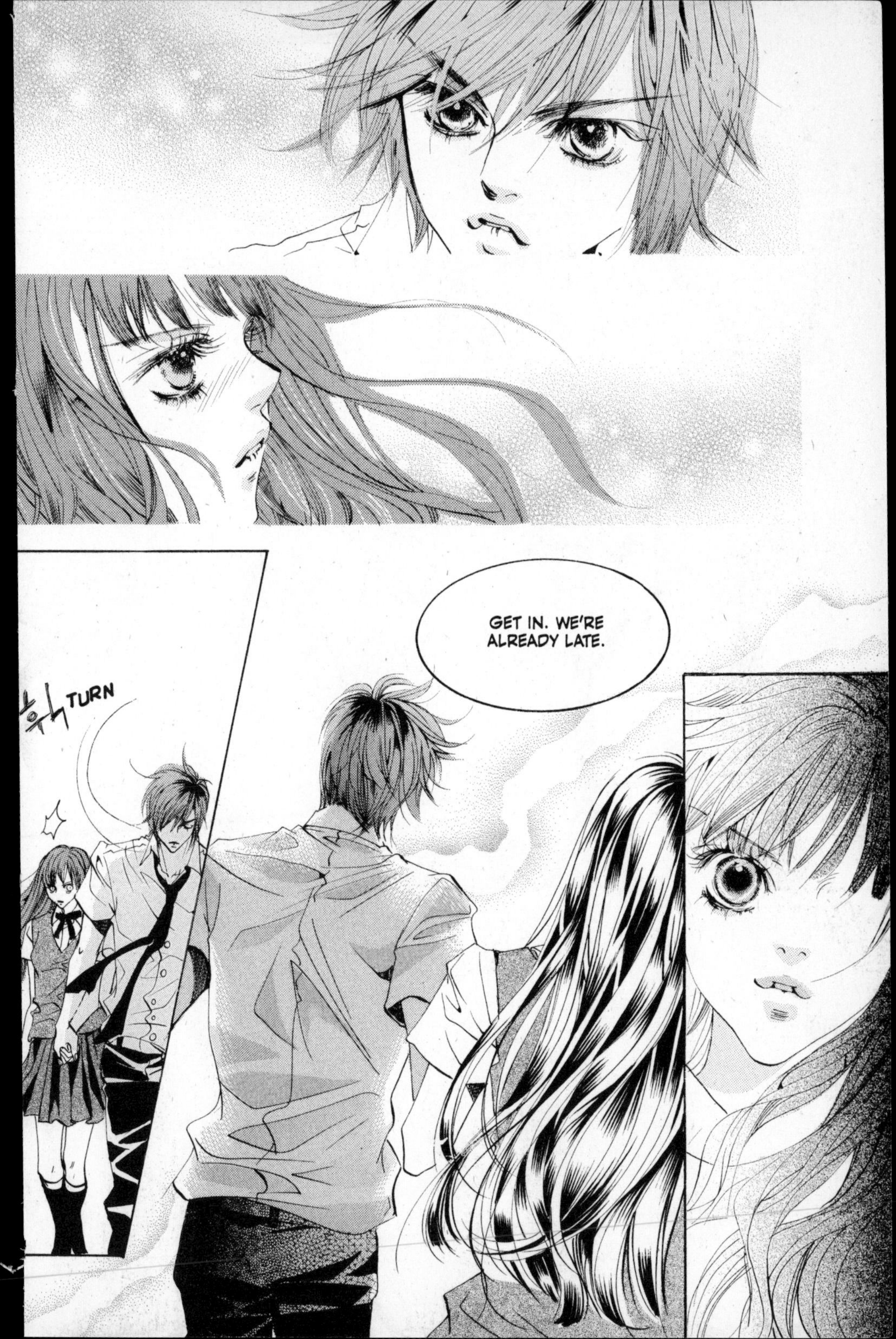
GET IN. WE'RE ALREADY LATE.
휘익 TURN

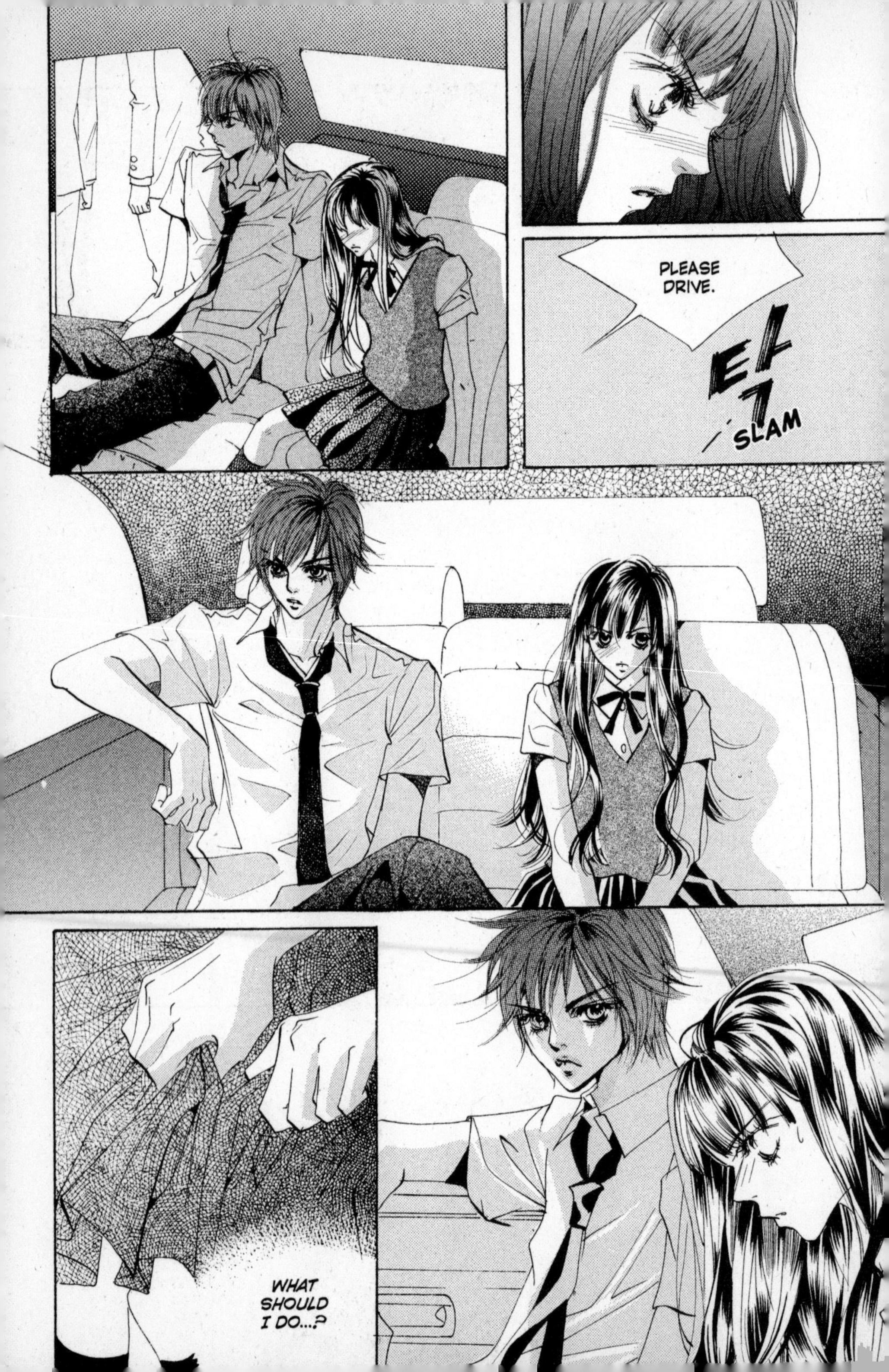
PLEASE DRIVE.
탁
SLAM
WHAT SHOULD I DO...?

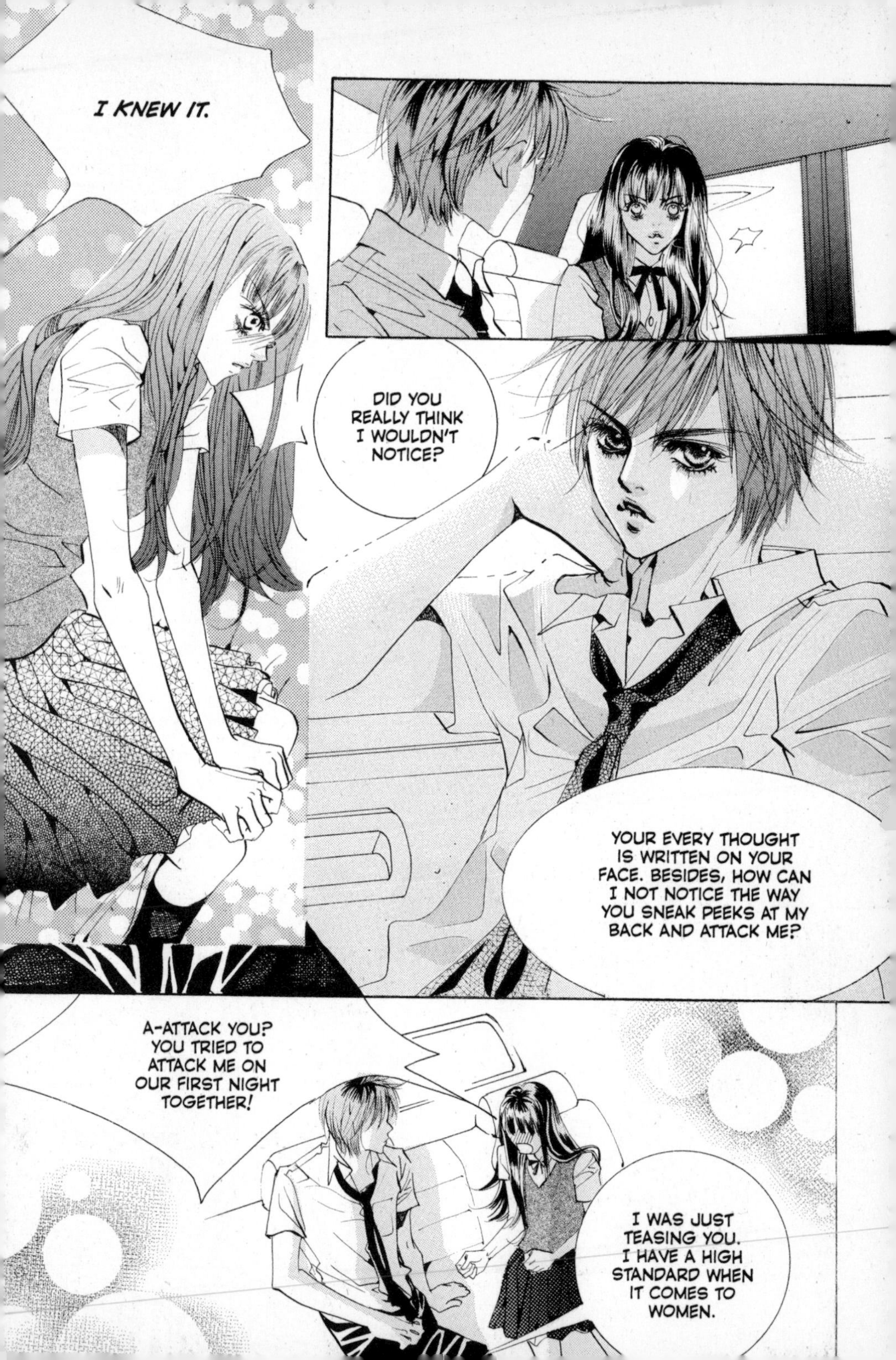
I KNEW IT.
DID YOU REALLY THINK I WOULDN'T NOTICE?
YOUR EVERY THOUGHT IS WRITTEN ON YOUR FACE. BESIDES, HOW CAN I NOT NOTICE THE WAY YOU SNEAK PEEKS AT MY BACK AND ATTACK ME?
A-ATTACK YOU? YOU TRIED TO ATTACK ME ON OUR FIRST NIGHT TOGETHER!
I WAS JUST TEASING YOU. I HAVE A HIGH STANDARD WHEN IT COMES TO WOMEN.

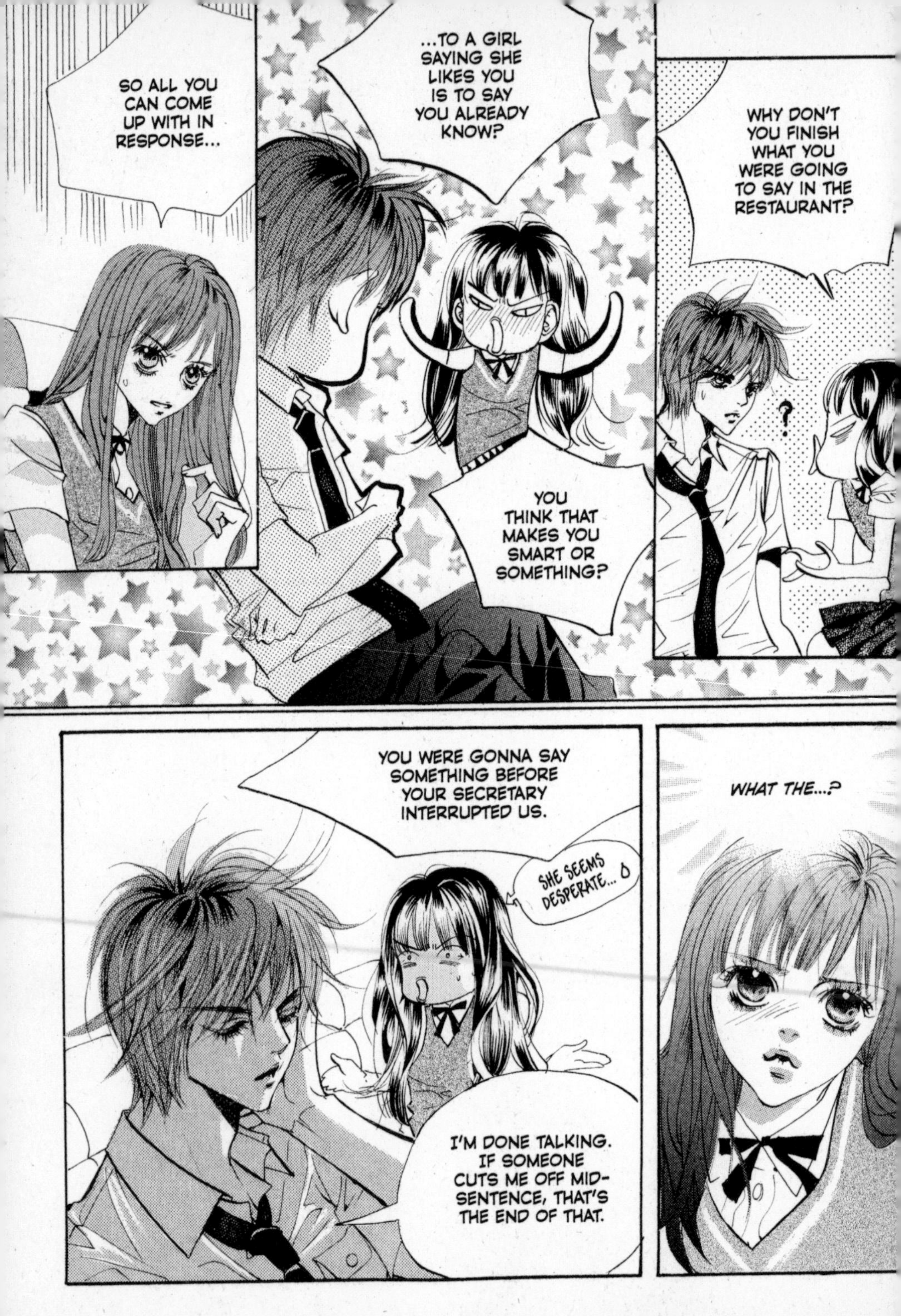

SO ALL YOU CAN COME UP WITH IN RESPONSE...
...TO A GIRL SAYING SHE LIKES YOU IS TO SAY YOU ALREADY KNOW?
YOU THINK THAT MAKES YOU SMART OR SOMETHING?
WHY DON'T YOU FINISH WHAT YOU WERE GOING TO SAY IN THE RESTAURANT?
?
YOU WERE GONNA SAY SOMETHING BEFORE YOUR SECRETARY INTERRUPTED US.
SHE SEEMS DESPERATE...
I'M DONE TALKING. IF SOMEONE CUTS ME OFF MID-SENTENCE, THAT'S THE END OF THAT.
WHAT THE...?

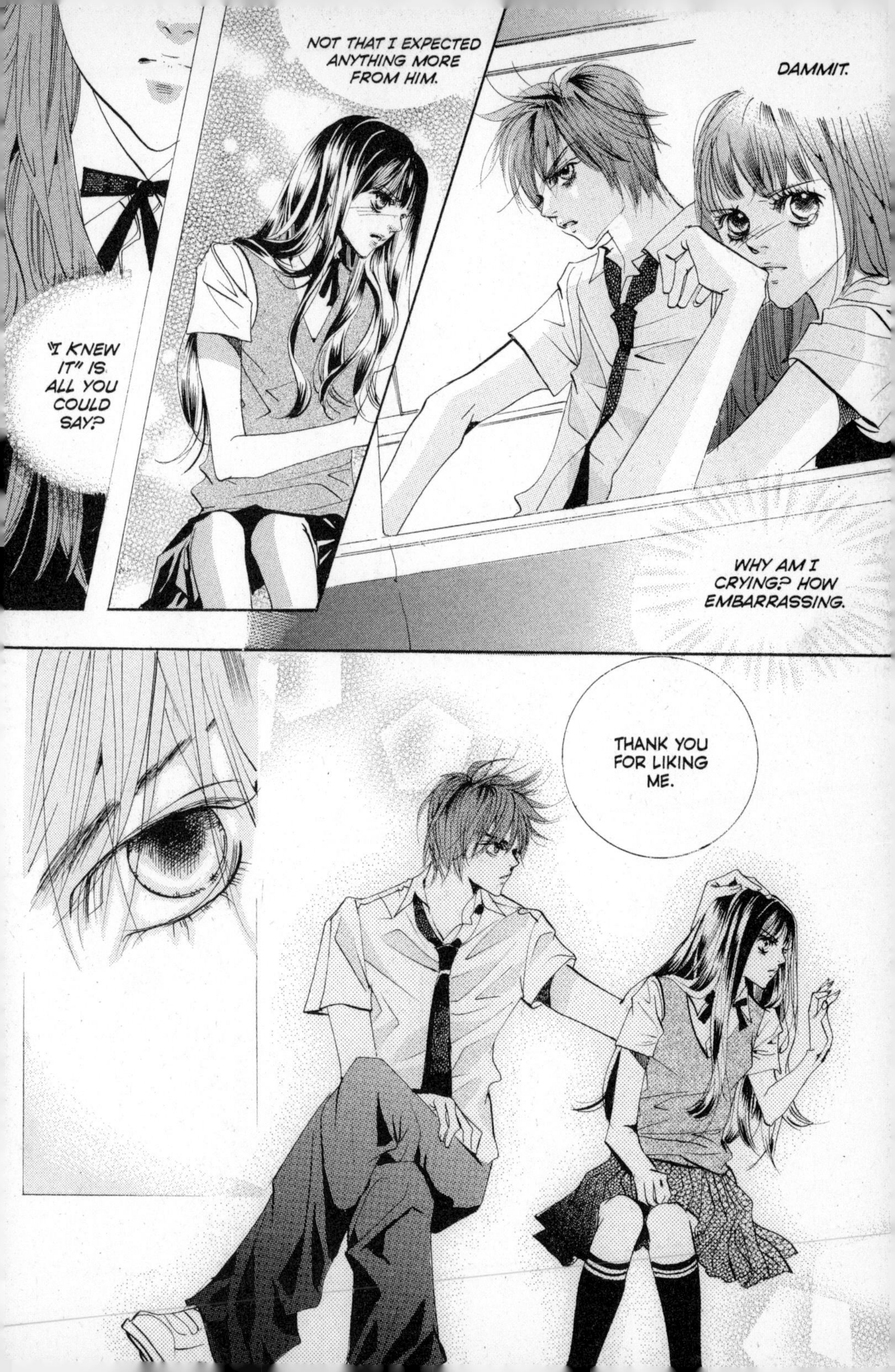
"I KNEW IT" IS ALL YOU COULD SAY?
NOT THAT I EXPECTED ANYTHING MORE FROM HIM.
DAMMIT.
WHY AM I CRYING? HOW EMBARRASSING.
THANK YOU FOR LIKING ME.

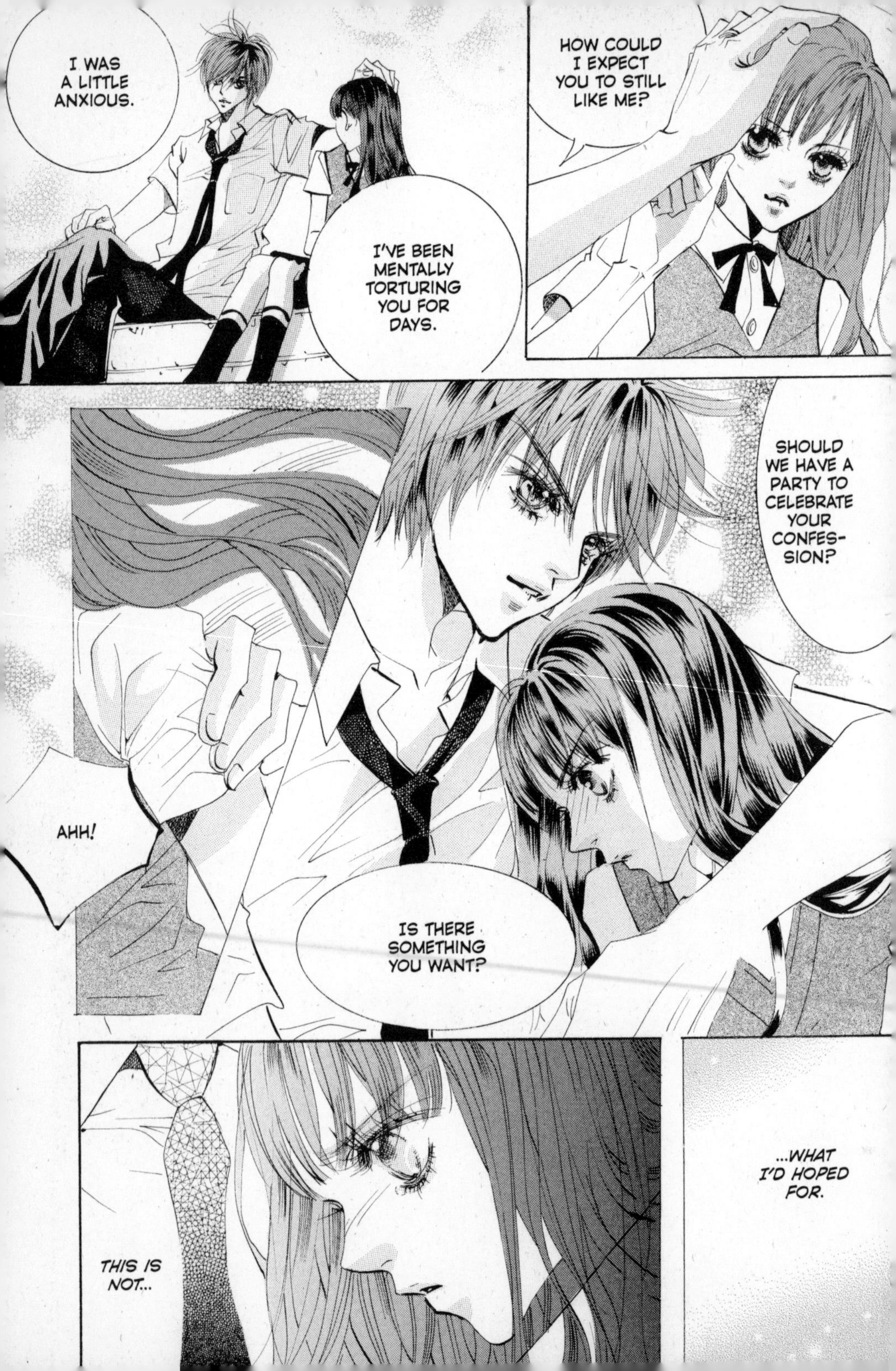
I WAS A LITTLE ANXIOUS.
I'VE BEEN MENTALLY TORTURING YOU FOR DAYS.
HOW COULD I EXPECT YOU TO STILL LIKE ME?
AHH!
IS THERE SOMETHING YOU WANT?
SHOULD WE HAVE A PARTY TO CELEBRATE YOUR CONFES-SION?
THIS IS NOT...
...WHAT I'D HOPED FOR.

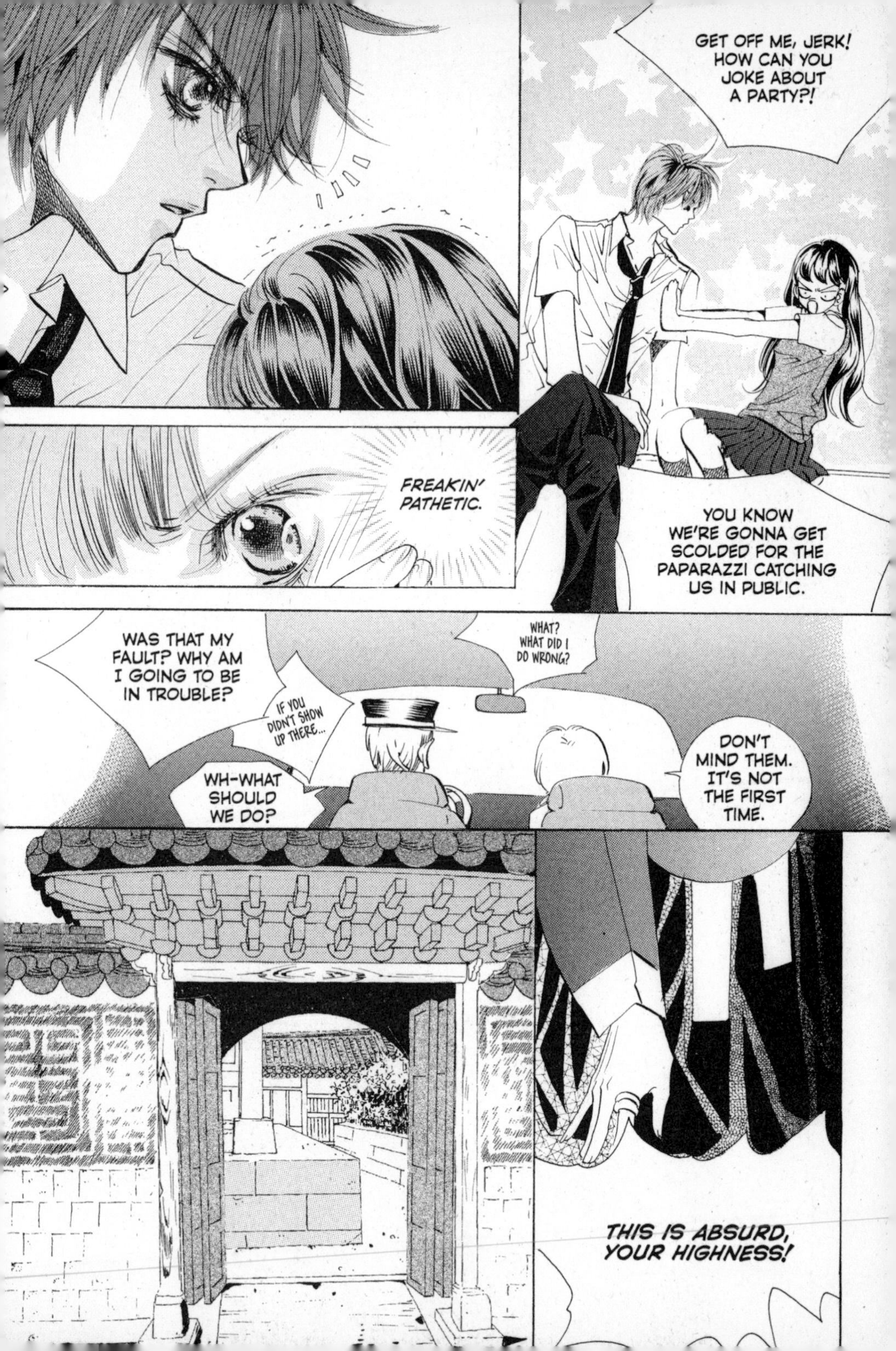
FREAKIN' PATHETIC.
GET OFF ME, JERK! HOW CAN YOU JOKE ABOUT A PARTY?!
YOU KNOW WE'RE GONNA GET SCOLDED FOR THE PAPARAZZI CATCHING US IN PUBLIC.
WAS THAT MY FAULT? WHY AM I GOING TO BE IN TROUBLE?
IF YOU DIDN'T SHOW UP THERE...
WH-WHAT SHOULD WE DO?
WHAT? WHAT DID I DO WRONG?
DON'T MIND THEM. IT'S NOT THE FIRST TIME.
THIS IS ABSURD, YOUR HIGHNESS!

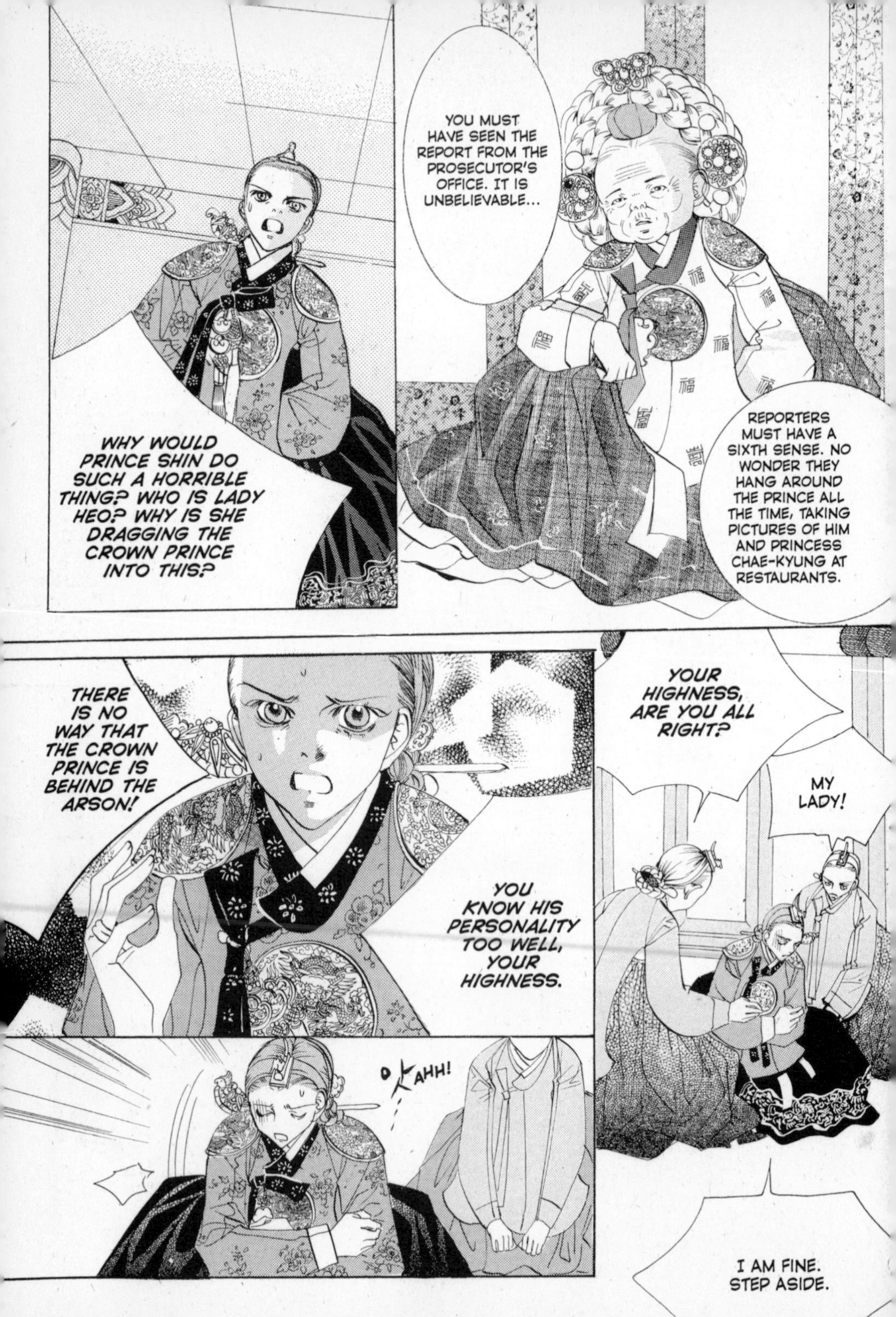

WHY WOULD PRINCE SHIN DO SUCH A HORRIBLE THING? WHO IS LADY HEO? WHY IS SHE DRAGGING THE CROWN PRINCE INTO THIS?
YOU MUST HAVE SEEN THE REPORT FROM THE PROSECUTOR'S OFFICE. IT IS UNBELIEVABLE...
REPORTERS MUST HAVE A SIXTH SENSE. NO WONDER THEY HANG AROUND THE PRINCE ALL THE TIME, TAKING PICTURES OF HIM AND PRINCESS CHAE-KYUNG AT RESTAURANTS.
THERE IS NO WAY THAT THE CROWN PRINCE IS BEHIND THE ARSON!
YOU KNOW HIS PERSONALITY TOO WELL, YOUR HIGHNESS.
KAHH!
YOUR HIGHNESS, ARE YOU ALL RIGHT?
MY LADY!
I AM FINE. STEP ASIDE.

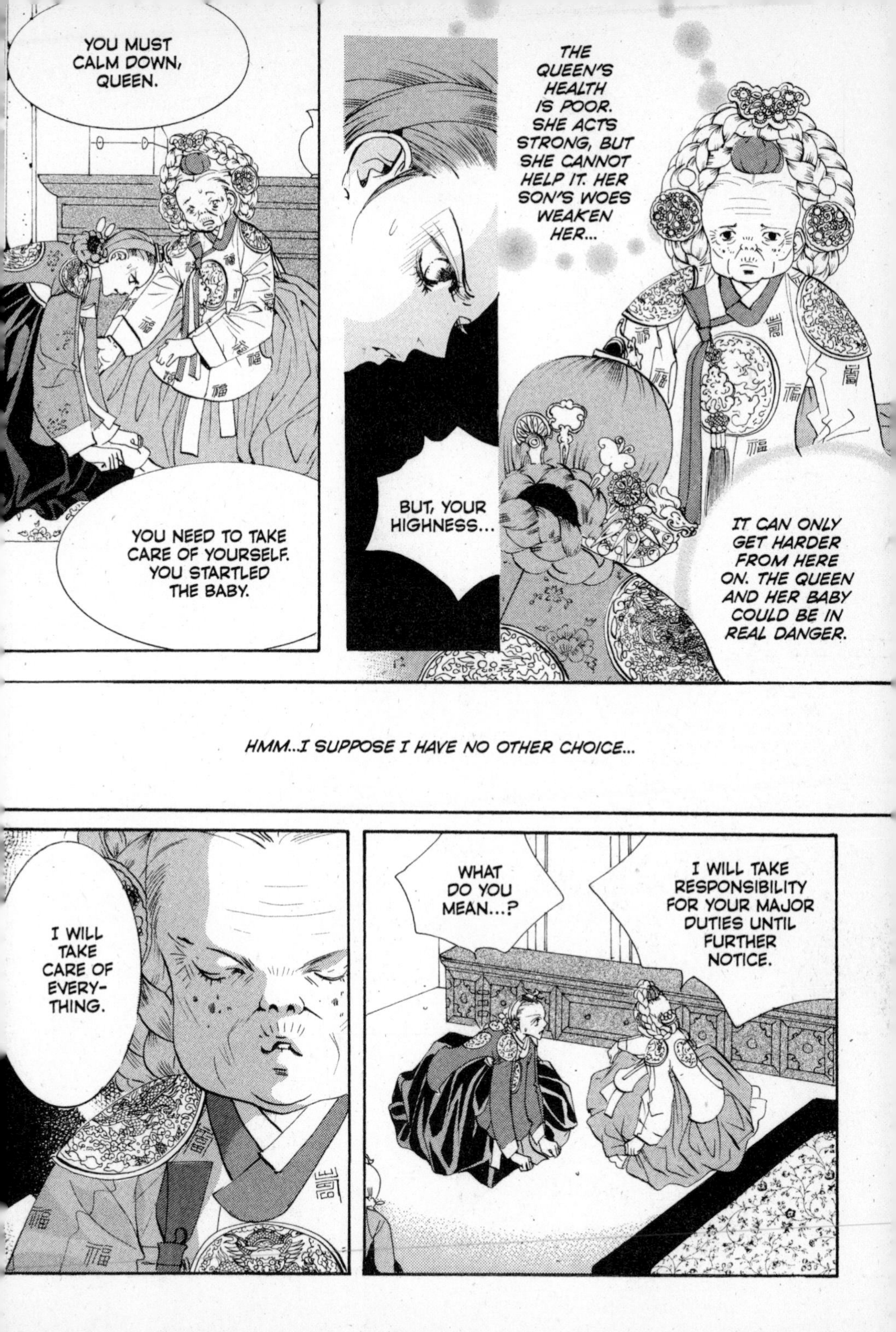
YOU MUST CALM DOWN, QUEEN.
YOU NEED TO TAKE CARE OF YOURSELF. YOU STARTLED THE BABY.
BUT, YOUR HIGHNESS...
THE QUEEN'S HEALTH IS POOR. SHE ACTS STRONG, BUT SHE CANNOT HELP IT. HER SON'S WOES WEAKEN HER...
IT CAN ONLY GET HARDER FROM HERE ON. THE QUEEN AND HER BABY COULD BE IN REAL DANGER.
HMM...I SUPPOSE I HAVE NO OTHER CHOICE...
I WILL TAKE CARE OF EVERY-THING.
WHAT DO YOU MEAN...?
I WILL TAKE RESPONSIBILITY FOR YOUR MAJOR DUTIES UNTIL FURTHER NOTICE.

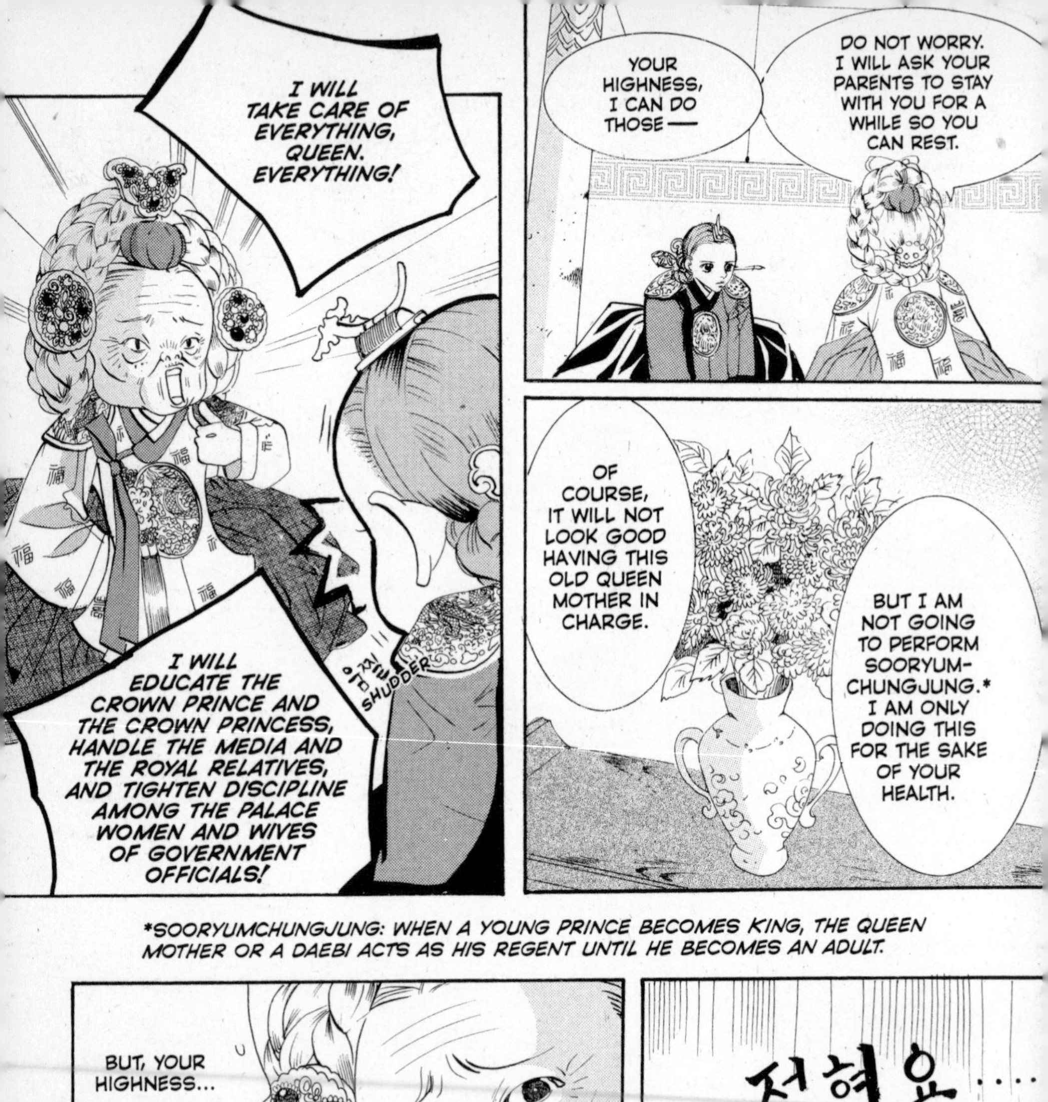
I WILL TAKE CARE OF EVERYTHING, QUEEN. EVERYTHING!
I WILL EDUCATE THE CROWN PRINCE AND THE CROWN PRINCESS, HANDLE THE MEDIA AND THE ROYAL RELATIVES, AND TIGHTEN DISCIPLINE AMONG THE PALACE WOMEN AND WIVES OF GOVERNMENT OFFICIALS!
SHUDDER
YOUR HIGHNESS, I CAN DO THOSE—
DO NOT WORRY. I WILL ASK YOUR PARENTS TO STAY WITH YOU FOR A WHILE SO YOU CAN REST.
OF COURSE, IT WILL NOT LOOK GOOD HAVING THIS OLD QUEEN MOTHER IN CHARGE.
BUT I AM NOT GOING TO PERFORM SOORYUM-CHUNGJUNG.* I AM ONLY DOING THIS FOR THE SAKE OF YOUR HEALTH.

*SOORYUMCHUNGJUNG: WHEN A YOUNG PRINCE BECOMES KING, THE QUEEN MOTHER OR A DAEBI ACTS AS HIS REGENT UNTIL HE BECOMES AN ADULT.

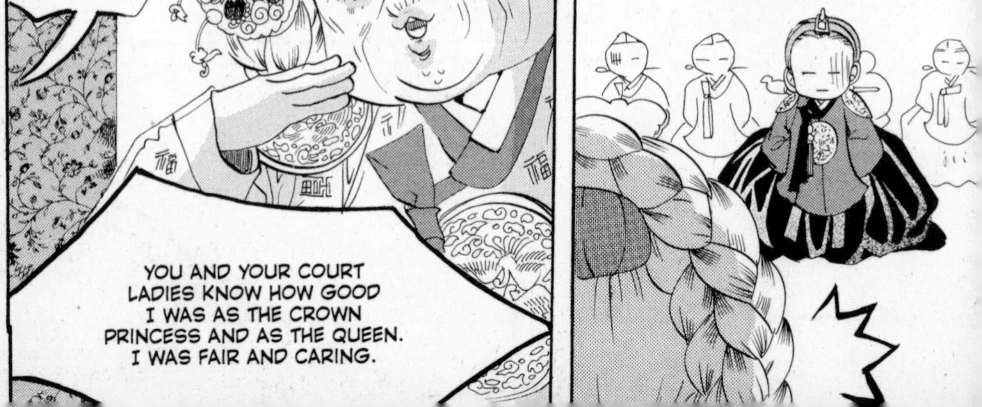
BUT, YOUR HIGHNESS...
YOU AND YOUR COURT LADIES KNOW HOW GOOD I WAS AS THE CROWN PRINCESS AND AS THE QUEEN. I WAS FAIR AND CARING.
전혀요....
NOT AT ALL...

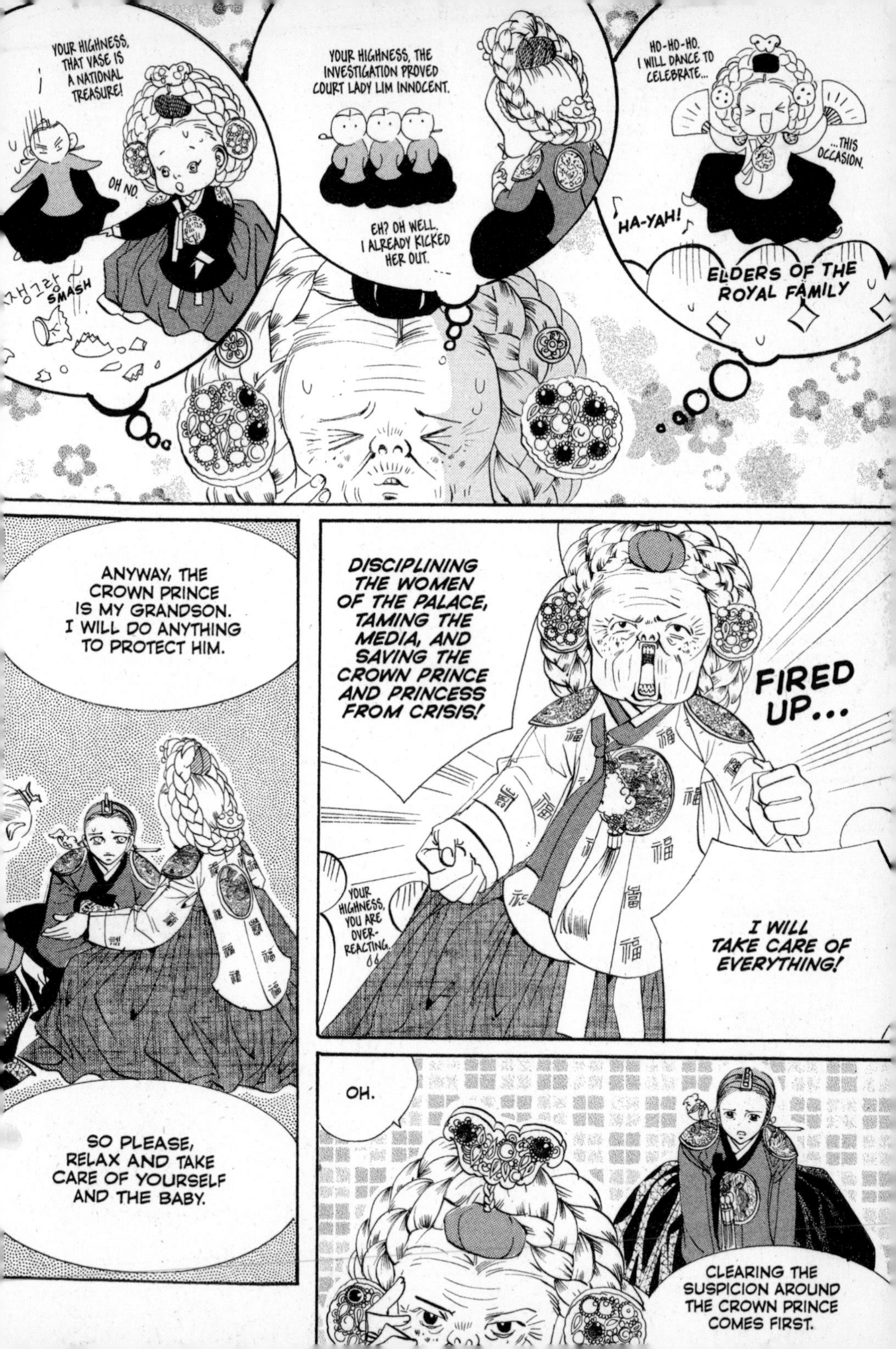

YOUR HIGHNESS, THAT VASE IS A NATIONAL TREASURE!
OH NO.
쨍그랑~
SMASH
YOUR HIGHNESS, THE INVESTIGATION PROVED COURT LADY LIM INNOCENT.
EH? OH WELL. I ALREADY KICKED HER OUT.
HO-HO-HO. I WILL DANCE TO CELEBRATE...
...THIS OCCASION.
HA-YAH!
ELDERS OF THE ROYAL FAMILY
ANYWAY, THE CROWN PRINCE IS MY GRANDSON. I WILL DO ANYTHING TO PROTECT HIM.
SO PLEASE, RELAX AND TAKE CARE OF YOURSELF AND THE BABY.
DISCIPLINING THE WOMEN OF THE PALACE, TAMING THE MEDIA, AND SAVING THE CROWN PRINCE AND PRINCESS FROM CRISIS!
FIRED UP...
YOUR HIGHNESS, YOU ARE OVER-REACTING.
I WILL TAKE CARE OF EVERYTHING!
OH.
CLEARING THE SUSPICION AROUND THE CROWN PRINCE COMES FIRST.

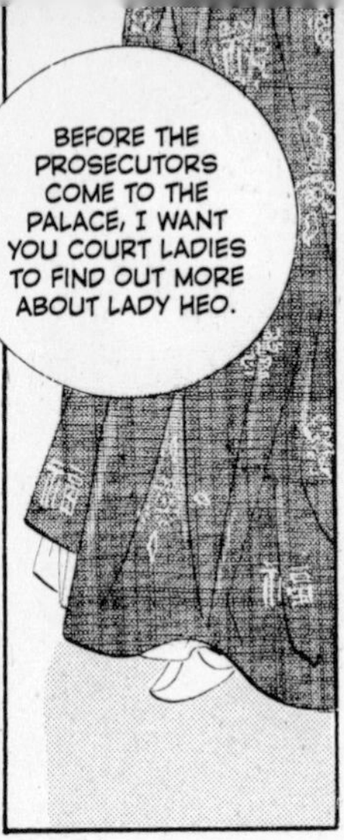
BEFORE THE PROSECUTORS COME TO THE PALACE, I WANT YOU COURT LADIES TO FIND OUT MORE ABOUT LADY HEO.

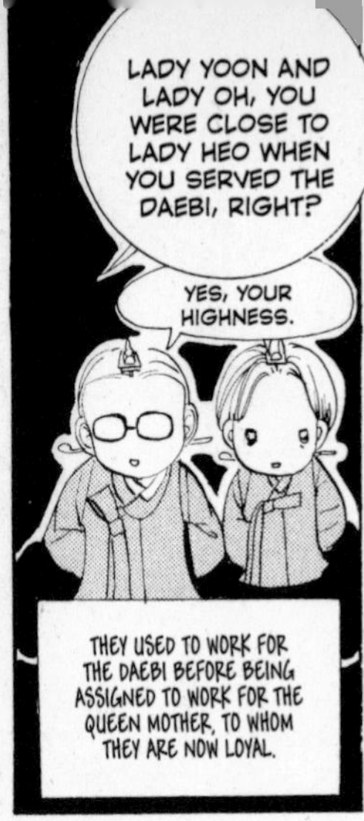
LADY YOON AND LADY OH, YOU WERE CLOSE TO LADY HEO WHEN YOU SERVED THE DAEBI, RIGHT?
YES, YOUR HIGHNESS.
THEY USED TO WORK FOR THE DAEBI BEFORE BEING ASSIGNED TO WORK FOR THE QUEEN MOTHER, TO WHOM THEY ARE NOW LOYAL.

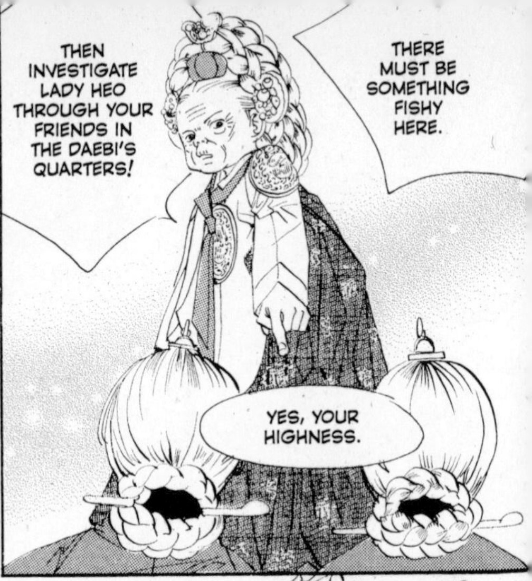
THEN INVESTIGATE LADY HEO THROUGH YOUR FRIENDS IN THE DAEBI'S QUARTERS!
THERE MUST BE SOMETHING FISHY HERE.
YES, YOUR HIGHNESS.

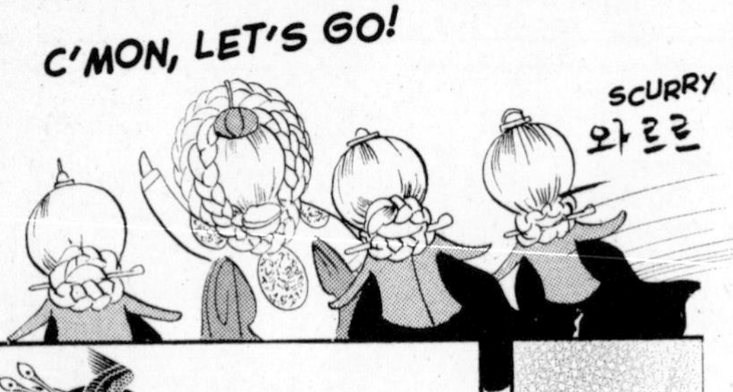
C'MON, LET'S GO!
SCURRY
와르르

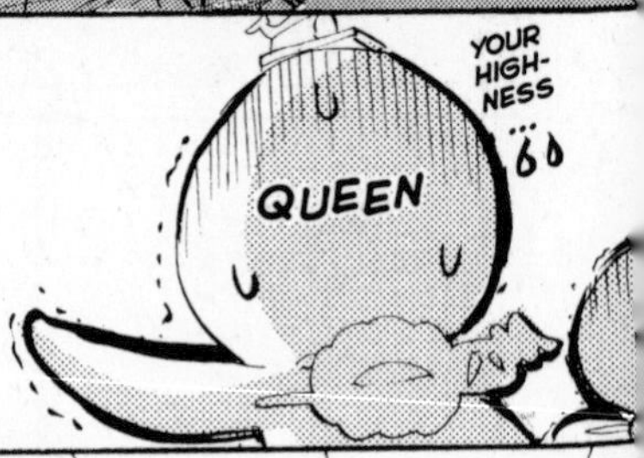
YOUR HIGH-NESS ...
QUEEN

THE POWER OF COURT LADIES

WHEN I WATCH HISTORICAL DRAMAS, ROYAL FAMILIES DISCUSS ALL OF THEIR SECRETS IN FRONT OF THE LADIES OF THE COURT. IT'S BECAUSE THE MOST IMPORTANT RESPONSIBILITY OF A COURT LADY IS TO NEVER TALK ABOUT ANYTHING THEY HEAR. EVEN IF A COURT LADY HAD A BABY WITH HER LOVER AND RAISED THAT LOVE CHILD IN THE PALACE, MEMBERS OF THE ROYAL FAMILY WOULDN'T KNOW. THIS SHOWS HOW STRICTLY SECRETS WERE KEPT AMONG COURT LADIES. (REFERENCE: THE STUDY OF PALACE CUSTOMS IN THE CHOSUN DYNASTY BY YONG-SOOK KIM)

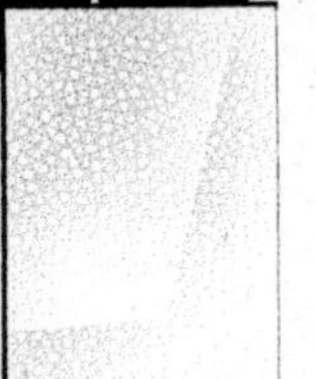

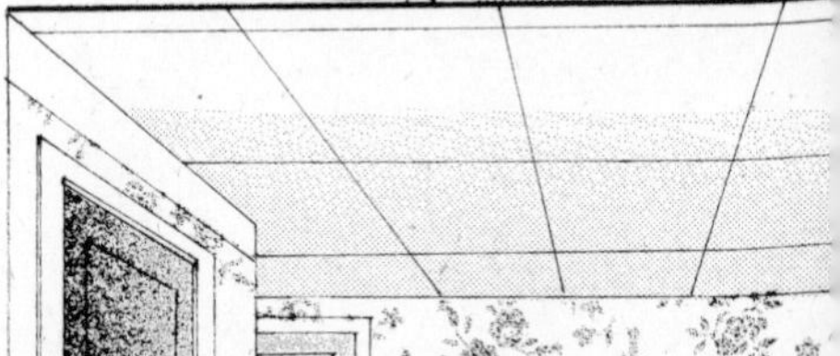
CHAE-KYUNG SHOULD BE INFORMED THAT YOUR ILLNESS IS GETTING WORSE, FATHER.

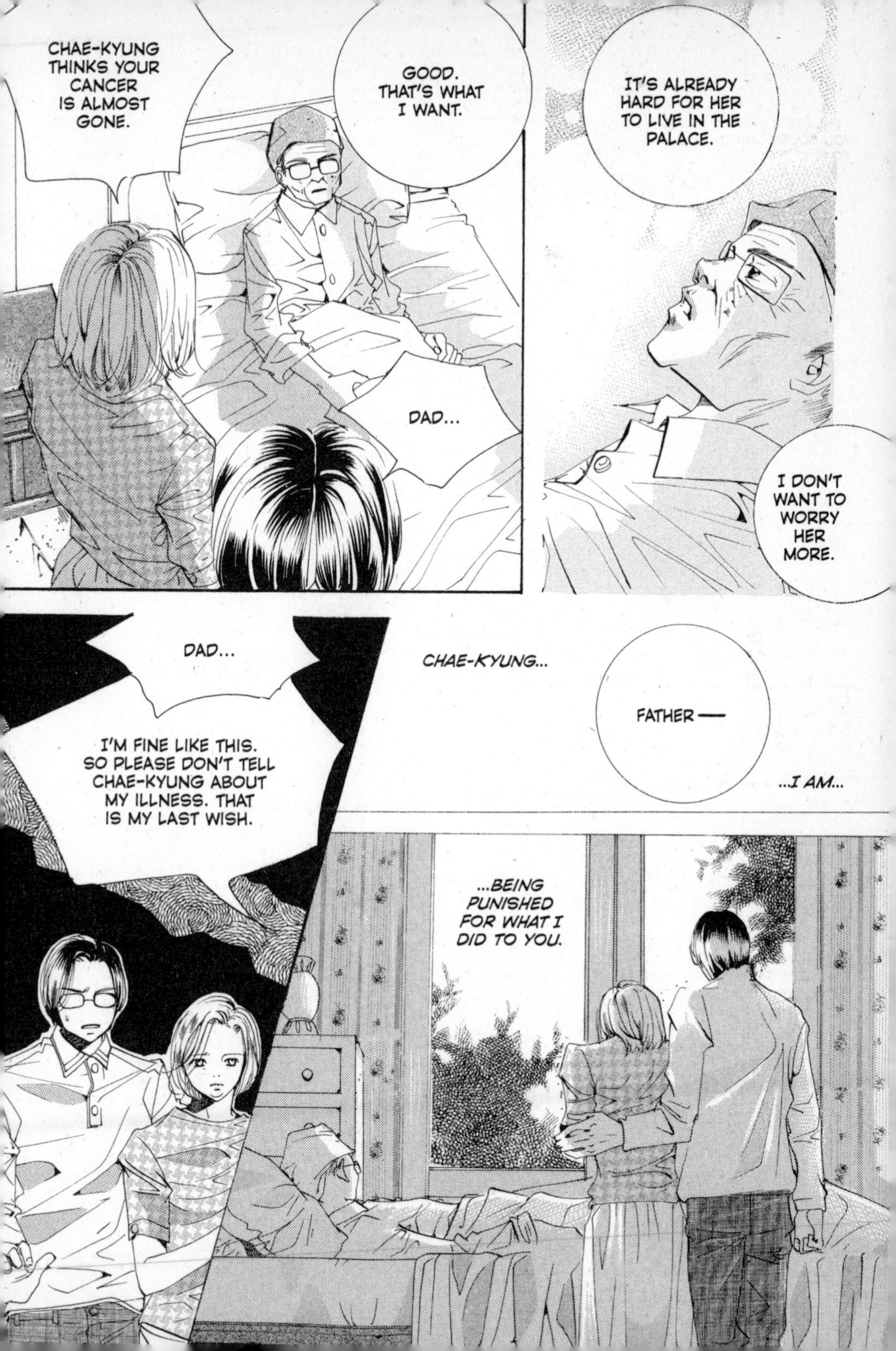
CHAE-KYUNG THINKS YOUR CANCER IS ALMOST GONE.
GOOD. THAT'S WHAT I WANT.
DAD...
IT'S ALREADY HARD FOR HER TO LIVE IN THE PALACE.
I DON'T WANT TO WORRY HER MORE.
DAD...
I'M FINE LIKE THIS. SO PLEASE DON'T TELL CHAE-KYUNG ABOUT MY ILLNESS. THAT IS MY LAST WISH.
CHAE-KYUNG...
FATHER —
...I AM...
...BEING PUNISHED FOR WHAT I DID TO YOU.

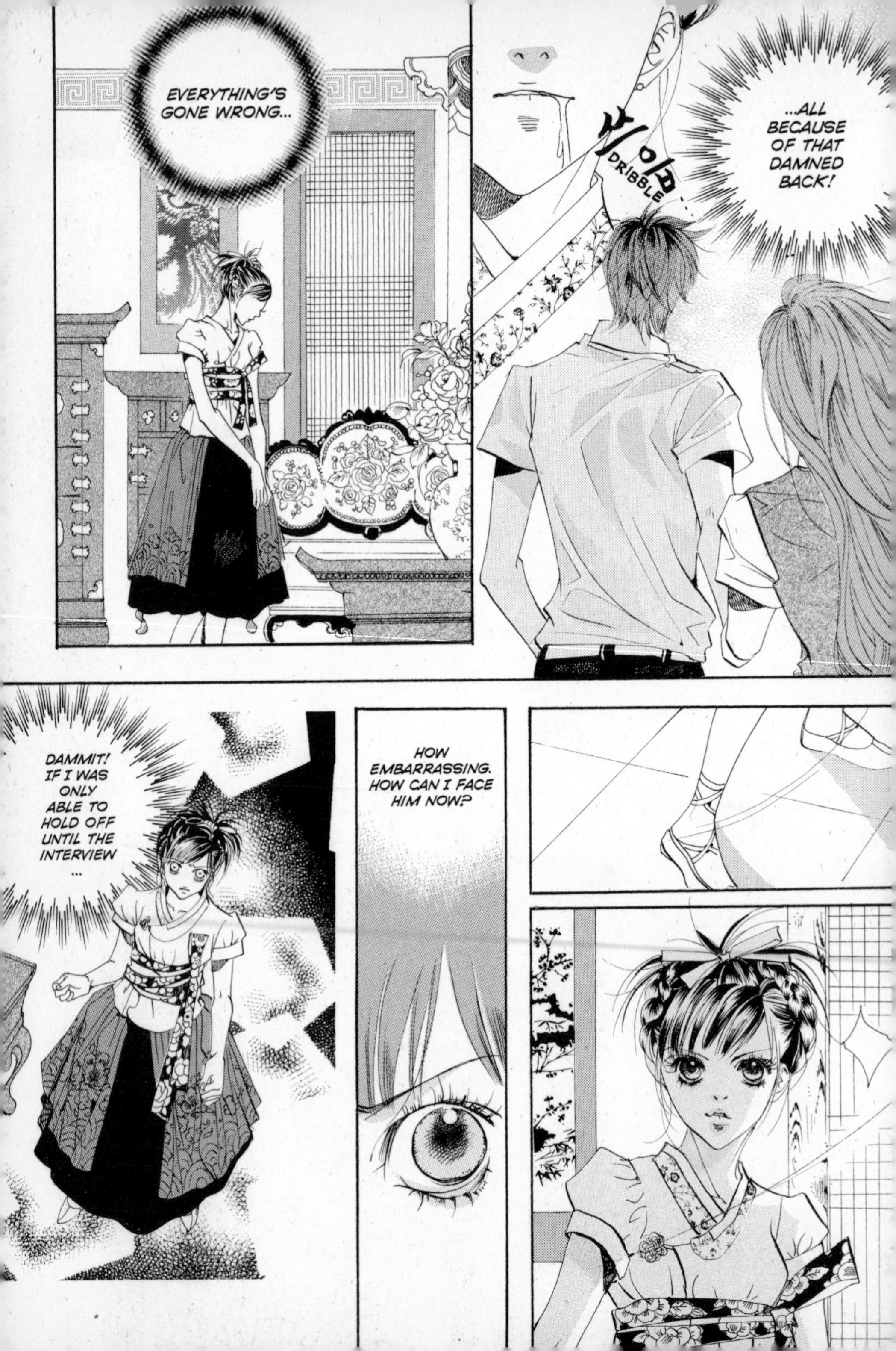
EVERYTHING'S GONE WRONG...
DRIBBLE
...ALL BECAUSE OF THAT DAMNED BACK!
DAMMIT! IF I WAS ONLY ABLE TO HOLD OFF UNTIL THE INTERVIEW ...
HOW EMBARRASSING. HOW CAN I FACE HIM NOW?

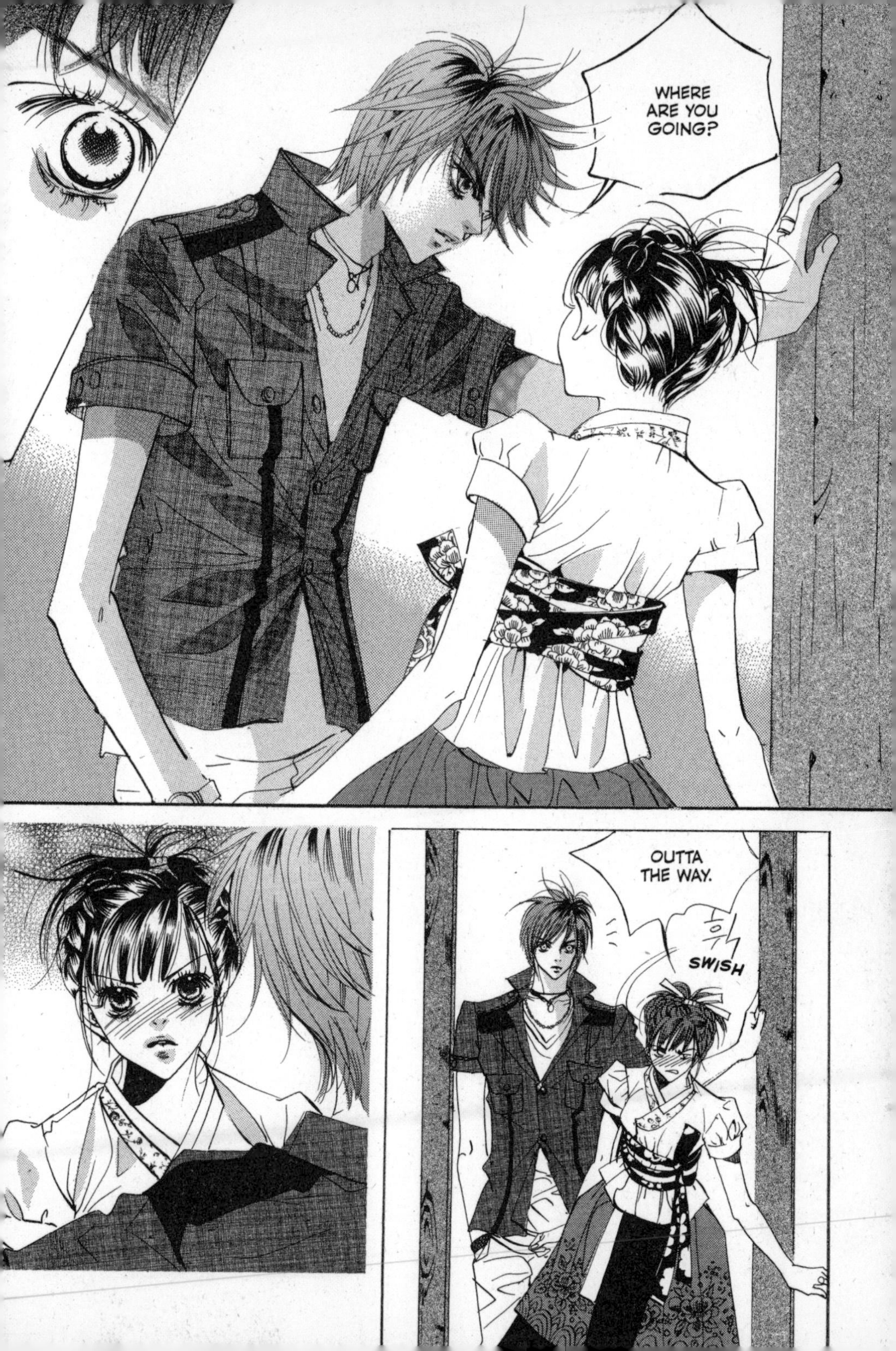
WHERE ARE YOU GOING?
OUTTA THE WAY.
SWISH

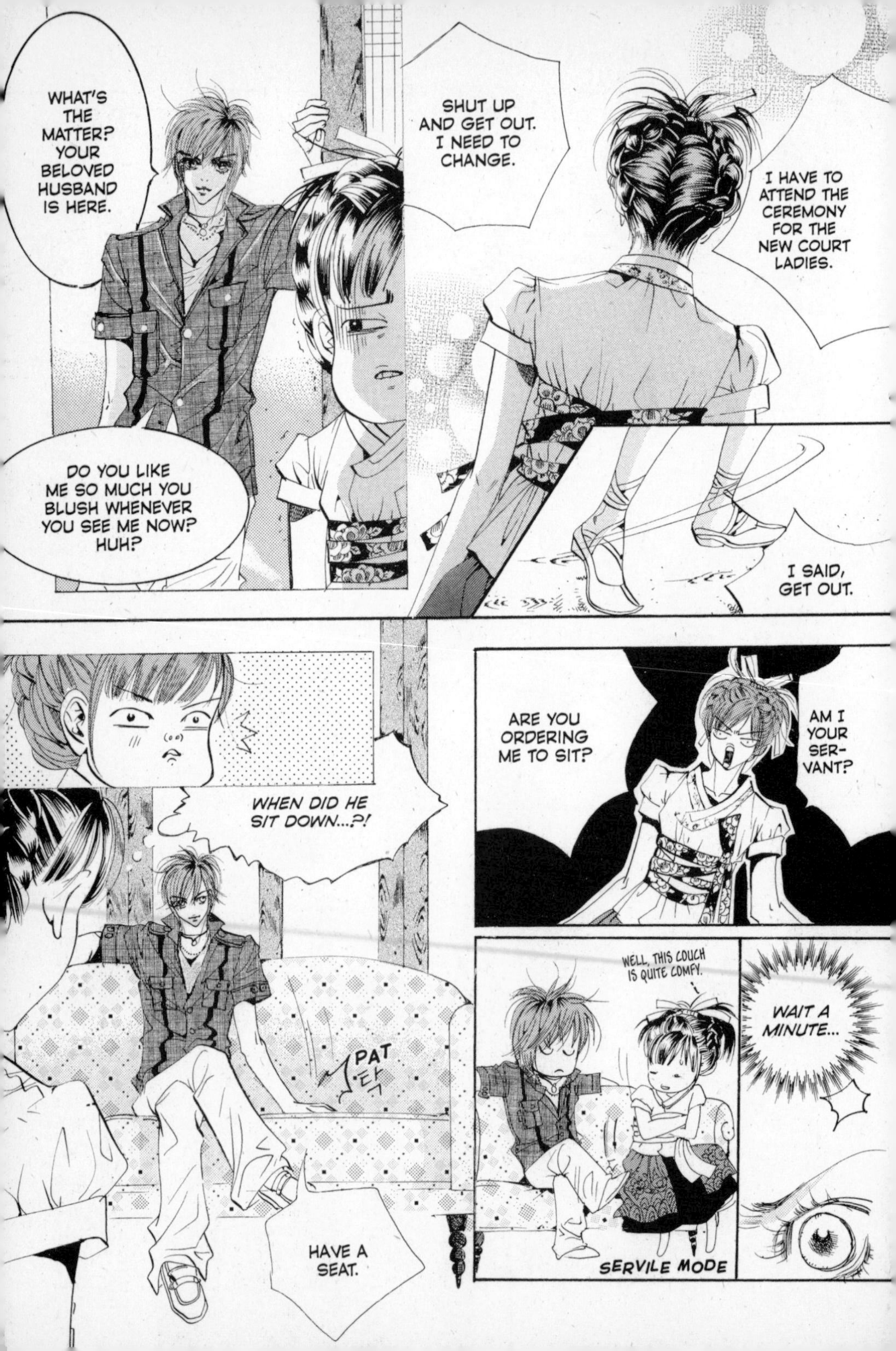
WHAT'S THE MATTER? YOUR BELOVED HUSBAND IS HERE.
DO YOU LIKE ME SO MUCH YOU BLUSH WHENEVER YOU SEE ME NOW? HUH?
SHUT UP AND GET OUT. I NEED TO CHANGE.
I HAVE TO ATTEND THE CEREMONY FOR THE NEW COURT LADIES.
I SAID, GET OUT.
WHEN DID HE SIT DOWN...?!
PAT
탁
HAVE A SEAT.
ARE YOU ORDERING ME TO SIT?
AM I YOUR SER-VANT?
WELL, THIS COUCH IS QUITE COMFY.
SERVILE MODE
WAIT A MINUTE...

HAVE I GOTTEN MORE PATHETIC SINCE I TOLD HIM HOW I FELT?

I DIDN'T DO ANYTHING WRONG!

RISE

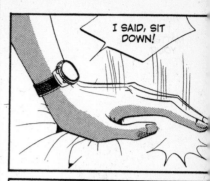

I SAID, SIT DOWN!

YES, SIR.

I LIKE YOU, SHIN...

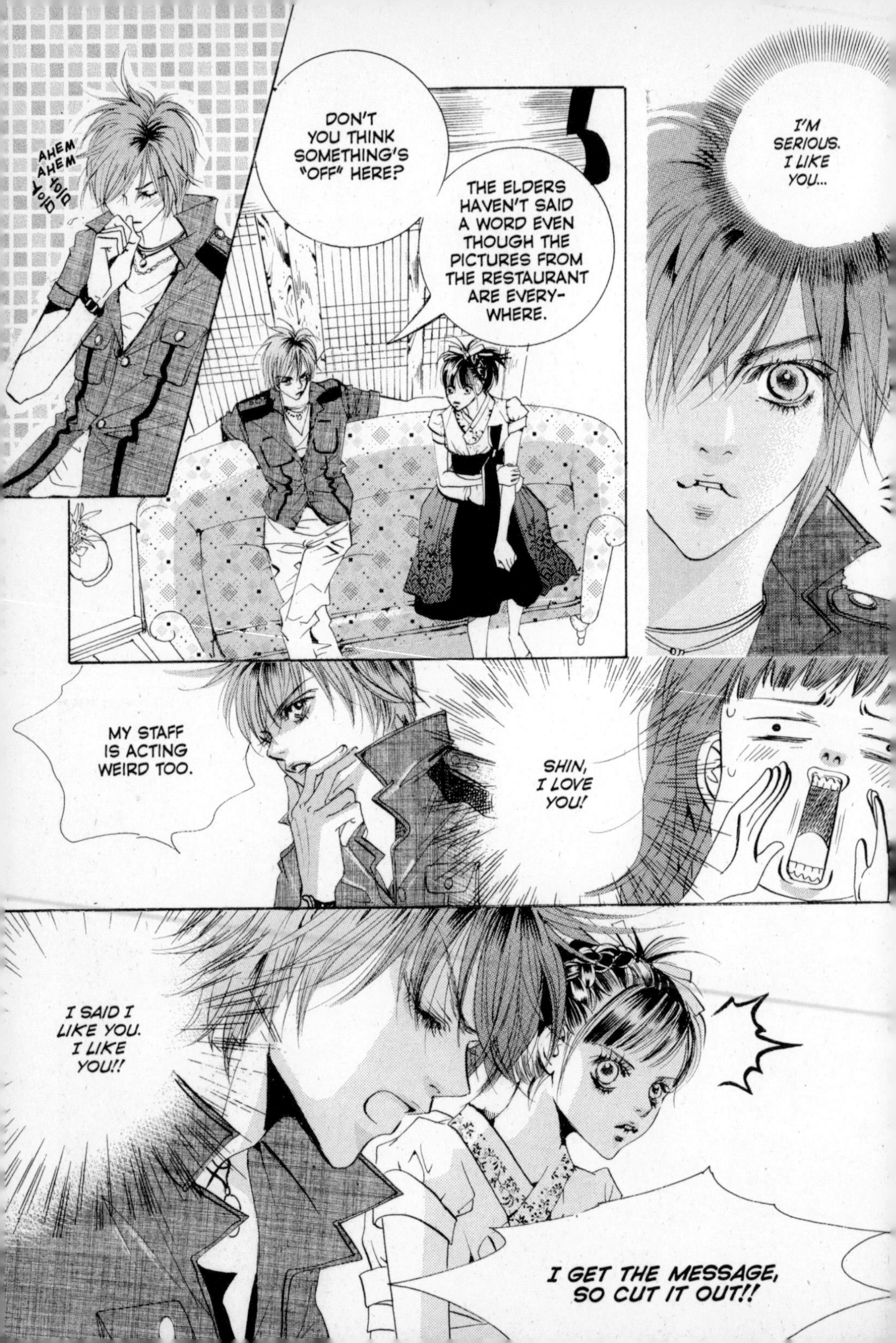
AHEM AHEM
DON'T YOU THINK SOMETHING'S "OFF" HERE?
THE ELDERS HAVEN'T SAID A WORD EVEN THOUGH THE PICTURES FROM THE RESTAURANT ARE EVERY-WHERE.
I'M SERIOUS. I LIKE YOU...
MY STAFF IS ACTING WEIRD TOO.
SHIN, I LOVE YOU!
I SAID I LIKE YOU. I LIKE YOU!!
I GET THE MESSAGE, SO CUT IT OUT!!

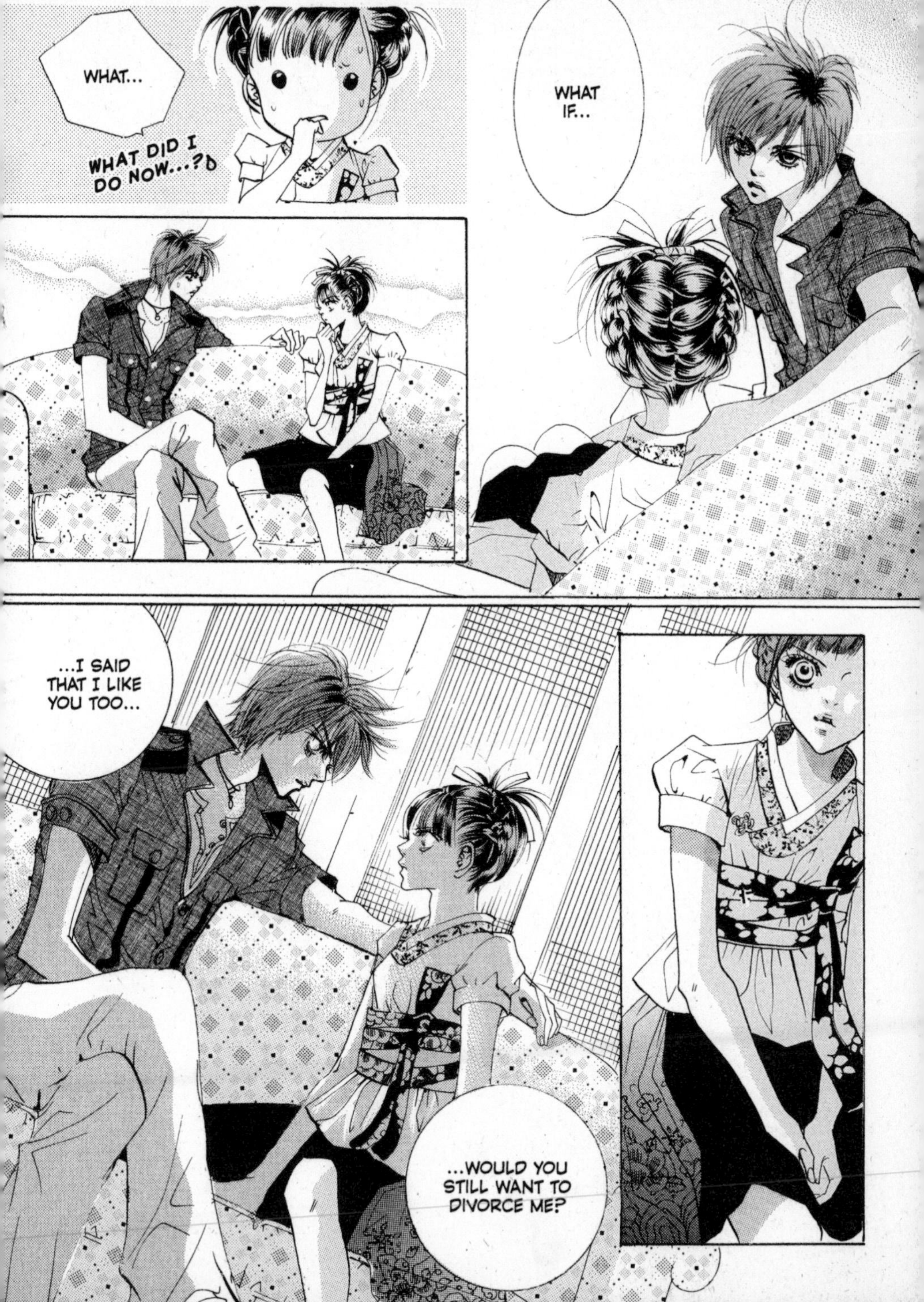
WHAT...
WHAT DID I DO NOW...?
WHAT IF...
...I SAID THAT I LIKE YOU TOO...
...WOULD YOU STILL WANT TO DIVORCE ME?

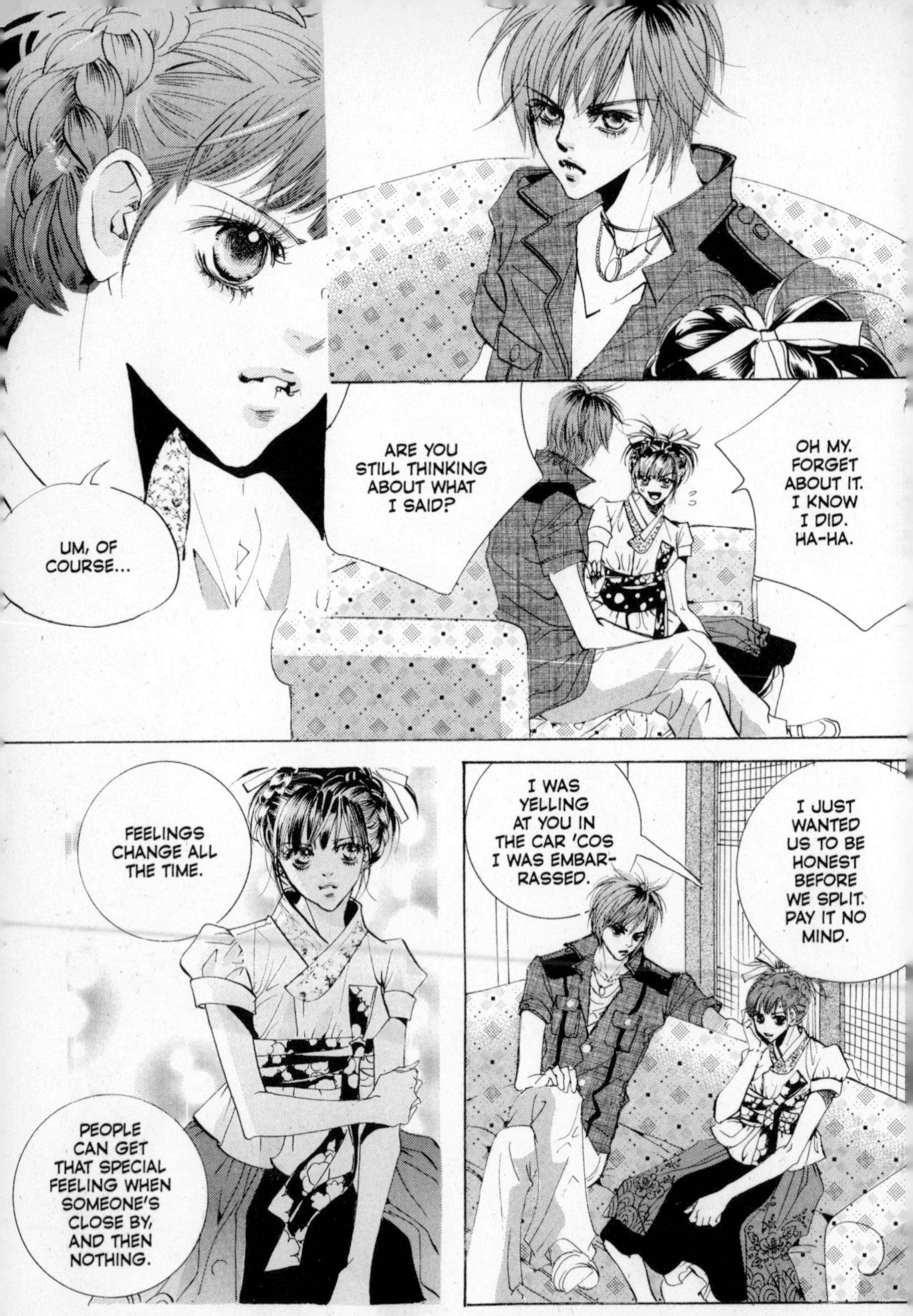
UM, OF COURSE...
ARE YOU STILL THINKING ABOUT WHAT I SAID?
OH MY. FORGET ABOUT IT. I KNOW I DID. HA-HA.
FEELINGS CHANGE ALL THE TIME.
PEOPLE CAN GET THAT SPECIAL FEELING WHEN SOMEONE'S CLOSE BY, AND THEN NOTHING.
I WAS YELLING AT YOU IN THE CAR 'COS I WAS EMBAR-RASSED.
I JUST WANTED US TO BE HONEST BEFORE WE SPLIT. PAY IT NO MIND.

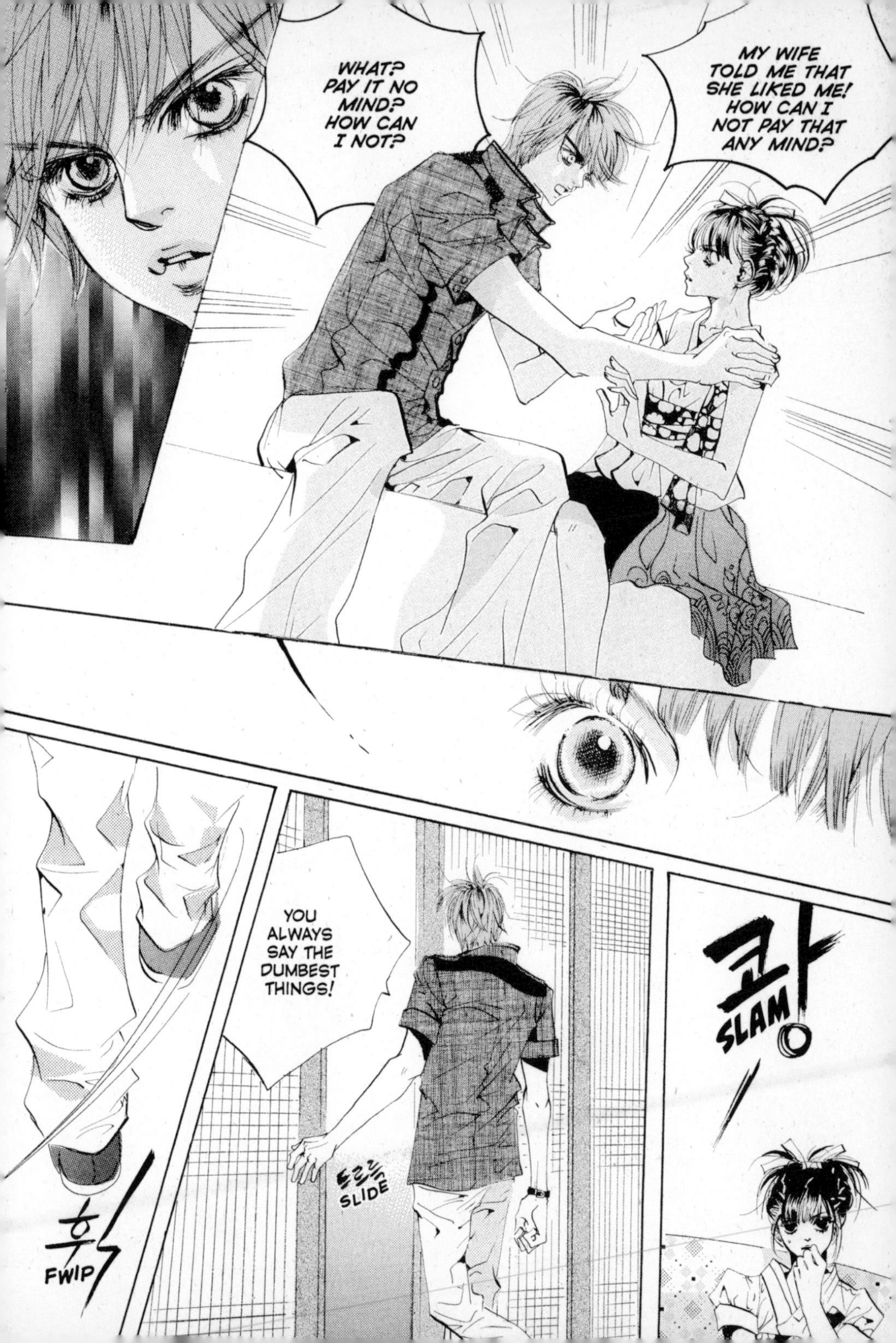
WHAT? PAY IT NO MIND? HOW CAN I NOT?
MY WIFE TOLD ME THAT SHE LIKED ME! HOW CAN I NOT PAY THAT ANY MIND?
FWIP
YOU ALWAYS SAY THE DUMBEST THINGS!
SLIDE
쾅
SLAM

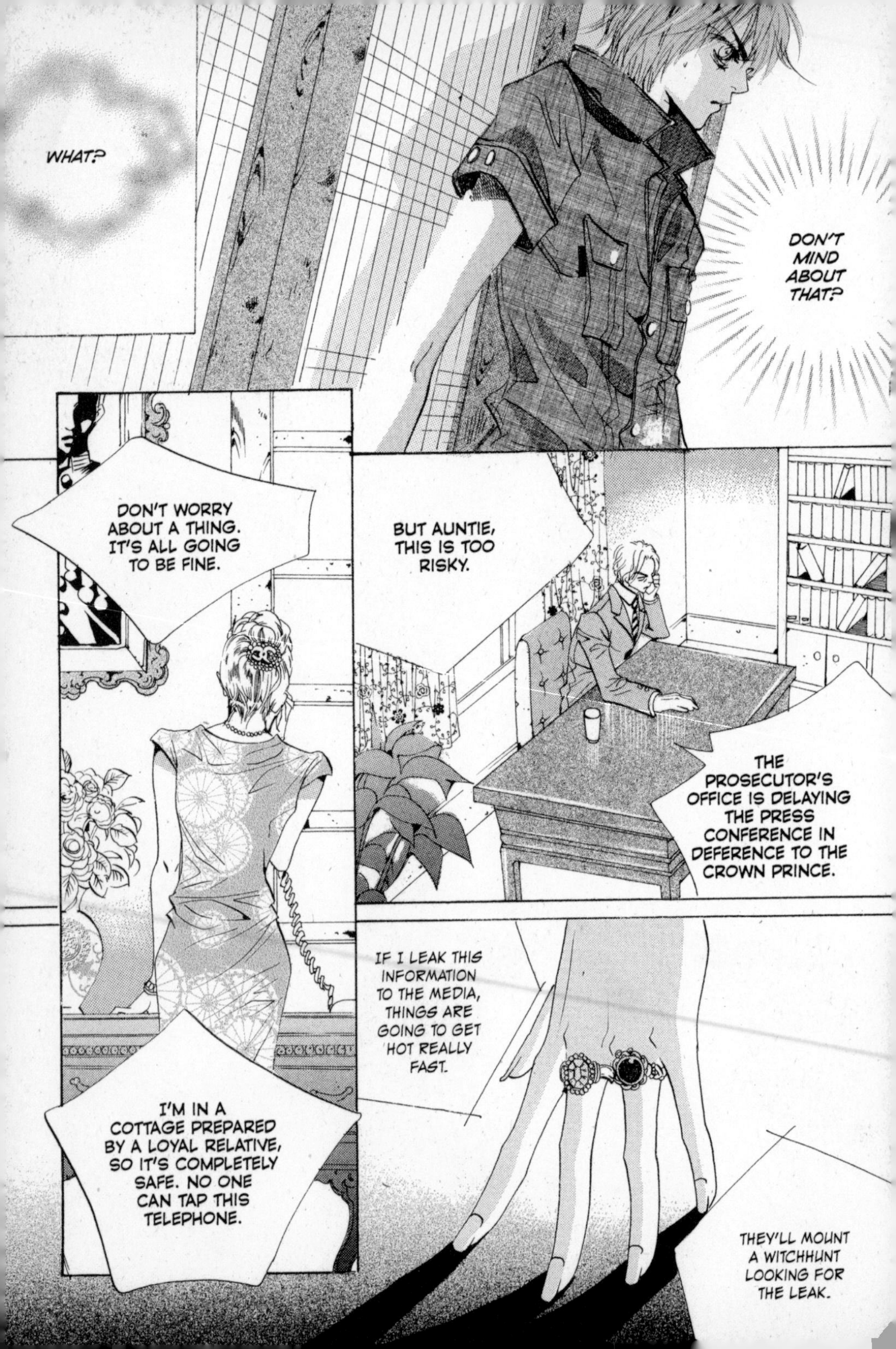
WHAT?
DON'T MIND ABOUT THAT?
DON'T WORRY ABOUT A THING. IT'S ALL GOING TO BE FINE.
I'M IN A COTTAGE PREPARED BY A LOYAL RELATIVE, SO IT'S COMPLETELY SAFE. NO ONE CAN TAP THIS TELEPHONE.
BUT AUNTIE, THIS IS TOO RISKY.
THE PROSECUTOR'S OFFICE IS DELAYING THE PRESS CONFERENCE IN DEFERENCE TO THE CROWN PRINCE.
IF I LEAK THIS INFORMATION TO THE MEDIA, THINGS ARE GOING TO GET HOT REALLY FAST.
THEY'LL MOUNT A WITCHHUNT LOOKING FOR THE LEAK.

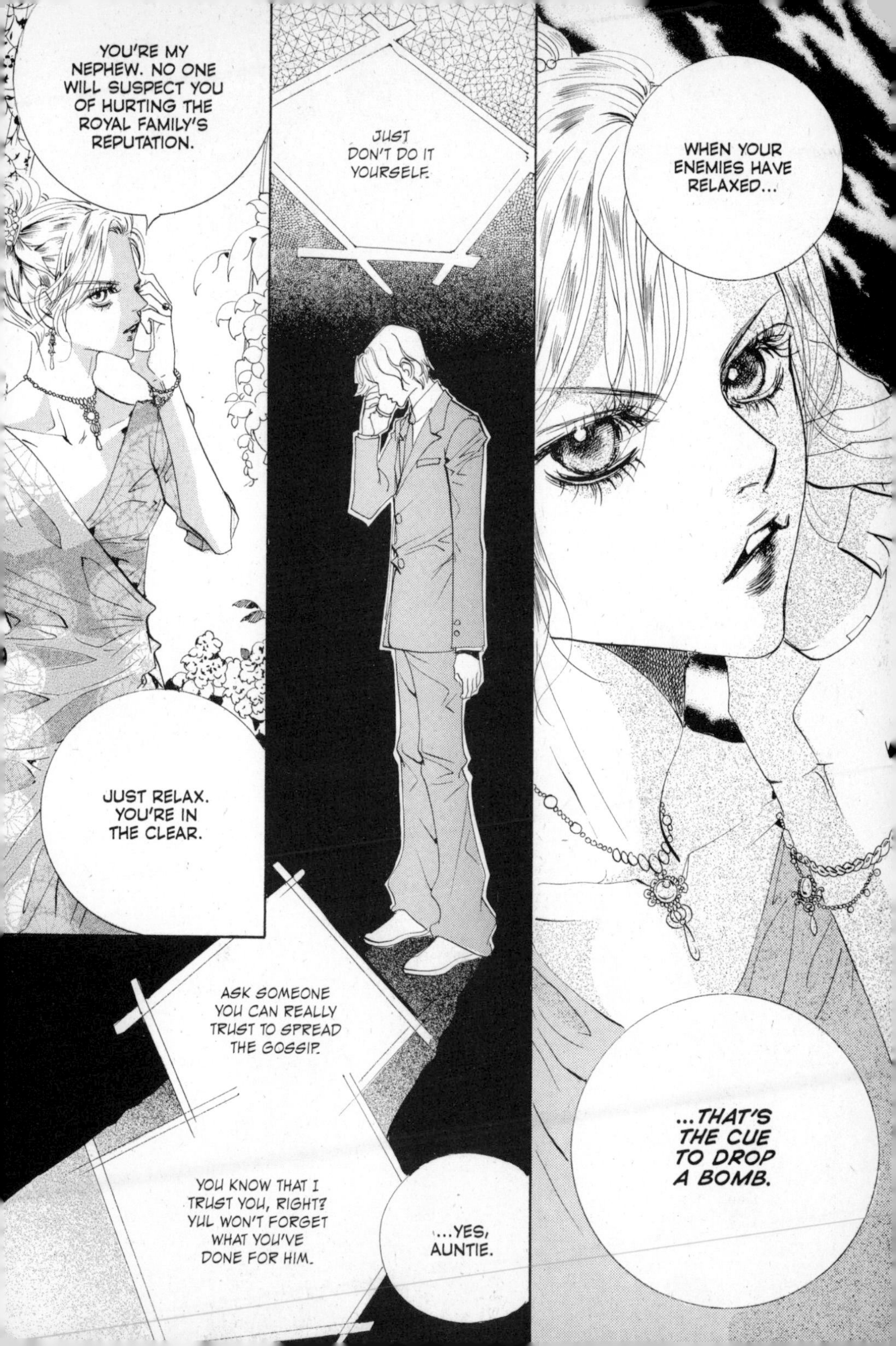
YOU'RE MY NEPHEW. NO ONE WILL SUSPECT YOU OF HURTING THE ROYAL FAMILY'S REPUTATION.
JUST RELAX. YOU'RE IN THE CLEAR.
JUST DON'T DO IT YOURSELF.
ASK SOMEONE YOU CAN REALLY TRUST TO SPREAD THE GOSSIP.
YOU KNOW THAT I TRUST YOU, RIGHT? YUL WON'T FORGET WHAT YOU'VE DONE FOR HIM.
...YES, AUNTIE.
WHEN YOUR ENEMIES HAVE RELAXED...
...THAT'S THE CUE TO DROP A BOMB.

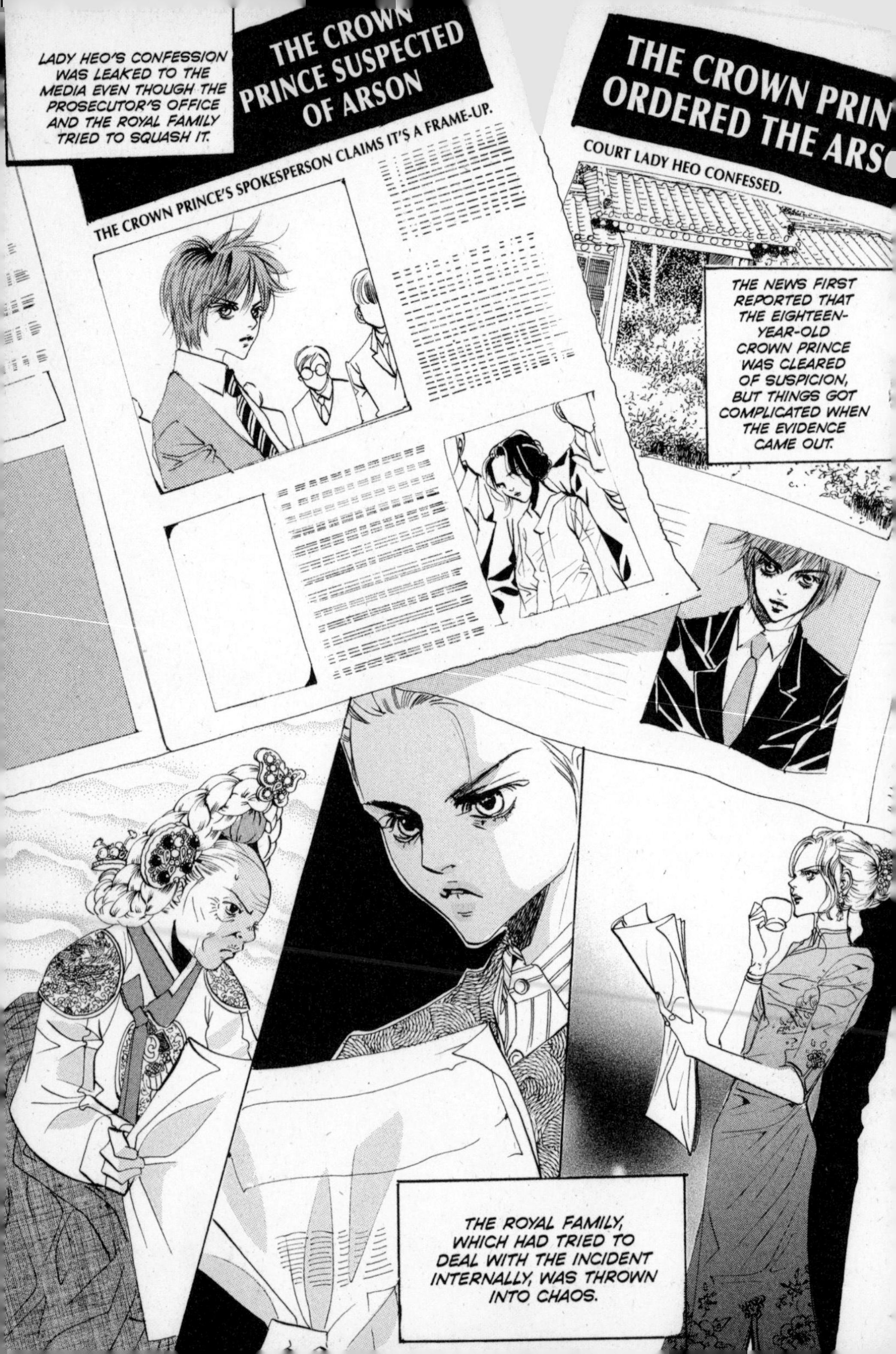
LADY HEO'S CONFESSION WAS LEAKED TO THE MEDIA EVEN THOUGH THE PROSECUTOR'S OFFICE AND THE ROYAL FAMILY TRIED TO SQUASH IT.
THE CROWN PRINCE SUSPECTED OF ARSON
THE CROWN PRINCE'S SPOKESPERSON CLAIMS IT'S A FRAME-UP.
THE CROWN PRIN
ORDERED THE ARSO
COURT LADY HEO CONFESSED.
THE NEWS FIRST REPORTED THAT THE EIGHTEEN-YEAR-OLD CROWN PRINCE WAS CLEARED OF SUSPICION, BUT THINGS GOT COMPLICATED WHEN THE EVIDENCE CAME OUT.
THE ROYAL FAMILY, WHICH HAD TRIED TO DEAL WITH THE INCIDENT INTERNALLY, WAS THROWN INTO CHAOS.

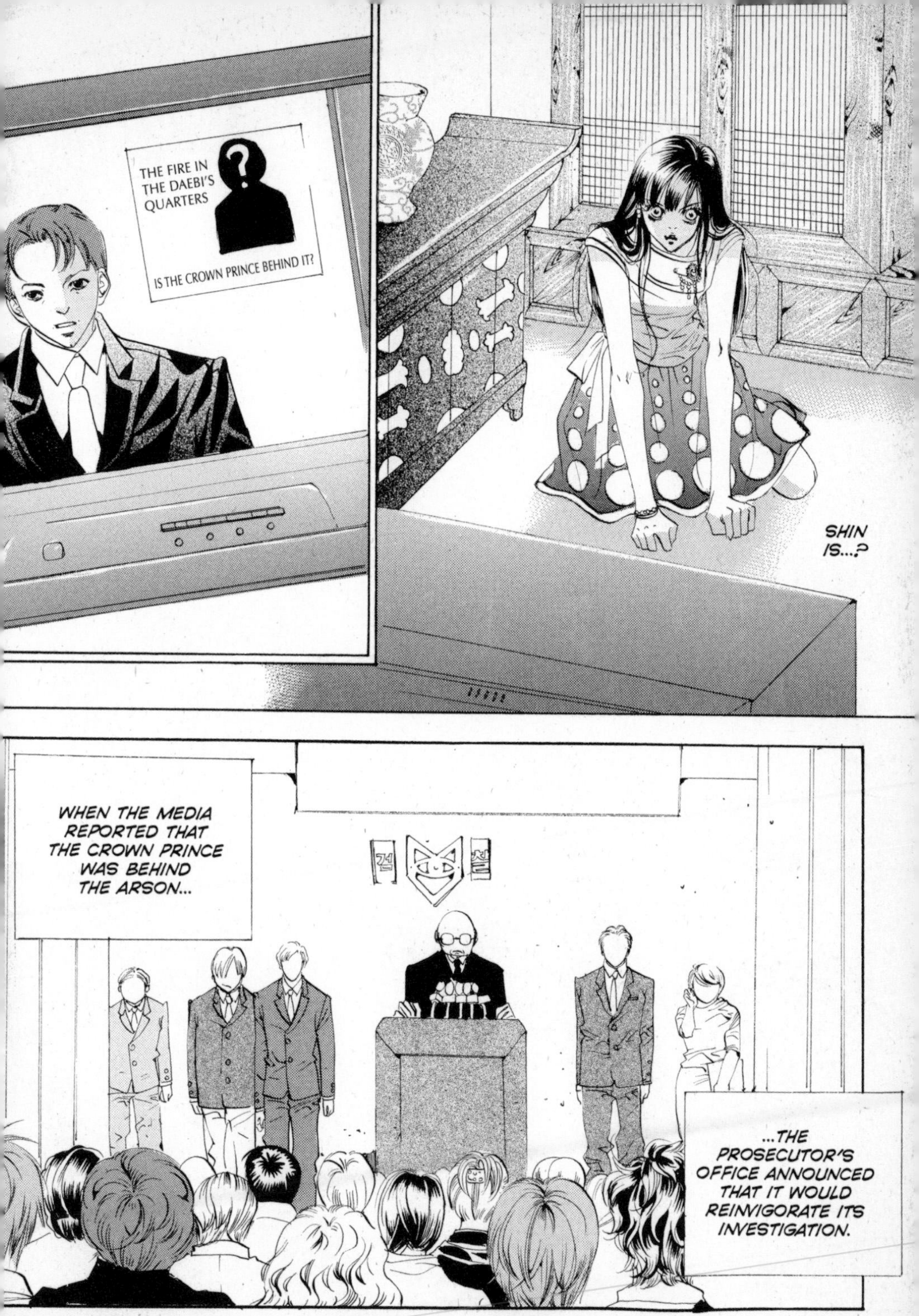
THE FIRE IN THE DAEBI'S QUARTERS
IS THE CROWN PRINCE BEHIND IT?
SHIN IS...?
WHEN THE MEDIA REPORTED THAT THE CROWN PRINCE WAS BEHIND THE ARSON...
...THE PROSECUTOR'S OFFICE ANNOUNCED THAT IT WOULD REINVIGORATE ITS INVESTIGATION.

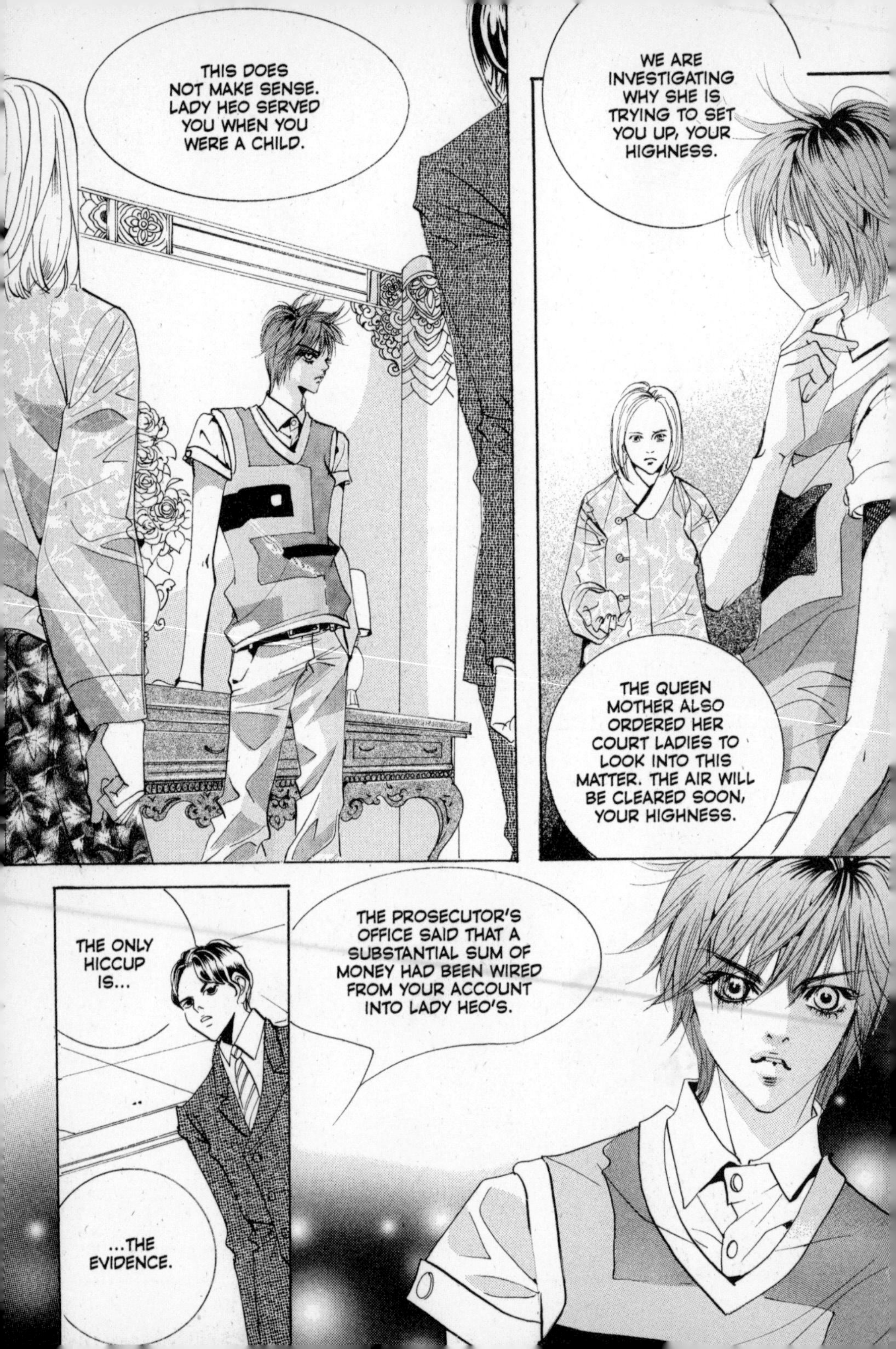
THIS DOES NOT MAKE SENSE. LADY HEO SERVED YOU WHEN YOU WERE A CHILD.
WE ARE INVESTIGATING WHY SHE IS TRYING TO SET YOU UP, YOUR HIGHNESS.
THE QUEEN MOTHER ALSO ORDERED HER COURT LADIES TO LOOK INTO THIS MATTER. THE AIR WILL BE CLEARED SOON, YOUR HIGHNESS.
THE ONLY HICCUP IS...
...THE EVIDENCE.
THE PROSECUTOR'S OFFICE SAID THAT A SUBSTANTIAL SUM OF MONEY HAD BEEN WIRED FROM YOUR ACCOUNT INTO LADY HEO'S.

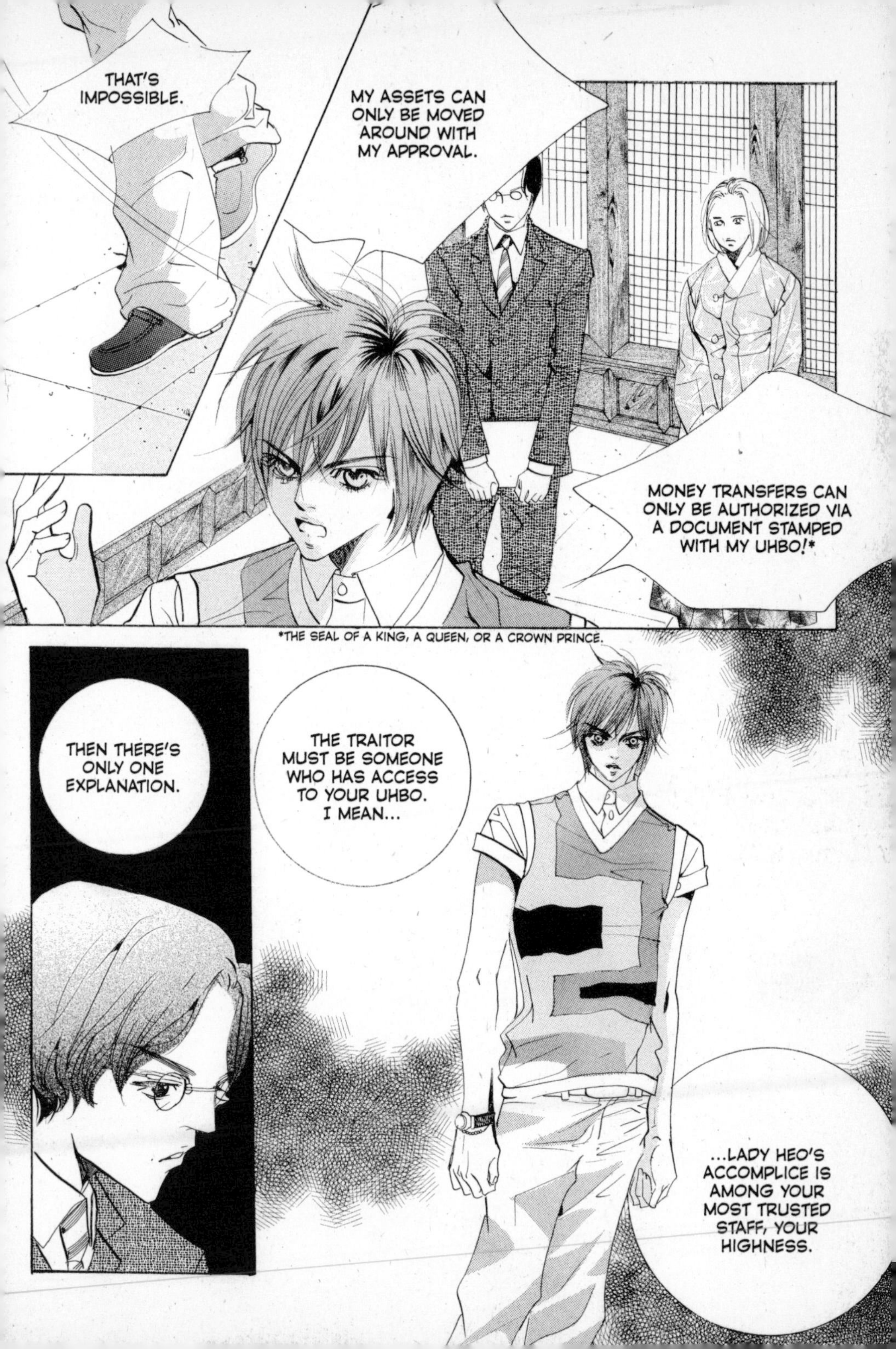
THAT'S IMPOSSIBLE.
MY ASSETS CAN ONLY BE MOVED AROUND WITH MY APPROVAL.
MONEY TRANSFERS CAN ONLY BE AUTHORIZED VIA A DOCUMENT STAMPED WITH MY UHBO!*
*THE SEAL OF A KING, A QUEEN, OR A CROWN PRINCE.
THEN THERE'S ONLY ONE EXPLANATION.
THE TRAITOR MUST BE SOMEONE WHO HAS ACCESS TO YOUR UHBO. I MEAN...
...LADY HEO'S ACCOMPLICE IS AMONG YOUR MOST TRUSTED STAFF, YOUR HIGHNESS.

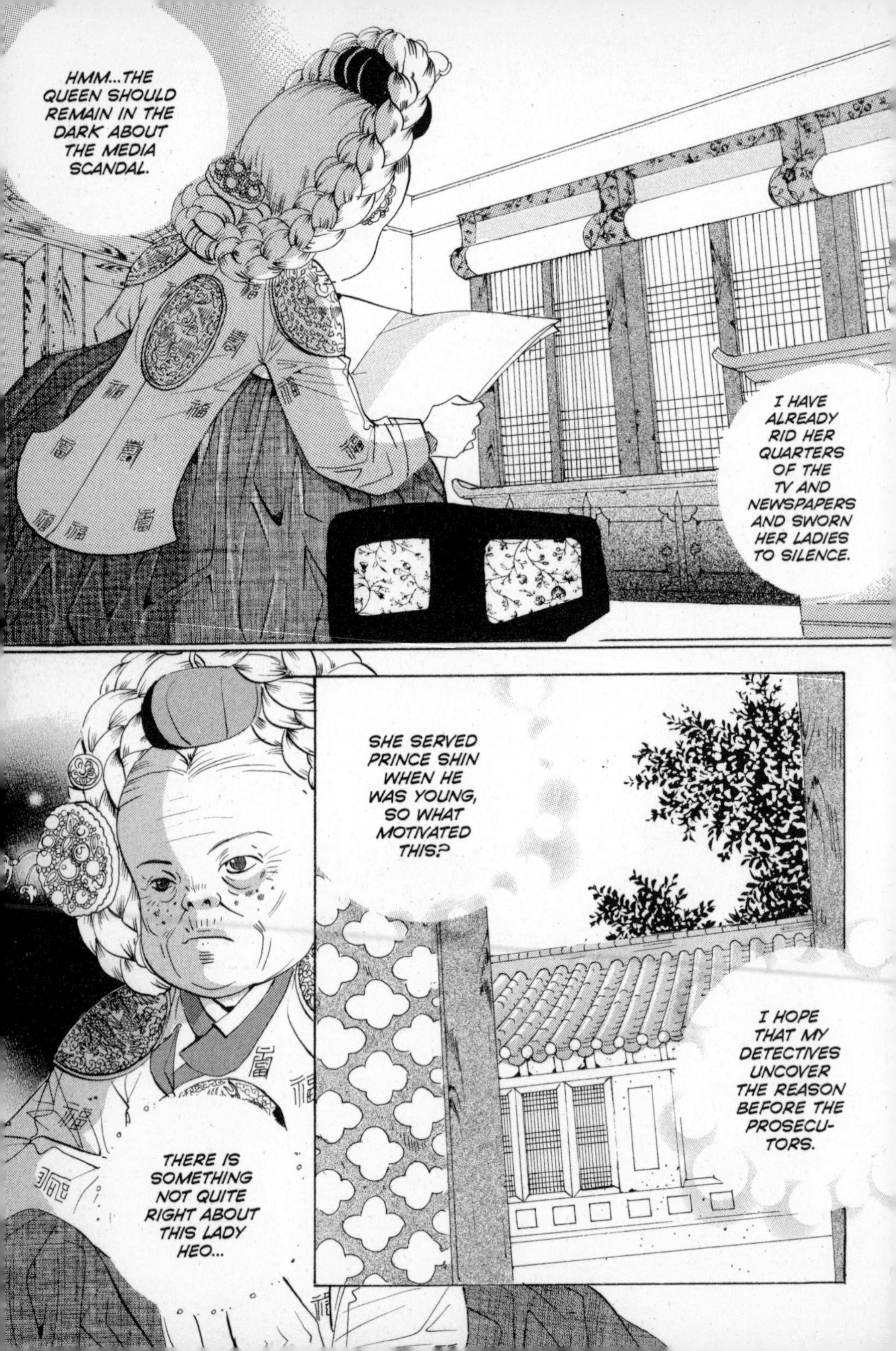
HMM...THE QUEEN SHOULD REMAIN IN THE DARK ABOUT THE MEDIA SCANDAL.
I HAVE ALREADY RID HER QUARTERS OF THE TV AND NEWSPAPERS AND SWORN HER LADIES TO SILENCE.
THERE IS SOMETHING NOT QUITE RIGHT ABOUT THIS LADY HEO...
SHE SERVED PRINCE SHIN WHEN HE WAS YOUNG, SO WHAT MOTIVATED THIS?
I HOPE THAT MY DETECTIVES UNCOVER THE REASON BEFORE THE PROSECU-TORS.

I AM THE ONLY ONE WHO CAN PROTECT THE CROWN PRINCE NOW.

BUT THE DAEBI AND THE QUEEN MOTHER ARE NOT ALLOWED TO USE THEIR POWER EXCEPT IN AN EMERGENCY...

...LIKE THE DEATH OF A KING.

BUT MANY DAEBI'S EMPLOY THEIR POWER UNDER A KING'S KIND APPROVAL.

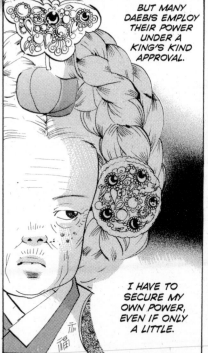

I HAVE TO SECURE MY OWN POWER, EVEN IF ONLY A LITTLE.

AND I WILL HAVE TO FIND A WAY TO SAVE THE CROWN PRINCE.

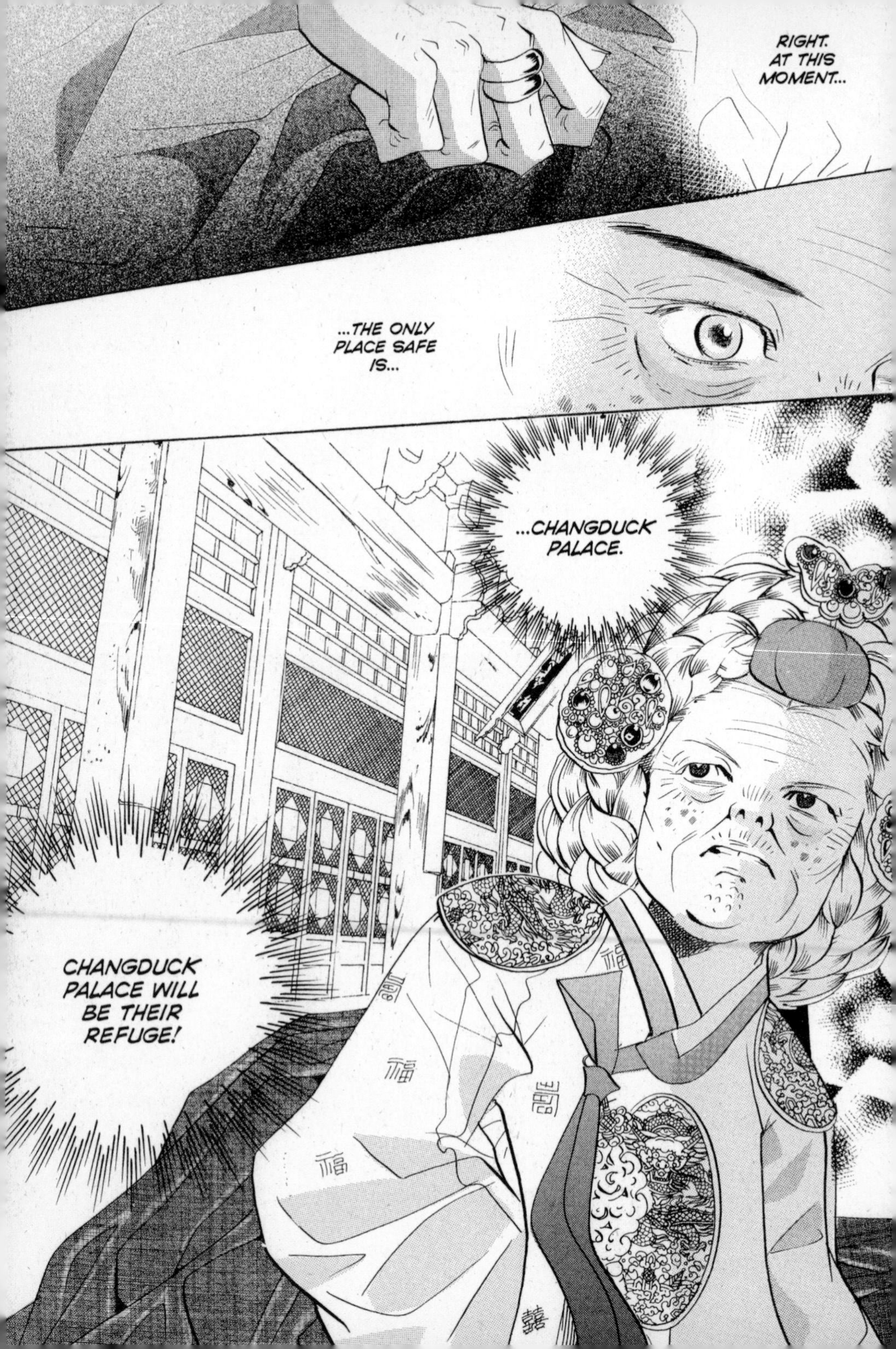
RIGHT. AT THIS MOMENT...
...THE ONLY PLACE SAFE IS...
...CHANGDUCK PALACE.
CHANGDUCK PALACE WILL BE THEIR REFUGE!
福
福
福

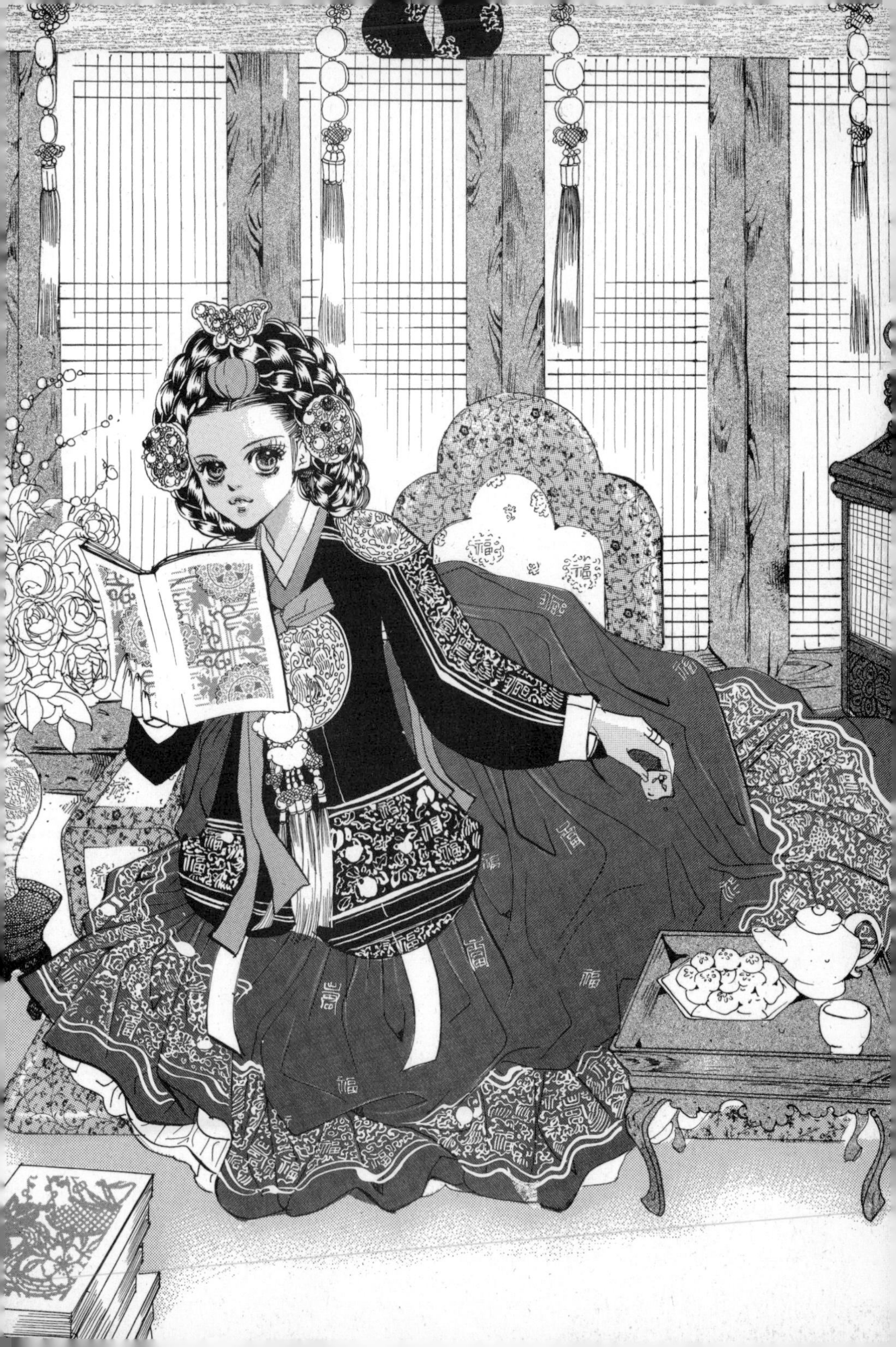

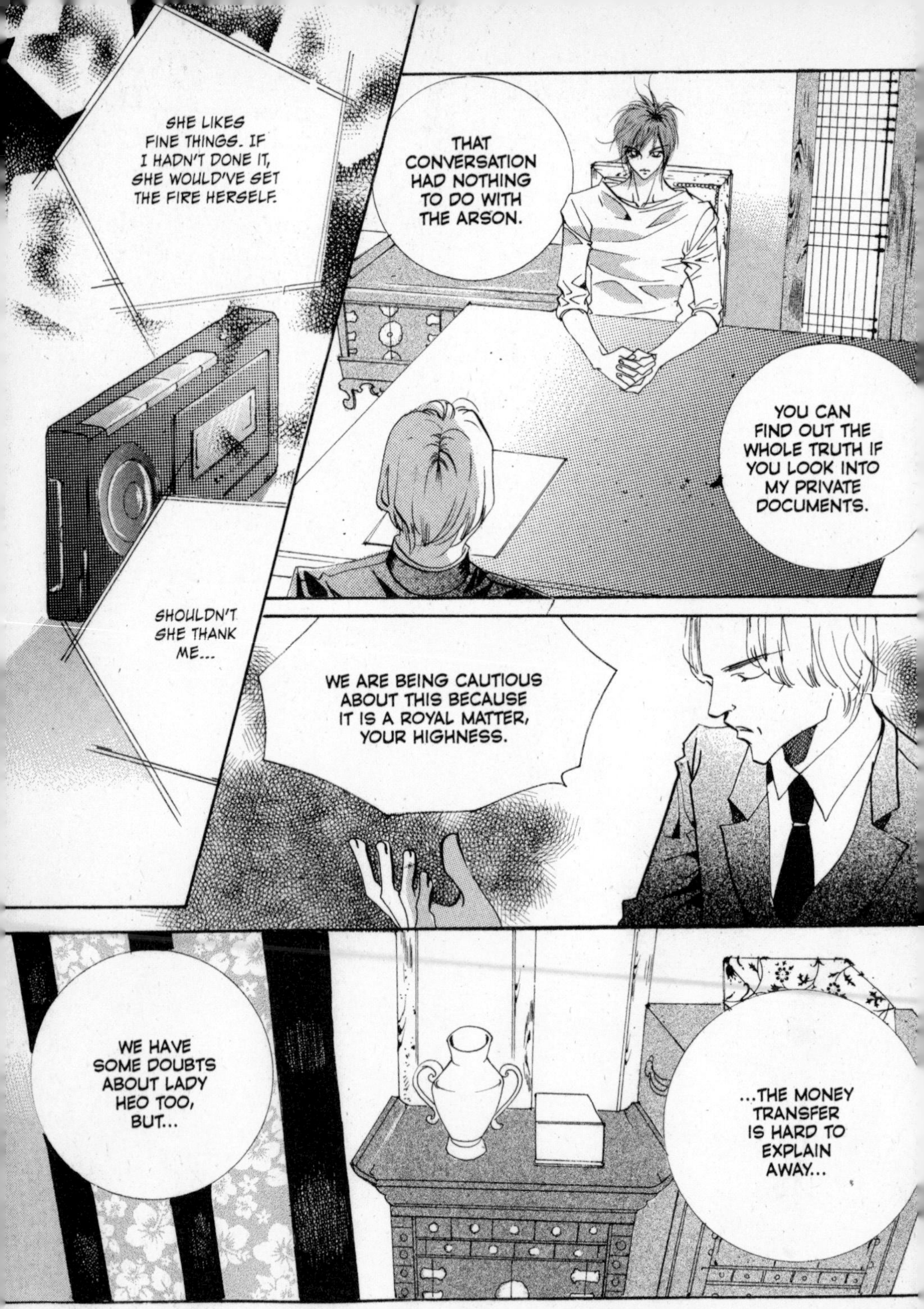
SHE LIKES FINE THINGS. IF I HADN'T DONE IT, SHE WOULD'VE SET THE FIRE HERSELF.
SHOULDN'T SHE THANK ME...
THAT CONVERSATION HAD NOTHING TO DO WITH THE ARSON.
YOU CAN FIND OUT THE WHOLE TRUTH IF YOU LOOK INTO MY PRIVATE DOCUMENTS.
WE ARE BEING CAUTIOUS ABOUT THIS BECAUSE IT IS A ROYAL MATTER, YOUR HIGHNESS.
WE HAVE SOME DOUBTS ABOUT LADY HEO TOO, BUT...
...THE MONEY TRANSFER IS HARD TO EXPLAIN AWAY...

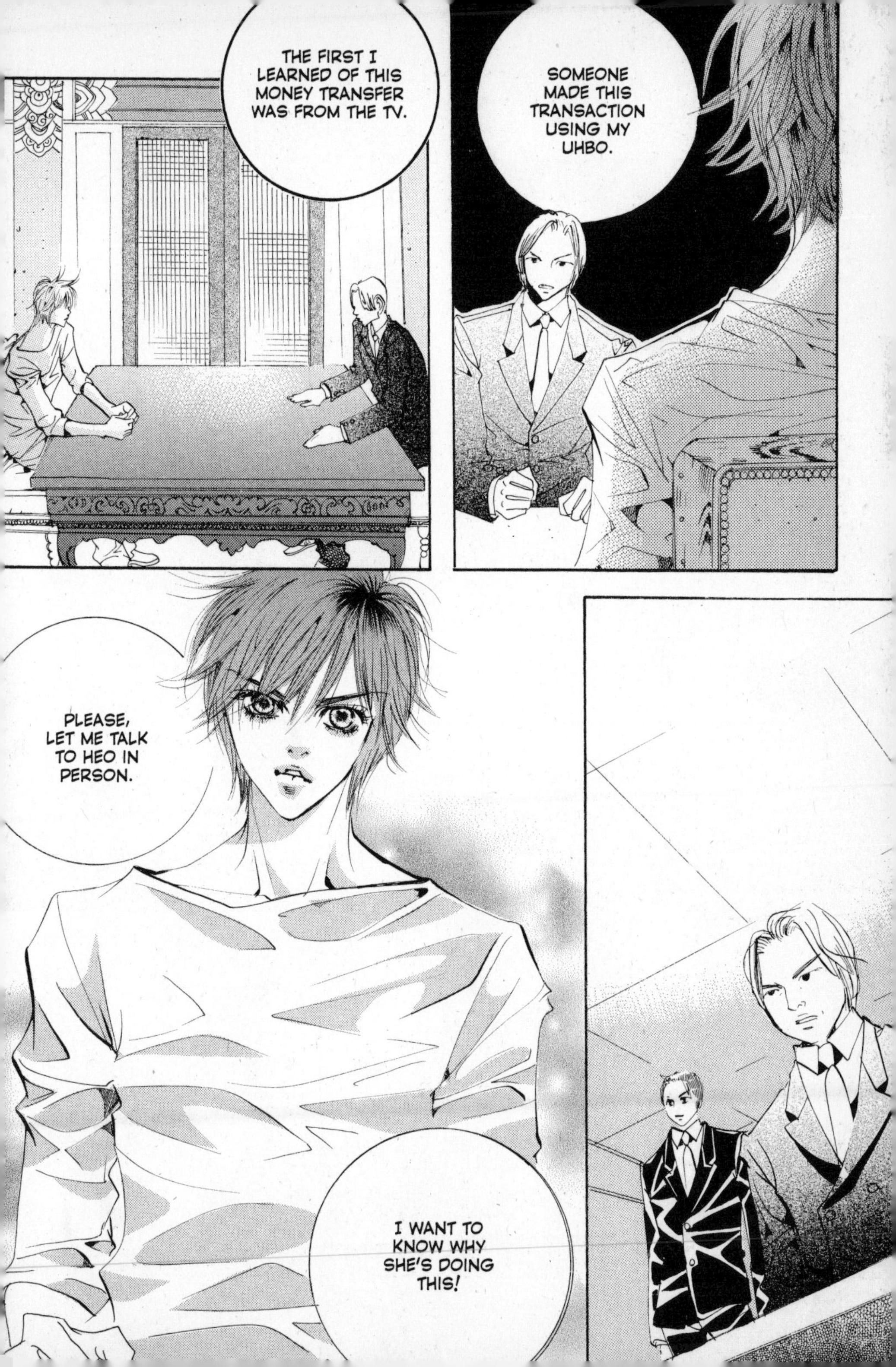
THE FIRST I LEARNED OF THIS MONEY TRANSFER WAS FROM THE TV.
SOMEONE MADE THIS TRANSACTION USING MY UHBO.
PLEASE, LET ME TALK TO HEO IN PERSON.
I WANT TO KNOW WHY SHE'S DOING THIS!

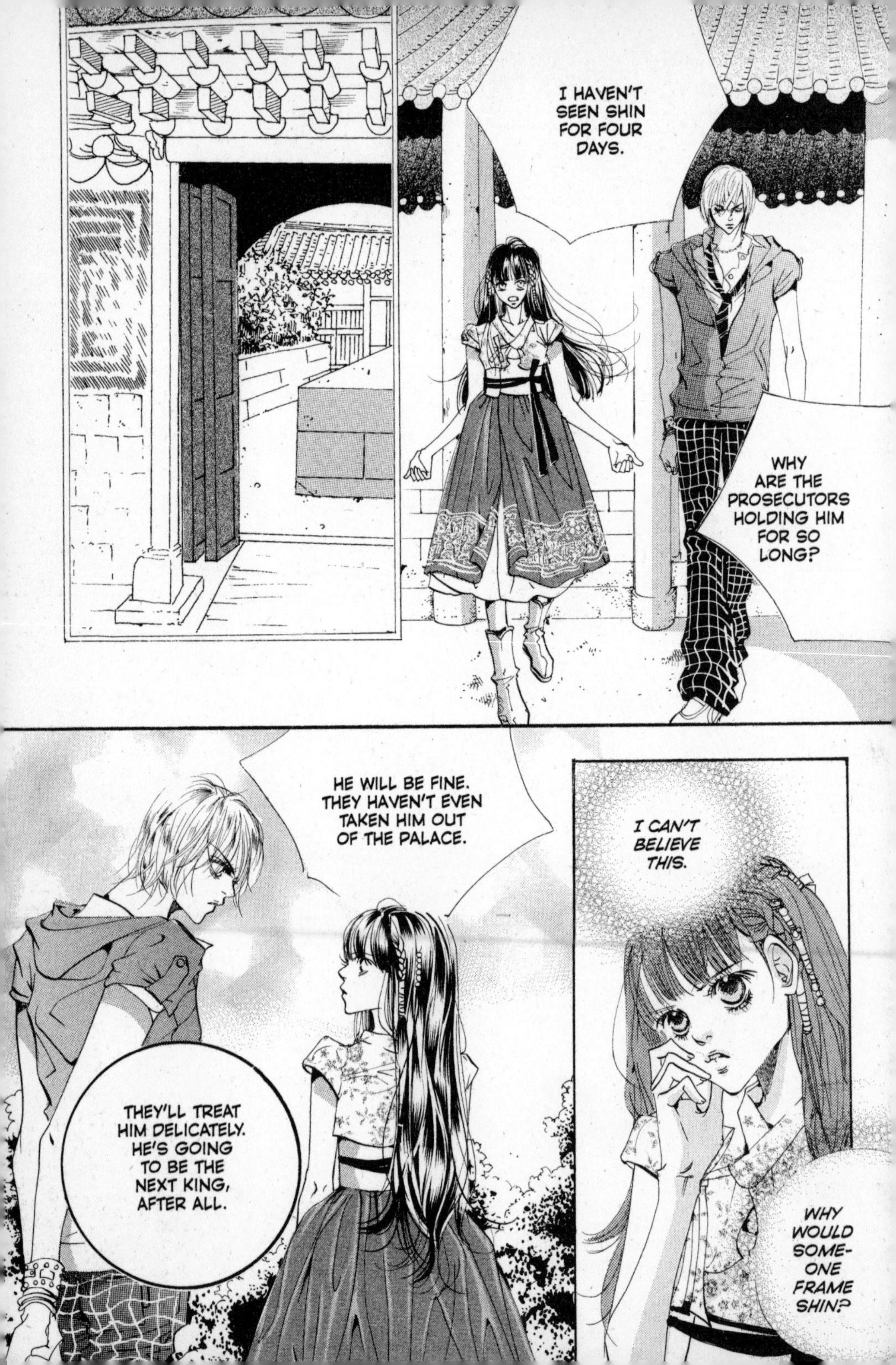

I HAVEN'T SEEN SHIN FOR FOUR DAYS.
WHY ARE THE PROSECUTORS HOLDING HIM FOR SO LONG?
HE WILL BE FINE. THEY HAVEN'T EVEN TAKEN HIM OUT OF THE PALACE.
THEY'LL TREAT HIM DELICATELY. HE'S GOING TO BE THE NEXT KING, AFTER ALL.
I CAN'T BELIEVE THIS.
WHY WOULD SOME-ONE FRAME SHIN?

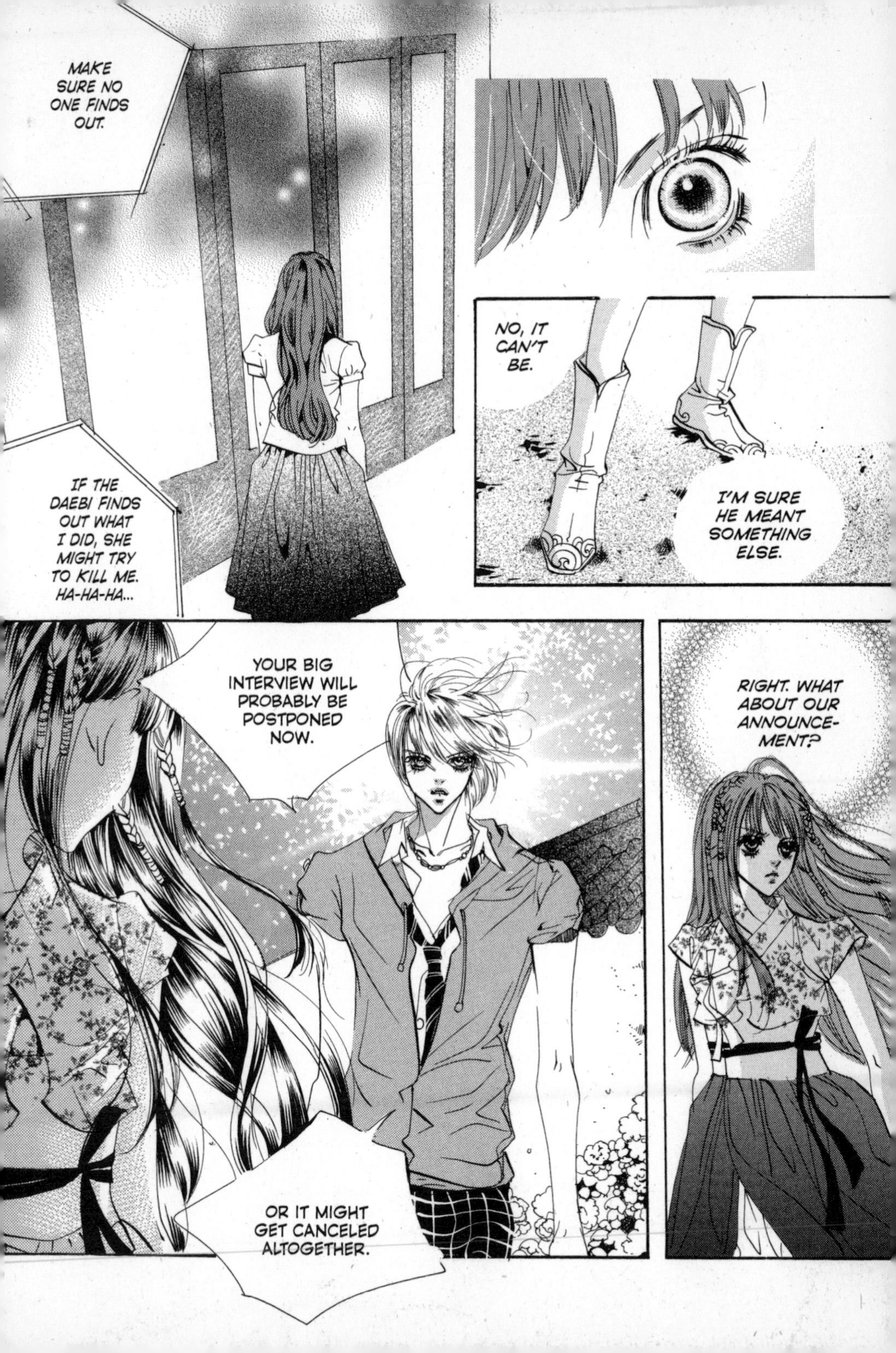
MAKE SURE NO ONE FINDS OUT.
IF THE DAEBI FINDS OUT WHAT I DID, SHE MIGHT TRY TO KILL ME. HA-HA-HA...
NO, IT CAN'T BE.
I'M SURE HE MEANT SOMETHING ELSE.
YOUR BIG INTERVIEW WILL PROBABLY BE POSTPONED NOW.
OR IT MIGHT GET CANCELED ALTOGETHER.
RIGHT. WHAT ABOUT OUR ANNOUNCE-MENT?

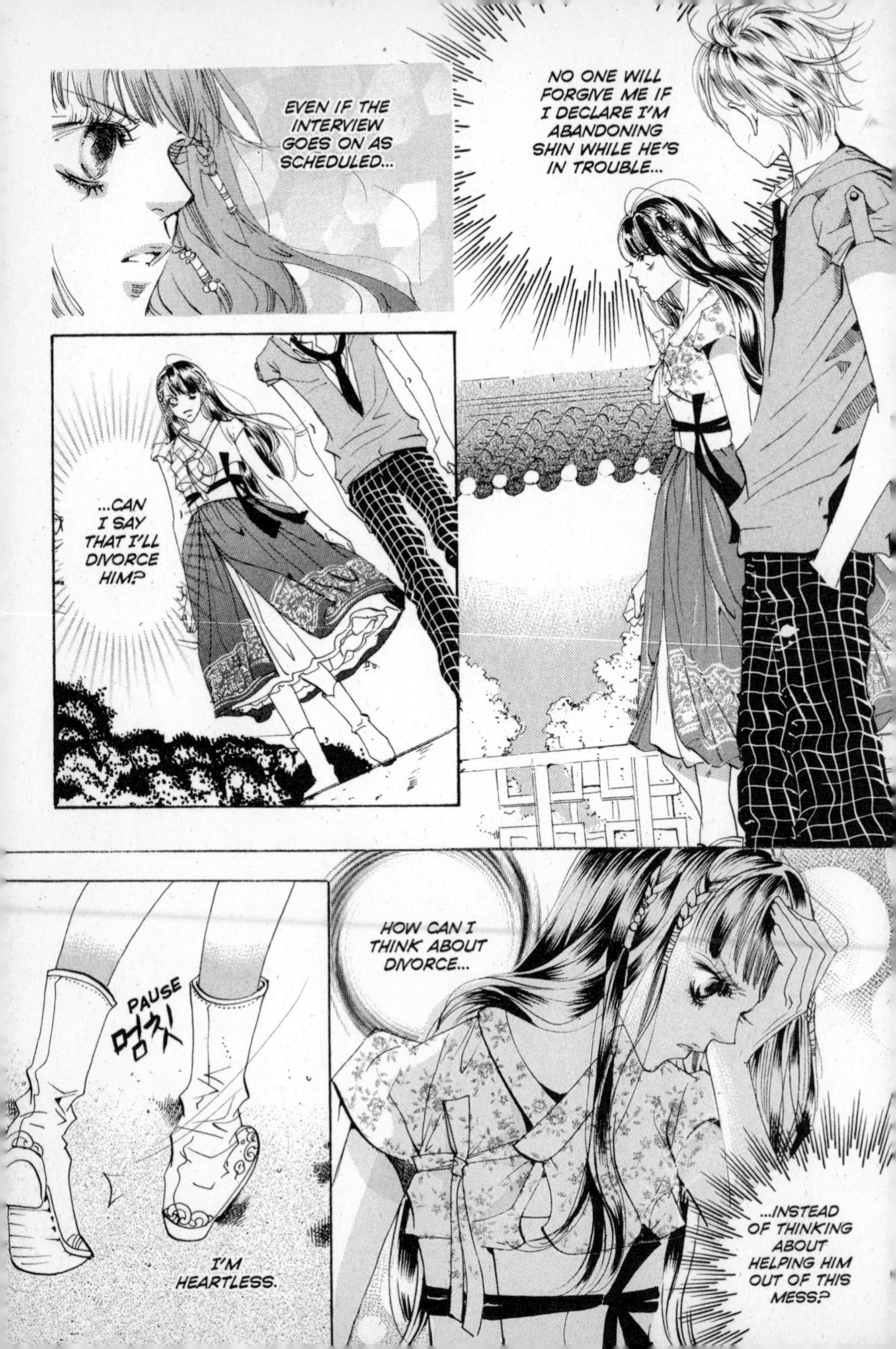
EVEN IF THE INTERVIEW GOES ON AS SCHEDULED...
NO ONE WILL FORGIVE ME IF I DECLARE I'M ABANDONING SHIN WHILE HE'S IN TROUBLE...
...CAN I SAY THAT I'LL DIVORCE HIM?
PAUSE
멈칫
I'M HEARTLESS.
HOW CAN I THINK ABOUT DIVORCE...
...INSTEAD OF THINKING ABOUT HELPING HIM OUT OF THIS MESS?

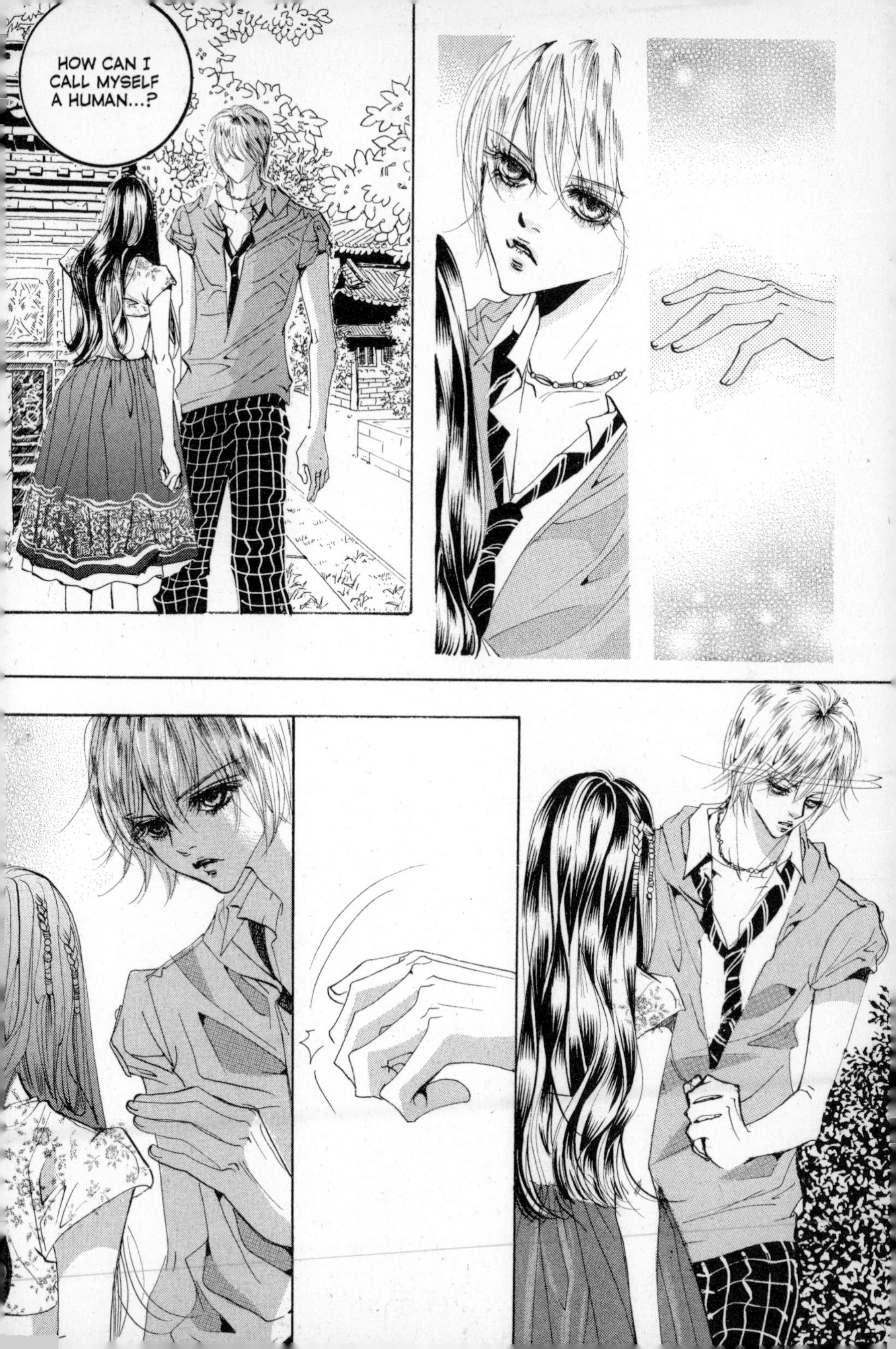
HOW CAN I CALL MYSELF A HUMAN...?

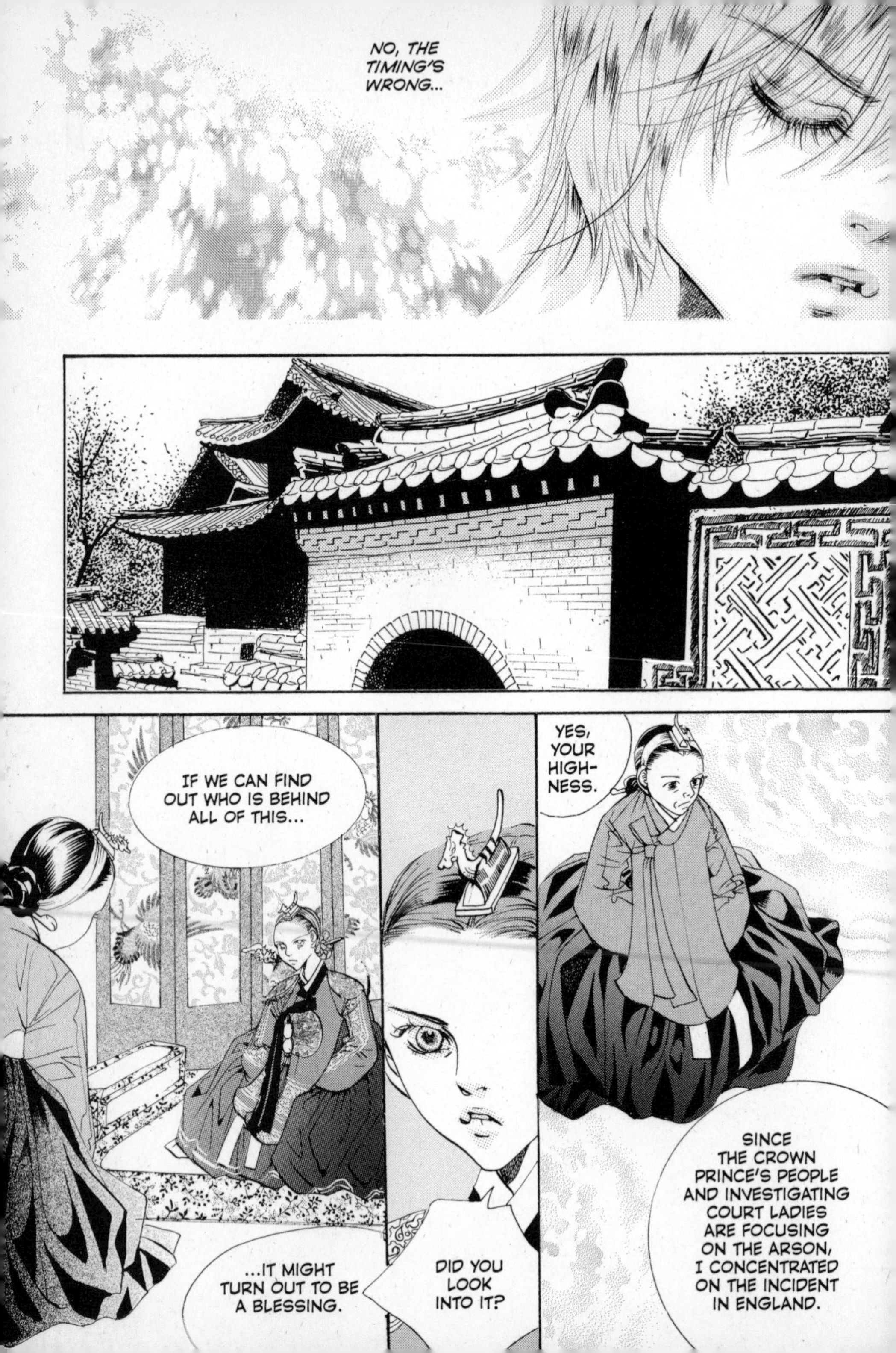
NO, THE TIMING'S WRONG...
IF WE CAN FIND OUT WHO IS BEHIND ALL OF THIS...
...IT MIGHT TURN OUT TO BE A BLESSING.
DID YOU LOOK INTO IT?
YES, YOUR HIGH-NESS.
SINCE THE CROWN PRINCE'S PEOPLE AND INVESTIGATING COURT LADIES ARE FOCUSING ON THE ARSON, I CONCENTRATED ON THE INCIDENT IN ENGLAND.

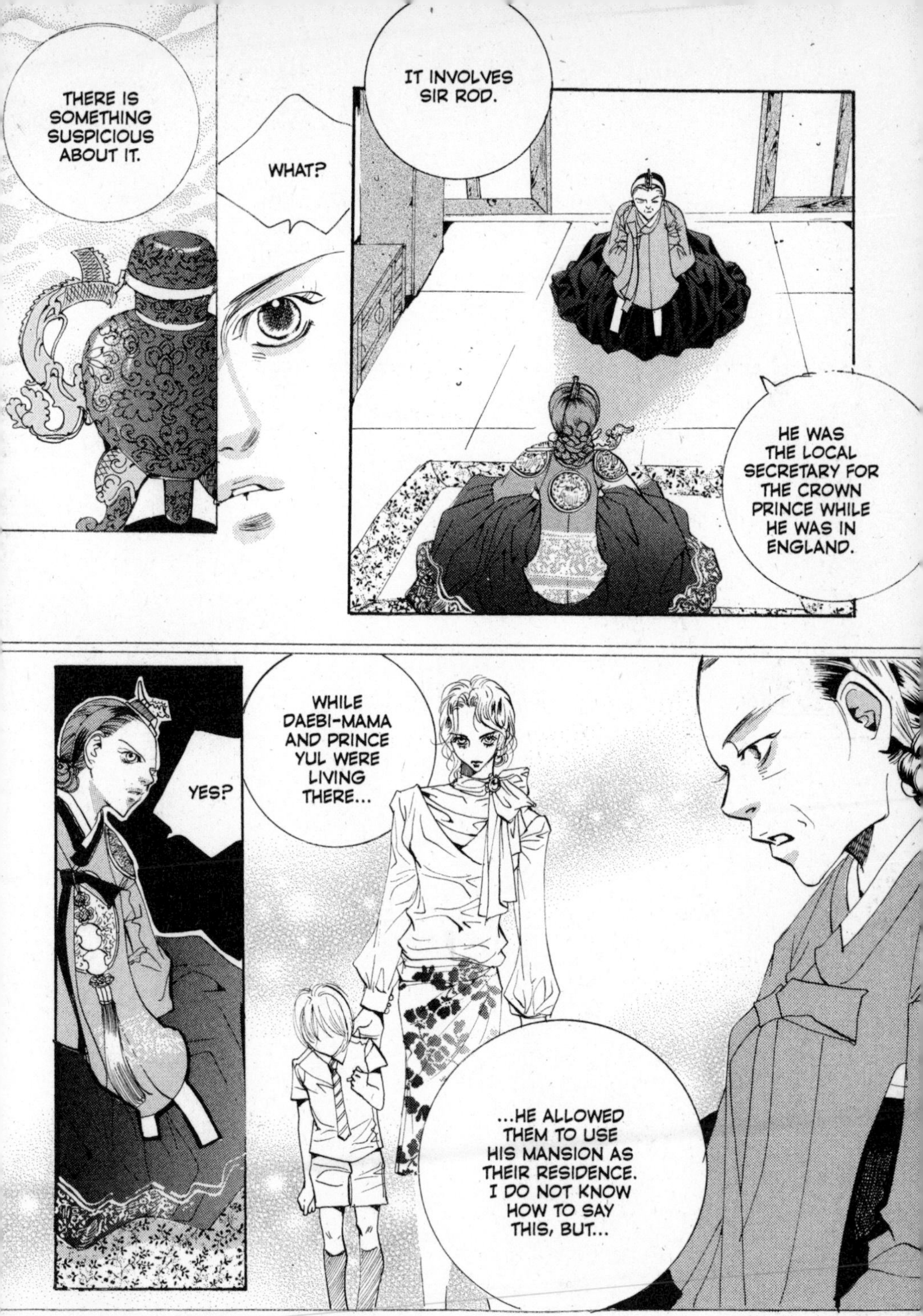
THERE IS SOMETHING SUSPICIOUS ABOUT IT.
WHAT?
IT INVOLVES SIR ROD.
HE WAS THE LOCAL SECRETARY FOR THE CROWN PRINCE WHILE HE WAS IN ENGLAND.
YES?
WHILE DAEBI-MAMA AND PRINCE YUL WERE LIVING THERE...
...HE ALLOWED THEM TO USE HIS MANSION AS THEIR RESIDENCE. I DO NOT KNOW HOW TO SAY THIS, BUT...

...THERE WAS A RUMOR AMONG MEMBERS OF THE ENGLISH UPPER CRUST THAT DAEBI-MAMA AND SIR ROD WERE LOVERS.

NO...!

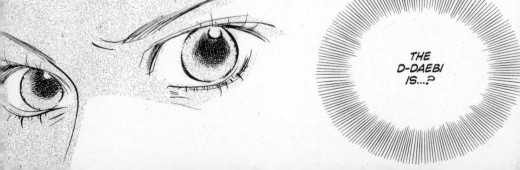

THE D-DAEBI IS...?

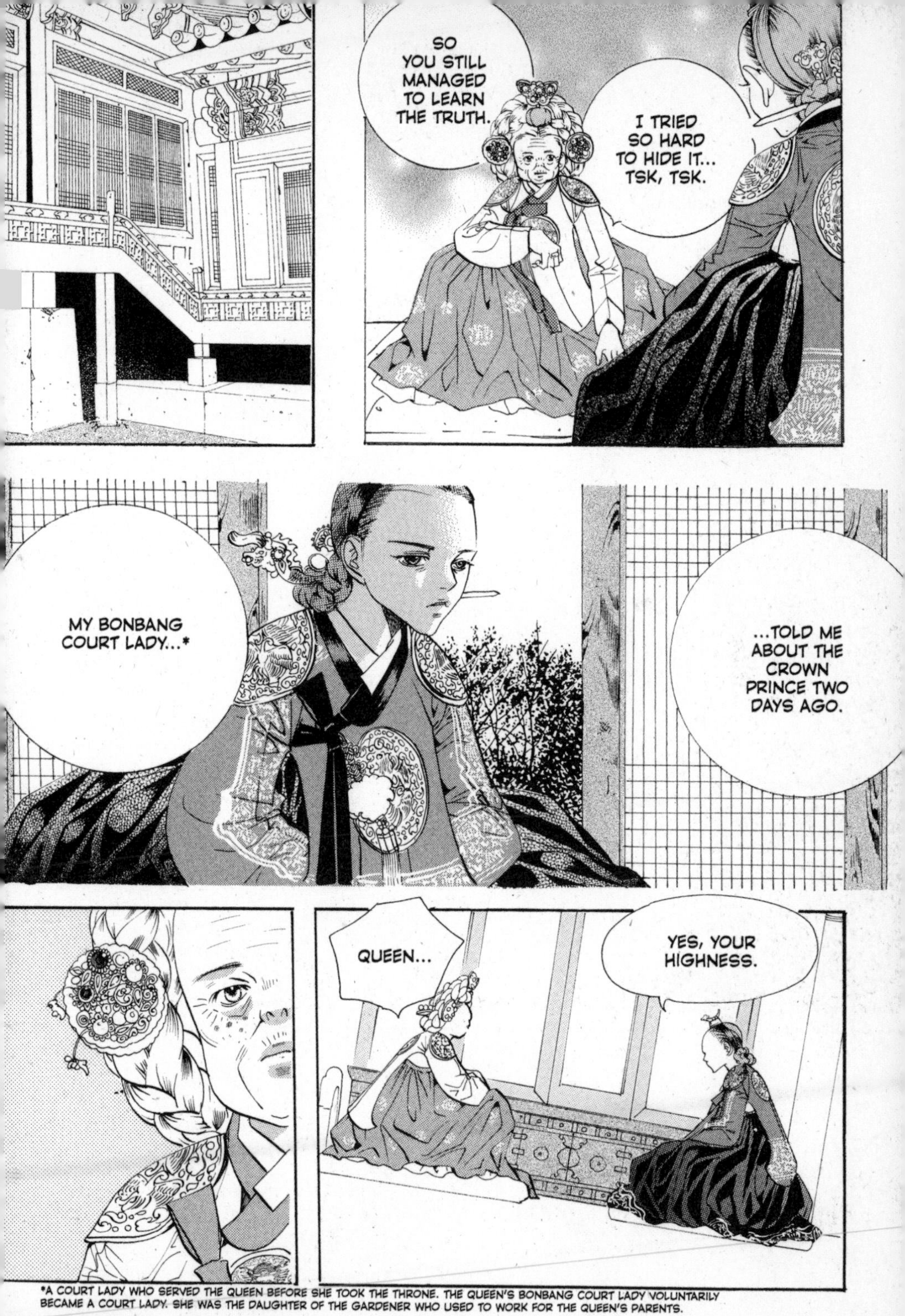
SO YOU STILL MANAGED TO LEARN THE TRUTH.
I TRIED SO HARD TO HIDE IT... TSK, TSK.
MY BONBANG COURT LADY...*
...TOLD ME ABOUT THE CROWN PRINCE TWO DAYS AGO.
QUEEN...
YES, YOUR HIGHNESS.

*A COURT LADY WHO SERVED THE QUEEN BEFORE SHE TOOK THE THRONE. THE QUEEN'S BONBANG COURT LADY VOLUNTARILY BECAME A COURT LADY. SHE WAS THE DAUGHTER OF THE GARDENER WHO USED TO WORK FOR THE QUEEN'S PARENTS.

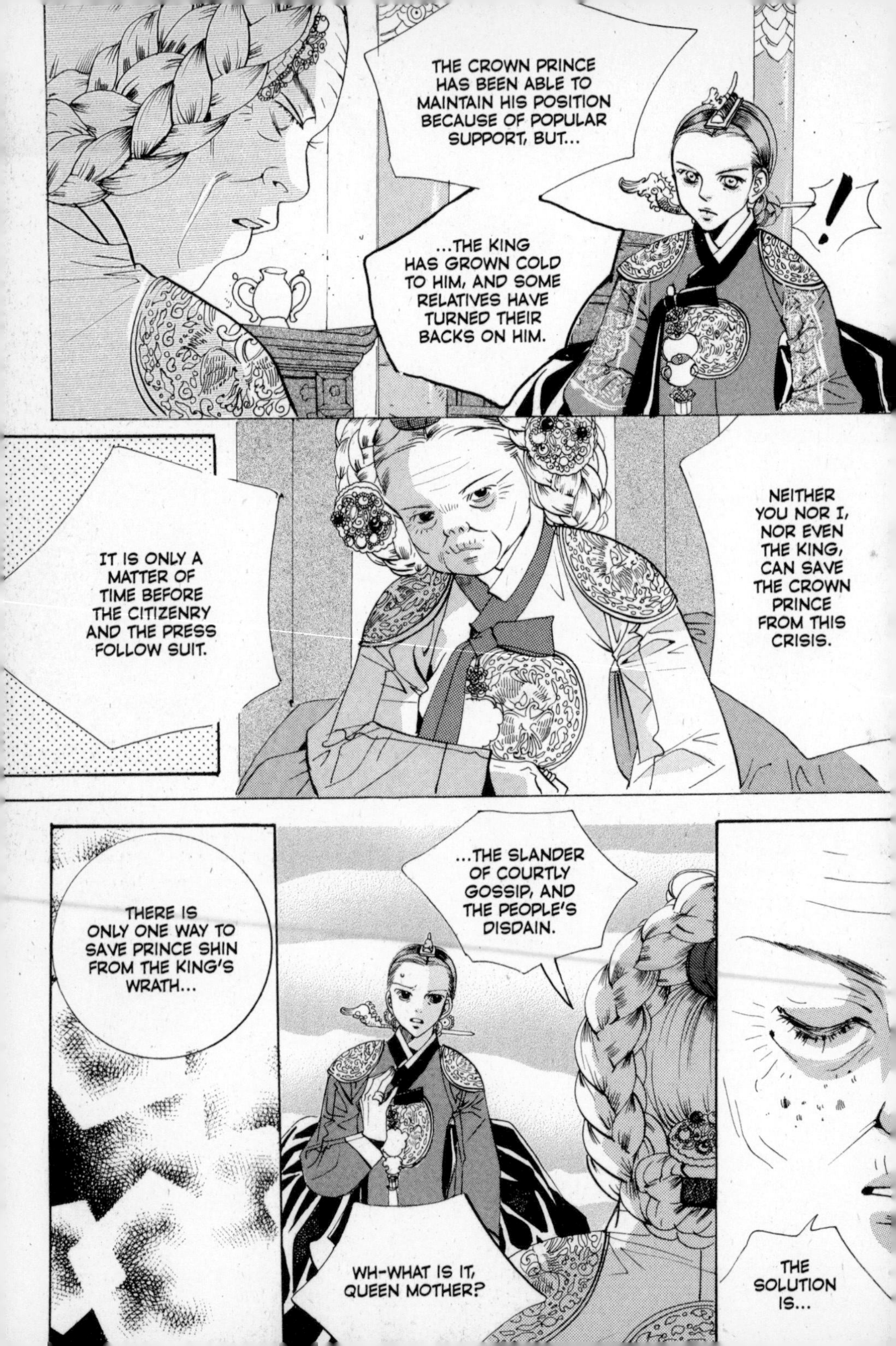
THE CROWN PRINCE HAS BEEN ABLE TO MAINTAIN HIS POSITION BECAUSE OF POPULAR SUPPORT, BUT...
...THE KING HAS GROWN COLD TO HIM, AND SOME RELATIVES HAVE TURNED THEIR BACKS ON HIM.
!
IT IS ONLY A MATTER OF TIME BEFORE THE CITIZENRY AND THE PRESS FOLLOW SUIT.
NEITHER YOU NOR I, NOR EVEN THE KING, CAN SAVE THE CROWN PRINCE FROM THIS CRISIS.
THERE IS ONLY ONE WAY TO SAVE PRINCE SHIN FROM THE KING'S WRATH...
...THE SLANDER OF COURTLY GOSSIP, AND THE PEOPLE'S DISDAIN.
WH-WHAT IS IT, QUEEN MOTHER?
THE SOLUTION IS...

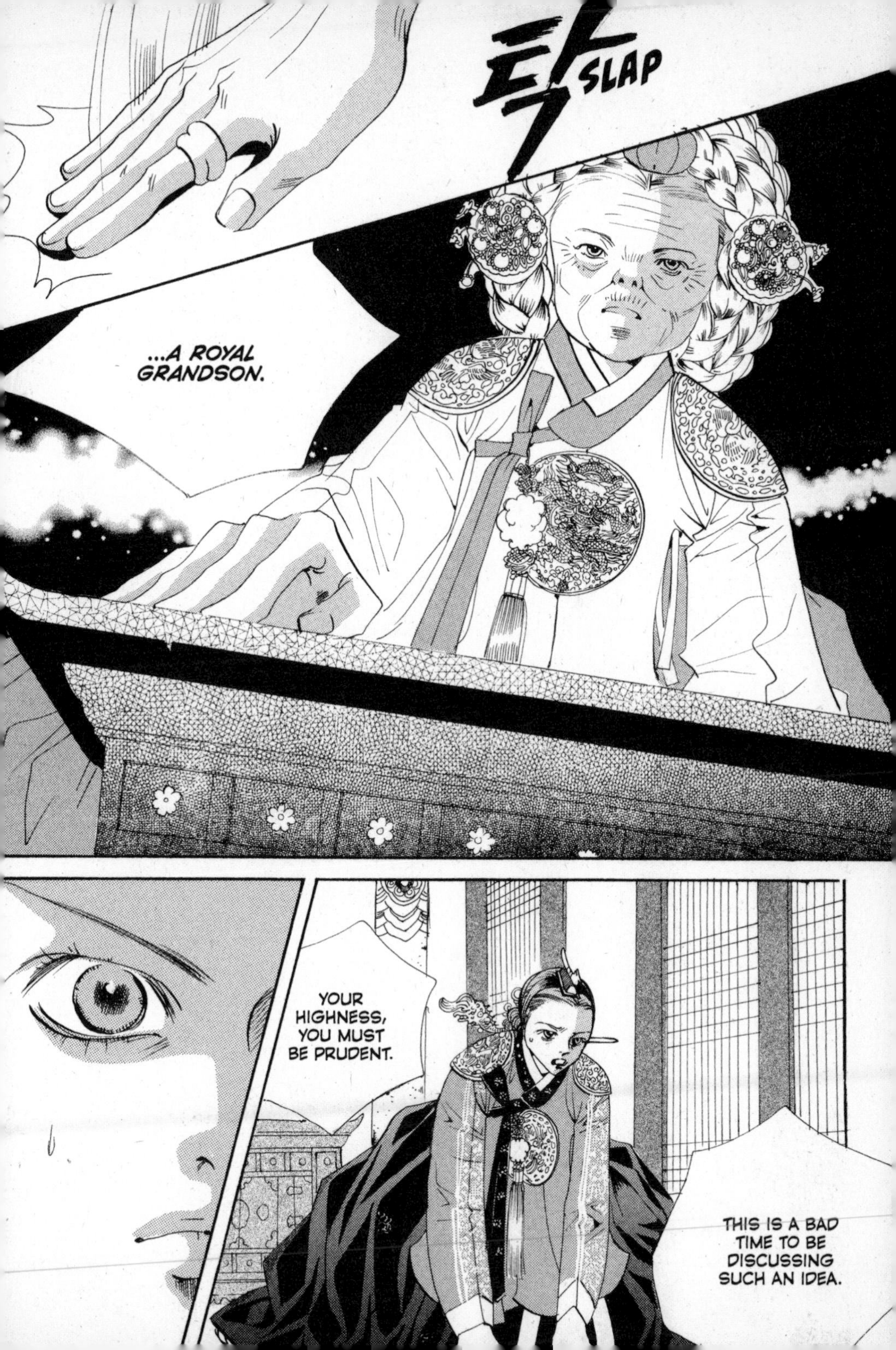
탁
SLAP
...A ROYAL GRANDSON.
YOUR HIGHNESS, YOU MUST BE PRUDENT.
THIS IS A BAD TIME TO BE DISCUSSING SUCH AN IDEA.

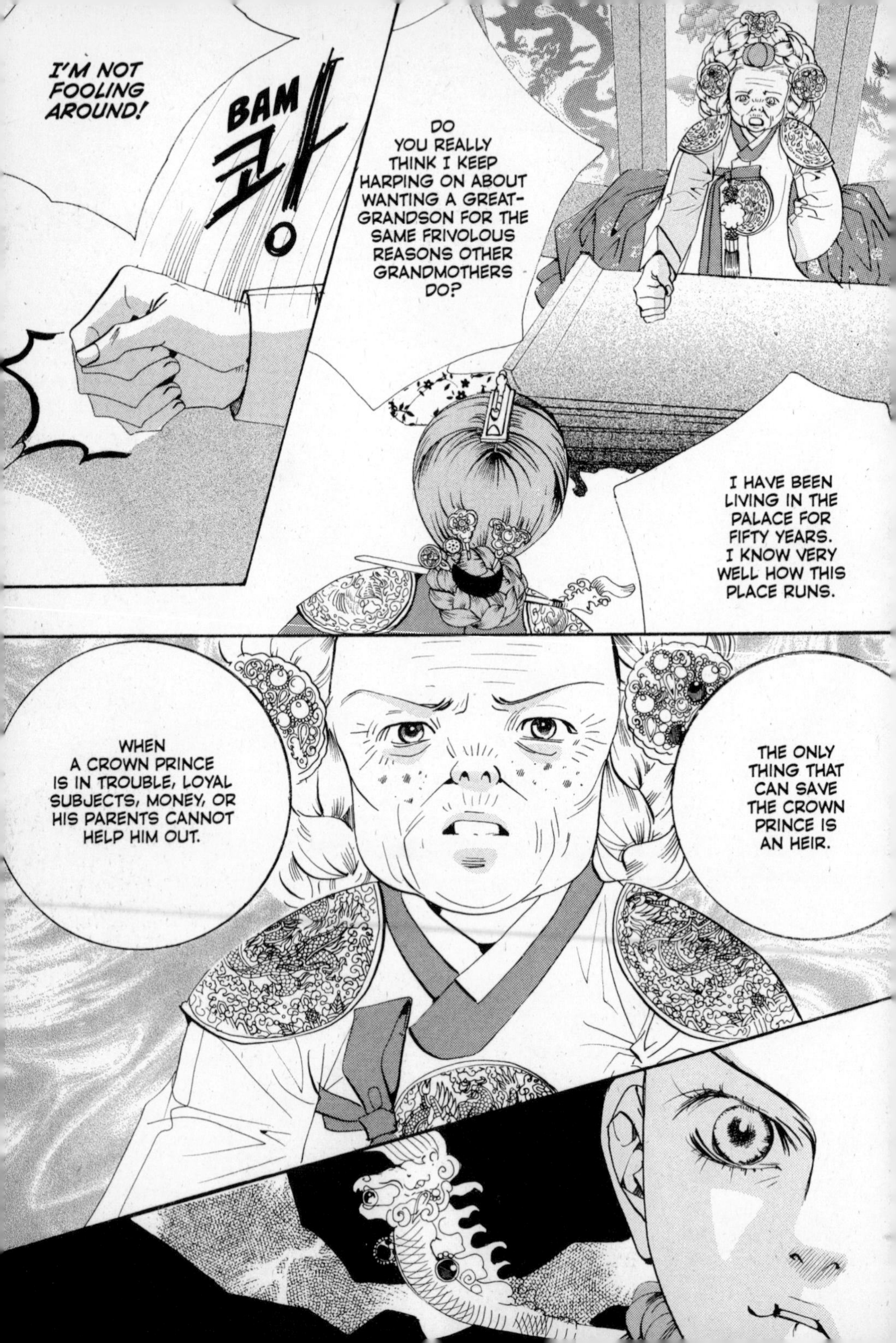
I'M NOT FOOLING AROUND!
BAM 쾅!
DO YOU REALLY THINK I KEEP HARPING ON ABOUT WANTING A GREAT-GRANDSON FOR THE SAME FRIVOLOUS REASONS OTHER GRANDMOTHERS DO?
I HAVE BEEN LIVING IN THE PALACE FOR FIFTY YEARS. I KNOW VERY WELL HOW THIS PLACE RUNS.
WHEN A CROWN PRINCE IS IN TROUBLE, LOYAL SUBJECTS, MONEY, OR HIS PARENTS CANNOT HELP HIM OUT.
THE ONLY THING THAT CAN SAVE THE CROWN PRINCE IS AN HEIR.

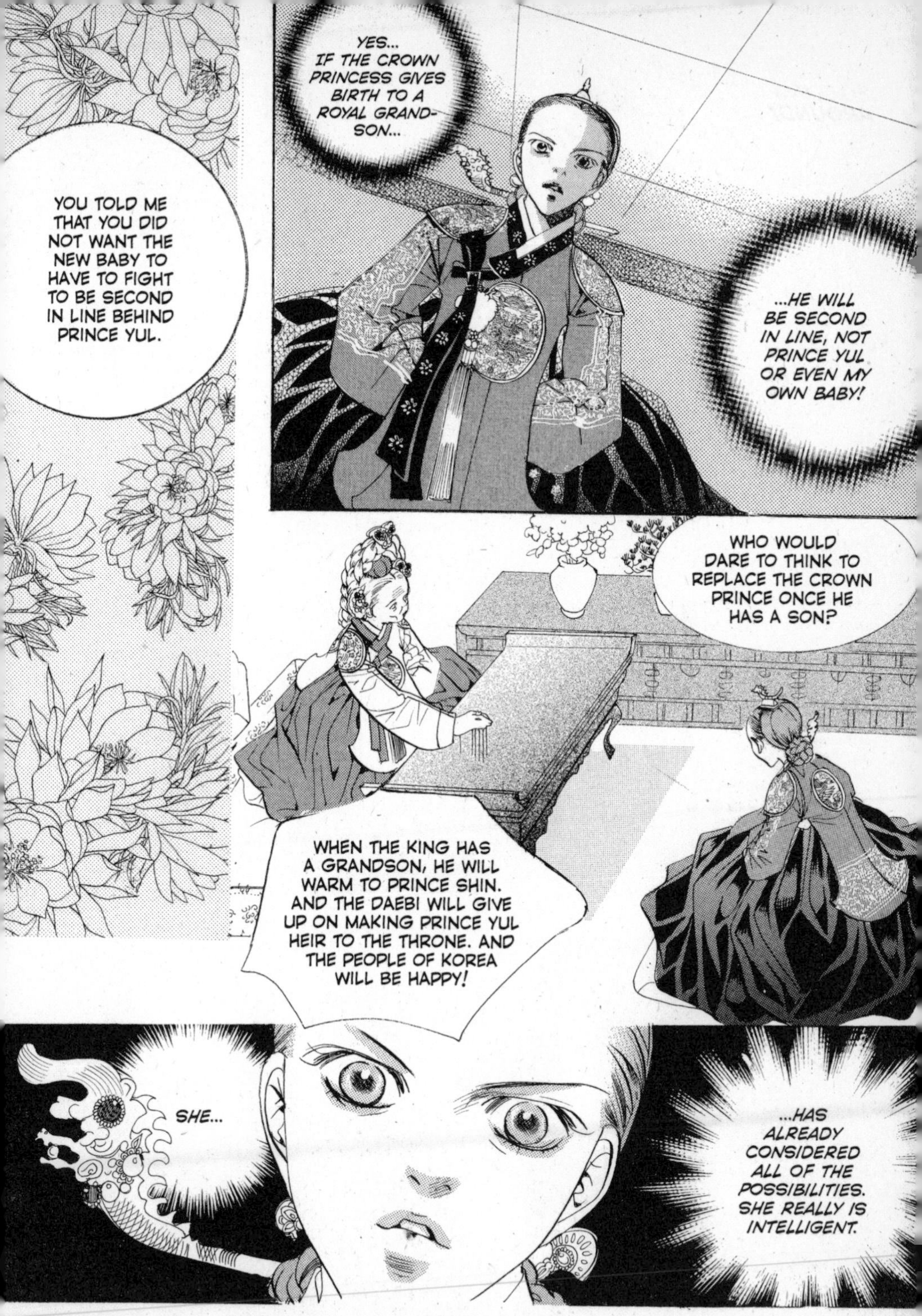
YOU TOLD ME THAT YOU DID NOT WANT THE NEW BABY TO HAVE TO FIGHT TO BE SECOND IN LINE BEHIND PRINCE YUL.
YES... IF THE CROWN PRINCESS GIVES BIRTH TO A ROYAL GRAND-SON...
...HE WILL BE SECOND IN LINE, NOT PRINCE YUL OR EVEN MY OWN BABY!
WHO WOULD DARE TO THINK TO REPLACE THE CROWN PRINCE ONCE HE HAS A SON?
WHEN THE KING HAS A GRANDSON, HE WILL WARM TO PRINCE SHIN. AND THE DAEBI WILL GIVE UP ON MAKING PRINCE YUL HEIR TO THE THRONE. AND THE PEOPLE OF KOREA WILL BE HAPPY!
SHE...
...HAS ALREADY CONSIDERED ALL OF THE POSSIBILITIES. SHE REALLY IS INTELLIGENT.

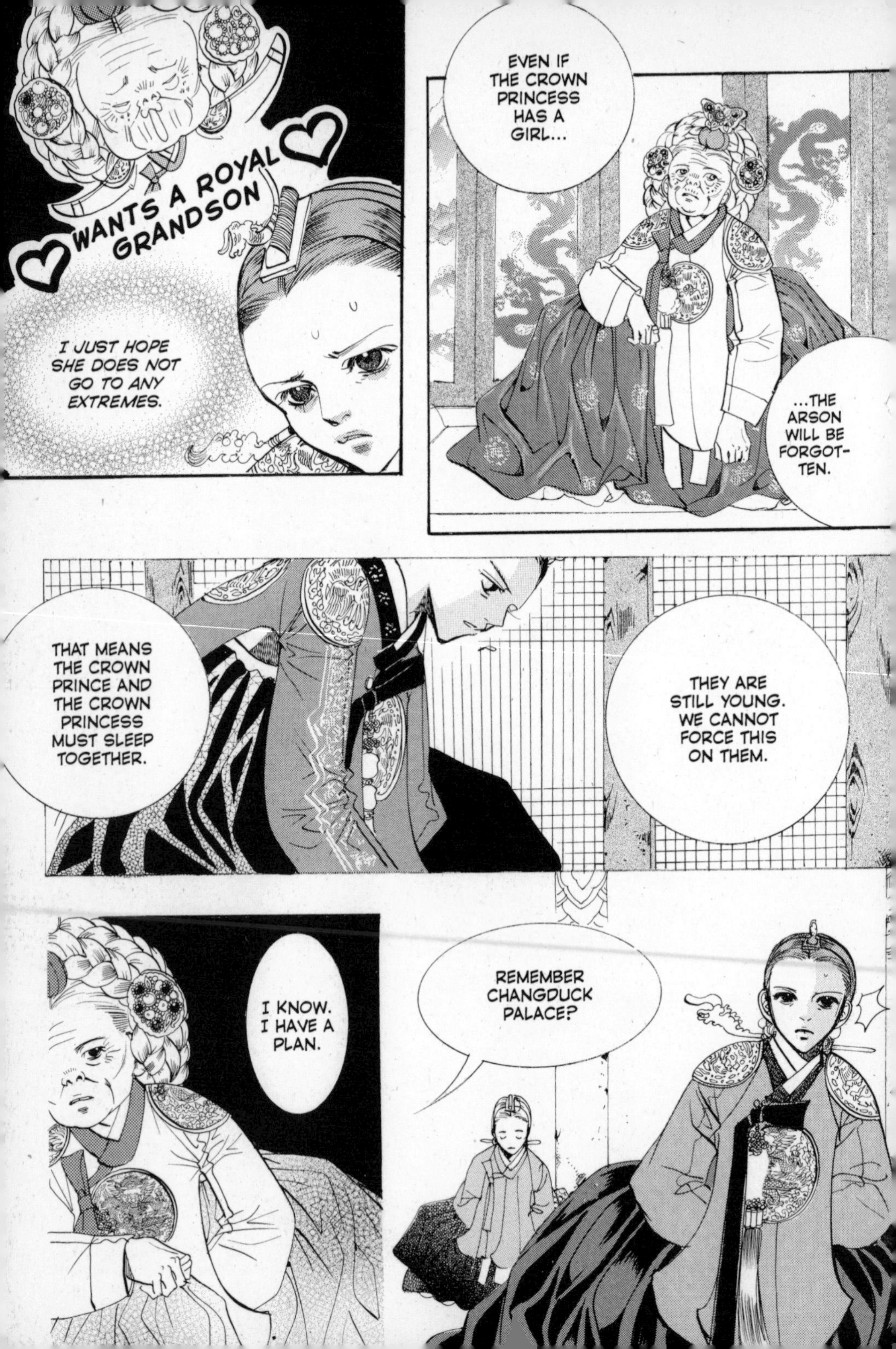
WANTS A ROYAL GRANDSON
I JUST HOPE SHE DOES NOT GO TO ANY EXTREMES.
EVEN IF THE CROWN PRINCESS HAS A GIRL...
...THE ARSON WILL BE FORGOT-TEN.
THAT MEANS THE CROWN PRINCE AND THE CROWN PRINCESS MUST SLEEP TOGETHER.
THEY ARE STILL YOUNG. WE CANNOT FORCE THIS ON THEM.
I KNOW. I HAVE A PLAN.
REMEMBER CHANGDUCK PALACE?

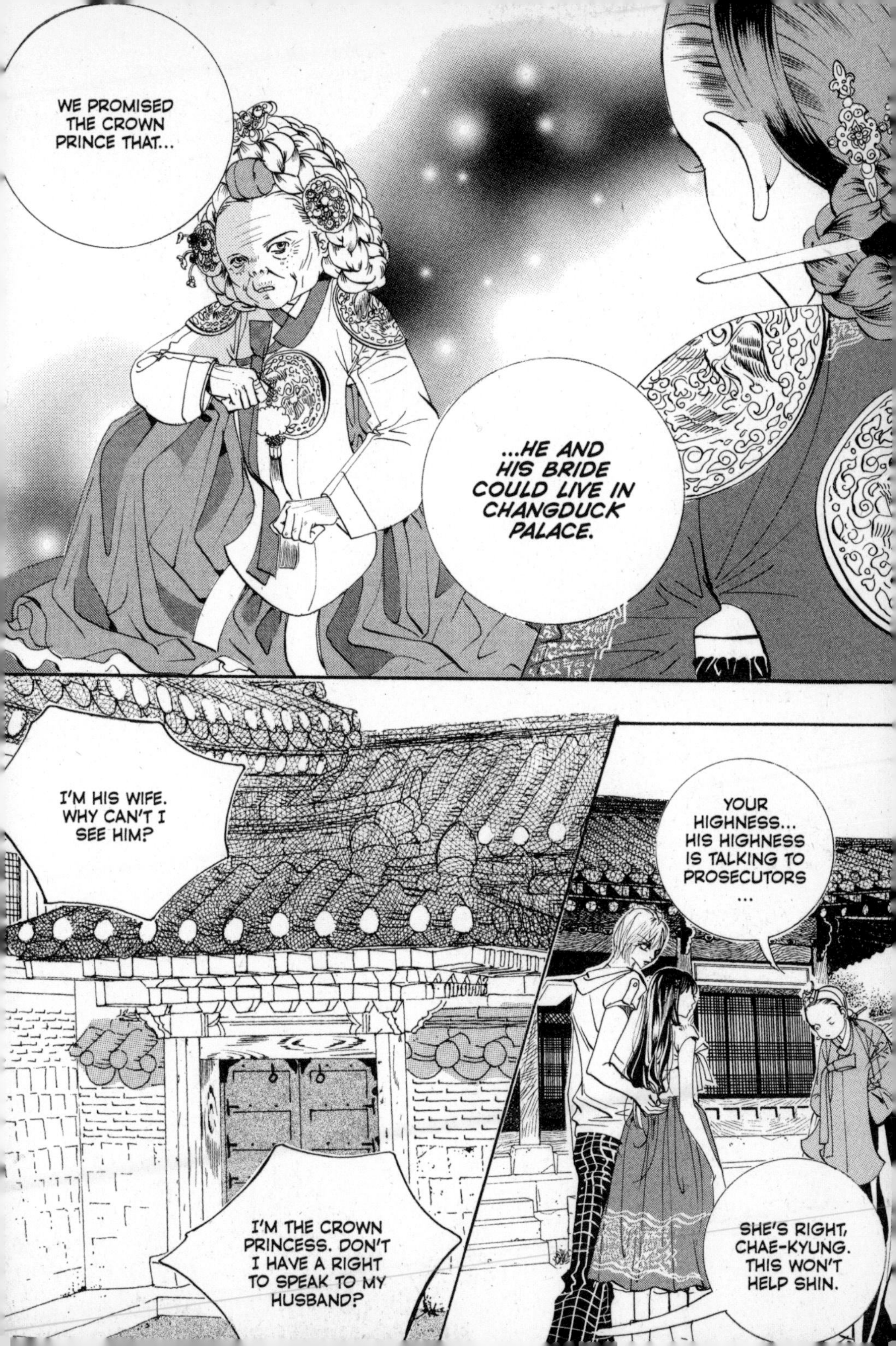

WE PROMISED THE CROWN PRINCE THAT...
...HE AND HIS BRIDE COULD LIVE IN CHANGDUCK PALACE.
I'M HIS WIFE. WHY CAN'T I SEE HIM?
I'M THE CROWN PRINCESS. DON'T I HAVE A RIGHT TO SPEAK TO MY HUSBAND?
YOUR HIGHNESS... HIS HIGHNESS IS TALKING TO PROSECUTORS ...
SHE'S RIGHT, CHAE-KYUNG. THIS WON'T HELP SHIN.

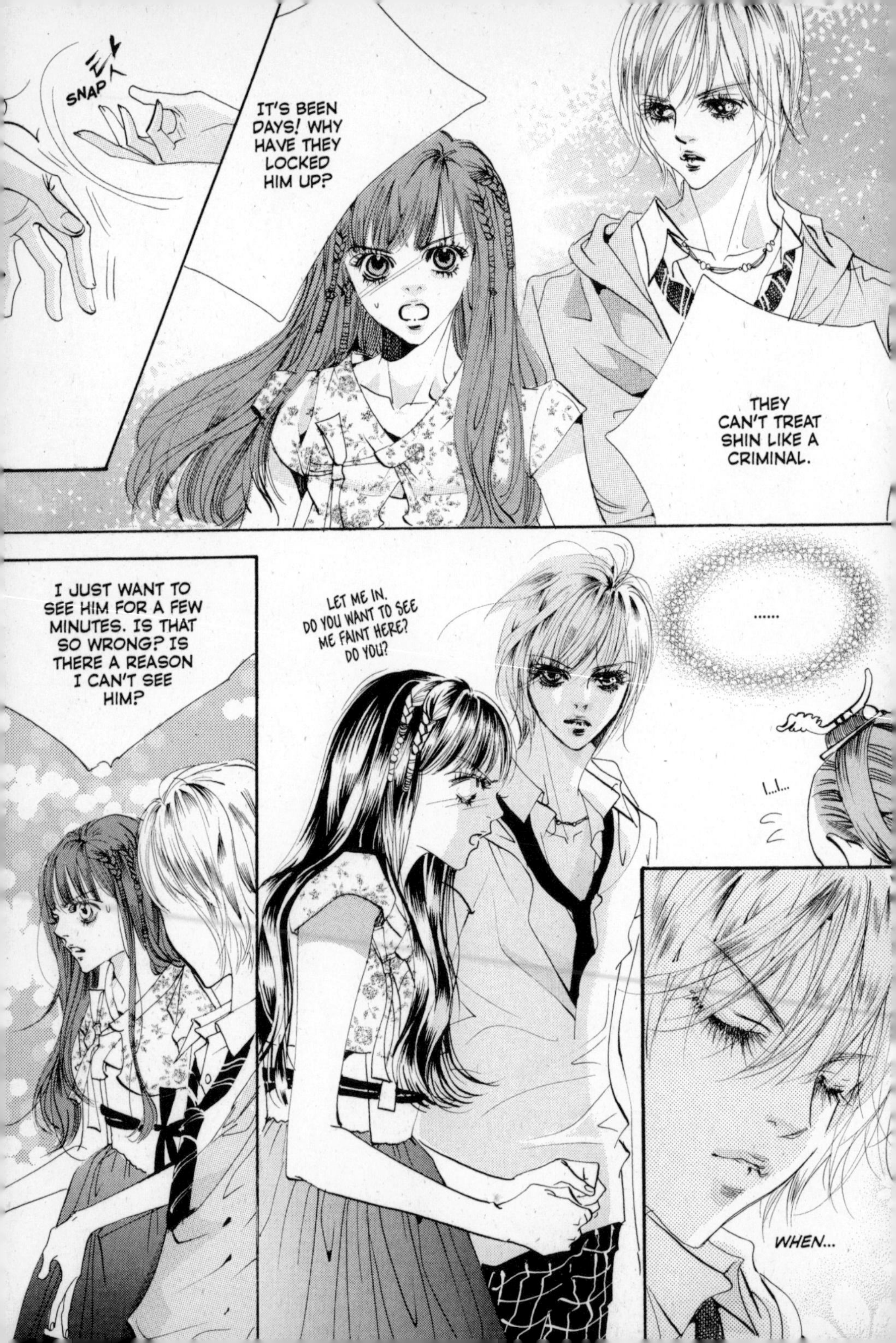
SNAP
IT'S BEEN DAYS! WHY HAVE THEY LOCKED HIM UP?
THEY CAN'T TREAT SHIN LIKE A CRIMINAL.
I JUST WANT TO SEE HIM FOR A FEW MINUTES. IS THAT SO WRONG? IS THERE A REASON I CAN'T SEE HIM?
LET ME IN. DO YOU WANT TO SEE ME FAINT HERE? DO YOU?
......
I...I...
WHEN...

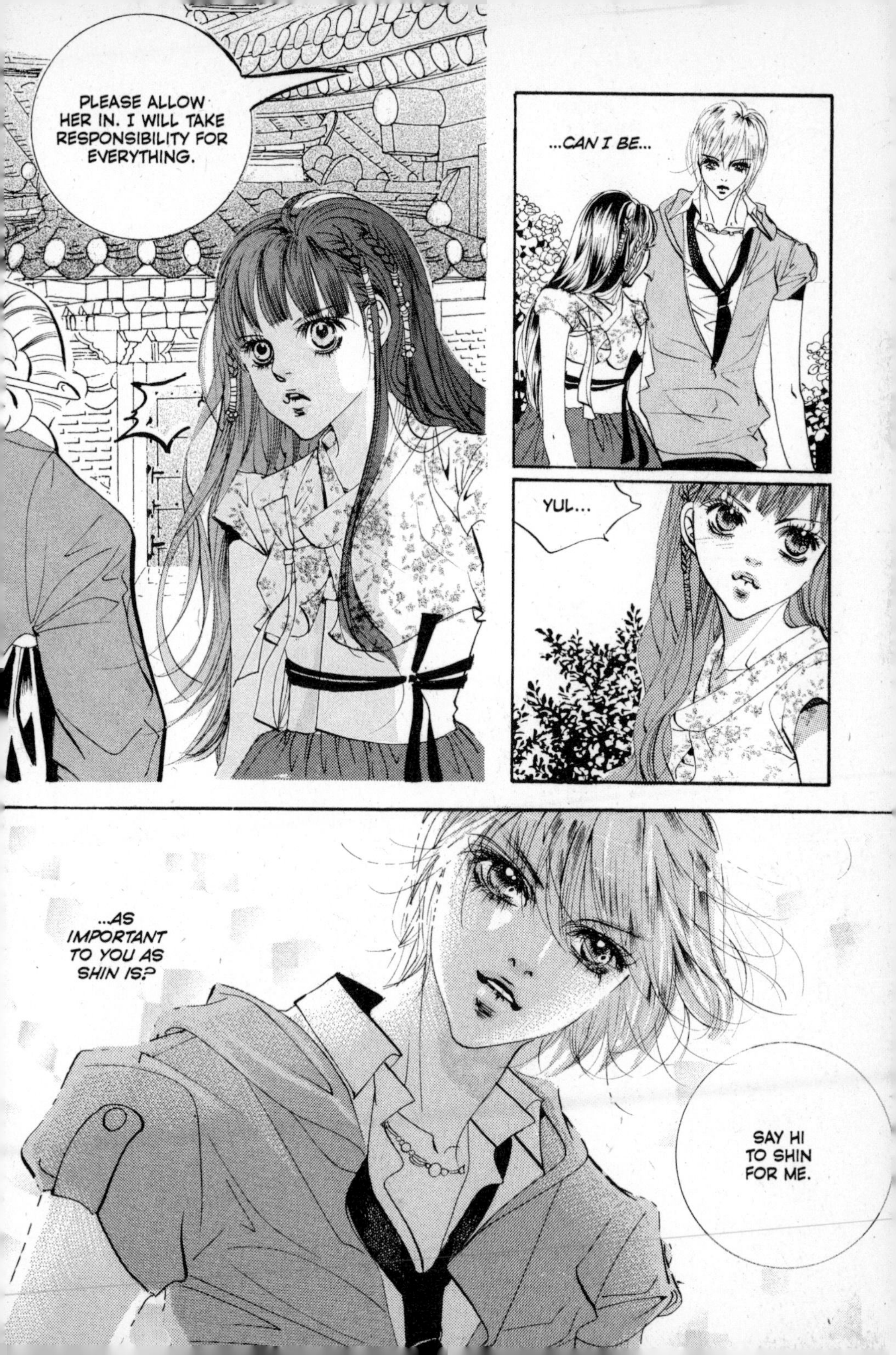
PLEASE ALLOW HER IN. I WILL TAKE RESPONSIBILITY FOR EVERYTHING.
...CAN I BE...
YUL...
...AS IMPORTANT TO YOU AS SHIN IS?
SAY HI TO SHIN FOR ME.

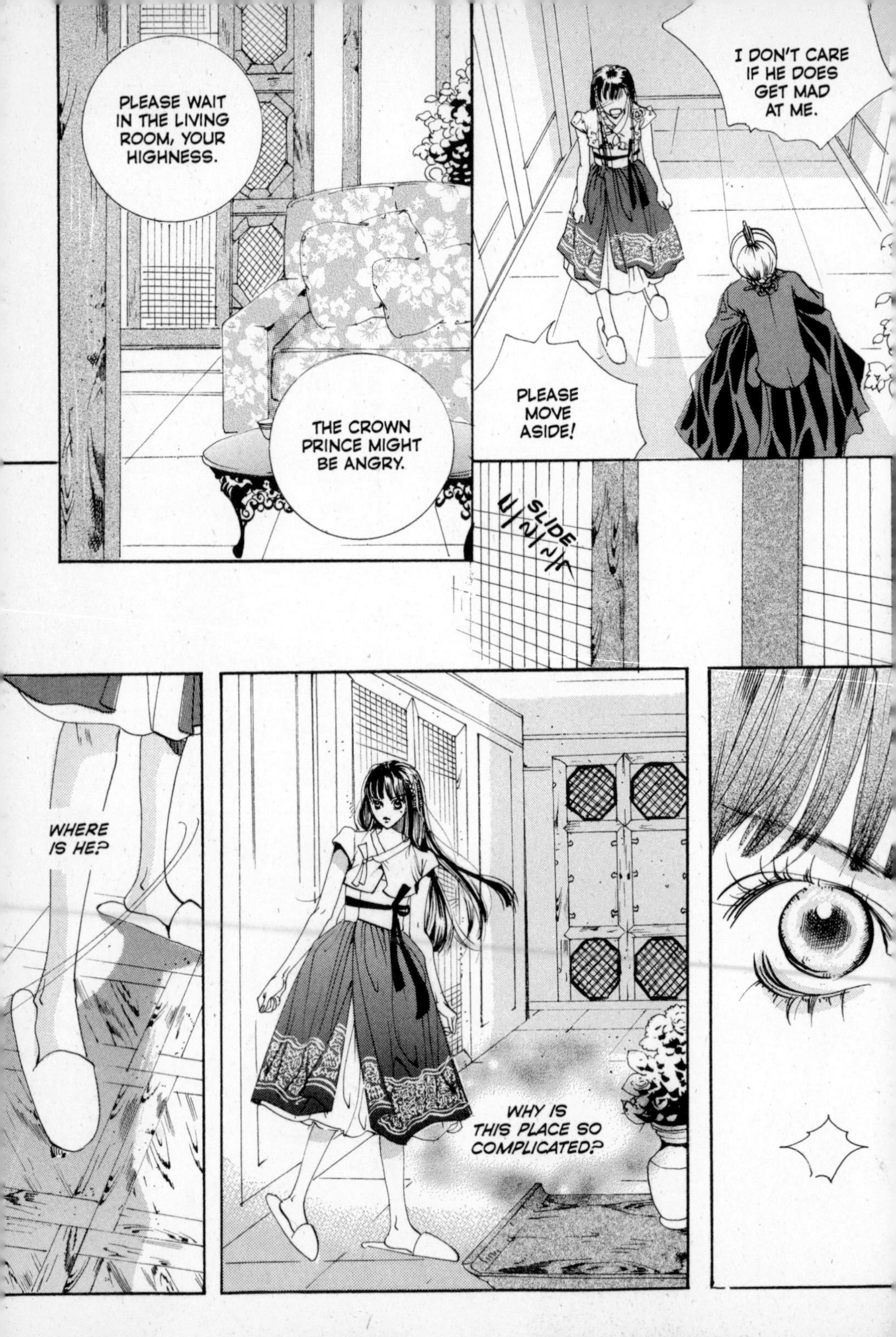
PLEASE WAIT IN THE LIVING ROOM, YOUR HIGHNESS.
THE CROWN PRINCE MIGHT BE ANGRY.
I DON'T CARE IF HE DOES GET MAD AT ME.
PLEASE MOVE ASIDE!
SLIDE
WHERE IS HE?
WHY IS THIS PLACE SO COMPLICATED?

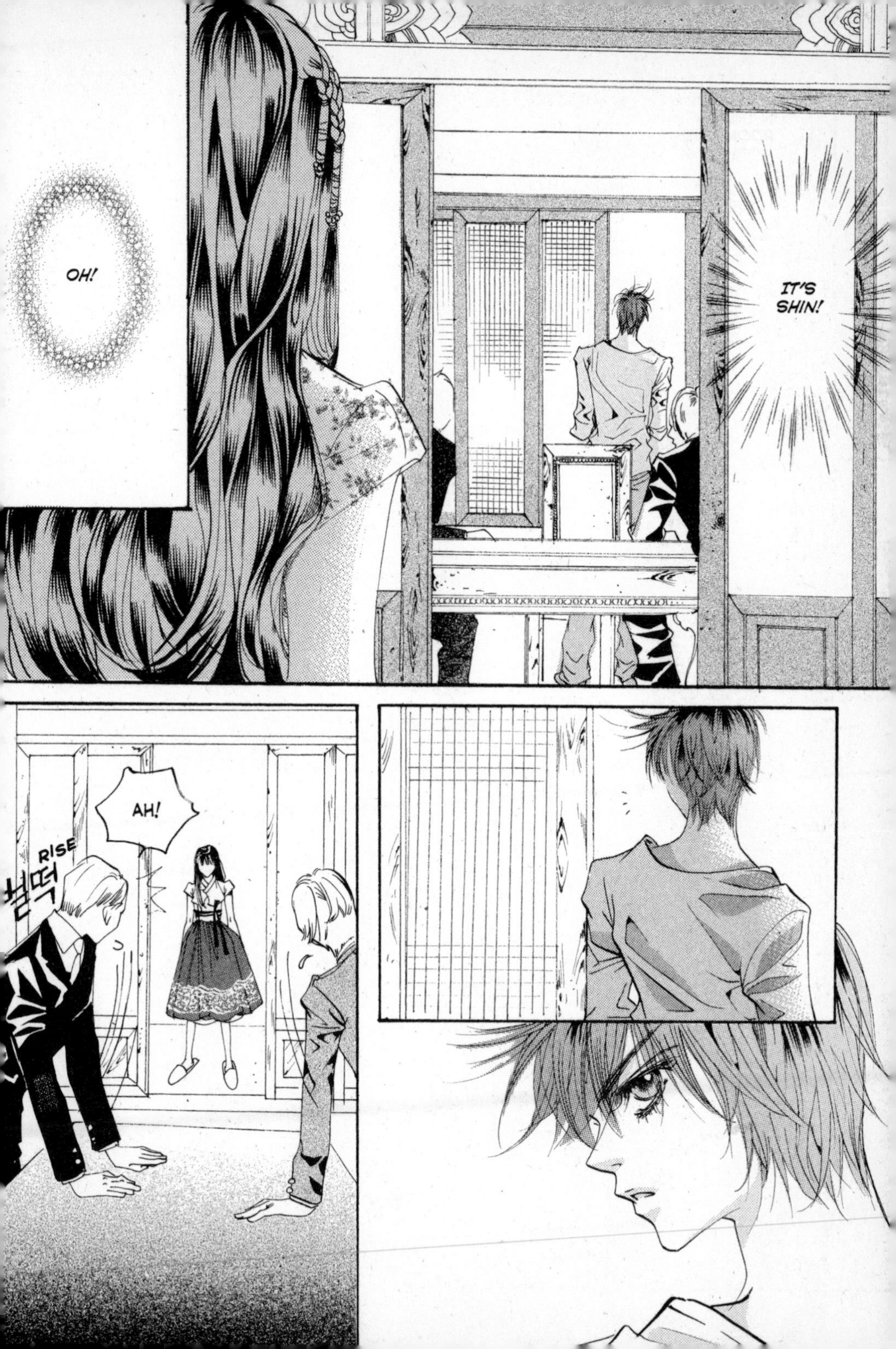
OH!
IT'S SHIN!
RISE
벌떡
AH!

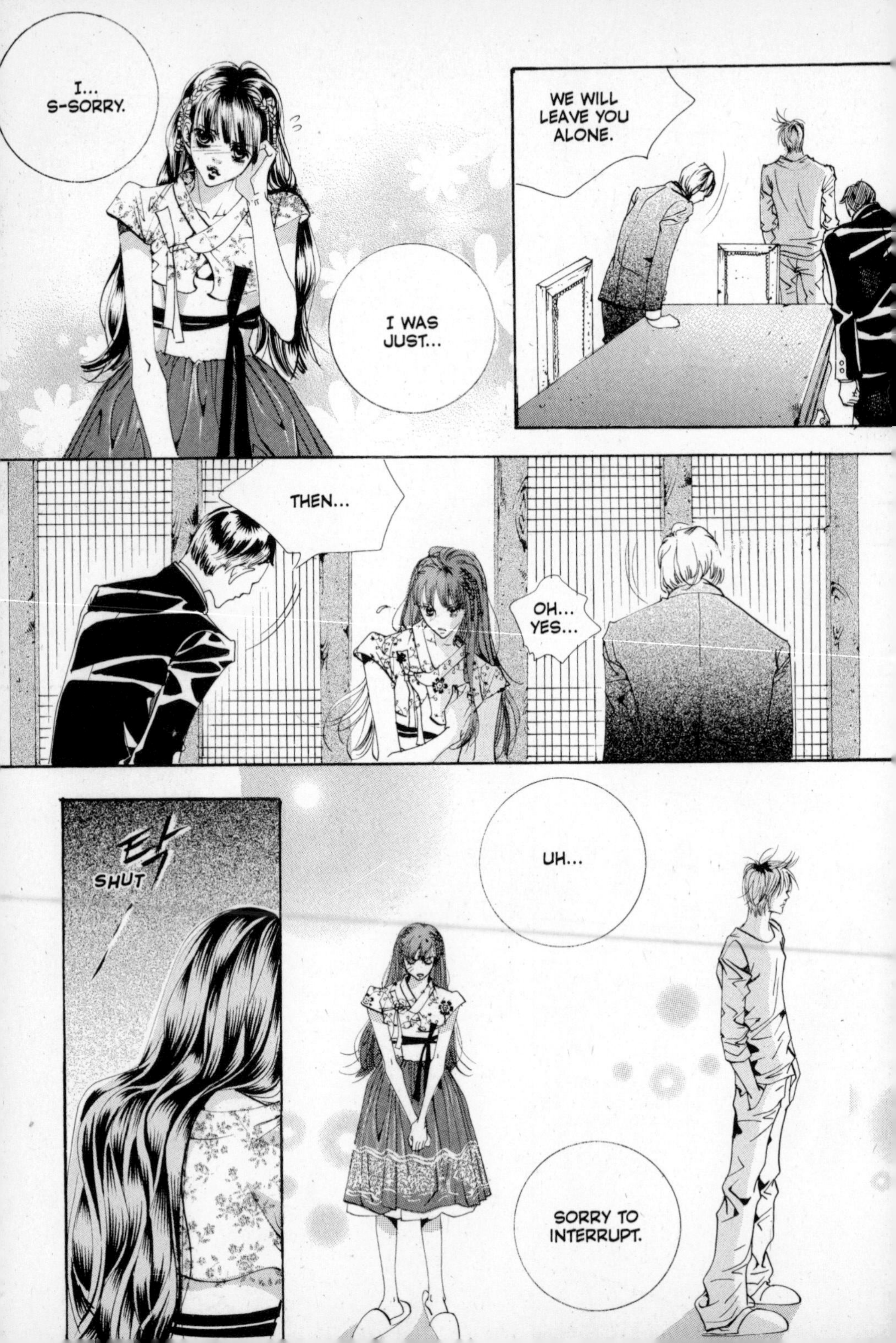
I...
S-SORRY.
I WAS
JUST...
WE WILL
LEAVE YOU
ALONE.
THEN...
OH...
YES...
SHUT
UH...
SORRY TO
INTERRUPT.

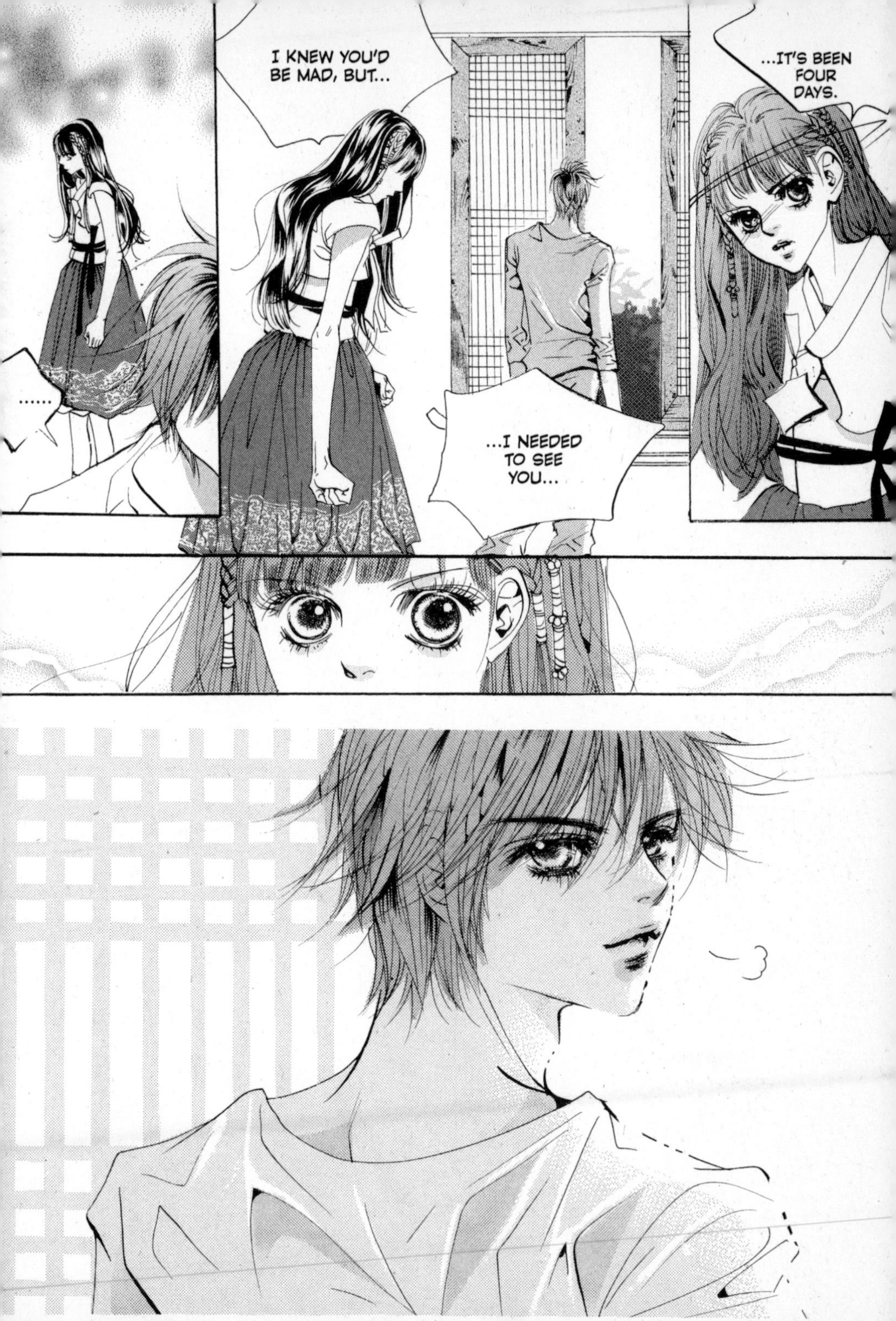
......
I KNEW YOU'D BE MAD, BUT...
...I NEEDED TO SEE YOU...
...IT'S BEEN FOUR DAYS.

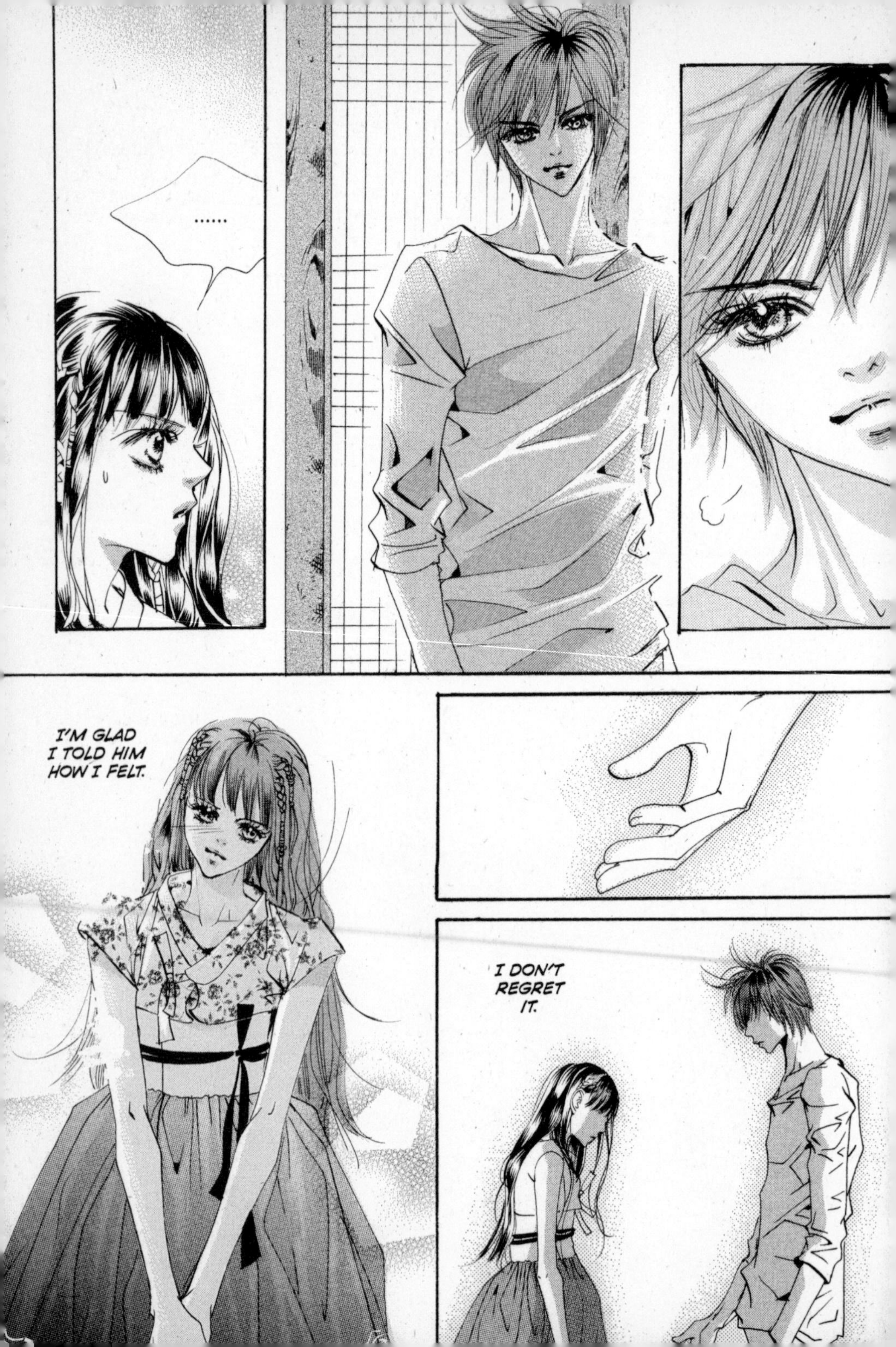
......
I'M GLAD I TOLD HIM HOW I FELT.
I DON'T REGRET IT.

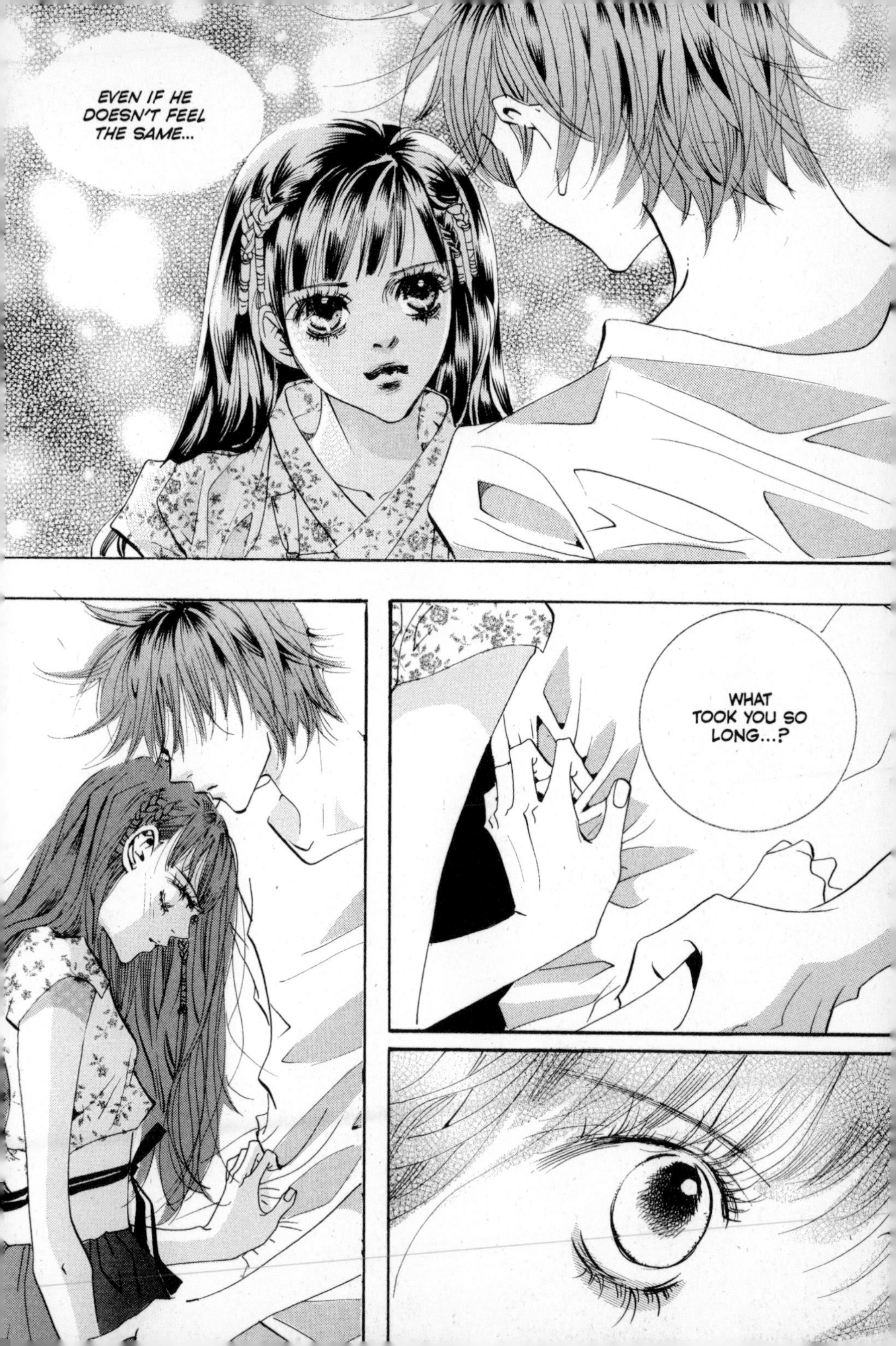
EVEN IF HE DOESN'T FEEL THE SAME...
WHAT TOOK YOU SO LONG...?

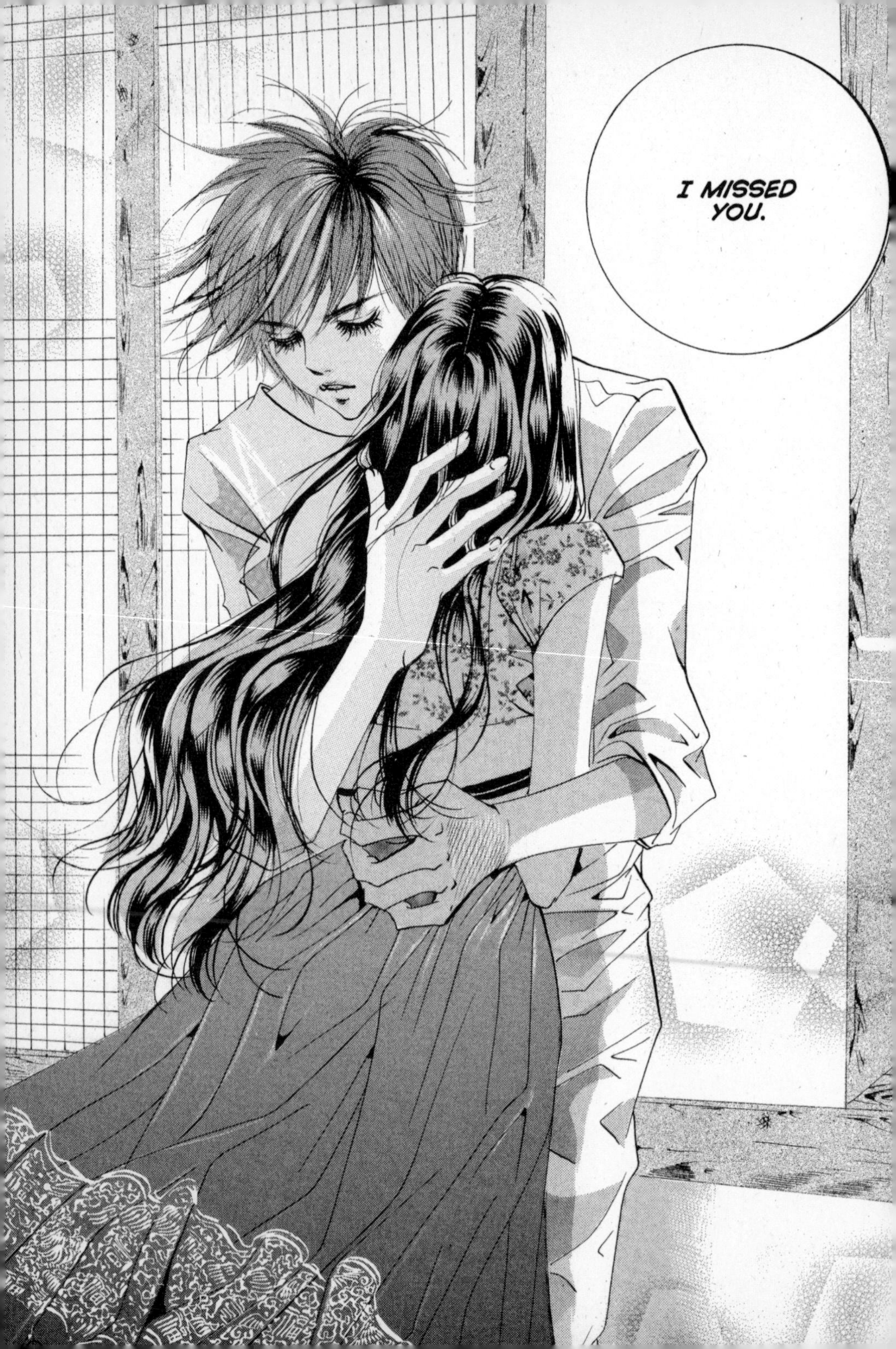
I MISSED YOU.

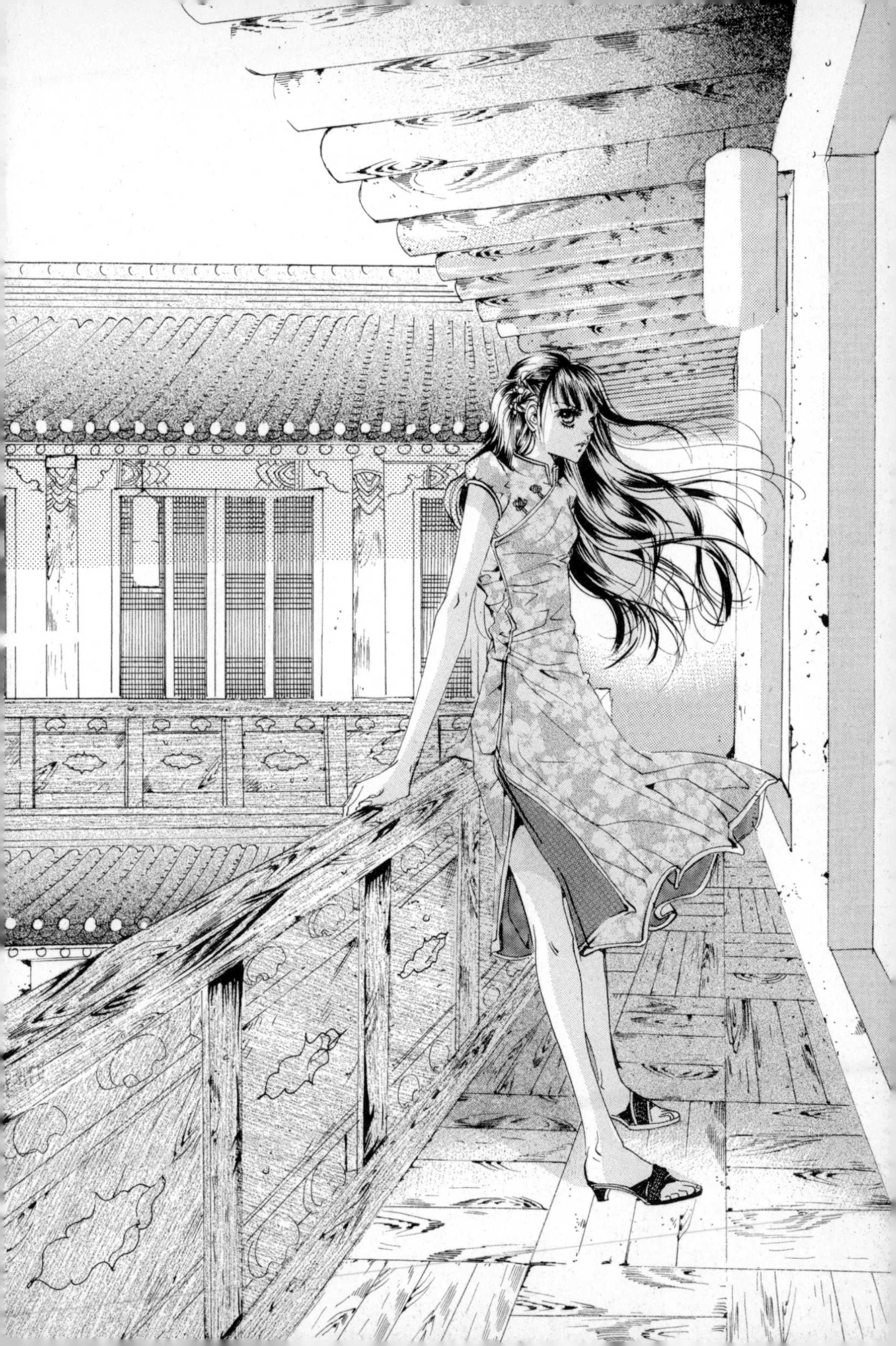

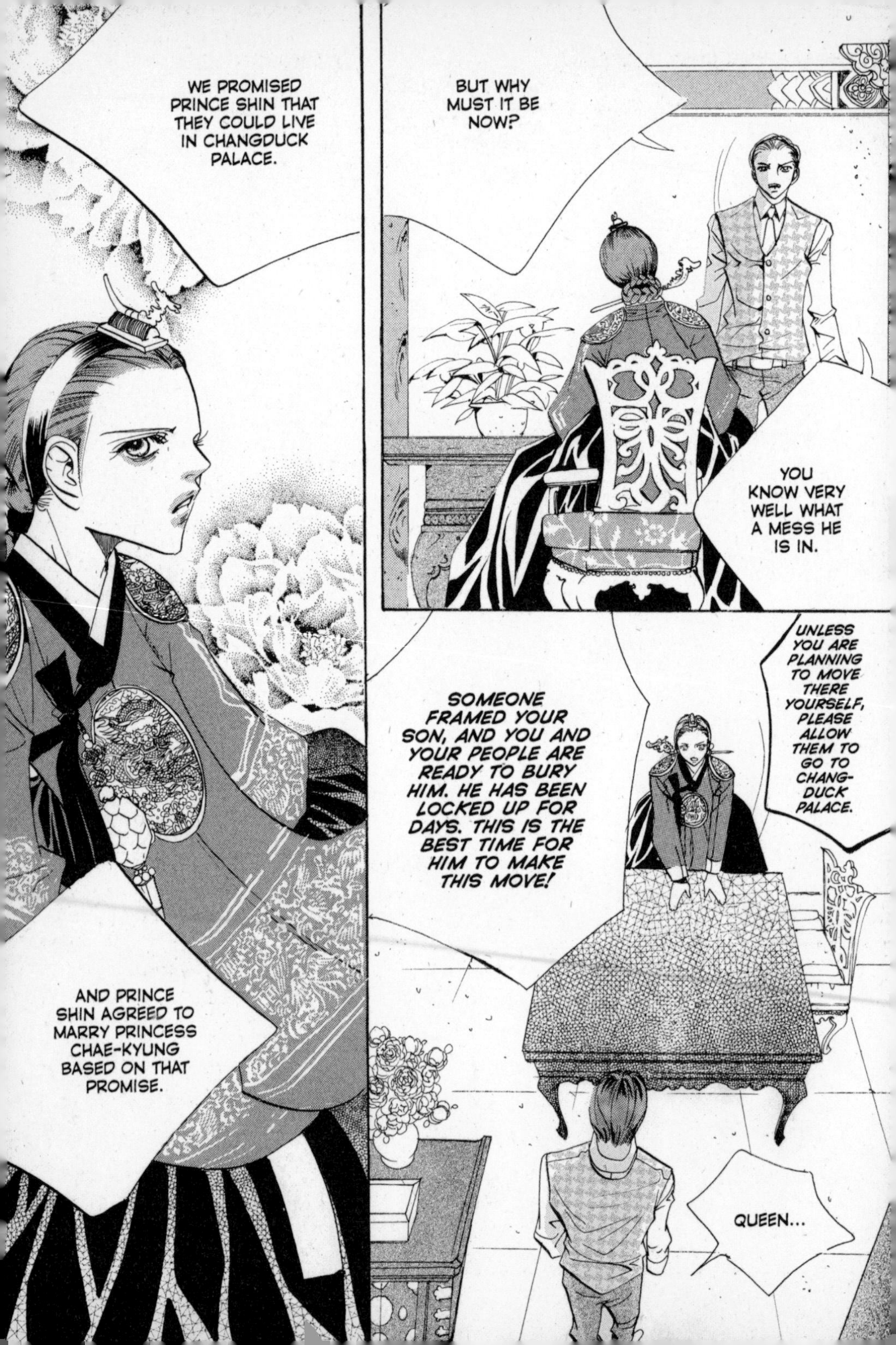
WE PROMISED PRINCE SHIN THAT THEY COULD LIVE IN CHANGDUCK PALACE.
AND PRINCE SHIN AGREED TO MARRY PRINCESS CHAE-KYUNG BASED ON THAT PROMISE.
BUT WHY MUST IT BE NOW?
YOU KNOW VERY WELL WHAT A MESS HE IS IN.
SOMEONE FRAMED YOUR SON, AND YOU AND YOUR PEOPLE ARE READY TO BURY HIM. HE HAS BEEN LOCKED UP FOR DAYS. THIS IS THE BEST TIME FOR HIM TO MAKE THIS MOVE!
UNLESS YOU ARE PLANNING TO MOVE THERE YOURSELF, PLEASE ALLOW THEM TO GO TO CHANG-DUCK PALACE.
QUEEN...

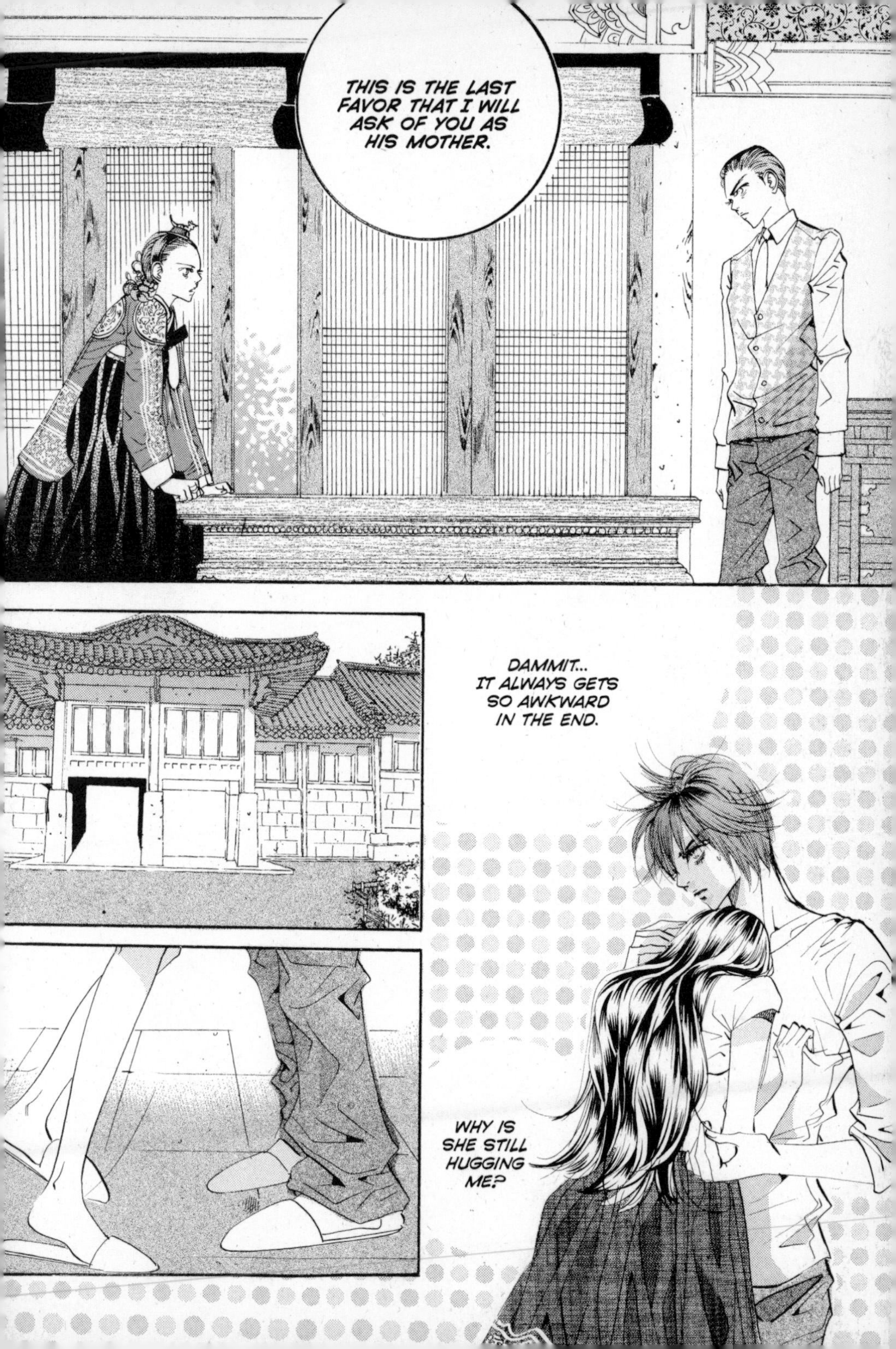
THIS IS THE LAST FAVOR THAT I WILL ASK OF YOU AS HIS MOTHER.
DAMMIT... IT ALWAYS GETS SO AWKWARD IN THE END.
WHY IS SHE STILL HUGGING ME?

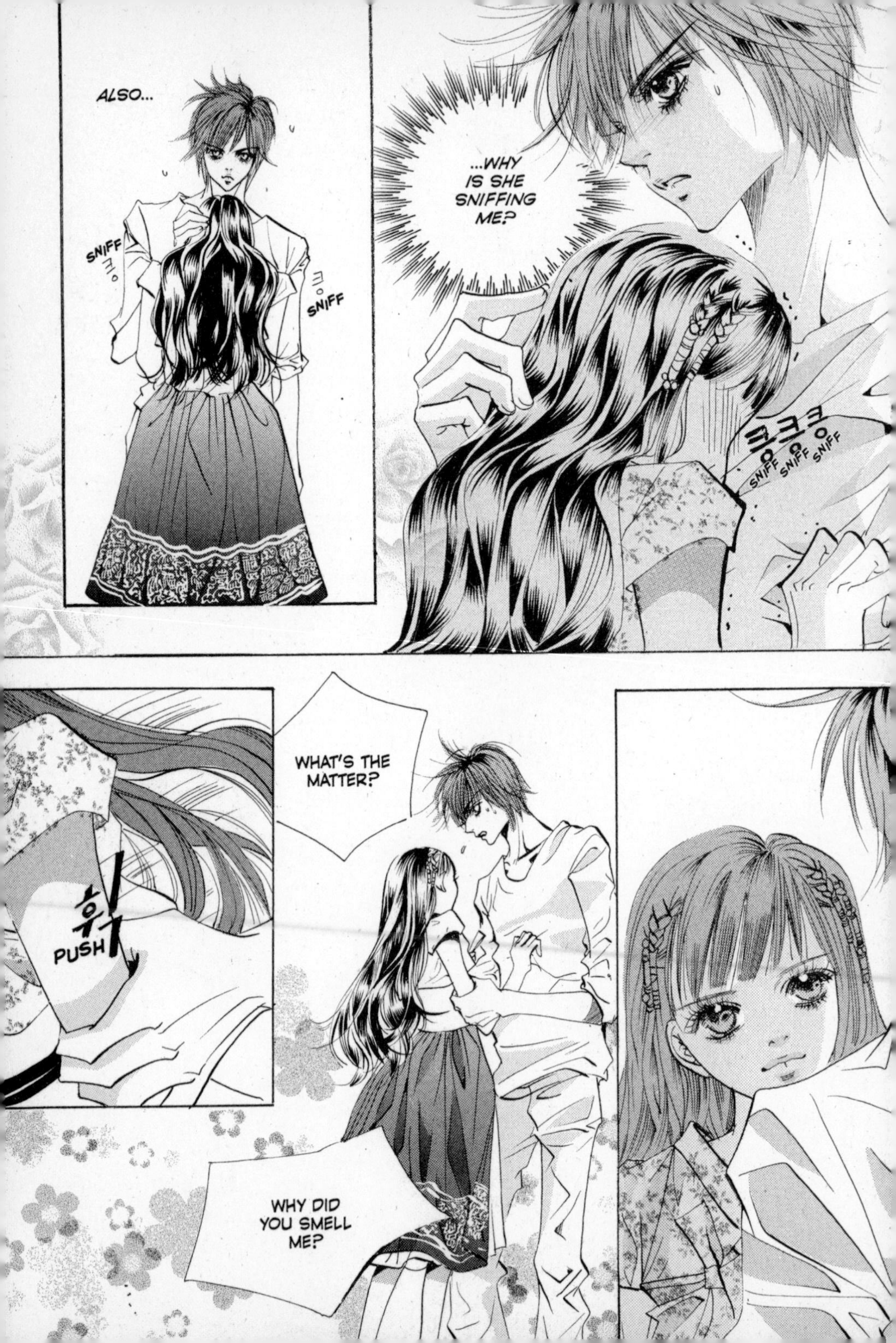
ALSO...
SNIFF 킁
킁 SNIFF
...WHY IS SHE SNIFFING ME?
킁킁킁
SNIFF SNIFF SNIFF
휙
PUSH
WHAT'S THE MATTER?
WHY DID YOU SMELL ME?

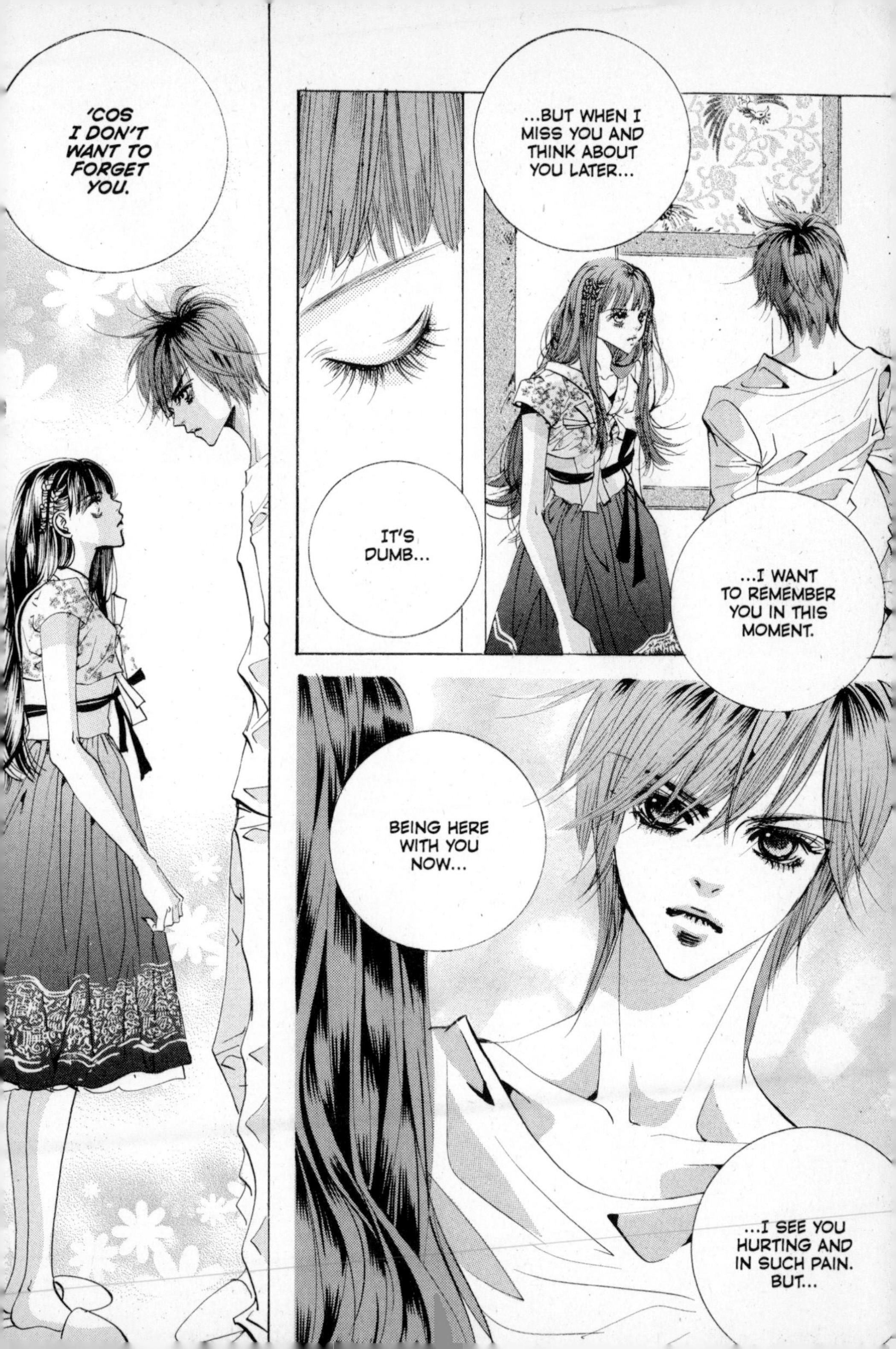
'COS I DON'T WANT TO FORGET YOU.
IT'S DUMB...
...BUT WHEN I MISS YOU AND THINK ABOUT YOU LATER...
...I WANT TO REMEMBER YOU IN THIS MOMENT.
BEING HERE WITH YOU NOW...
...I SEE YOU HURTING AND IN SUCH PAIN. BUT...

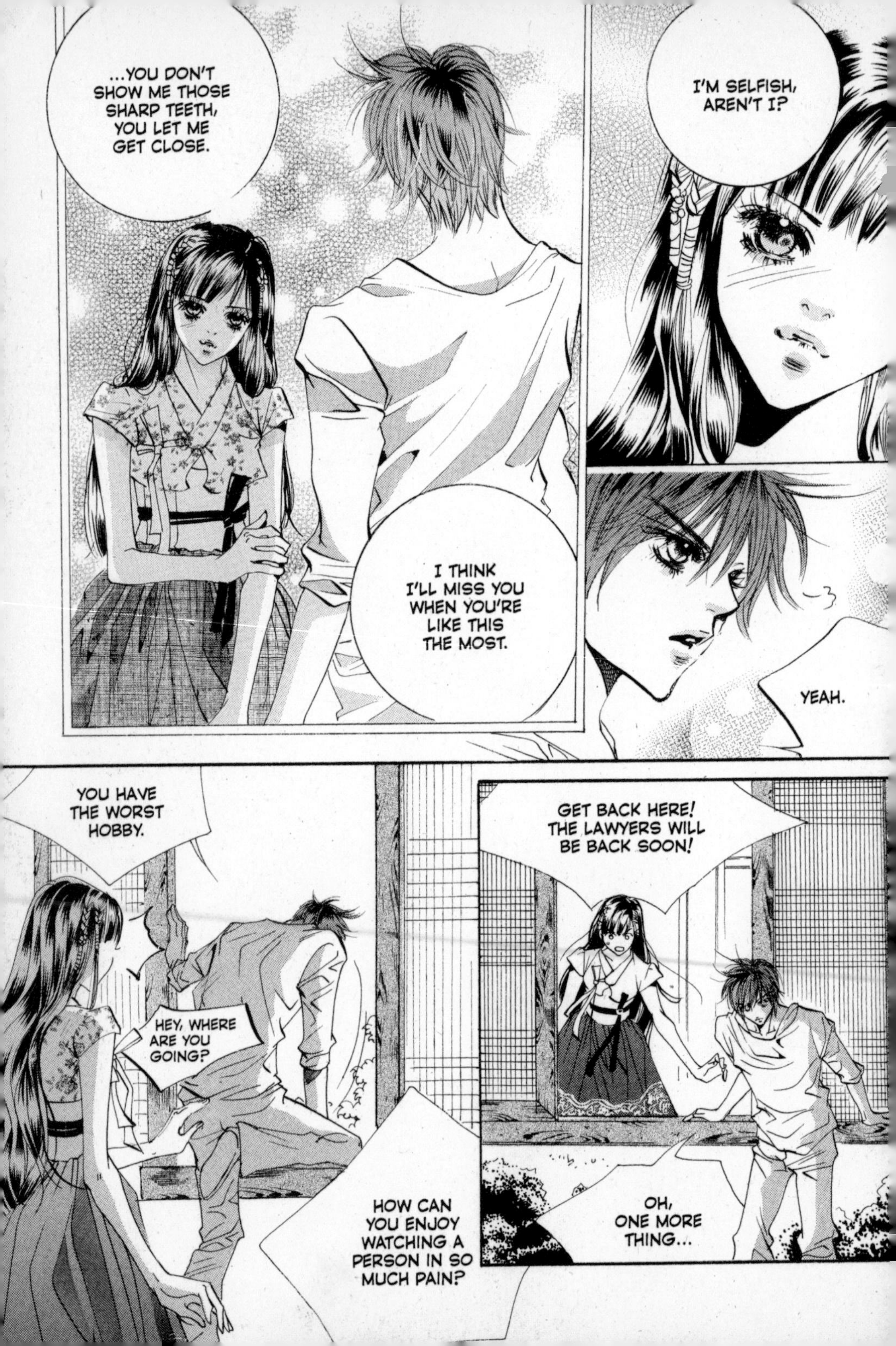
...YOU DON'T SHOW ME THOSE SHARP TEETH, YOU LET ME GET CLOSE.
I THINK I'LL MISS YOU WHEN YOU'RE LIKE THIS THE MOST.
I'M SELFISH, AREN'T I?
YEAH.
YOU HAVE THE WORST HOBBY.
HEY, WHERE ARE YOU GOING?
HOW CAN YOU ENJOY WATCHING A PERSON IN SO MUCH PAIN?
GET BACK HERE! THE LAWYERS WILL BE BACK SOON!
OH, ONE MORE THING...

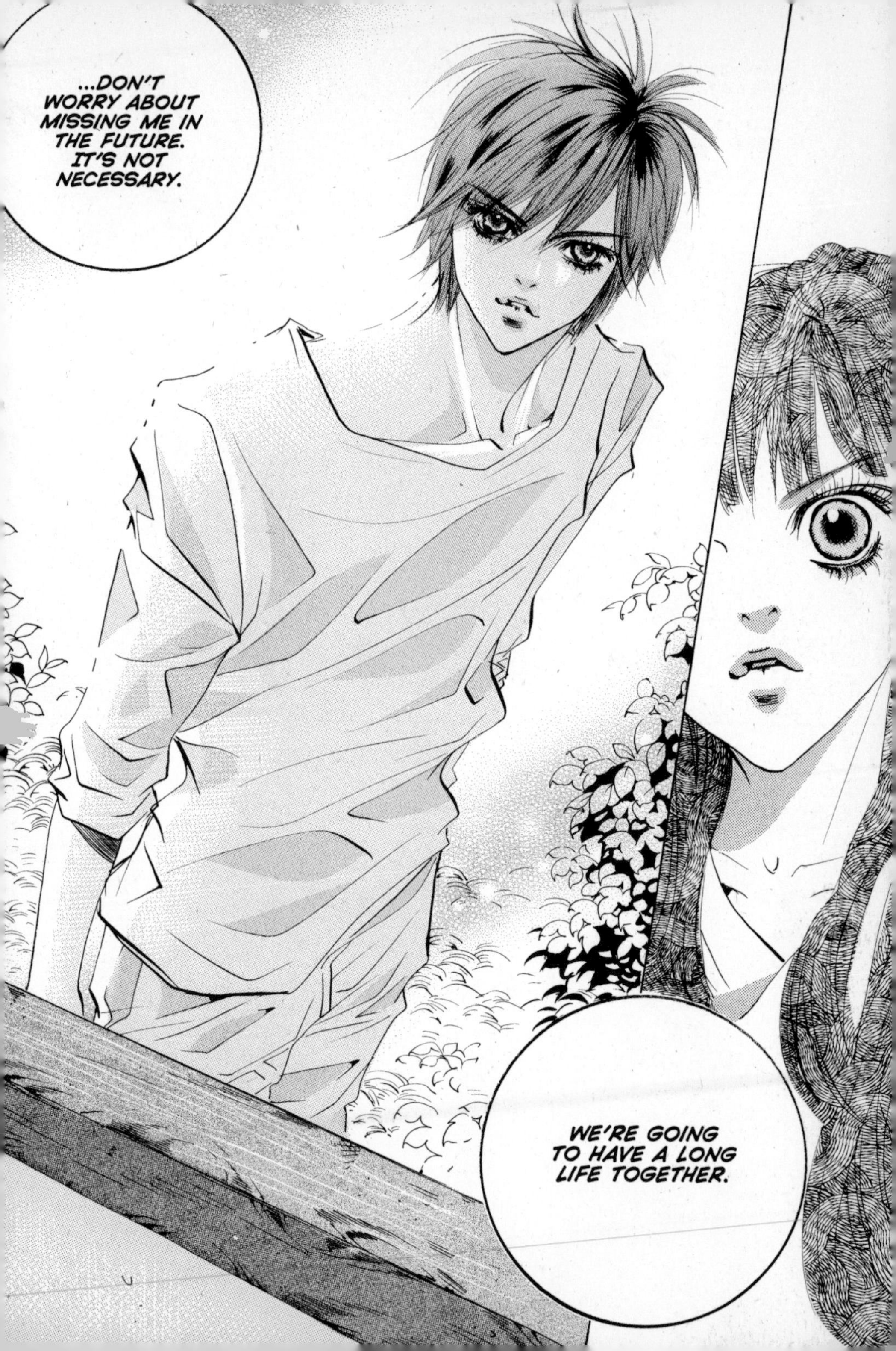
...DON'T WORRY ABOUT MISSING ME IN THE FUTURE. IT'S NOT NECESSARY.
WE'RE GOING TO HAVE A LONG LIFE TOGETHER.

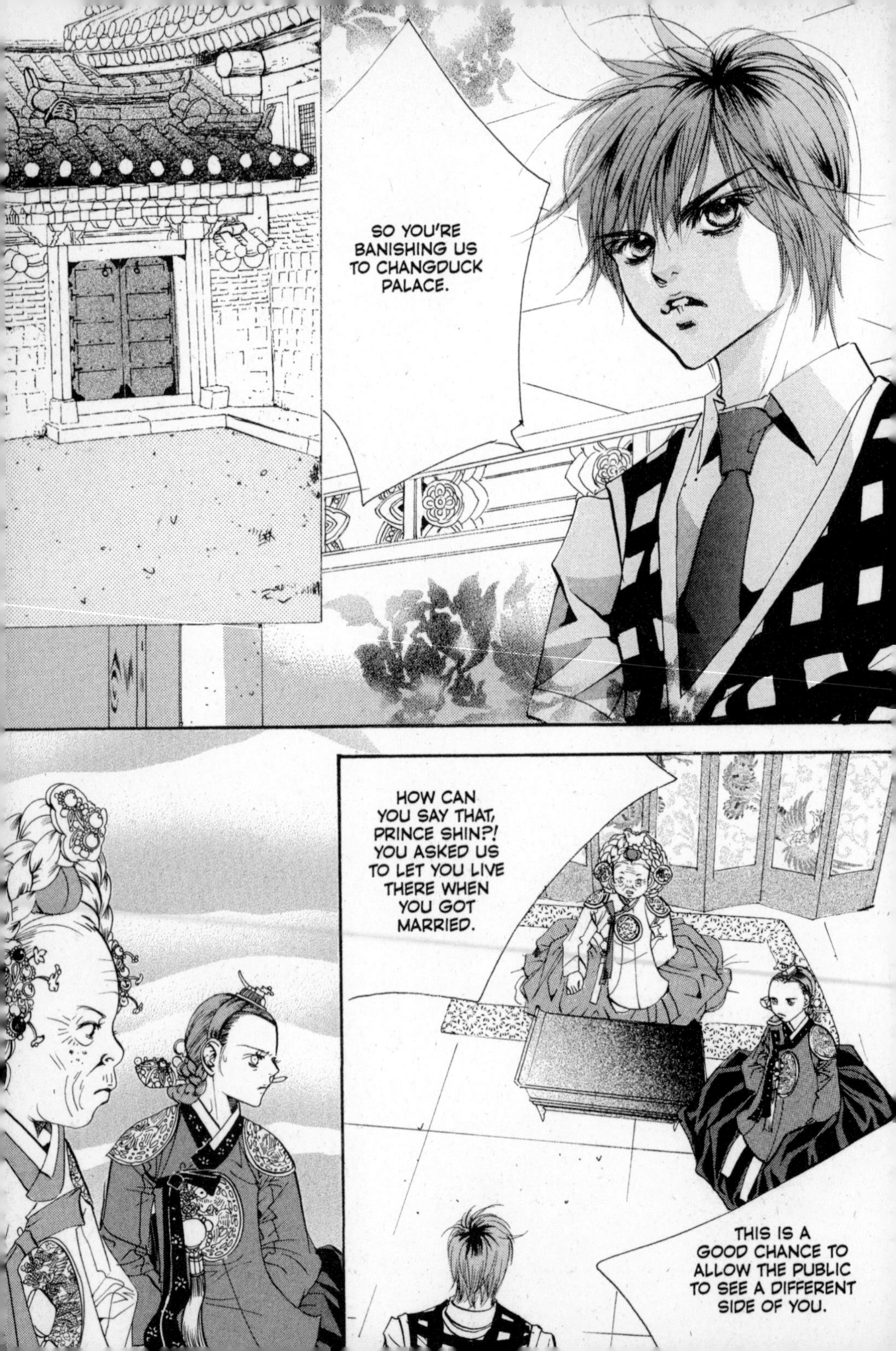
SO YOU'RE BANISHING US TO CHANGDUCK PALACE.
HOW CAN YOU SAY THAT, PRINCE SHIN?! YOU ASKED US TO LET YOU LIVE THERE WHEN YOU GOT MARRIED.
THIS IS A GOOD CHANCE TO ALLOW THE PUBLIC TO SEE A DIFFERENT SIDE OF YOU.

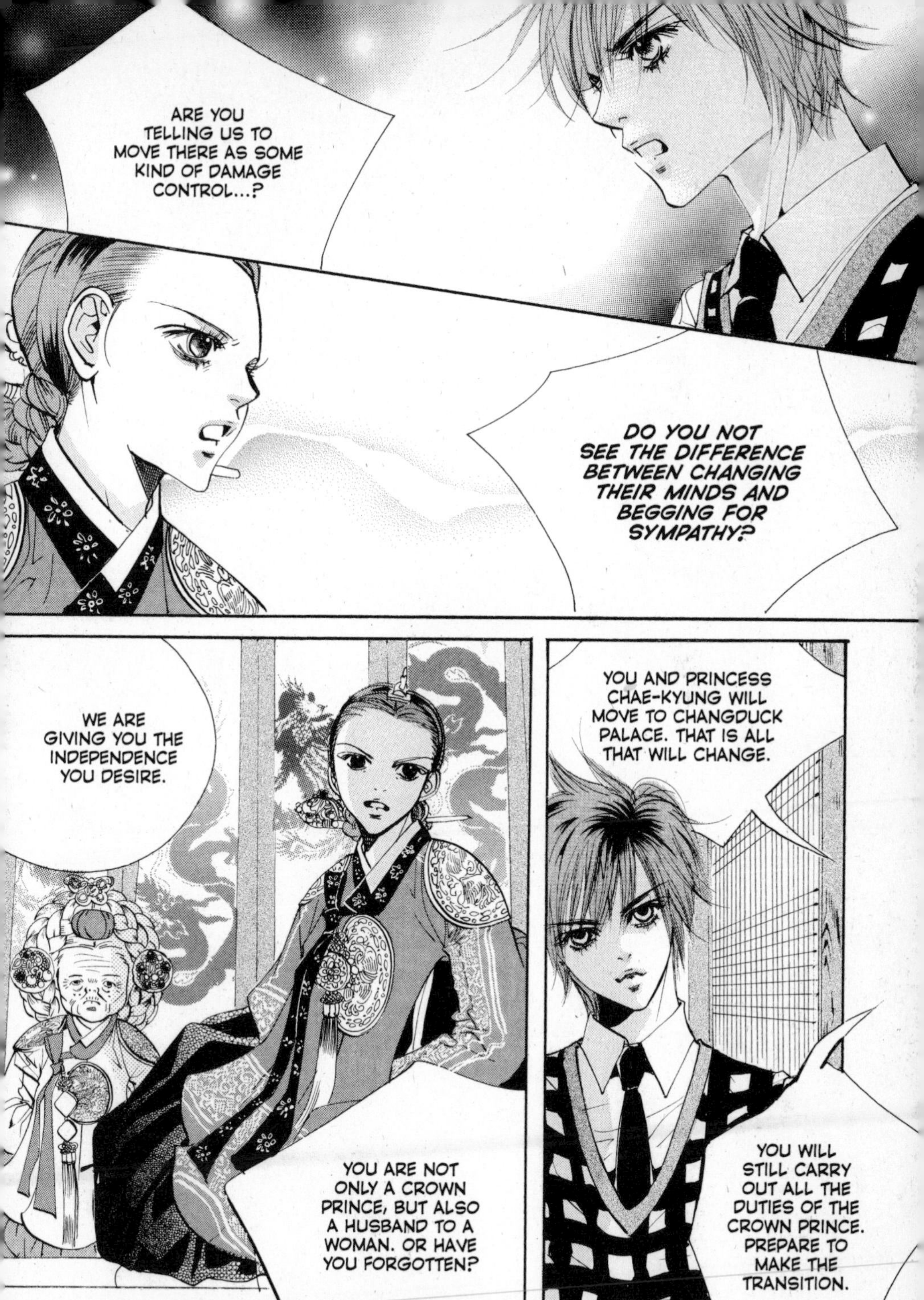
ARE YOU TELLING US TO MOVE THERE AS SOME KIND OF DAMAGE CONTROL...?
DO YOU NOT SEE THE DIFFERENCE BETWEEN CHANGING THEIR MINDS AND BEGGING FOR SYMPATHY?
WE ARE GIVING YOU THE INDEPENDENCE YOU DESIRE.
YOU ARE NOT ONLY A CROWN PRINCE, BUT ALSO A HUSBAND TO A WOMAN. OR HAVE YOU FORGOTTEN?
YOU AND PRINCESS CHAE-KYUNG WILL MOVE TO CHANGDUCK PALACE. THAT IS ALL THAT WILL CHANGE.
YOU WILL STILL CARRY OUT ALL THE DUTIES OF THE CROWN PRINCE. PREPARE TO MAKE THE TRANSITION.

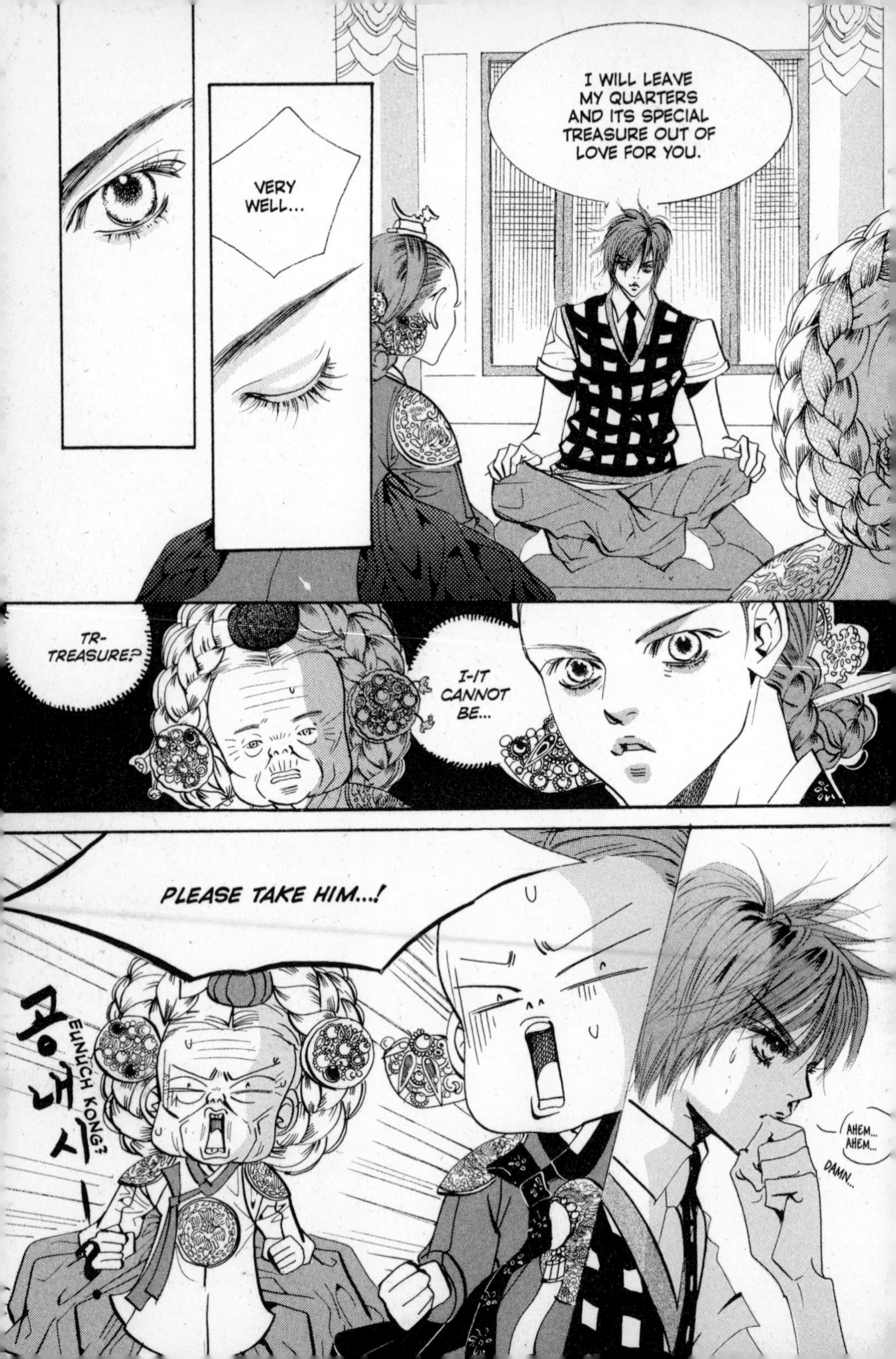
VERY WELL...
I WILL LEAVE MY QUARTERS AND ITS SPECIAL TREASURE OUT OF LOVE FOR YOU.
TR-TREASURE?
I-IT CANNOT BE...
PLEASE TAKE HIM...!
EUNUCH KONG?
AHEM... AHEM...
DAMN...

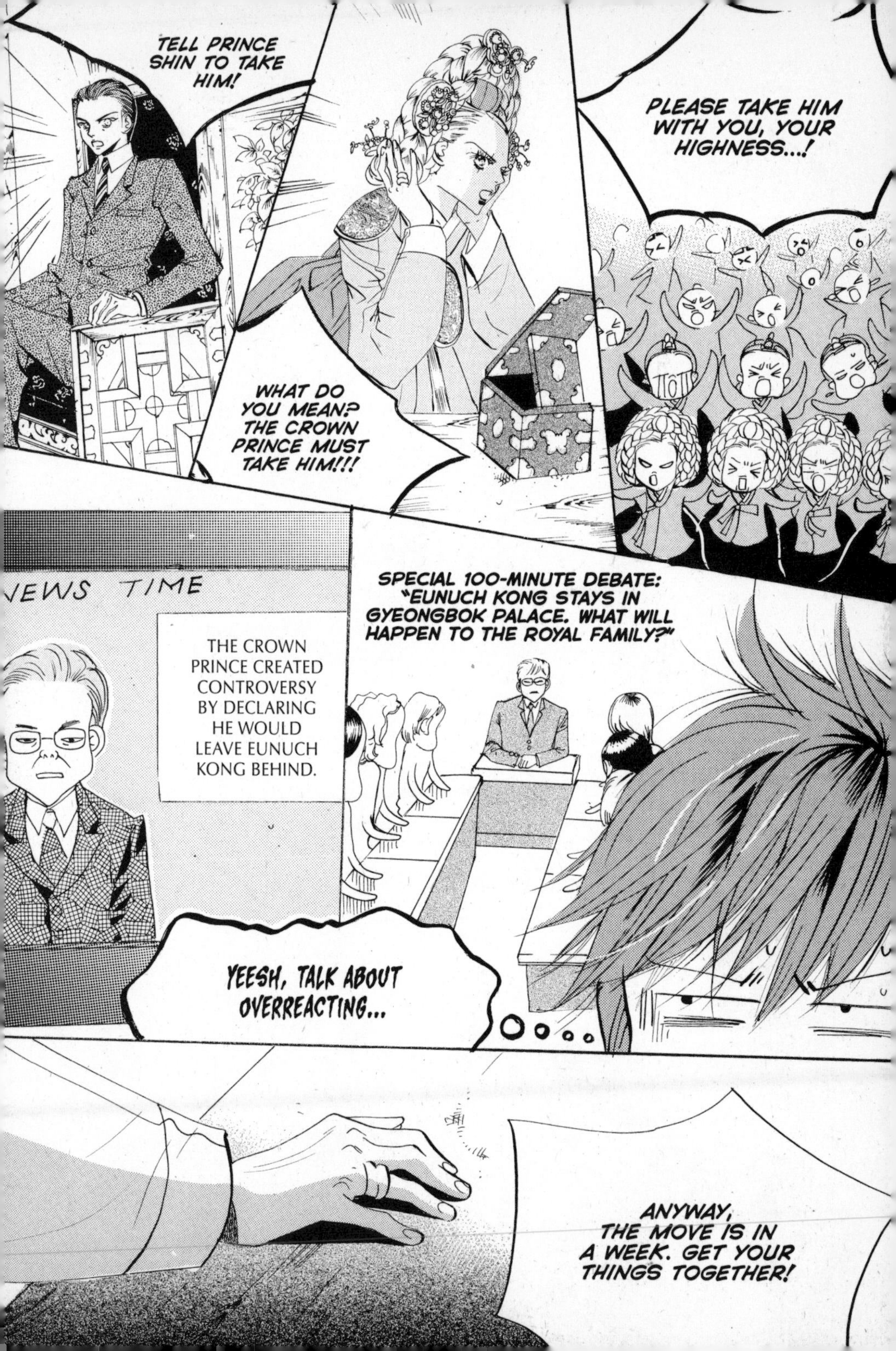
TELL PRINCE SHIN TO TAKE HIM!
WHAT DO YOU MEAN? THE CROWN PRINCE MUST TAKE HIM!!!
PLEASE TAKE HIM WITH YOU, YOUR HIGHNESS...!
NEWS TIME
THE CROWN PRINCE CREATED CONTROVERSY BY DECLARING HE WOULD LEAVE EUNUCH KONG BEHIND.
SPECIAL 100-MINUTE DEBATE: "EUNUCH KONG STAYS IN GYEONGBOK PALACE. WHAT WILL HAPPEN TO THE ROYAL FAMILY?"
YEESH, TALK ABOUT OVERREACTING...
ANYWAY, THE MOVE IS IN A WEEK. GET YOUR THINGS TOGETHER!

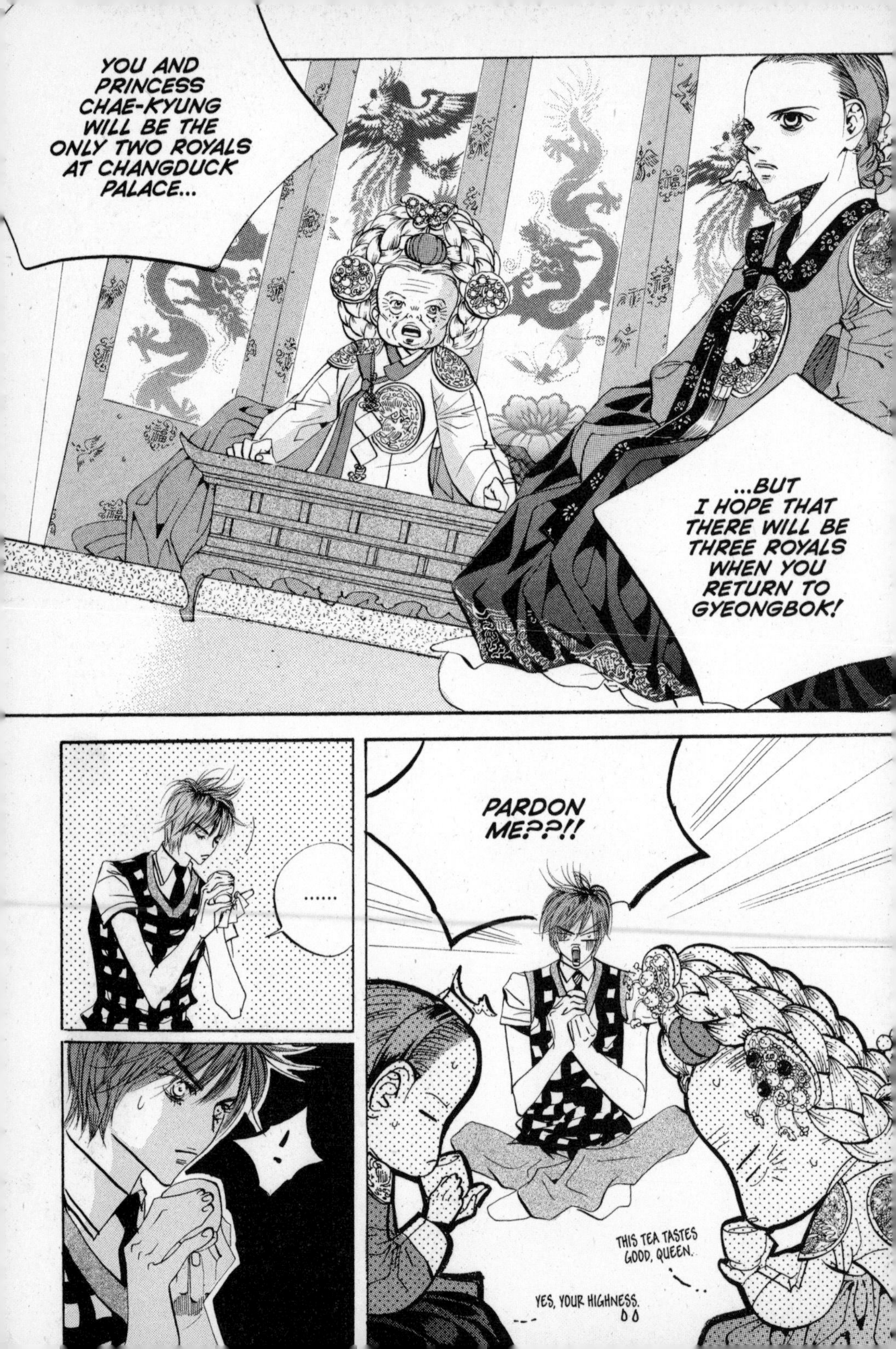
YOU AND PRINCESS CHAE-KYUNG WILL BE THE ONLY TWO ROYALS AT CHANGDUCK PALACE...
...BUT I HOPE THAT THERE WILL BE THREE ROYALS WHEN YOU RETURN TO GYEONGBOK!
......
PARDON ME??!!
THIS TEA TASTES GOOD, QUEEN.
YES, YOUR HIGHNESS.

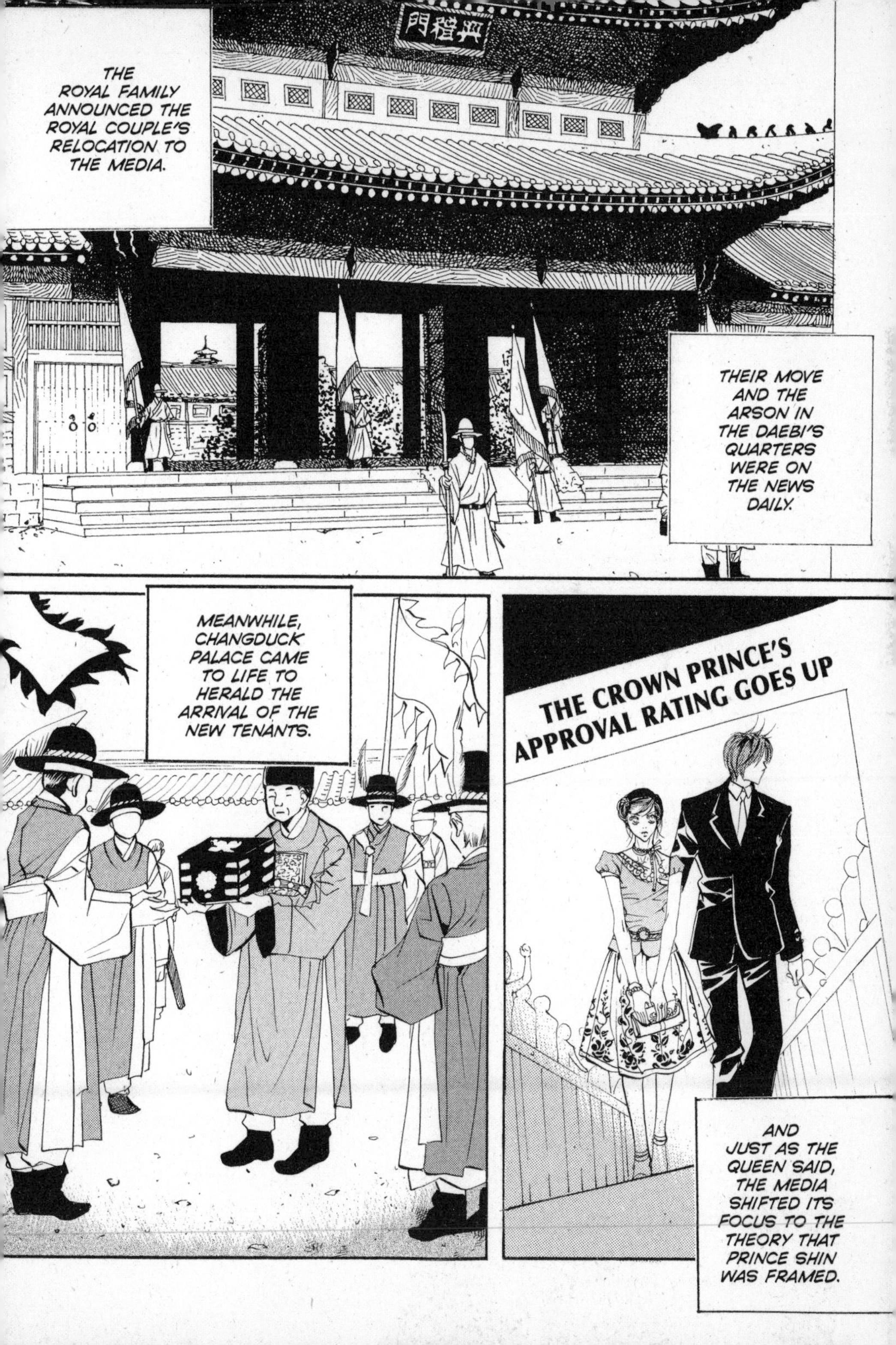
THE ROYAL FAMILY ANNOUNCED THE ROYAL COUPLE'S RELOCATION TO THE MEDIA.
THEIR MOVE AND THE ARSON IN THE DAEBI'S QUARTERS WERE ON THE NEWS DAILY.
MEANWHILE, CHANGDUCK PALACE CAME TO LIFE TO HERALD THE ARRIVAL OF THE NEW TENANTS.
THE CROWN PRINCE'S APPROVAL RATING GOES UP
AND JUST AS THE QUEEN SAID, THE MEDIA SHIFTED ITS FOCUS TO THE THEORY THAT PRINCE SHIN WAS FRAMED.

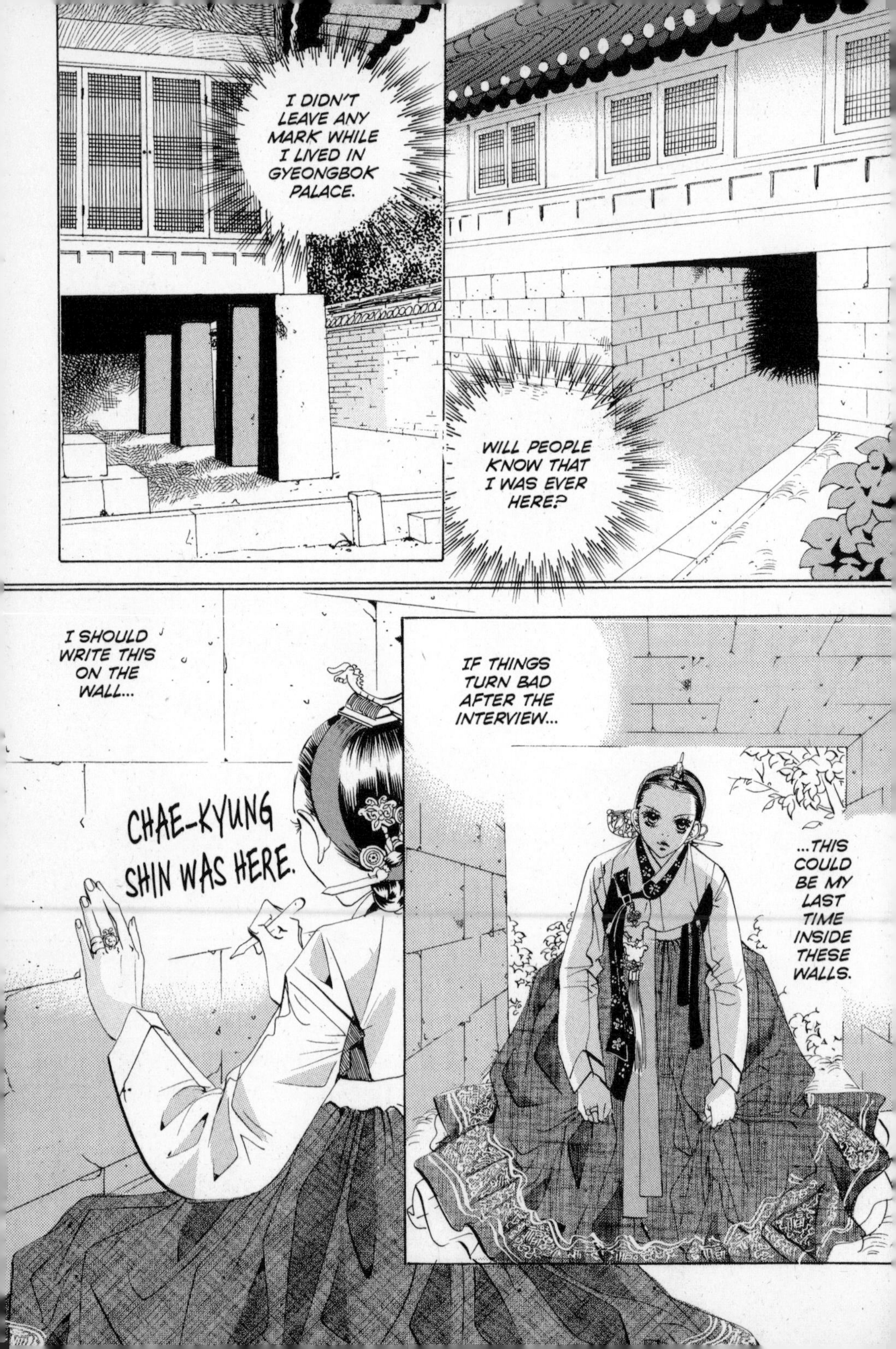
I DIDN'T LEAVE ANY MARK WHILE I LIVED IN GYEONGBOK PALACE.
WILL PEOPLE KNOW THAT I WAS EVER HERE?
I SHOULD WRITE THIS ON THE WALL...
CHAE-KYUNG SHIN WAS HERE.
IF THINGS TURN BAD AFTER THE INTERVIEW...
...THIS COULD BE MY LAST TIME INSIDE THESE WALLS.

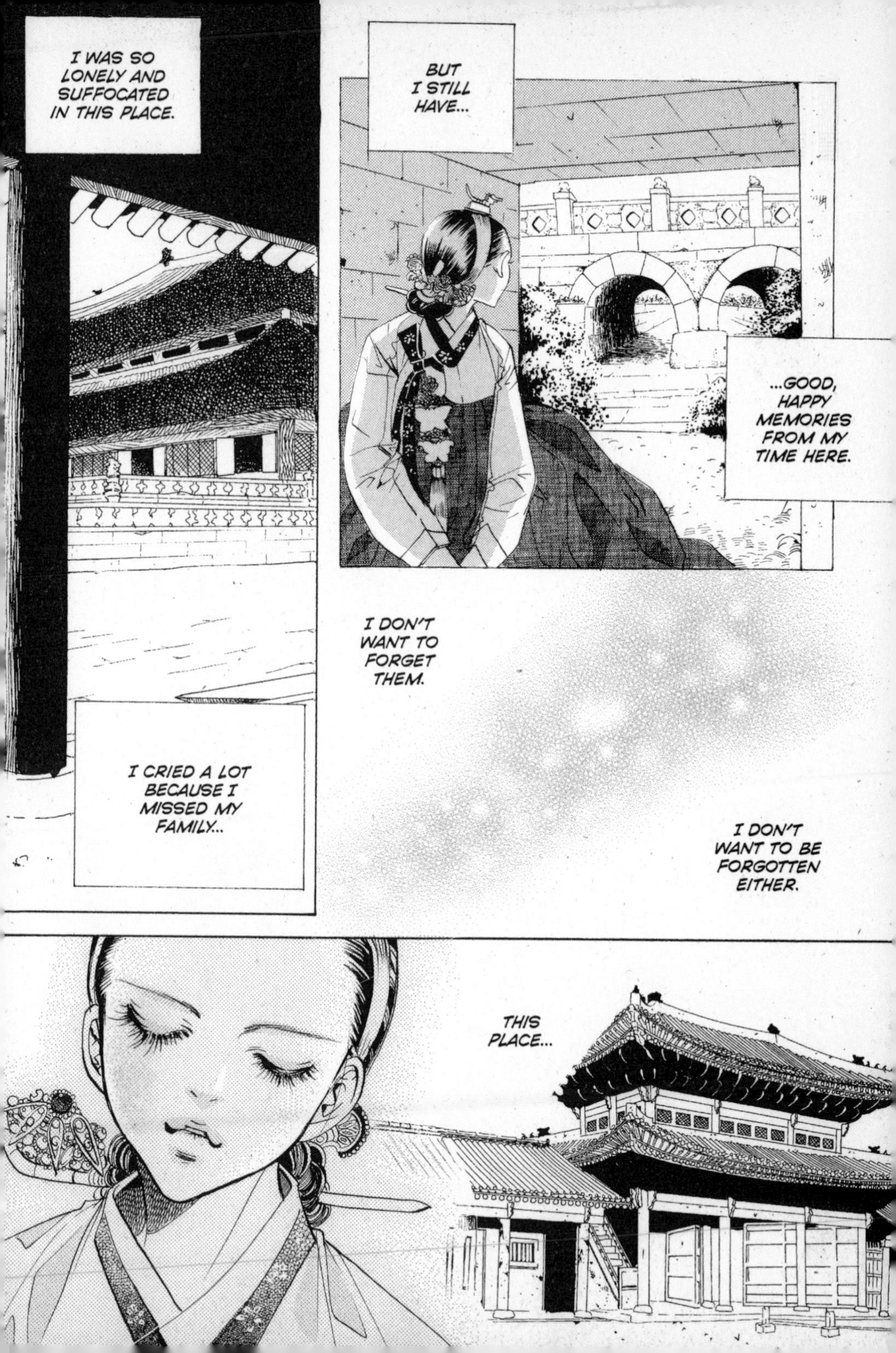
I WAS SO LONELY AND SUFFOCATED IN THIS PLACE.
I CRIED A LOT BECAUSE I MISSED MY FAMILY...
BUT I STILL HAVE...
...GOOD, HAPPY MEMORIES FROM MY TIME HERE.
I DON'T WANT TO FORGET THEM.
I DON'T WANT TO BE FORGOTTEN EITHER.
THIS PLACE...

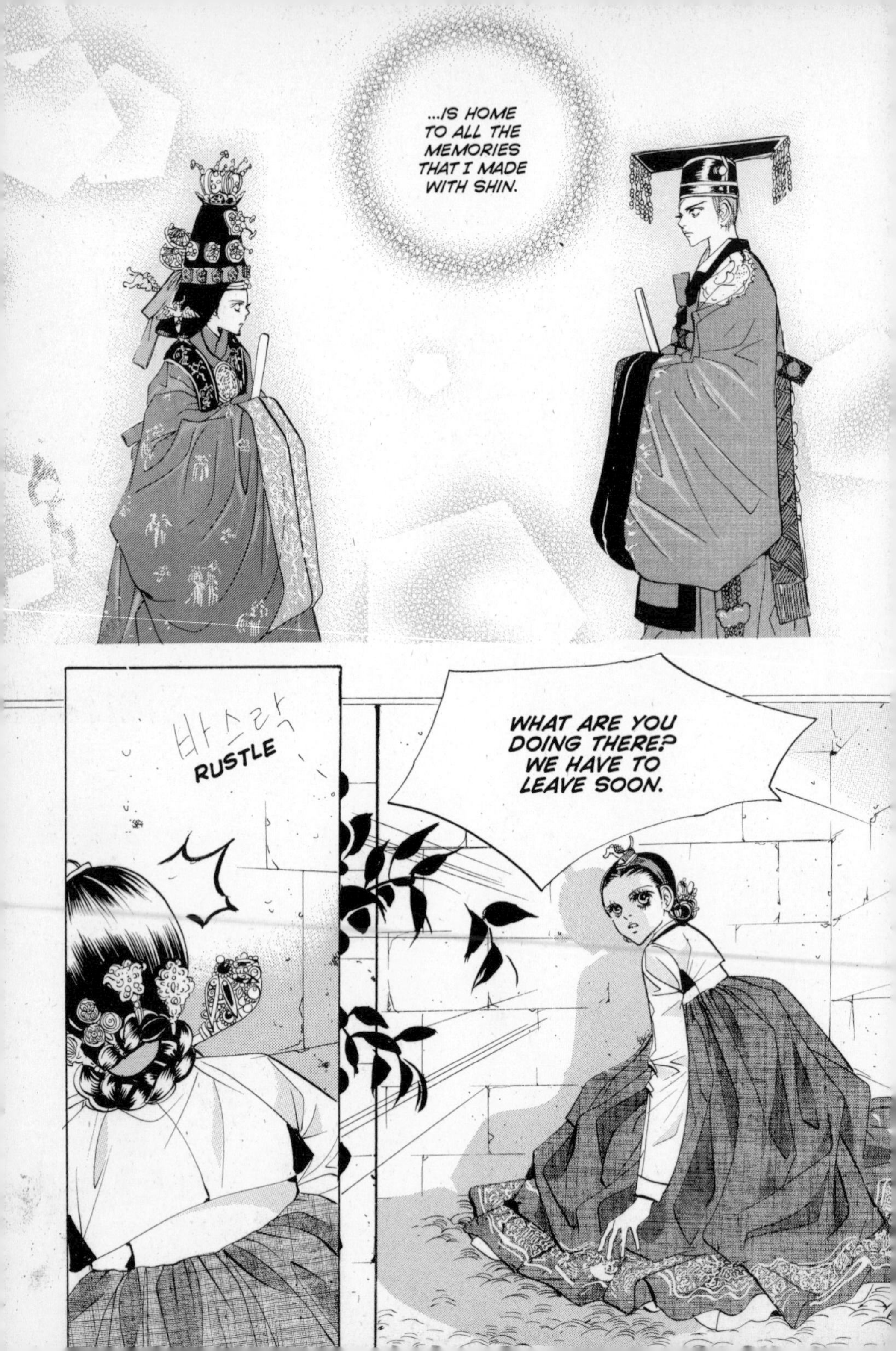
...IS HOME TO ALL THE MEMORIES THAT I MADE WITH SHIN.
바스락
RUSTLE
WHAT ARE YOU DOING THERE? WE HAVE TO LEAVE SOON.

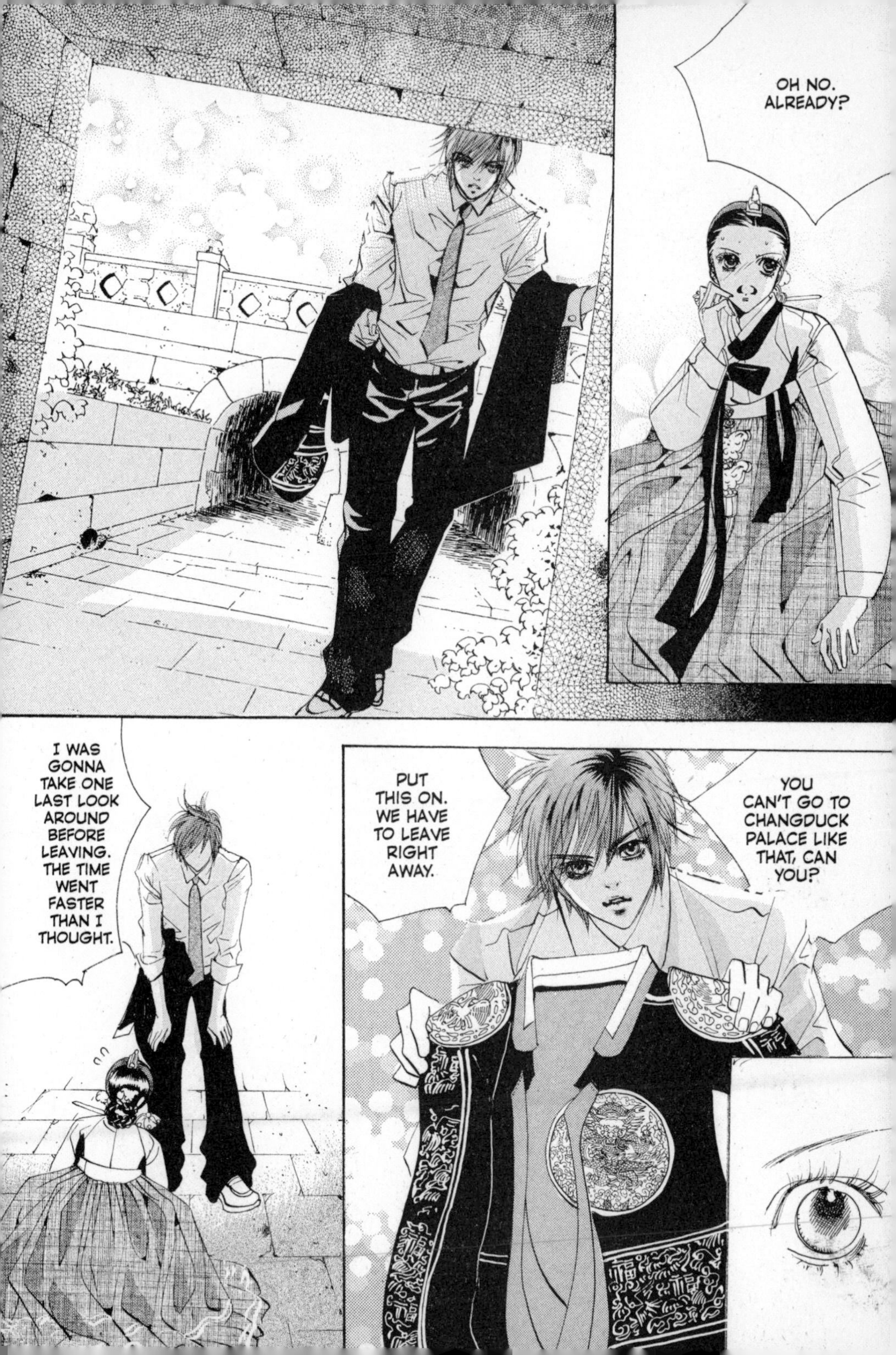
OH NO. ALREADY?
I WAS GONNA TAKE ONE LAST LOOK AROUND BEFORE LEAVING. THE TIME WENT FASTER THAN I THOUGHT.
PUT THIS ON. WE HAVE TO LEAVE RIGHT AWAY.
YOU CAN'T GO TO CHANGDUCK PALACE LIKE THAT, CAN YOU?

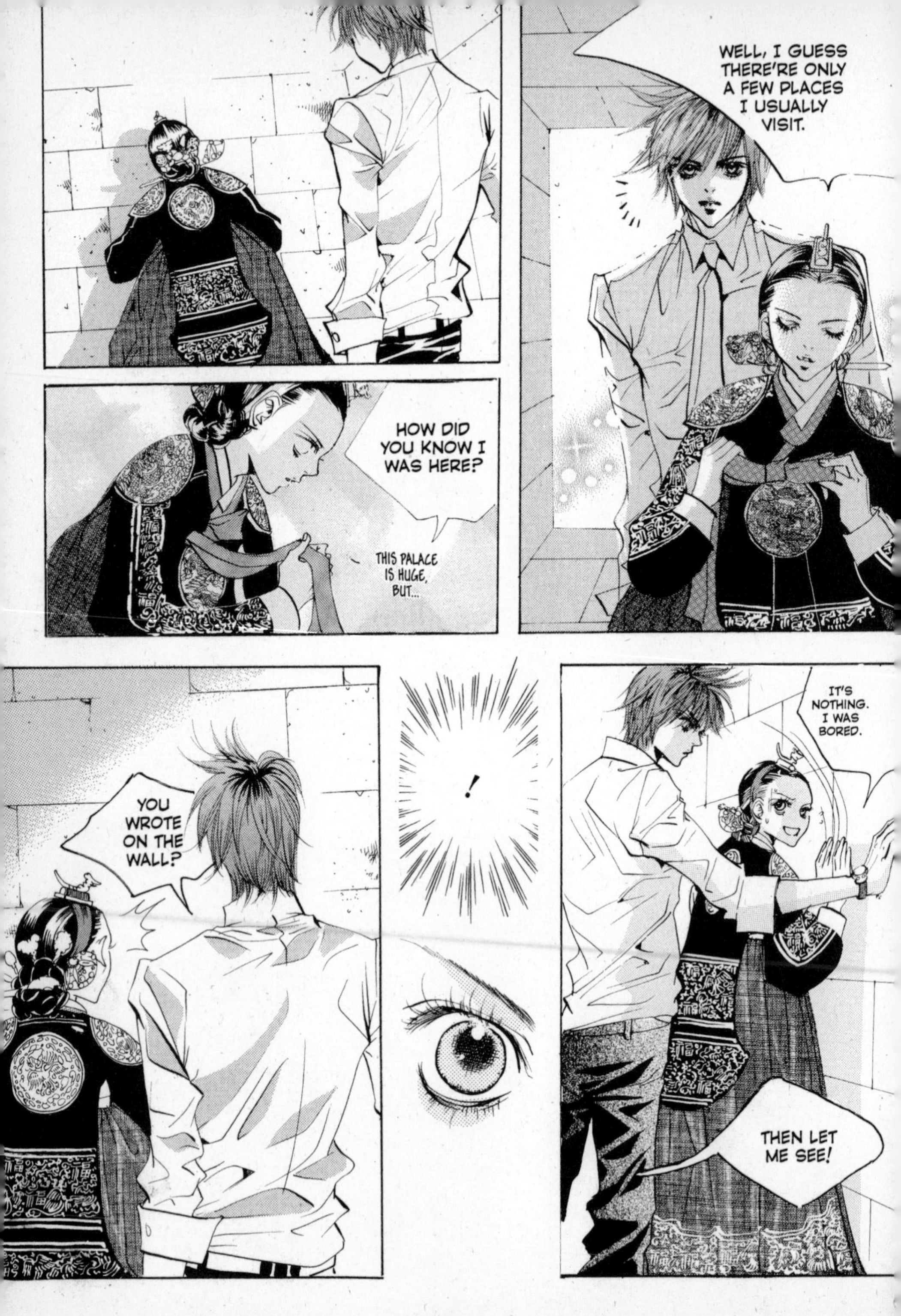
HOW DID YOU KNOW I WAS HERE?
WELL, I GUESS THERE'RE ONLY A FEW PLACES I USUALLY VISIT.
THIS PALACE IS HUGE, BUT...
YOU WROTE ON THE WALL?
!
IT'S NOTHING. I WAS BORED.
THEN LET ME SEE!

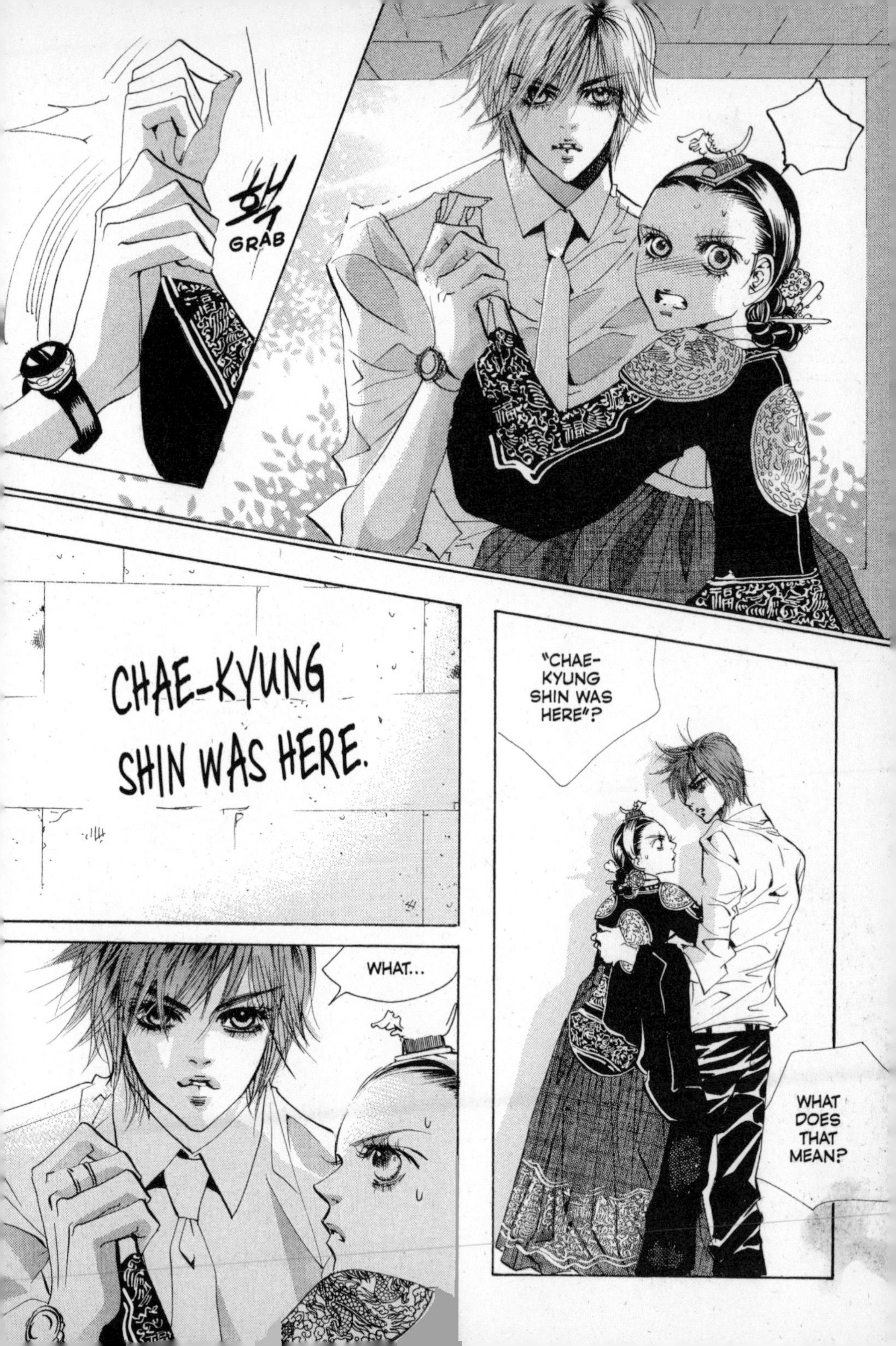
홱
GRAB
CHAE-KYUNG SHIN WAS HERE.
WHAT...
"CHAE-KYUNG SHIN WAS HERE"?
WHAT DOES THAT MEAN?

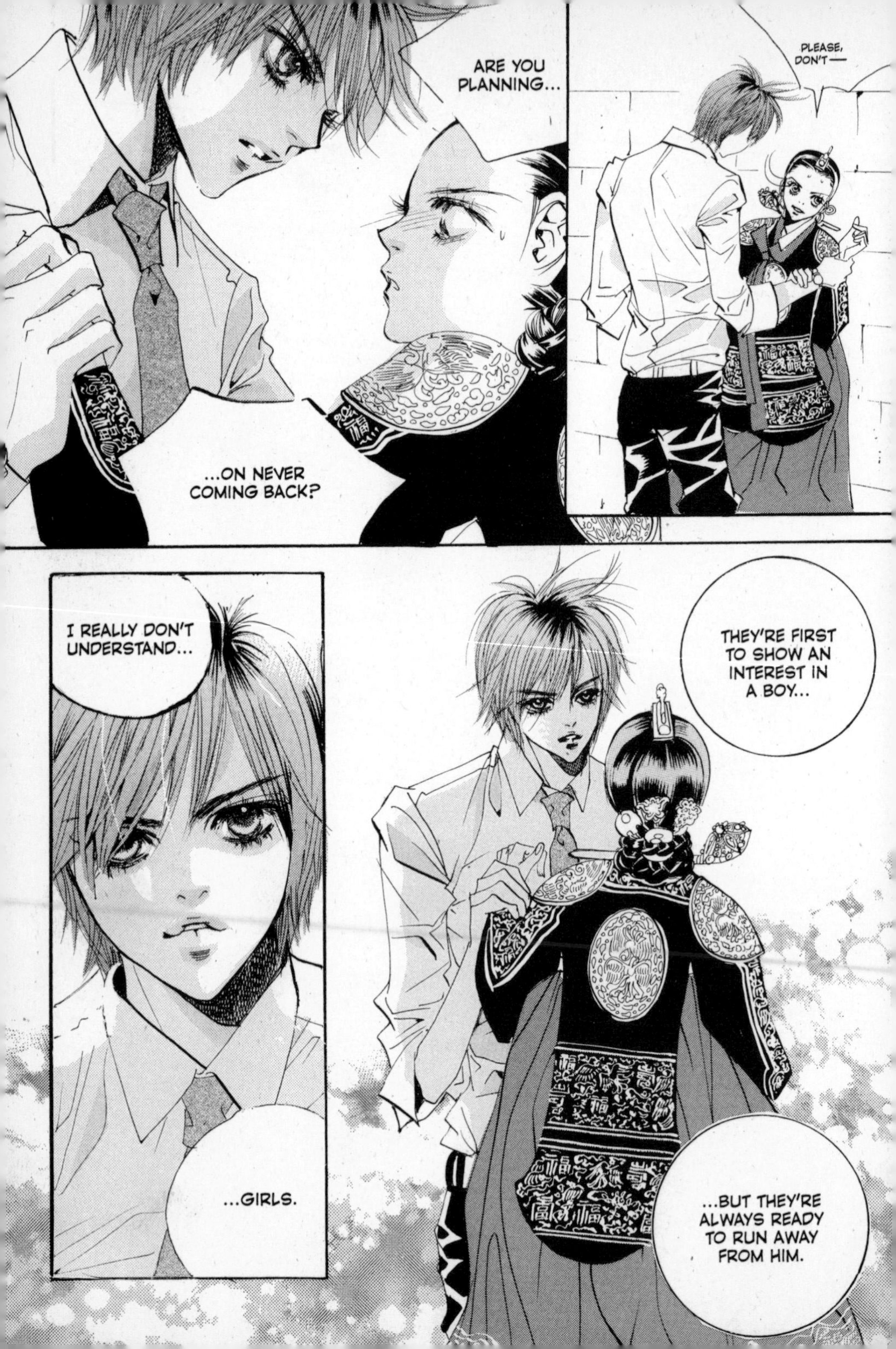

ARE YOU PLANNING...
...ON NEVER COMING BACK?
PLEASE, DON'T—
I REALLY DON'T UNDERSTAND...
...GIRLS.
THEY'RE FIRST TO SHOW AN INTEREST IN A BOY...
...BUT THEY'RE ALWAYS READY TO RUN AWAY FROM HIM.

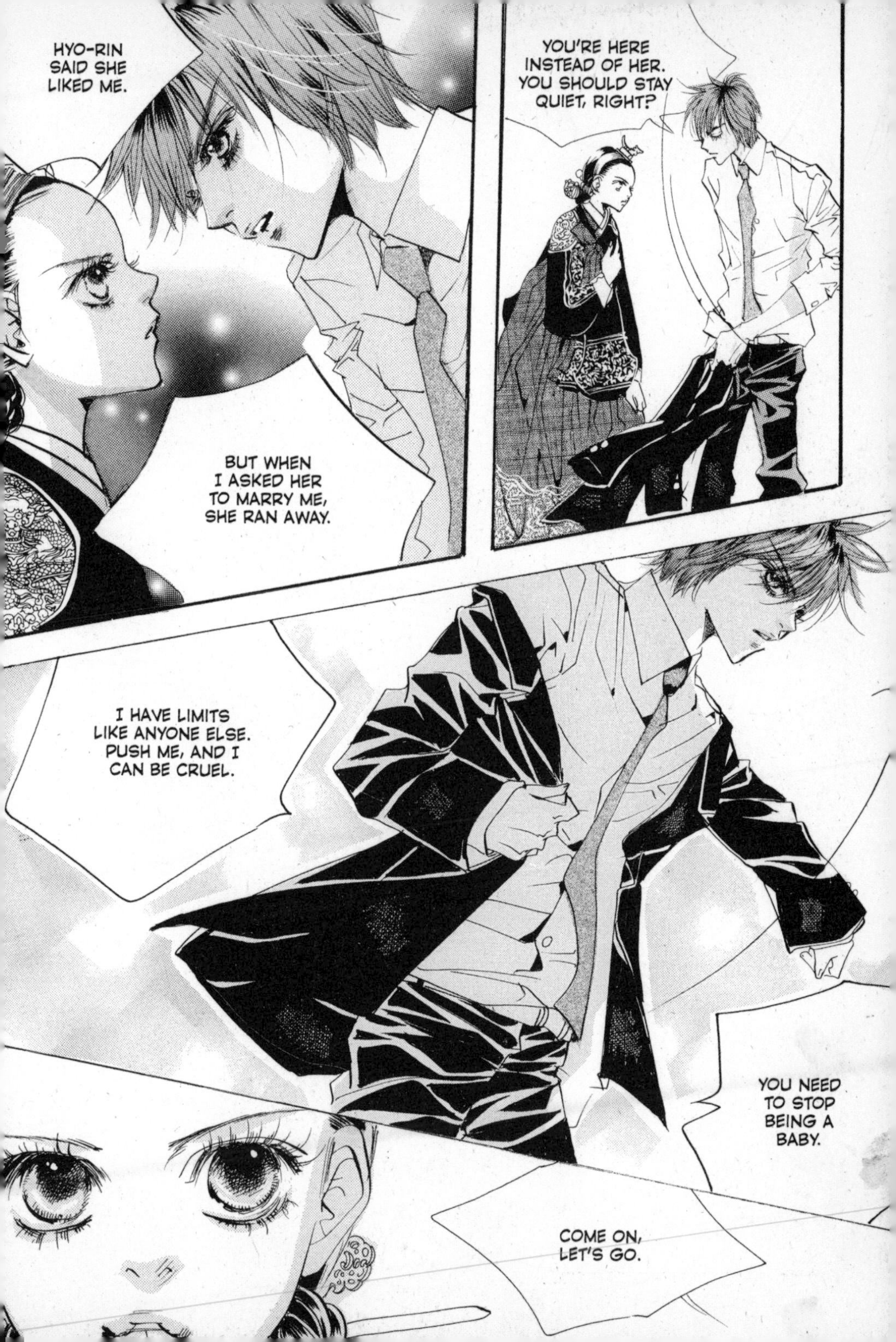
HYO-RIN SAID SHE LIKED ME.
BUT WHEN I ASKED HER TO MARRY ME, SHE RAN AWAY.
YOU'RE HERE INSTEAD OF HER. YOU SHOULD STAY QUIET, RIGHT?
I HAVE LIMITS LIKE ANYONE ELSE. PUSH ME, AND I CAN BE CRUEL.
YOU NEED TO STOP BEING A BABY.
COME ON, LET'S GO.

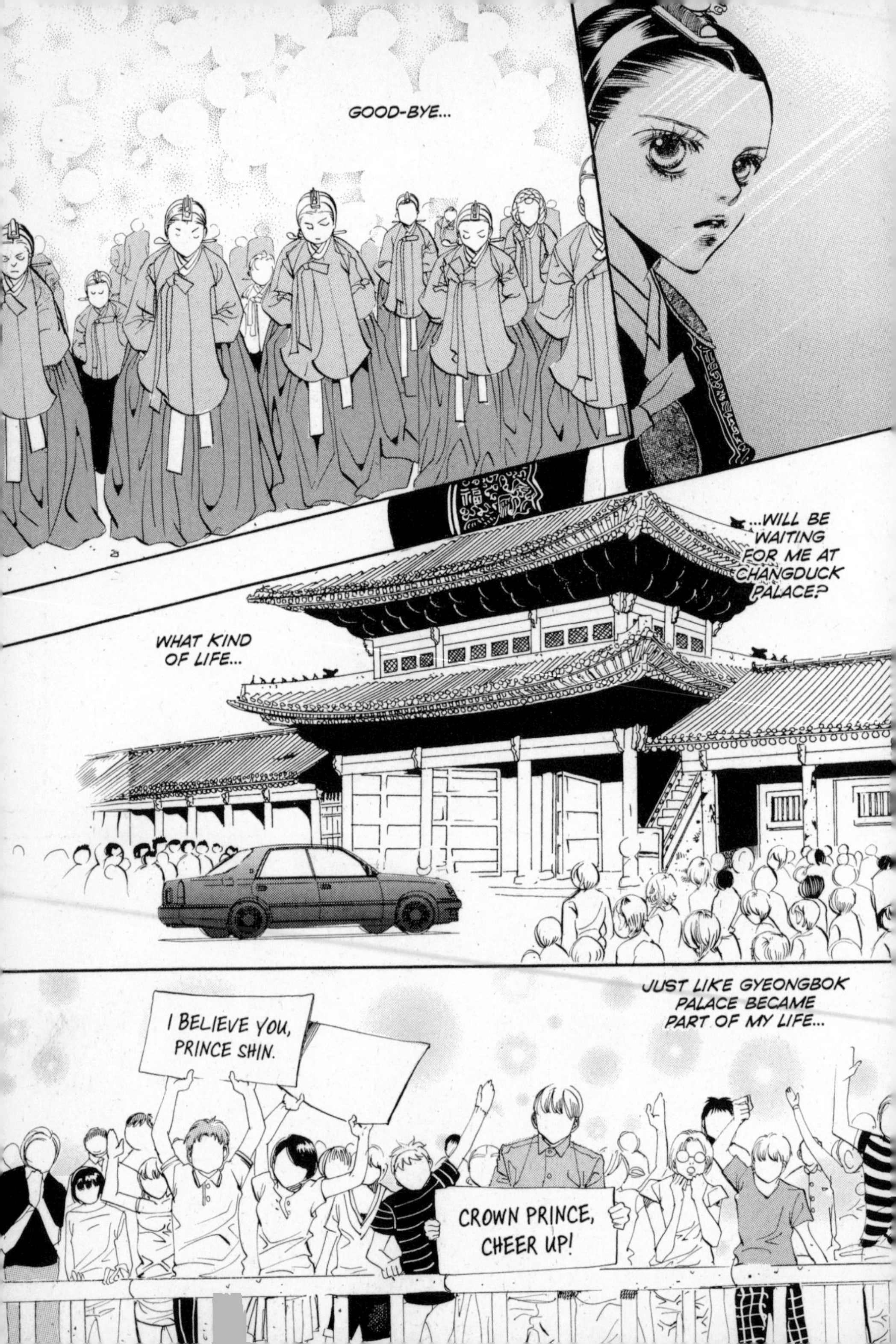
GOOD-BYE...
WHAT KIND OF LIFE...
...WILL BE WAITING FOR ME AT CHANGDUCK PALACE?
I BELIEVE YOU, PRINCE SHIN.
JUST LIKE GYEONGBOK PALACE BECAME PART OF MY LIFE...
CROWN PRINCE, CHEER UP!

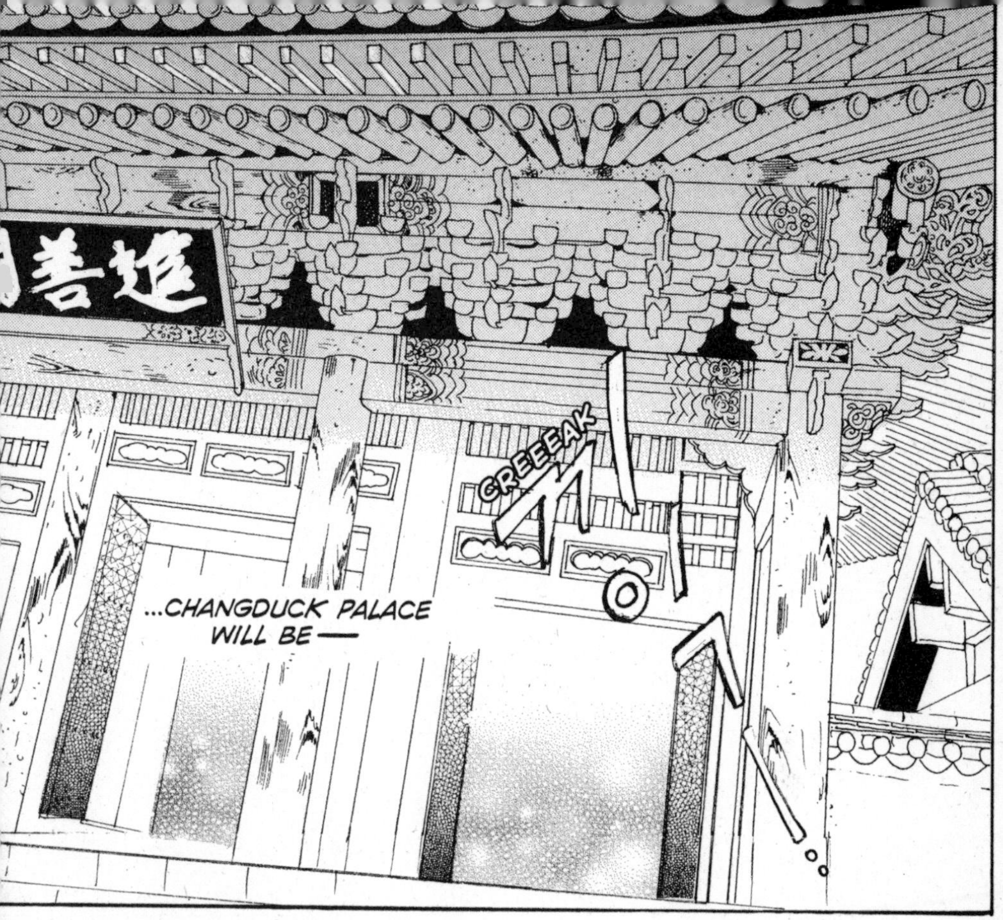
GREEEAK
...CHANGDUCK PALACE WILL BE—
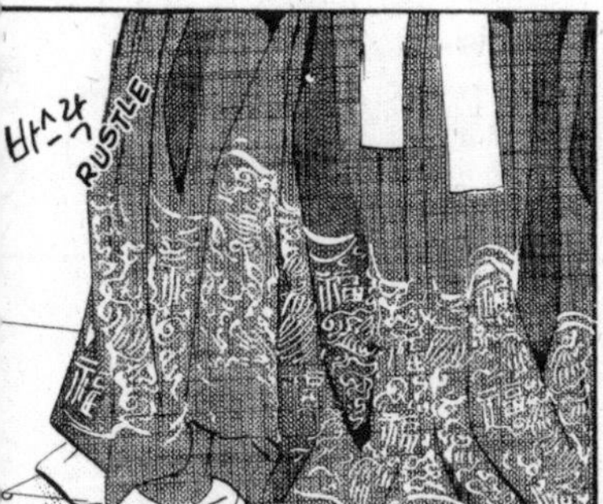
바스락
RUSTLE
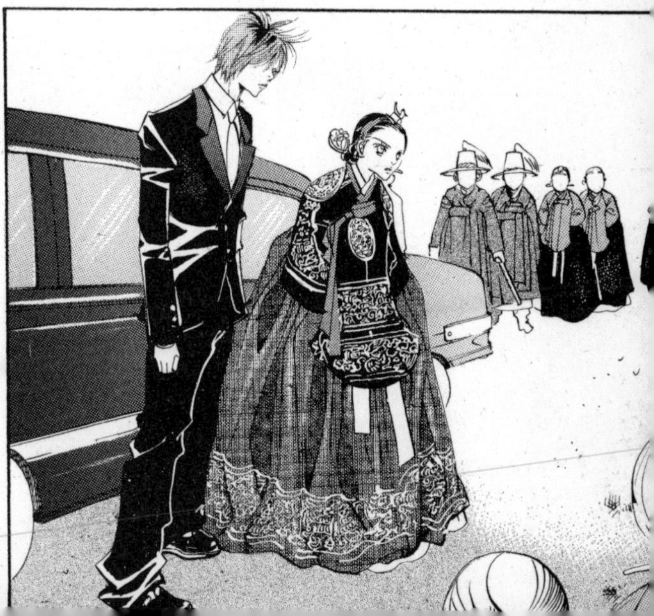

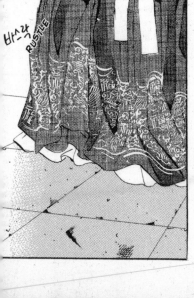

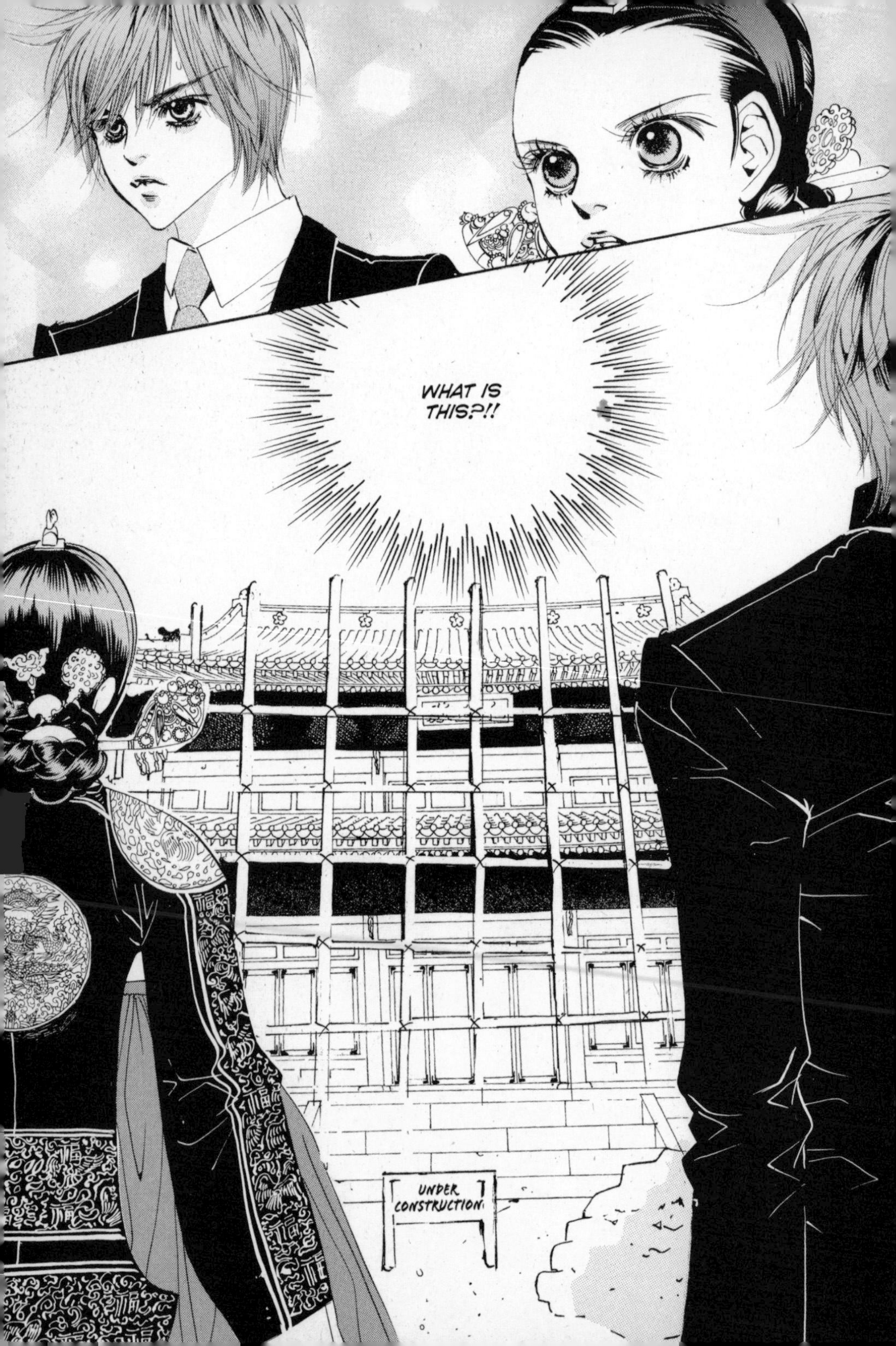
WHAT IS THIS?!!
UNDER CONSTRUCTION

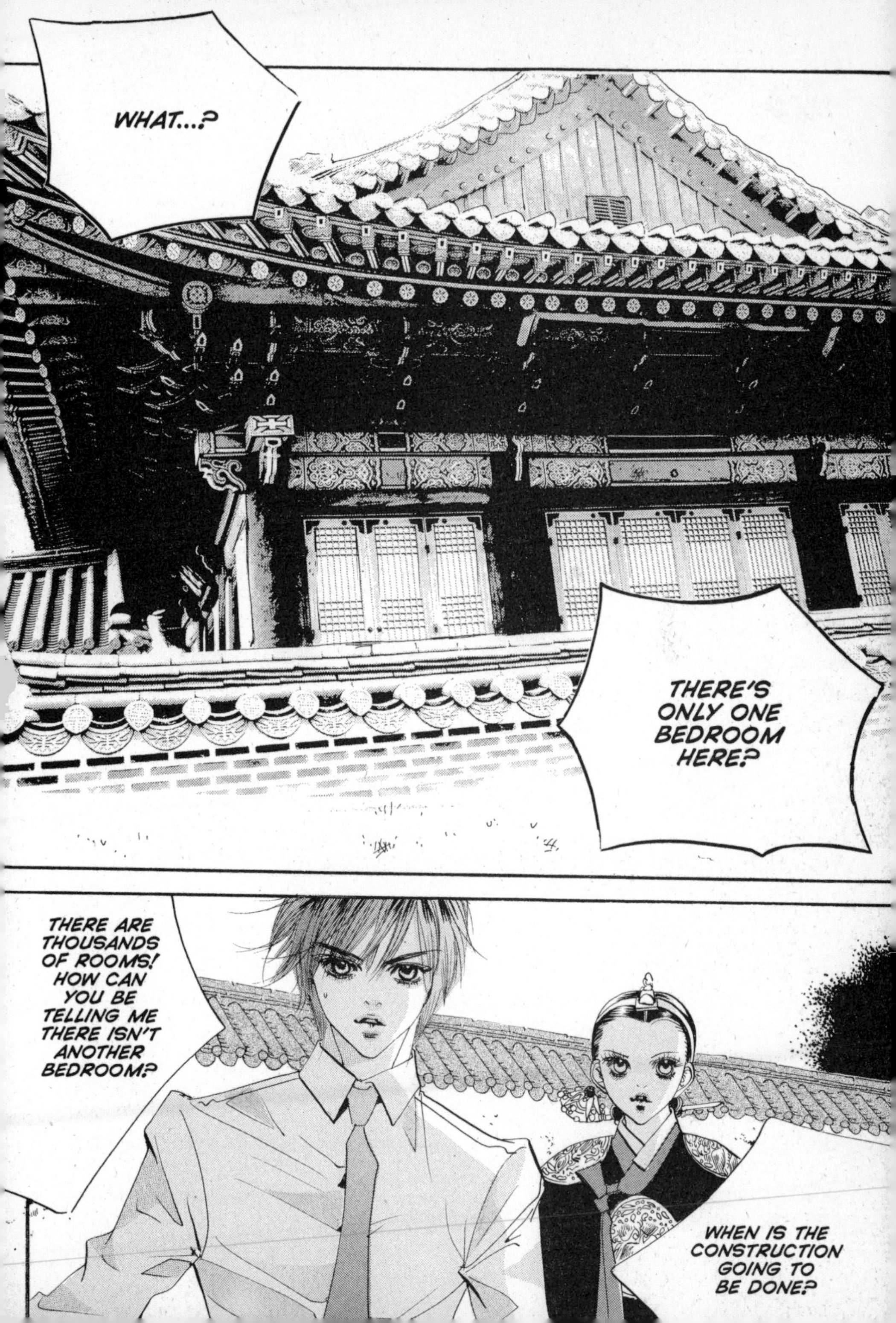
WHAT...?
THERE'S ONLY ONE BEDROOM HERE?
THERE ARE THOUSANDS OF ROOMS! HOW CAN YOU BE TELLING ME THERE ISN'T ANOTHER BEDROOM?
WHEN IS THE CONSTRUCTION GOING TO BE DONE?

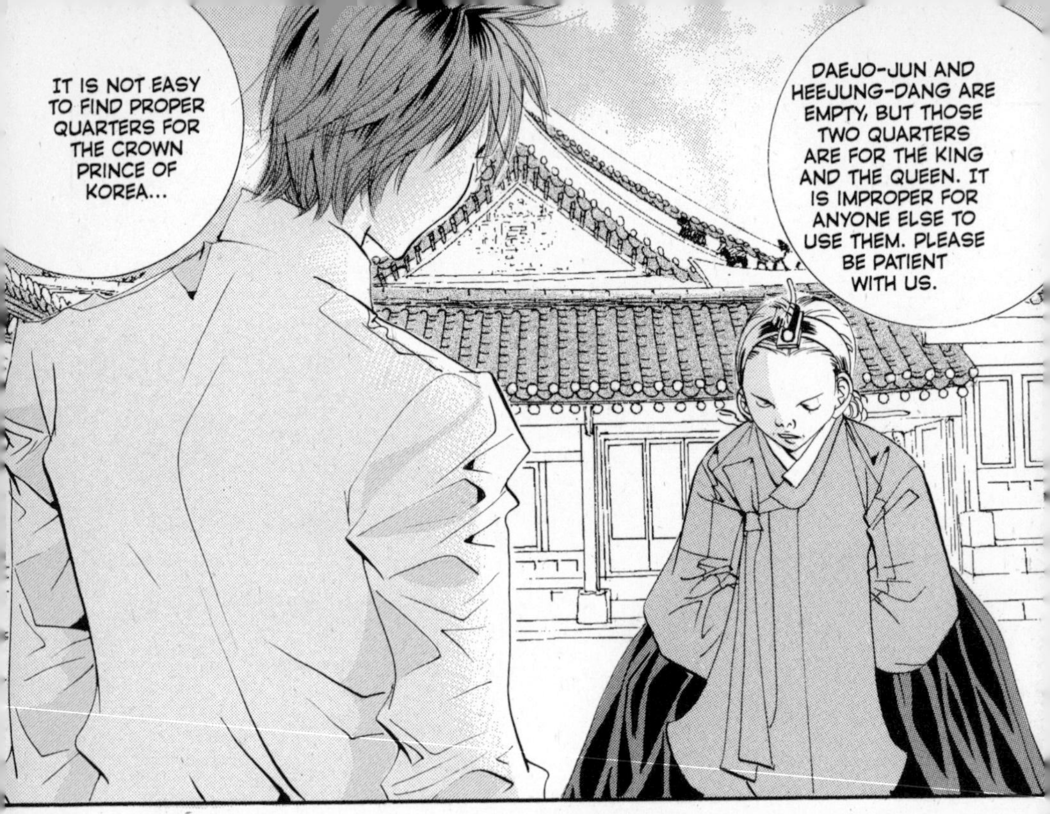
IT IS NOT EASY TO FIND PROPER QUARTERS FOR THE CROWN PRINCE OF KOREA...
DAEJO-JUN AND HEEJUNG-DANG ARE EMPTY, BUT THOSE TWO QUARTERS ARE FOR THE KING AND THE QUEEN. IT IS IMPROPER FOR ANYONE ELSE TO USE THEM. PLEASE BE PATIENT WITH US.

PALACE TERMINOLOGY

IF YOU EXAMINE THE NAMES OF PALACE BUILDINGS, YOU WILL SEE THEY END WITH JUN, DANG, HAP, GAK, JAE, HUN, NOO, OR JUNG. THERE WAS A PECKING ORDER FOR PALACES THE WAY THERE WAS FOR PEOPLE IN THE CHOSUN DYNASTY.

JUN: THE HIGHEST LEVEL OF PALACES. A KING AND QUEEN'S PUBLIC AND PRIVATE HOMES WERE CALLED JUN. A PALACE WHERE THE KING'S PARENTS STAYED WAS ALSO CALLED JUN (EXAMPLE: JAKYUNG-JUN). THESE PALACES WERE BIG AND LUXURIOUSLY DECORATED.

DANG: ONE LEVEL LOWER THAN JUN. A PRINCE'S HOUSE (EXAMPLE: JASUN-DANG) OR A PUBLIC SPACE USED BY A GOVERNMENT OFFICIAL WAS CALLED DANG. A KING AND A QUEEN COULD USE DANG, BUT A PRINCE COULD NOT USE JUN.

HAP: A BUILDING THAT IS PART OF JUN OR DANG.

GAK: A BUILDING THAT IS PART OF JUN OR DANG.

JAE: A ROYAL FAMILY'S RESTING OR LIVING AREA AND GOVERNMENTAL WORKPLACES WERE BOTH CALLED JAE. THESE BUILDINGS WERE USUALLY USED FOR READING OR THINKING.

HUN: WHILE THESE BUILDINGS WERE USED FOR EVERYDAY LIFE AS WELL, THEY WERE MOSTLY USED FOR PUBLIC GATHERINGS.

NOO: THESE PLACES WERE USUALLY FOR RESTING AND PLEASURE AND LOCATED ON A SECOND FLOOR. THE FIRST-FLOOR AREA WAS CALLED GAK.

JUNG: THE PURPOSE OF THESE BUILDINGS WAS THE SAME AS THE NOO, BUT THEY WERE BUNGALOWS. THEY WERE ALSO CALLED JUNGJA.

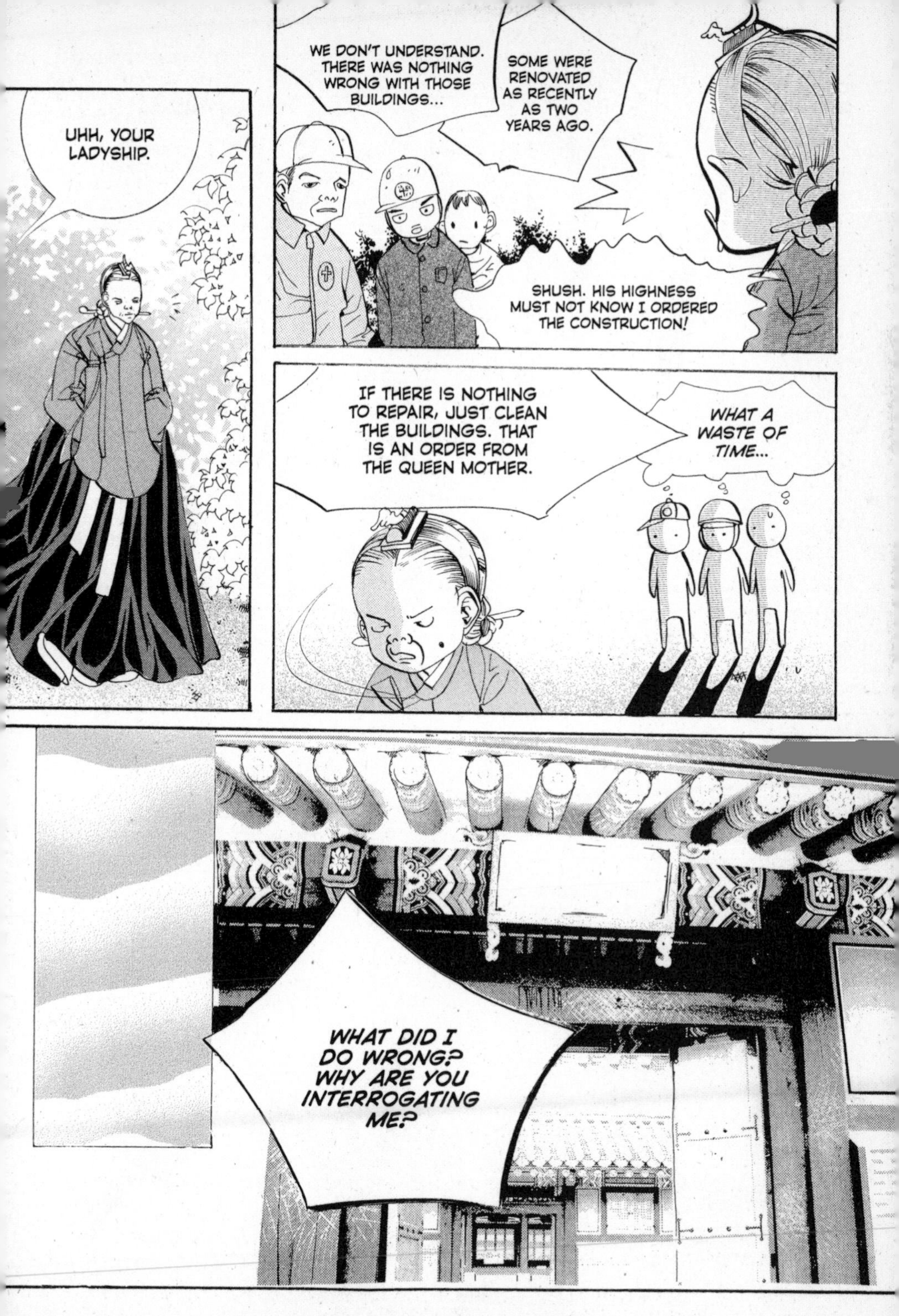
UHH, YOUR LADYSHIP.
WE DON'T UNDERSTAND. THERE WAS NOTHING WRONG WITH THOSE BUILDINGS...
SOME WERE RENOVATED AS RECENTLY AS TWO YEARS AGO.
SHUSH. HIS HIGHNESS MUST NOT KNOW I ORDERED THE CONSTRUCTION!
IF THERE IS NOTHING TO REPAIR, JUST CLEAN THE BUILDINGS. THAT IS AN ORDER FROM THE QUEEN MOTHER.
WHAT A WASTE OF TIME...
WHAT DID I DO WRONG? WHY ARE YOU INTERROGATING ME?

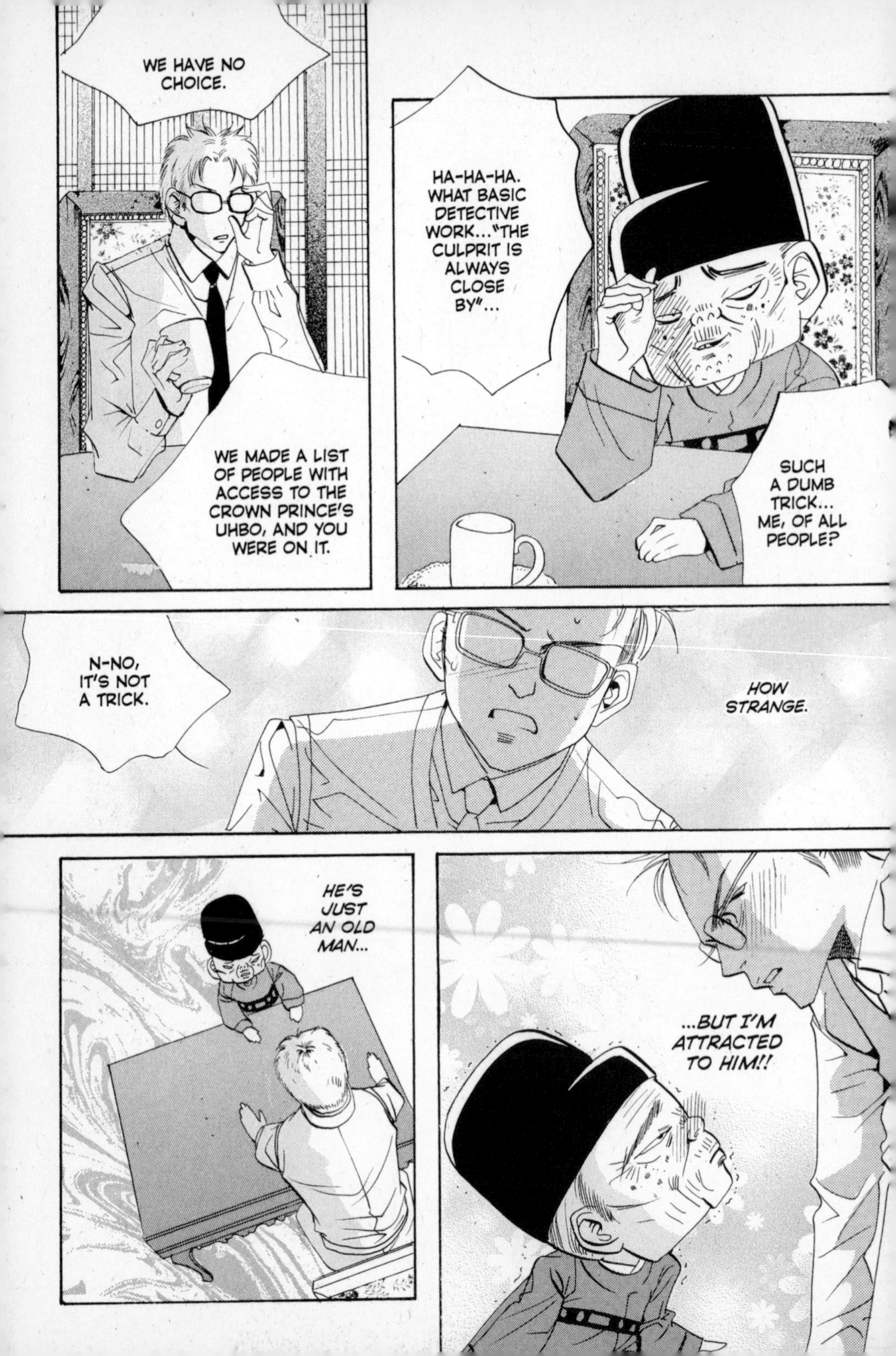
WE HAVE NO CHOICE.
WE MADE A LIST OF PEOPLE WITH ACCESS TO THE CROWN PRINCE'S UHBO, AND YOU WERE ON IT.
HA-HA-HA. WHAT BASIC DETECTIVE WORK..."THE CULPRIT IS ALWAYS CLOSE BY"...
SUCH A DUMB TRICK... ME, OF ALL PEOPLE?
N-NO, IT'S NOT A TRICK.
HOW STRANGE.
HE'S JUST AN OLD MAN...
...BUT I'M ATTRACTED TO HIM!!

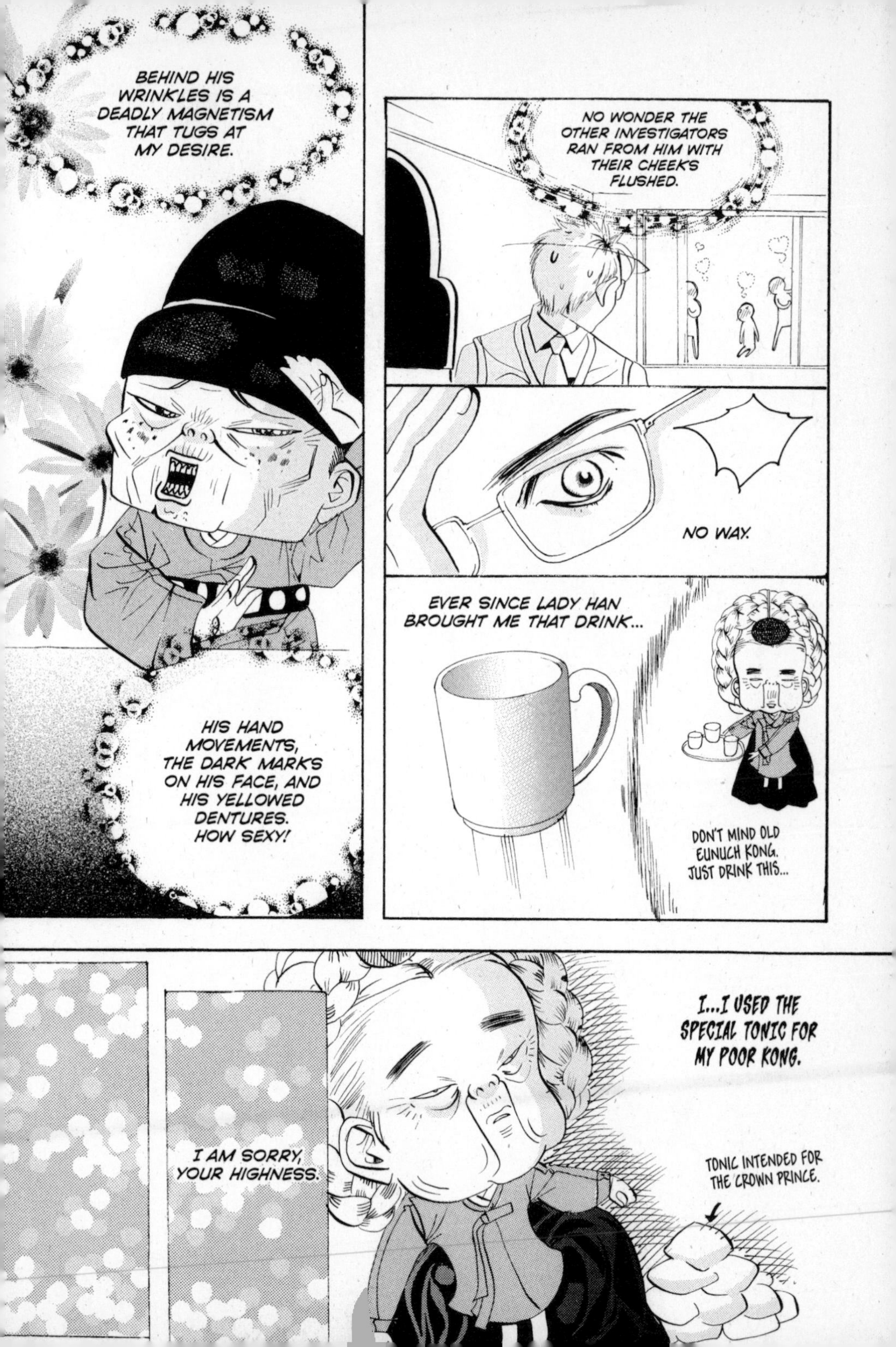
BEHIND HIS WRINKLES IS A DEADLY MAGNETISM THAT TUGS AT MY DESIRE.
HIS HAND MOVEMENTS, THE DARK MARKS ON HIS FACE, AND HIS YELLOWED DENTURES. HOW SEXY!
NO WONDER THE OTHER INVESTIGATORS RAN FROM HIM WITH THEIR CHEEKS FLUSHED.
NO WAY.
EVER SINCE LADY HAN BROUGHT ME THAT DRINK...
DON'T MIND OLD EUNUCH KONG. JUST DRINK THIS...
I AM SORRY, YOUR HIGHNESS.
I...I USED THE SPECIAL TONIC FOR MY POOR KONG.
TONIC INTENDED FOR THE CROWN PRINCE.

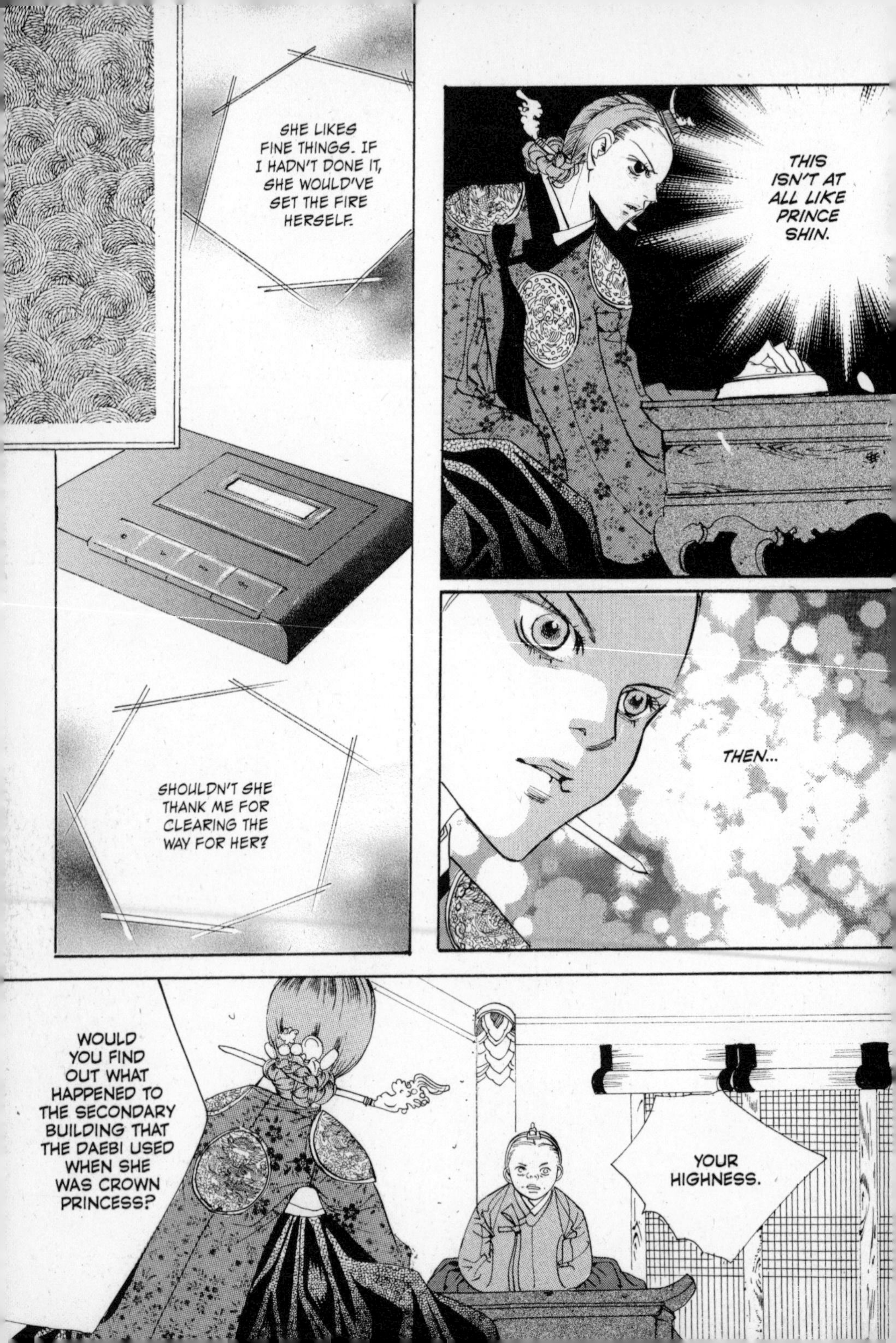
SHE LIKES FINE THINGS. IF I HADN'T DONE IT, SHE WOULD'VE SET THE FIRE HERSELF.
THIS ISN'T AT ALL LIKE PRINCE SHIN.
SHOULDN'T SHE THANK ME FOR CLEARING THE WAY FOR HER?
THEN...
WOULD YOU FIND OUT WHAT HAPPENED TO THE SECONDARY BUILDING THAT THE DAEBI USED WHEN SHE WAS CROWN PRINCESS?
YOUR HIGHNESS.

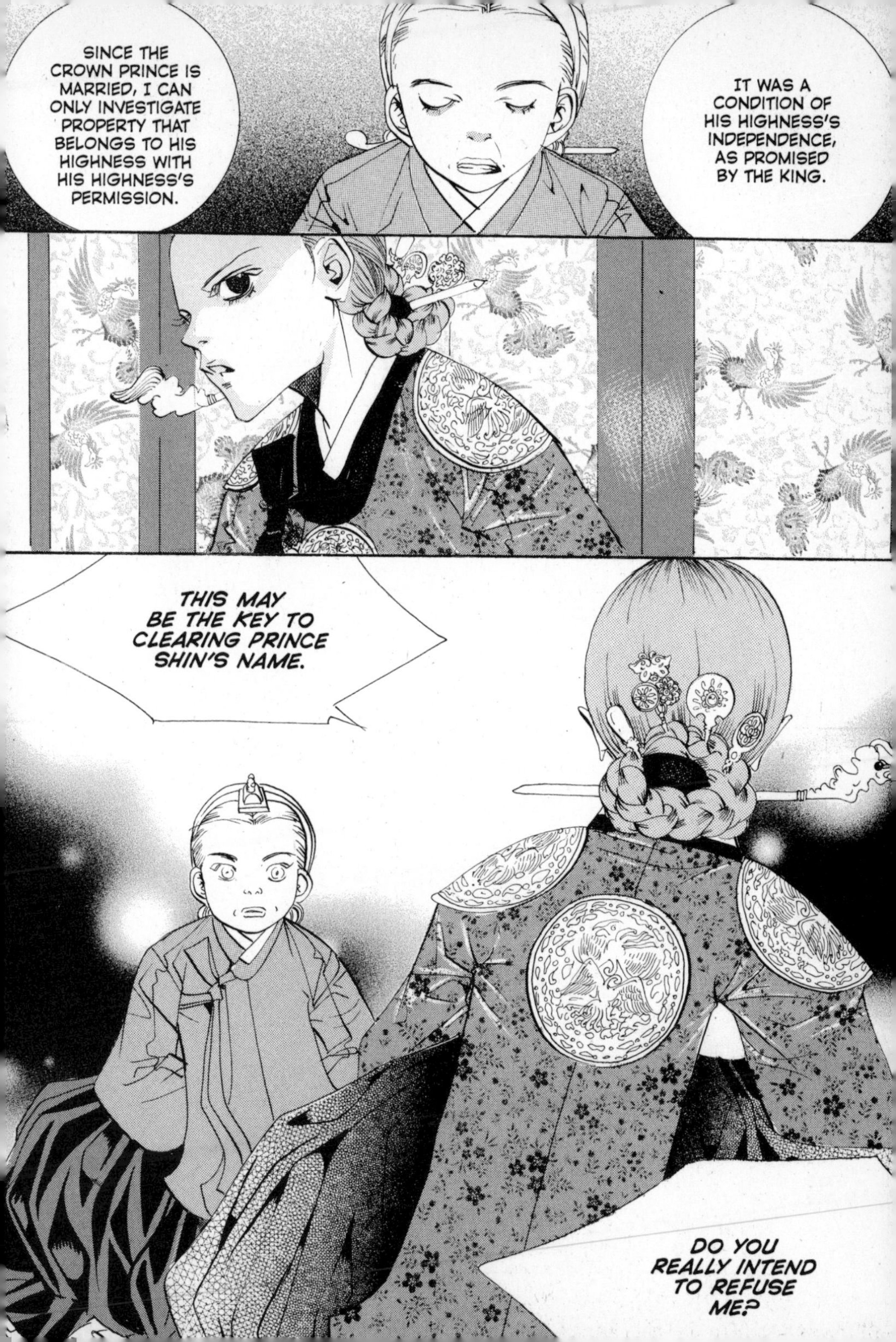
SINCE THE CROWN PRINCE IS MARRIED, I CAN ONLY INVESTIGATE PROPERTY THAT BELONGS TO HIS HIGHNESS WITH HIS HIGHNESS'S PERMISSION.
IT WAS A CONDITION OF HIS HIGHNESS'S INDEPENDENCE, AS PROMISED BY THE KING.
THIS MAY BE THE KEY TO CLEARING PRINCE SHIN'S NAME.
DO YOU REALLY INTEND TO REFUSE ME?

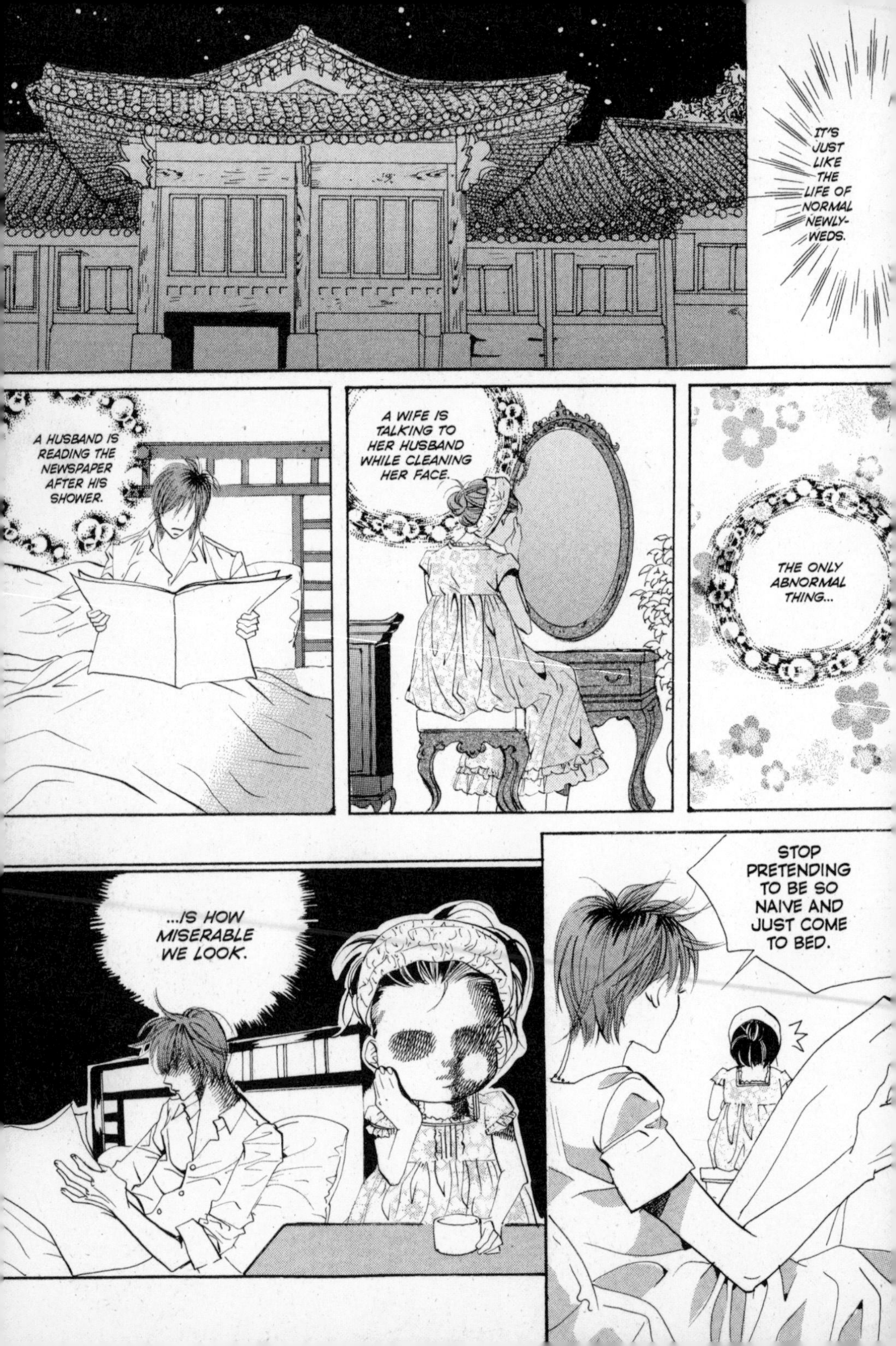
IT'S JUST LIKE THE LIFE OF NORMAL NEWLY-WEDS.
A HUSBAND IS READING THE NEWSPAPER AFTER HIS SHOWER.
A WIFE IS TALKING TO HER HUSBAND WHILE CLEANING HER FACE.
THE ONLY ABNORMAL THING...
...IS HOW MISERABLE WE LOOK.
STOP PRETENDING TO BE SO NAIVE AND JUST COME TO BED.

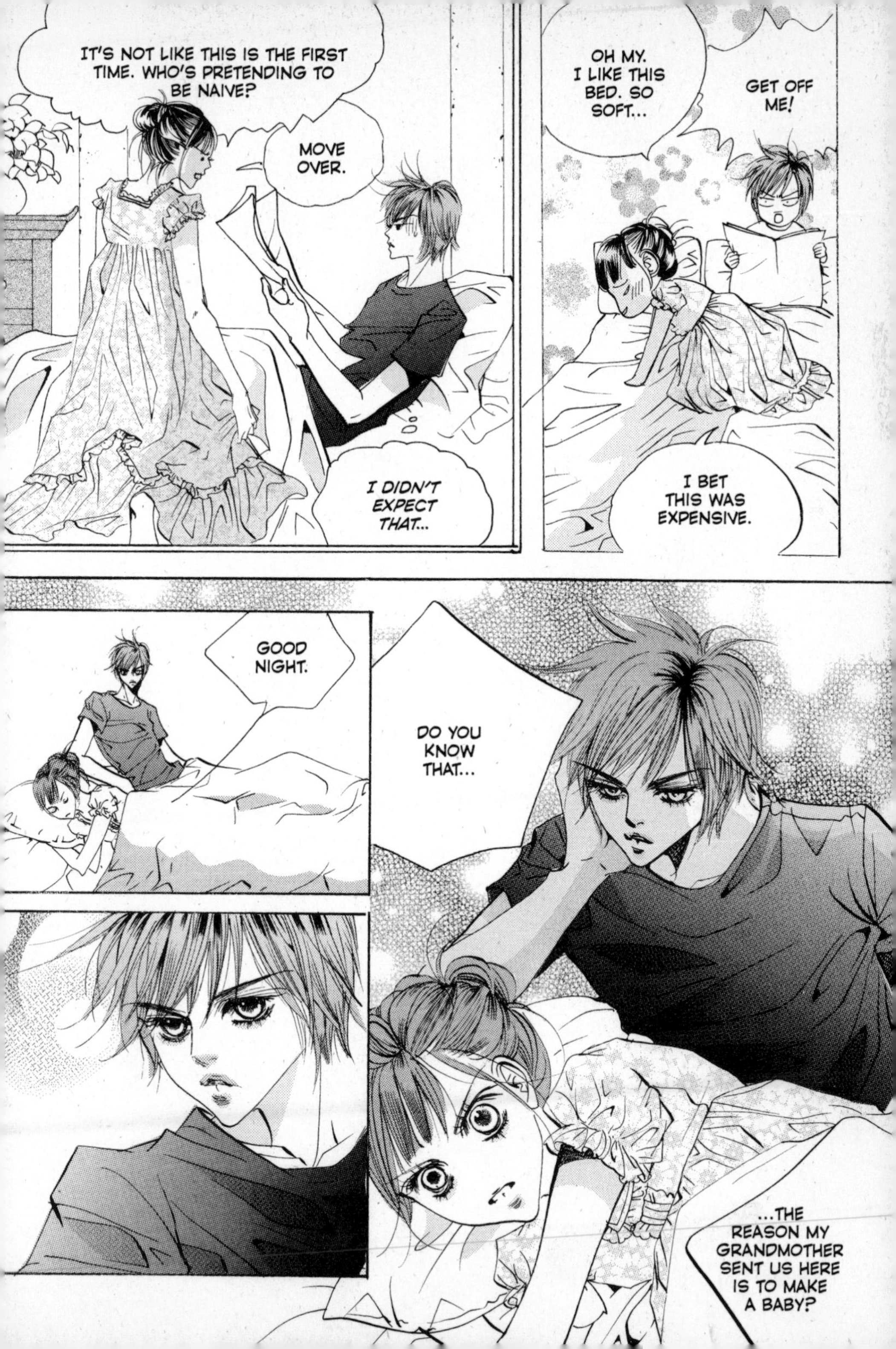
IT'S NOT LIKE THIS IS THE FIRST TIME. WHO'S PRETENDING TO BE NAIVE?
MOVE OVER.
I DIDN'T EXPECT THAT...
OH MY. I LIKE THIS BED. SO SOFT...
GET OFF ME!
I BET THIS WAS EXPENSIVE.
GOOD NIGHT.
DO YOU KNOW THAT...
...THE REASON MY GRANDMOTHER SENT US HERE IS TO MAKE A BABY?

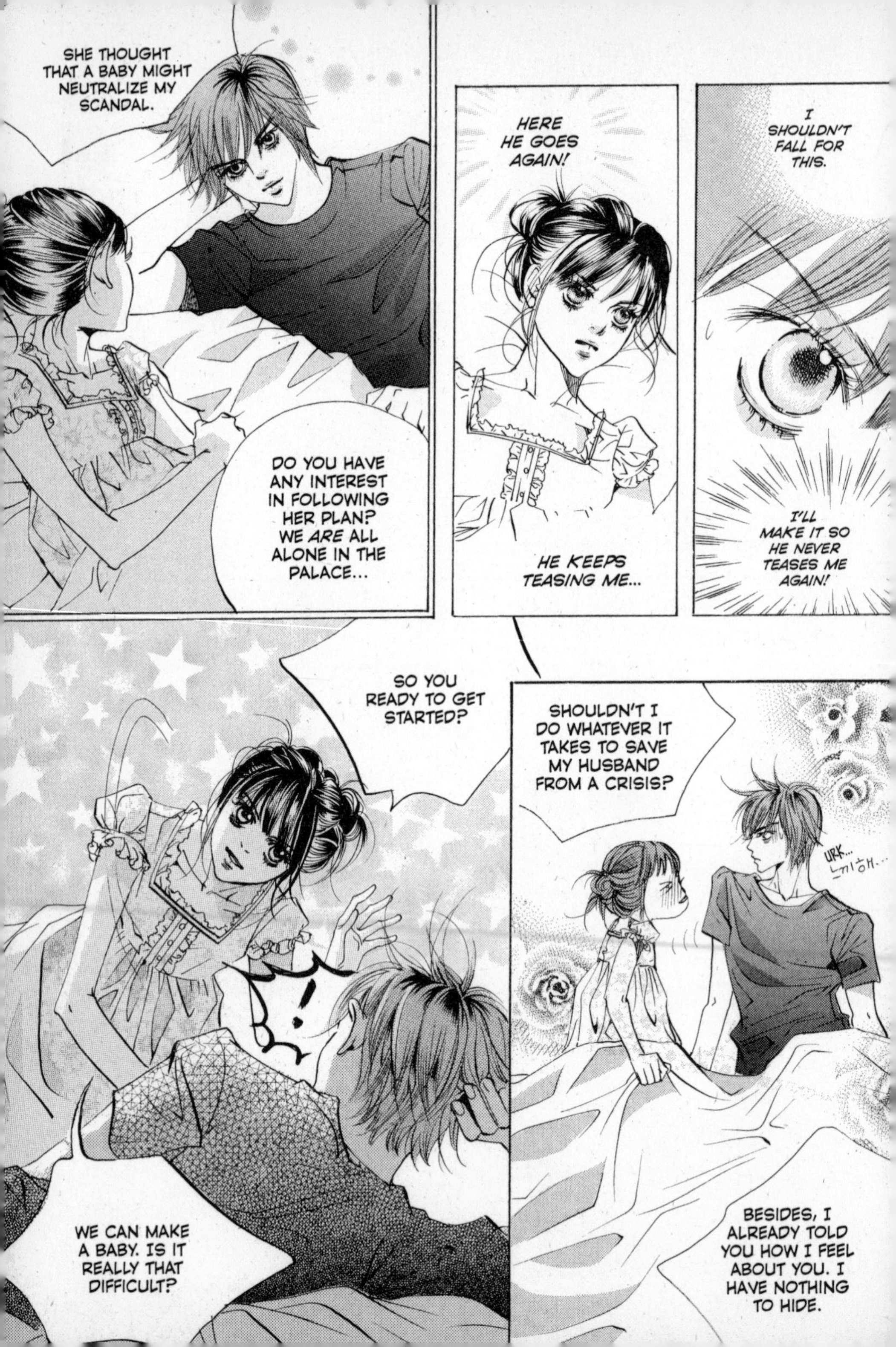
SHE THOUGHT THAT A BABY MIGHT NEUTRALIZE MY SCANDAL.
DO YOU HAVE ANY INTEREST IN FOLLOWING HER PLAN? WE *ARE* ALL ALONE IN THE PALACE...
HERE HE GOES AGAIN!
HE KEEPS TEASING ME...
I SHOULDN'T FALL FOR THIS.
I'LL MAKE IT SO HE NEVER TEASES ME AGAIN!
SO YOU READY TO GET STARTED?
!
WE CAN MAKE A BABY. IS IT REALLY THAT DIFFICULT?
SHOULDN'T I DO WHATEVER IT TAKES TO SAVE MY HUSBAND FROM A CRISIS?
URK...
느끼해...
BESIDES, I ALREADY TOLD YOU HOW I FEEL ABOUT YOU. I HAVE NOTHING TO HIDE.

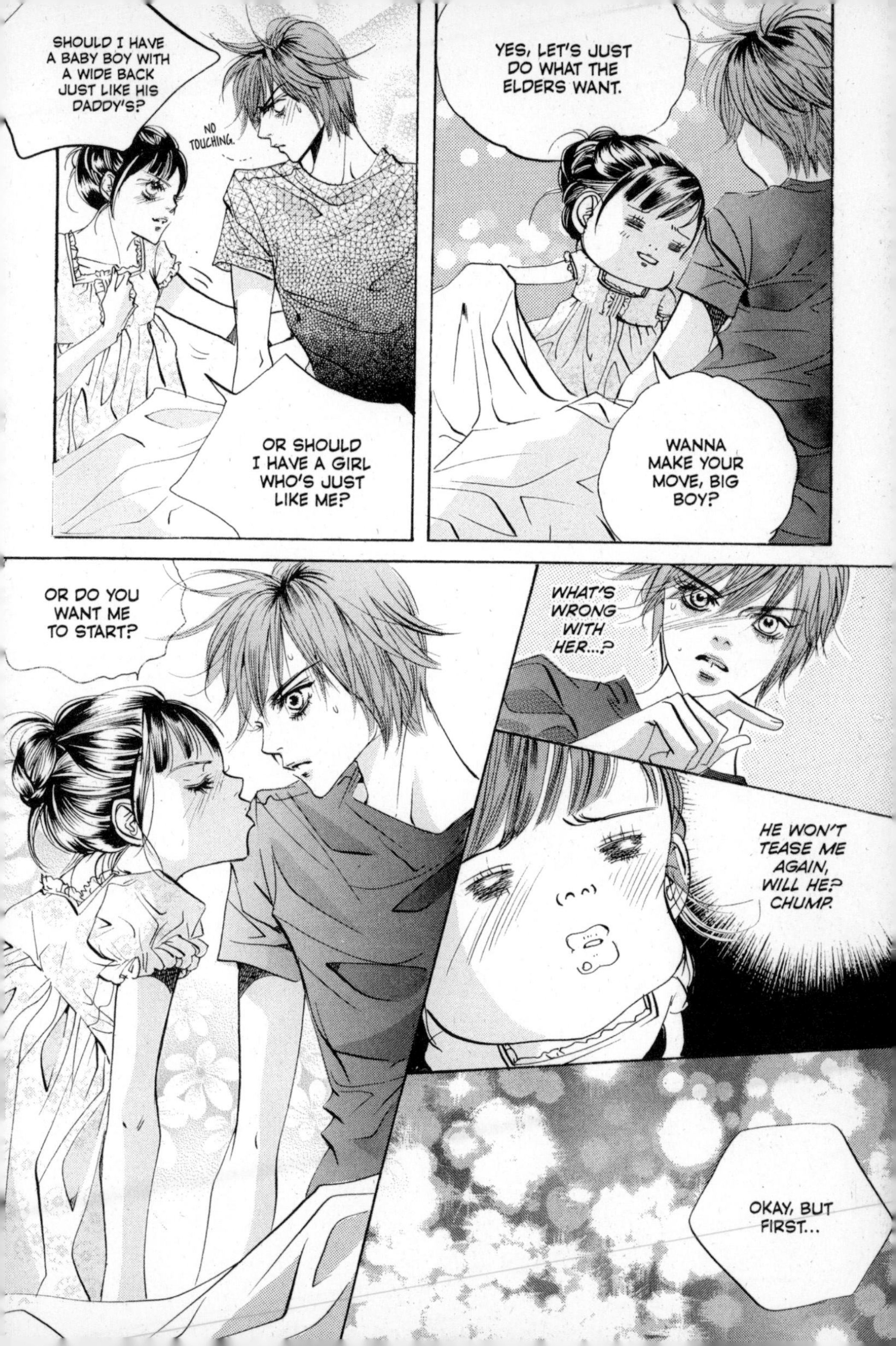
SHOULD I HAVE A BABY BOY WITH A WIDE BACK JUST LIKE HIS DADDY'S?
NO TOUCHING.
OR SHOULD I HAVE A GIRL WHO'S JUST LIKE ME?
YES, LET'S JUST DO WHAT THE ELDERS WANT.
WANNA MAKE YOUR MOVE, BIG BOY?
OR DO YOU WANT ME TO START?
WHAT'S WRONG WITH HER...?
HE WON'T TEASE ME AGAIN, WILL HE? CHUMP.
OKAY, BUT FIRST...

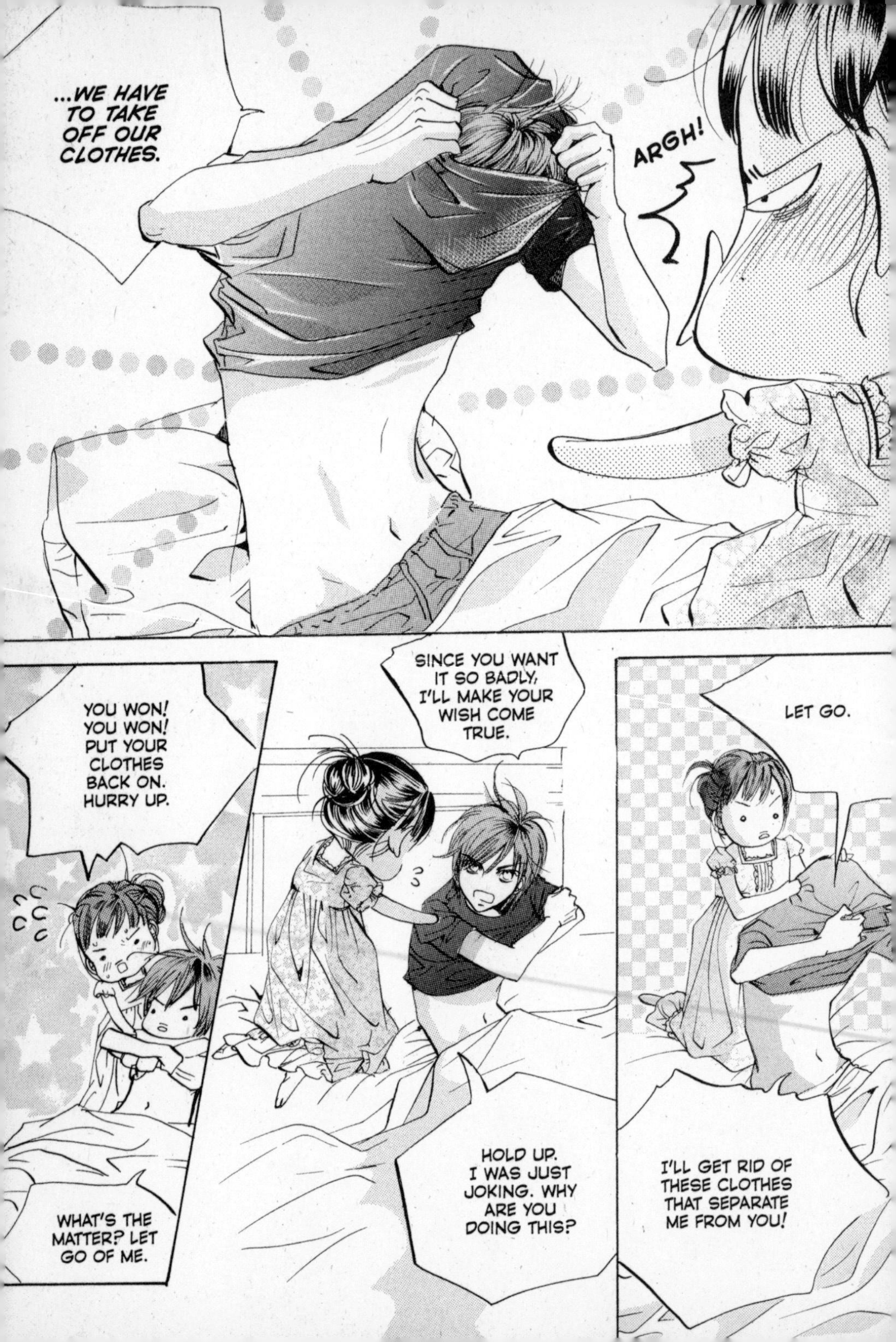
...WE HAVE TO TAKE OFF OUR CLOTHES.
ARGH!
YOU WON! YOU WON! PUT YOUR CLOTHES BACK ON. HURRY UP.
WHAT'S THE MATTER? LET GO OF ME.
SINCE YOU WANT IT SO BADLY, I'LL MAKE YOUR WISH COME TRUE.
HOLD UP. I WAS JUST JOKING. WHY ARE YOU DOING THIS?
LET GO.
I'LL GET RID OF THESE CLOTHES THAT SEPARATE ME FROM YOU!

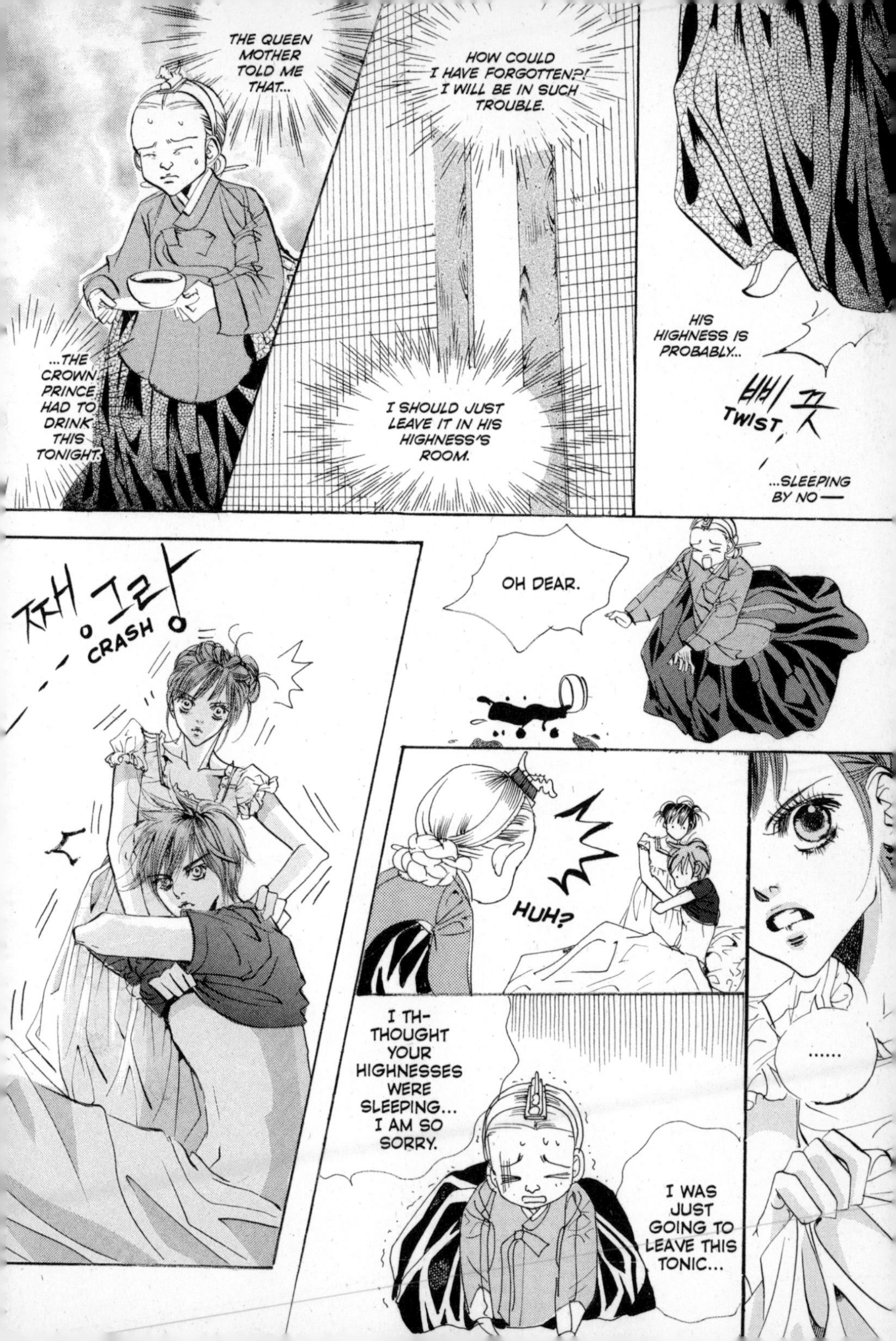
THE QUEEN MOTHER TOLD ME THAT...
...THE CROWN PRINCE HAD TO DRINK THIS TONIGHT.
HOW COULD I HAVE FORGOTTEN?! I WILL BE IN SUCH TROUBLE.
I SHOULD JUST LEAVE IT IN HIS HIGHNESS'S ROOM.
HIS HIGHNESS IS PROBABLY...
삐끗
TWIST,
...SLEEPING BY NO—
쨍그랑
CRASH
OH DEAR.
HUH?
I TH-THOUGHT YOUR HIGHNESSES WERE SLEEPING... I AM SO SORRY.
I WAS JUST GOING TO LEAVE THIS TONIC...
......

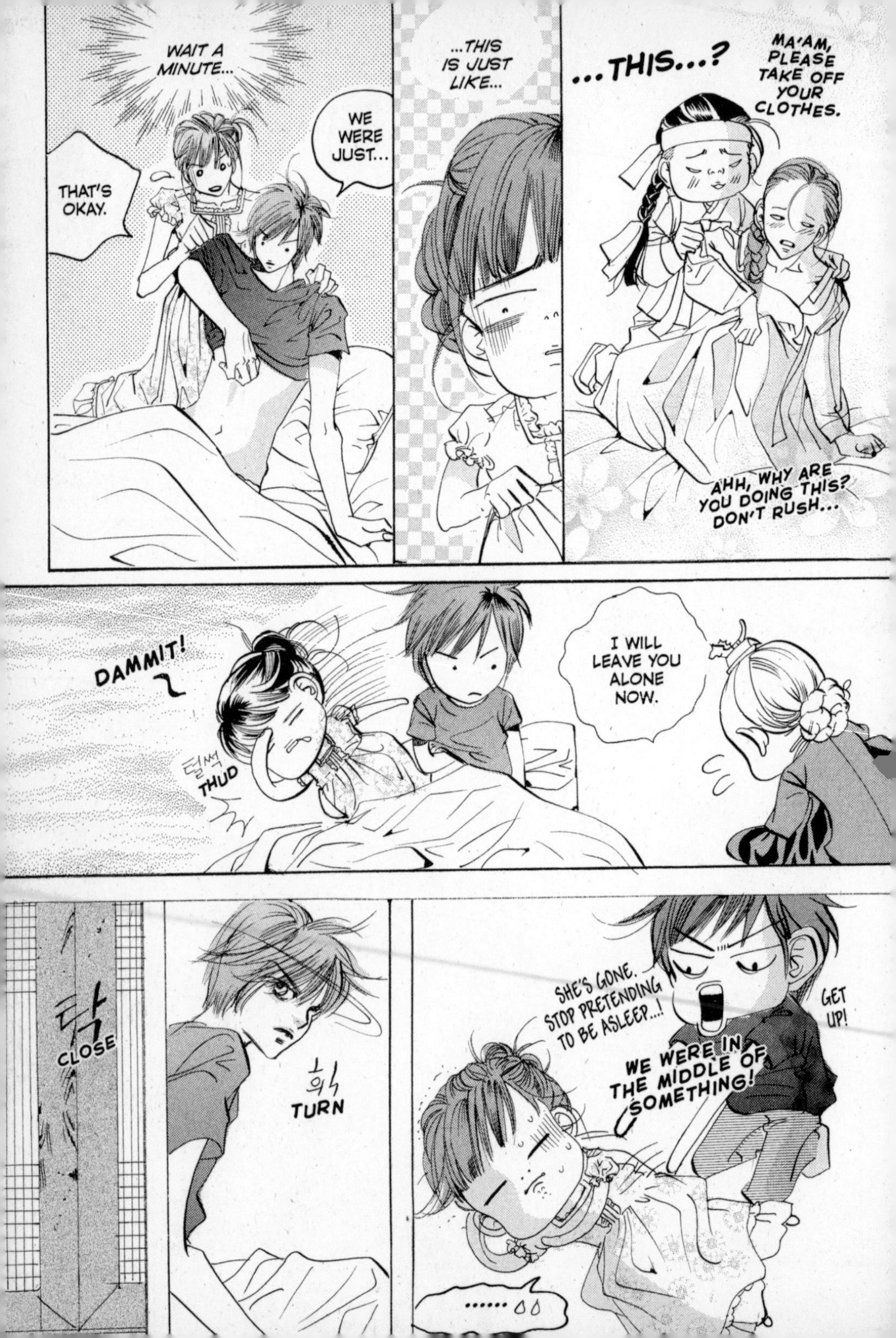
WAIT A MINUTE...
THAT'S OKAY.
WE WERE JUST...
...THIS IS JUST LIKE...
...THIS...?
MA'AM, PLEASE TAKE OFF YOUR CLOTHES.
AHH, WHY ARE YOU DOING THIS? DON'T RUSH...
DAMMIT!
털썩
THUD
I WILL LEAVE YOU ALONE NOW.
닥
CLOSE
획
TURN
SHE'S GONE. STOP PRETENDING TO BE ASLEEP...!
GET UP!
WE WERE IN THE MIDDLE OF SOMETHING!
....

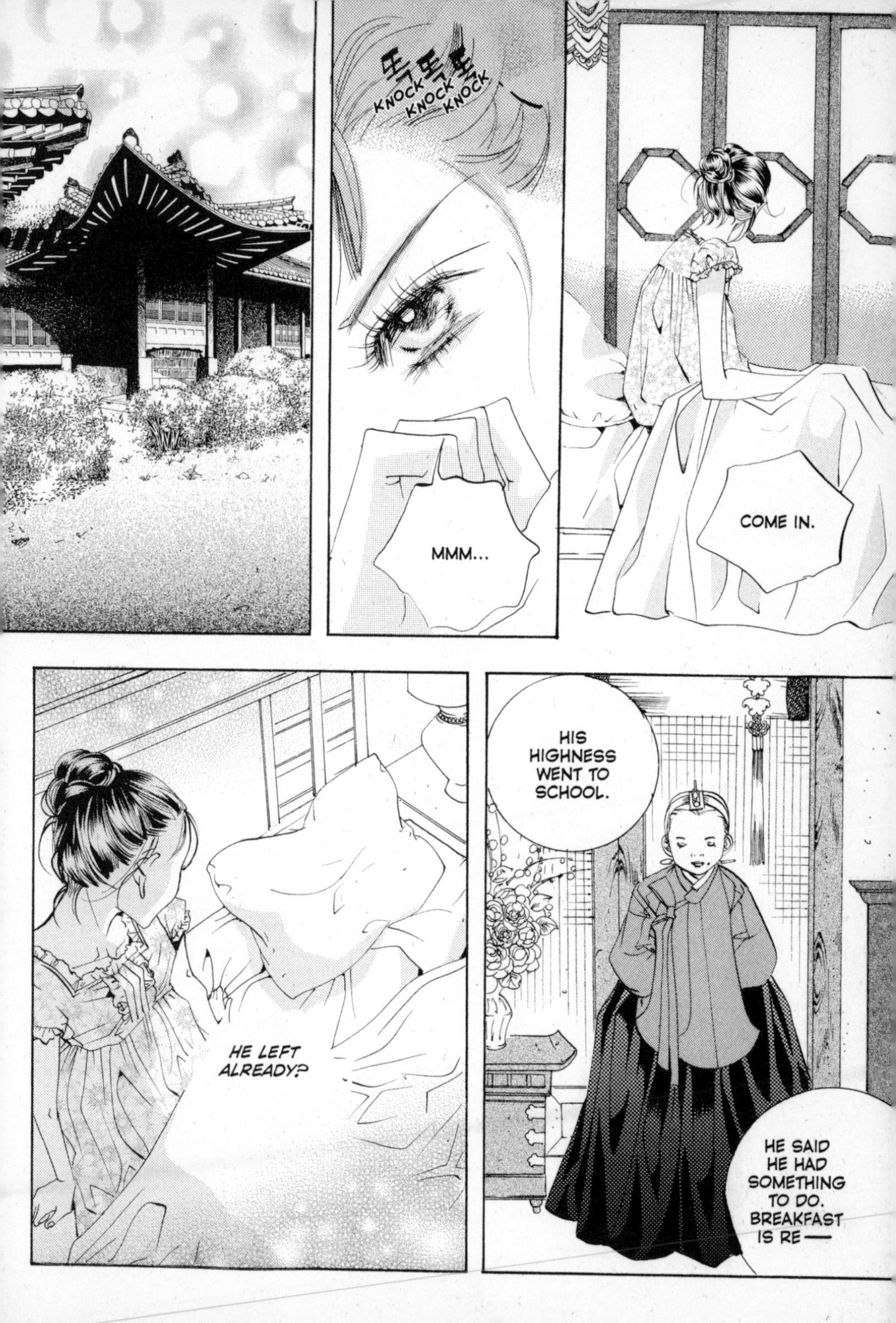
똑똑똑
KNOCK KNOCK KNOCK
MMM...
COME IN.
HE LEFT ALREADY?
HIS HIGHNESS WENT TO SCHOOL.
HE SAID HE HAD SOMETHING TO DO. BREAKFAST IS RE—

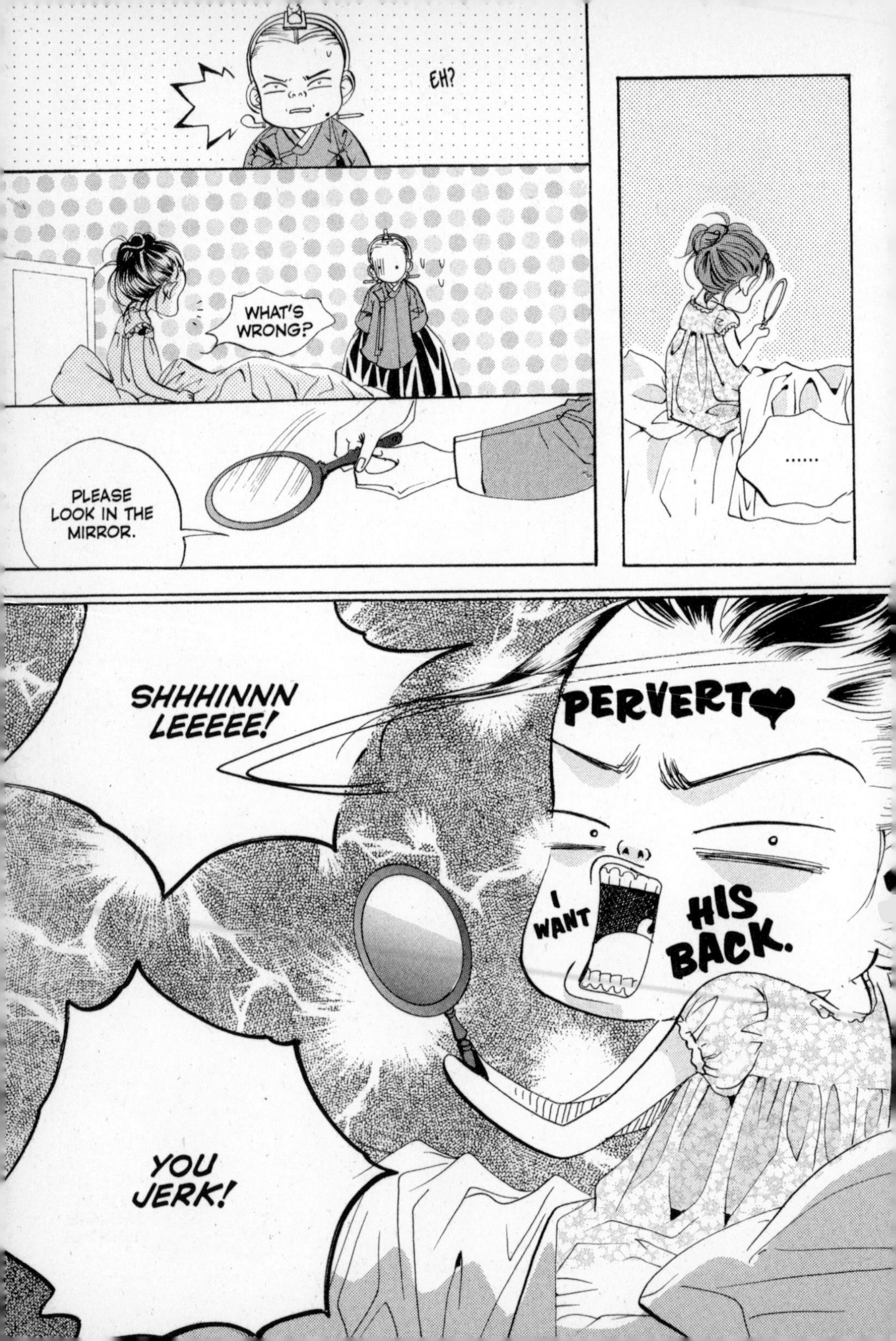
EH?
WHAT'S WRONG?
PLEASE LOOK IN THE MIRROR.
......
SHHHINNN LEEEEE!
PERVERT♥
I WANT HIS BACK.
YOU JERK!

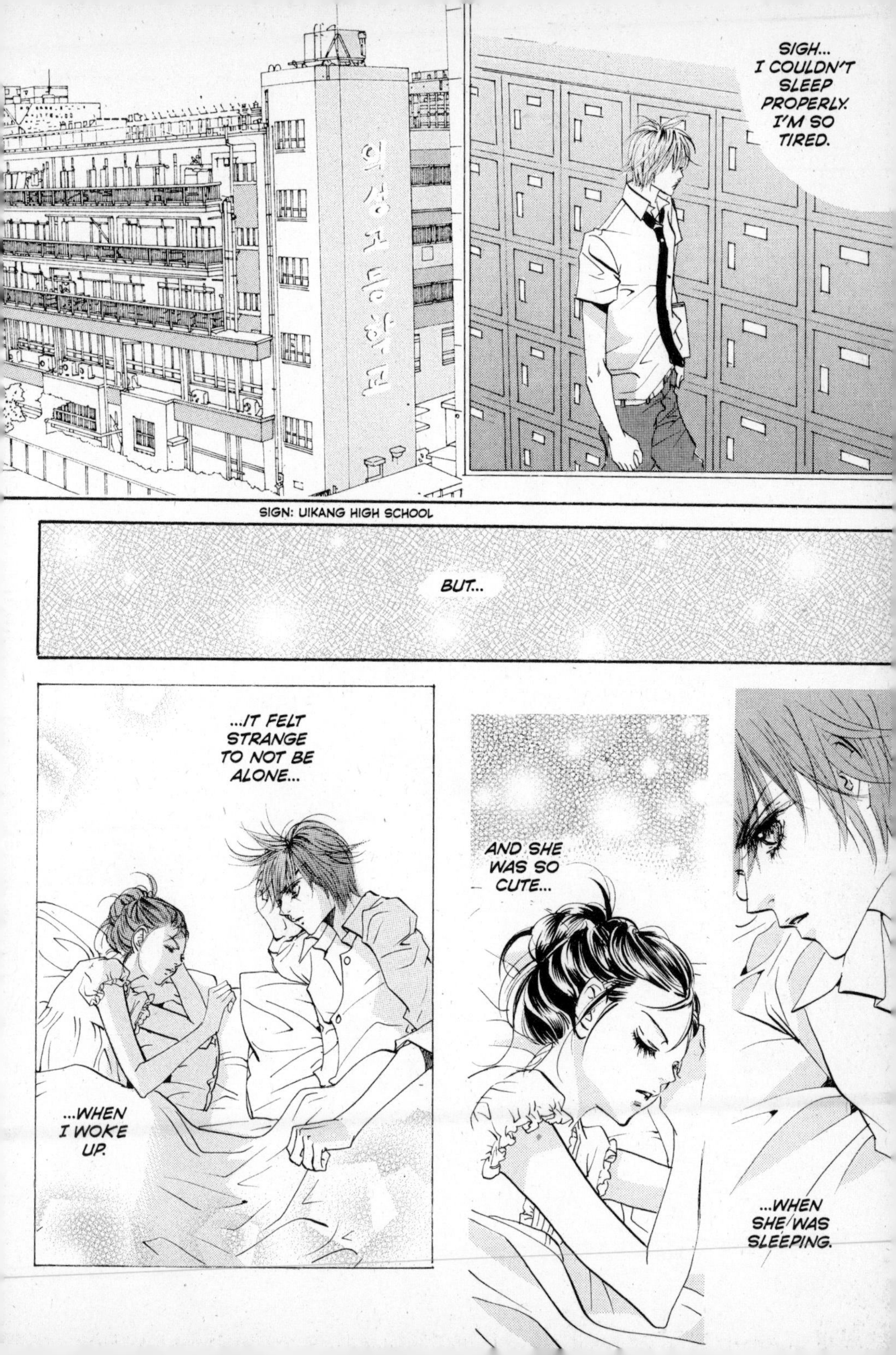
SIGN: UIKANG HIGH SCHOOL
SIGH... I COULDN'T SLEEP PROPERLY. I'M SO TIRED.
BUT...
...IT FELT STRANGE TO NOT BE ALONE...
...WHEN I WOKE UP.
AND SHE WAS SO CUTE...
...WHEN SHE WAS SLEEPING.

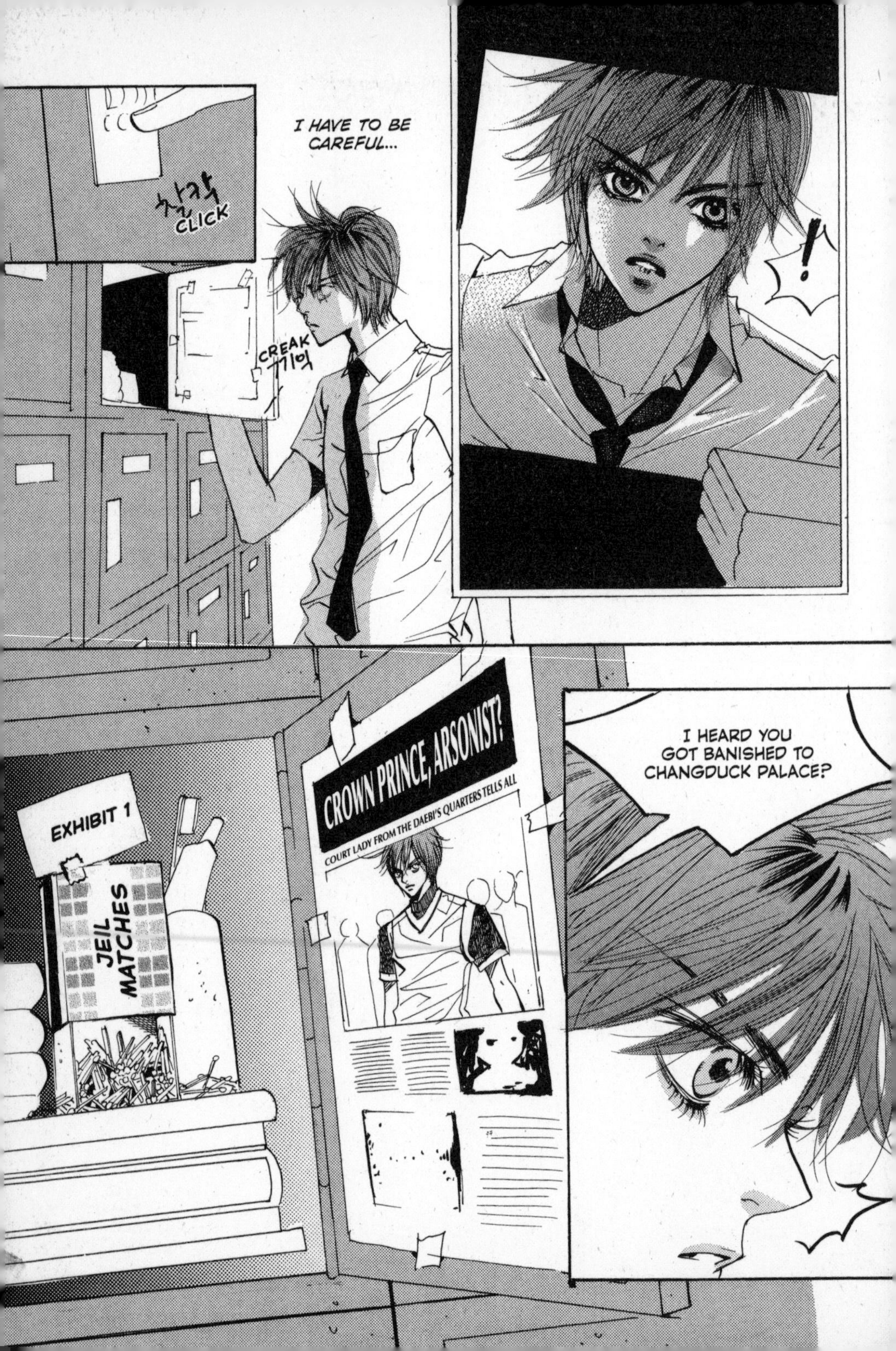
CLICK
I HAVE TO BE CAREFUL...
CREAK
!
EXHIBIT 1
JEIL MATCHES
CROWN PRINCE, ARSONIST?
COURT LADY FROM THE DAEBI'S QUARTERS TELLS ALL
I HEARD YOU GOT BANISHED TO CHANGDUCK PALACE?

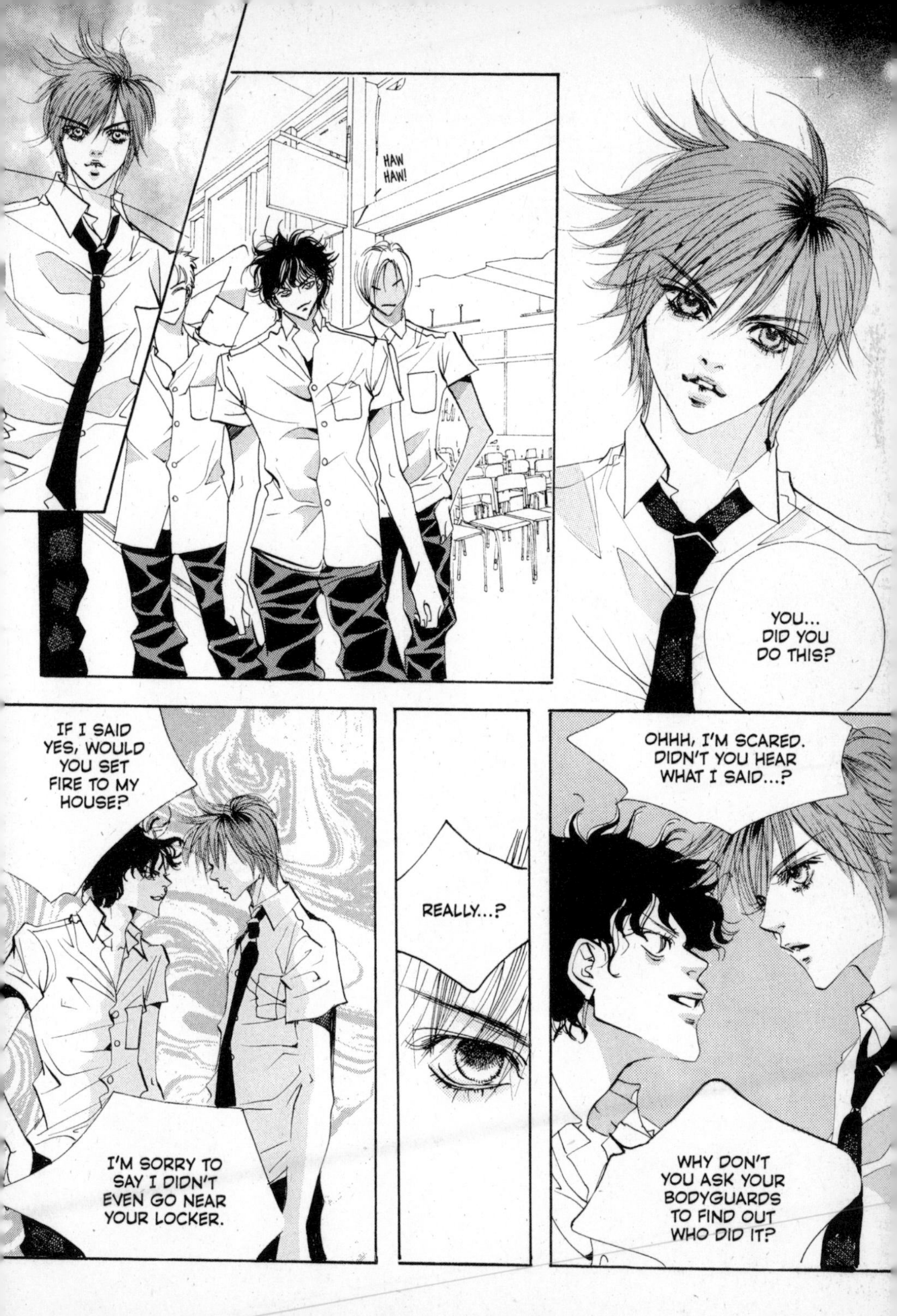
HAW HAW!
YOU... DID YOU DO THIS?
IF I SAID YES, WOULD YOU SET FIRE TO MY HOUSE?
I'M SORRY TO SAY I DIDN'T EVEN GO NEAR YOUR LOCKER.
REALLY...?
OHHH, I'M SCARED. DIDN'T YOU HEAR WHAT I SAID...?
WHY DON'T YOU ASK YOUR BODYGUARDS TO FIND OUT WHO DID IT?

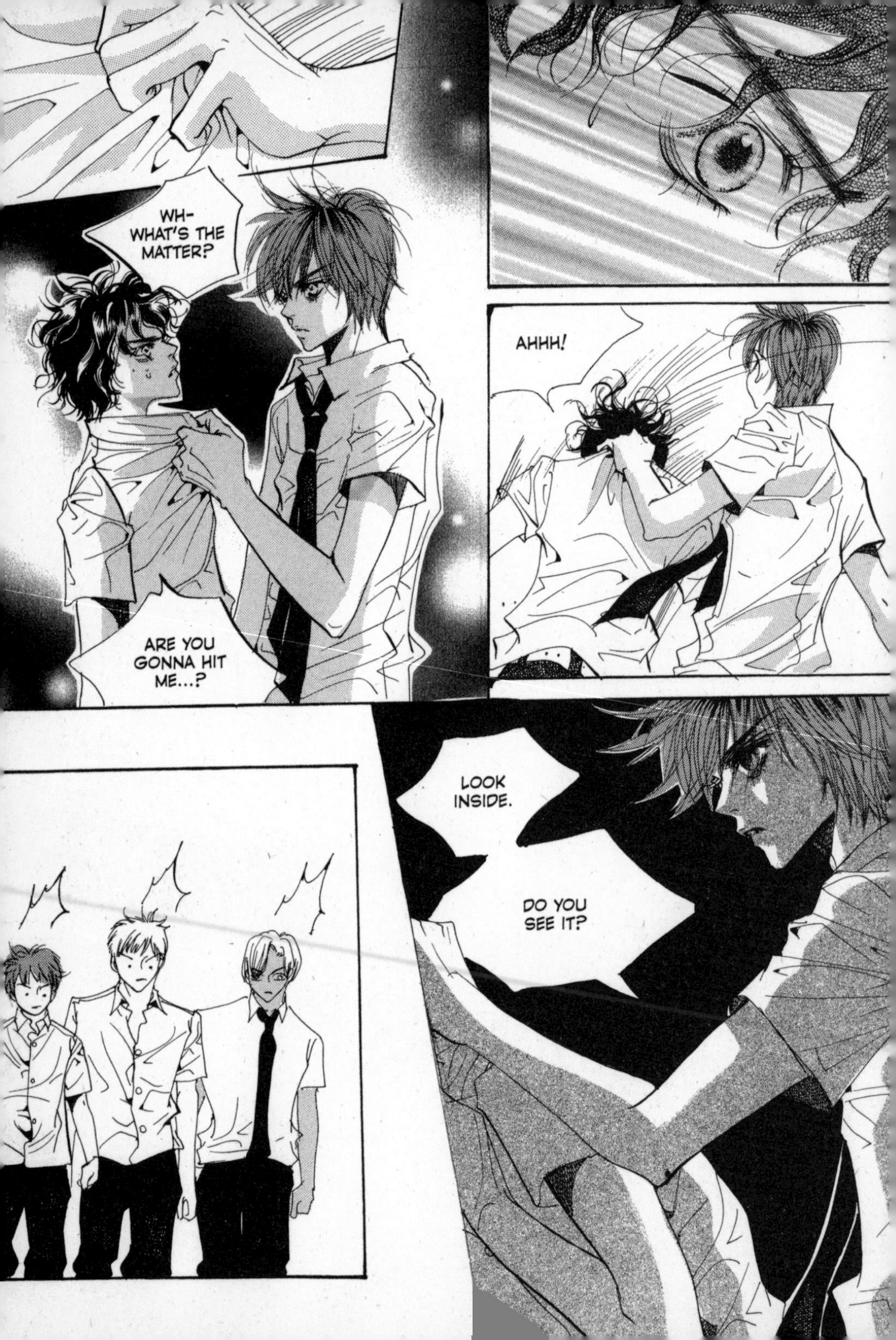
WH- WHAT'S THE MATTER?
ARE YOU GONNA HIT ME...?
AHHH!
LOOK INSIDE.
DO YOU SEE IT?

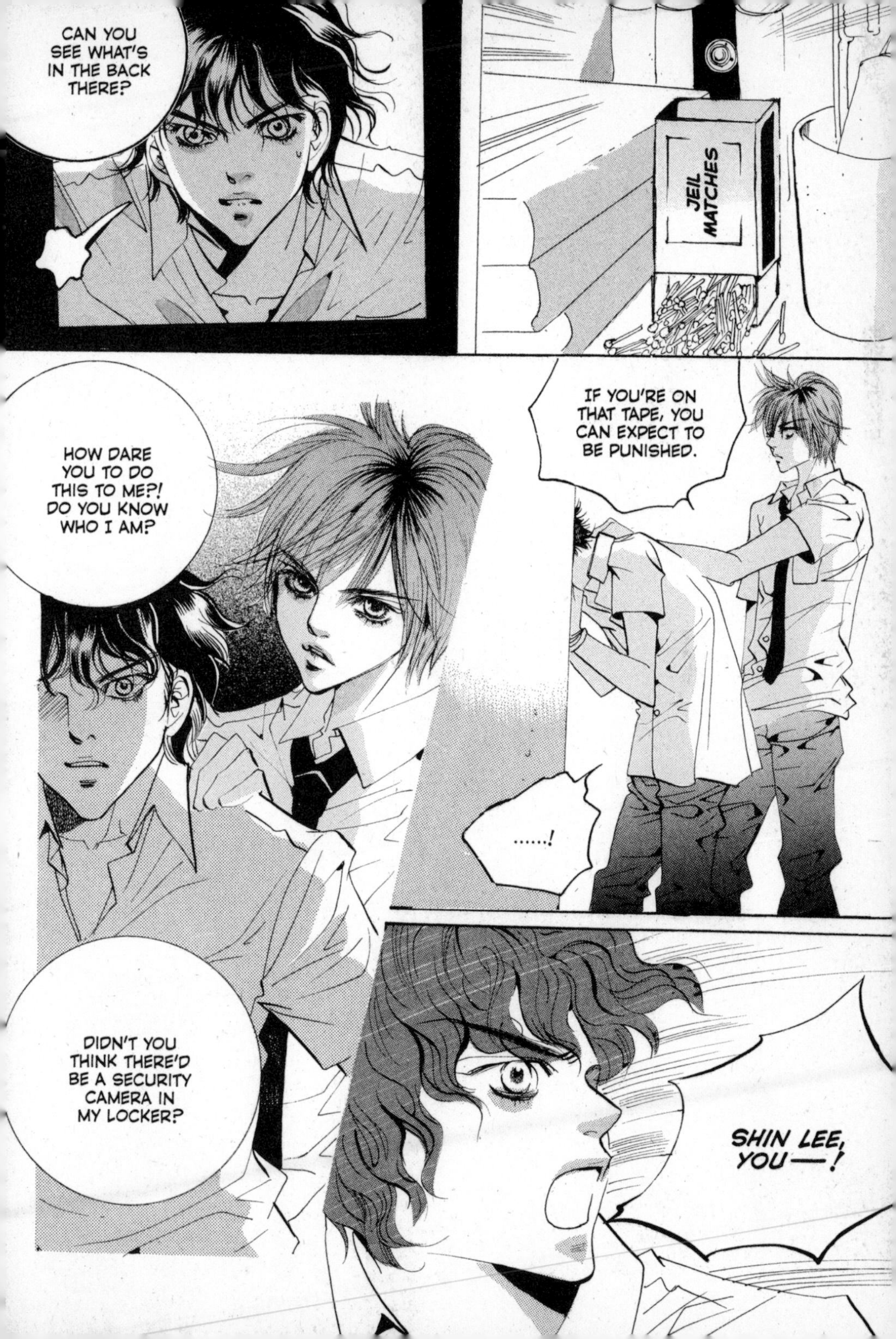
CAN YOU SEE WHAT'S IN THE BACK THERE?
JEIL MATCHES
HOW DARE YOU TO DO THIS TO ME?! DO YOU KNOW WHO I AM?
IF YOU'RE ON THAT TAPE, YOU CAN EXPECT TO BE PUNISHED.
......!
DIDN'T YOU THINK THERE'D BE A SECURITY CAMERA IN MY LOCKER?
SHIN LEE, YOU—!

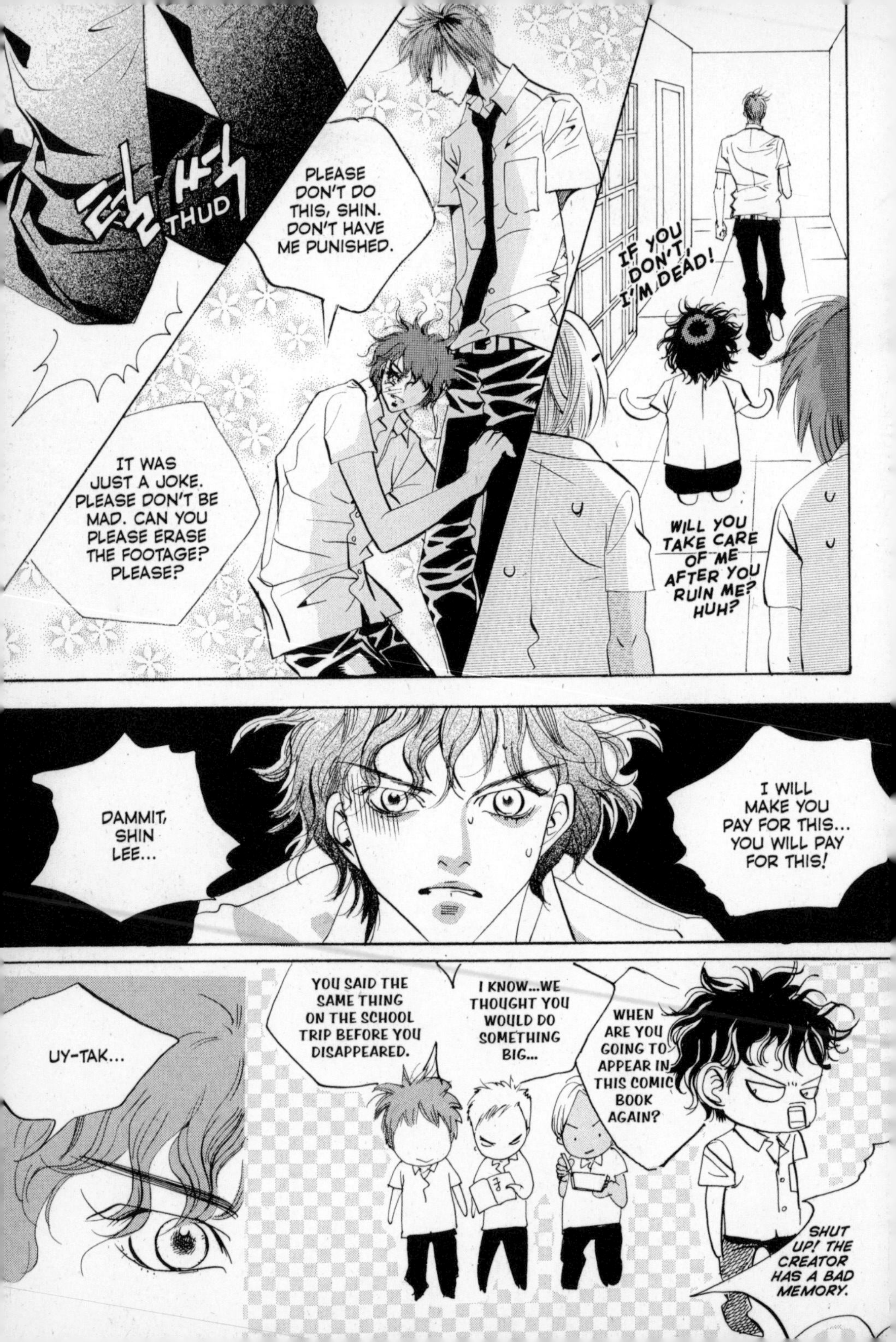
털썩
THUD
PLEASE DON'T DO THIS, SHIN. DON'T HAVE ME PUNISHED.
IT WAS JUST A JOKE. PLEASE DON'T BE MAD. CAN YOU PLEASE ERASE THE FOOTAGE? PLEASE?
IF YOU DON'T, I'M DEAD!
WILL YOU TAKE CARE OF ME AFTER YOU RUIN ME? HUH?
DAMMIT, SHIN LEE...
I WILL MAKE YOU PAY FOR THIS... YOU WILL PAY FOR THIS!
UY-TAK...
YOU SAID THE SAME THING ON THE SCHOOL TRIP BEFORE YOU DISAPPEARED.
I KNOW...WE THOUGHT YOU WOULD DO SOMETHING BIG...
WHEN ARE YOU GOING TO APPEAR IN THIS COMIC BOOK AGAIN?
SHUT UP! THE CREATOR HAS A BAD MEMORY.

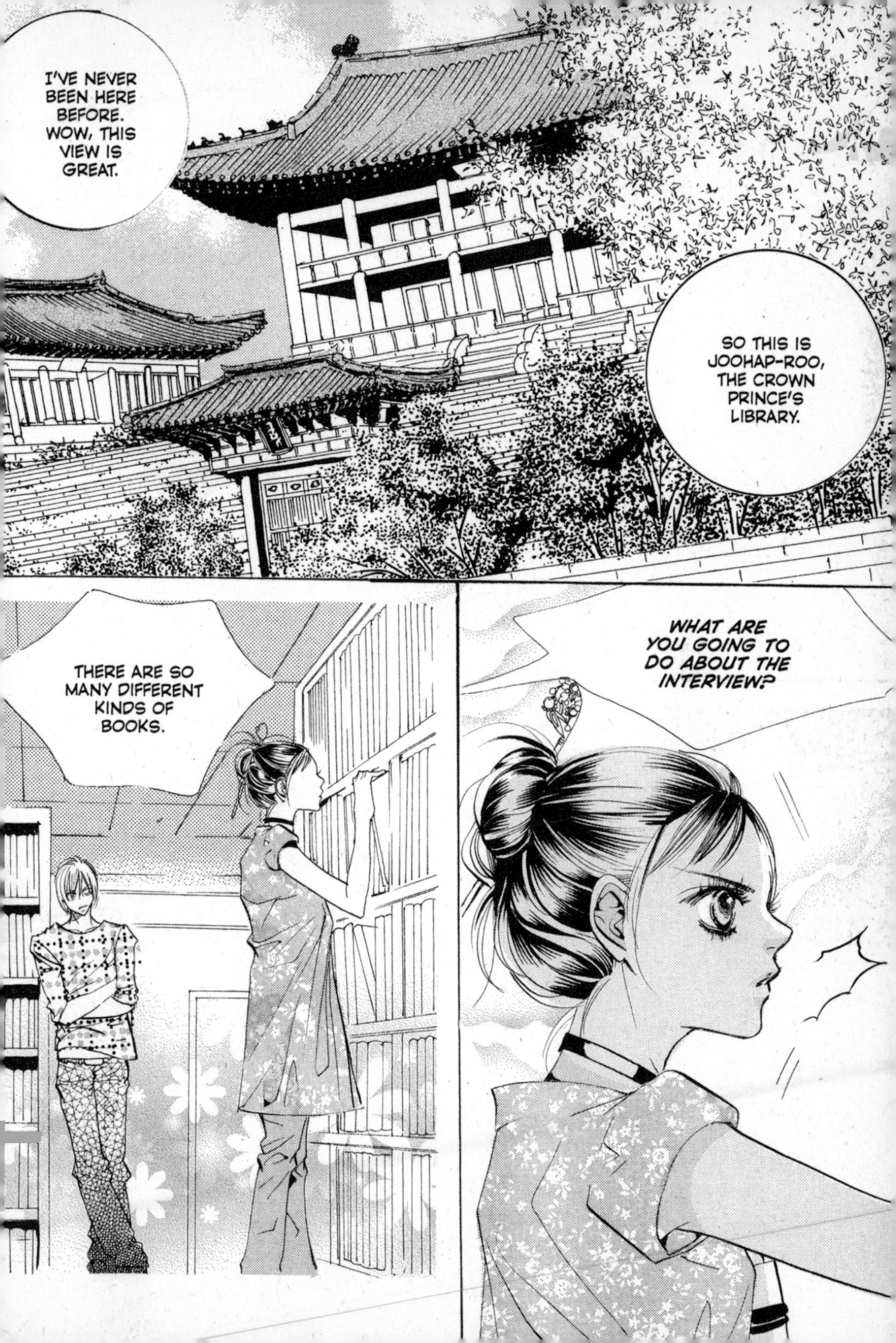
I'VE NEVER BEEN HERE BEFORE. WOW, THIS VIEW IS GREAT.
SO THIS IS JOOHAP-ROO, THE CROWN PRINCE'S LIBRARY.
THERE ARE SO MANY DIFFERENT KINDS OF BOOKS.
WHAT ARE YOU GOING TO DO ABOUT THE INTERVIEW?

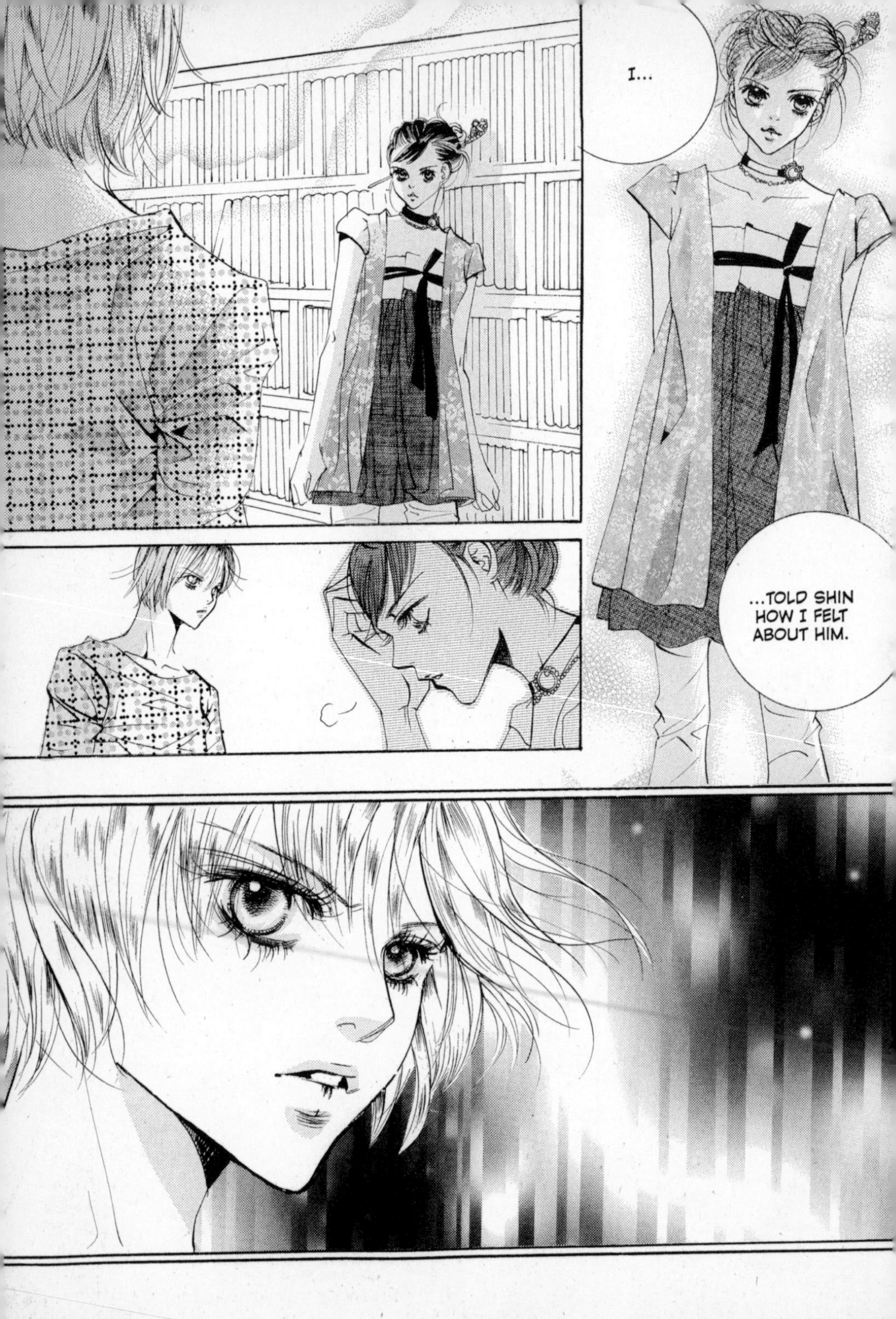
I...
...TOLD SHIN HOW I FELT ABOUT HIM.

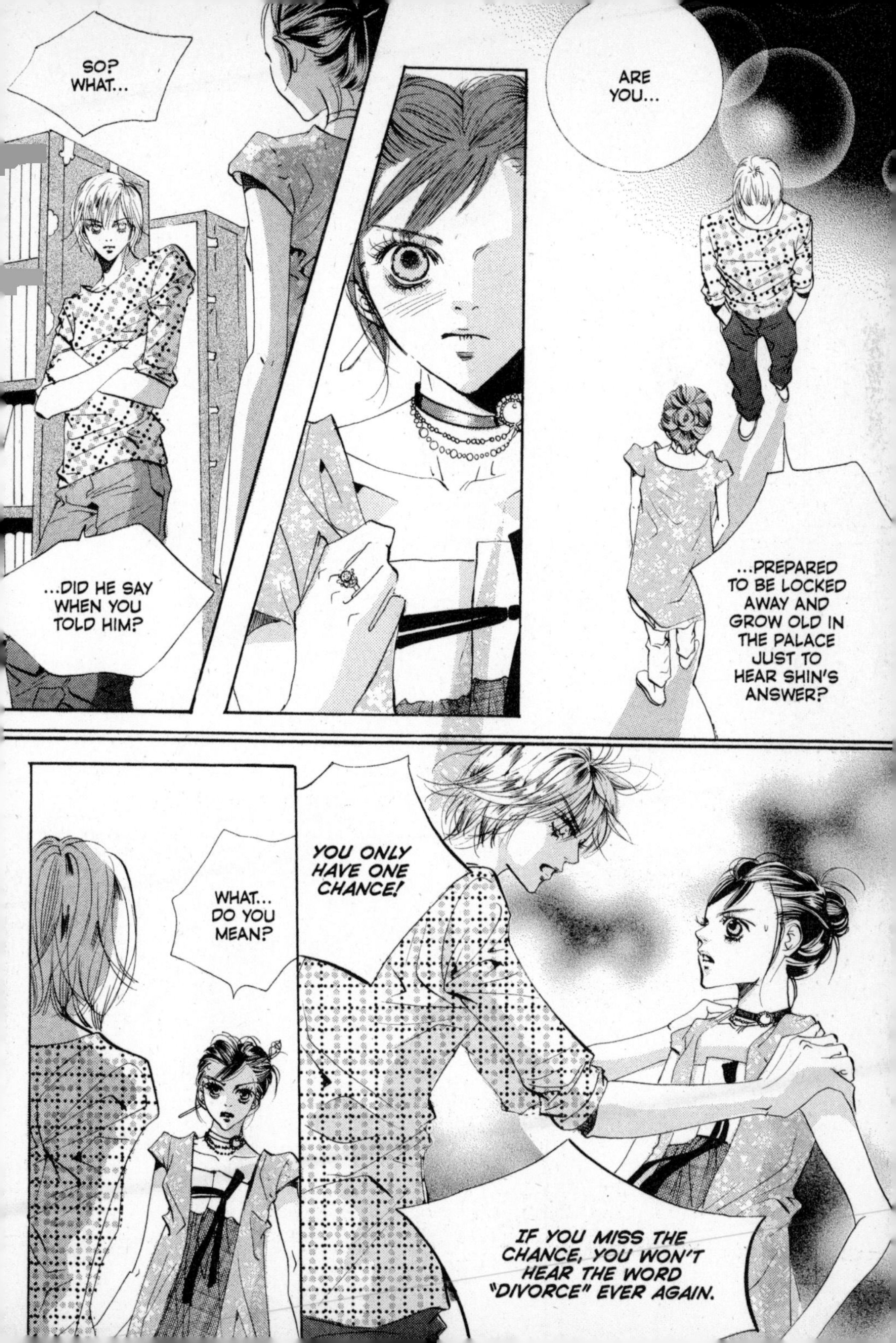
SO? WHAT...
...DID HE SAY WHEN YOU TOLD HIM?
ARE YOU...
...PREPARED TO BE LOCKED AWAY AND GROW OLD IN THE PALACE JUST TO HEAR SHIN'S ANSWER?
WHAT... DO YOU MEAN?
YOU ONLY HAVE ONE CHANCE!
IF YOU MISS THE CHANCE, YOU WON'T HEAR THE WORD "DIVORCE" EVER AGAIN.

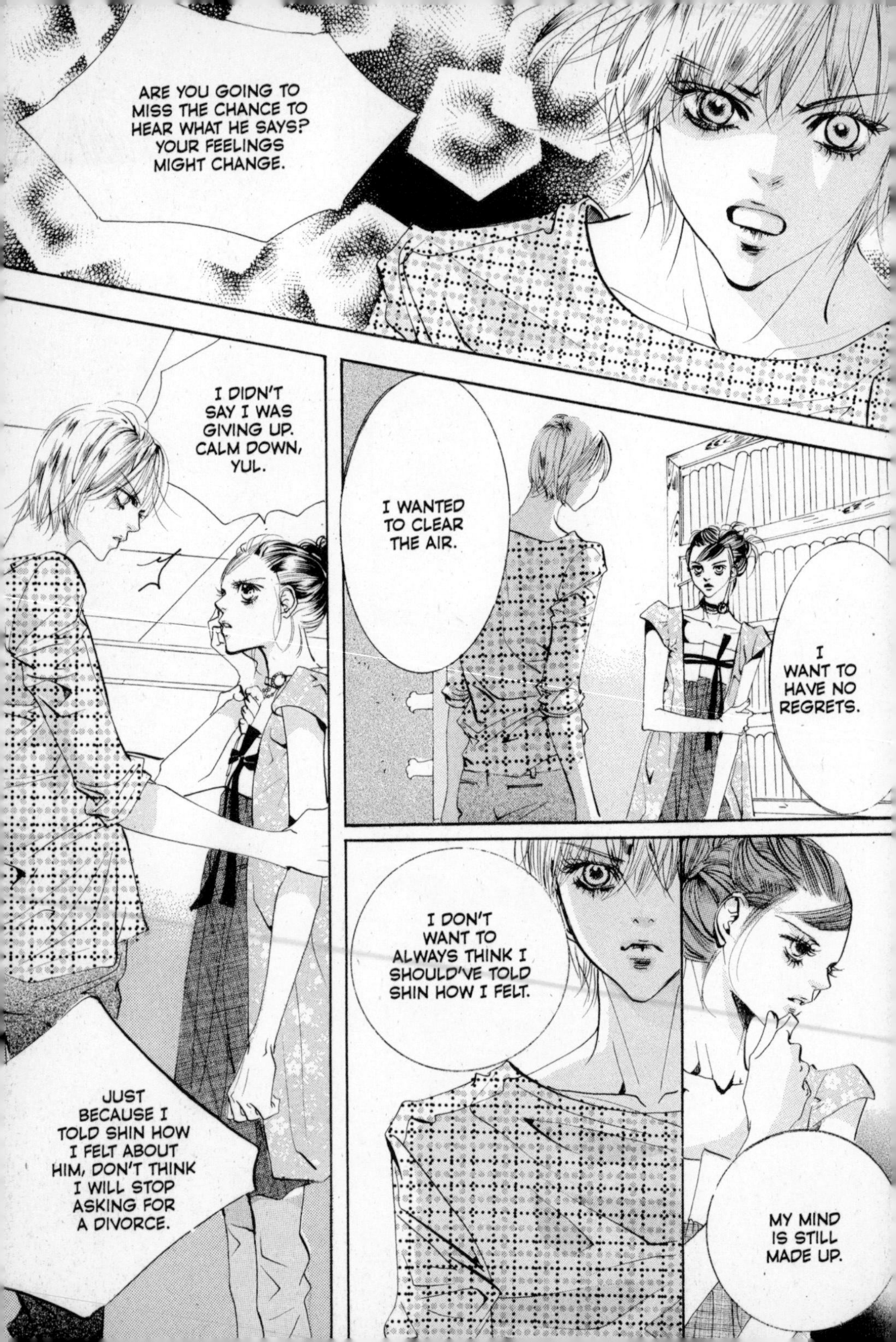
ARE YOU GOING TO MISS THE CHANCE TO HEAR WHAT HE SAYS? YOUR FEELINGS MIGHT CHANGE.
I DIDN'T SAY I WAS GIVING UP. CALM DOWN, YUL.
JUST BECAUSE I TOLD SHIN HOW I FELT ABOUT HIM, DON'T THINK I WILL STOP ASKING FOR A DIVORCE.
I WANTED TO CLEAR THE AIR.
I WANT TO HAVE NO REGRETS.
I DON'T WANT TO ALWAYS THINK I SHOULD'VE TOLD SHIN HOW I FELT.
MY MIND IS STILL MADE UP.

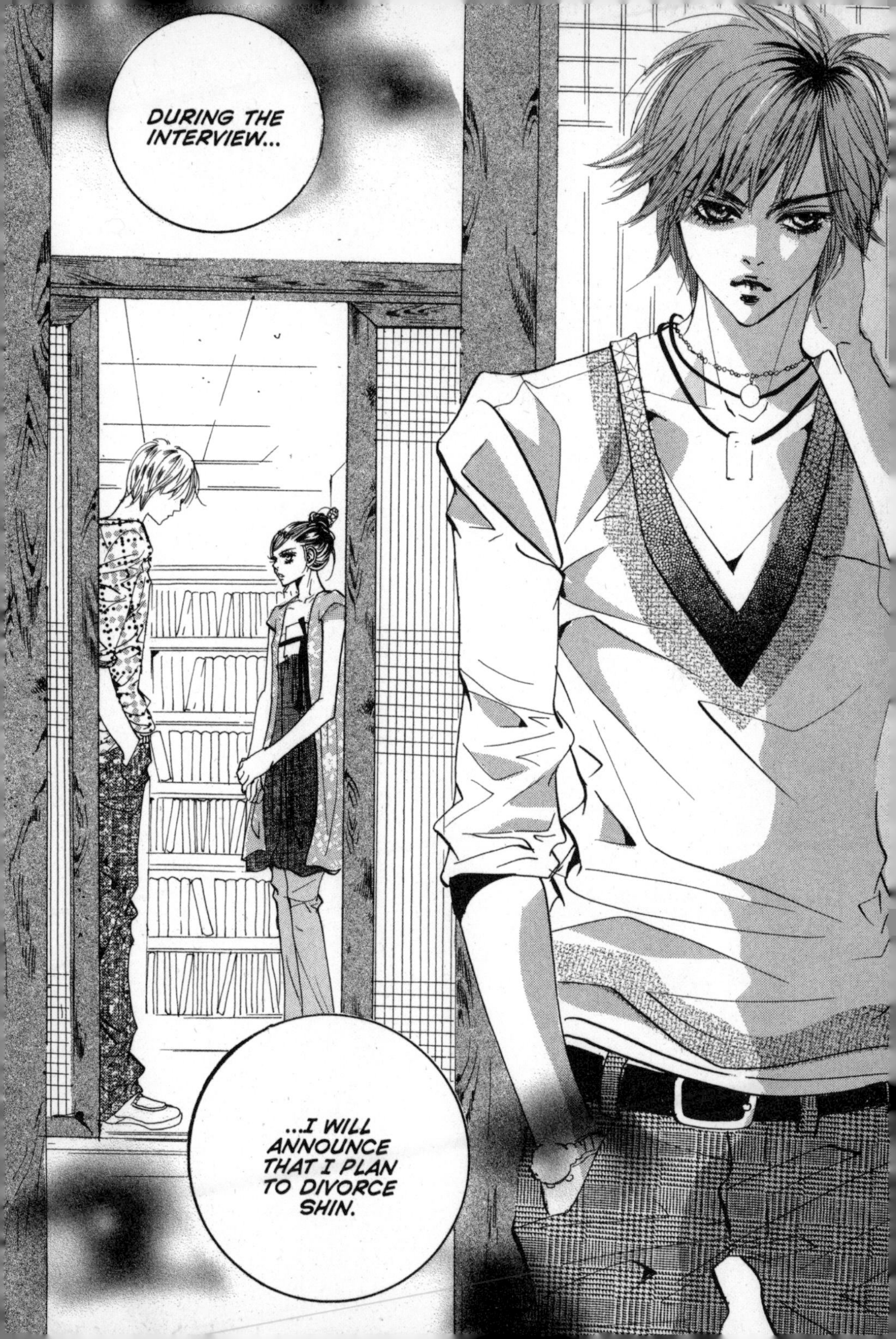
DURING THE INTERVIEW...
...I WILL ANNOUNCE THAT I PLAN TO DIVORCE SHIN.

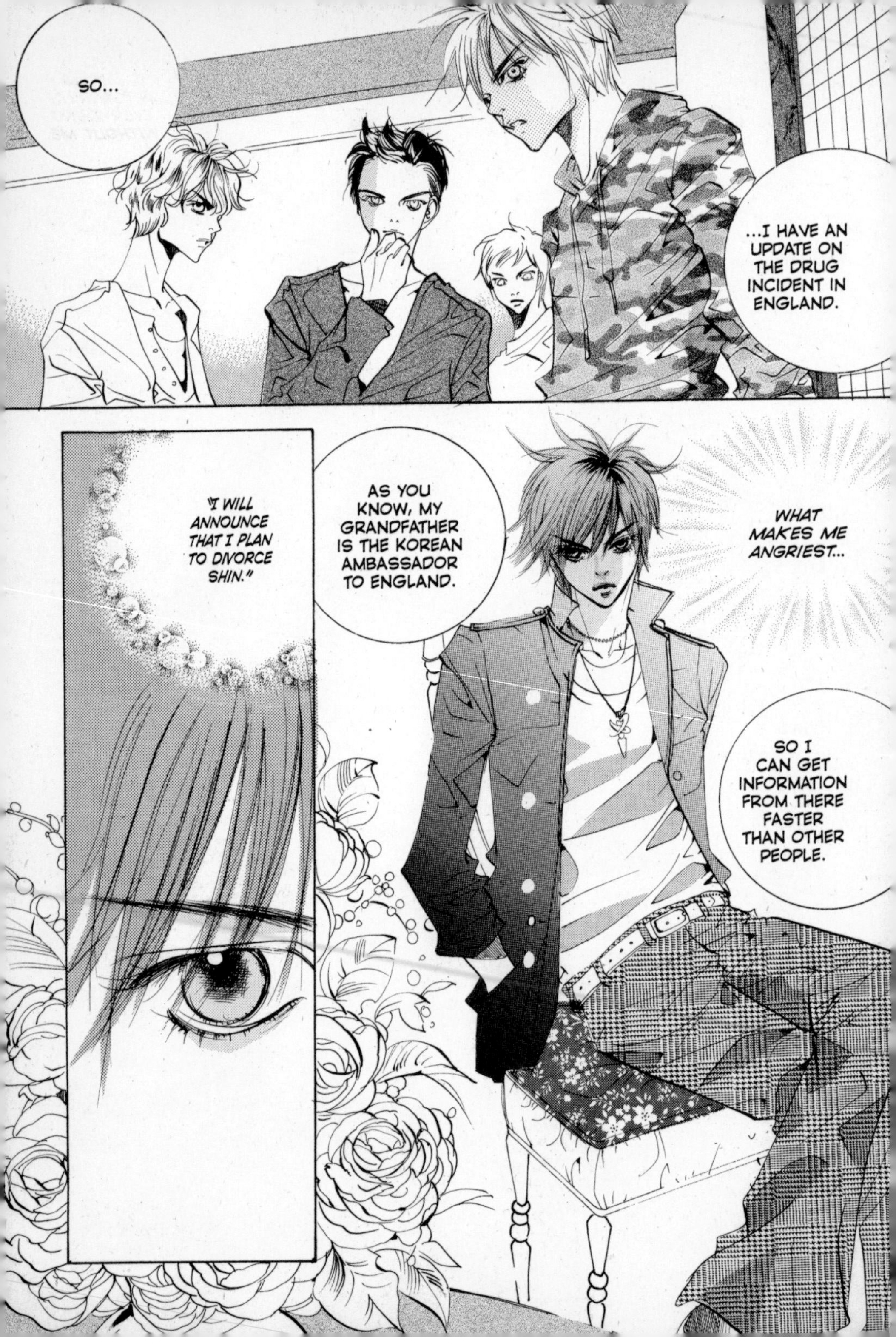
SO...
...I HAVE AN UPDATE ON THE DRUG INCIDENT IN ENGLAND.
"I WILL ANNOUNCE THAT I PLAN TO DIVORCE SHIN."
AS YOU KNOW, MY GRANDFATHER IS THE KOREAN AMBASSADOR TO ENGLAND.
WHAT MAKES ME ANGRIEST...
SO I CAN GET INFORMATION FROM THERE FASTER THAN OTHER PEOPLE.

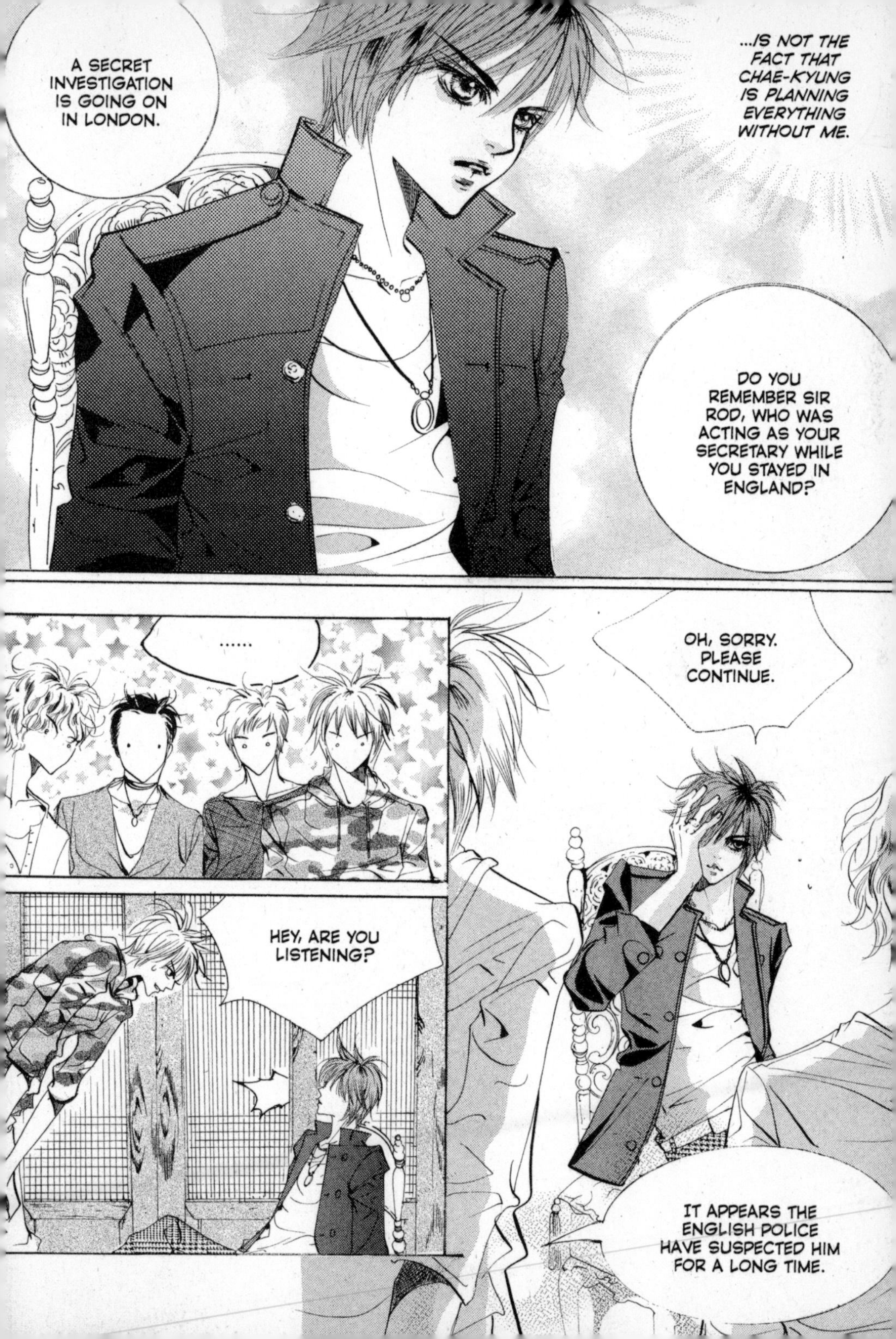
A SECRET INVESTIGATION IS GOING ON IN LONDON.
...IS NOT THE FACT THAT CHAE-KYUNG IS PLANNING EVERYTHING WITHOUT ME.
DO YOU REMEMBER SIR ROD, WHO WAS ACTING AS YOUR SECRETARY WHILE YOU STAYED IN ENGLAND?
......
HEY, ARE YOU LISTENING?
OH, SORRY. PLEASE CONTINUE.
IT APPEARS THE ENGLISH POLICE HAVE SUSPECTED HIM FOR A LONG TIME.

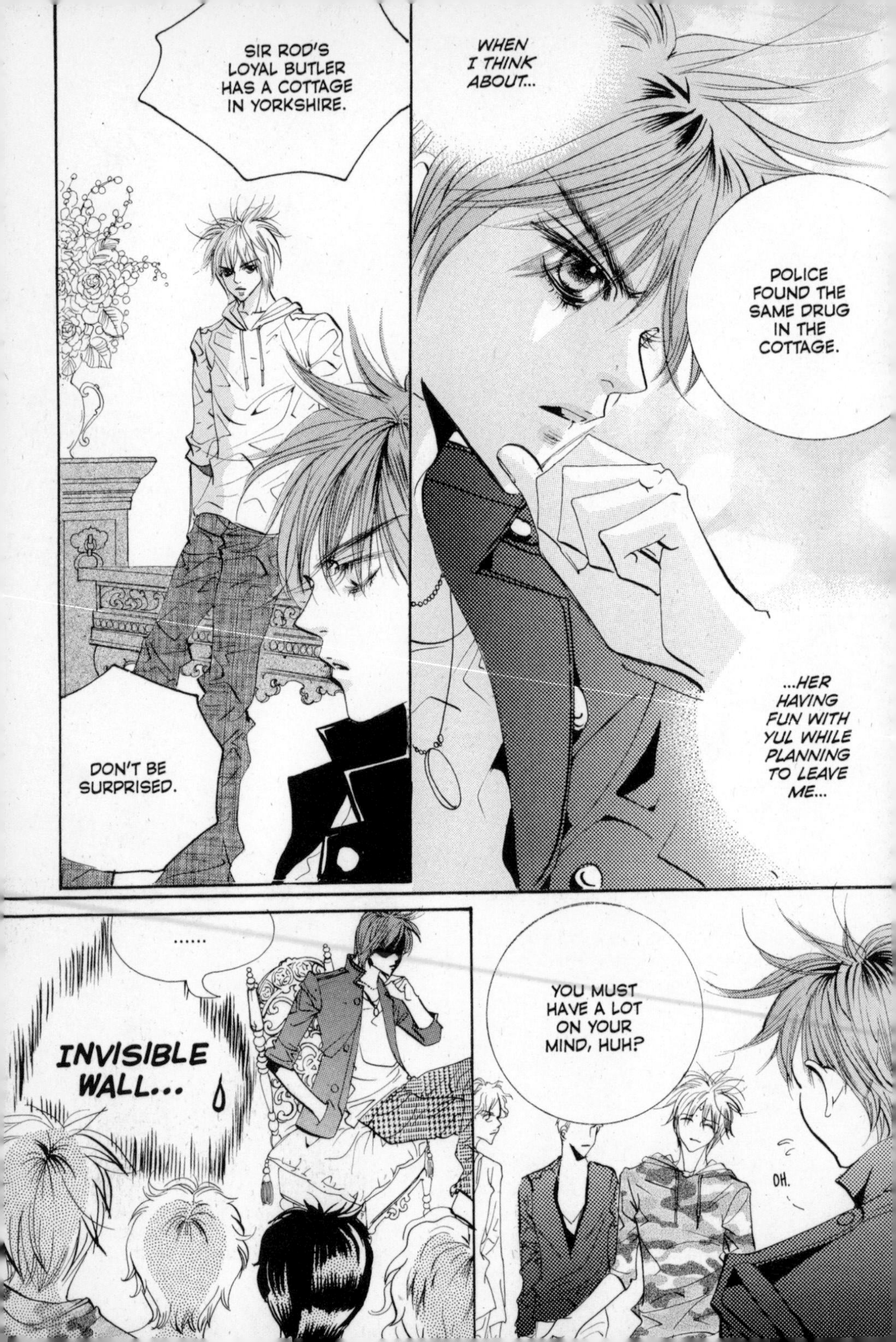
SIR ROD'S LOYAL BUTLER HAS A COTTAGE IN YORKSHIRE.
DON'T BE SURPRISED.
WHEN I THINK ABOUT...
POLICE FOUND THE SAME DRUG IN THE COTTAGE.
...HER HAVING FUN WITH YUL WHILE PLANNING TO LEAVE ME...
......
INVISIBLE WALL...
YOU MUST HAVE A LOT ON YOUR MIND, HUH?
OH.

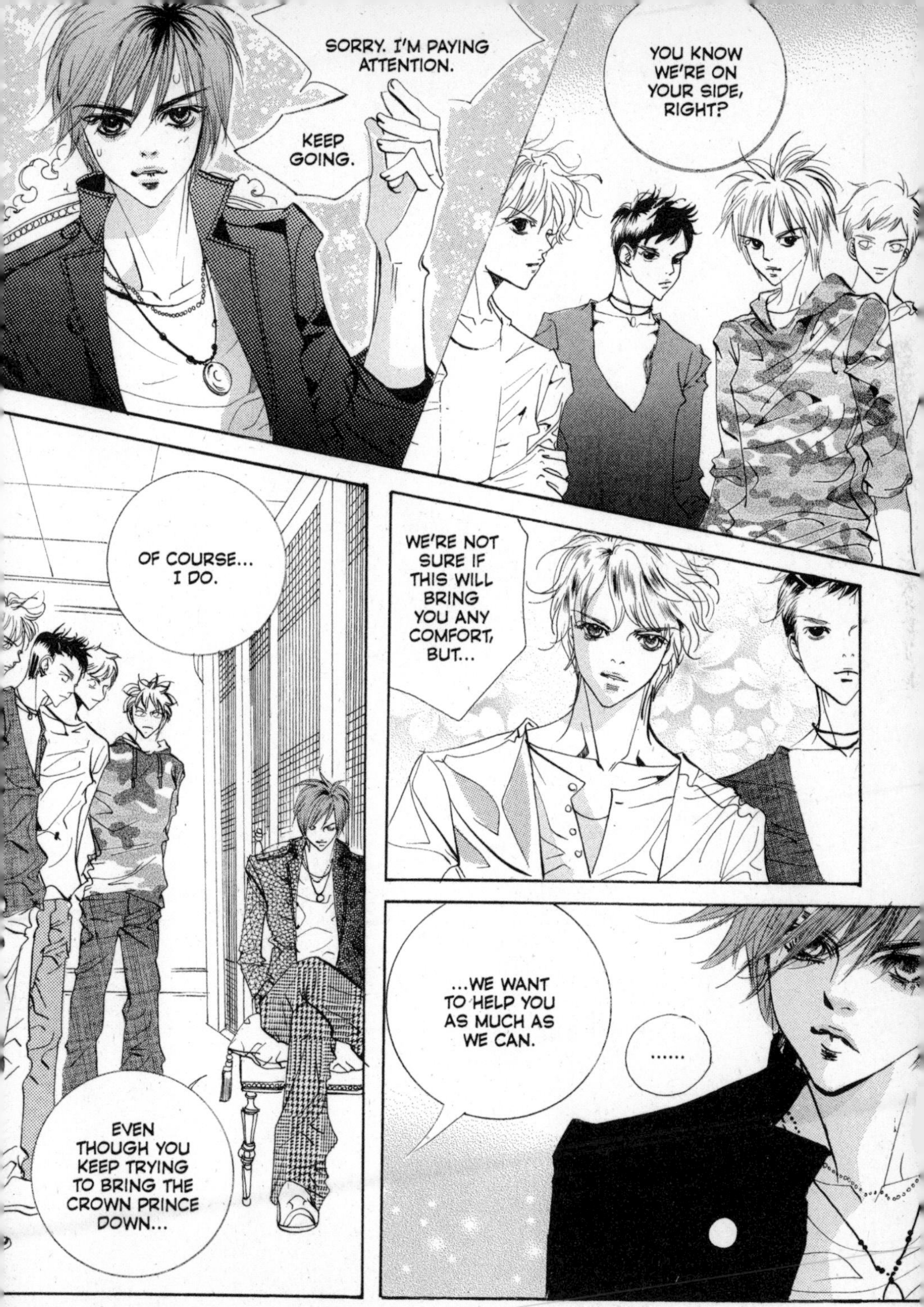
SORRY. I'M PAYING ATTENTION.
KEEP GOING.
YOU KNOW WE'RE ON YOUR SIDE, RIGHT?
OF COURSE... I DO.
EVEN THOUGH YOU KEEP TRYING TO BRING THE CROWN PRINCE DOWN...
WE'RE NOT SURE IF THIS WILL BRING YOU ANY COMFORT, BUT...
...WE WANT TO HELP YOU AS MUCH AS WE CAN.
......

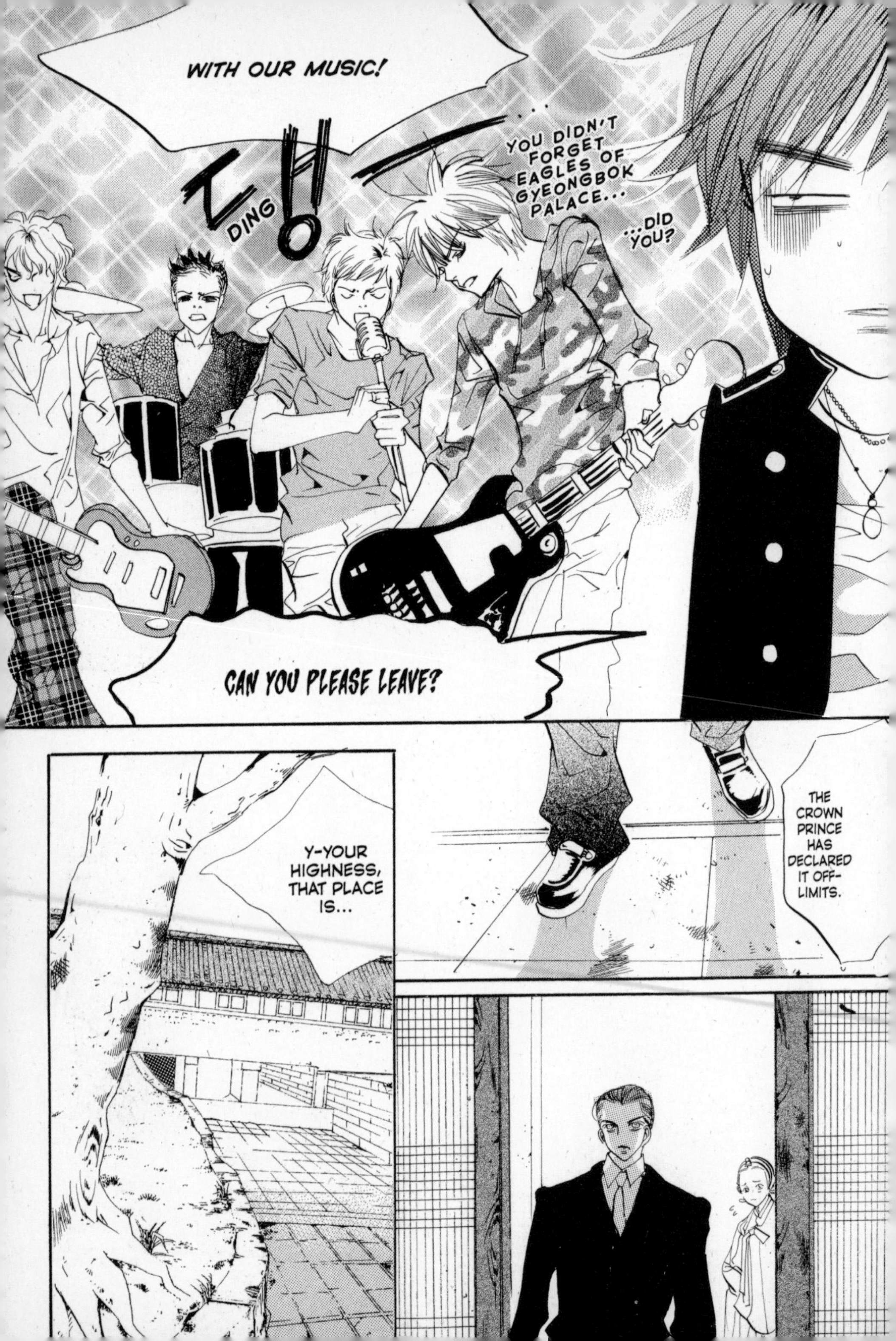
WITH OUR MUSIC!
DING
YOU DIDN'T FORGET EAGLES OF GYEONGBOK PALACE...
...DID YOU?
CAN YOU PLEASE LEAVE?
Y-YOUR HIGHNESS, THAT PLACE IS...
THE CROWN PRINCE HAS DECLARED IT OFF-LIMITS.

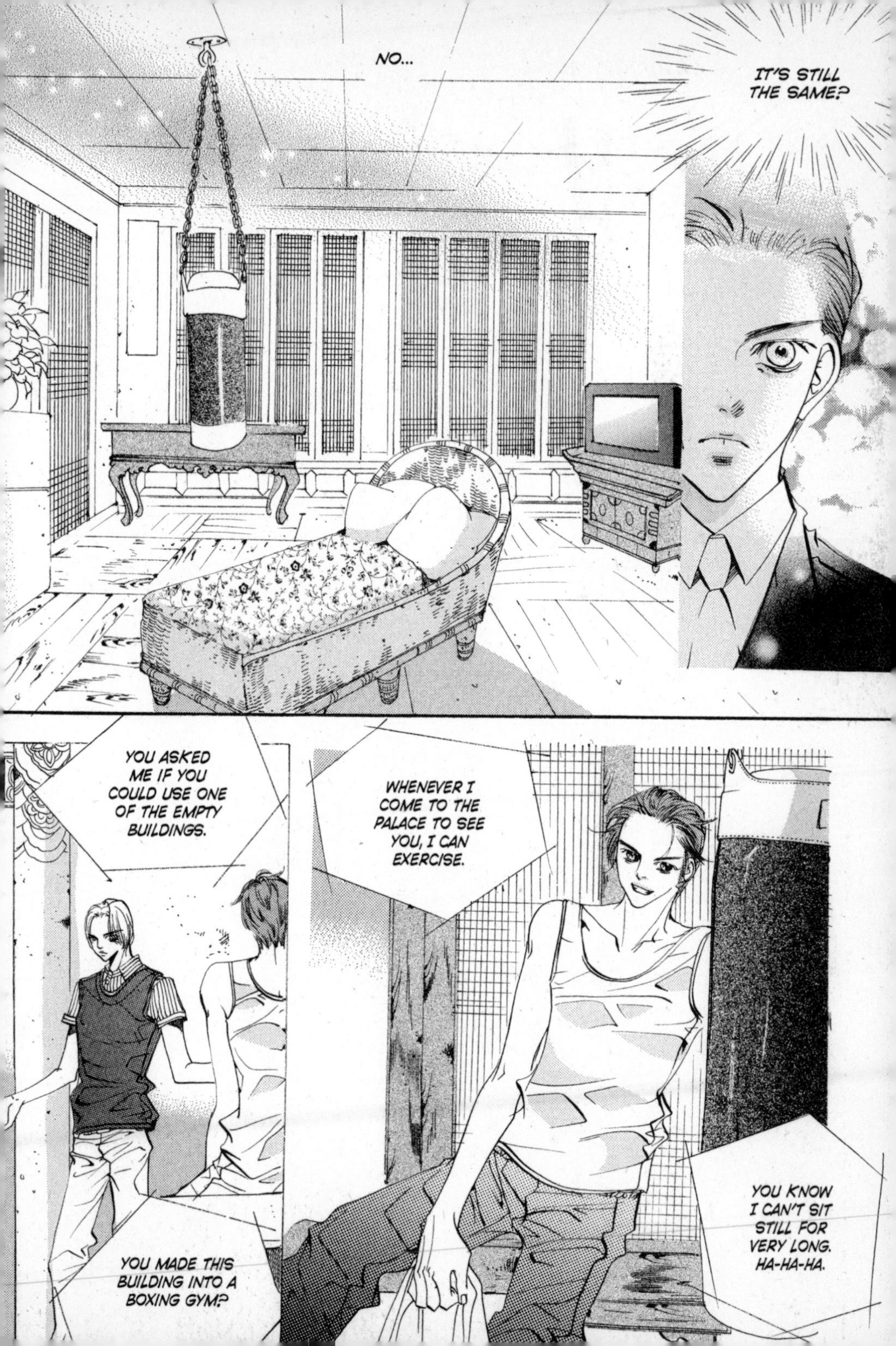
NO...
IT'S STILL THE SAME?
YOU ASKED ME IF YOU COULD USE ONE OF THE EMPTY BUILDINGS.
WHENEVER I COME TO THE PALACE TO SEE YOU, I CAN EXERCISE.
YOU MADE THIS BUILDING INTO A BOXING GYM?
YOU KNOW I CAN'T SIT STILL FOR VERY LONG. HA-HA-HA.

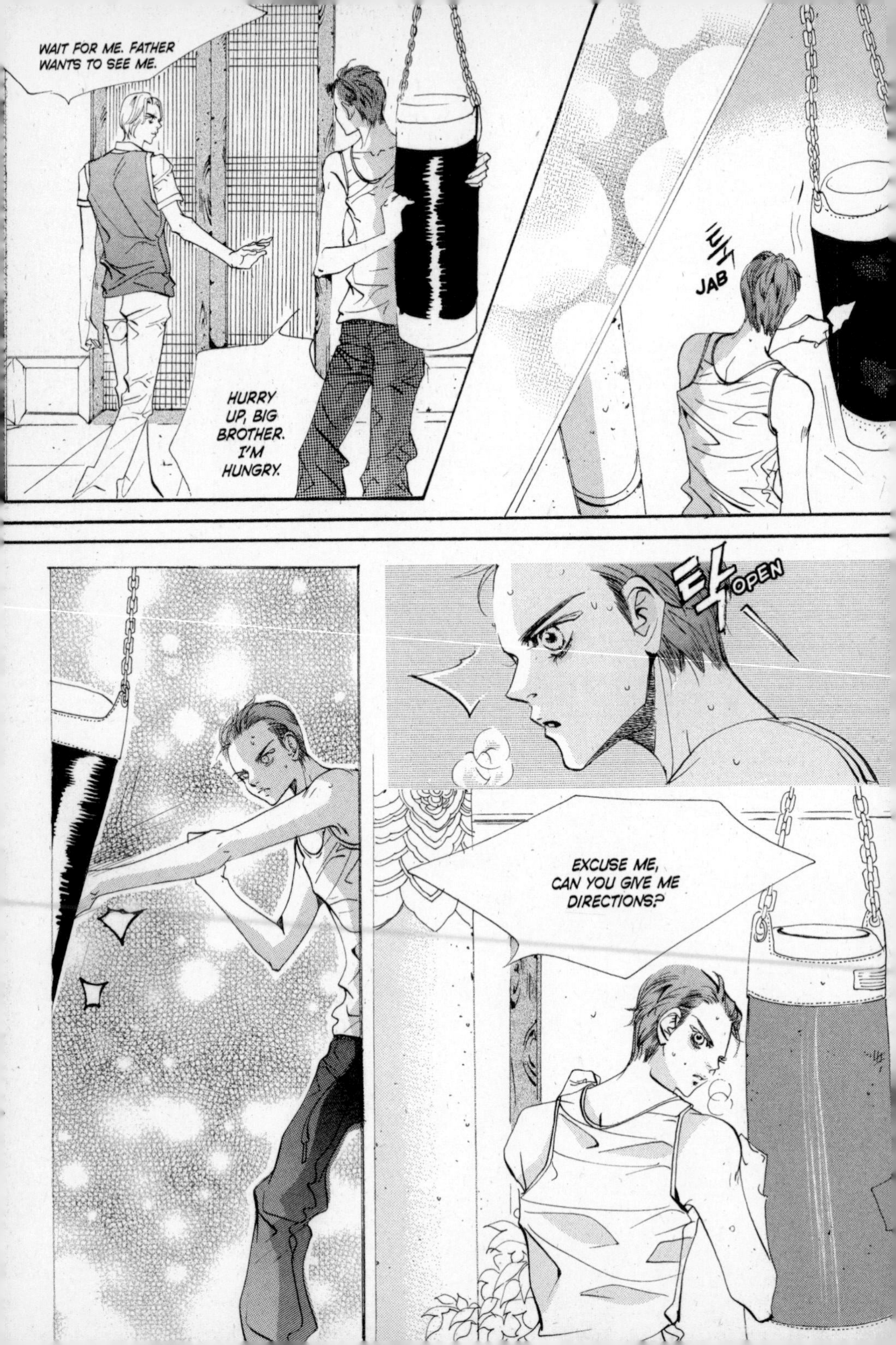

WAIT FOR ME. FATHER WANTS TO SEE ME.
HURRY UP, BIG BROTHER. I'M HUNGRY.
JAB
OPEN
EXCUSE ME, CAN YOU GIVE ME DIRECTIONS?

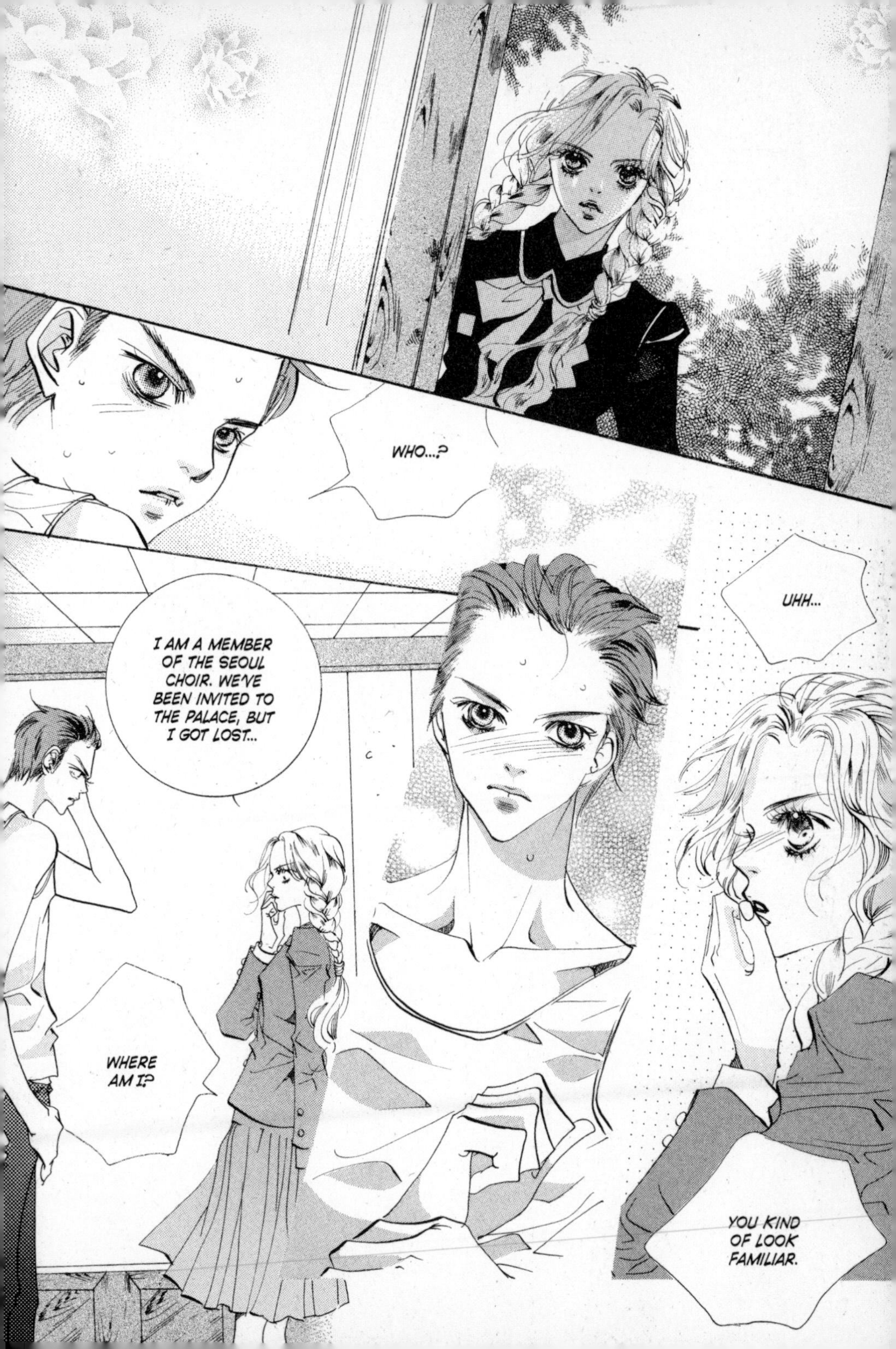
WHO...?
I AM A MEMBER OF THE SEOUL CHOIR. WE'VE BEEN INVITED TO THE PALACE, BUT I GOT LOST...
WHERE AM I?
UHH...
YOU KIND OF LOOK FAMILIAR.

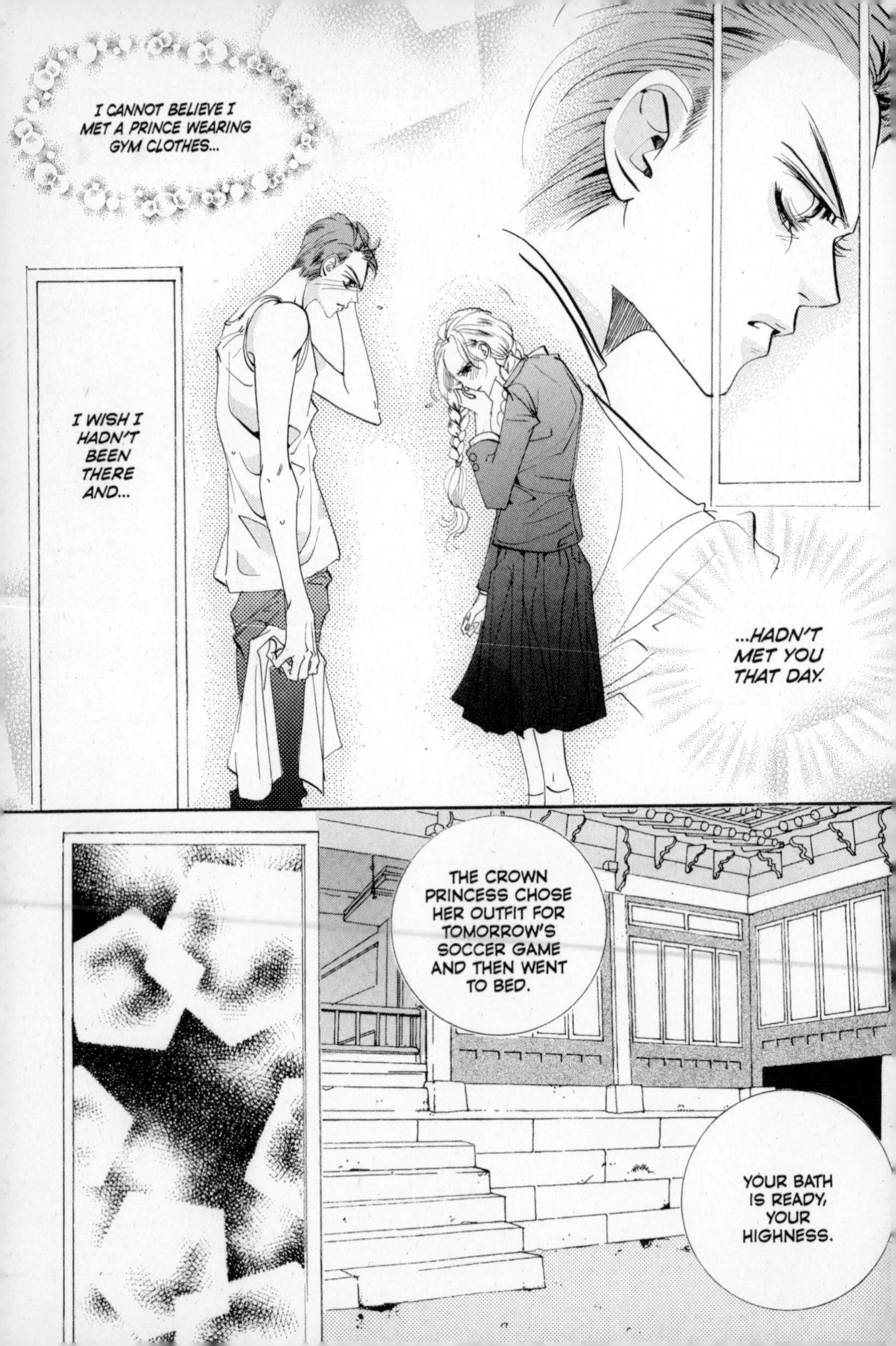
I CANNOT BELIEVE I MET A PRINCE WEARING GYM CLOTHES...
I WISH I HADN'T BEEN THERE AND...
...HADN'T MET YOU THAT DAY.
THE CROWN PRINCESS CHOSE HER OUTFIT FOR TOMORROW'S SOCCER GAME AND THEN WENT TO BED.
YOUR BATH IS READY, YOUR HIGHNESS.

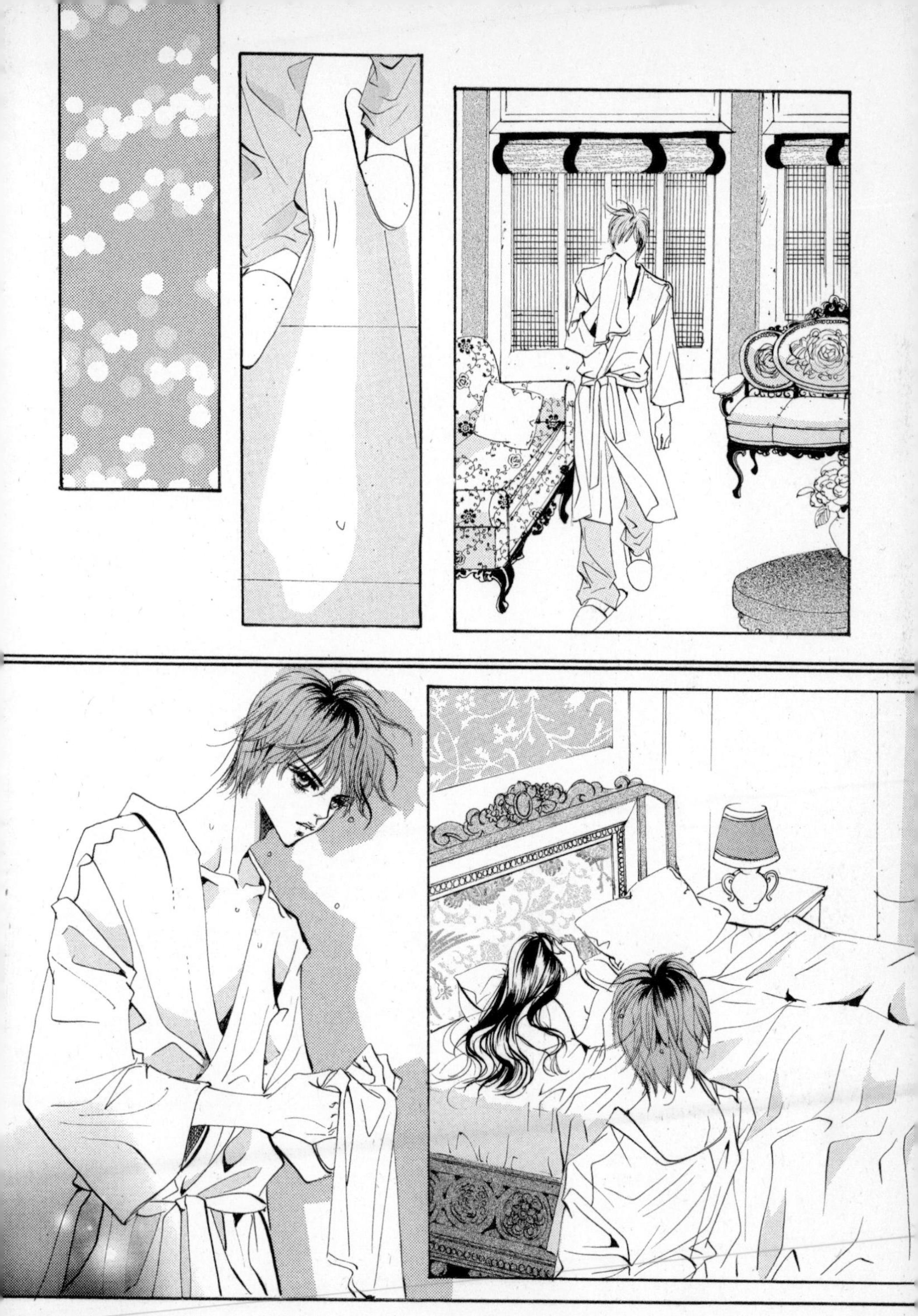

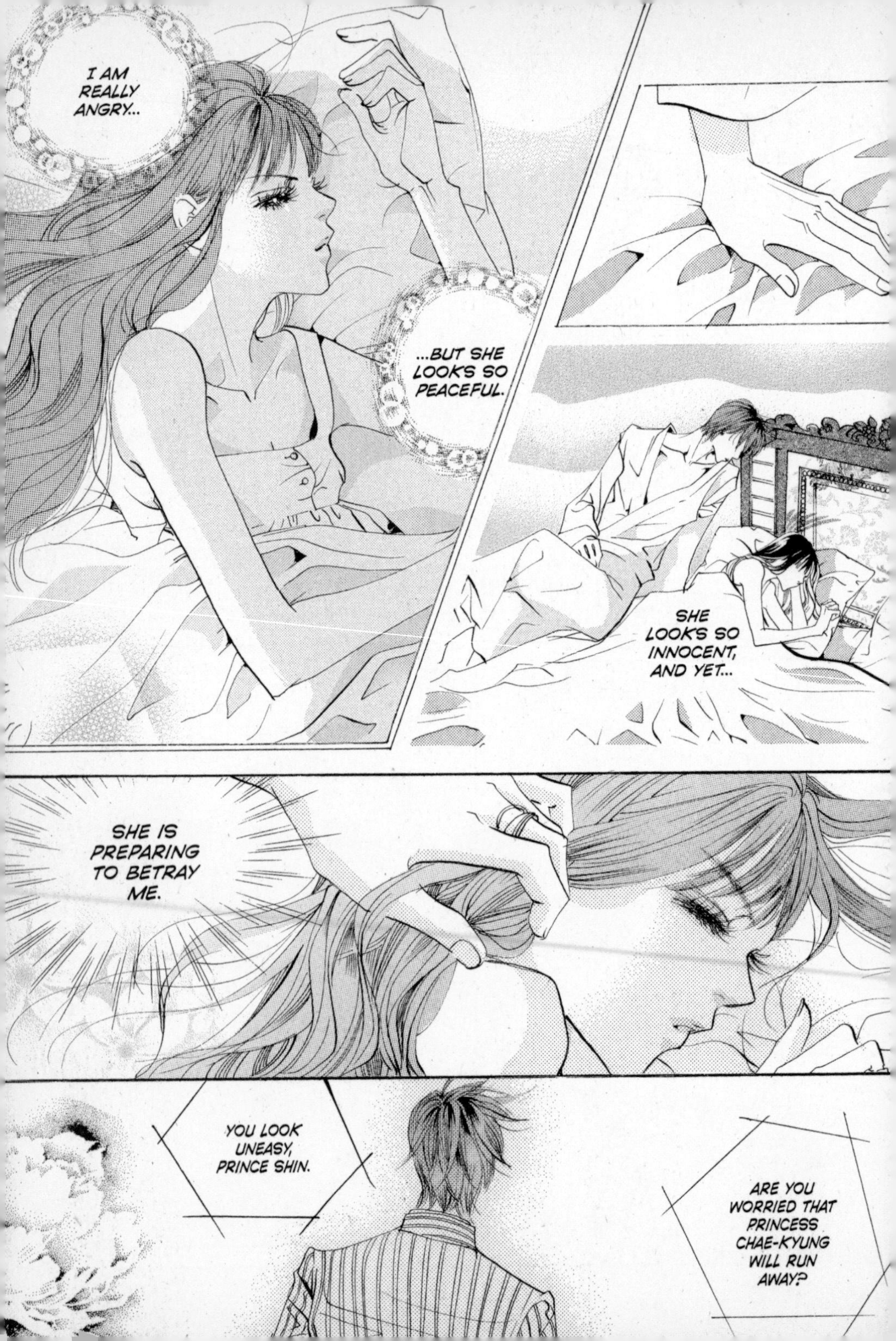
I AM REALLY ANGRY...
...BUT SHE LOOKS SO PEACEFUL.
SHE LOOKS SO INNOCENT, AND YET...
SHE IS PREPARING TO BETRAY ME.
YOU LOOK UNEASY, PRINCE SHIN.
ARE YOU WORRIED THAT PRINCESS CHAE-KYUNG WILL RUN AWAY?

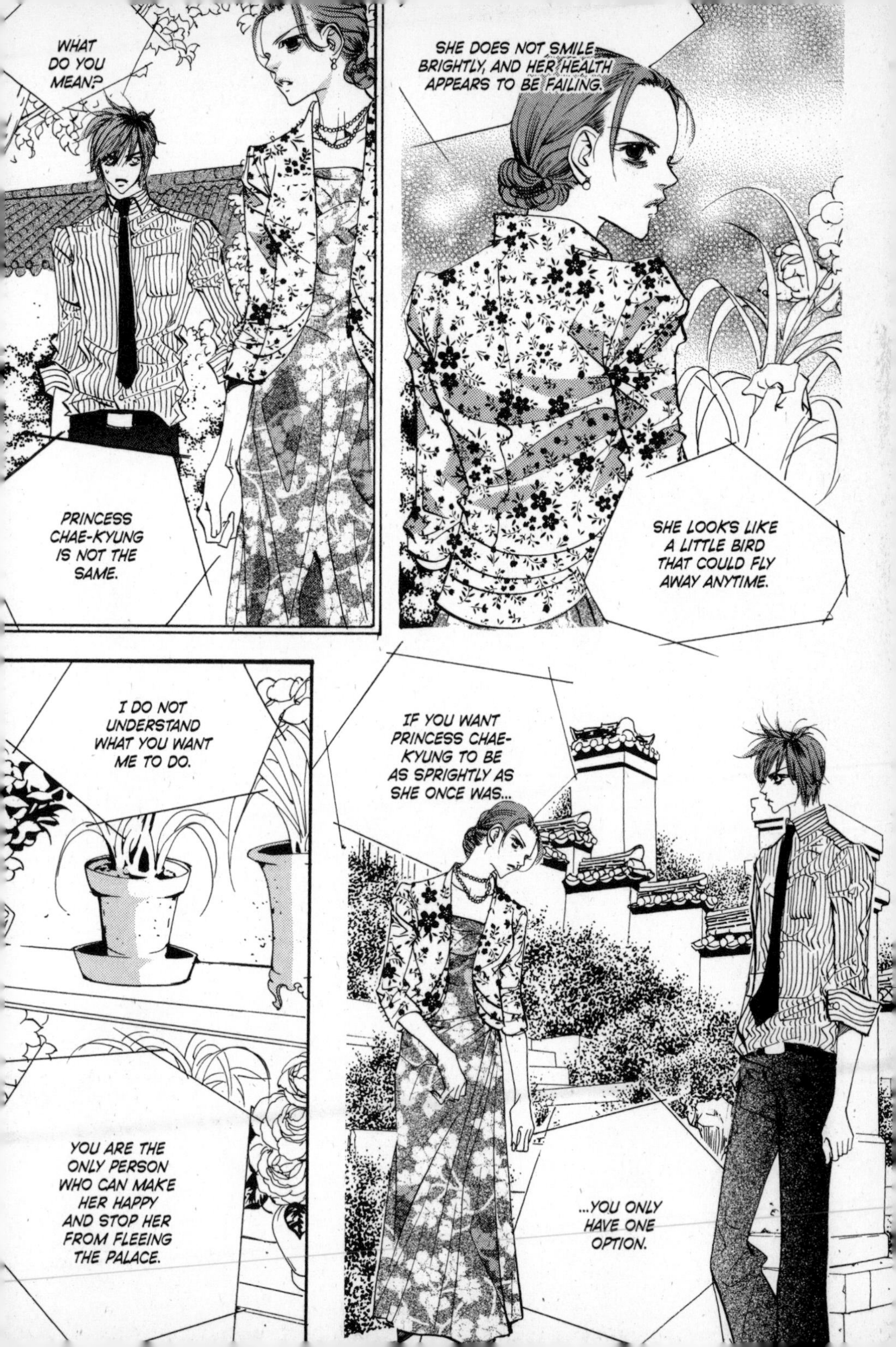
WHAT DO YOU MEAN?
PRINCESS CHAE-KYUNG IS NOT THE SAME.
SHE DOES NOT SMILE BRIGHTLY, AND HER HEALTH APPEARS TO BE FAILING.
SHE LOOKS LIKE A LITTLE BIRD THAT COULD FLY AWAY ANYTIME.
I DO NOT UNDERSTAND WHAT YOU WANT ME TO DO.
YOU ARE THE ONLY PERSON WHO CAN MAKE HER HAPPY AND STOP HER FROM FLEEING THE PALACE.
IF YOU WANT PRINCESS CHAE-KYUNG TO BE AS SPRIGHTLY AS SHE ONCE WAS...
...YOU ONLY HAVE ONE OPTION.

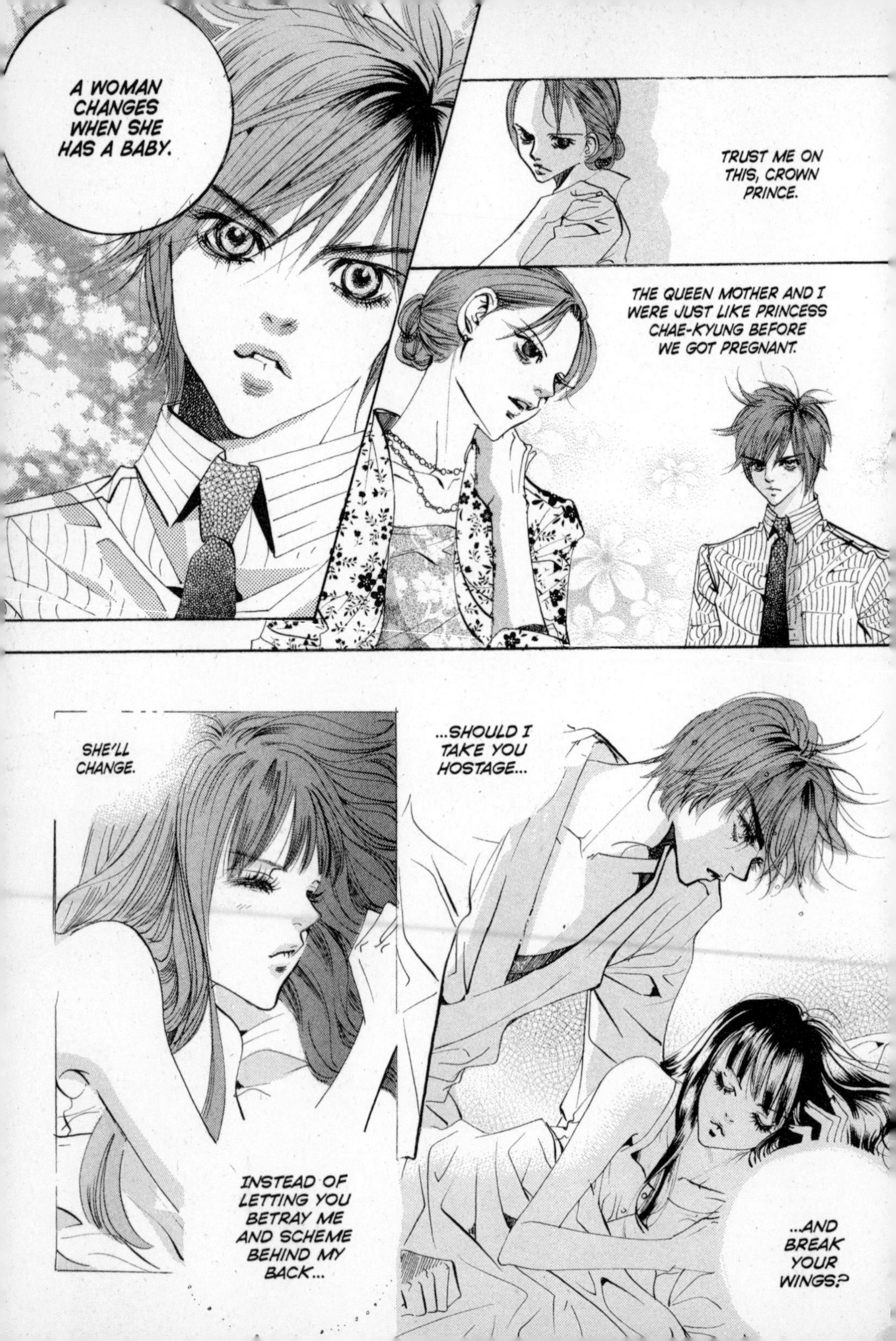

A WOMAN CHANGES WHEN SHE HAS A BABY.
TRUST ME ON THIS, CROWN PRINCE.
THE QUEEN MOTHER AND I WERE JUST LIKE PRINCESS CHAE-KYUNG BEFORE WE GOT PREGNANT.
SHE'LL CHANGE.
INSTEAD OF LETTING YOU BETRAY ME AND SCHEME BEHIND MY BACK...
...SHOULD I TAKE YOU HOSTAGE...
...AND BREAK YOUR WINGS?

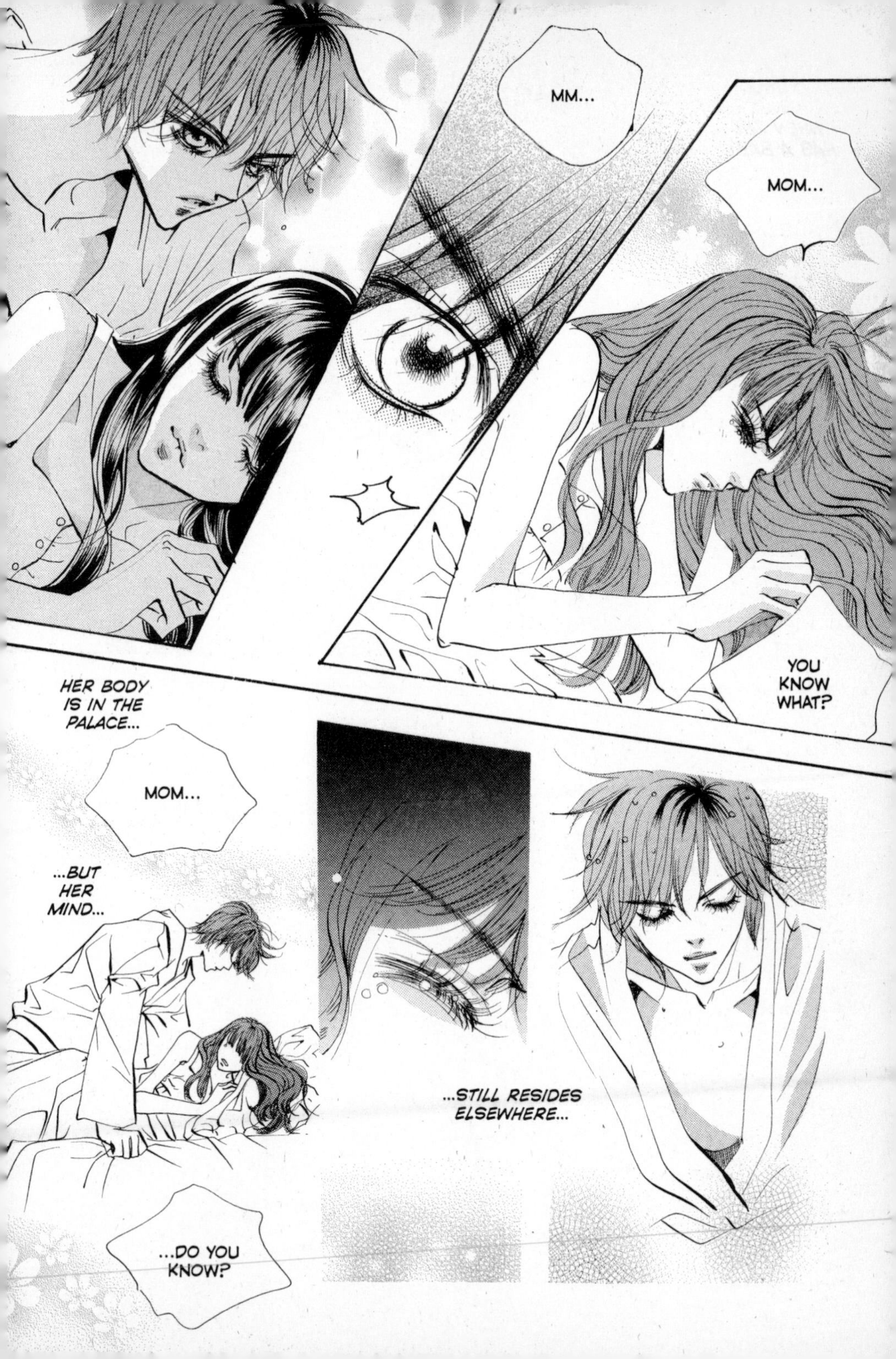
MM...
MOM...
YOU KNOW WHAT?
HER BODY IS IN THE PALACE...
MOM...
...BUT HER MIND...
...DO YOU KNOW?
...STILL RESIDES ELSEWHERE...

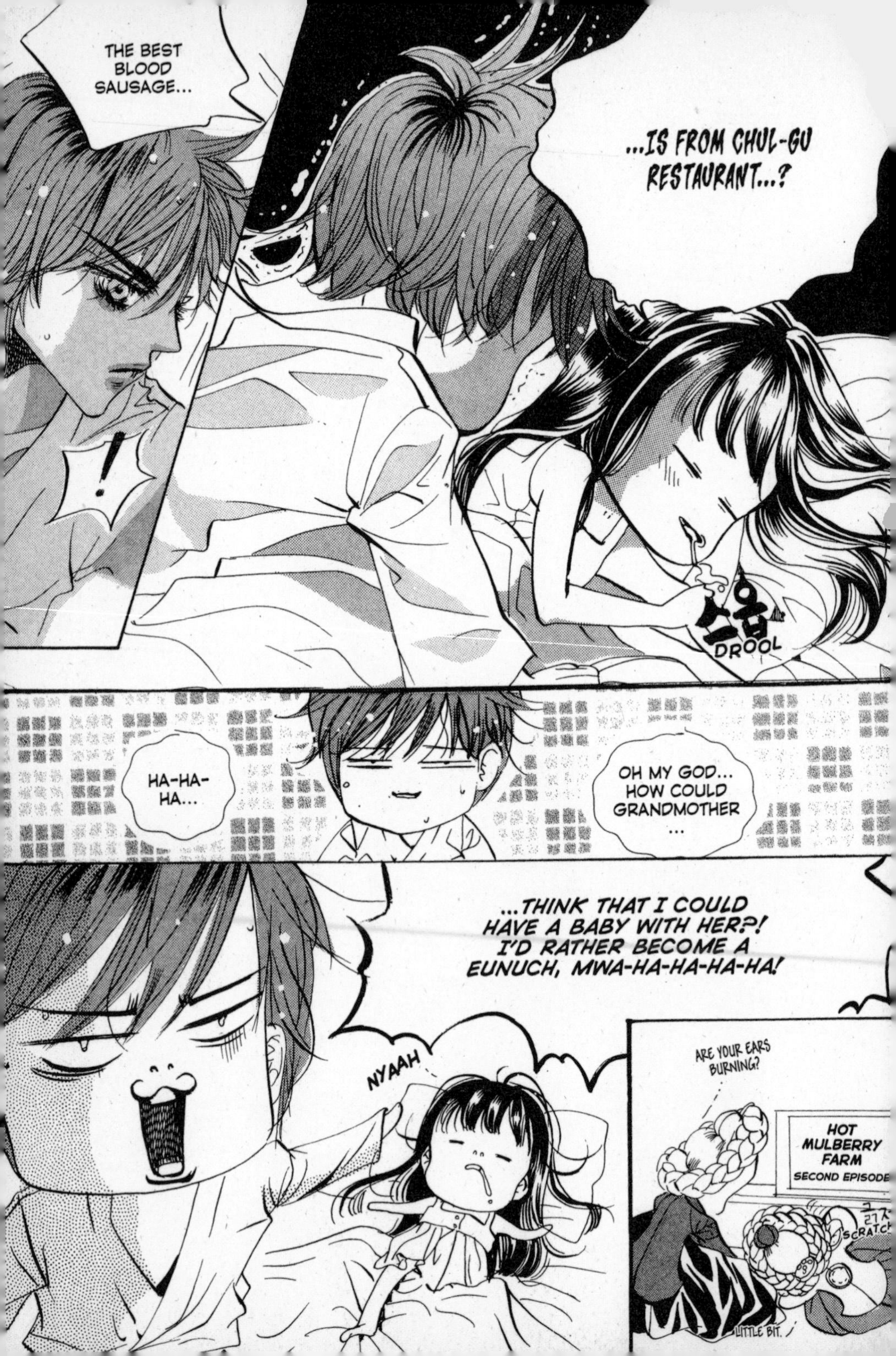
THE BEST BLOOD SAUSAGE...
...IS FROM CHUL-GU RESTAURANT...?
!
DROOL
HA-HA-HA...
OH MY GOD... HOW COULD GRANDMOTHER ...
...THINK THAT I COULD HAVE A BABY WITH HER?! I'D RATHER BECOME A EUNUCH, MWA-HA-HA-HA-HA!
NYAAH
ARE YOUR EARS BURNING?
HOT MULBERRY FARM
SECOND EPISODE
SCRATCH
LITTLE BIT.

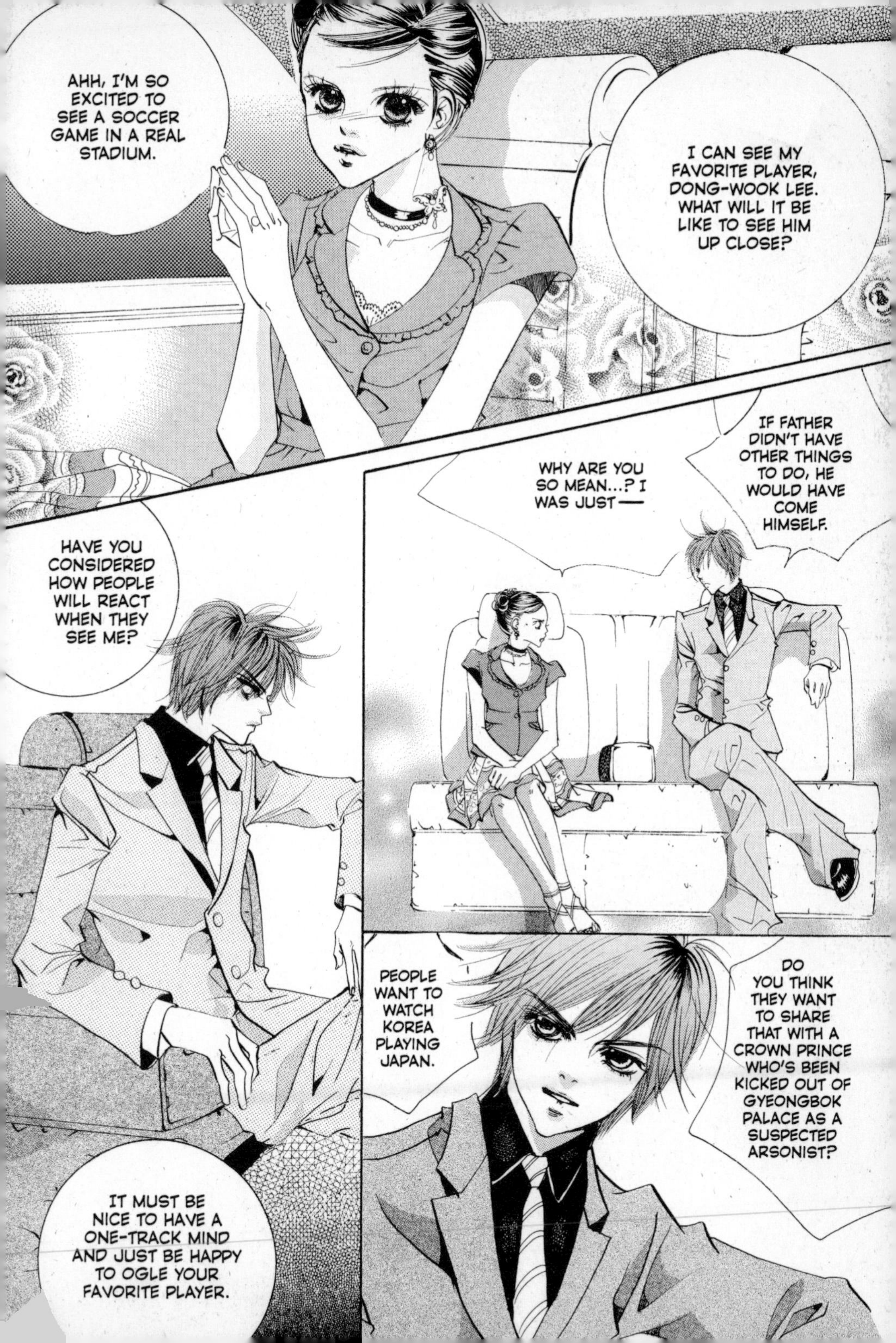
AHH, I'M SO EXCITED TO SEE A SOCCER GAME IN A REAL STADIUM.
I CAN SEE MY FAVORITE PLAYER, DONG-WOOK LEE. WHAT WILL IT BE LIKE TO SEE HIM UP CLOSE?
HAVE YOU CONSIDERED HOW PEOPLE WILL REACT WHEN THEY SEE ME?
IT MUST BE NICE TO HAVE A ONE-TRACK MIND AND JUST BE HAPPY TO OGLE YOUR FAVORITE PLAYER.
WHY ARE YOU SO MEAN...? I WAS JUST—
IF FATHER DIDN'T HAVE OTHER THINGS TO DO, HE WOULD HAVE COME HIMSELF.
PEOPLE WANT TO WATCH KOREA PLAYING JAPAN.
DO YOU THINK THEY WANT TO SHARE THAT WITH A CROWN PRINCE WHO'S BEEN KICKED OUT OF GYEONGBOK PALACE AS A SUSPECTED ARSONIST?

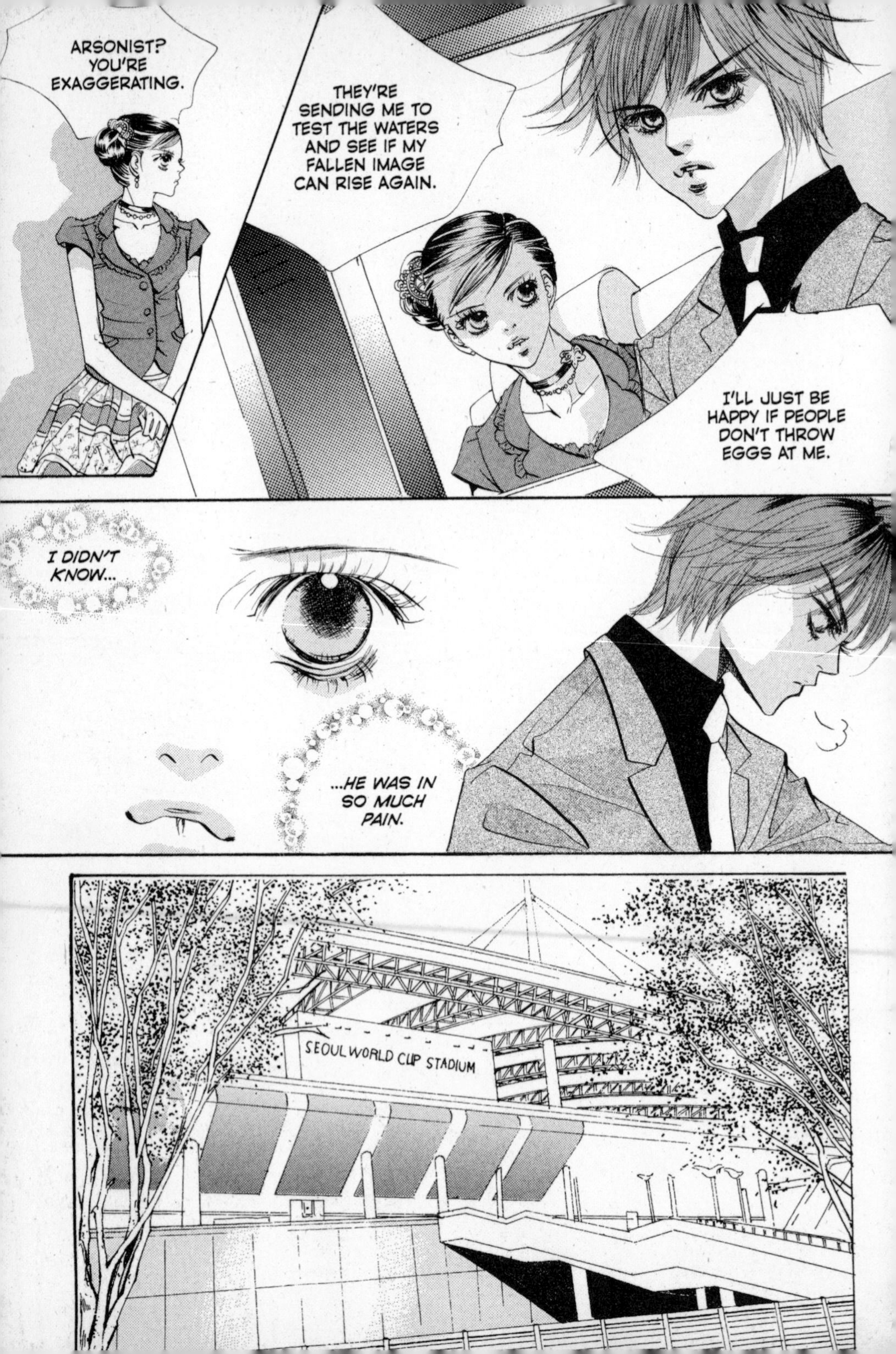
ARSONIST? YOU'RE EXAGGERATING.
THEY'RE SENDING ME TO TEST THE WATERS AND SEE IF MY FALLEN IMAGE CAN RISE AGAIN.
I'LL JUST BE HAPPY IF PEOPLE DON'T THROW EGGS AT ME.
I DIDN'T KNOW...
...HE WAS IN SO MUCH PAIN.
SEOUL WORLD CUP STADIUM

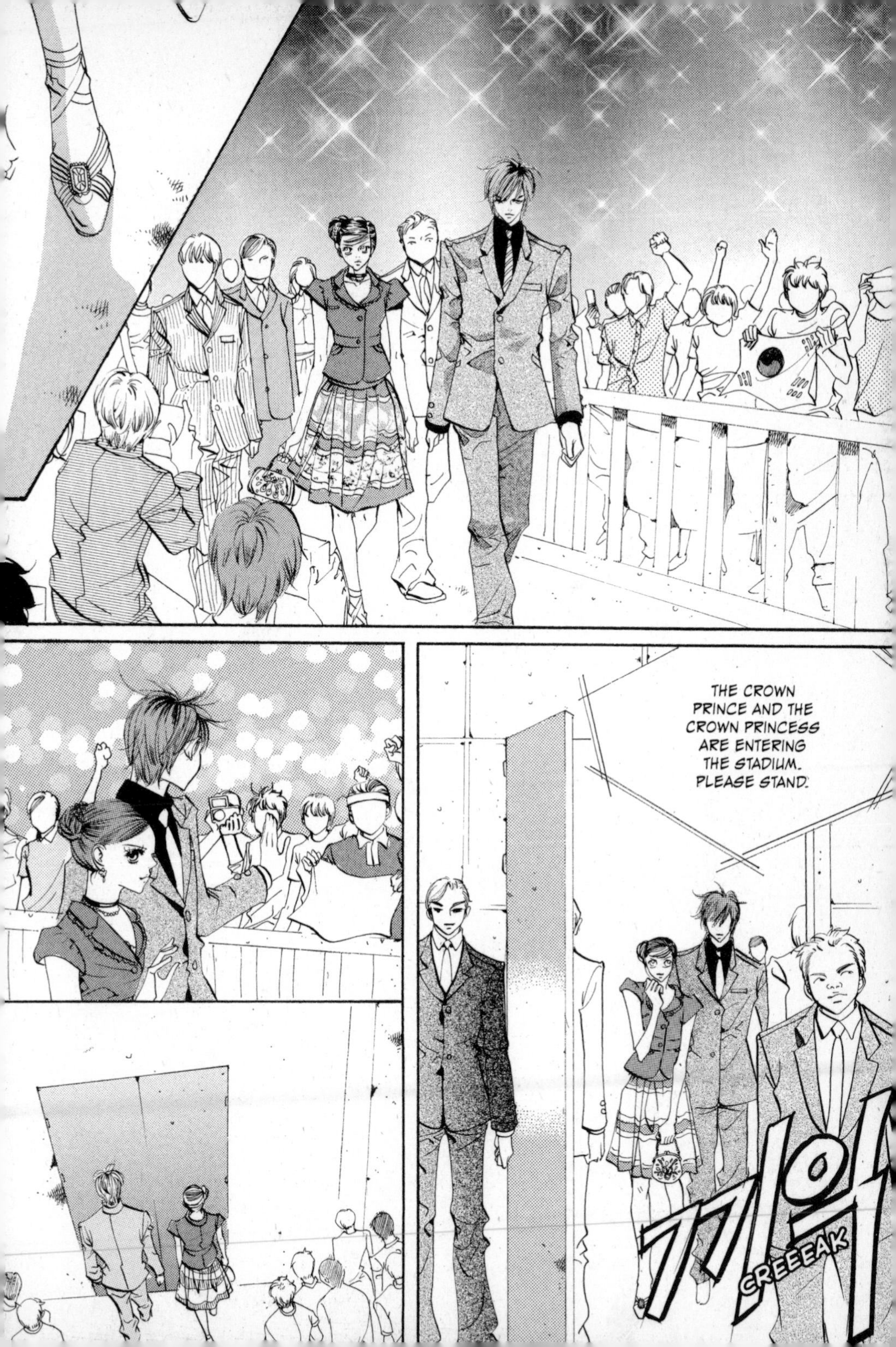
THE CROWN PRINCE AND THE CROWN PRINCESS ARE ENTERING THE STADIUM. PLEASE STAND.
CREEEAK

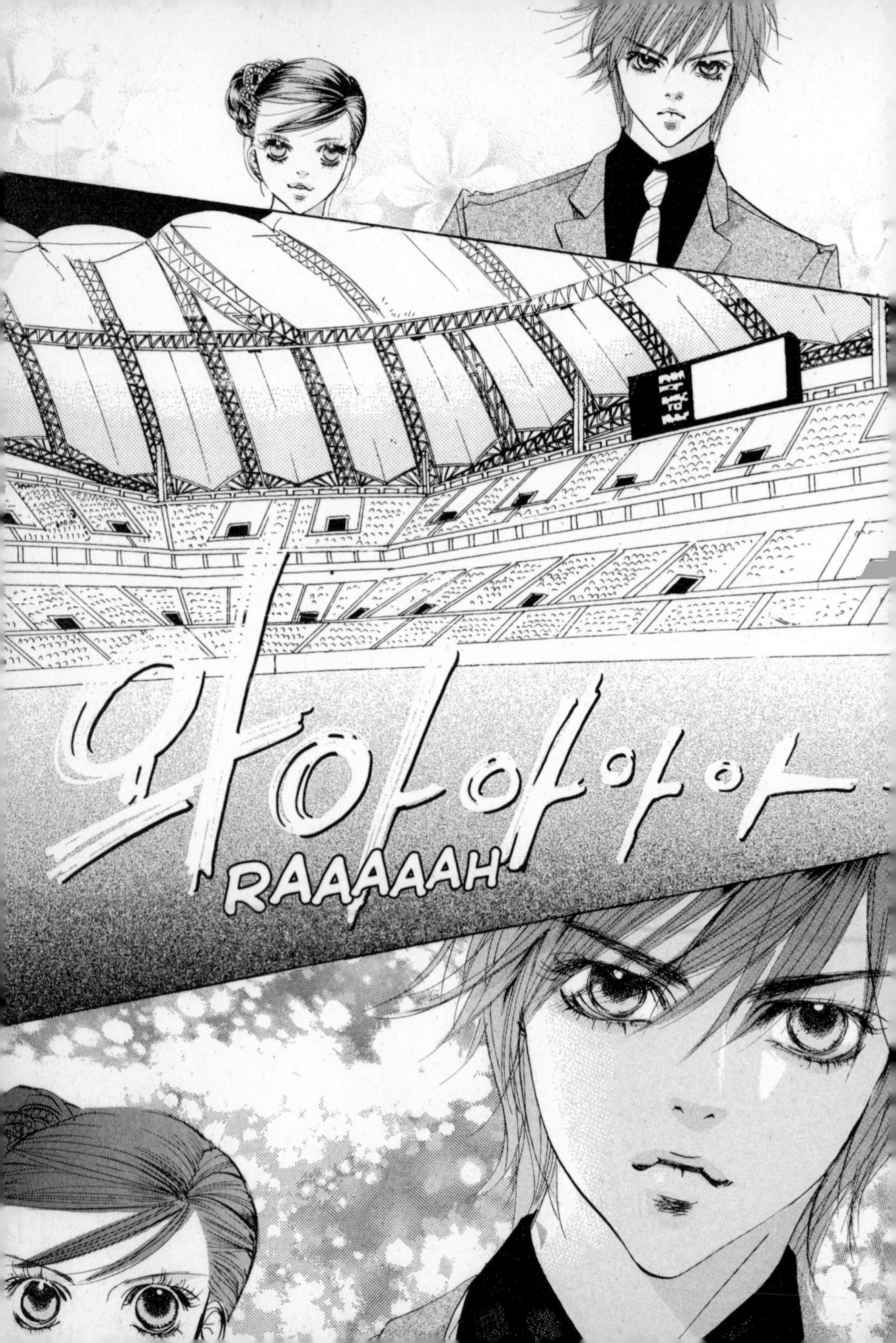
와아아아아
RAAAAAH

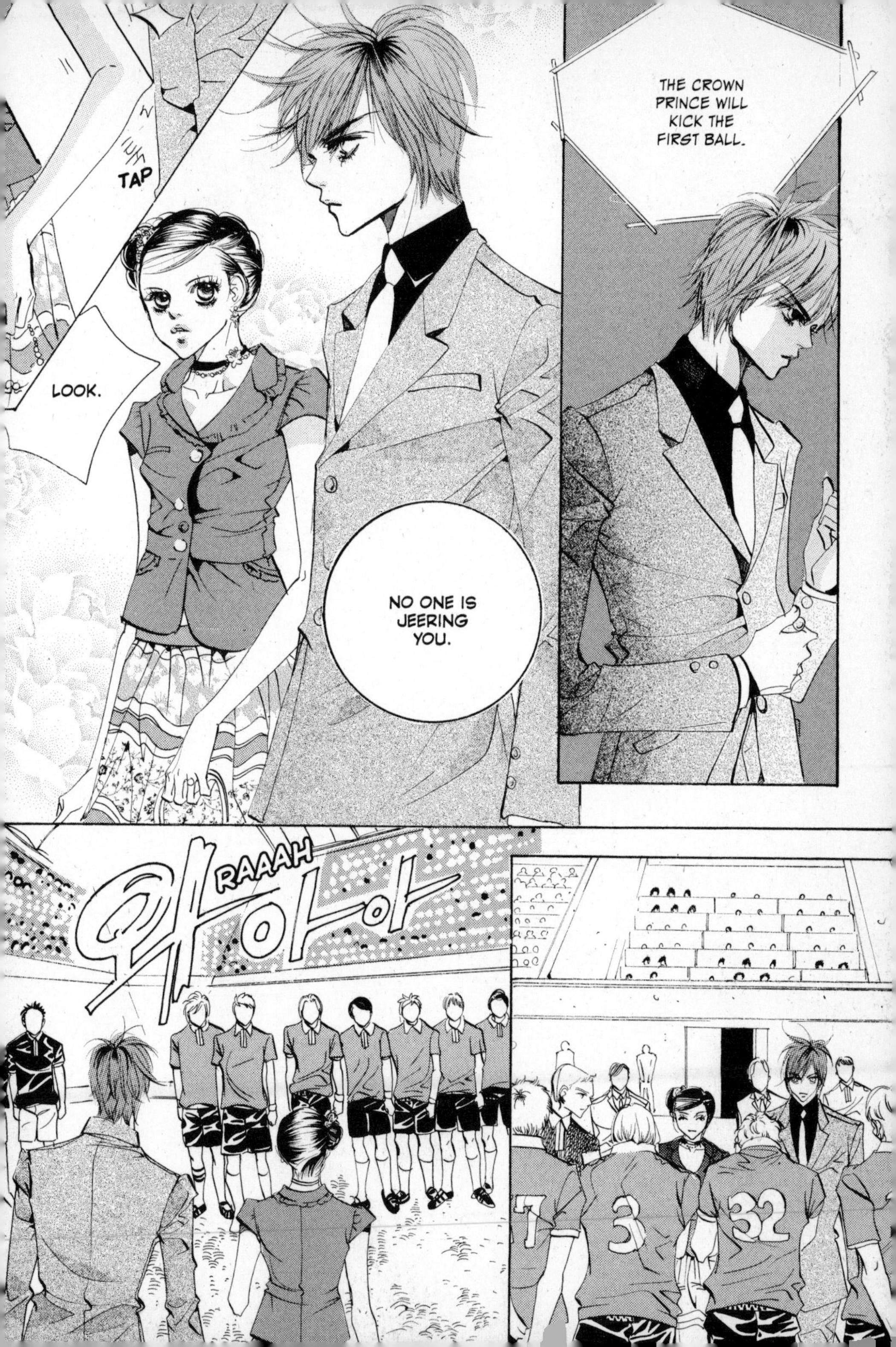
TAP
LOOK.
NO ONE IS JEERING YOU.
THE CROWN PRINCE WILL KICK THE FIRST BALL.
RAAAH

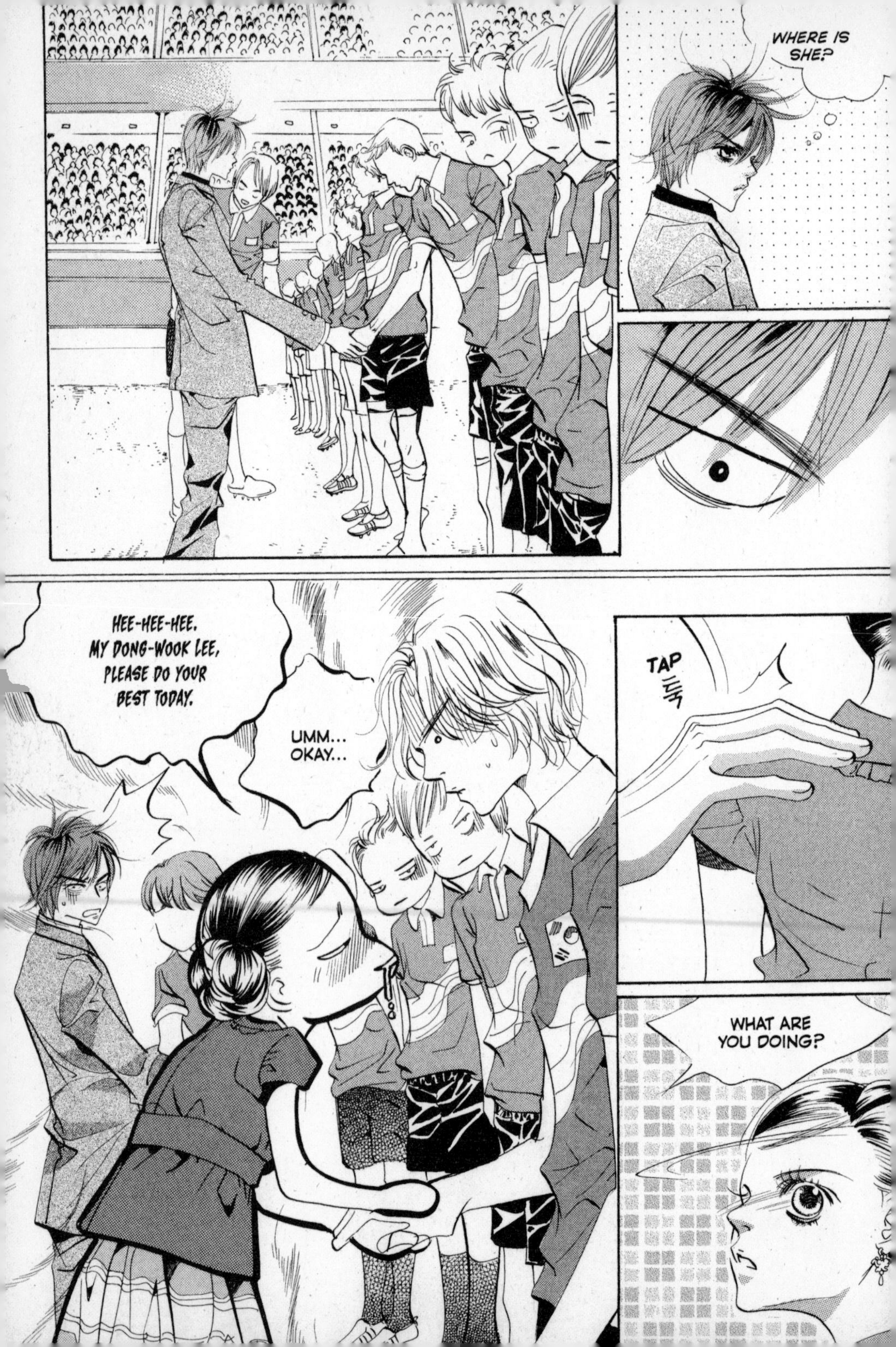
WHERE IS SHE?
HEE-HEE-HEE. MY DONG-WOOK LEE, PLEASE DO YOUR BEST TODAY.
UMM... OKAY...
TAP
WHAT ARE YOU DOING?

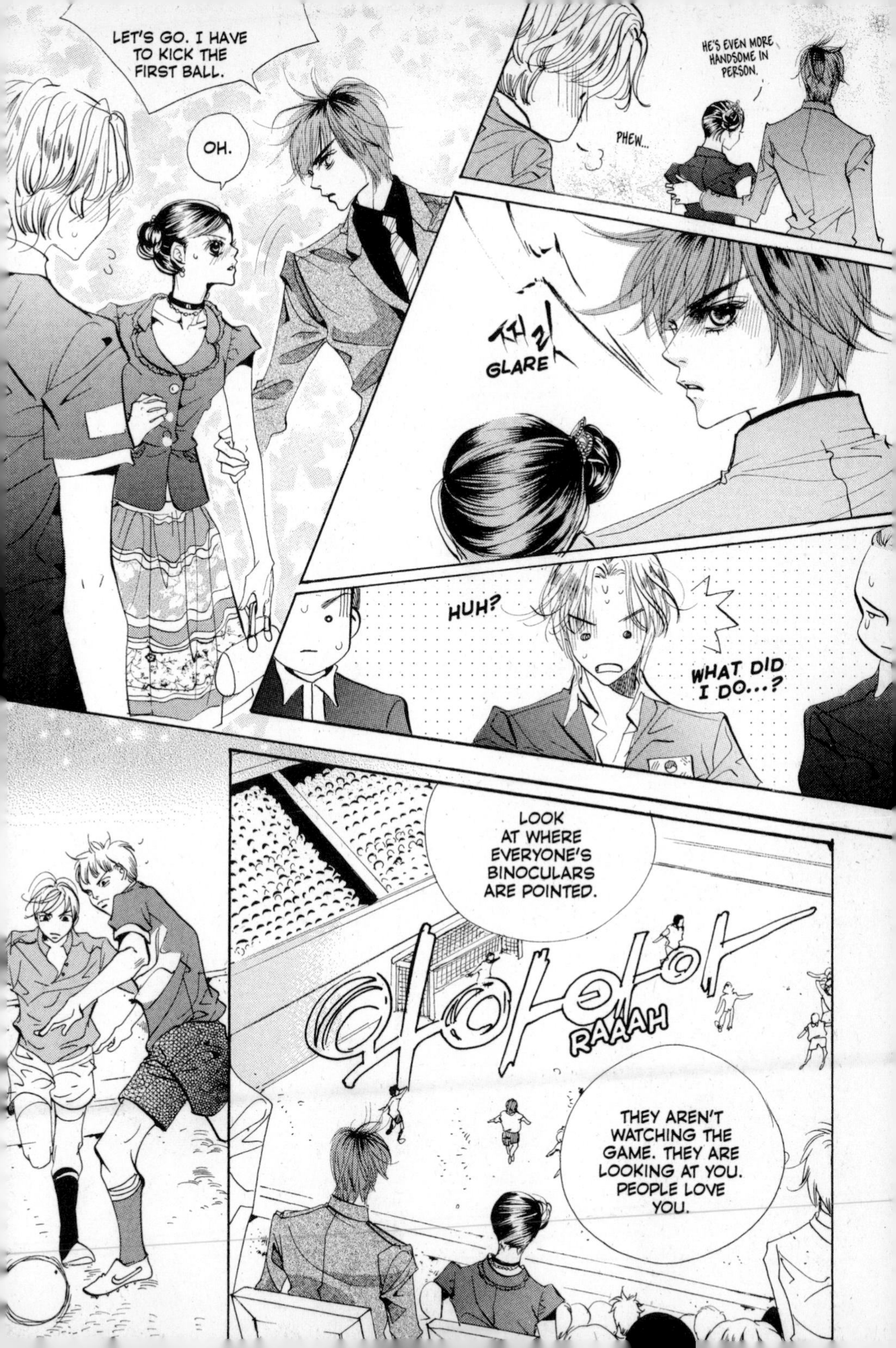
LET'S GO. I HAVE TO KICK THE FIRST BALL.
OH.
HE'S EVEN MORE HANDSOME IN PERSON.
PHEW...
GLARE
HUH?
WHAT DID I DO...?
LOOK AT WHERE EVERYONE'S BINOCULARS ARE POINTED.
RAAAH
THEY AREN'T WATCHING THE GAME. THEY ARE LOOKING AT YOU. PEOPLE LOVE YOU.

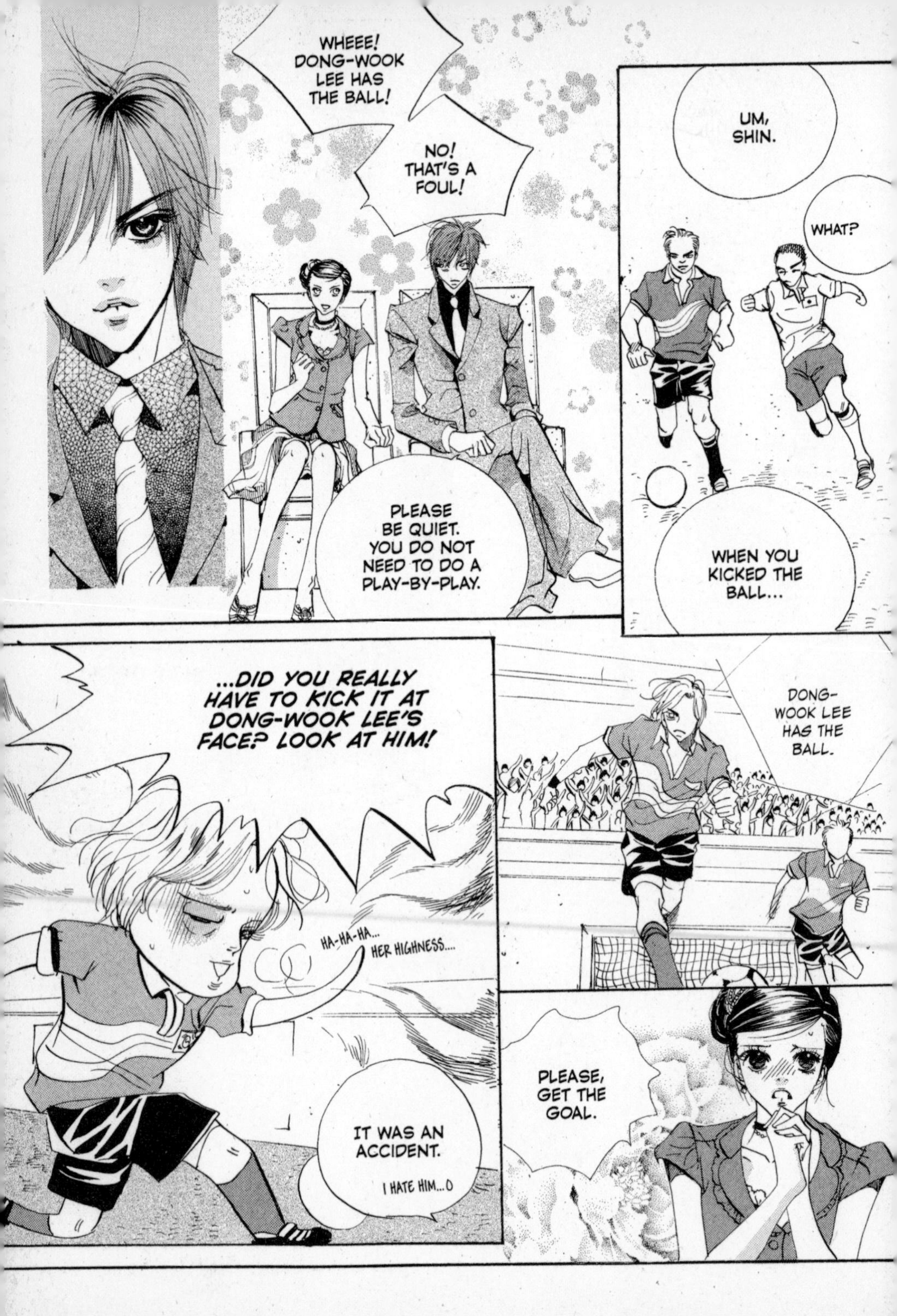
WHEEE! DONG-WOOK LEE HAS THE BALL!
NO! THAT'S A FOUL!
PLEASE BE QUIET. YOU DO NOT NEED TO DO A PLAY-BY-PLAY.
UM, SHIN.
WHAT?
WHEN YOU KICKED THE BALL...
...DID YOU REALLY HAVE TO KICK IT AT DONG-WOOK LEE'S FACE? LOOK AT HIM!
HA-HA-HA... HER HIGHNESS....
IT WAS AN ACCIDENT.
I HATE HIM...
DONG-WOOK LEE HAS THE BALL.
PLEASE, GET THE GOAL.

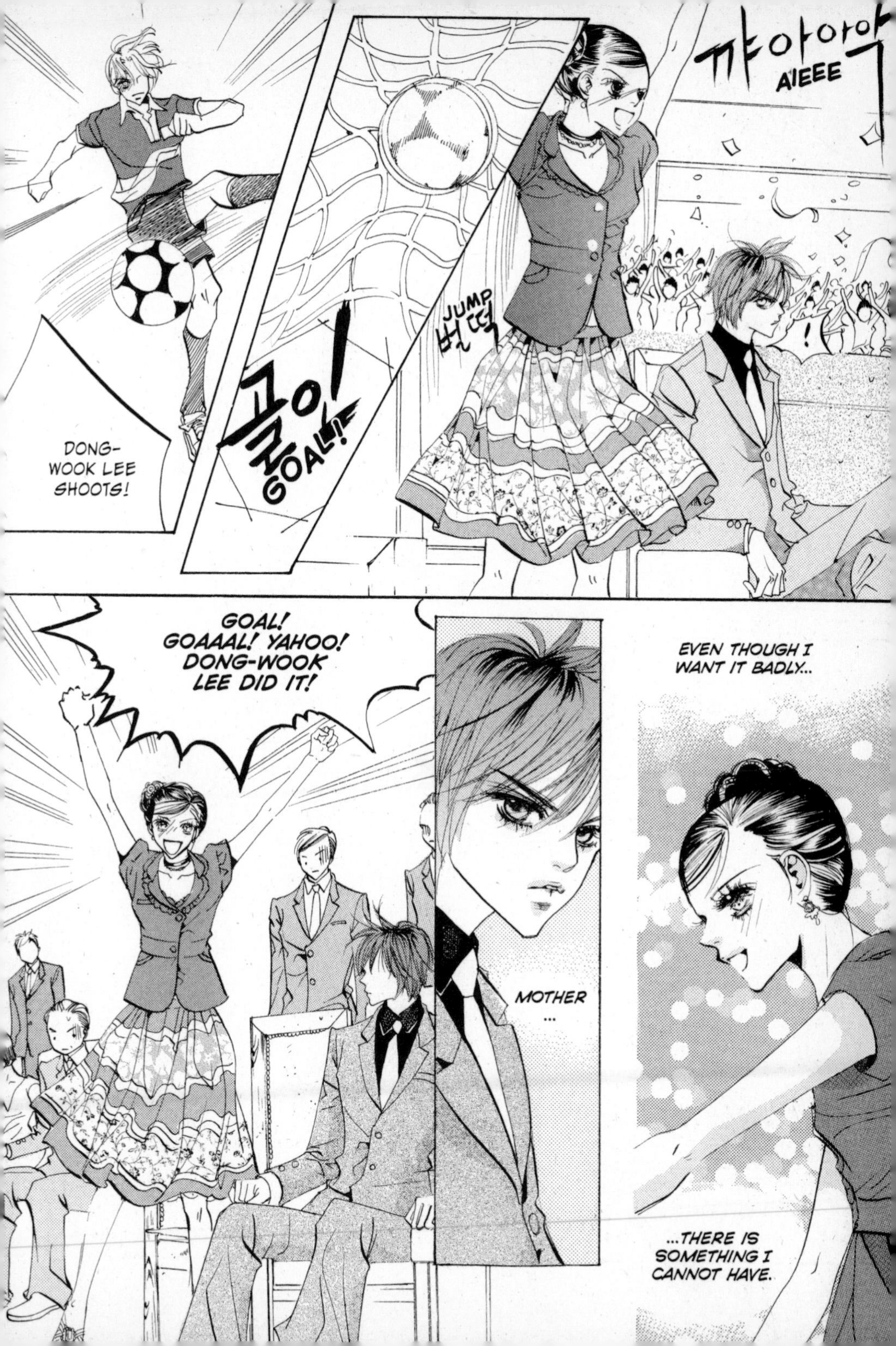
DONG-WOOK LEE SHOOTS!
골인
GOAL!!
벌떡
JUMP
꺄아아악
AIEEE
!
GOAL! GOAAAL! YAHOO! DONG-WOOK LEE DID IT!
MOTHER ...
EVEN THOUGH I WANT IT BADLY...
...THERE IS SOMETHING I CANNOT HAVE.

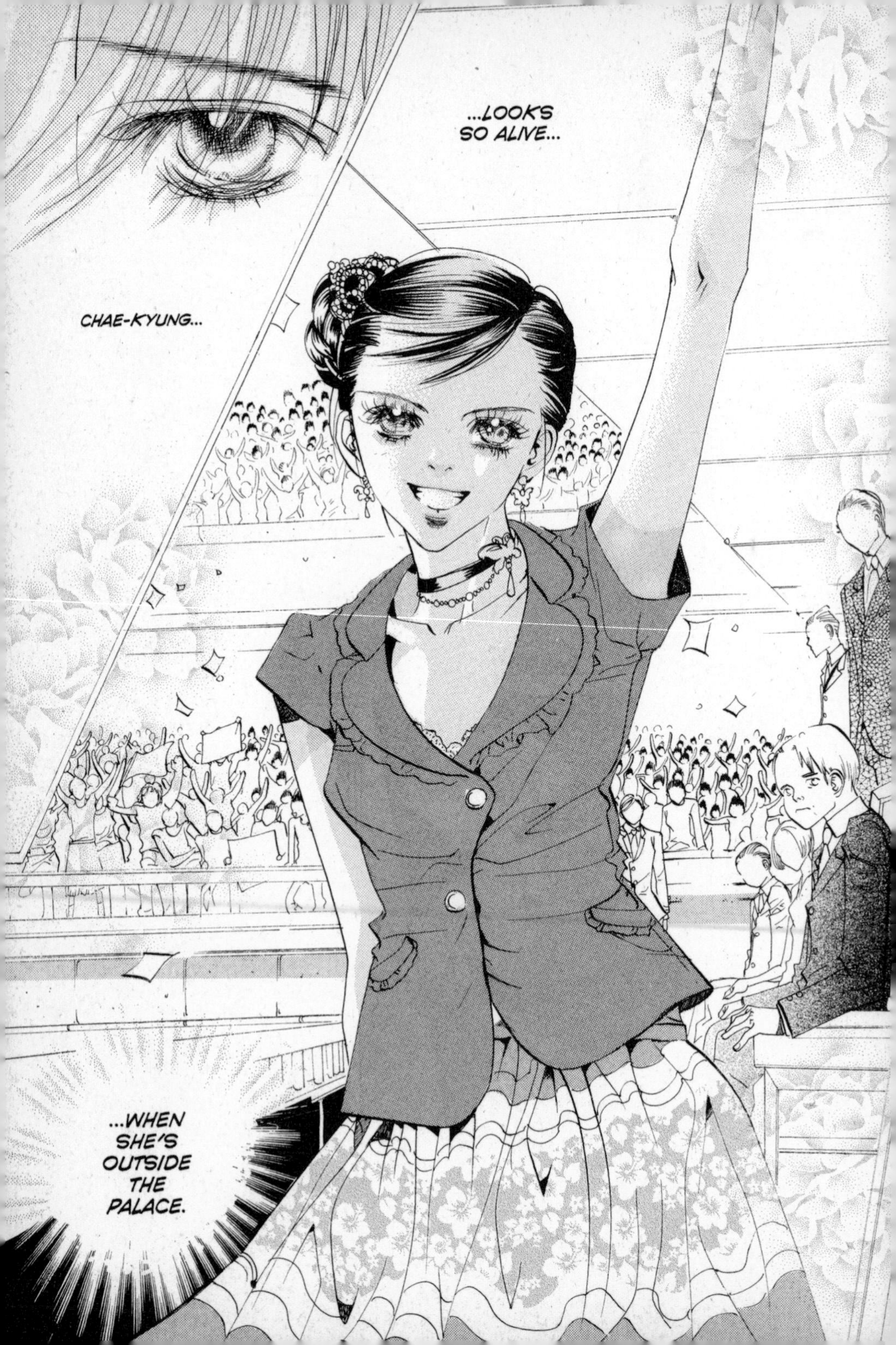
...LOOKS SO ALIVE...
CHAE-KYUNG...
...WHEN SHE'S OUTSIDE THE PALACE.

THE ROYAL PALACE

Goong

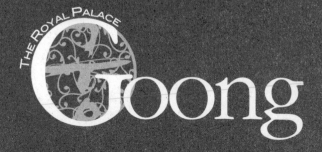

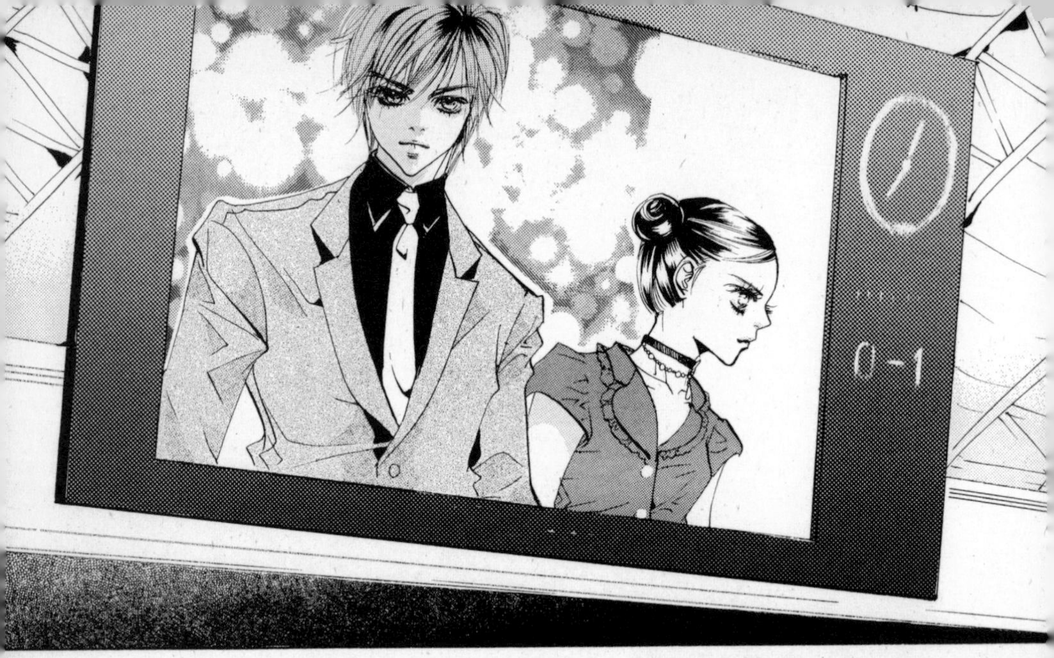
0-1

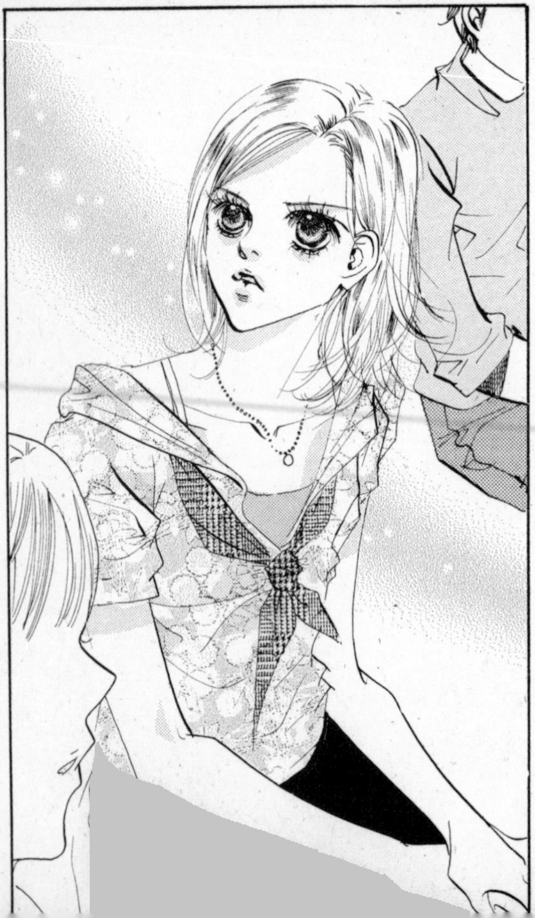

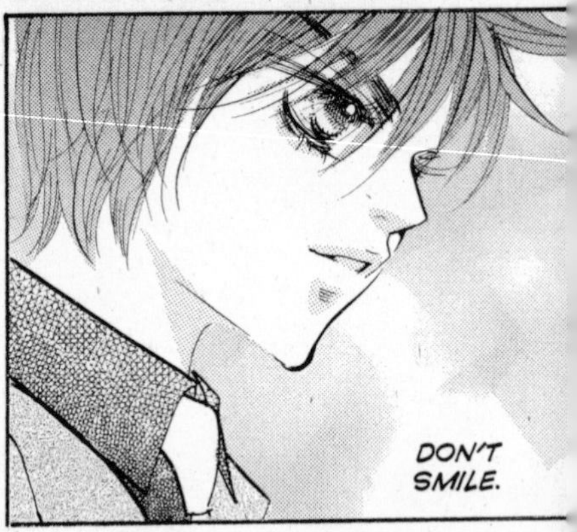
DON'T SMILE.

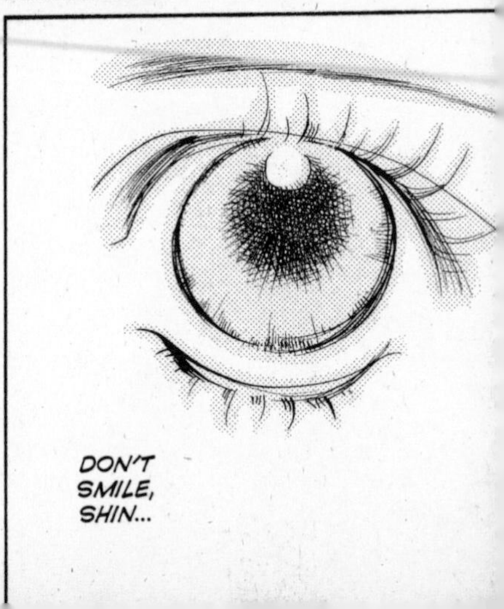
DON'T SMILE, SHIN...

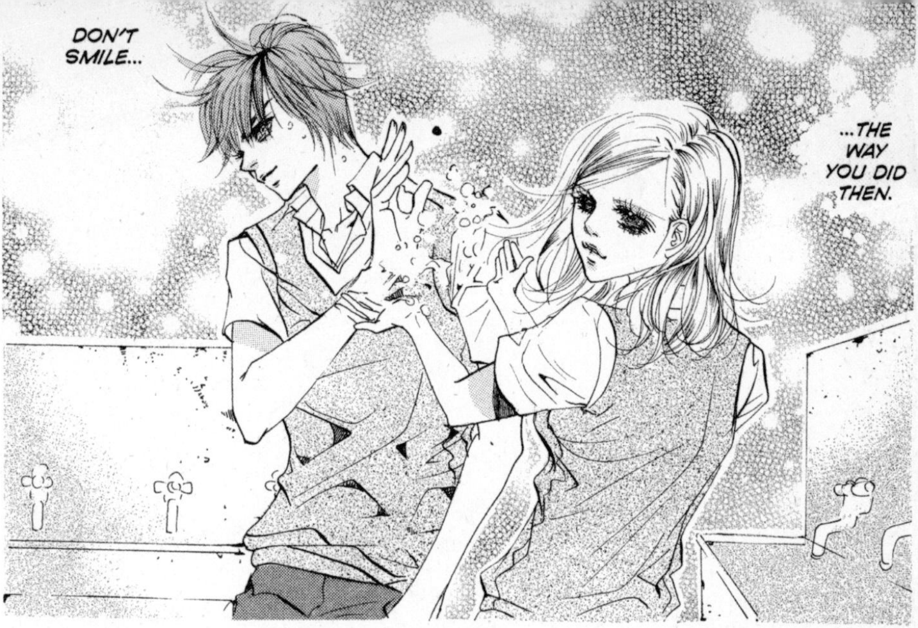
DON'T SMILE...
...THE WAY YOU DID THEN.

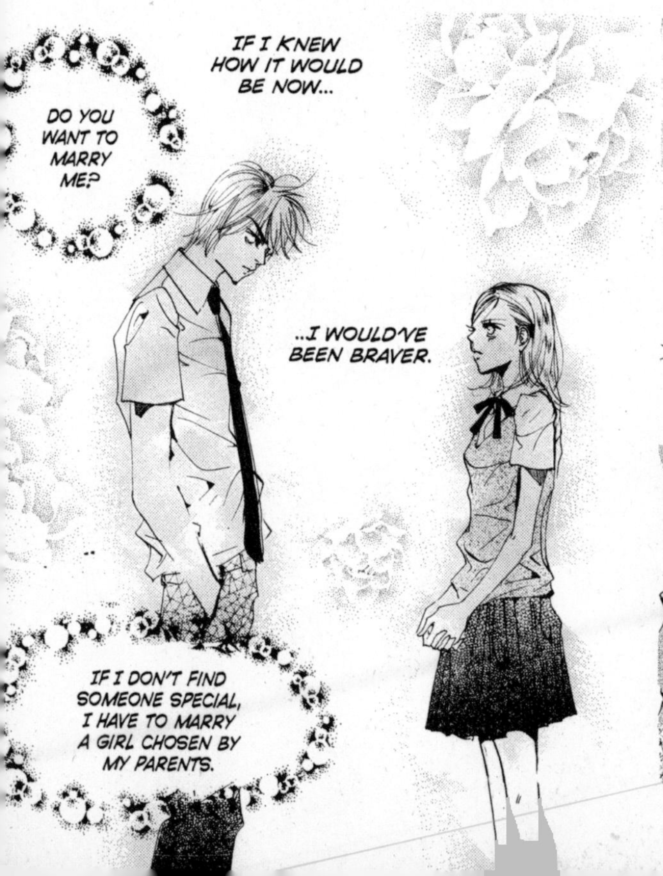
IF I KNEW HOW IT WOULD BE NOW...
DO YOU WANT TO MARRY ME?
..I WOULD'VE BEEN BRAVER.
IF I DON'T FIND SOMEONE SPECIAL, I HAVE TO MARRY A GIRL CHOSEN BY MY PARENTS.

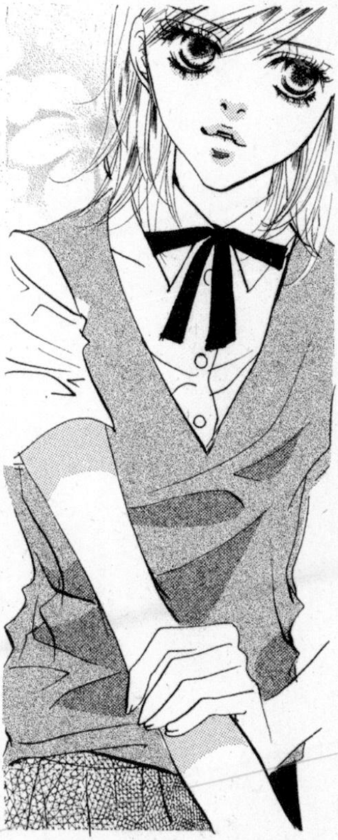

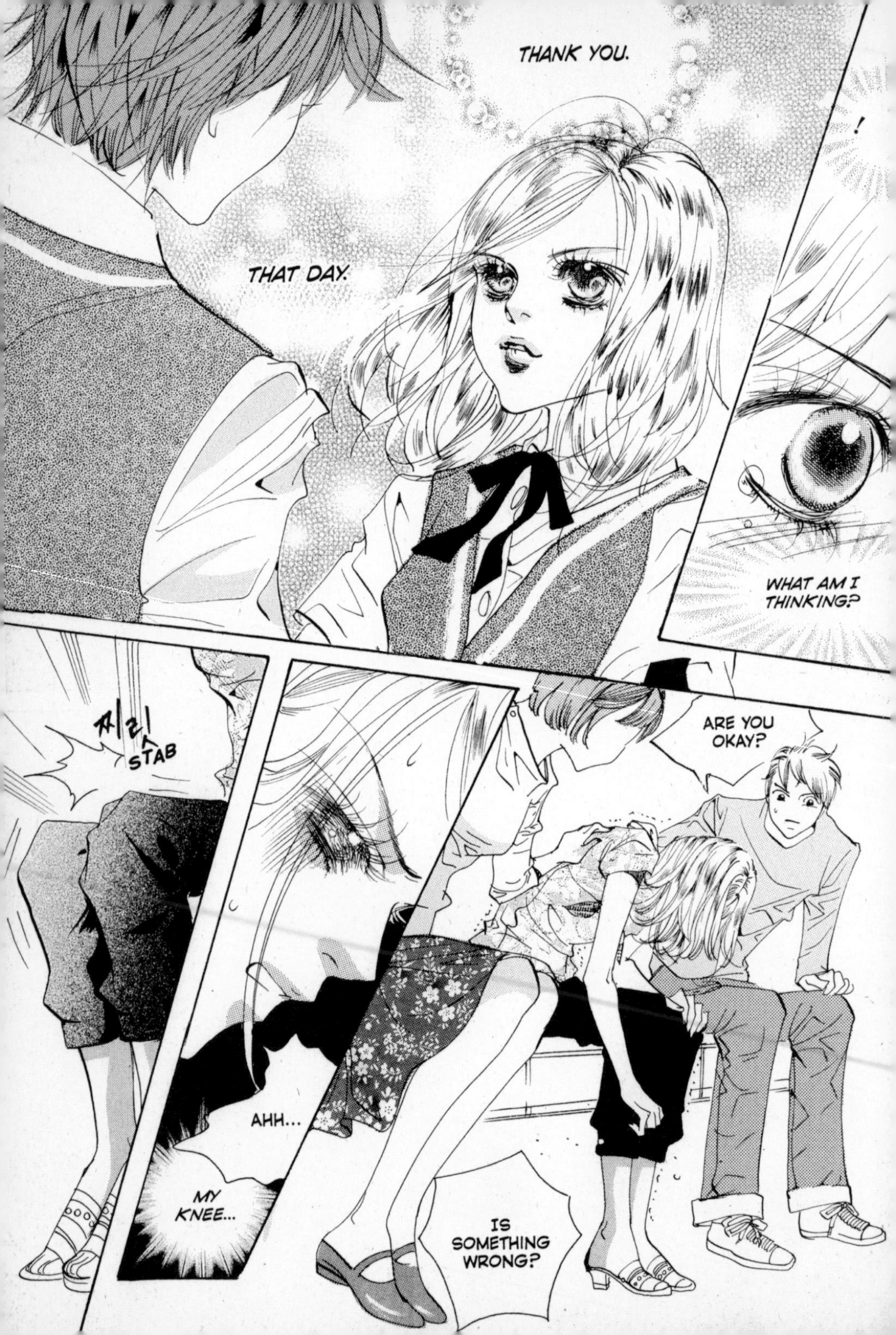
THAT DAY.
THANK YOU.
!
WHAT AM I THINKING?
찌릿
STAB
AHH...
MY KNEE...
ARE YOU OKAY?
IS SOMETHING WRONG?

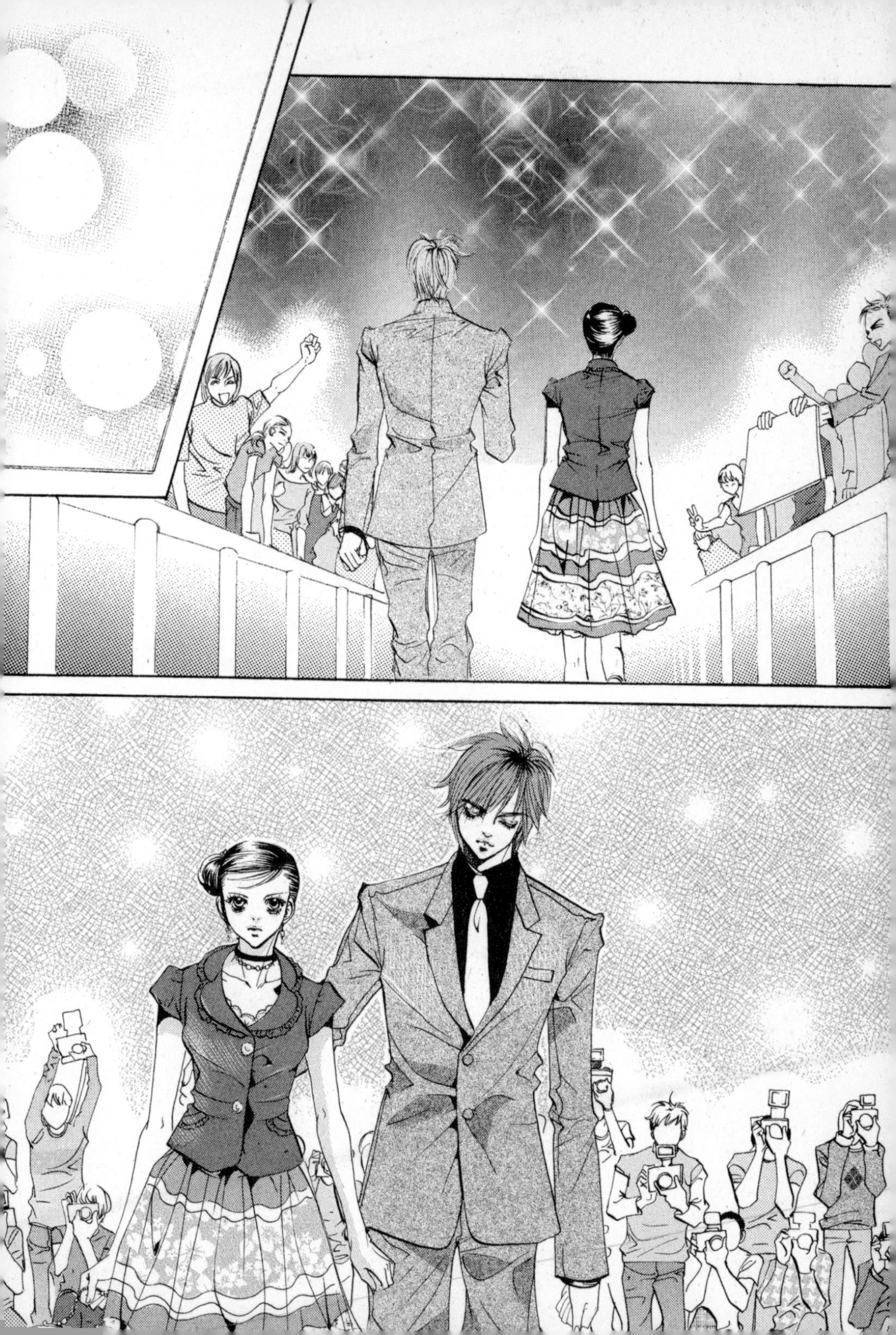

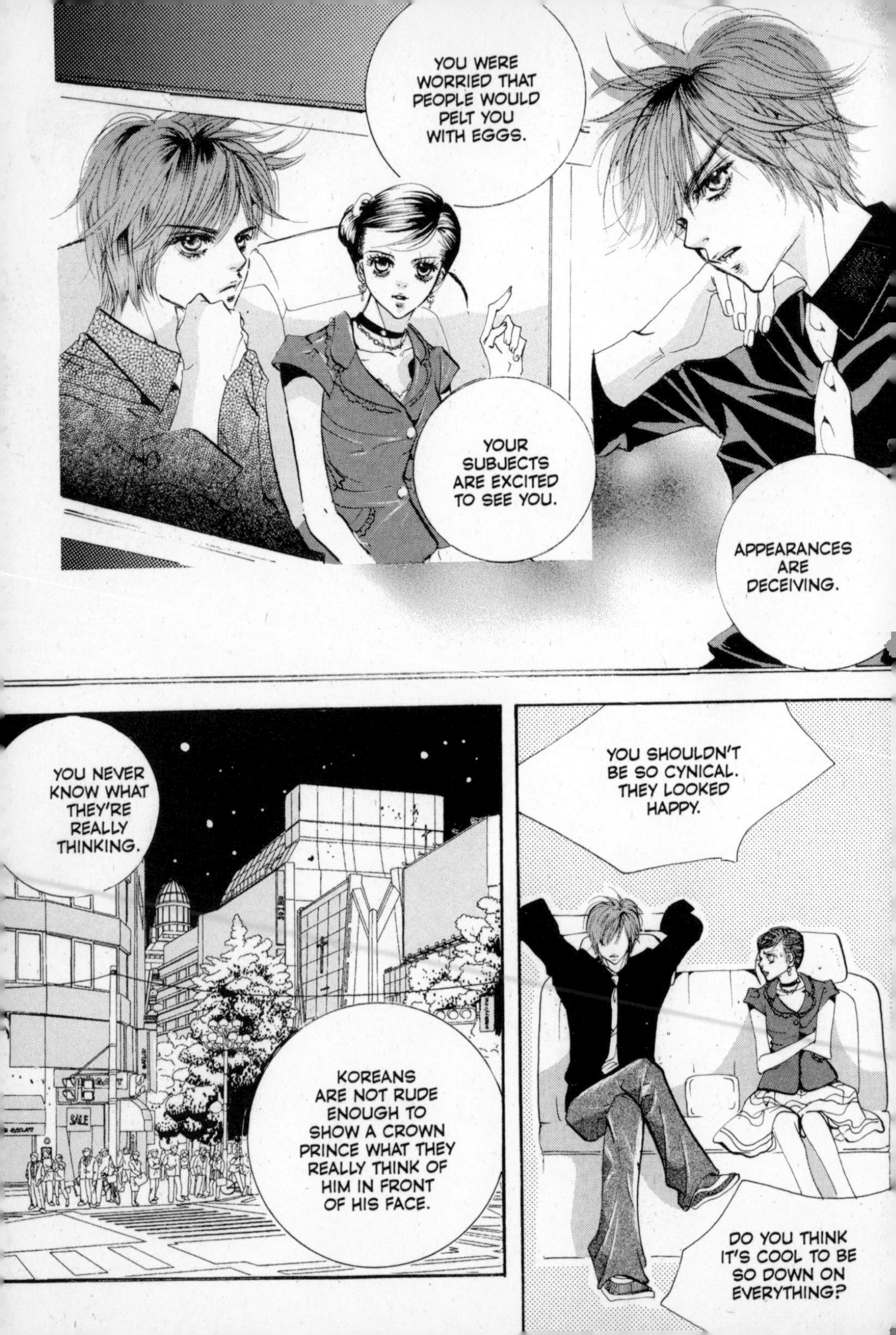
YOU WERE WORRIED THAT PEOPLE WOULD PELT YOU WITH EGGS.
YOUR SUBJECTS ARE EXCITED TO SEE YOU.
APPEARANCES ARE DECEIVING.
YOU NEVER KNOW WHAT THEY'RE REALLY THINKING.
KOREANS ARE NOT RUDE ENOUGH TO SHOW A CROWN PRINCE WHAT THEY REALLY THINK OF HIM IN FRONT OF HIS FACE.
SALE
YOU SHOULDN'T BE SO CYNICAL. THEY LOOKED HAPPY.
DO YOU THINK IT'S COOL TO BE SO DOWN ON EVERYTHING?

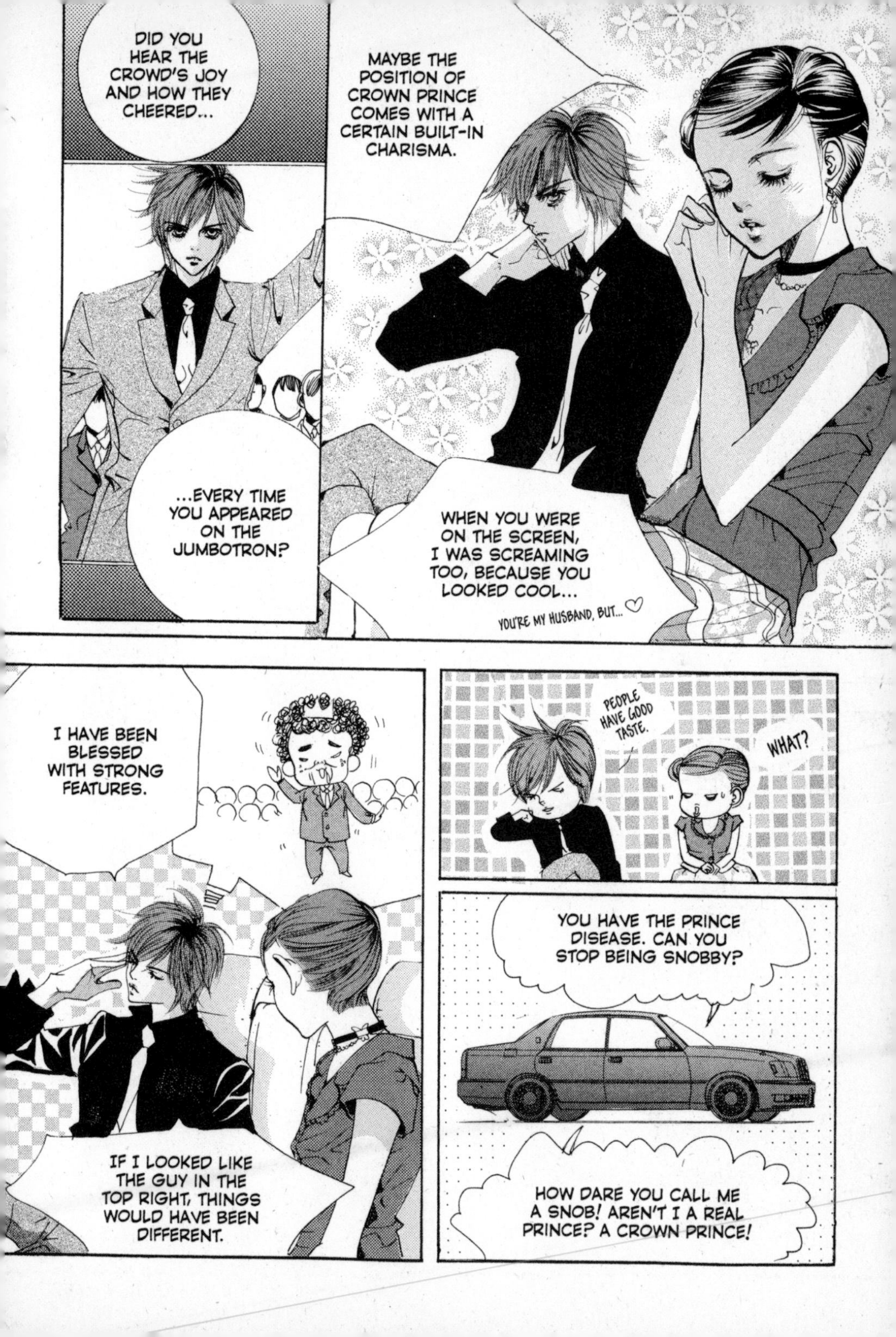

DID YOU HEAR THE CROWD'S JOY AND HOW THEY CHEERED...
...EVERY TIME YOU APPEARED ON THE JUMBOTRON?
MAYBE THE POSITION OF CROWN PRINCE COMES WITH A CERTAIN BUILT-IN CHARISMA.
WHEN YOU WERE ON THE SCREEN, I WAS SCREAMING TOO, BECAUSE YOU LOOKED COOL...
YOU'RE MY HUSBAND, BUT...
I HAVE BEEN BLESSED WITH STRONG FEATURES.
IF I LOOKED LIKE THE GUY IN THE TOP RIGHT, THINGS WOULD HAVE BEEN DIFFERENT.
PEOPLE HAVE GOOD TASTE.
WHAT?
YOU HAVE THE PRINCE DISEASE. CAN YOU STOP BEING SNOBBY?
HOW DARE YOU CALL ME A SNOB! AREN'T I A REAL PRINCE? A CROWN PRINCE!

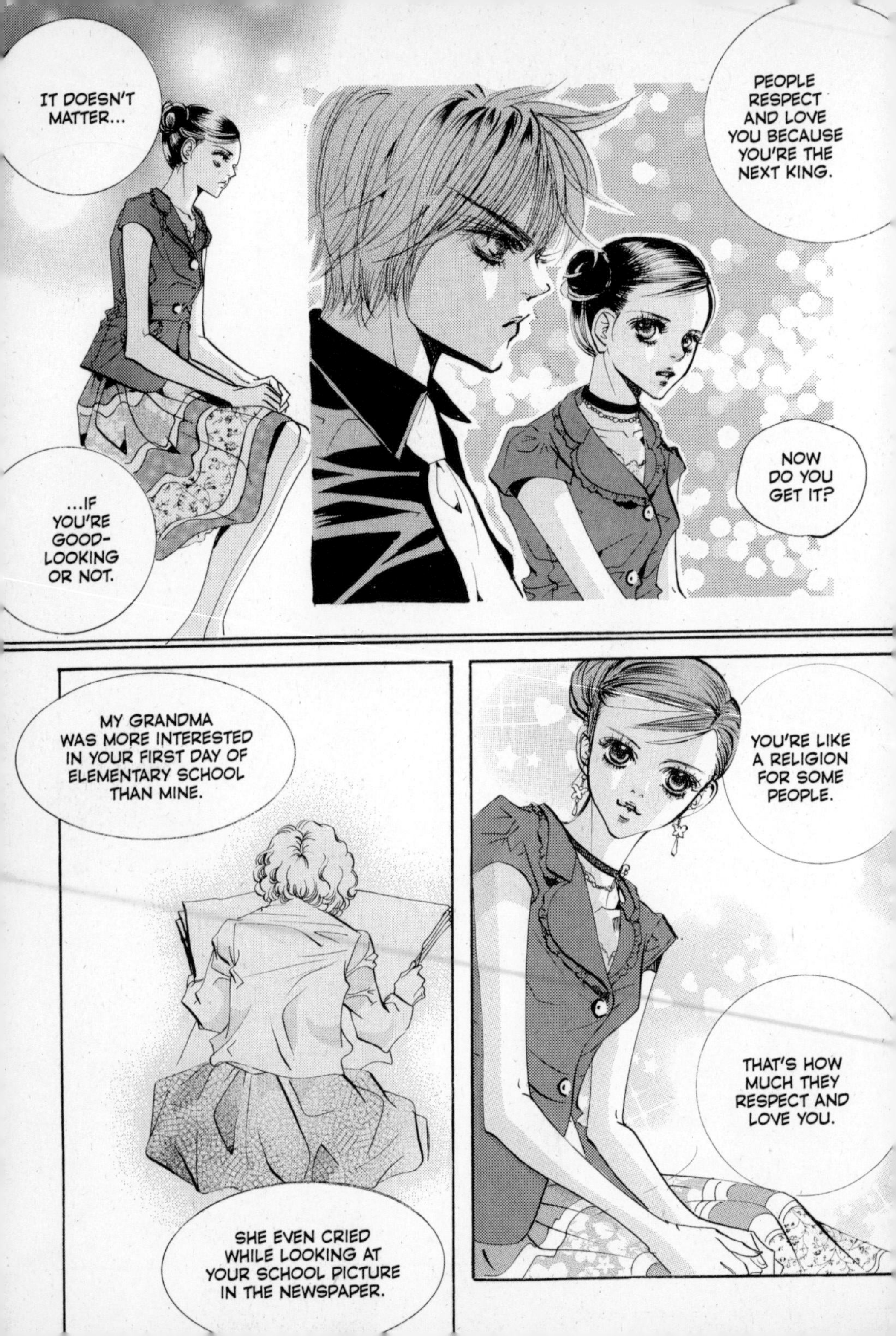
IT DOESN'T MATTER...
...IF YOU'RE GOOD-LOOKING OR NOT.
PEOPLE RESPECT AND LOVE YOU BECAUSE YOU'RE THE NEXT KING.
NOW DO YOU GET IT?
MY GRANDMA WAS MORE INTERESTED IN YOUR FIRST DAY OF ELEMENTARY SCHOOL THAN MINE.
SHE EVEN CRIED WHILE LOOKING AT YOUR SCHOOL PICTURE IN THE NEWSPAPER.
YOU'RE LIKE A RELIGION FOR SOME PEOPLE.
THAT'S HOW MUCH THEY RESPECT AND LOVE YOU.

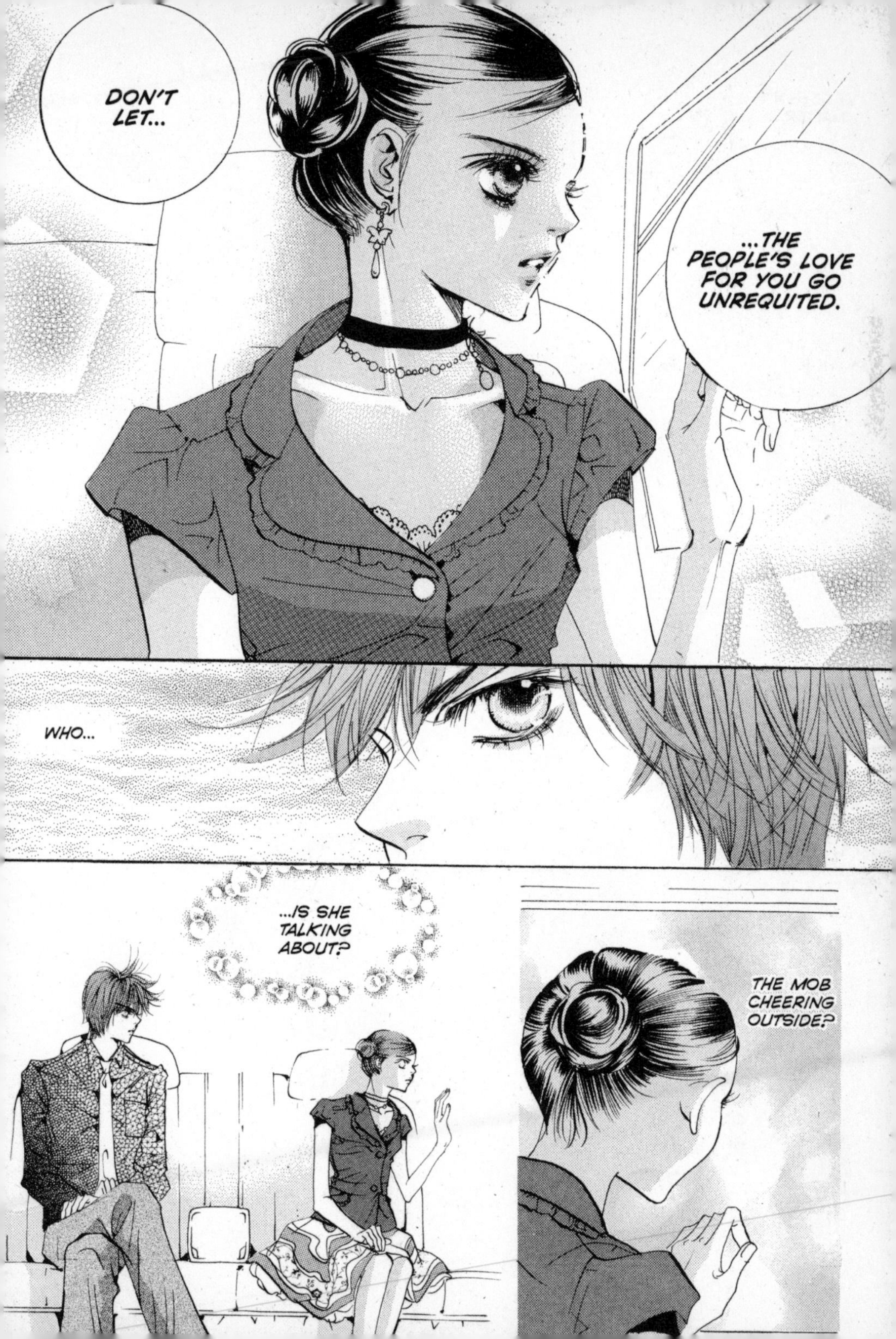
DON'T LET...
...THE PEOPLE'S LOVE FOR YOU GO UNREQUITED.
WHO...
...IS SHE TALKING ABOUT?
THE MOB CHEERING OUTSIDE?

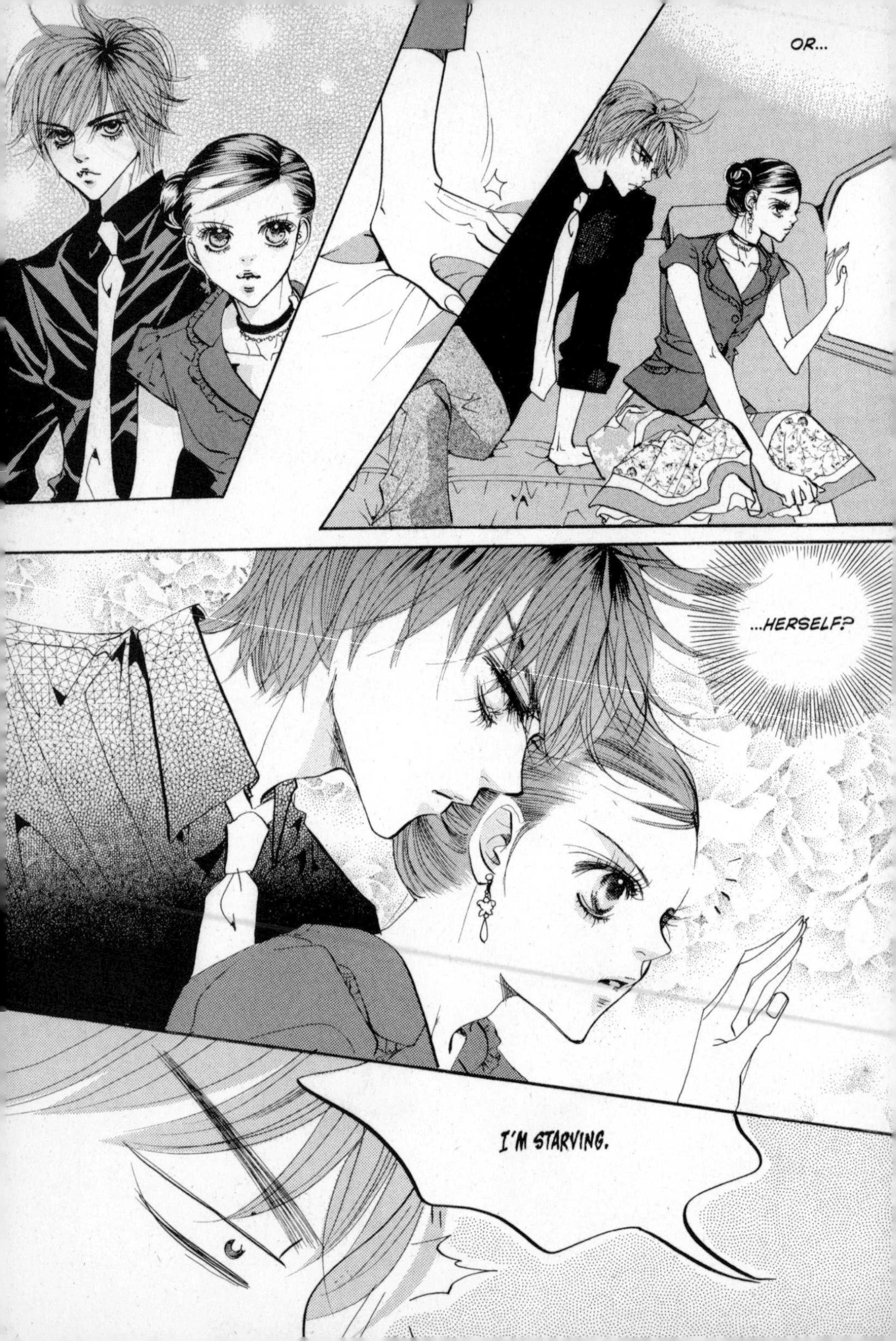
OR...
...HERSELF?
I'M STARVING.

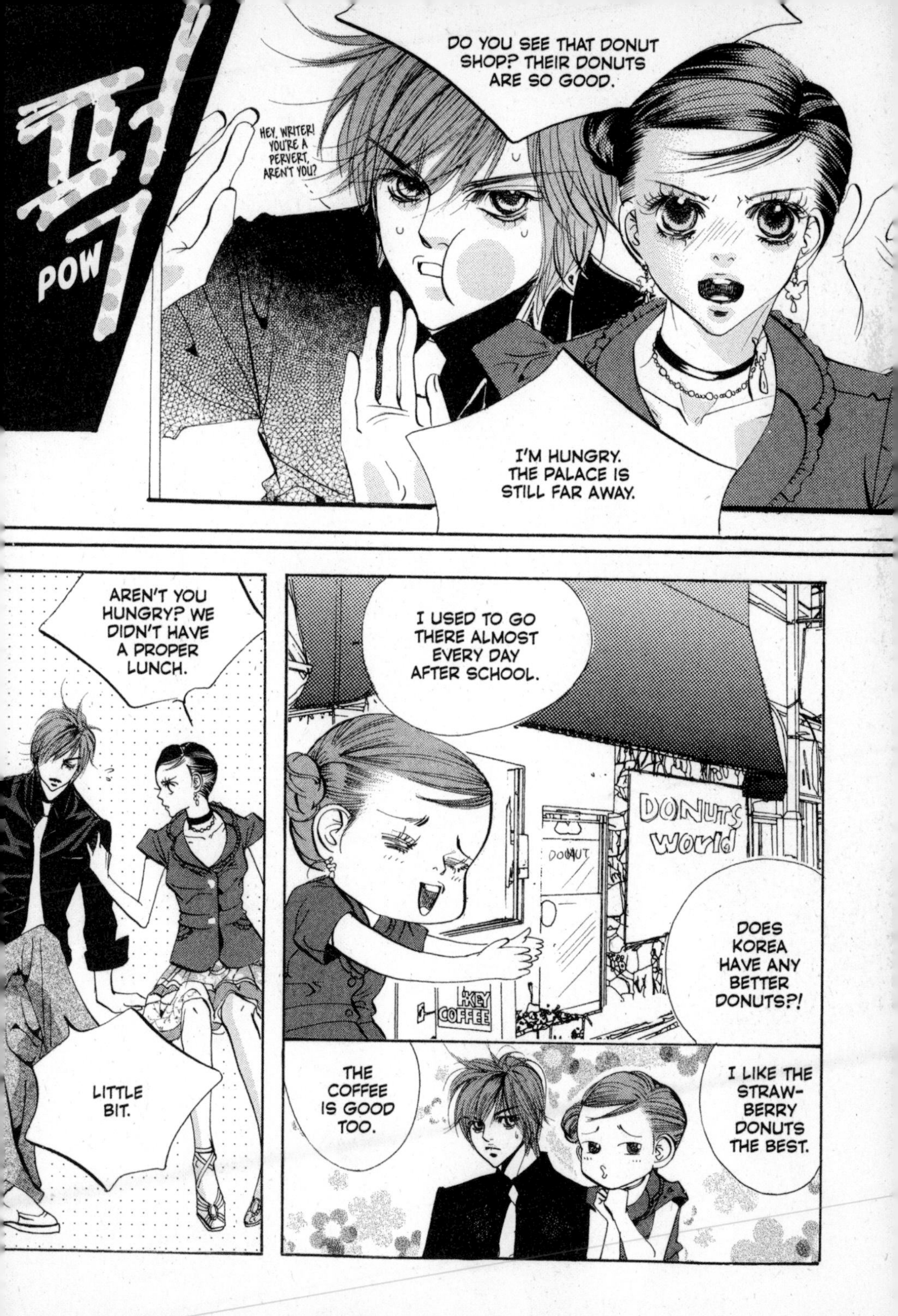

퍽
POW
HEY, WRITER! YOU'RE A PERVERT, AREN'T YOU?
DO YOU SEE THAT DONUT SHOP? THEIR DONUTS ARE SO GOOD.
I'M HUNGRY. THE PALACE IS STILL FAR AWAY.
AREN'T YOU HUNGRY? WE DIDN'T HAVE A PROPER LUNCH.
LITTLE BIT.
I USED TO GO THERE ALMOST EVERY DAY AFTER SCHOOL.
DONUTS world
DONUT
KEY COFFEE
DOES KOREA HAVE ANY BETTER DONUTS?!
THE COFFEE IS GOOD TOO.
I LIKE THE STRAW-BERRY DONUTS THE BEST.

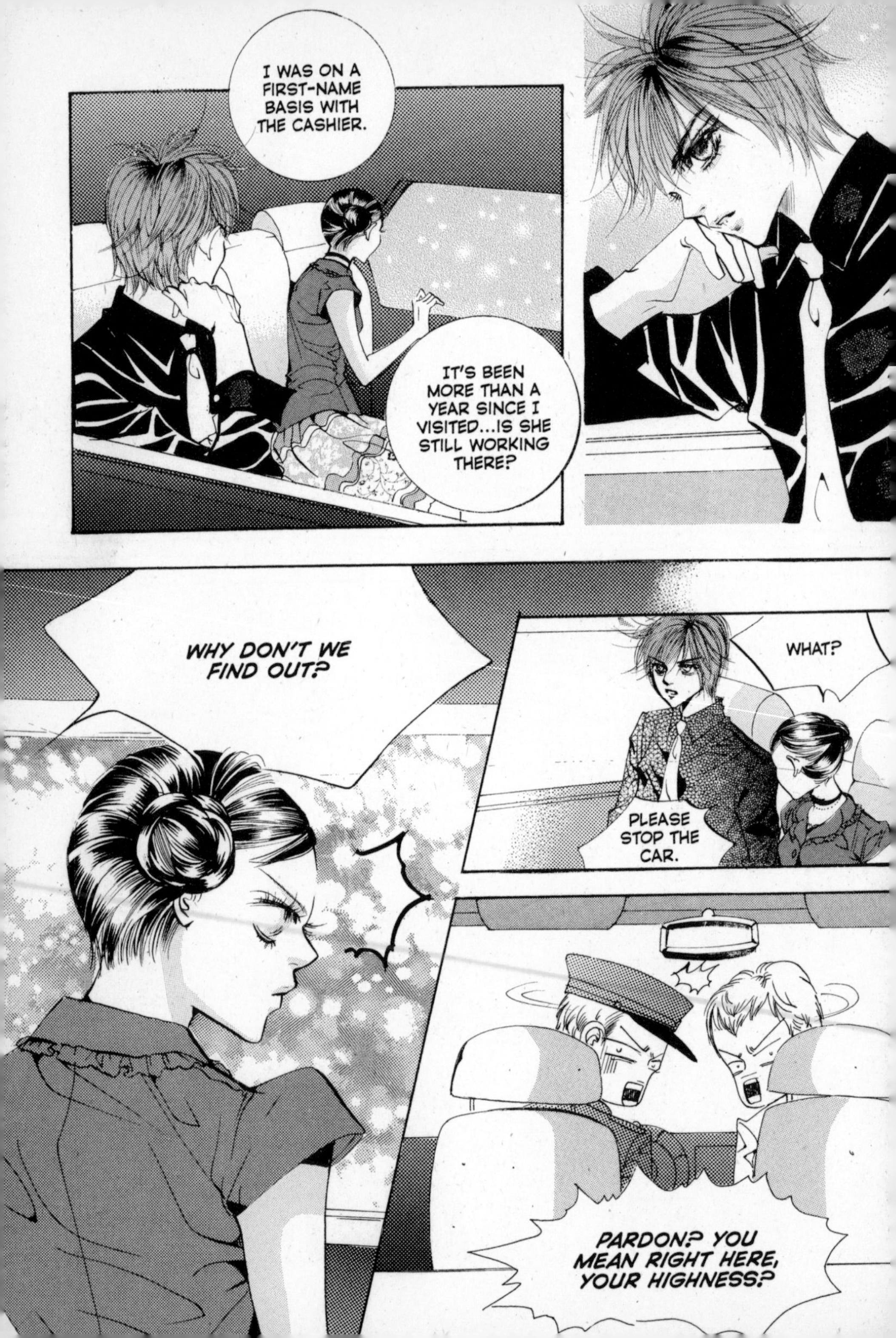
I WAS ON A FIRST-NAME BASIS WITH THE CASHIER.
IT'S BEEN MORE THAN A YEAR SINCE I VISITED...IS SHE STILL WORKING THERE?
WHY DON'T WE FIND OUT?
WHAT?
PLEASE STOP THE CAR.
PARDON? YOU MEAN RIGHT HERE, YOUR HIGHNESS?

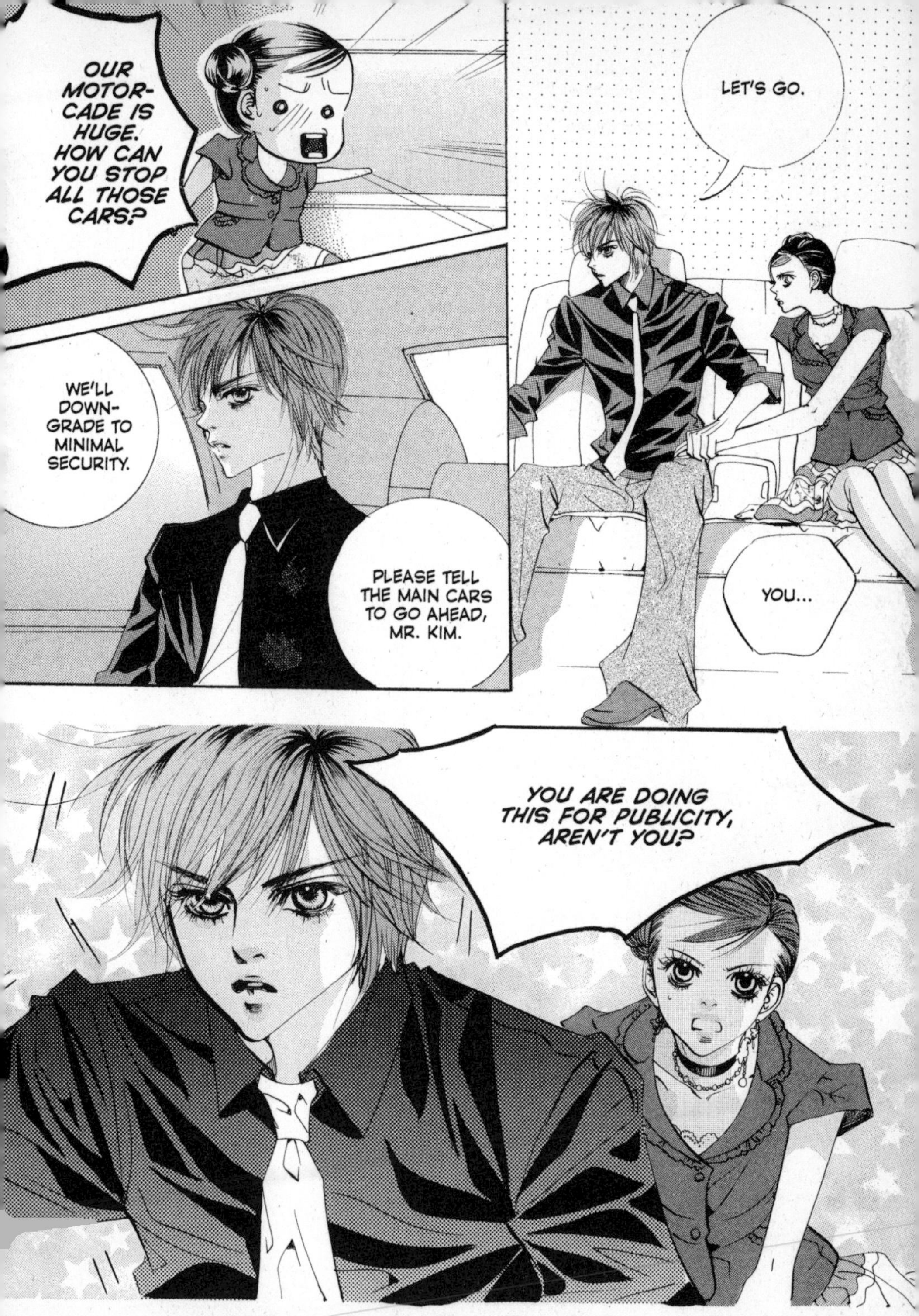
OUR MOTOR-CADE IS HUGE. HOW CAN YOU STOP ALL THOSE CARS?
WE'LL DOWN-GRADE TO MINIMAL SECURITY.
PLEASE TELL THE MAIN CARS TO GO AHEAD, MR. KIM.
LET'S GO.
YOU...
YOU ARE DOING THIS FOR PUBLICITY, AREN'T YOU?

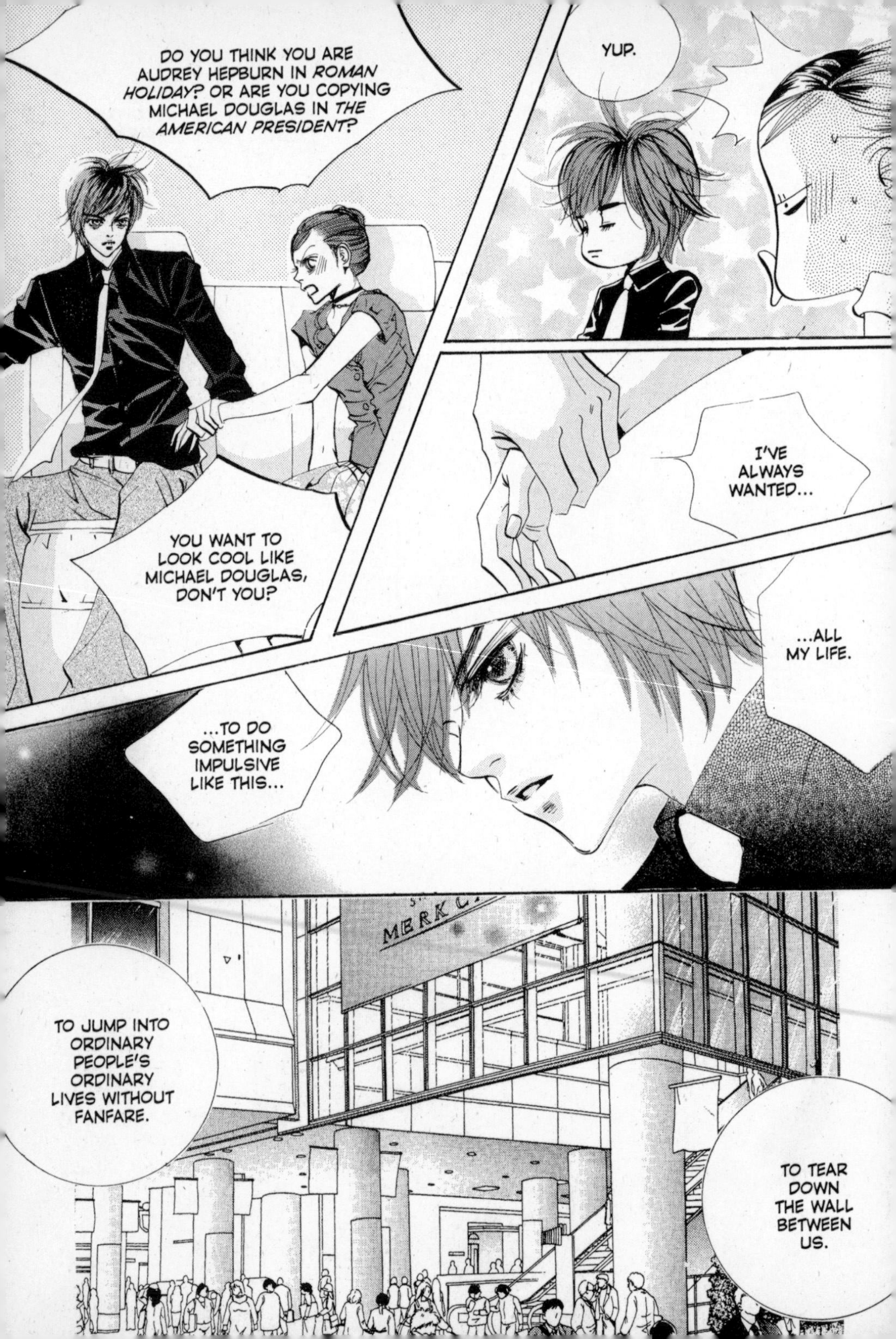
DO YOU THINK YOU ARE AUDREY HEPBURN IN *ROMAN HOLIDAY*? OR ARE YOU COPYING MICHAEL DOUGLAS IN *THE AMERICAN PRESIDENT*?
YUP.
YOU WANT TO LOOK COOL LIKE MICHAEL DOUGLAS, DON'T YOU?
I'VE ALWAYS WANTED...
...TO DO SOMETHING IMPULSIVE LIKE THIS...
...ALL MY LIFE.
MERK
TO JUMP INTO ORDINARY PEOPLE'S ORDINARY LIVES WITHOUT FANFARE.
TO TEAR DOWN THE WALL BETWEEN US.

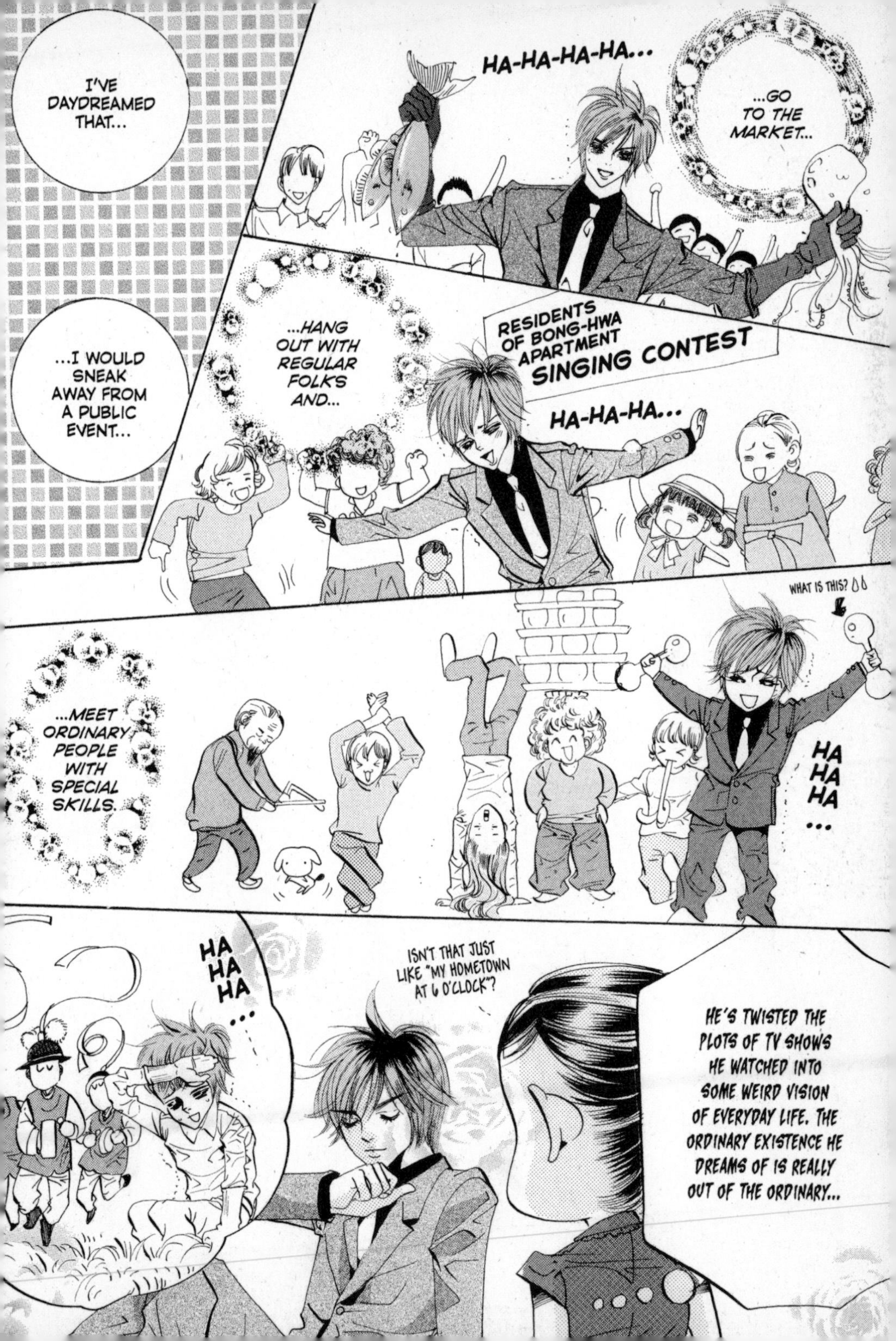
I'VE DAYDREAMED THAT...
HA-HA-HA-HA...
...GO TO THE MARKET...
...I WOULD SNEAK AWAY FROM A PUBLIC EVENT...
...HANG OUT WITH REGULAR FOLKS AND...
RESIDENTS OF BONG-HWA APARTMENT SINGING CONTEST
HA-HA-HA...
...MEET ORDINARY PEOPLE WITH SPECIAL SKILLS.
WHAT IS THIS?
HA HA HA ...
HA HA HA ...
ISN'T THAT JUST LIKE "MY HOMETOWN AT 6 O'CLOCK"?
HE'S TWISTED THE PLOTS OF TV SHOWS HE WATCHED INTO SOME WEIRD VISION OF EVERYDAY LIFE. THE ORDINARY EXISTENCE HE DREAMS OF IS REALLY OUT OF THE ORDINARY...

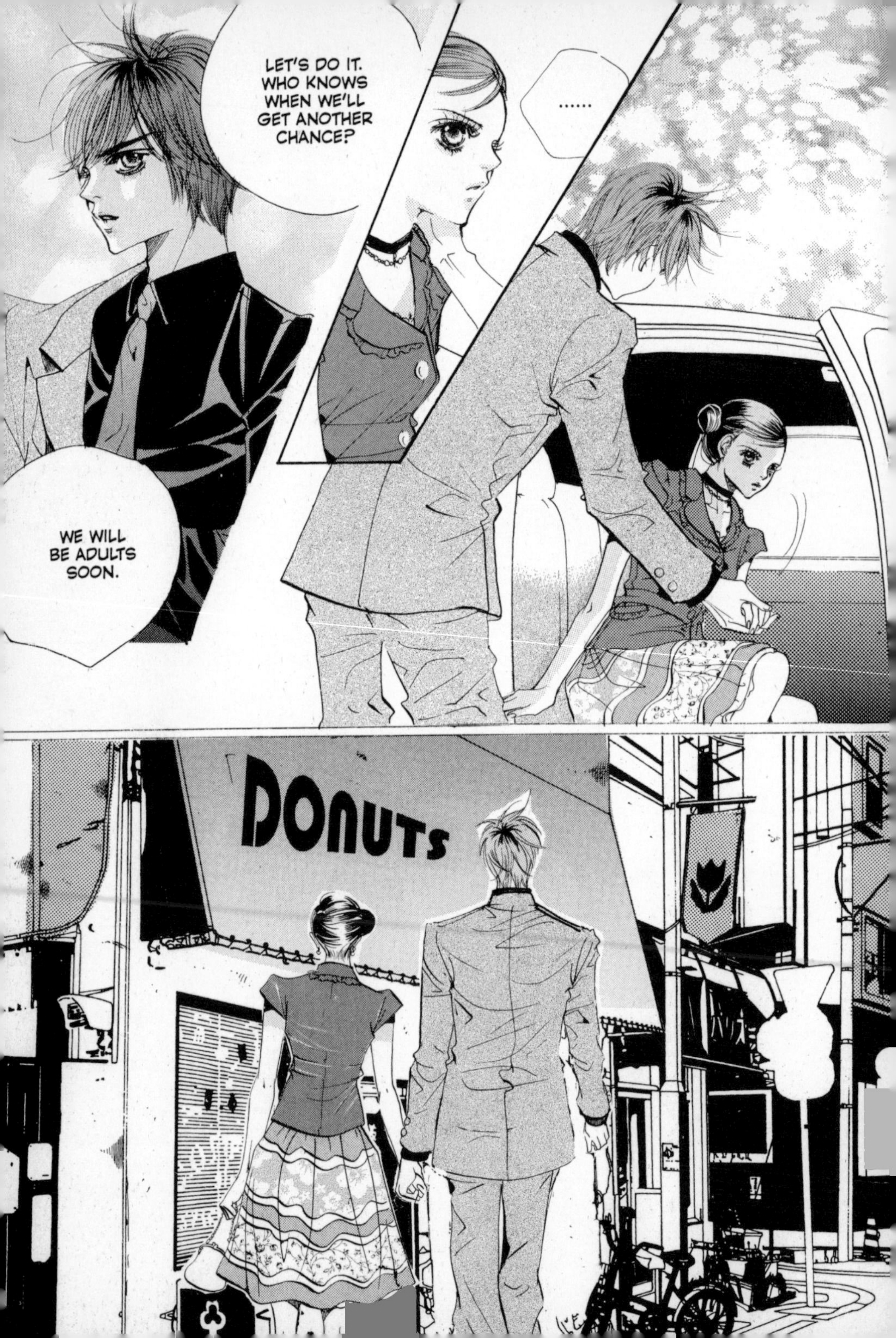
LET'S DO IT. WHO KNOWS WHEN WE'LL GET ANOTHER CHANCE?
WE WILL BE ADULTS SOON.
......
DONUTS

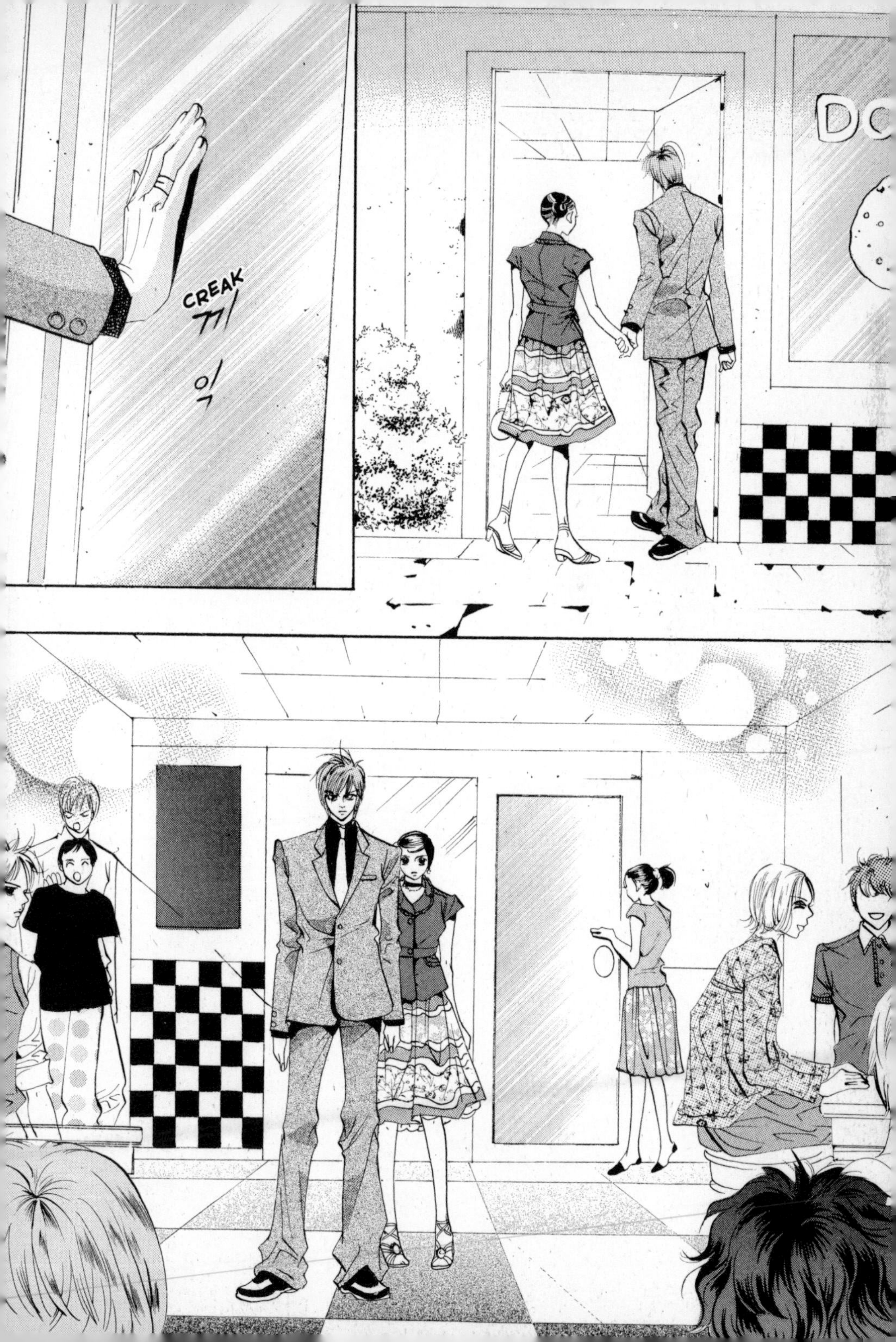
CREAK
끼익

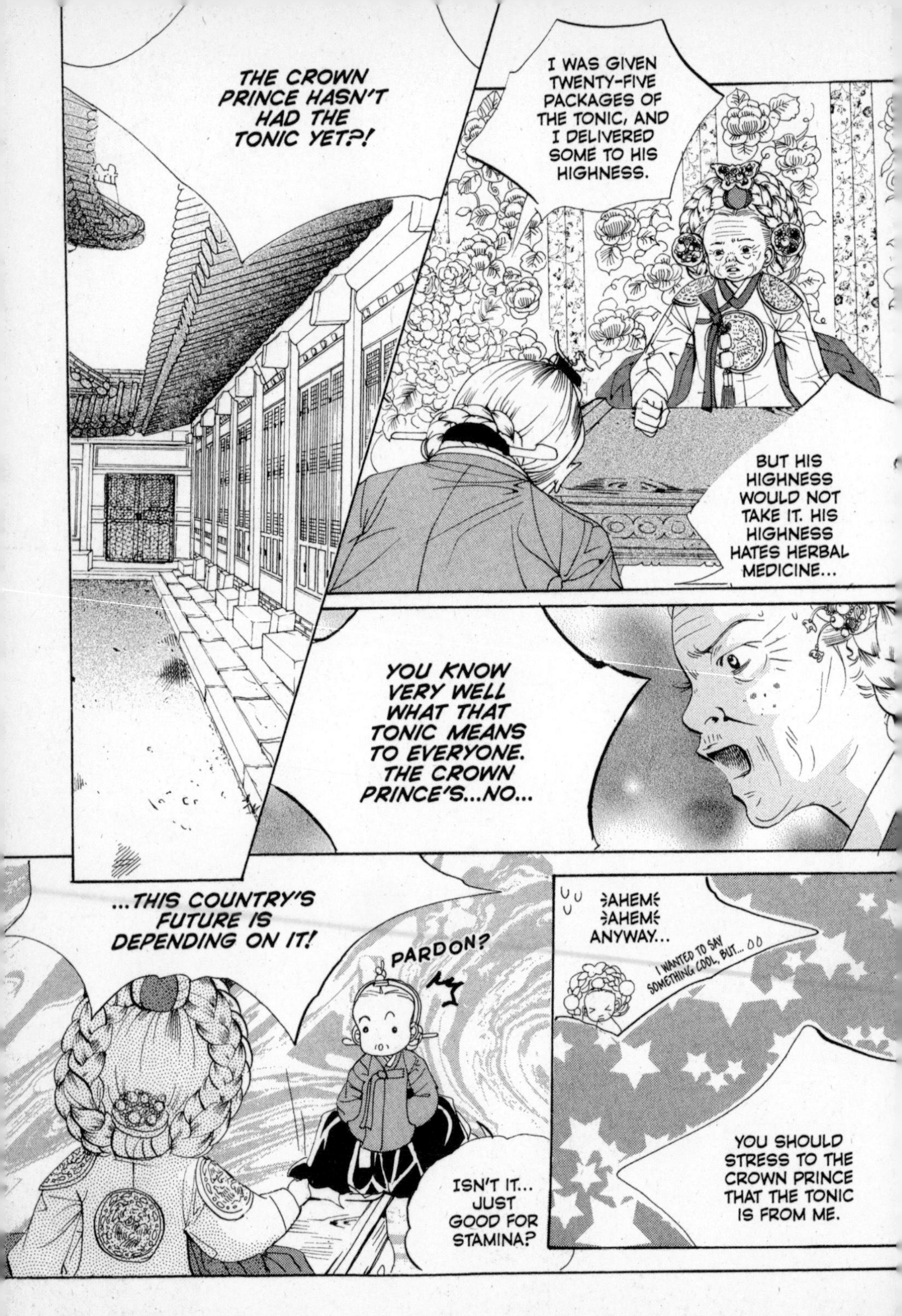
THE CROWN PRINCE HASN'T HAD THE TONIC YET?!
I WAS GIVEN TWENTY-FIVE PACKAGES OF THE TONIC, AND I DELIVERED SOME TO HIS HIGHNESS.
BUT HIS HIGHNESS WOULD NOT TAKE IT. HIS HIGHNESS HATES HERBAL MEDICINE...
YOU KNOW VERY WELL WHAT THAT TONIC MEANS TO EVERYONE. THE CROWN PRINCE'S...NO...
...THIS COUNTRY'S FUTURE IS DEPENDING ON IT!
PARDON?
ISN'T IT... JUST GOOD FOR STAMINA?
AHEM AHEM ANYWAY...
I WANTED TO SAY SOMETHING COOL, BUT...
YOU SHOULD STRESS TO THE CROWN PRINCE THAT THE TONIC IS FROM ME.

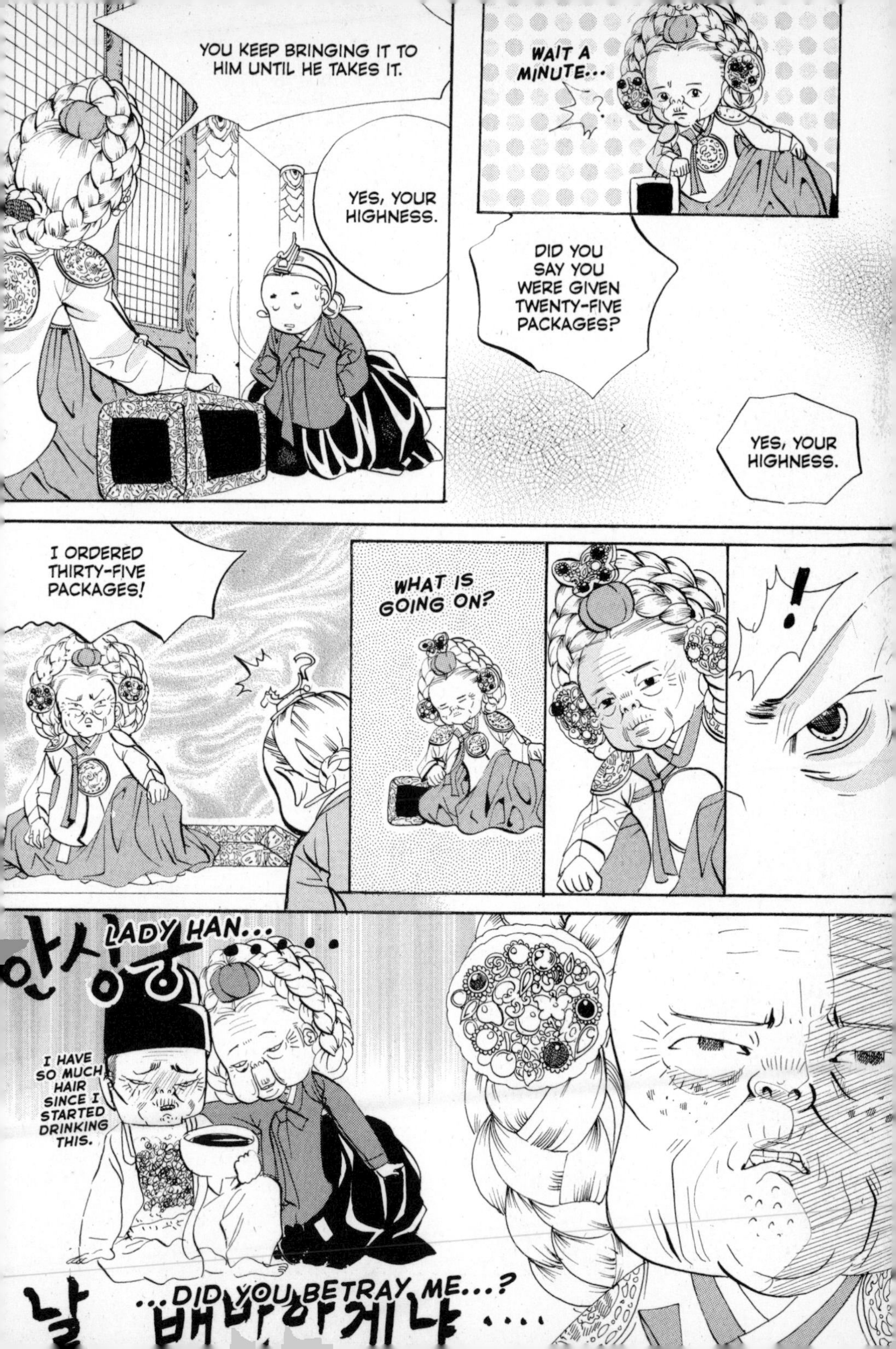

YOU KEEP BRINGING IT TO HIM UNTIL HE TAKES IT.
YES, YOUR HIGHNESS.
WAIT A MINUTE...
?
DID YOU SAY YOU WERE GIVEN TWENTY-FIVE PACKAGES?
YES, YOUR HIGHNESS.
I ORDERED THIRTY-FIVE PACKAGES!
WHAT IS GOING ON?
!
한상궁
LADY HAN...
I HAVE SO MUCH HAIR SINCE I STARTED DRINKING THIS.
날 배반하게냐 ....
...DID YOU BETRAY ME...?

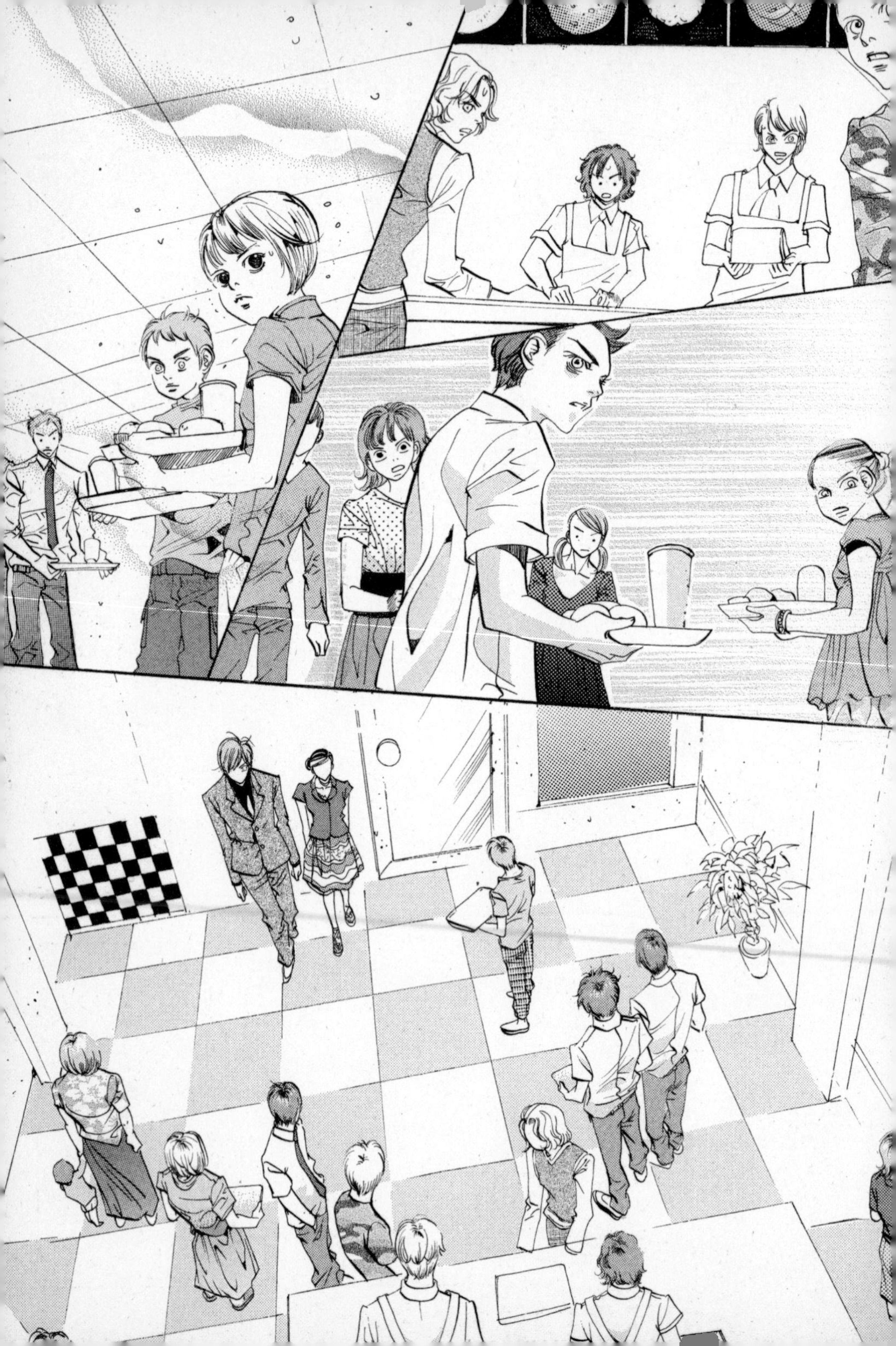

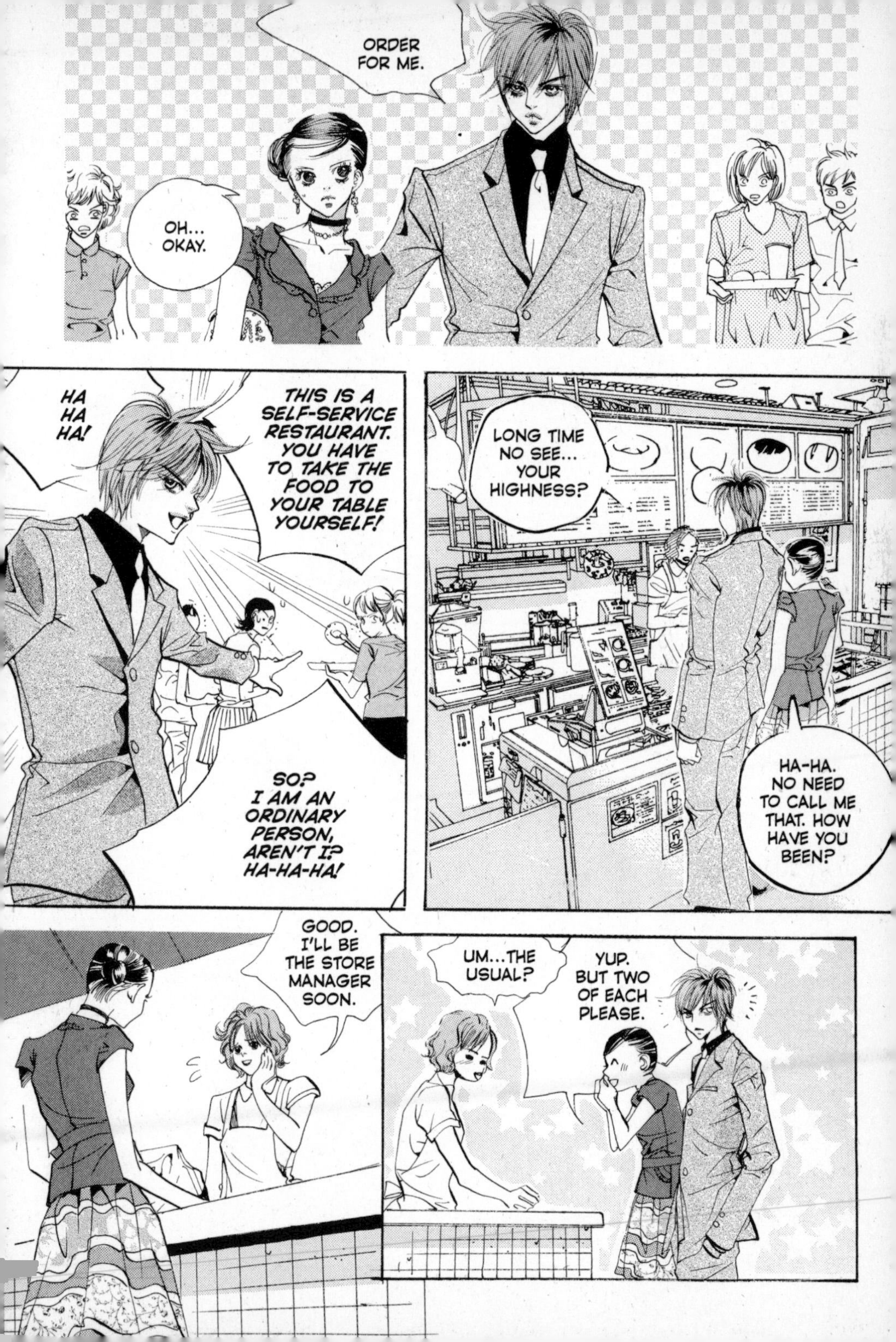
ORDER FOR ME.
OH... OKAY.
HA HA HA!
THIS IS A SELF-SERVICE RESTAURANT. YOU HAVE TO TAKE THE FOOD TO YOUR TABLE YOURSELF!
SO? I AM AN ORDINARY PERSON, AREN'T I? HA-HA-HA!
LONG TIME NO SEE... YOUR HIGHNESS?
HA-HA. NO NEED TO CALL ME THAT. HOW HAVE YOU BEEN?
GOOD. I'LL BE THE STORE MANAGER SOON.
UM...THE USUAL?
YUP. BUT TWO OF EACH PLEASE.

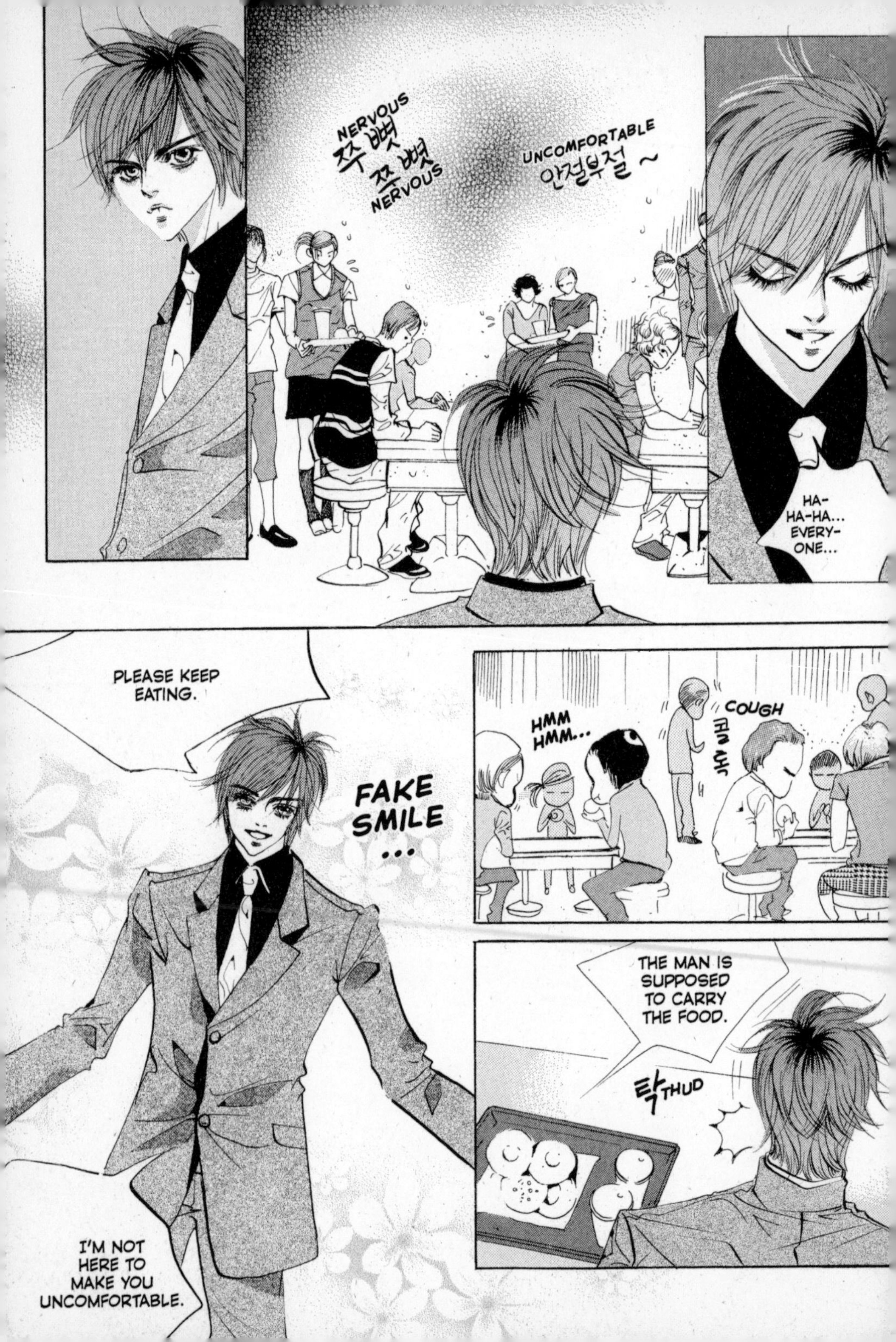
NERVOUS
쭈뼛
쭈뼛
NERVOUS
UNCOMFORTABLE
안절부절 ~
HA-HA-HA... EVERY-ONE...
PLEASE KEEP EATING.
FAKE SMILE...
I'M NOT HERE TO MAKE YOU UNCOMFORTABLE.
HMM HMM...
COUGH
THE MAN IS SUPPOSED TO CARRY THE FOOD.
탁 THUD

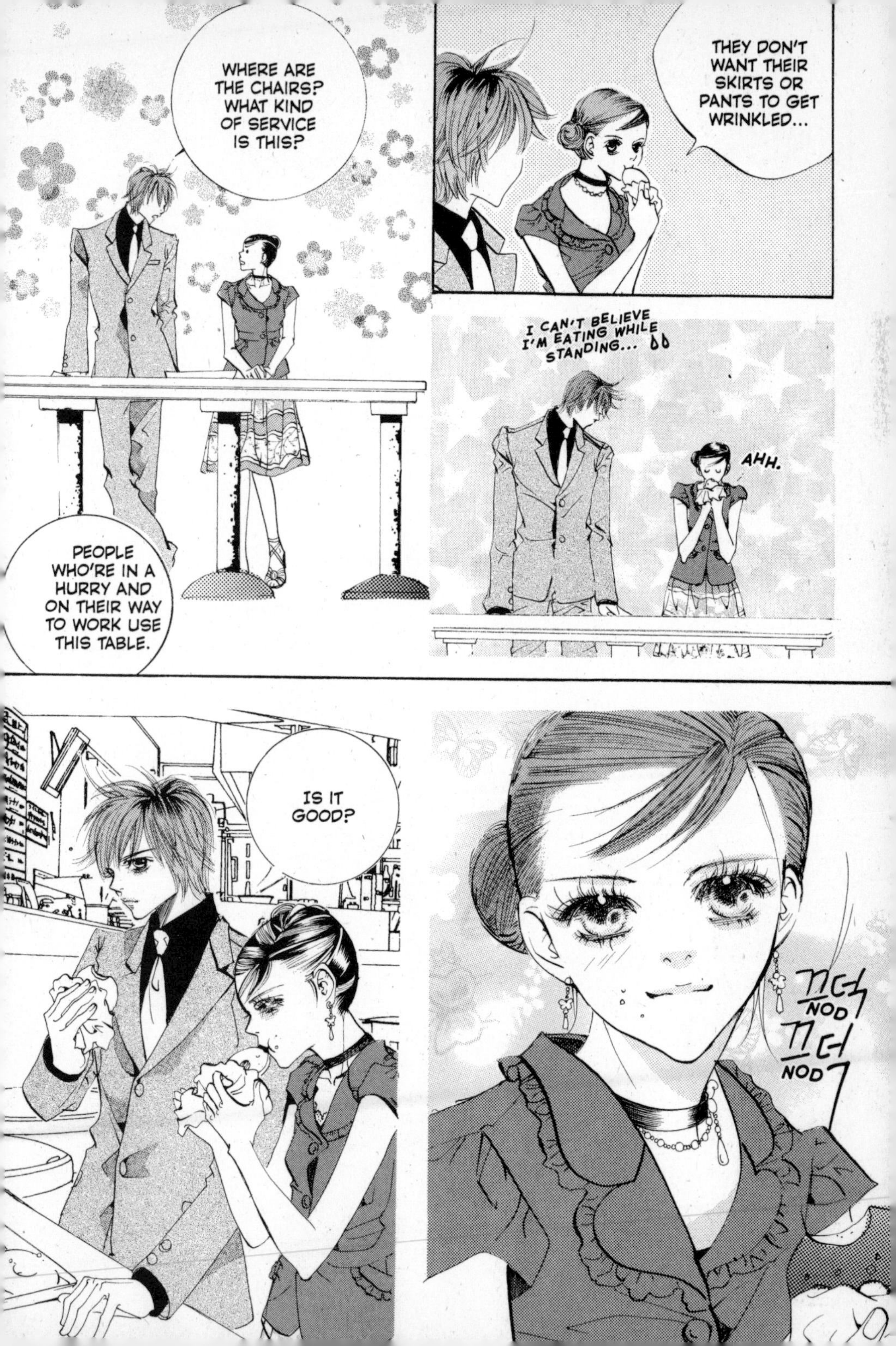
WHERE ARE THE CHAIRS? WHAT KIND OF SERVICE IS THIS?
PEOPLE WHO'RE IN A HURRY AND ON THEIR WAY TO WORK USE THIS TABLE.
THEY DON'T WANT THEIR SKIRTS OR PANTS TO GET WRINKLED...
I CAN'T BELIEVE I'M EATING WHILE STANDING...
AHH.
IS IT GOOD?
끄덕
NOD
끄덕
NOD

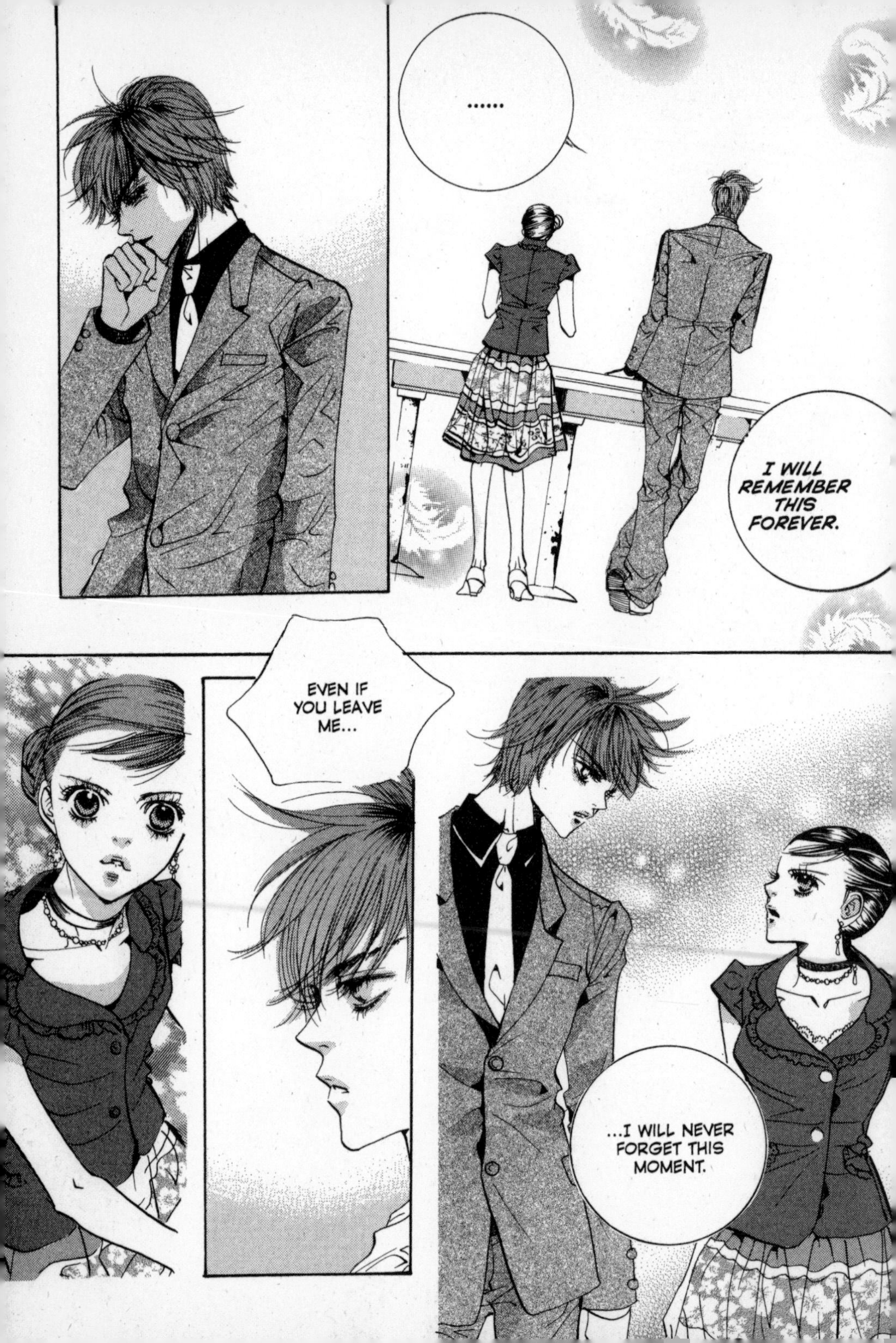
......
I WILL REMEMBER THIS FOREVER.
EVEN IF YOU LEAVE ME...
...I WILL NEVER FORGET THIS MOMENT.

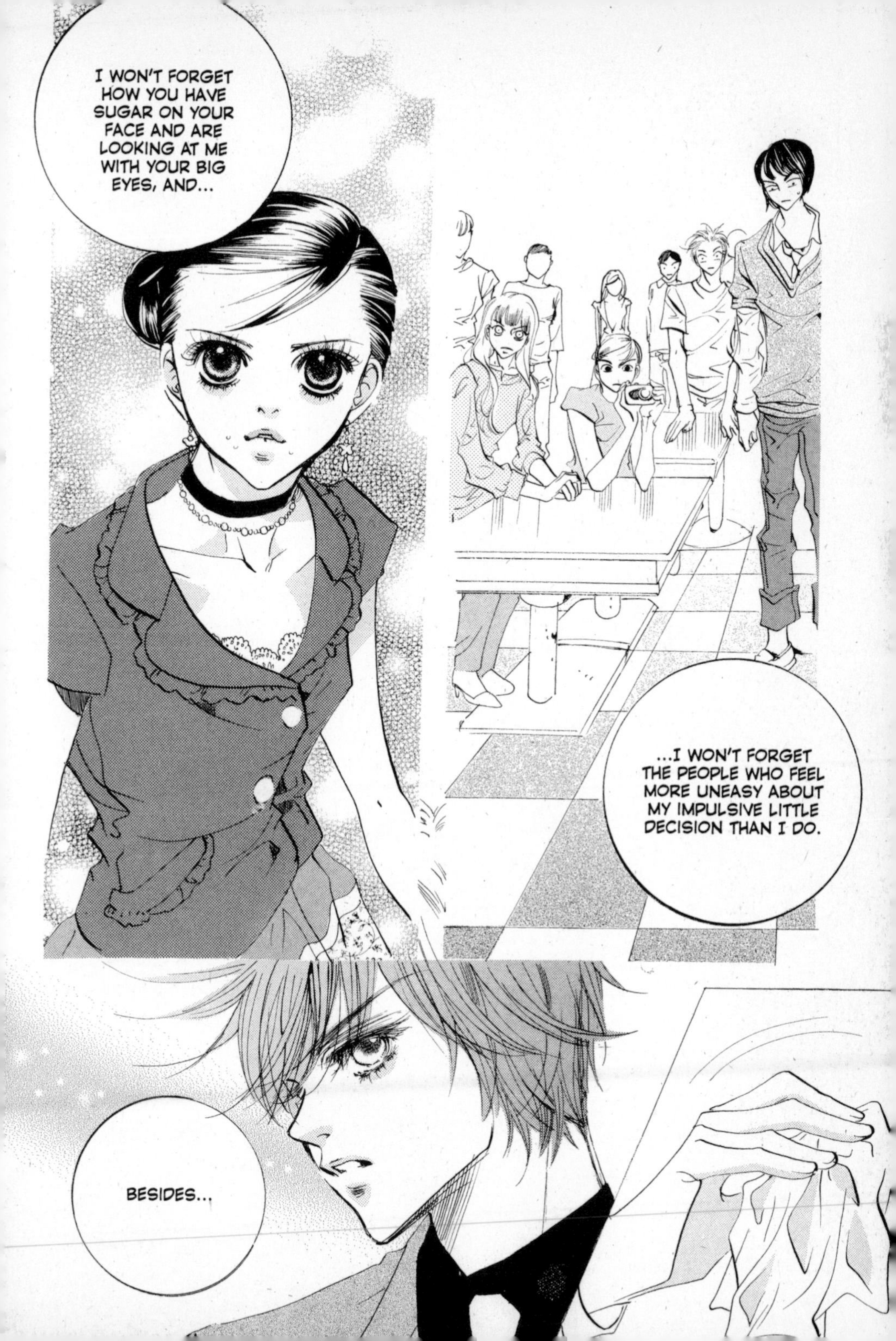
I WON'T FORGET HOW YOU HAVE SUGAR ON YOUR FACE AND ARE LOOKING AT ME WITH YOUR BIG EYES, AND...
...I WON'T FORGET THE PEOPLE WHO FEEL MORE UNEASY ABOUT MY IMPULSIVE LITTLE DECISION THAN I DO.
BESIDES...

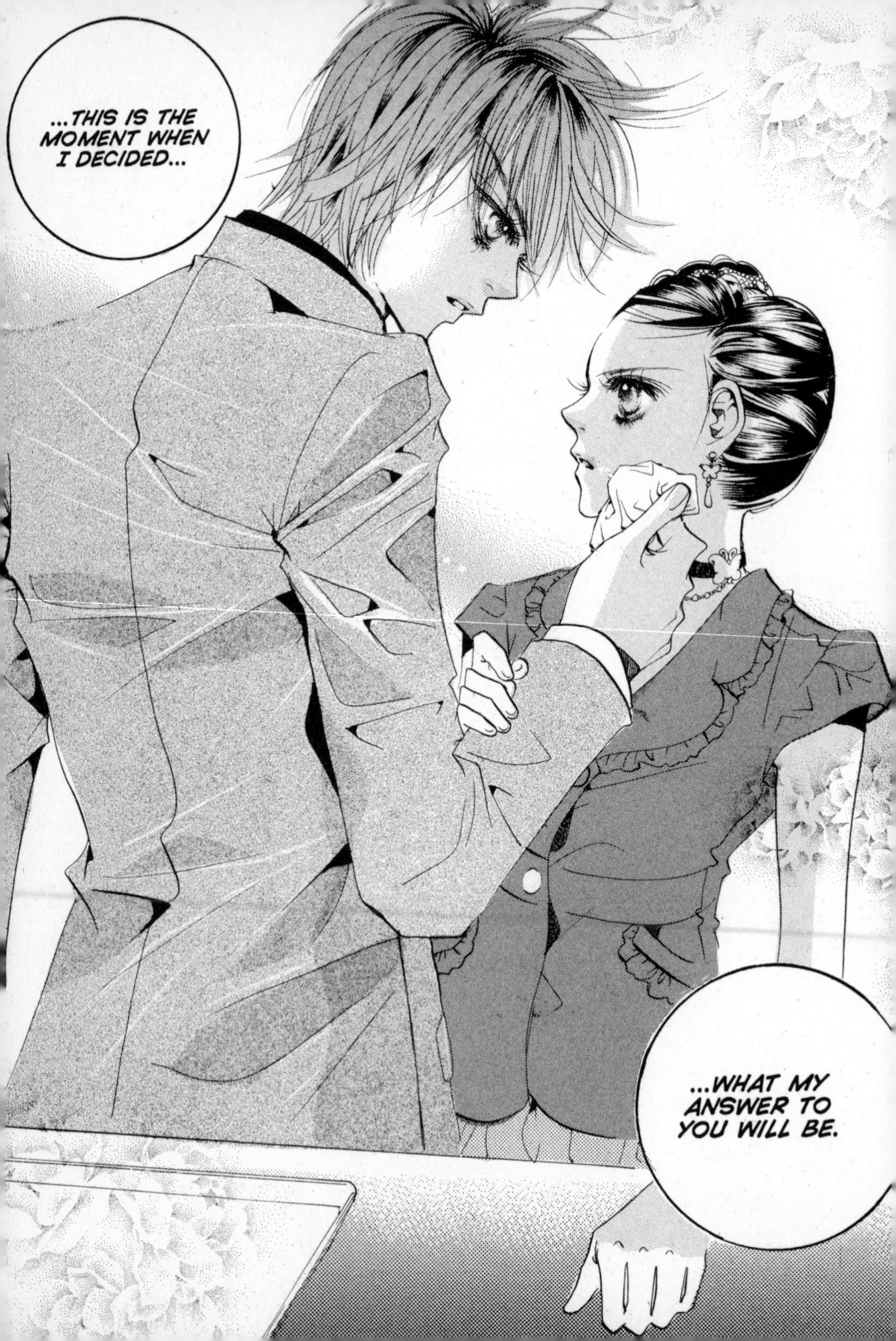
...THIS IS THE MOMENT WHEN I DECIDED...
...WHAT MY ANSWER TO YOU WILL BE.

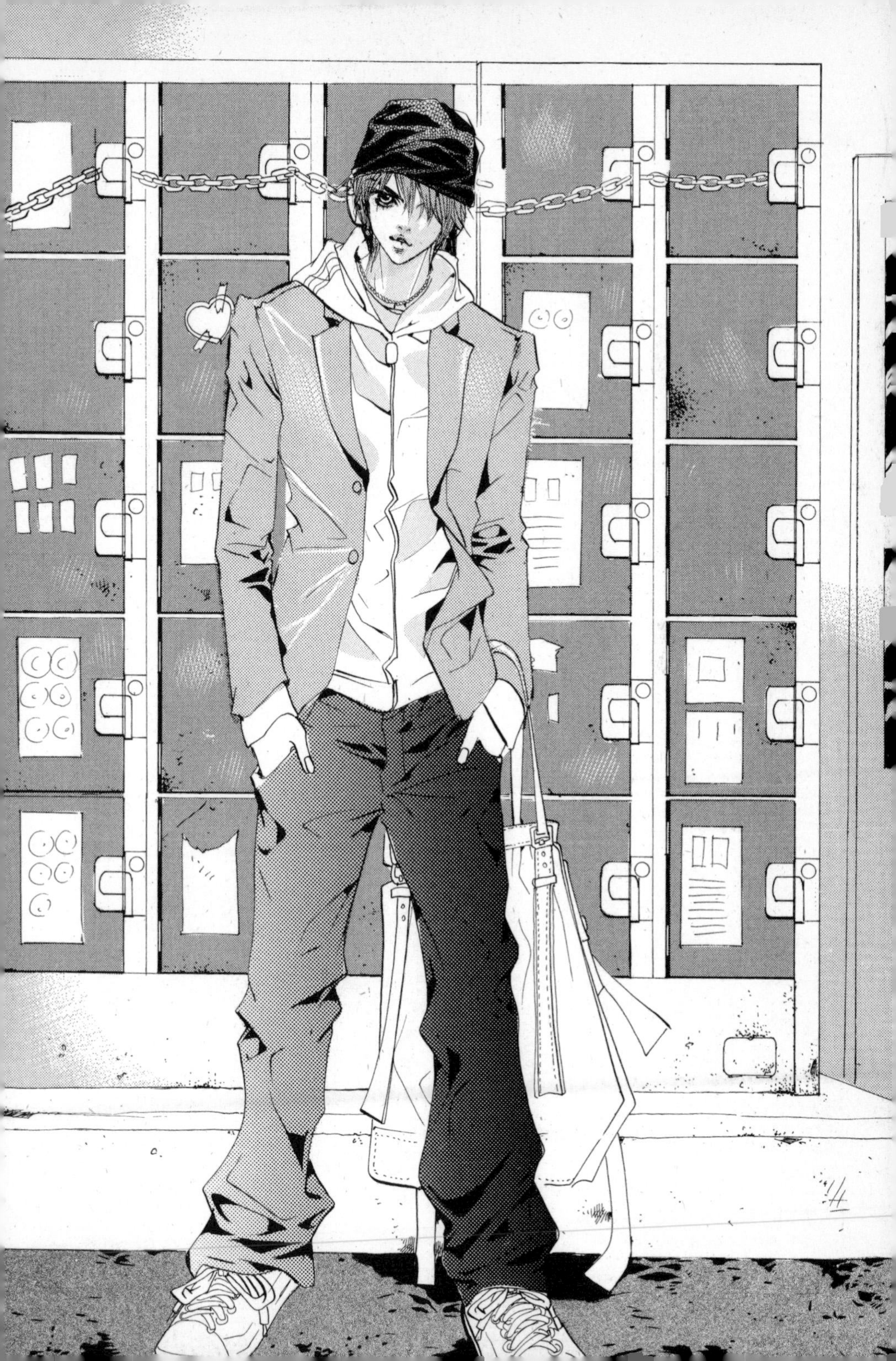

WHAT KIND OF PLACE IS SHIN AND CHAE-KYUNG'S NEW RESIDENCE, CHANGDUCK PALACE?

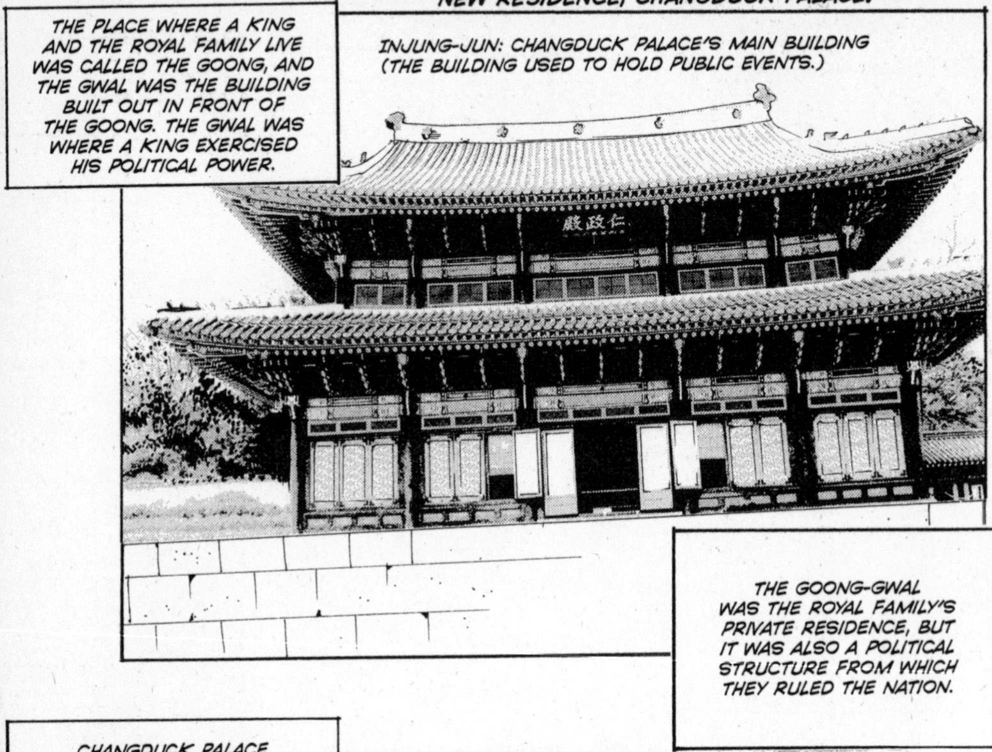

THE PLACE WHERE A KING AND THE ROYAL FAMILY LIVE WAS CALLED THE GOONG, AND THE GWAL WAS THE BUILDING BUILT OUT IN FRONT OF THE GOONG. THE GWAL WAS WHERE A KING EXERCISED HIS POLITICAL POWER.
INJUNG-JUN: CHANGDUCK PALACE'S MAIN BUILDING (THE BUILDING USED TO HOLD PUBLIC EVENTS.)
仁政殿
THE GOONG-GWAL WAS THE ROYAL FAMILY'S PRIVATE RESIDENCE, BUT IT WAS ALSO A POLITICAL STRUCTURE FROM WHICH THEY RULED THE NATION.

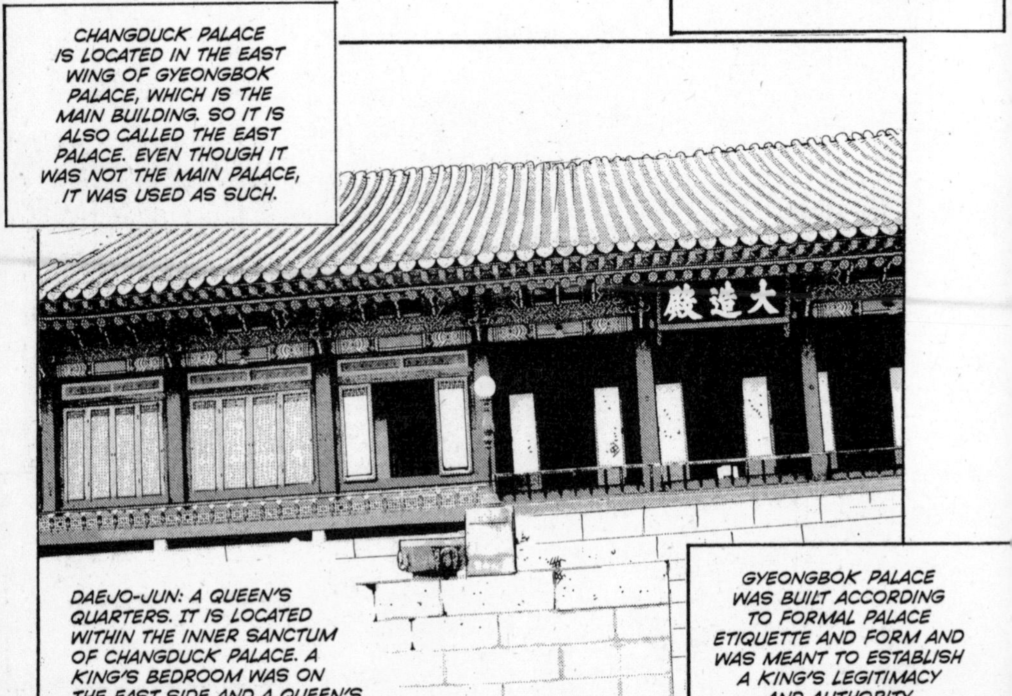

CHANGDUCK PALACE IS LOCATED IN THE EAST WING OF GYEONGBOK PALACE, WHICH IS THE MAIN BUILDING. SO IT IS ALSO CALLED THE EAST PALACE. EVEN THOUGH IT WAS NOT THE MAIN PALACE, IT WAS USED AS SUCH.
大造殿
DAEJO-JUN: A QUEEN'S QUARTERS. IT IS LOCATED WITHIN THE INNER SANCTUM OF CHANGDUCK PALACE. A KING'S BEDROOM WAS ON THE EAST SIDE AND A QUEEN'S BEDROOM WAS ON THE WEST.
GYEONGBOK PALACE WAS BUILT ACCORDING TO FORMAL PALACE ETIQUETTE AND FORM AND WAS MEANT TO ESTABLISH A KING'S LEGITIMACY AND AUTHORITY.

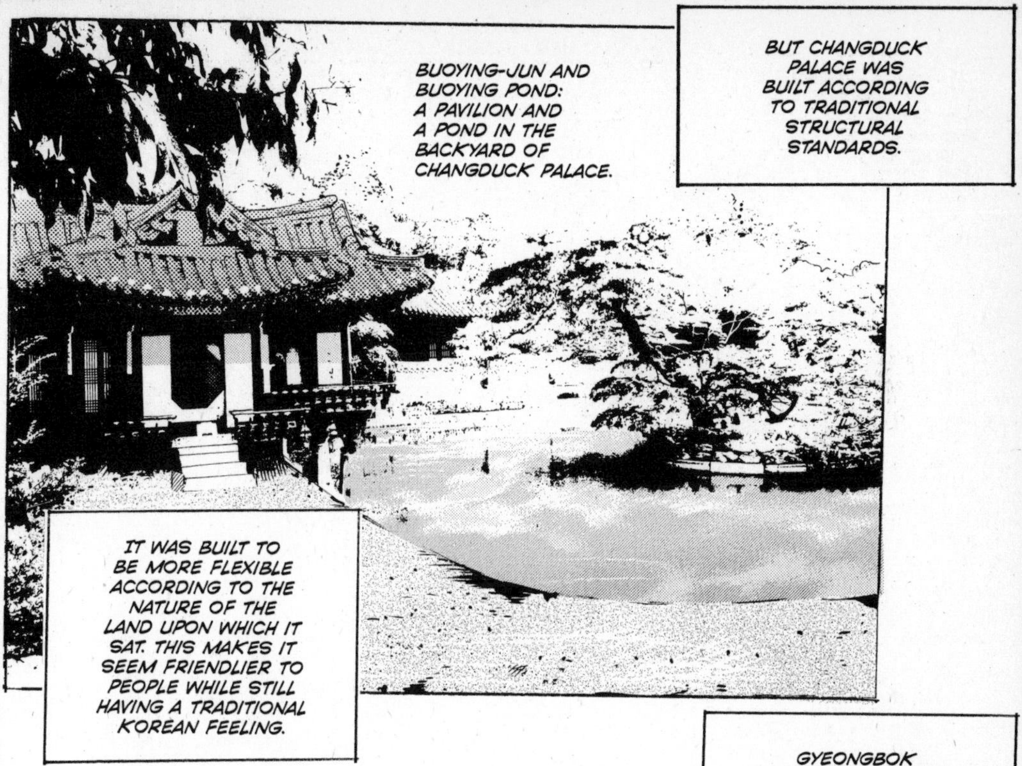
BUOYING-JUN AND BUOYING POND: A PAVILION AND A POND IN THE BACKYARD OF CHANGDUCK PALACE.
BUT CHANGDUCK PALACE WAS BUILT ACCORDING TO TRADITIONAL STRUCTURAL STANDARDS.
IT WAS BUILT TO BE MORE FLEXIBLE ACCORDING TO THE NATURE OF THE LAND UPON WHICH IT SAT. THIS MAKES IT SEEM FRIENDLIER TO PEOPLE WHILE STILL HAVING A TRADITIONAL KOREAN FEELING.

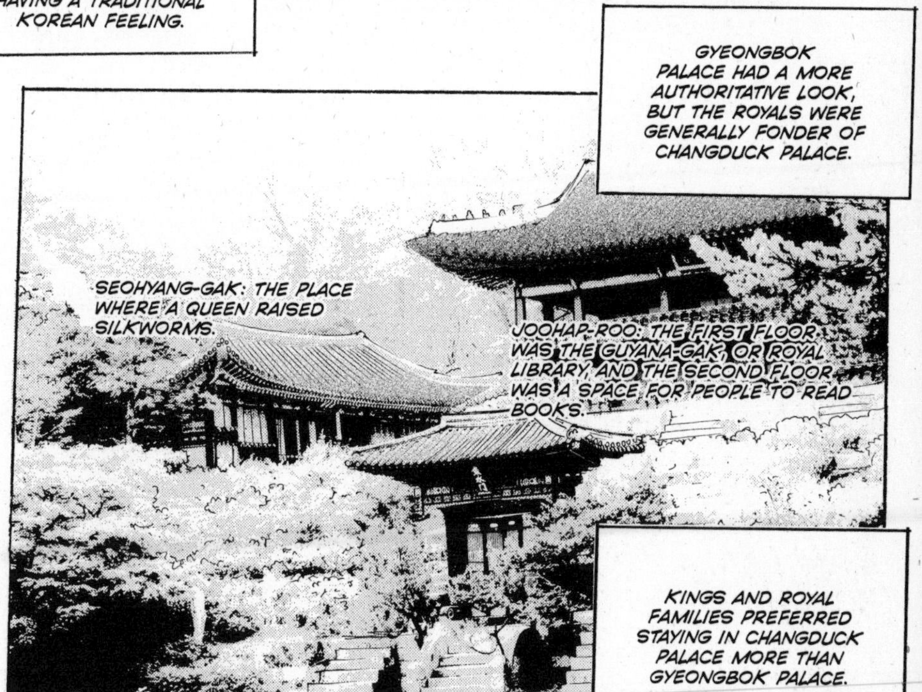
GYEONGBOK PALACE HAD A MORE AUTHORITATIVE LOOK, BUT THE ROYALS WERE GENERALLY FONDER OF CHANGDUCK PALACE.
SEOHYANG-GAK: THE PLACE WHERE A QUEEN RAISED SILKWORMS.
JOOHAP-ROO: THE FIRST FLOOR WAS THE GUYANA-GAK, OR ROYAL LIBRARY, AND THE SECOND FLOOR WAS A SPACE FOR PEOPLE TO READ BOOKS.
KINGS AND ROYAL FAMILIES PREFERRED STAYING IN CHANGDUCK PALACE MORE THAN GYEONGBOK PALACE.

REFERENCE: CHANGDUCK PALACE BY GANG-GUN LEE

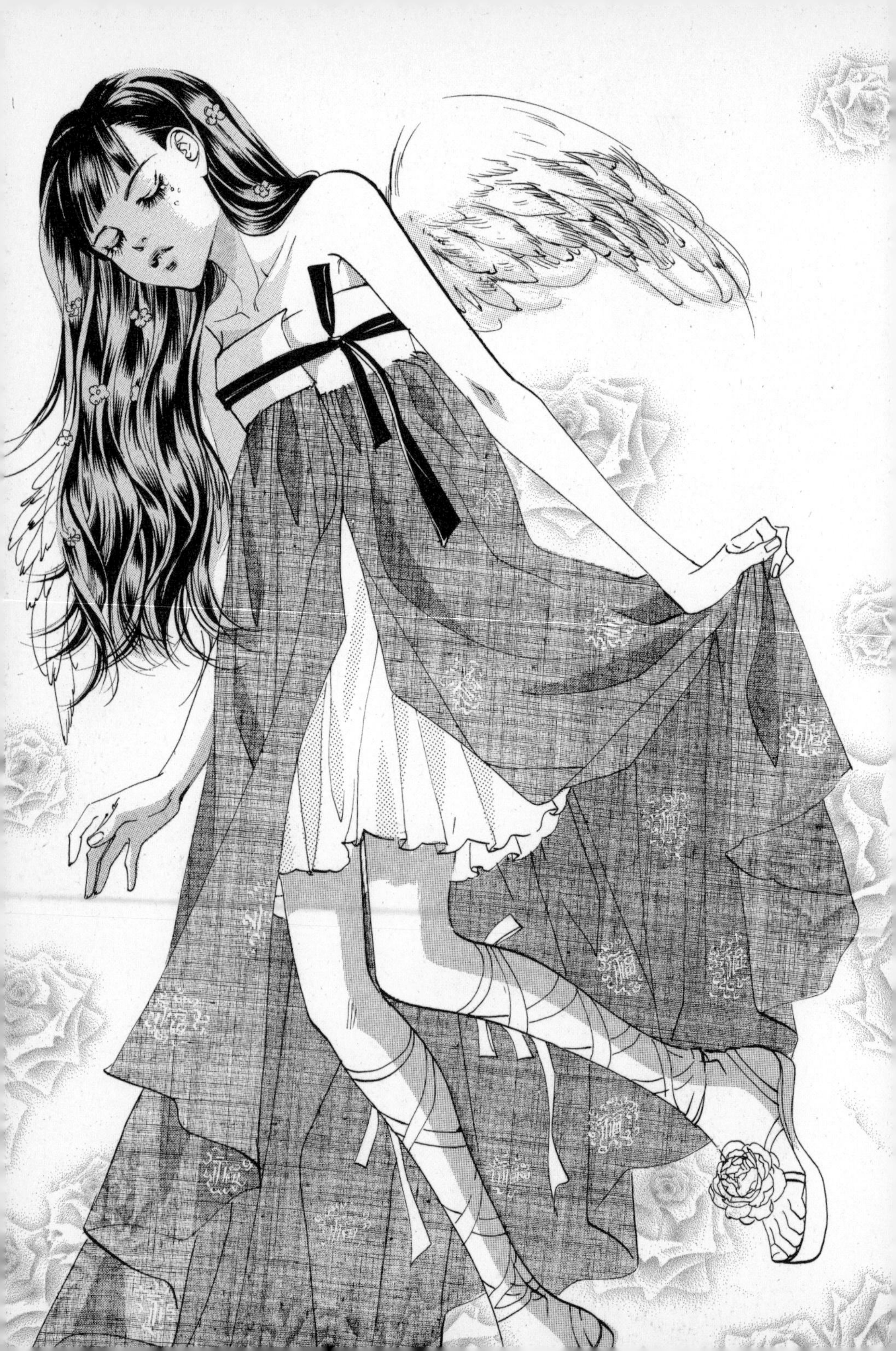

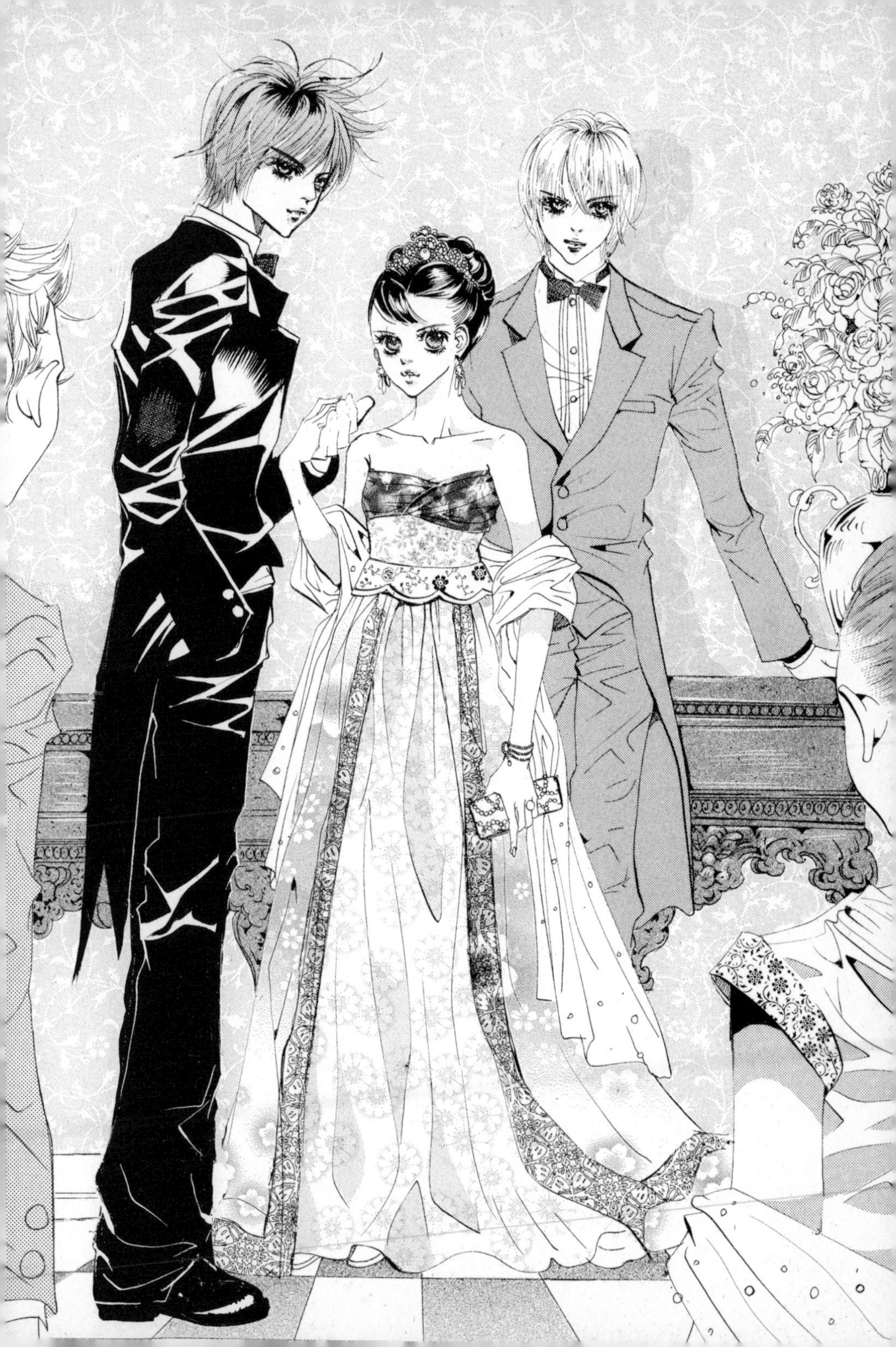

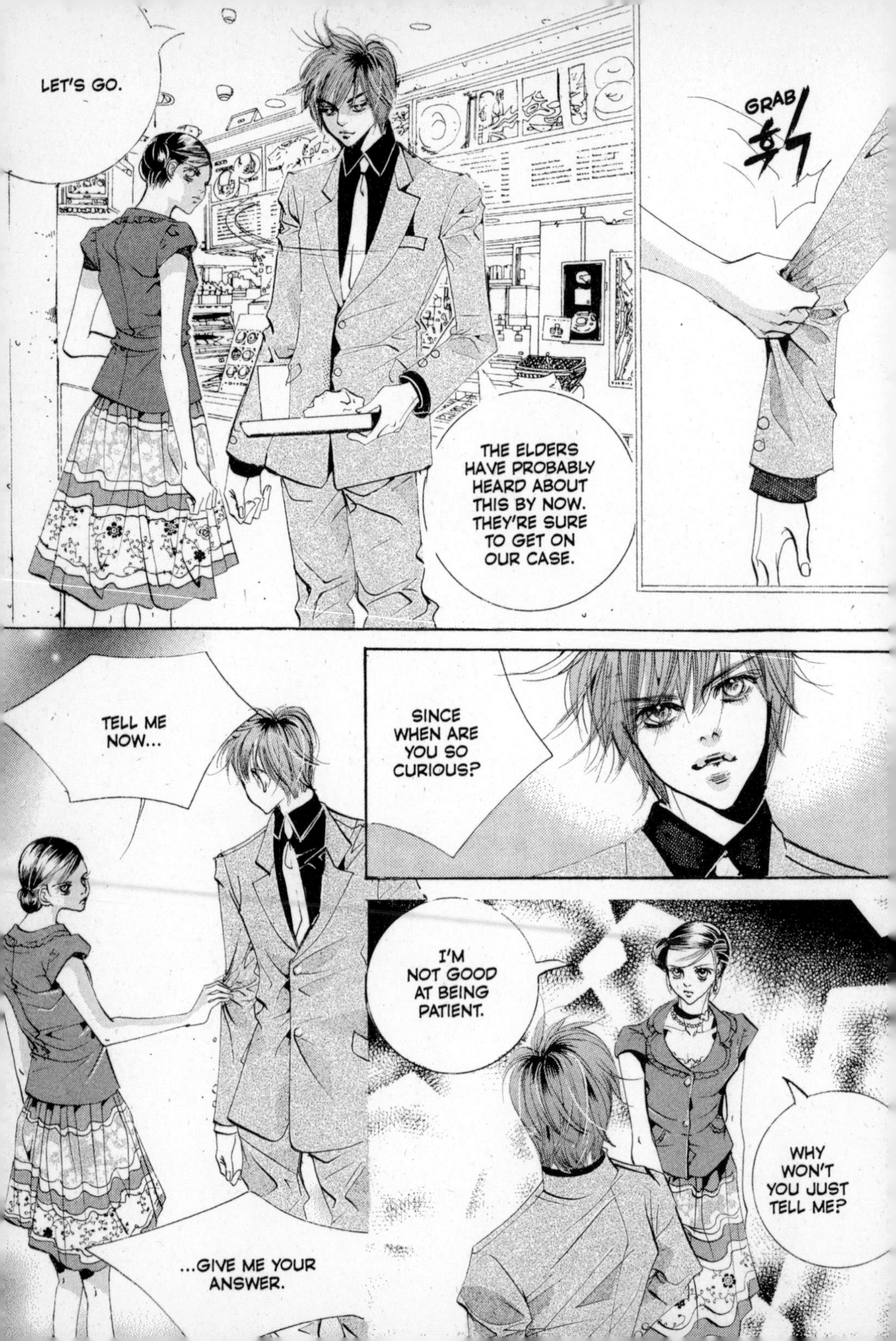
LET'S GO.
THE ELDERS HAVE PROBABLY HEARD ABOUT THIS BY NOW. THEY'RE SURE TO GET ON OUR CASE.
GRAB
확
TELL ME NOW...
...GIVE ME YOUR ANSWER.
SINCE WHEN ARE YOU SO CURIOUS?
I'M NOT GOOD AT BEING PATIENT.
WHY WON'T YOU JUST TELL ME?

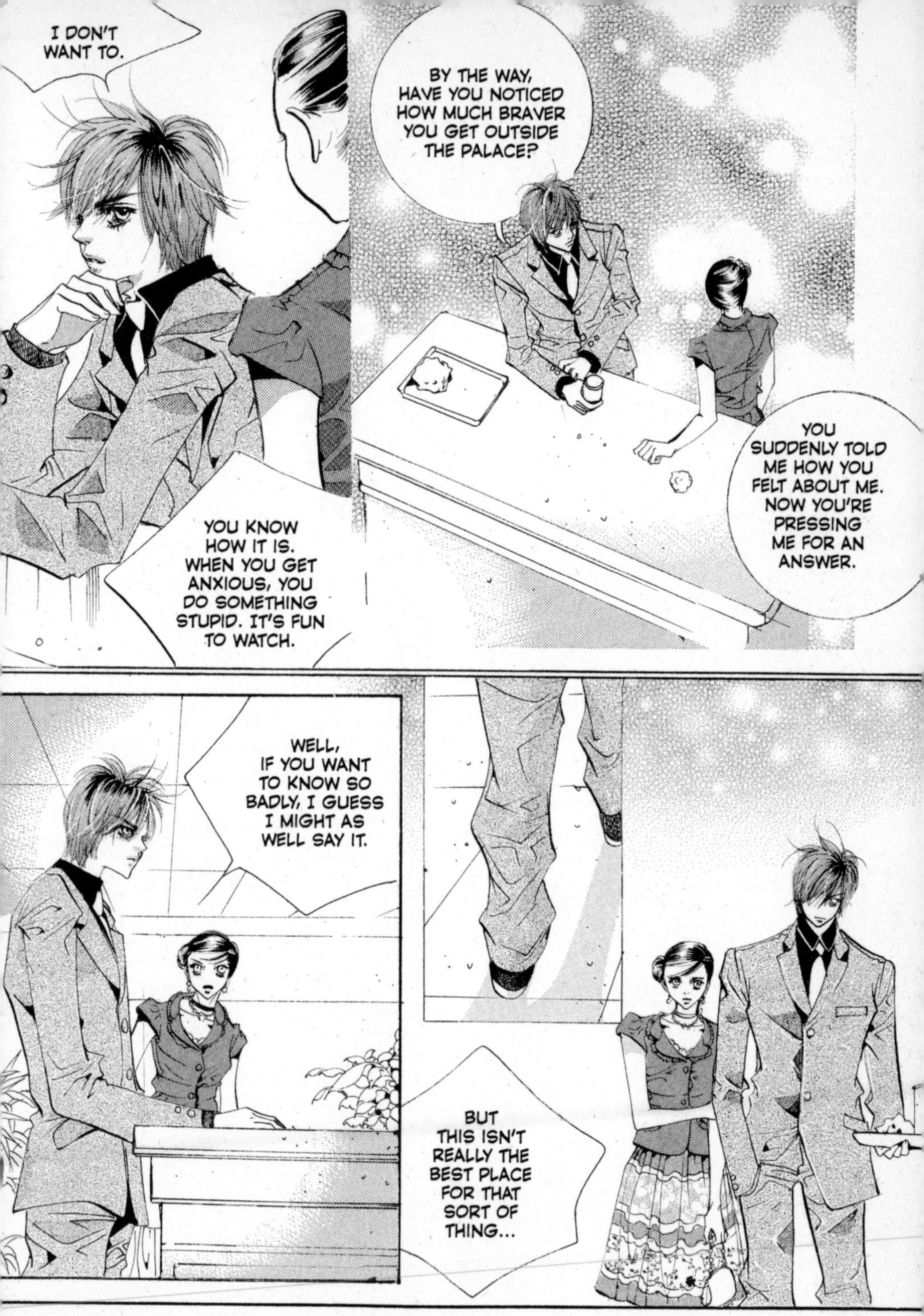
I DON'T WANT TO.
YOU KNOW HOW IT IS. WHEN YOU GET ANXIOUS, YOU DO SOMETHING STUPID. IT'S FUN TO WATCH.
BY THE WAY, HAVE YOU NOTICED HOW MUCH BRAVER YOU GET OUTSIDE THE PALACE?
YOU SUDDENLY TOLD ME HOW YOU FELT ABOUT ME. NOW YOU'RE PRESSING ME FOR AN ANSWER.
WELL, IF YOU WANT TO KNOW SO BADLY, I GUESS I MIGHT AS WELL SAY IT.
BUT THIS ISN'T REALLY THE BEST PLACE FOR THAT SORT OF THING...

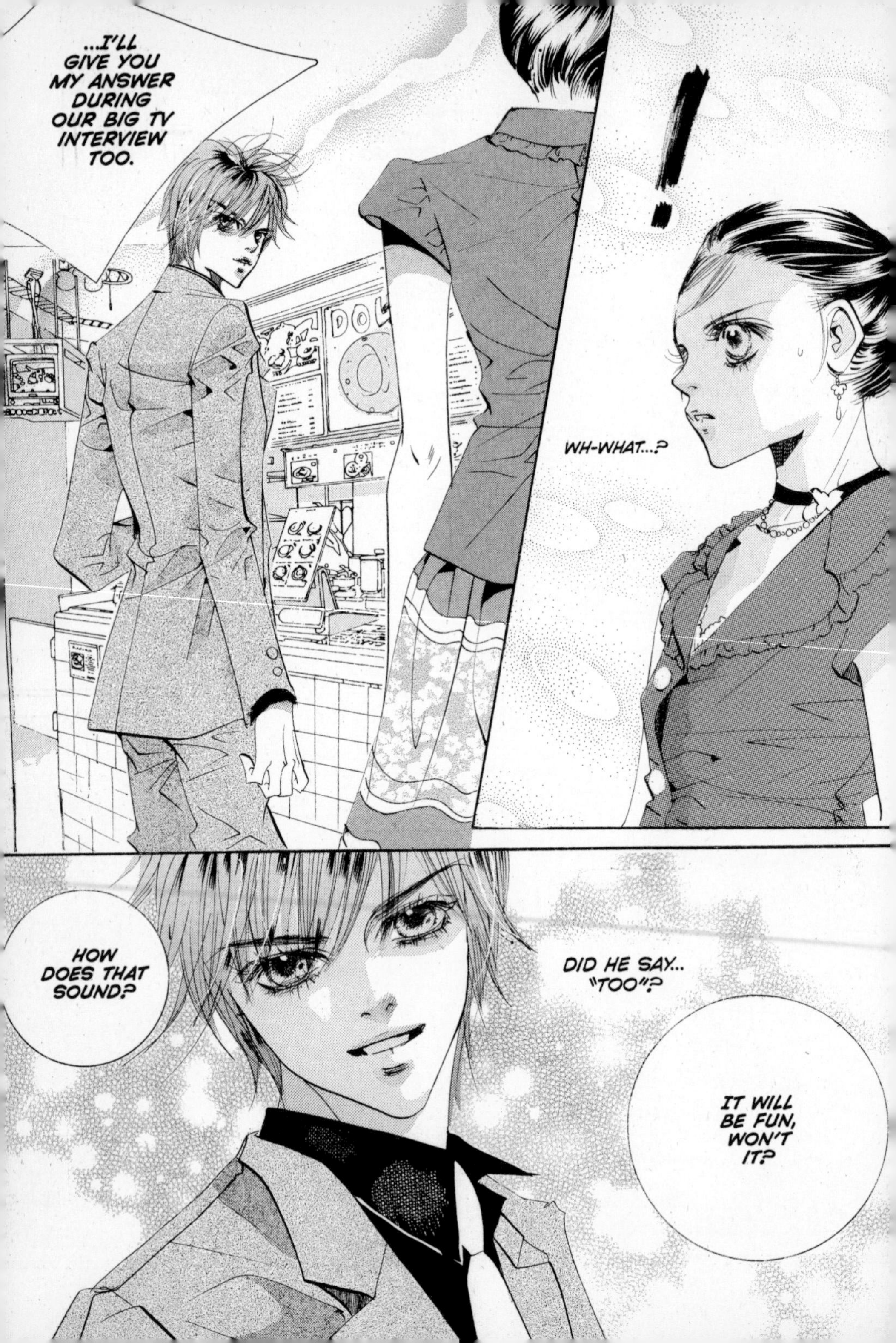
...I'LL GIVE YOU MY ANSWER DURING OUR BIG TV INTERVIEW TOO.
!
WH-WHAT...?
HOW DOES THAT SOUND?
DID HE SAY... "TOO"?
IT WILL BE FUN, WON'T IT?

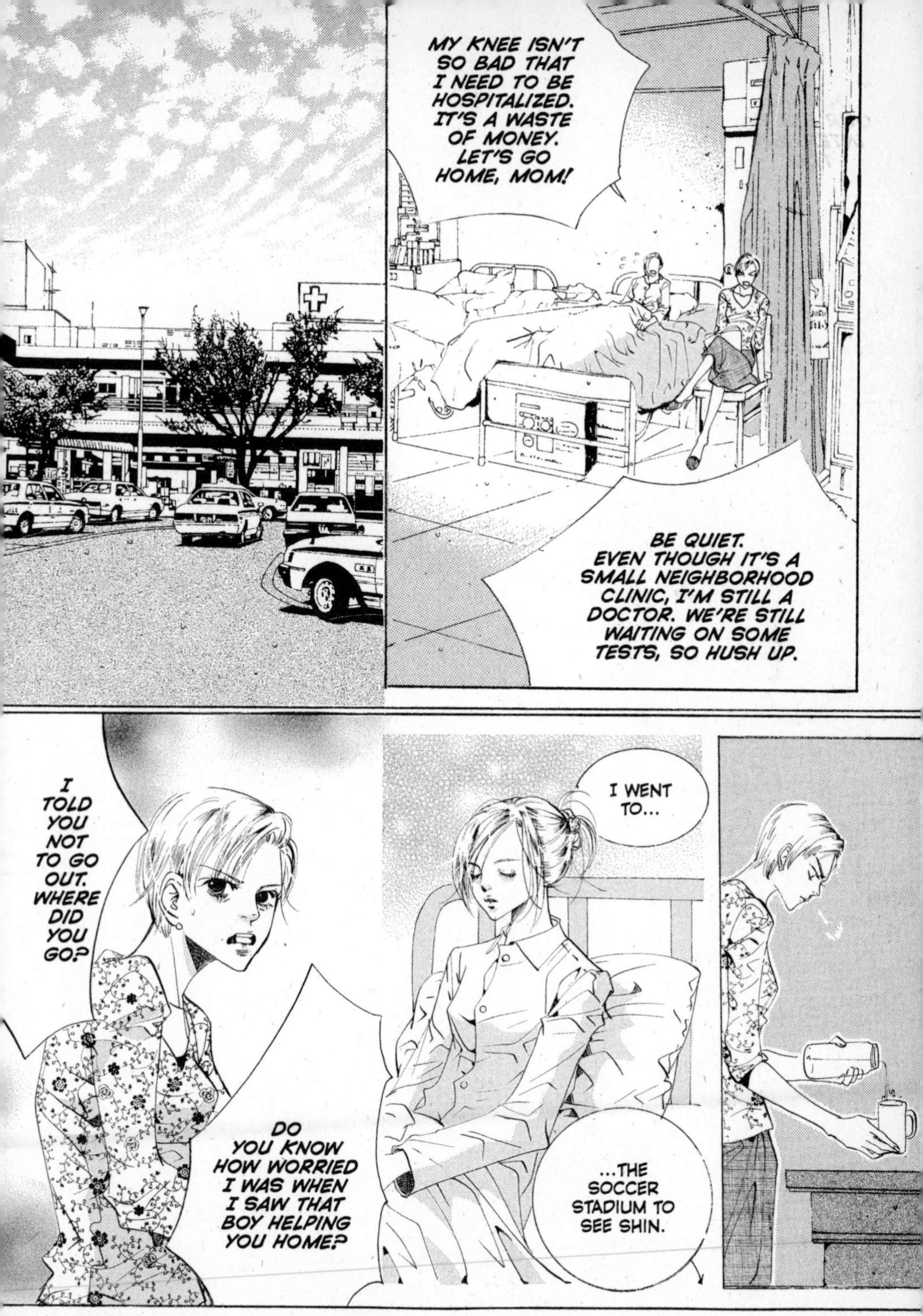
MY KNEE ISN'T SO BAD THAT I NEED TO BE HOSPITALIZED. IT'S A WASTE OF MONEY. LET'S GO HOME, MOM!
BE QUIET. EVEN THOUGH IT'S A SMALL NEIGHBORHOOD CLINIC, I'M STILL A DOCTOR. WE'RE STILL WAITING ON SOME TESTS, SO HUSH UP.
I TOLD YOU NOT TO GO OUT. WHERE DID YOU GO?
DO YOU KNOW HOW WORRIED I WAS WHEN I SAW THAT BOY HELPING YOU HOME?
I WENT TO...
...THE SOCCER STADIUM TO SEE SHIN.

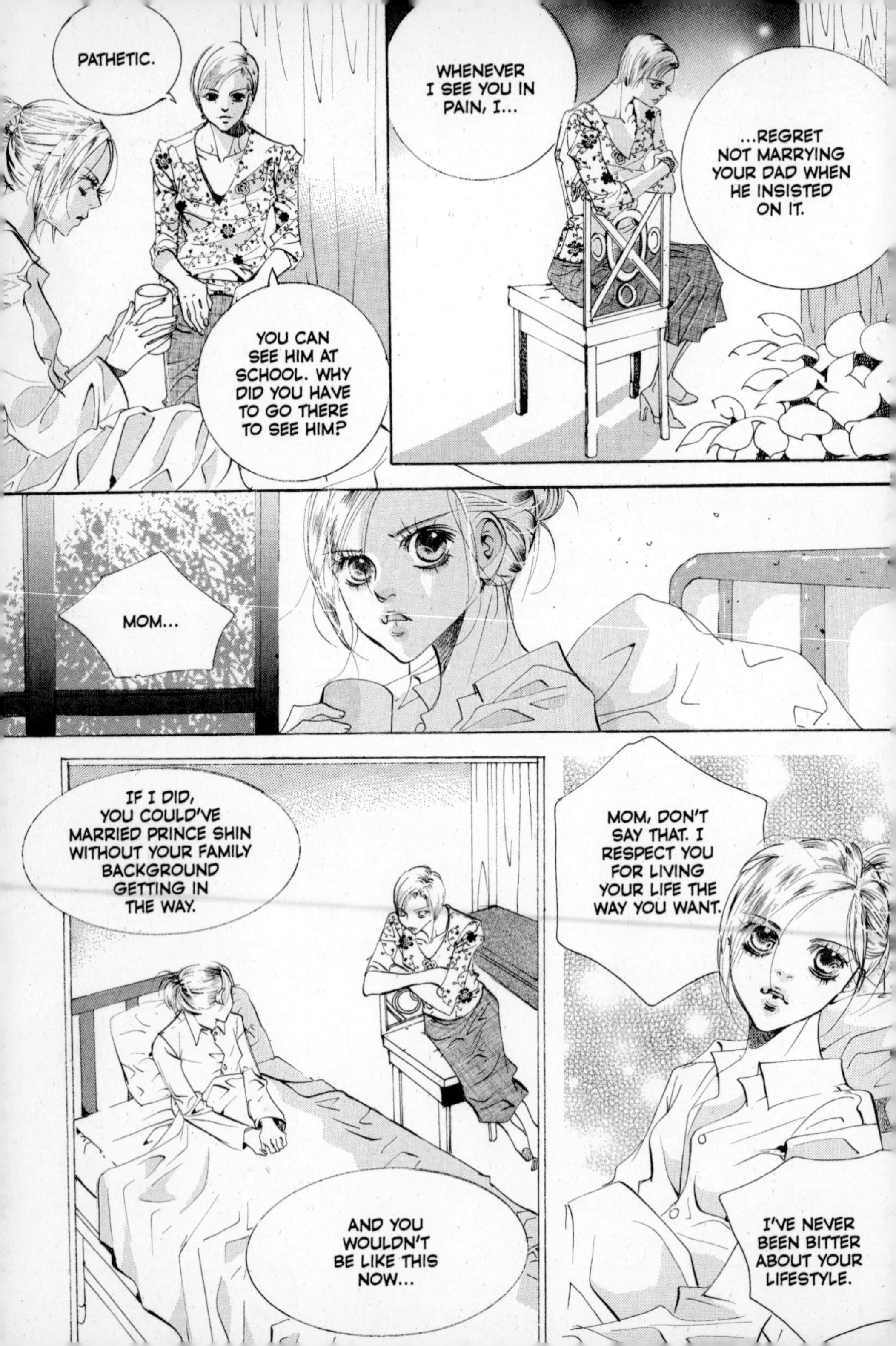
PATHETIC.
YOU CAN SEE HIM AT SCHOOL. WHY DID YOU HAVE TO GO THERE TO SEE HIM?
WHENEVER I SEE YOU IN PAIN, I...
...REGRET NOT MARRYING YOUR DAD WHEN HE INSISTED ON IT.
MOM...
IF I DID, YOU COULD'VE MARRIED PRINCE SHIN WITHOUT YOUR FAMILY BACKGROUND GETTING IN THE WAY.
AND YOU WOULDN'T BE LIKE THIS NOW...
MOM, DON'T SAY THAT. I RESPECT YOU FOR LIVING YOUR LIFE THE WAY YOU WANT.
I'VE NEVER BEEN BITTER ABOUT YOUR LIFESTYLE.

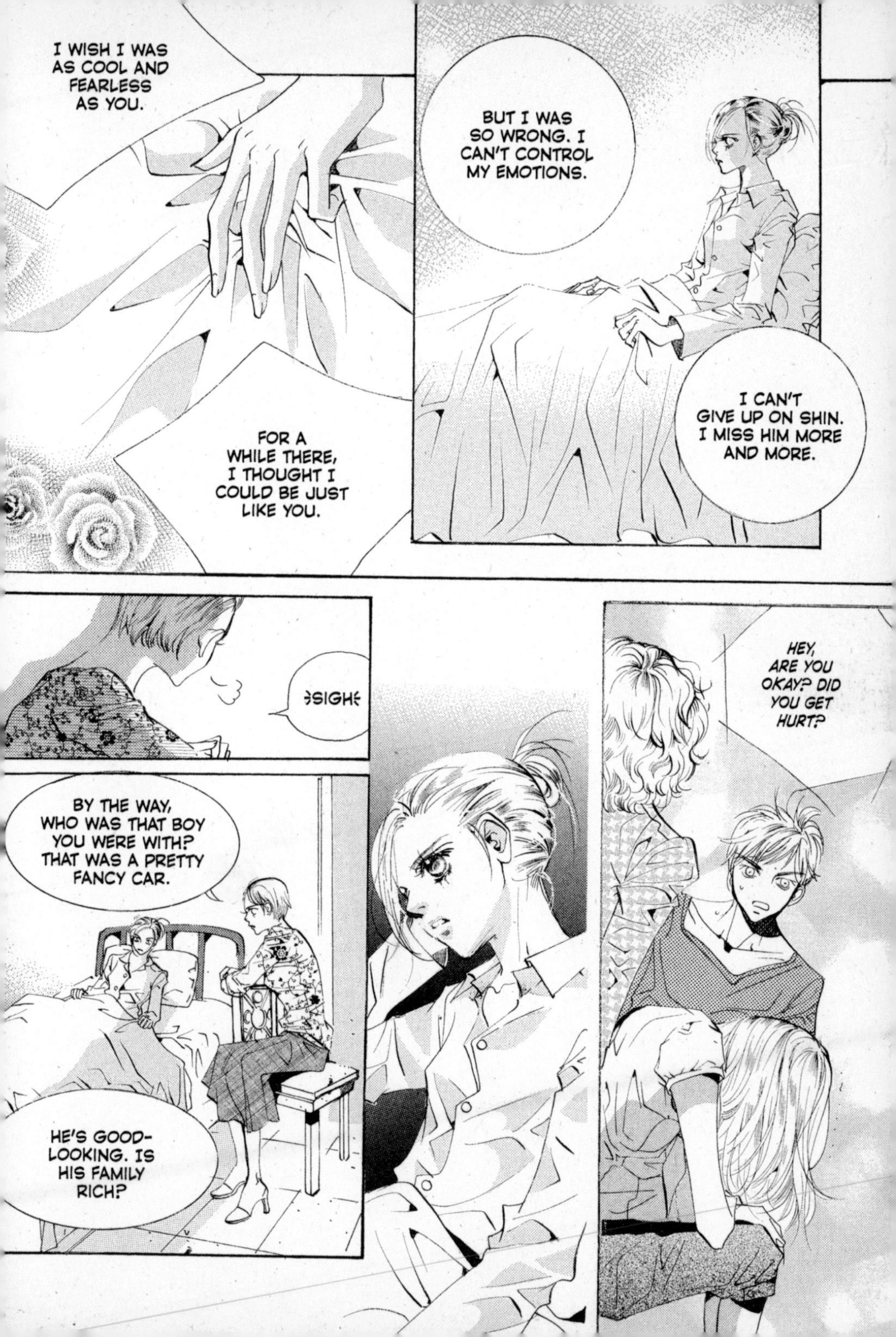
I WISH I WAS AS COOL AND FEARLESS AS YOU.
FOR A WHILE THERE, I THOUGHT I COULD BE JUST LIKE YOU.
BUT I WAS SO WRONG. I CAN'T CONTROL MY EMOTIONS.
I CAN'T GIVE UP ON SHIN. I MISS HIM MORE AND MORE.
SIGH
BY THE WAY, WHO WAS THAT BOY YOU WERE WITH? THAT WAS A PRETTY FANCY CAR.
HE'S GOOD-LOOKING. IS HIS FAMILY RICH?
HEY, ARE YOU OKAY? DID YOU GET HURT?

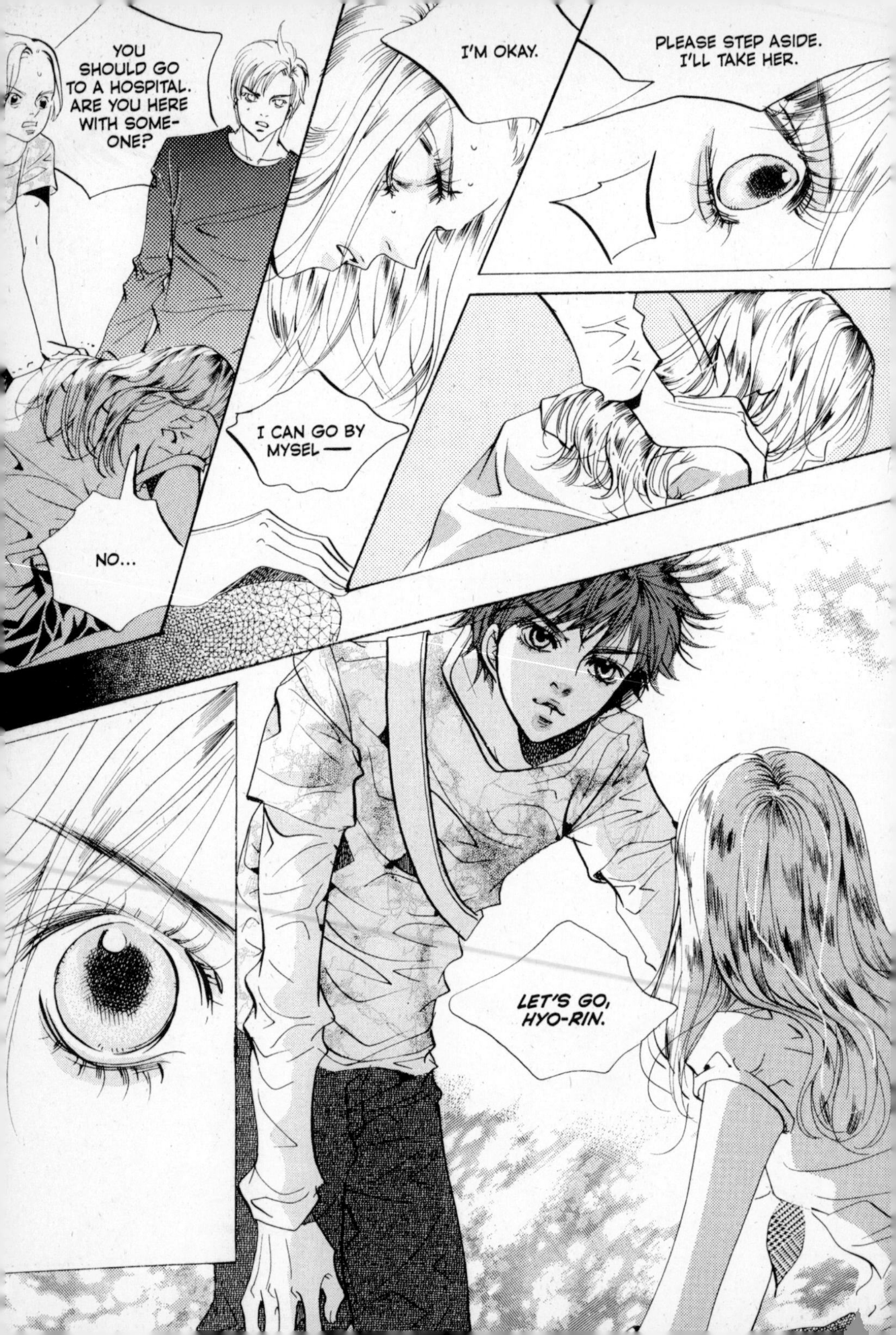
YOU SHOULD GO TO A HOSPITAL. ARE YOU HERE WITH SOME-ONE?
I'M OKAY.
PLEASE STEP ASIDE. I'LL TAKE HER.
I CAN GO BY MYSEL—
NO...
LET'S GO, HYO-RIN.

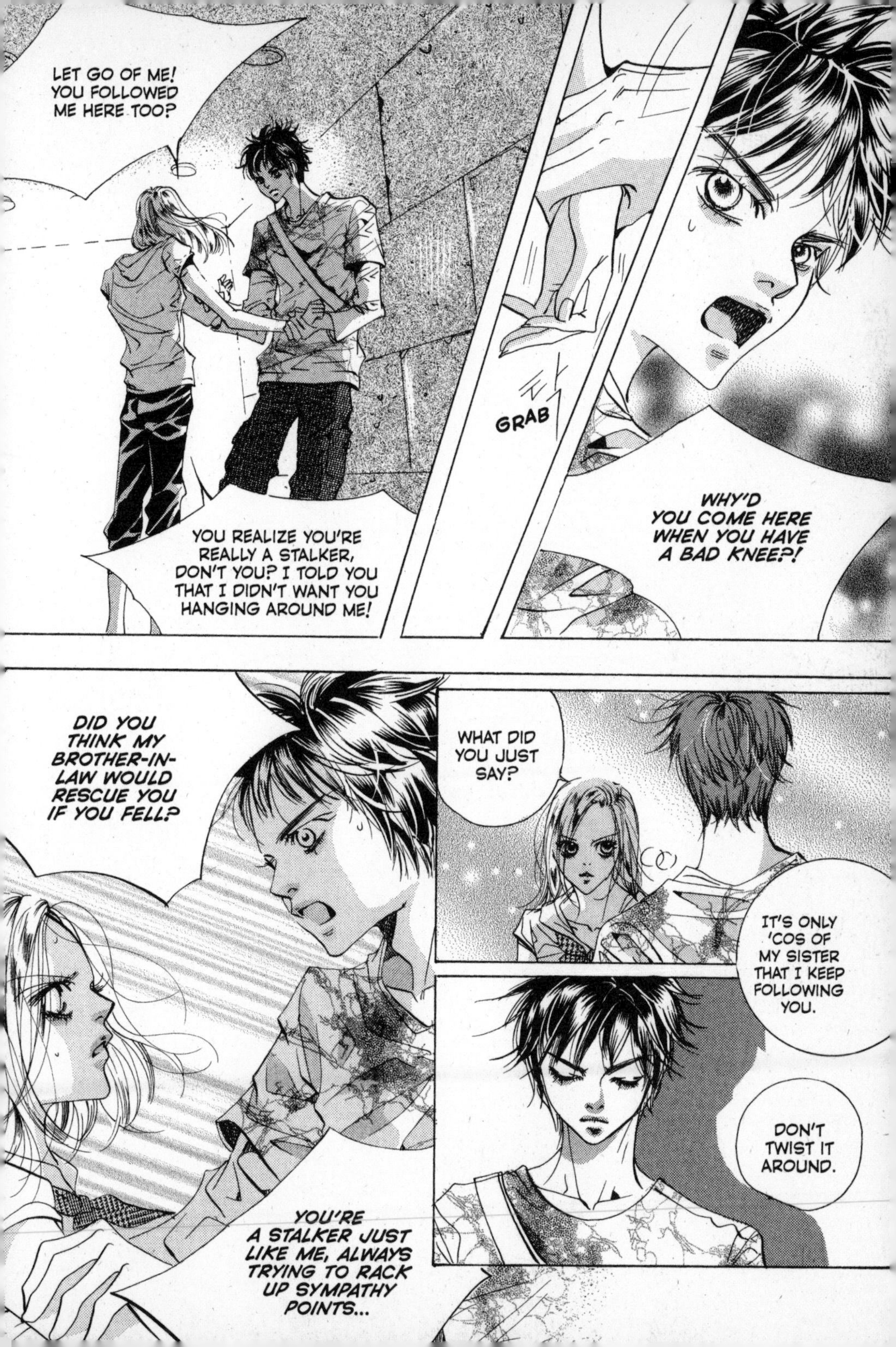

LET GO OF ME! YOU FOLLOWED ME HERE TOO?
YOU REALIZE YOU'RE REALLY A STALKER, DON'T YOU? I TOLD YOU THAT I DIDN'T WANT YOU HANGING AROUND ME!
GRAB
WHY'D YOU COME HERE WHEN YOU HAVE A BAD KNEE?!
DID YOU THINK MY BROTHER-IN-LAW WOULD RESCUE YOU IF YOU FELL?
YOU'RE A STALKER JUST LIKE ME, ALWAYS TRYING TO RACK UP SYMPATHY POINTS...
WHAT DID YOU JUST SAY?
IT'S ONLY 'COS OF MY SISTER THAT I KEEP FOLLOWING YOU.
DON'T TWIST IT AROUND.

I DON'T KNOW...

...WHAT CHAE-JUN IS REALLY LIKE.

PLEASE, DON'T TELL HER YET. IF I SEE CHAE-KYUNG NOW...

FATHER, PLEASE STOP BEING STUBBORN.

WE HAVE TO TELL CHAE-KYUNG ABOUT YOUR CONDITION.

...I JUST KNOW I'LL GET WORSE. HOW CAN I FACE HER?

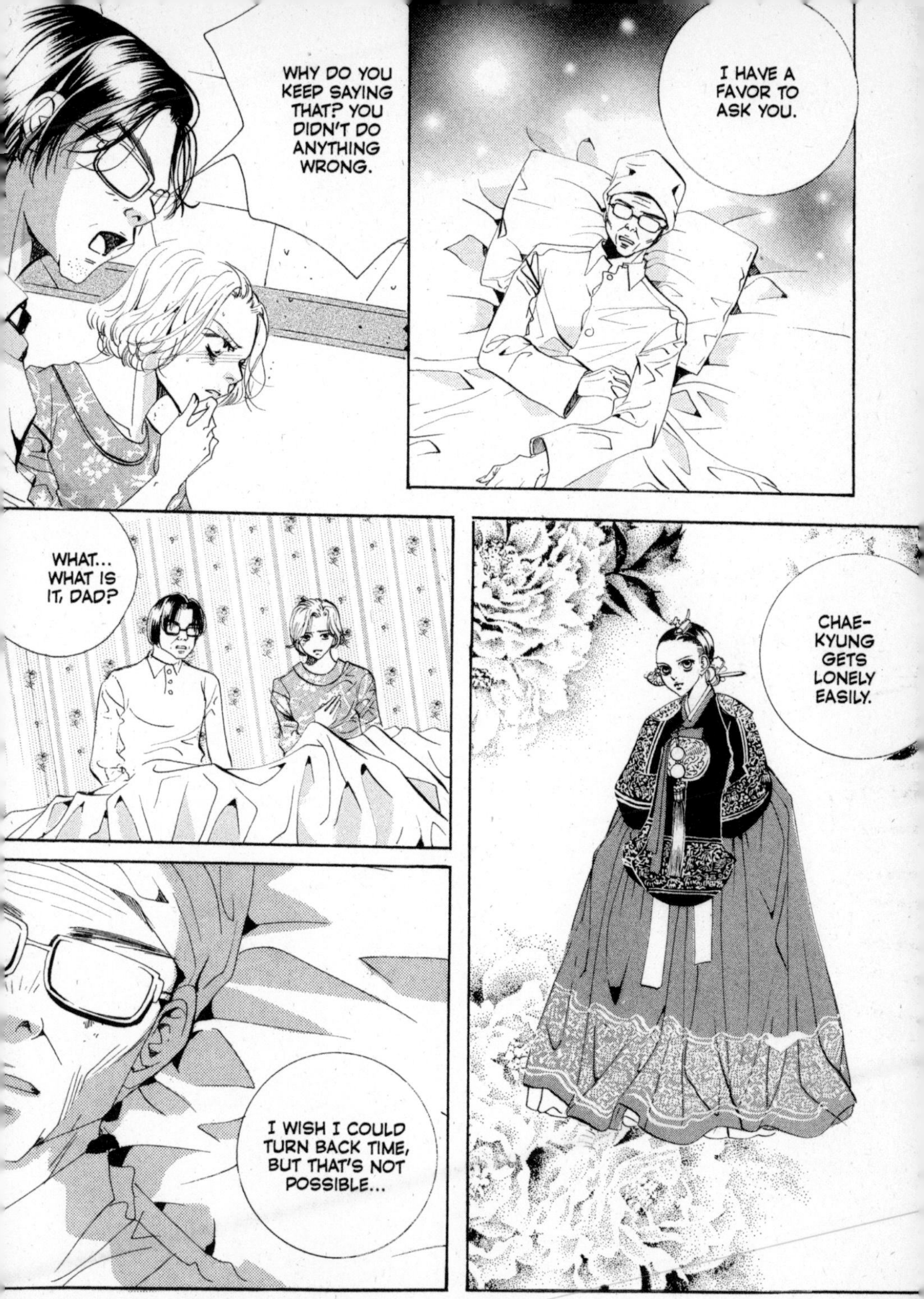
WHY DO YOU KEEP SAYING THAT? YOU DIDN'T DO ANYTHING WRONG.
I HAVE A FAVOR TO ASK YOU.
WHAT... WHAT IS IT, DAD?
I WISH I COULD TURN BACK TIME, BUT THAT'S NOT POSSIBLE...
CHAE-KYUNG GETS LONELY EASILY.

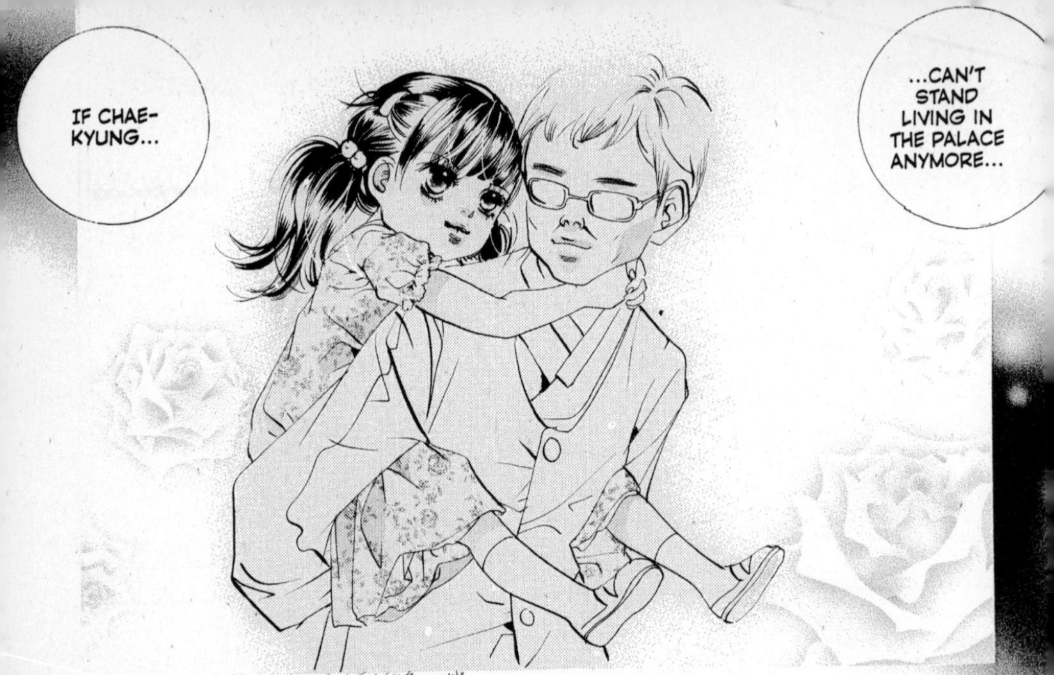
IF CHAE-KYUNG...
...CAN'T STAND LIVING IN THE PALACE ANYMORE...
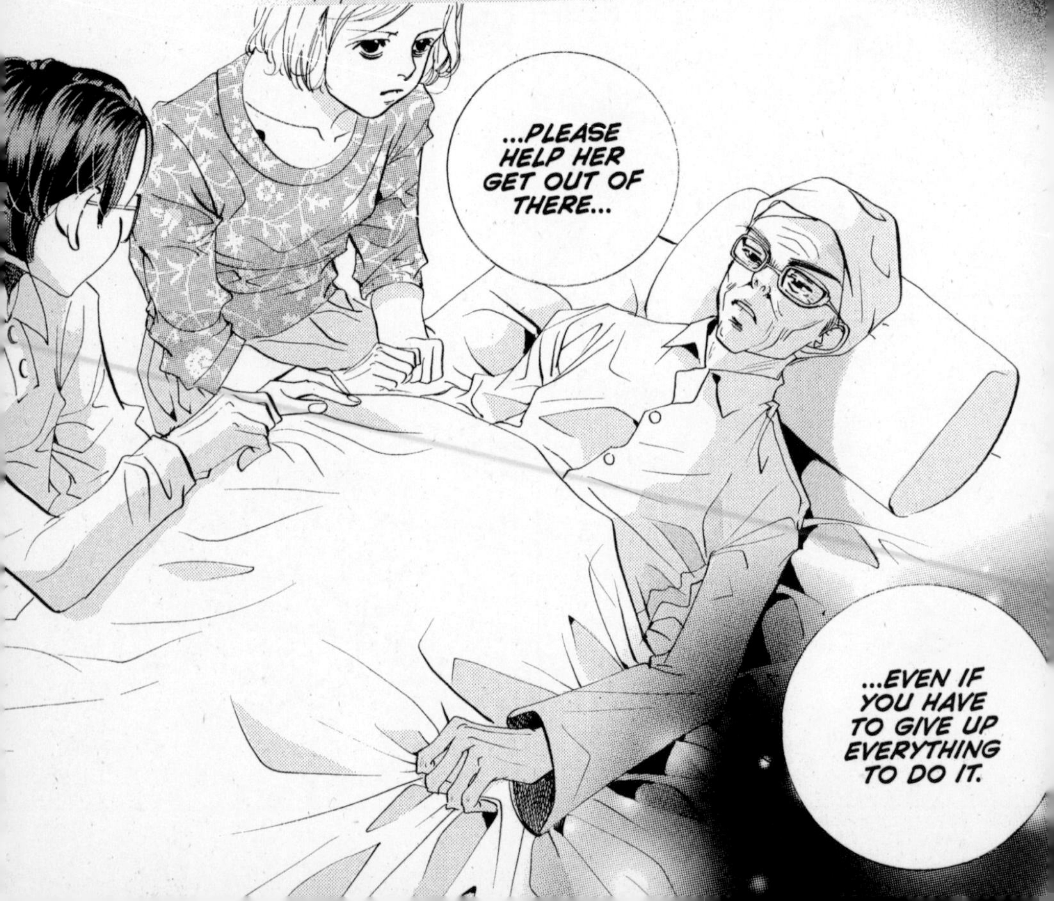
...PLEASE HELP HER GET OUT OF THERE...
...EVEN IF YOU HAVE TO GIVE UP EVERYTHING TO DO IT.

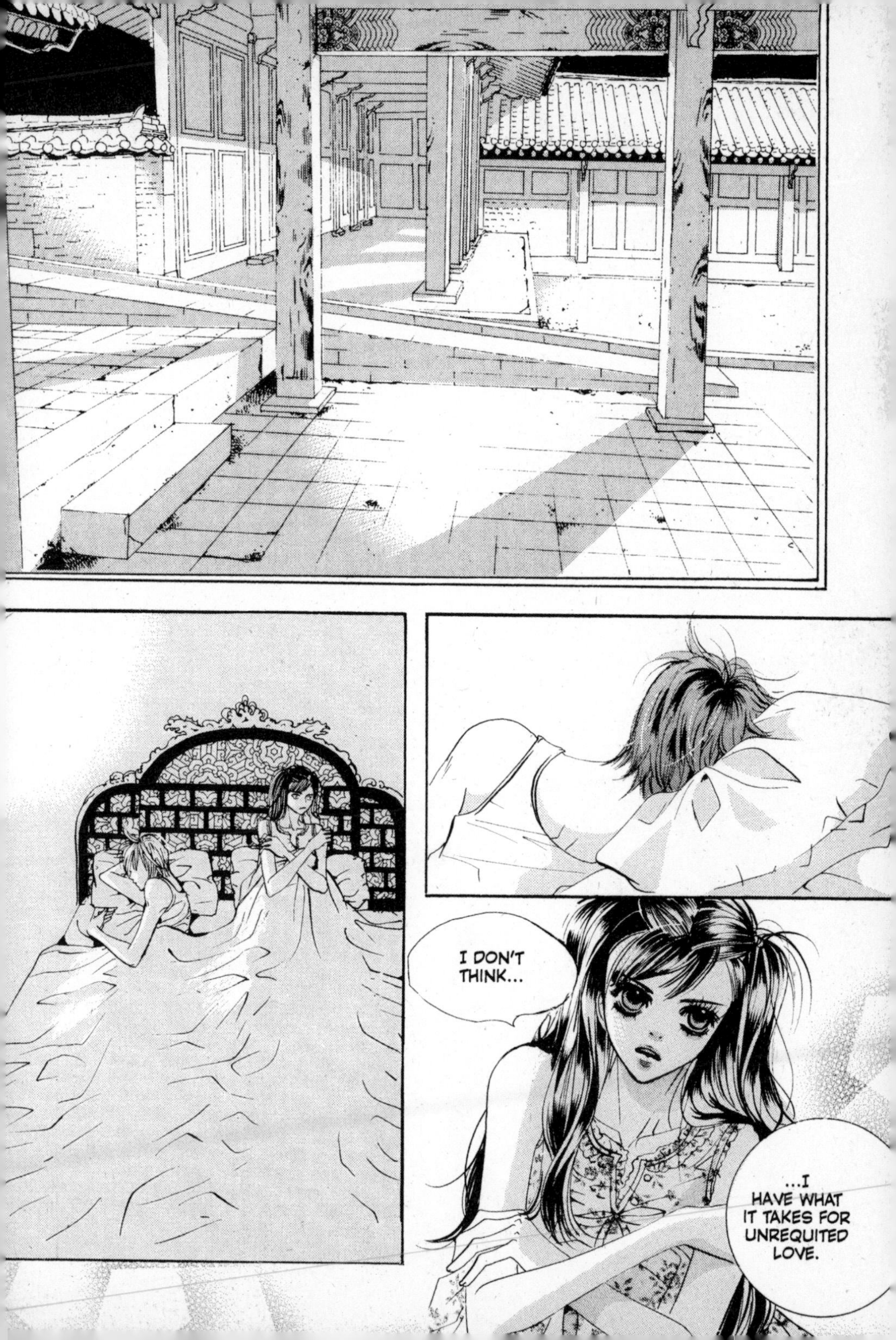
I DON'T THINK...
...I HAVE WHAT IT TAKES FOR UNREQUITED LOVE.

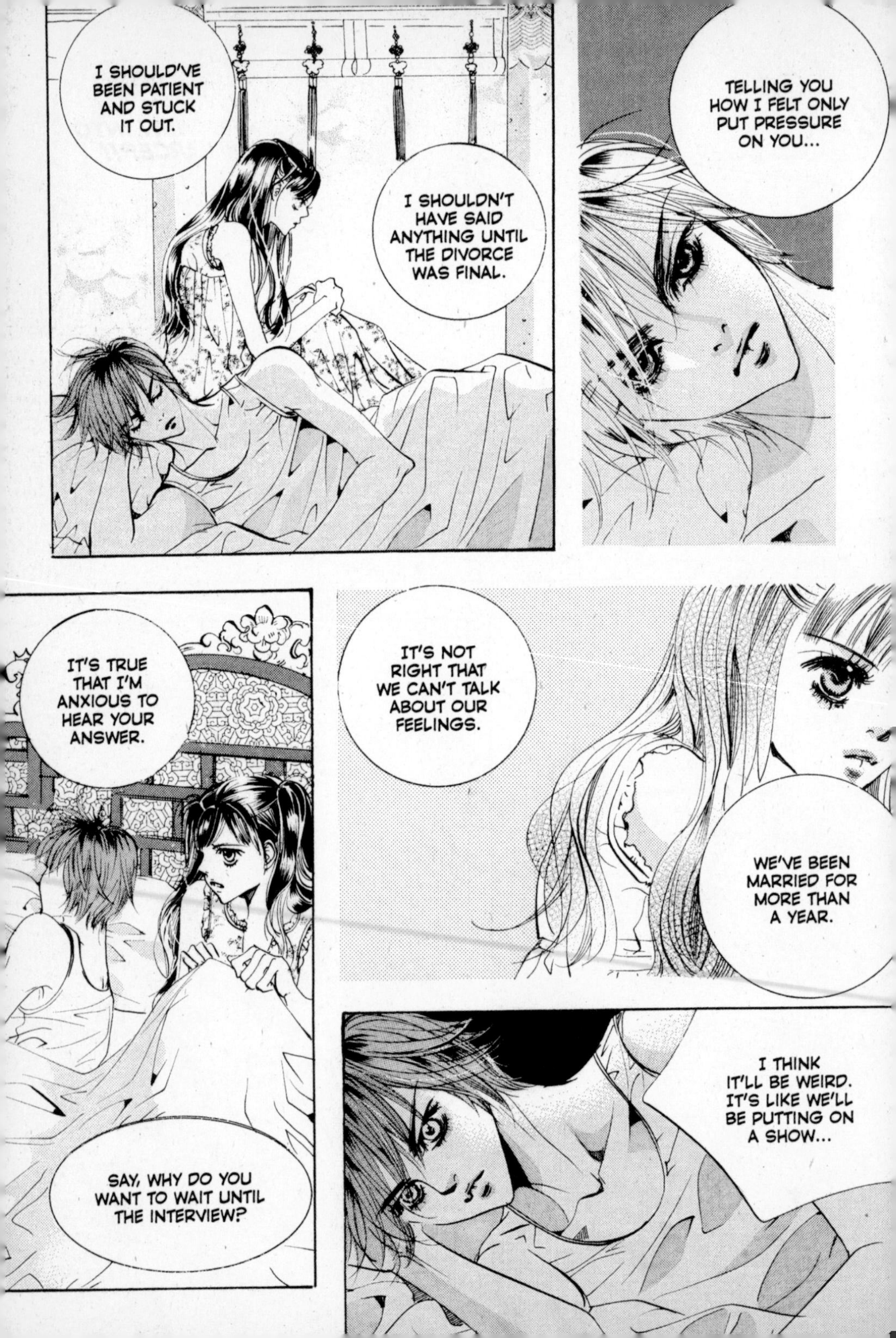
I SHOULD'VE BEEN PATIENT AND STUCK IT OUT.
I SHOULDN'T HAVE SAID ANYTHING UNTIL THE DIVORCE WAS FINAL.
TELLING YOU HOW I FELT ONLY PUT PRESSURE ON YOU...
IT'S TRUE THAT I'M ANXIOUS TO HEAR YOUR ANSWER.
SAY, WHY DO YOU WANT TO WAIT UNTIL THE INTERVIEW?
IT'S NOT RIGHT THAT WE CAN'T TALK ABOUT OUR FEELINGS.
WE'VE BEEN MARRIED FOR MORE THAN A YEAR.
I THINK IT'LL BE WEIRD. IT'S LIKE WE'LL BE PUTTING ON A SHOW...

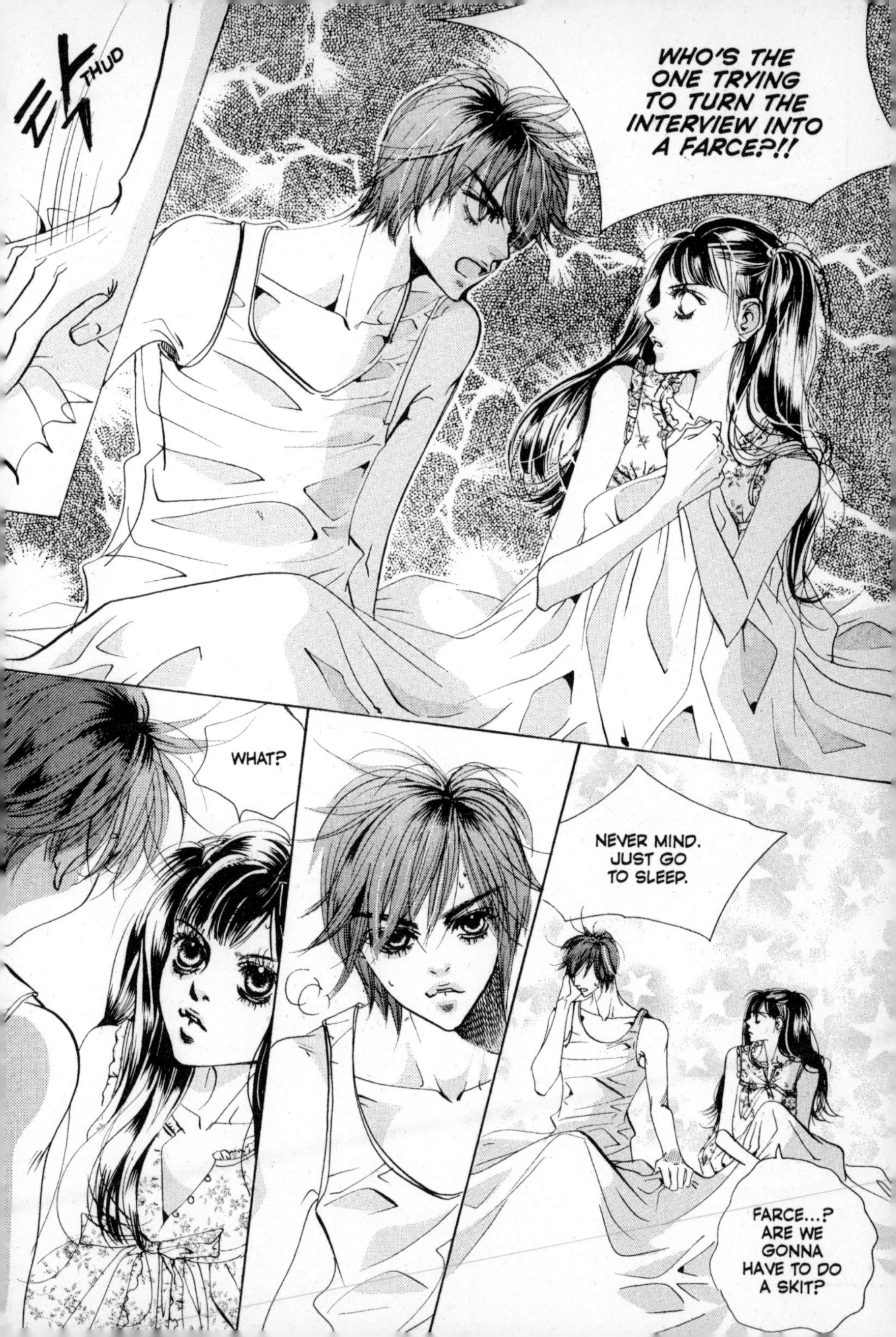
THUD
WHO'S THE ONE TRYING TO TURN THE INTERVIEW INTO A FARCE?!!
WHAT?
NEVER MIND. JUST GO TO SLEEP.
FARCE...? ARE WE GONNA HAVE TO DO A SKIT?

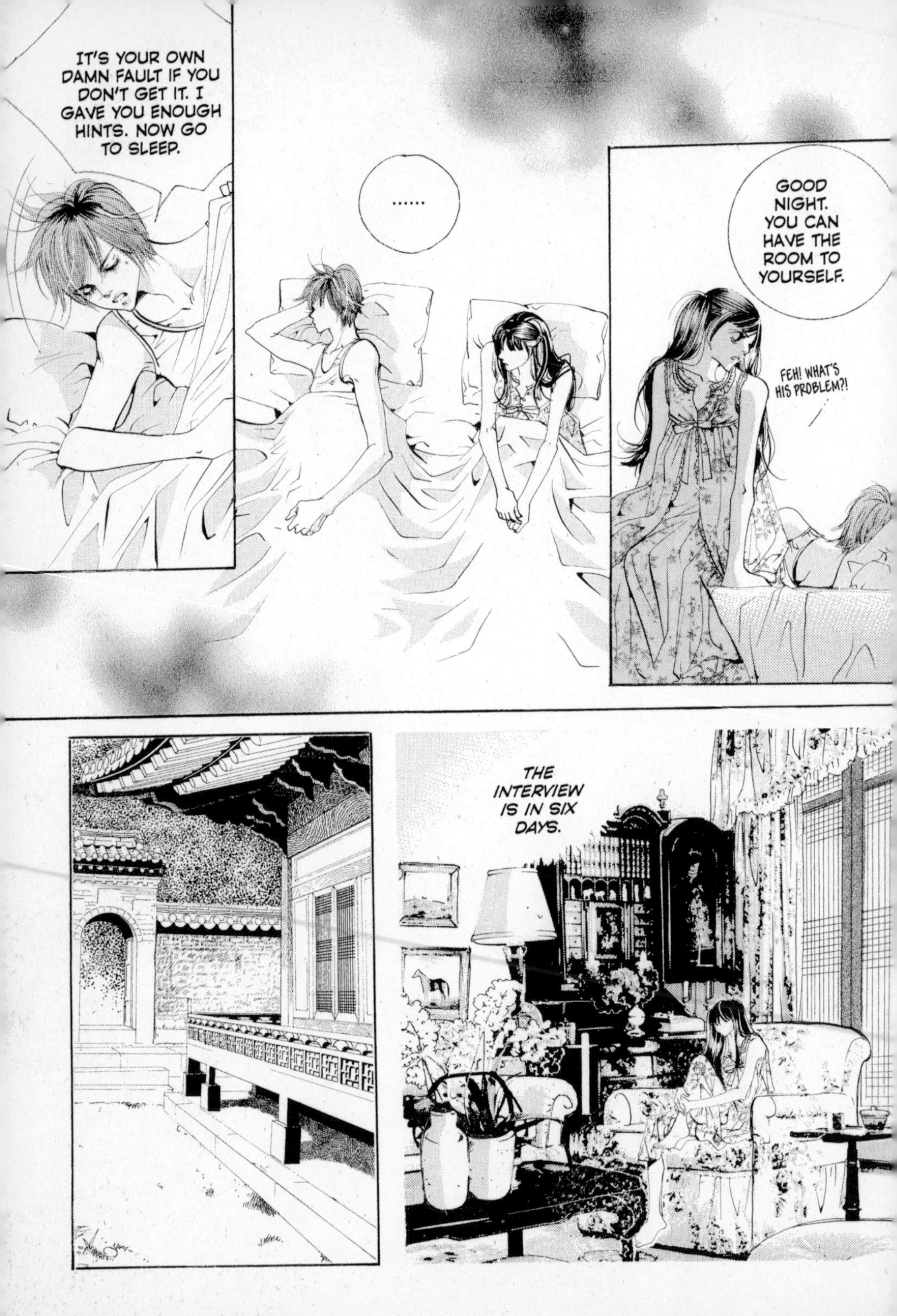
IT'S YOUR OWN DAMN FAULT IF YOU DON'T GET IT. I GAVE YOU ENOUGH HINTS. NOW GO TO SLEEP.
......
GOOD NIGHT. YOU CAN HAVE THE ROOM TO YOURSELF.
FEH! WHAT'S HIS PROBLEM?!
THE INTERVIEW IS IN SIX DAYS.

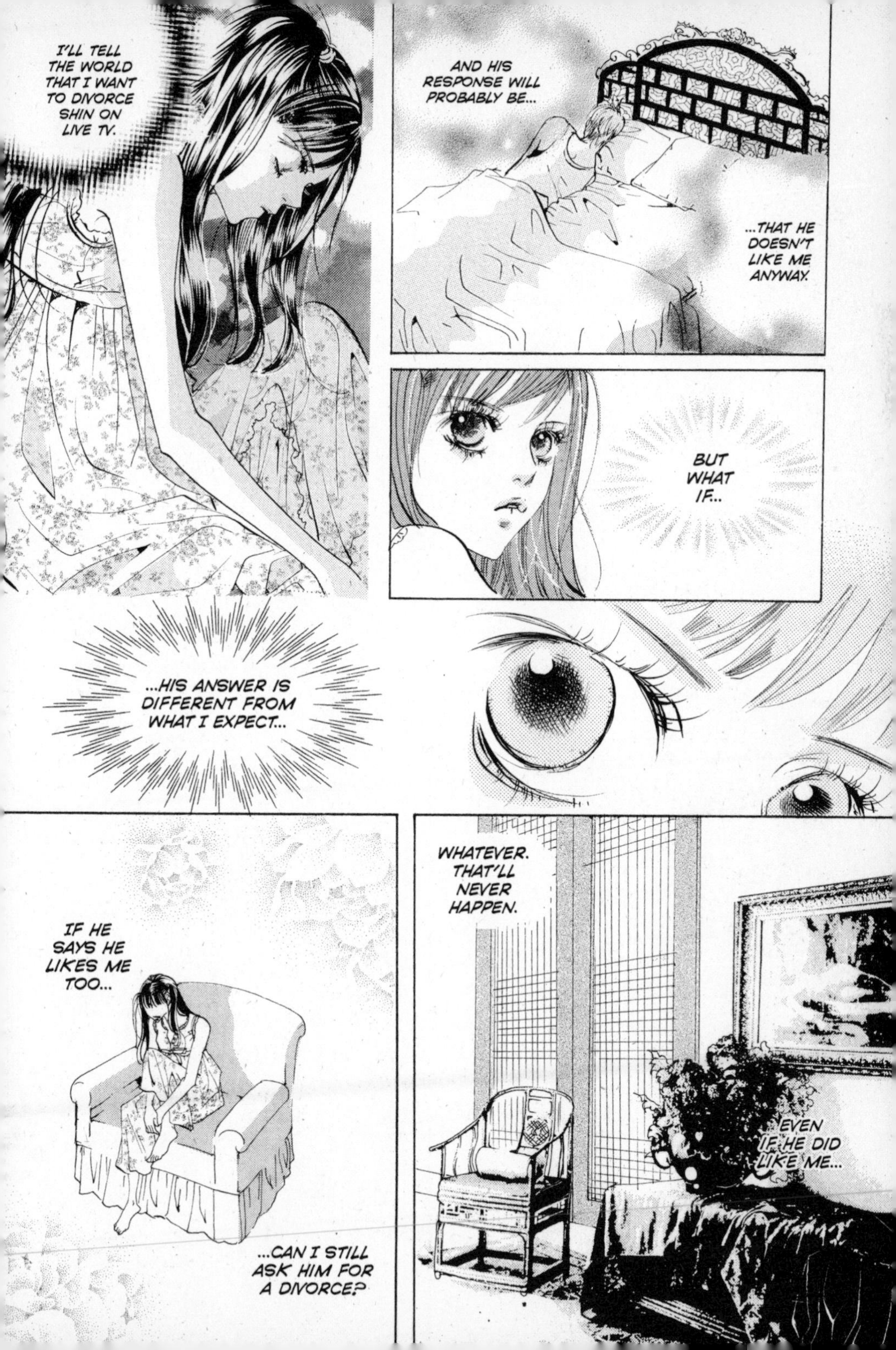
I'LL TELL THE WORLD THAT I WANT TO DIVORCE SHIN ON LIVE TV.
AND HIS RESPONSE WILL PROBABLY BE...
...THAT HE DOESN'T LIKE ME ANYWAY.
BUT WHAT IF...
...HIS ANSWER IS DIFFERENT FROM WHAT I EXPECT...
IF HE SAYS HE LIKES ME TOO...
...CAN I STILL ASK HIM FOR A DIVORCE?
WHATEVER. THAT'LL NEVER HAPPEN.
EVEN IF HE DID LIKE ME...

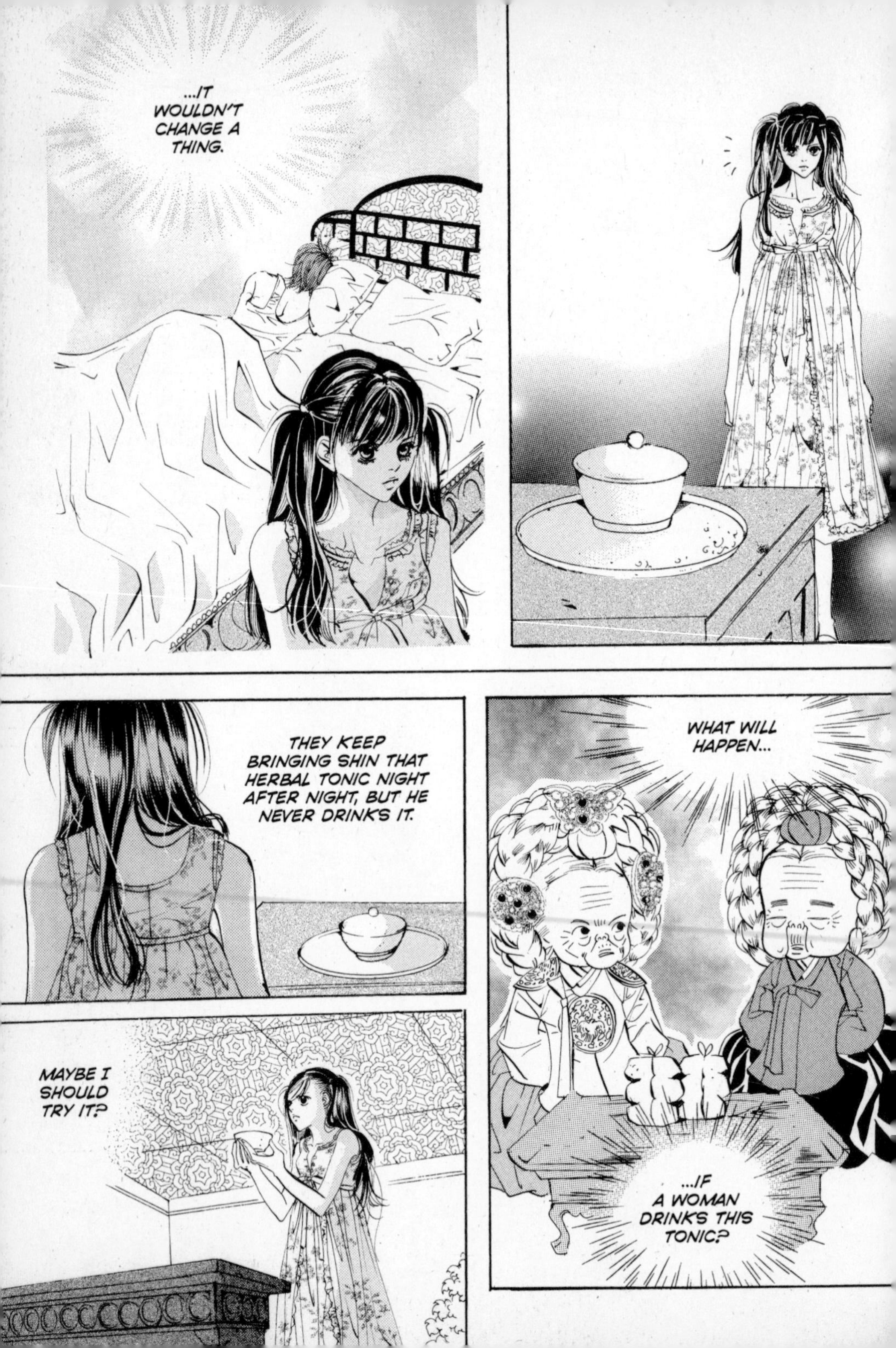
...IT WOULDN'T CHANGE A THING.
THEY KEEP BRINGING SHIN THAT HERBAL TONIC NIGHT AFTER NIGHT, BUT HE NEVER DRINKS IT.
MAYBE I SHOULD TRY IT?
WHAT WILL HAPPEN...
...IF A WOMAN DRINKS THIS TONIC?

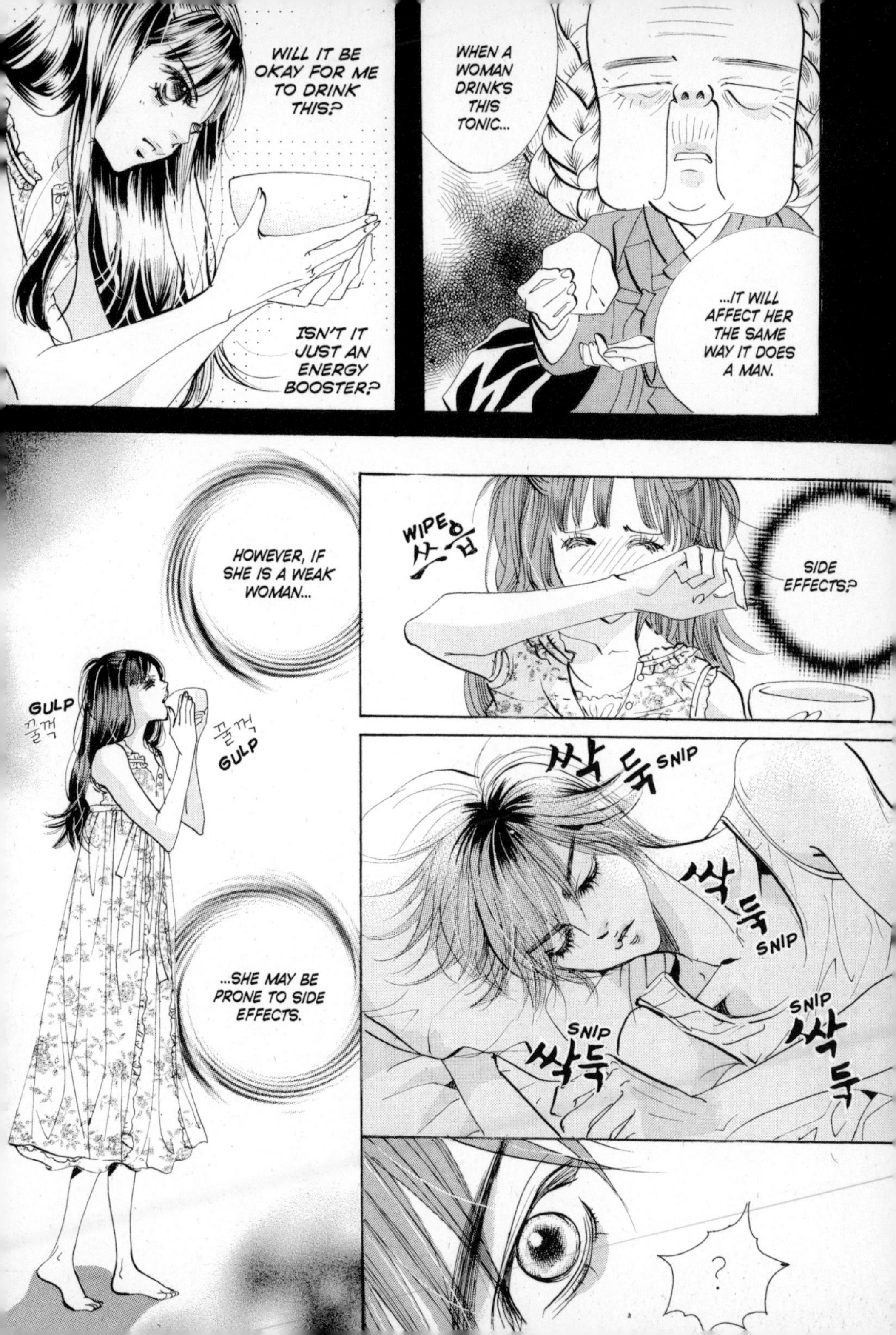
WILL IT BE OKAY FOR ME TO DRINK THIS?
ISN'T IT JUST AN ENERGY BOOSTER?
WHEN A WOMAN DRINKS THIS TONIC...
...IT WILL AFFECT HER THE SAME WAY IT DOES A MAN.
HOWEVER, IF SHE IS A WEAK WOMAN...
GULP
꿀꺽
꿀꺽
GULP
...SHE MAY BE PRONE TO SIDE EFFECTS.
WIPE
쓰읍
SIDE EFFECTS?
싹둑
SNIP
싹둑
SNIP
SNIP
싹둑
SNIP
싹둑
?

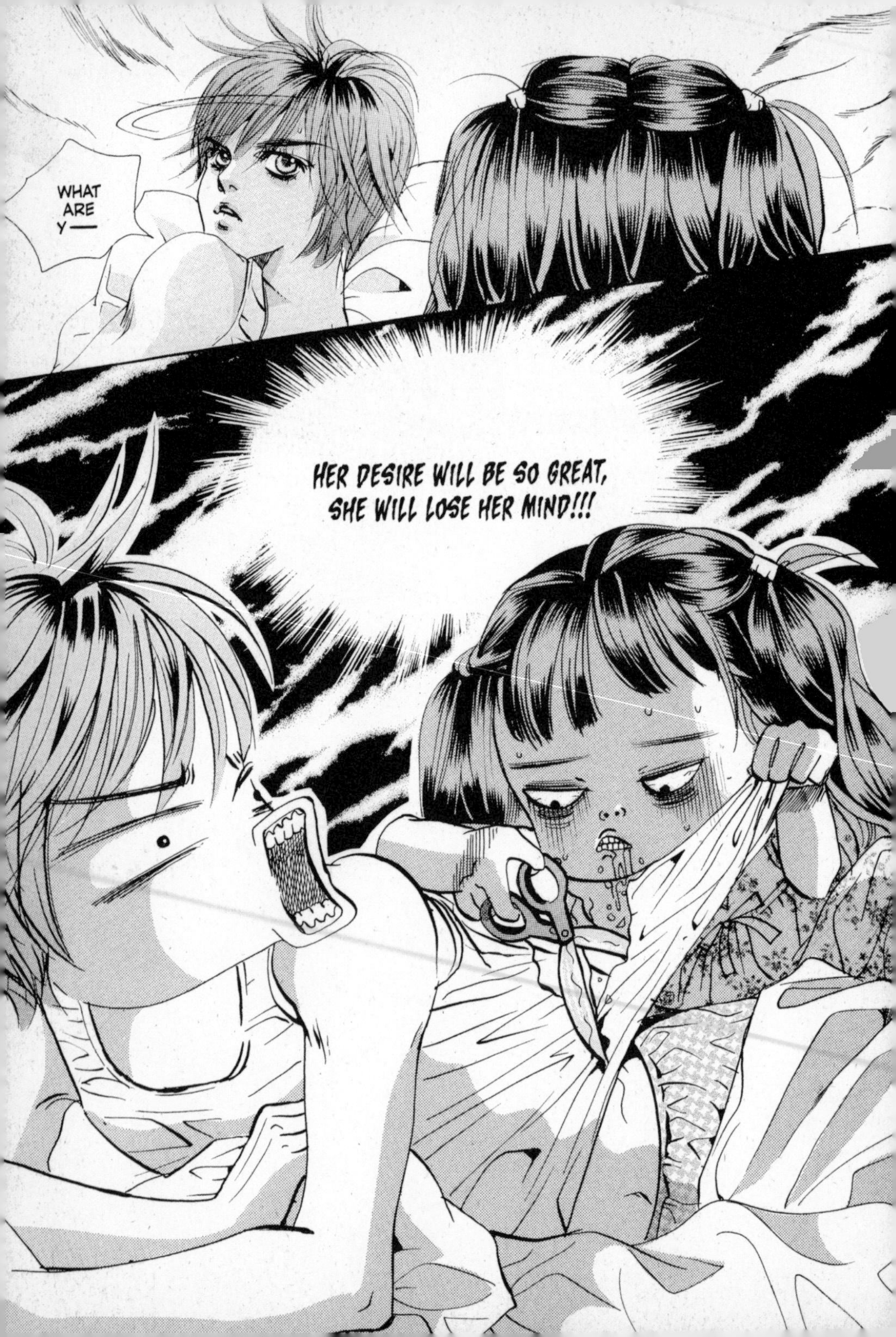
WHAT ARE Y—
HER DESIRE WILL BE SO GREAT, SHE WILL LOSE HER MIND!!!

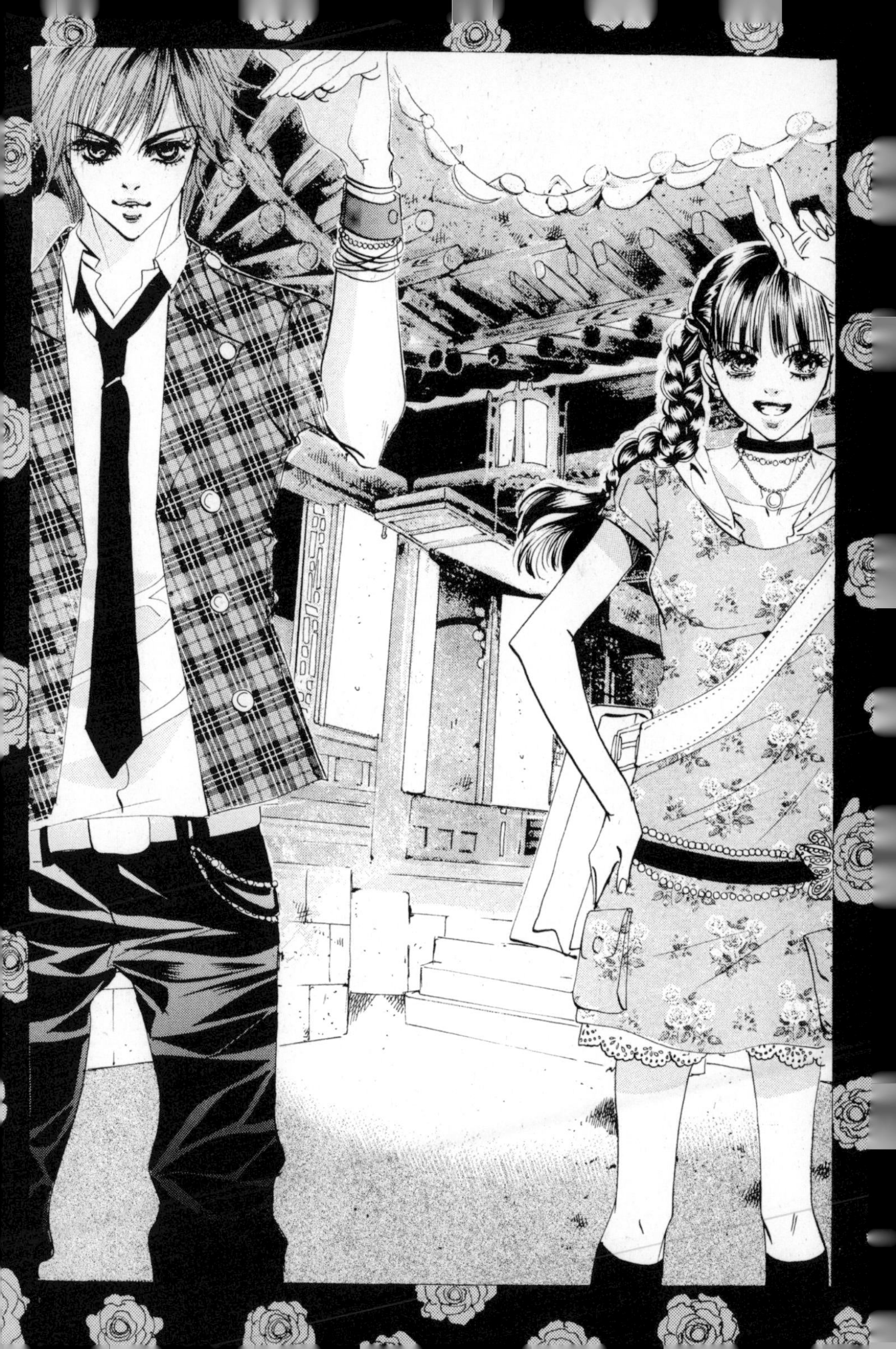

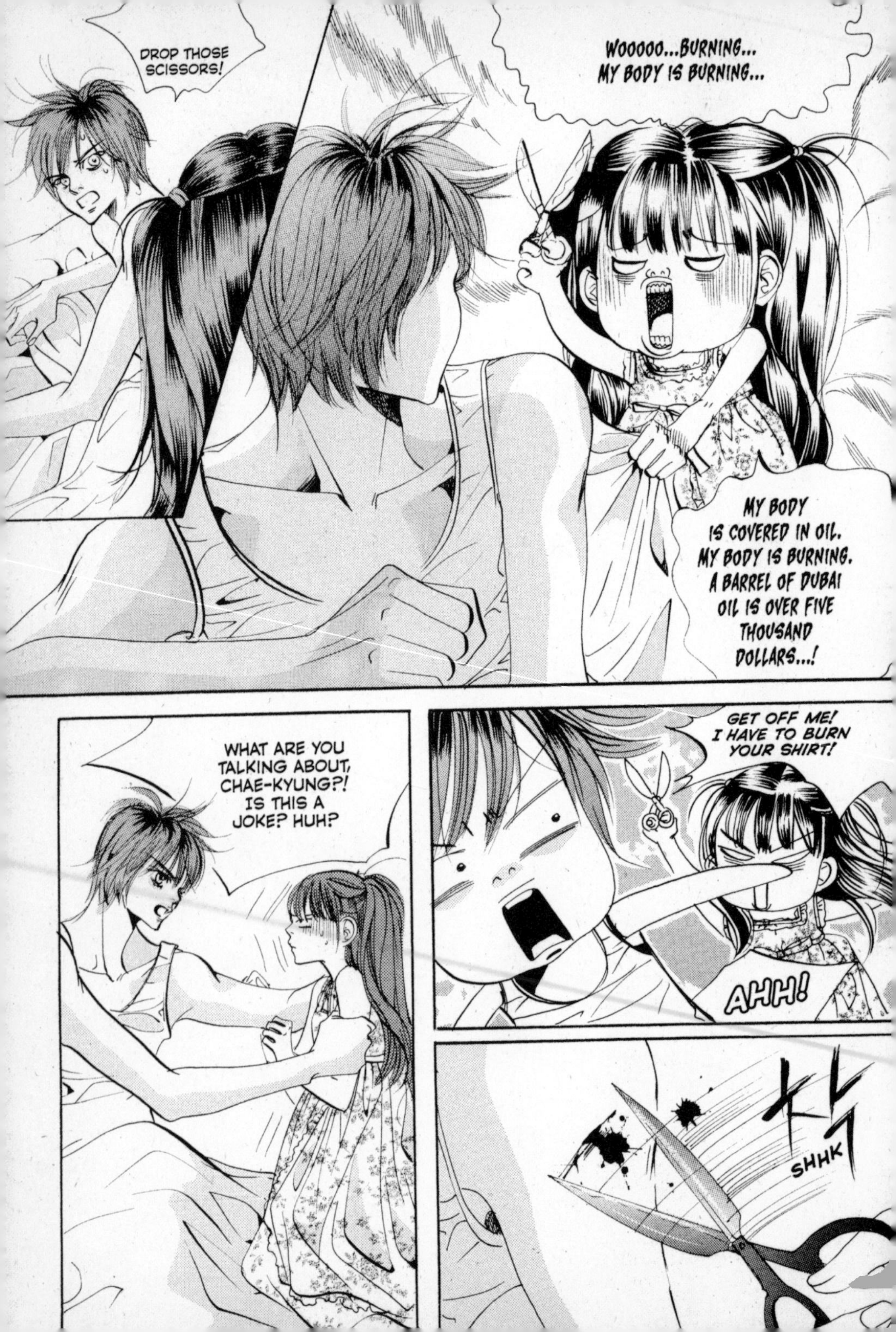
DROP THOSE SCISSORS!
WOOOOO...BURNING... MY BODY IS BURNING...
MY BODY IS COVERED IN OIL. MY BODY IS BURNING. A BARREL OF DUBAI OIL IS OVER FIVE THOUSAND DOLLARS...!
WHAT ARE YOU TALKING ABOUT, CHAE-KYUNG?! IS THIS A JOKE? HUH?
GET OFF ME! I HAVE TO BURN YOUR SHIRT!
AHH!
SHHK

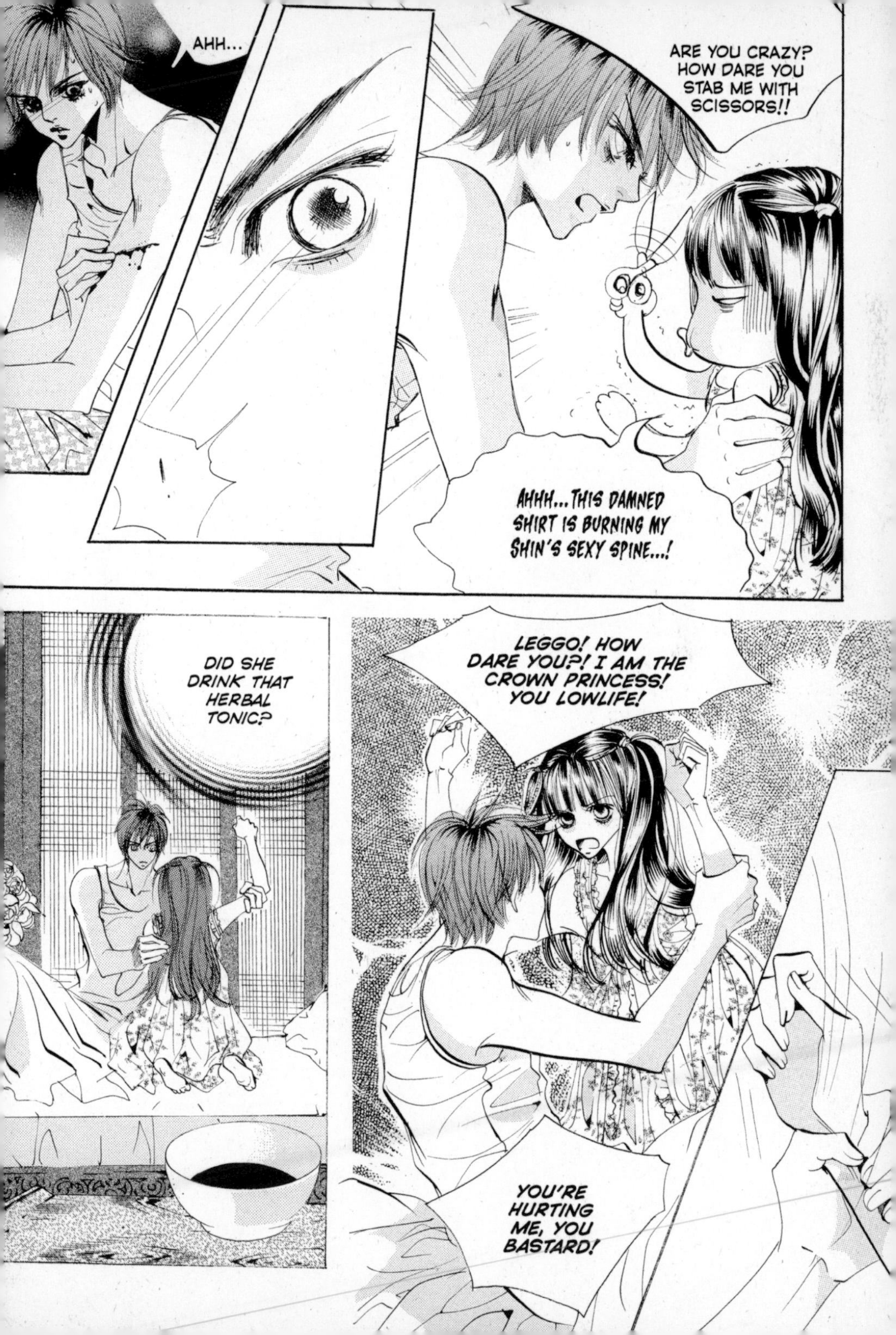
AHH...
ARE YOU CRAZY? HOW DARE YOU STAB ME WITH SCISSORS!!
AHHH...THIS DAMNED SHIRT IS BURNING MY SHIN'S SEXY SPINE...!
DID SHE DRINK THAT HERBAL TONIC?
LEGGO! HOW DARE YOU?! I AM THE CROWN PRINCESS! YOU LOWLIFE!
YOU'RE HURTING ME, YOU BASTARD!

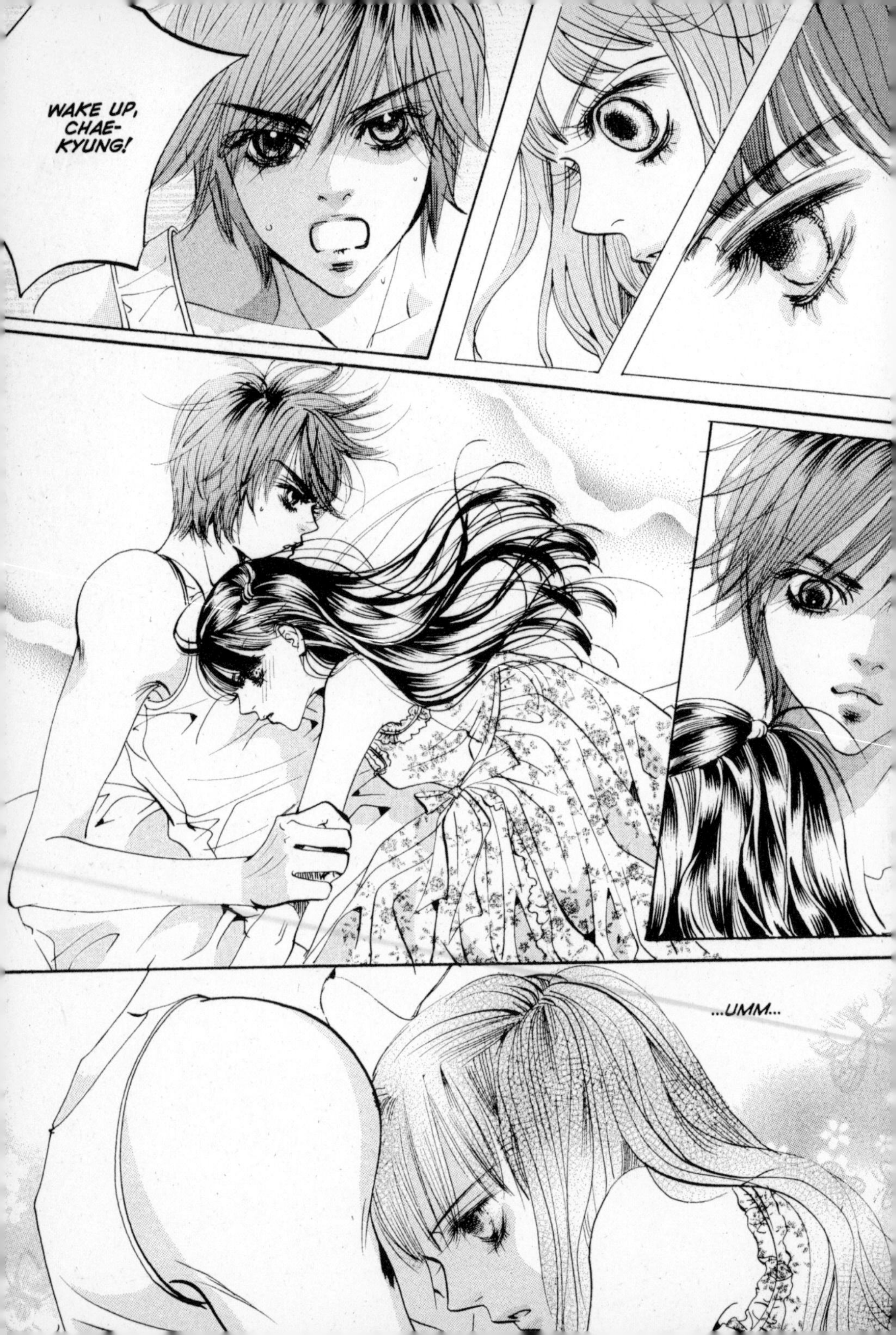
WAKE UP, CHAE-KYUNG!
...UMM...

HUH?

JERK! WHAT DID YOU DO?

YOU'RE THE ONE WHO JUMPED ME...66

BLOOOOOD!

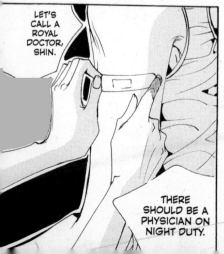

LET'S CALL A ROYAL DOCTOR, SHIN.

THERE SHOULD BE A PHYSICIAN ON NIGHT DUTY.

WE CAN'T. A DOCTOR WILL ASK HOW I GOT HURT, AND YOU'LL GET IN TROUBLE.

ST-STILL...

OH NO. I HURT THE CROWN PRINCE OF KOREA.....

YOU DID...

AHHHHH...

HEY!

SIDE EFFECT

OH, SORRY. THE TONIC IS STILL IN MY BODY.

MM-HMM.

OOOOOH...

LOOK AT THIS SPINE.

CHAE-KYUNG SHIN!!

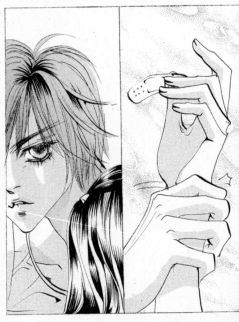

......

YOU...

...ARE LIKE THE LAST PIECE OF A PUZZLE.

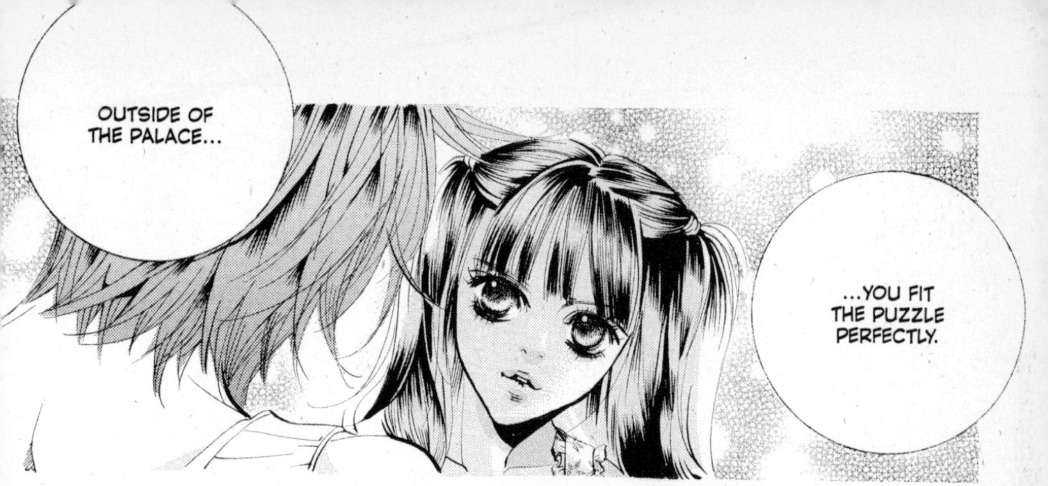
OUTSIDE OF THE PALACE...
...YOU FIT THE PUZZLE PERFECTLY.
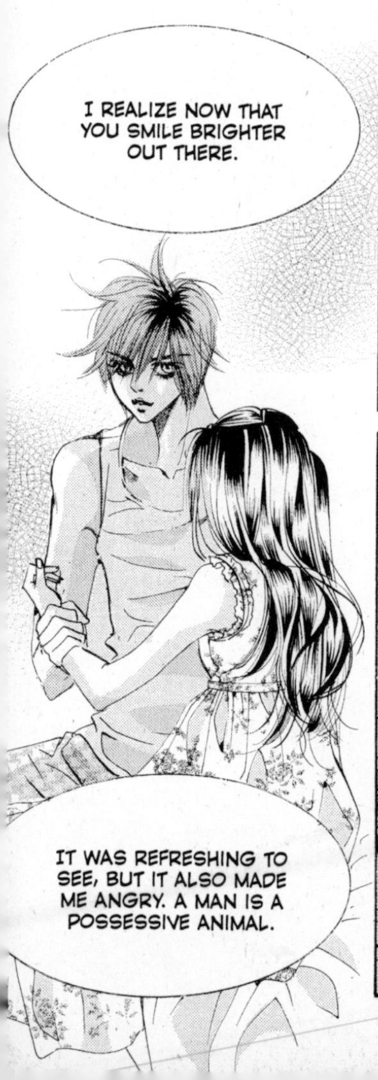
I REALIZE NOW THAT YOU SMILE BRIGHTER OUT THERE.
IT WAS REFRESHING TO SEE, BUT IT ALSO MADE ME ANGRY. A MAN IS A POSSESSIVE ANIMAL.
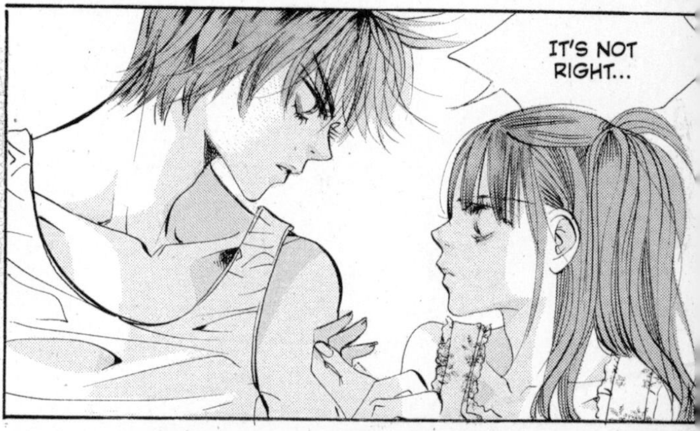
IT'S NOT RIGHT...
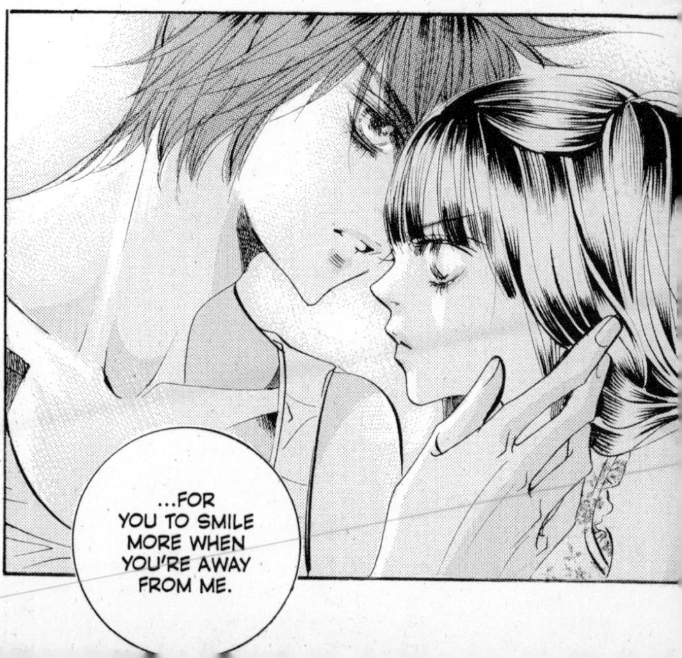
...FOR YOU TO SMILE MORE WHEN YOU'RE AWAY FROM ME.

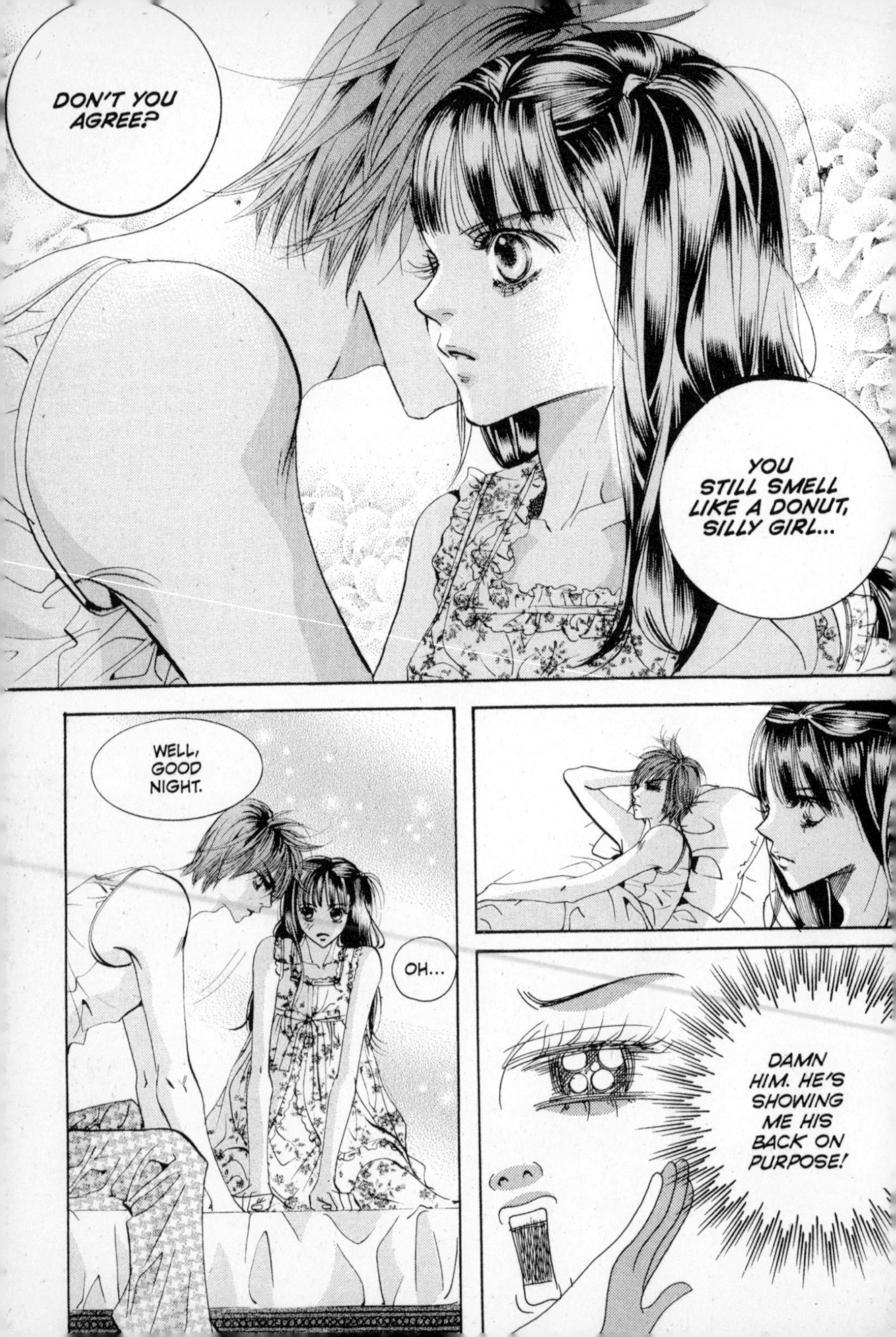
DON'T YOU AGREE?
YOU STILL SMELL LIKE A DONUT, SILLY GIRL...
WELL, GOOD NIGHT.
OH...
DAMN HIM. HE'S SHOWING ME HIS BACK ON PURPOSE!

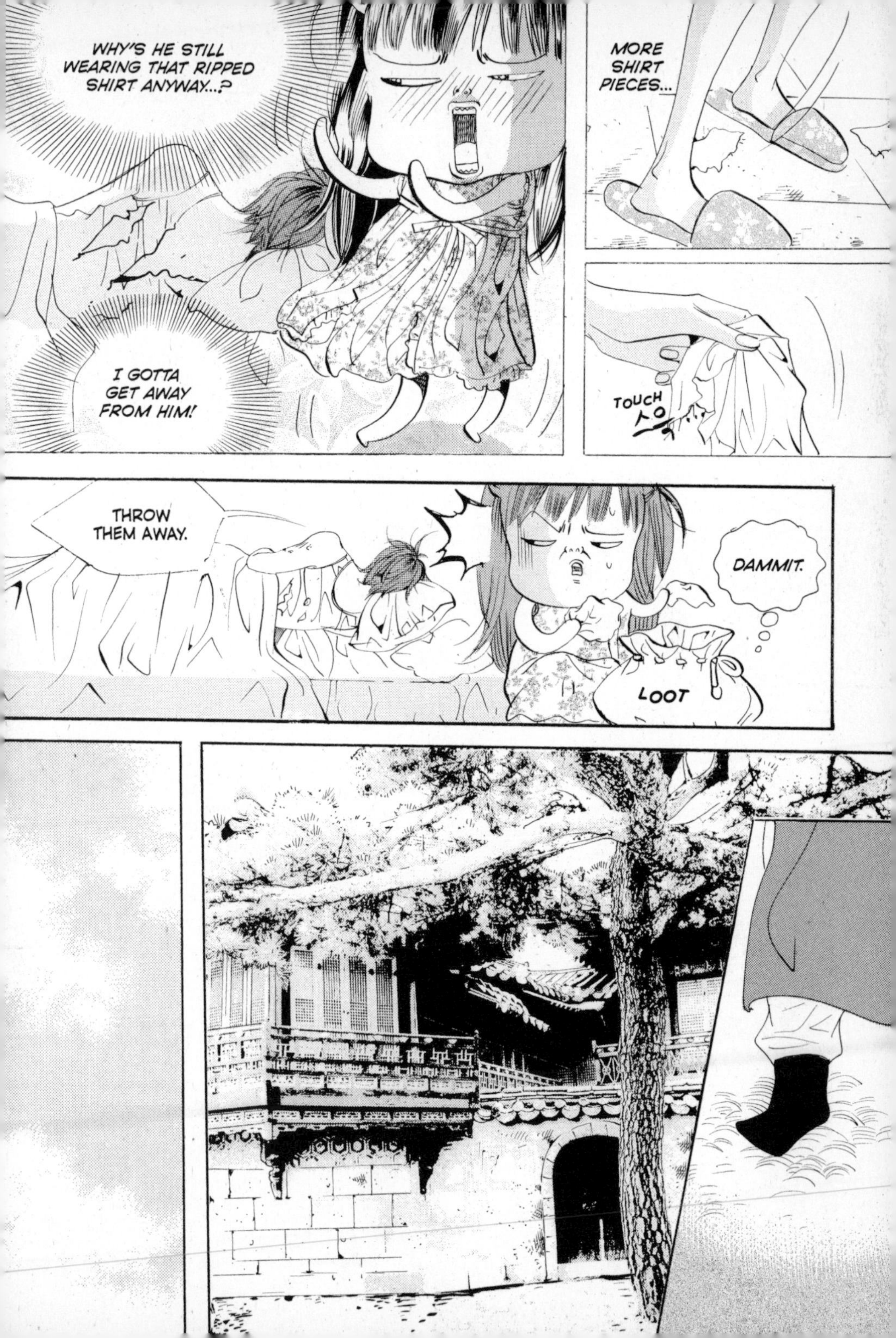
WHY'S HE STILL WEARING THAT RIPPED SHIRT ANYWAY...?
I GOTTA GET AWAY FROM HIM!
MORE SHIRT PIECES...
TOUCH
스윽
THROW THEM AWAY.
DAMMIT.
LOOT

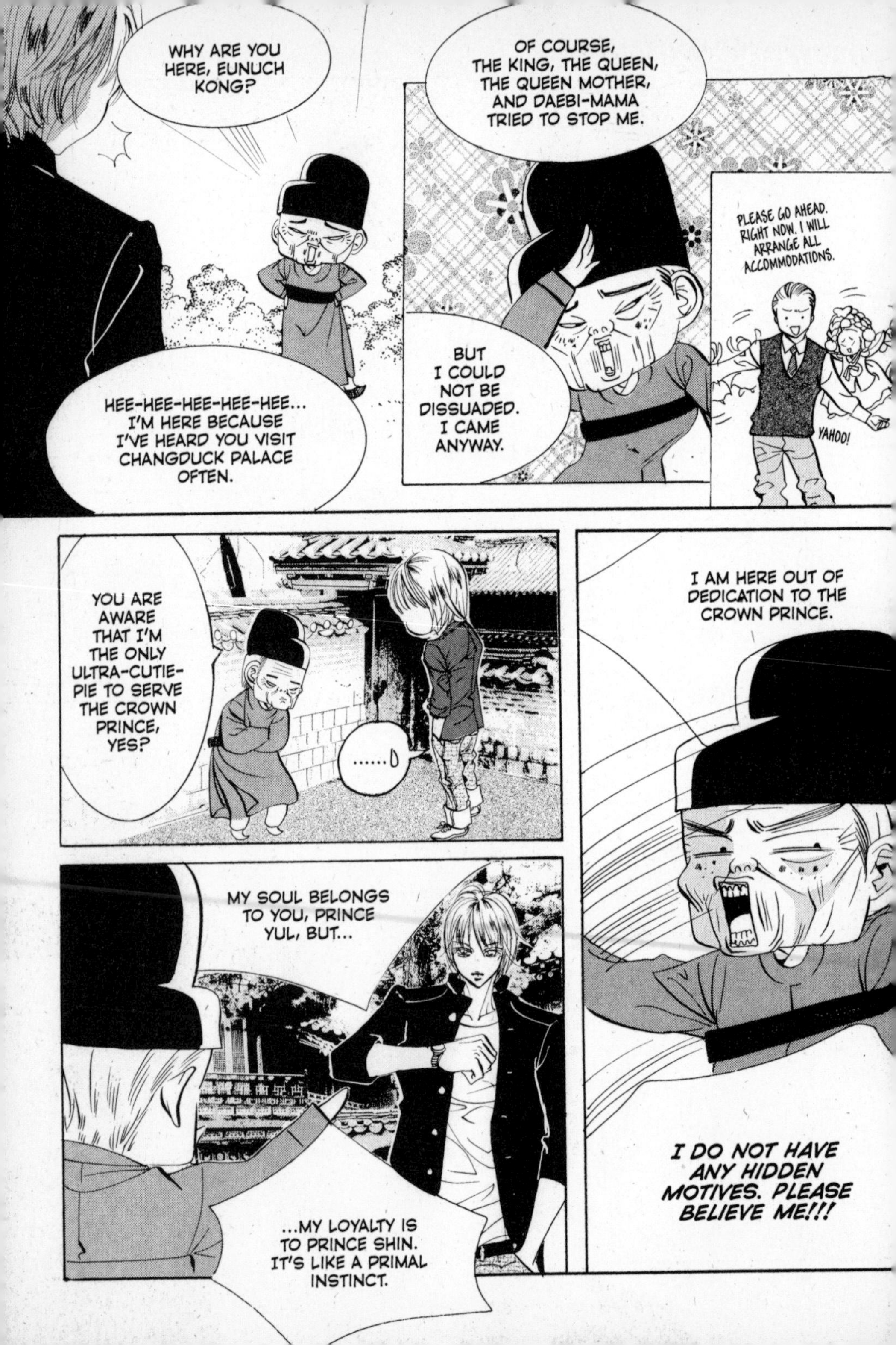
WHY ARE YOU HERE, EUNUCH KONG?
HEE-HEE-HEE-HEE-HEE... I'M HERE BECAUSE I'VE HEARD YOU VISIT CHANGDUCK PALACE OFTEN.
OF COURSE, THE KING, THE QUEEN, THE QUEEN MOTHER, AND DAEBI-MAMA TRIED TO STOP ME.
BUT I COULD NOT BE DISSUADED. I CAME ANYWAY.
PLEASE GO AHEAD. RIGHT NOW. I WILL ARRANGE ALL ACCOMMODATIONS.
YAHOO!
YOU ARE AWARE THAT I'M THE ONLY ULTRA-CUTIE-PIE TO SERVE THE CROWN PRINCE, YES?
......
MY SOUL BELONGS TO YOU, PRINCE YUL, BUT...
...MY LOYALTY IS TO PRINCE SHIN. IT'S LIKE A PRIMAL INSTINCT.
I AM HERE OUT OF DEDICATION TO THE CROWN PRINCE.
I DO NOT HAVE ANY HIDDEN MOTIVES. PLEASE BELIEVE ME!!!

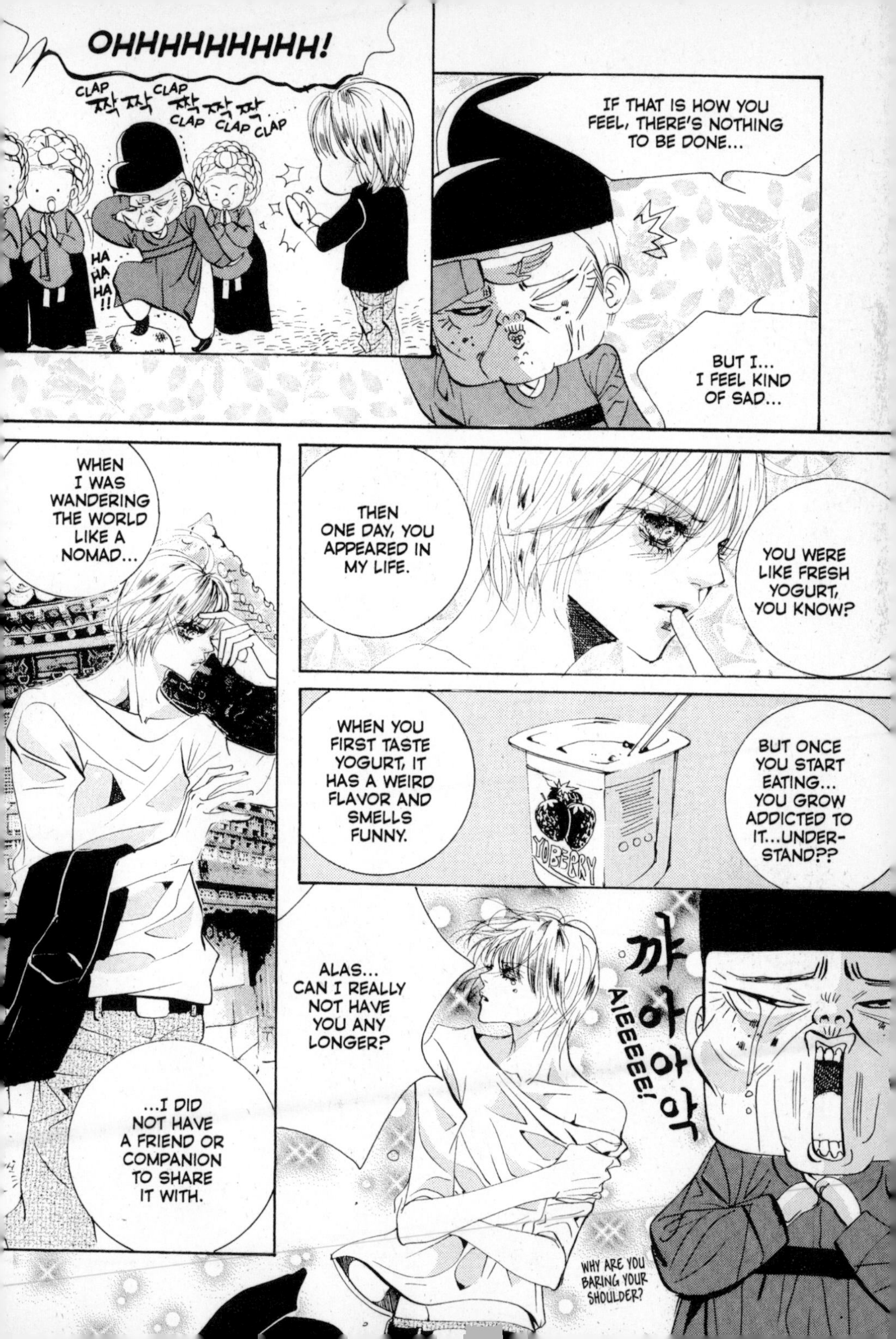
OHHHHHHHHH!
CLAP 짝짝 CLAP
짝짝짝 CLAP CLAP CLAP
HA HA HA!!
IF THAT IS HOW YOU FEEL, THERE'S NOTHING TO BE DONE...
BUT I... I FEEL KIND OF SAD...
WHEN I WAS WANDERING THE WORLD LIKE A NOMAD...
...I DID NOT HAVE A FRIEND OR COMPANION TO SHARE IT WITH.
THEN ONE DAY, YOU APPEARED IN MY LIFE.
YOU WERE LIKE FRESH YOGURT, YOU KNOW?
WHEN YOU FIRST TASTE YOGURT, IT HAS A WEIRD FLAVOR AND SMELLS FUNNY.
YOBERRY
BUT ONCE YOU START EATING... YOU GROW ADDICTED TO IT...UNDER-STAND??
ALAS... CAN I REALLY NOT HAVE YOU ANY LONGER?
꺄아아악
AIEEEEEE!
WHY ARE YOU BARING YOUR SHOULDER?

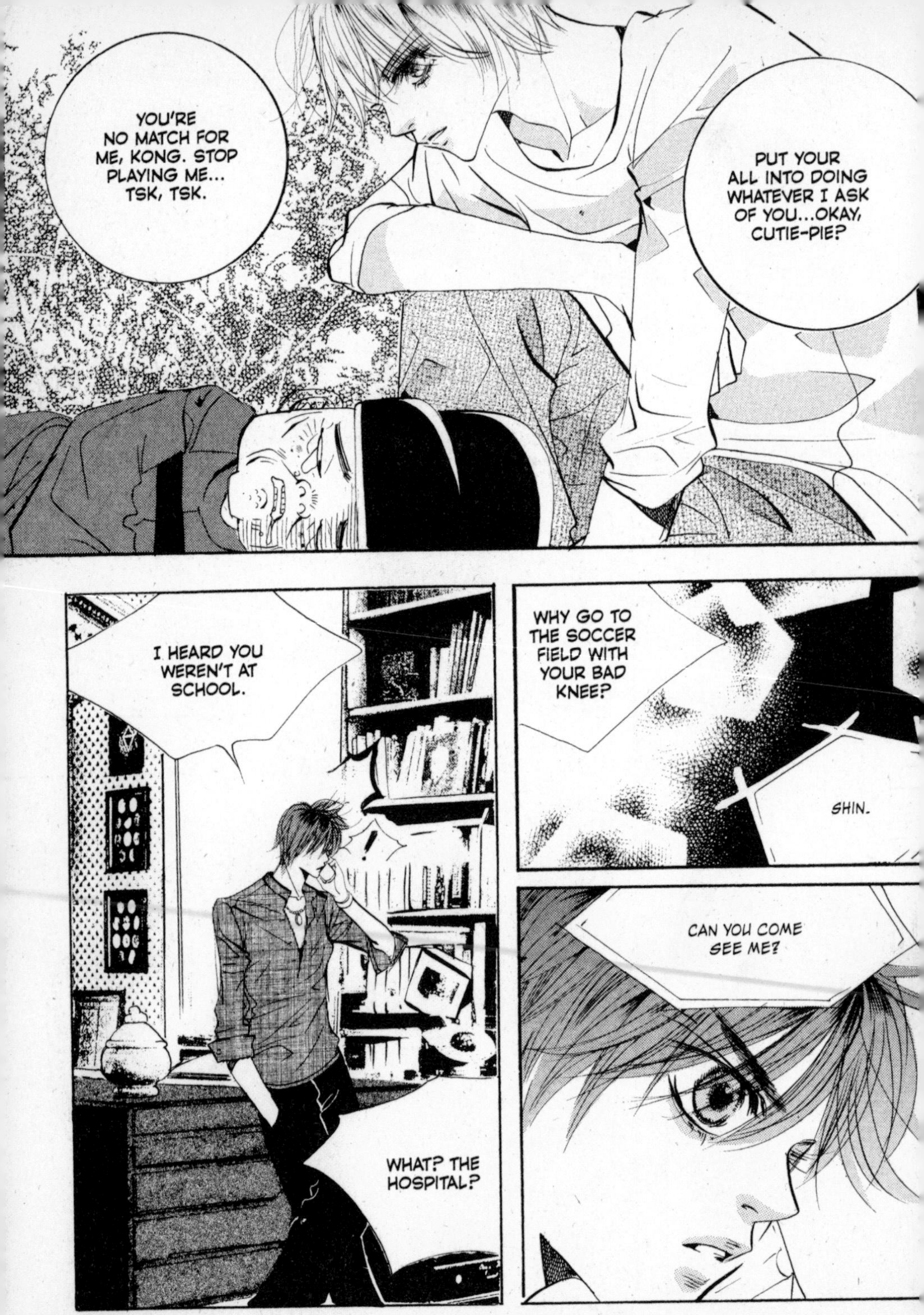

YOU'RE NO MATCH FOR ME, KONG. STOP PLAYING ME... TSK, TSK.
PUT YOUR ALL INTO DOING WHATEVER I ASK OF YOU...OKAY, CUTIE-PIE?
I HEARD YOU WEREN'T AT SCHOOL.
!
WHAT? THE HOSPITAL?
WHY GO TO THE SOCCER FIELD WITH YOUR BAD KNEE?
SHIN.
CAN YOU COME SEE ME?

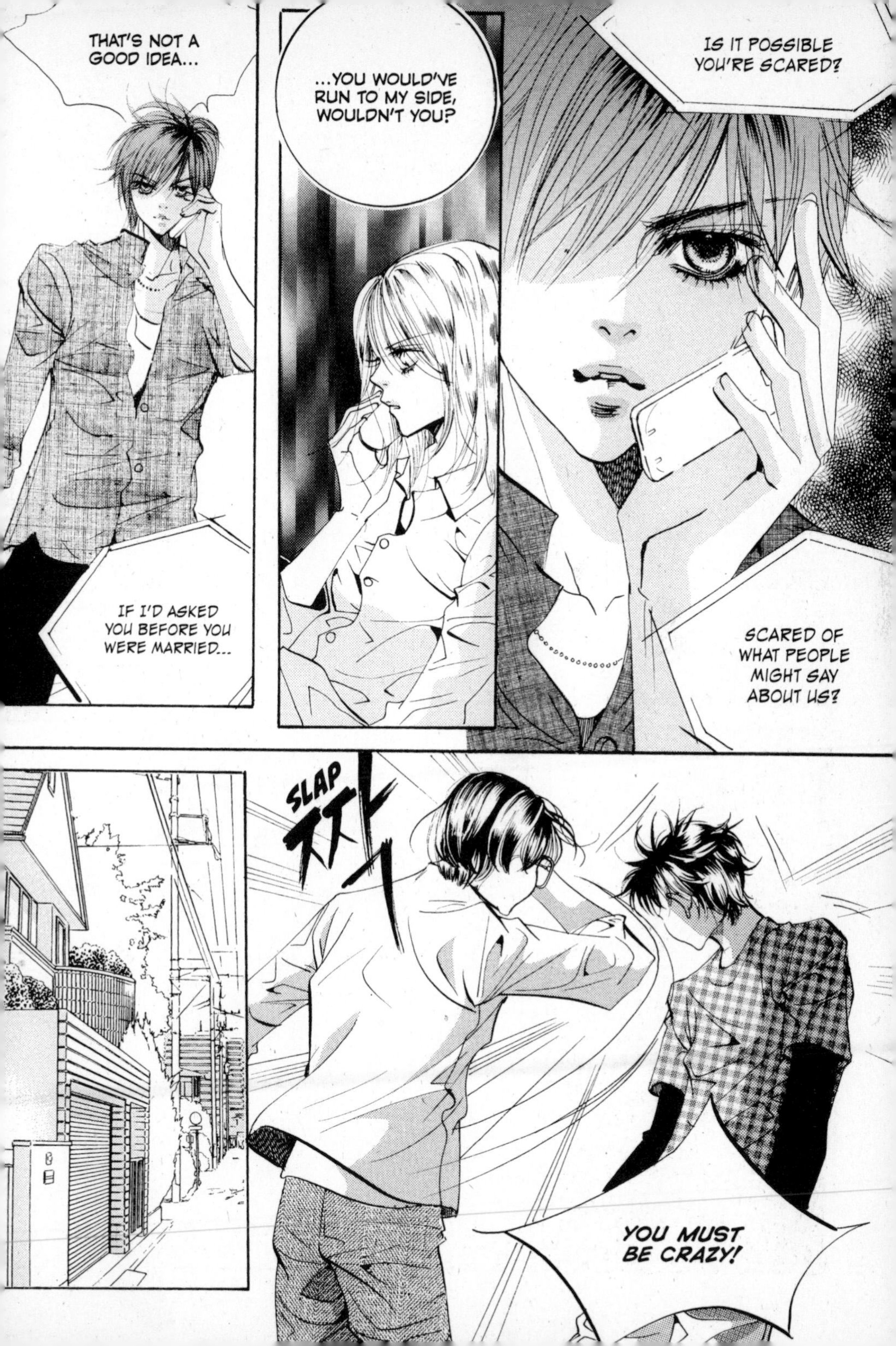
THAT'S NOT A GOOD IDEA...
IF I'D ASKED YOU BEFORE YOU WERE MARRIED...
...YOU WOULD'VE RUN TO MY SIDE, WOULDN'T YOU?
IS IT POSSIBLE YOU'RE SCARED?
SCARED OF WHAT PEOPLE MIGHT SAY ABOUT US?
SLAP
YOU MUST BE CRAZY!

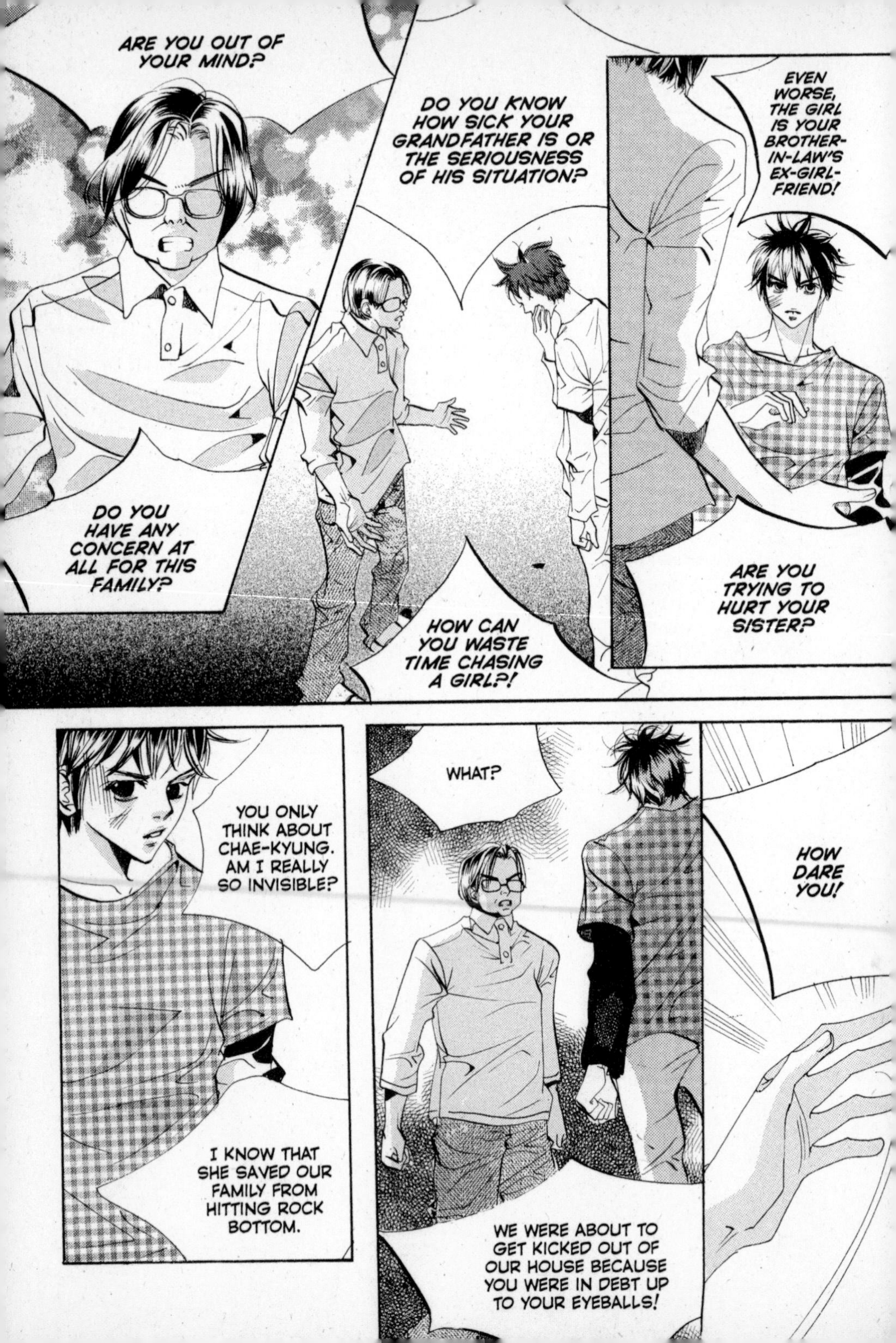
ARE YOU OUT OF YOUR MIND?
DO YOU HAVE ANY CONCERN AT ALL FOR THIS FAMILY?
DO YOU KNOW HOW SICK YOUR GRANDFATHER IS OR THE SERIOUSNESS OF HIS SITUATION?
HOW CAN YOU WASTE TIME CHASING A GIRL?!
EVEN WORSE, THE GIRL IS YOUR BROTHER-IN-LAW'S EX-GIRL-FRIEND!
ARE YOU TRYING TO HURT YOUR SISTER?
YOU ONLY THINK ABOUT CHAE-KYUNG. AM I REALLY SO INVISIBLE?
I KNOW THAT SHE SAVED OUR FAMILY FROM HITTING ROCK BOTTOM.
WHAT?
WE WERE ABOUT TO GET KICKED OUT OF OUR HOUSE BECAUSE YOU WERE IN DEBT UP TO YOUR EYEBALLS!
HOW DARE YOU!

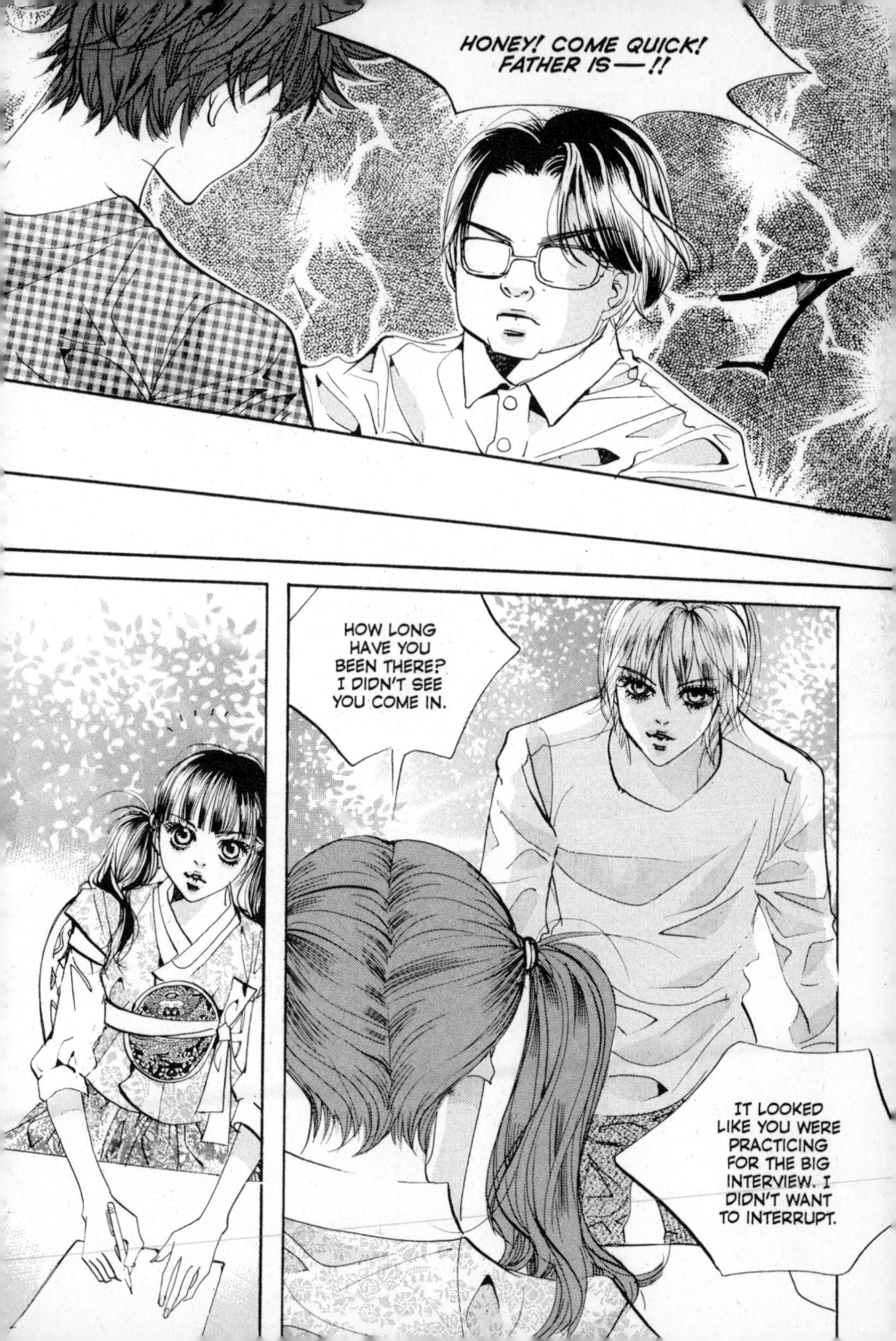
HONEY! COME QUICK! FATHER IS—!!
HOW LONG HAVE YOU BEEN THERE? I DIDN'T SEE YOU COME IN.
IT LOOKED LIKE YOU WERE PRACTICING FOR THE BIG INTERVIEW. I DIDN'T WANT TO INTERRUPT.

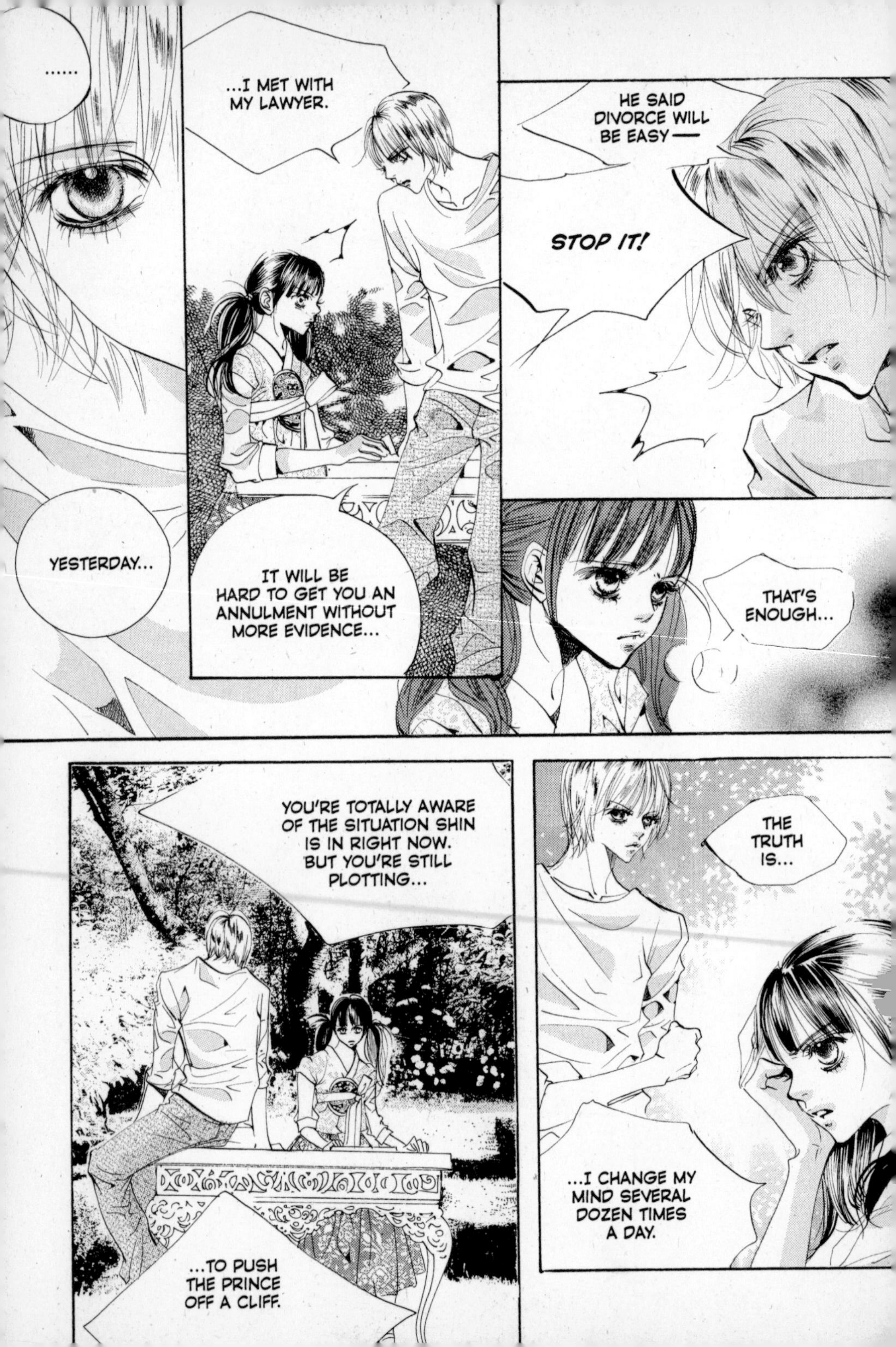
......
YESTERDAY...
...I MET WITH MY LAWYER.
IT WILL BE HARD TO GET YOU AN ANNULMENT WITHOUT MORE EVIDENCE...
HE SAID DIVORCE WILL BE EASY—
STOP IT!
THAT'S ENOUGH...
YOU'RE TOTALLY AWARE OF THE SITUATION SHIN IS IN RIGHT NOW. BUT YOU'RE STILL PLOTTING...
...TO PUSH THE PRINCE OFF A CLIFF.
THE TRUTH IS...
...I CHANGE MY MIND SEVERAL DOZEN TIMES A DAY.

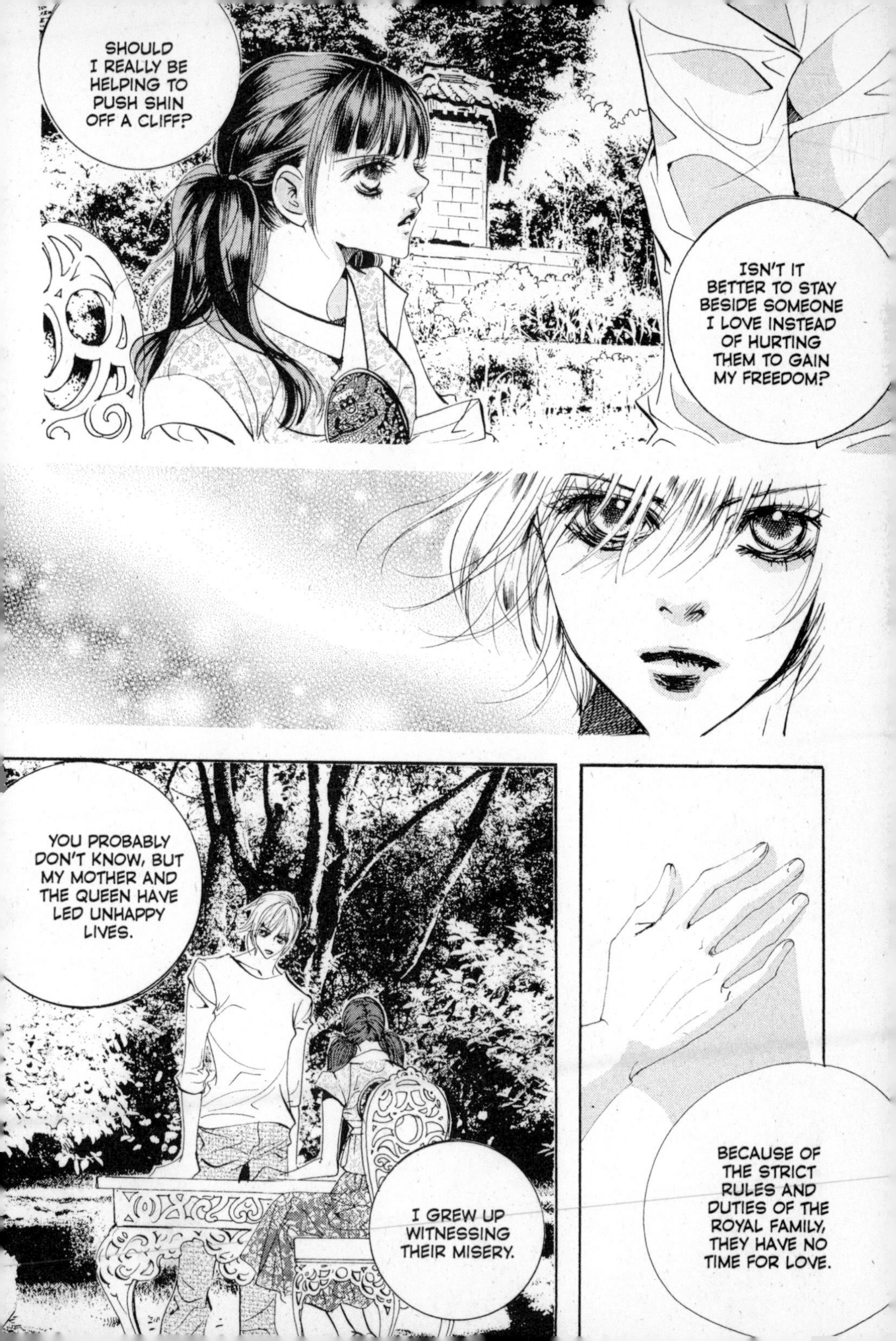
SHOULD I REALLY BE HELPING TO PUSH SHIN OFF A CLIFF?
ISN'T IT BETTER TO STAY BESIDE SOMEONE I LOVE INSTEAD OF HURTING THEM TO GAIN MY FREEDOM?
YOU PROBABLY DON'T KNOW, BUT MY MOTHER AND THE QUEEN HAVE LED UNHAPPY LIVES.
I GREW UP WITNESSING THEIR MISERY.
BECAUSE OF THE STRICT RULES AND DUTIES OF THE ROYAL FAMILY, THEY HAVE NO TIME FOR LOVE.

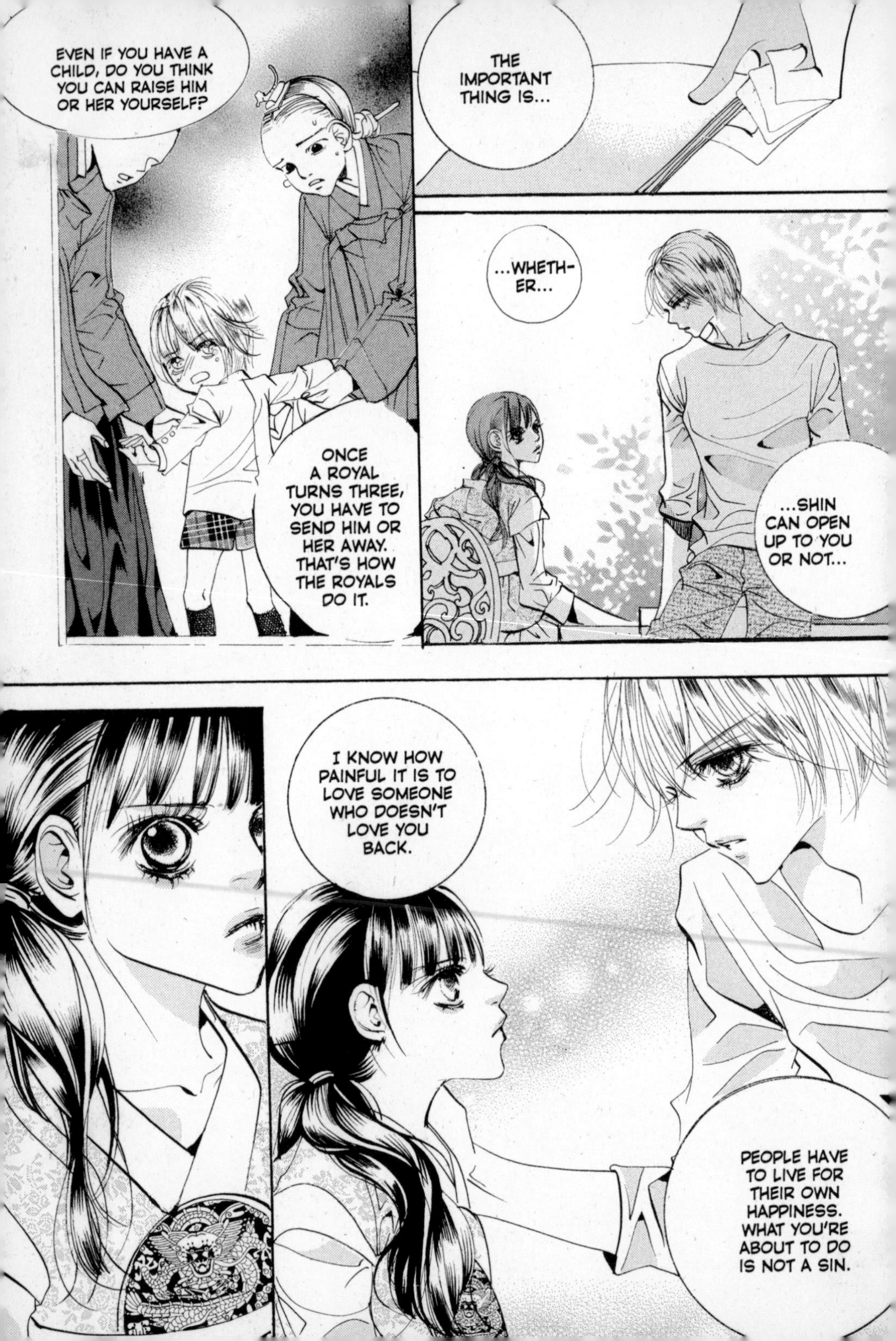
EVEN IF YOU HAVE A CHILD, DO YOU THINK YOU CAN RAISE HIM OR HER YOURSELF?
ONCE A ROYAL TURNS THREE, YOU HAVE TO SEND HIM OR HER AWAY. THAT'S HOW THE ROYALS DO IT.
THE IMPORTANT THING IS...
...WHETH-ER...
...SHIN CAN OPEN UP TO YOU OR NOT...
I KNOW HOW PAINFUL IT IS TO LOVE SOMEONE WHO DOESN'T LOVE YOU BACK.
PEOPLE HAVE TO LIVE FOR THEIR OWN HAPPINESS. WHAT YOU'RE ABOUT TO DO IS NOT A SIN.

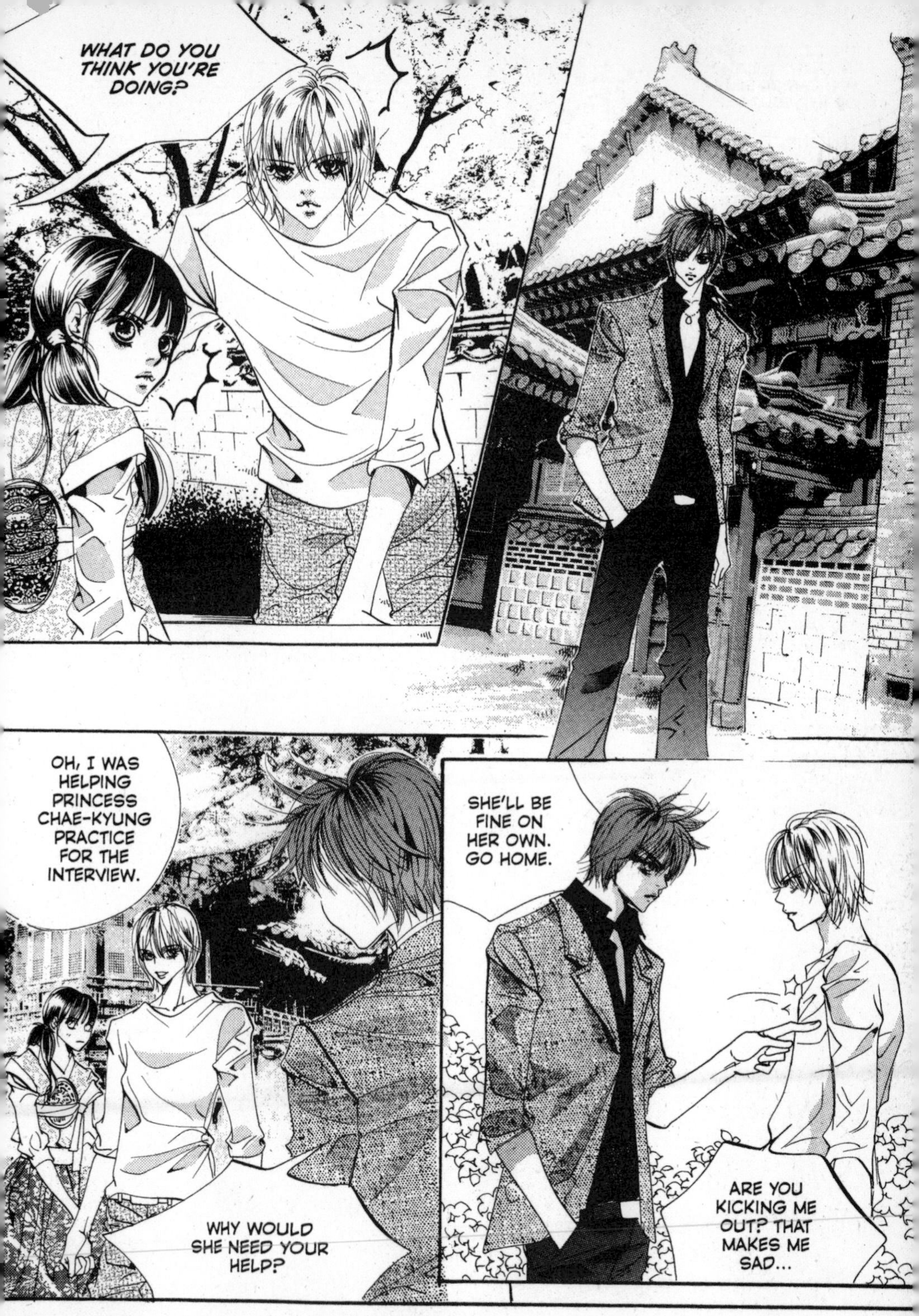
WHAT DO YOU THINK YOU'RE DOING?
OH, I WAS HELPING PRINCESS CHAE-KYUNG PRACTICE FOR THE INTERVIEW.
WHY WOULD SHE NEED YOUR HELP?
SHE'LL BE FINE ON HER OWN. GO HOME.
ARE YOU KICKING ME OUT? THAT MAKES ME SAD...

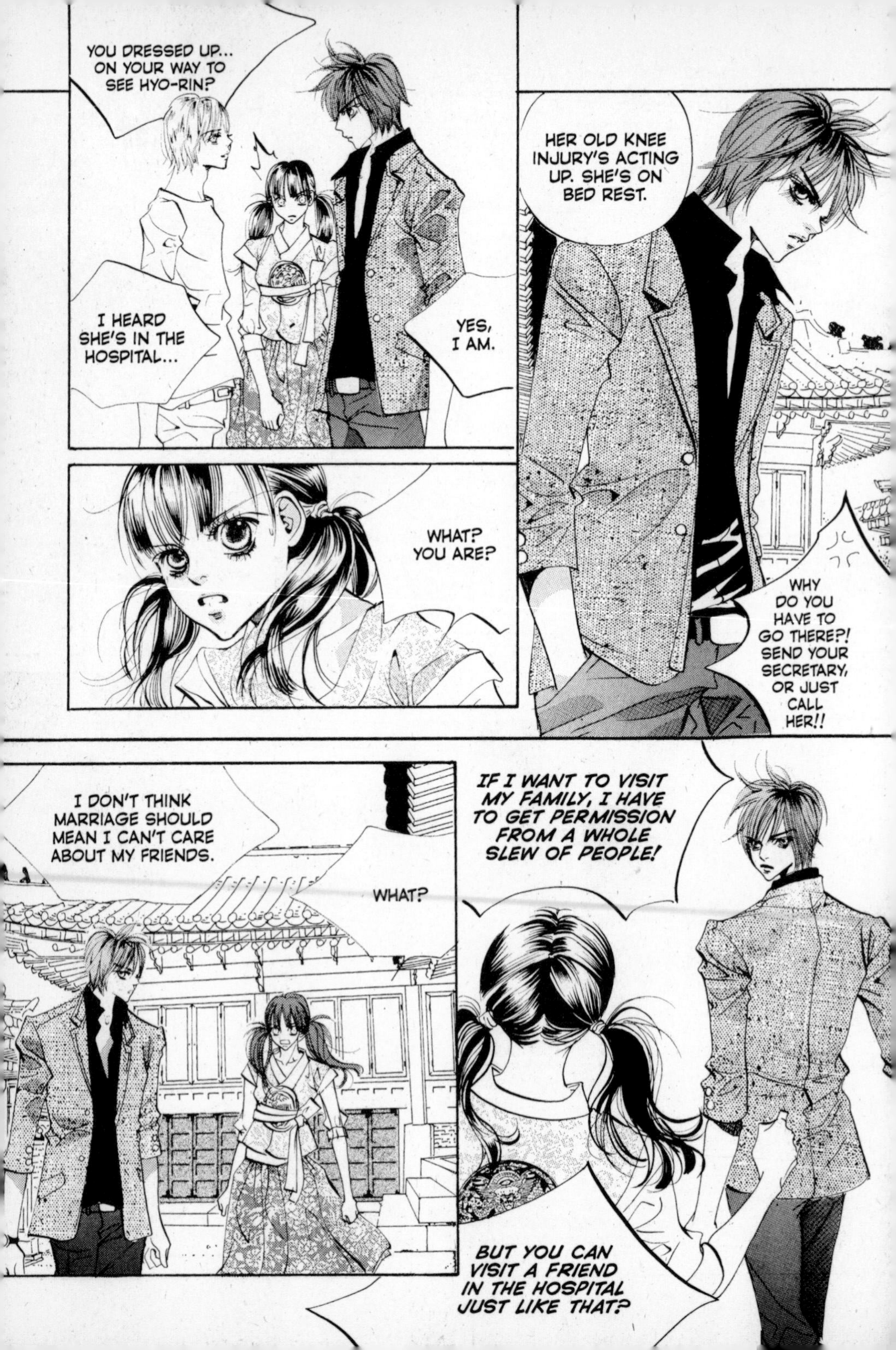
YOU DRESSED UP... ON YOUR WAY TO SEE HYO-RIN?
I HEARD SHE'S IN THE HOSPITAL...
YES, I AM.
HER OLD KNEE INJURY'S ACTING UP. SHE'S ON BED REST.
WHAT? YOU ARE?
WHY DO YOU HAVE TO GO THERE?! SEND YOUR SECRETARY, OR JUST CALL HER!!
I DON'T THINK MARRIAGE SHOULD MEAN I CAN'T CARE ABOUT MY FRIENDS.
WHAT?
IF I WANT TO VISIT MY FAMILY, I HAVE TO GET PERMISSION FROM A WHOLE SLEW OF PEOPLE!
BUT YOU CAN VISIT A FRIEND IN THE HOSPITAL JUST LIKE THAT?

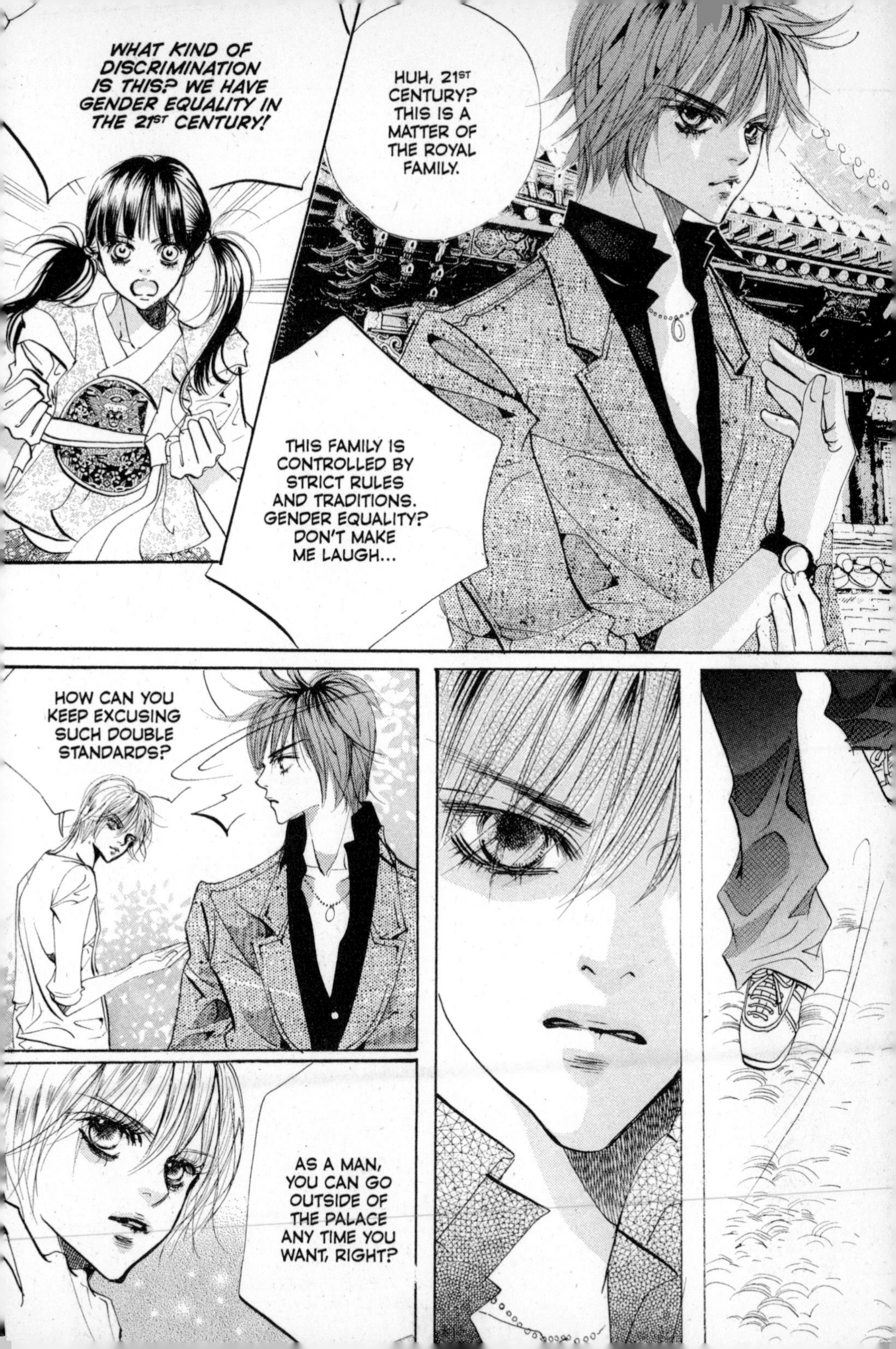
WHAT KIND OF DISCRIMINATION IS THIS? WE HAVE GENDER EQUALITY IN THE 21ST CENTURY!
HUH, 21ST CENTURY? THIS IS A MATTER OF THE ROYAL FAMILY.
THIS FAMILY IS CONTROLLED BY STRICT RULES AND TRADITIONS. GENDER EQUALITY? DON'T MAKE ME LAUGH...
HOW CAN YOU KEEP EXCUSING SUCH DOUBLE STANDARDS?
AS A MAN, YOU CAN GO OUTSIDE OF THE PALACE ANY TIME YOU WANT, RIGHT?

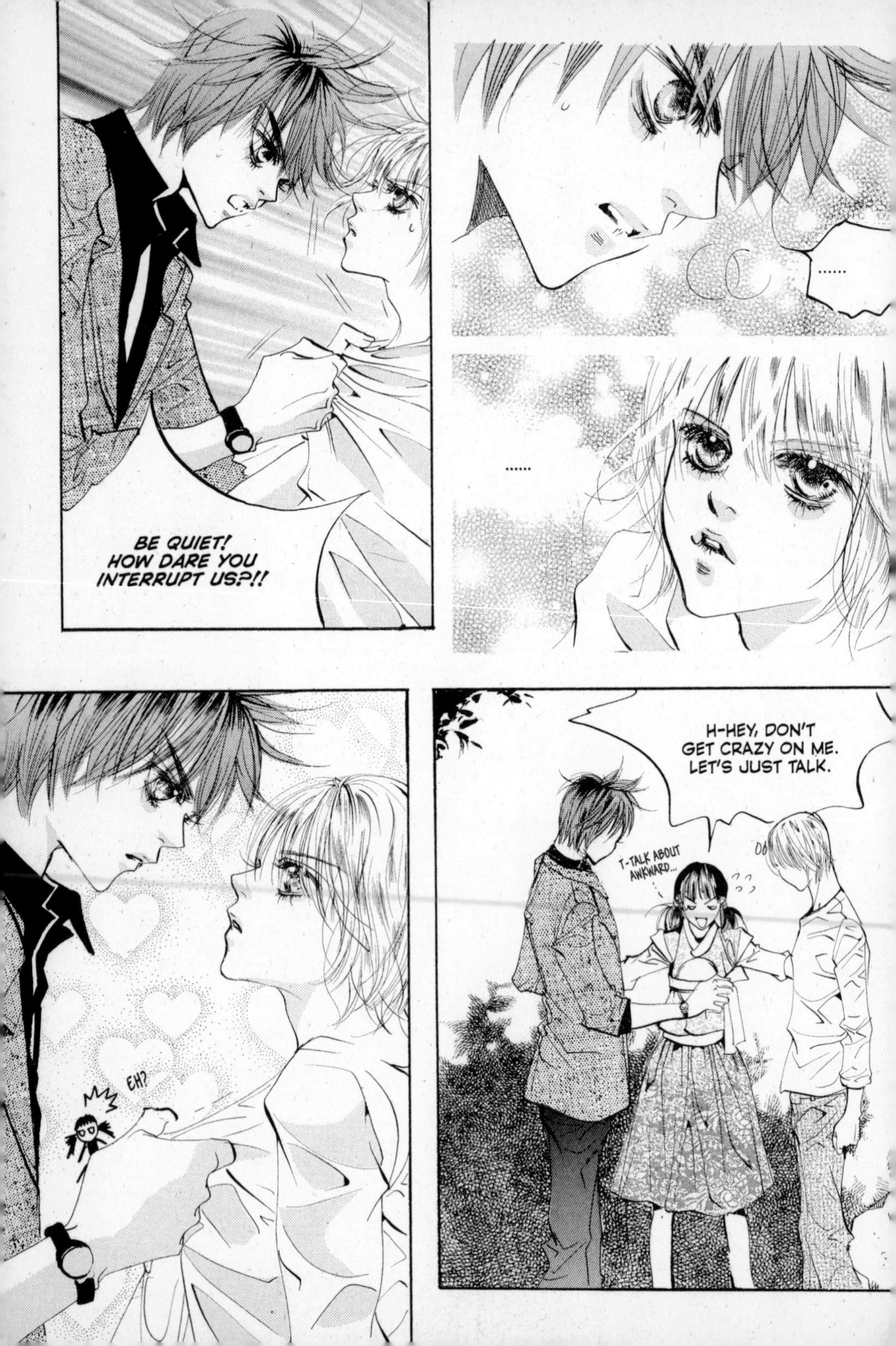
BE QUIET!
HOW DARE YOU
INTERRUPT US?!!
......
......
EH?
H-HEY, DON'T
GET CRAZY ON ME.
LET'S JUST TALK.
T-TALK ABOUT
AWKWARD...

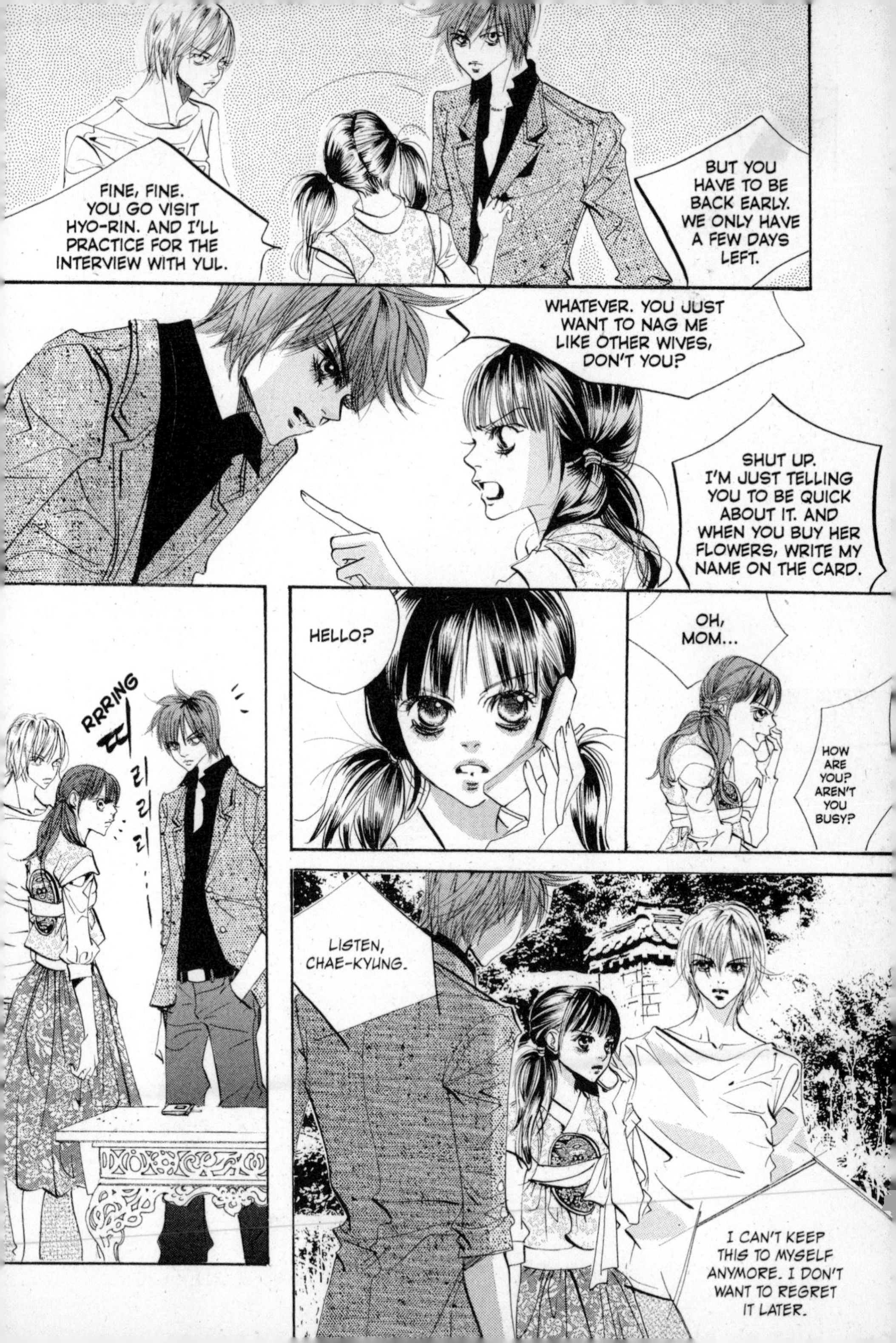
FINE, FINE. YOU GO VISIT HYO-RIN. AND I'LL PRACTICE FOR THE INTERVIEW WITH YUL.
BUT YOU HAVE TO BE BACK EARLY. WE ONLY HAVE A FEW DAYS LEFT.
WHATEVER. YOU JUST WANT TO NAG ME LIKE OTHER WIVES, DON'T YOU?
SHUT UP. I'M JUST TELLING YOU TO BE QUICK ABOUT IT. AND WHEN YOU BUY HER FLOWERS, WRITE MY NAME ON THE CARD.
RRRING
띠리리리...
HELLO?
OH, MOM...
HOW ARE YOU? AREN'T YOU BUSY?
LISTEN, CHAE-KYUNG.
I CAN'T KEEP THIS TO MYSELF ANYMORE. I DON'T WANT TO REGRET IT LATER.

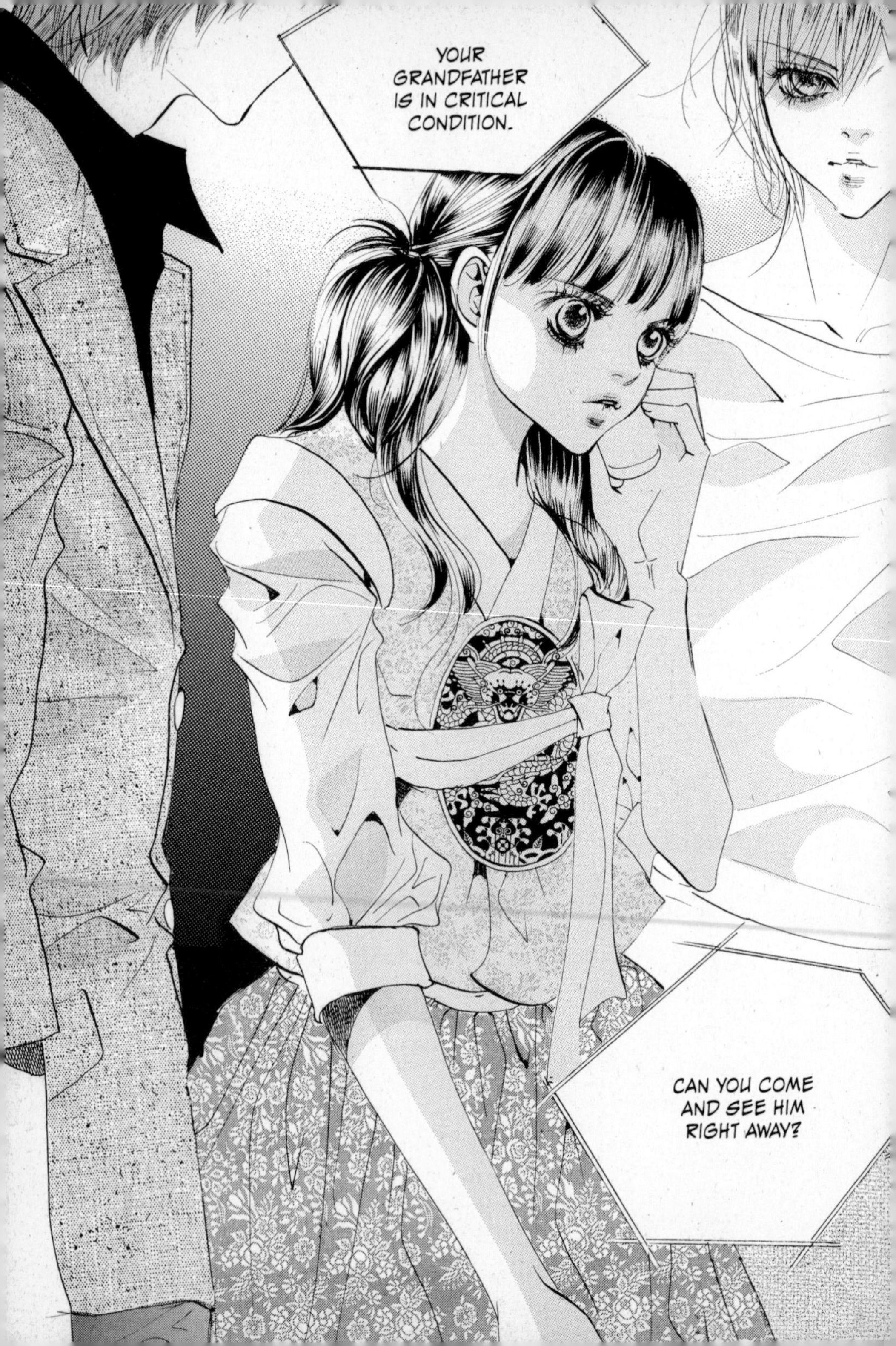
YOUR GRANDFATHER IS IN CRITICAL CONDITION.
CAN YOU COME AND SEE HIM RIGHT AWAY?

THE ROYAL PALACE
Goong

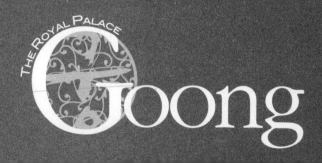

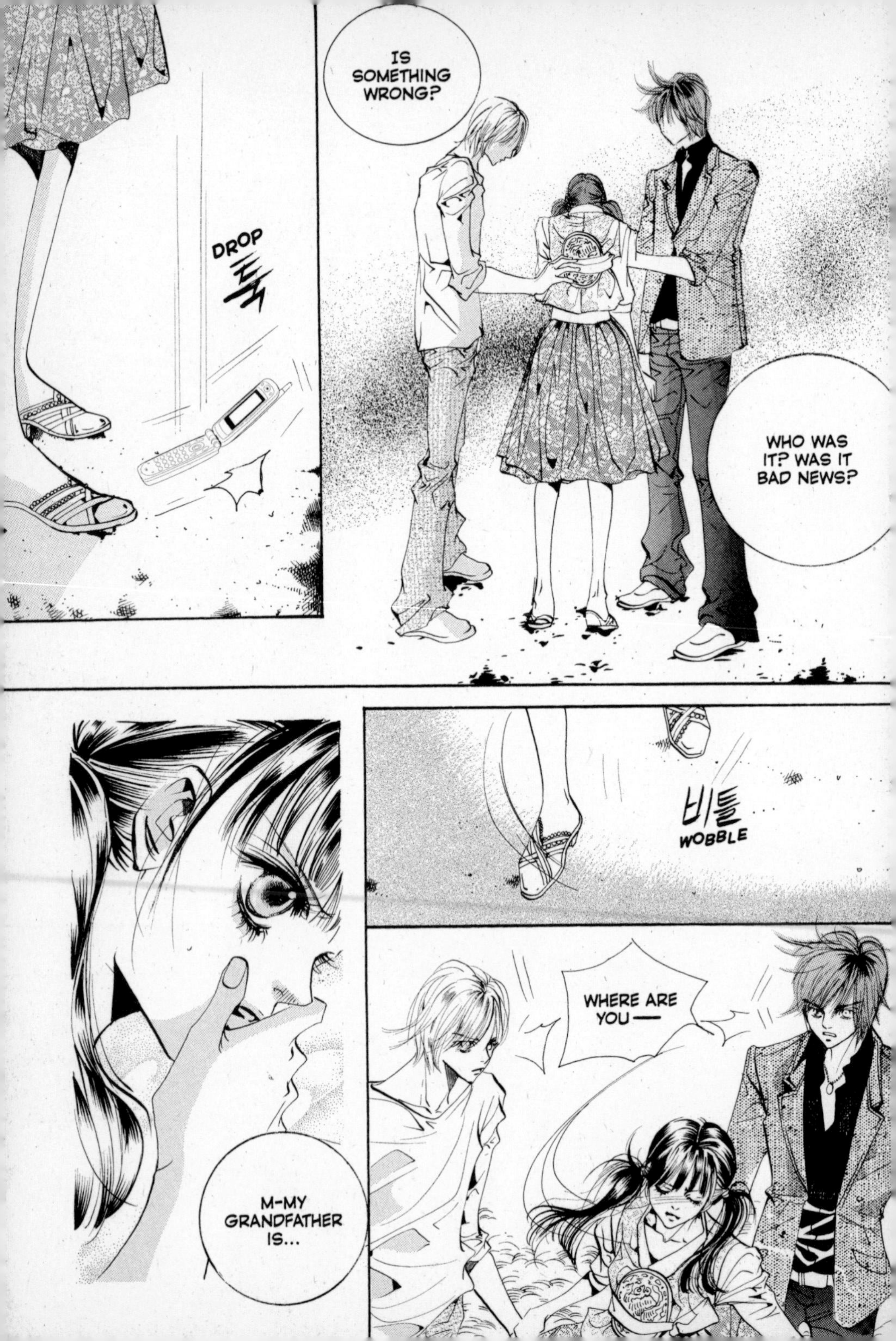
DROP
툭
IS SOMETHING WRONG?
WHO WAS IT? WAS IT BAD NEWS?
M-MY GRANDFATHER IS...
비틀
WOBBLE
WHERE ARE YOU—

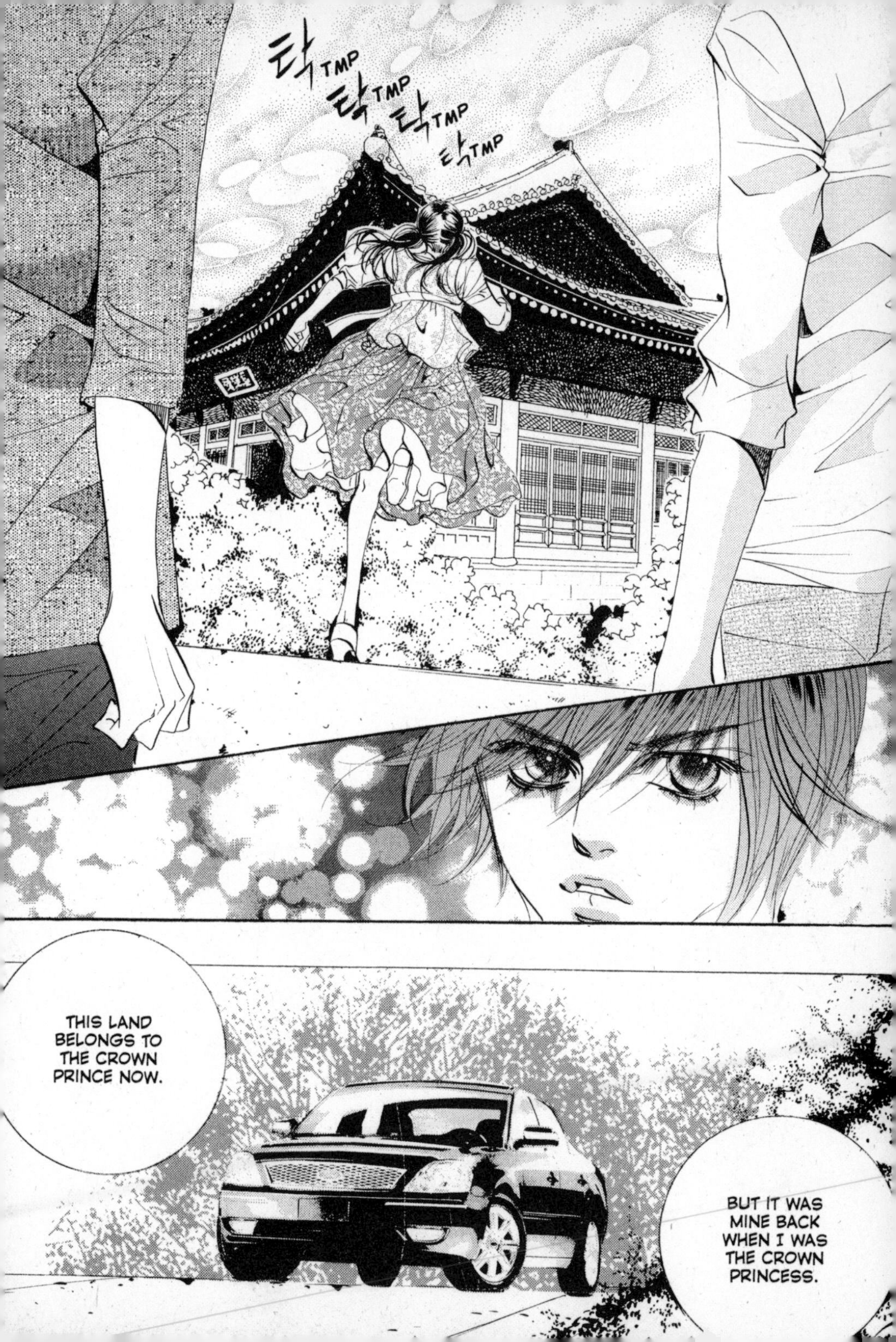

탁 TMP 탁 TMP 탁 TMP 탁 TMP
THIS LAND BELONGS TO THE CROWN PRINCE NOW.
BUT IT WAS MINE BACK WHEN I WAS THE CROWN PRINCESS.

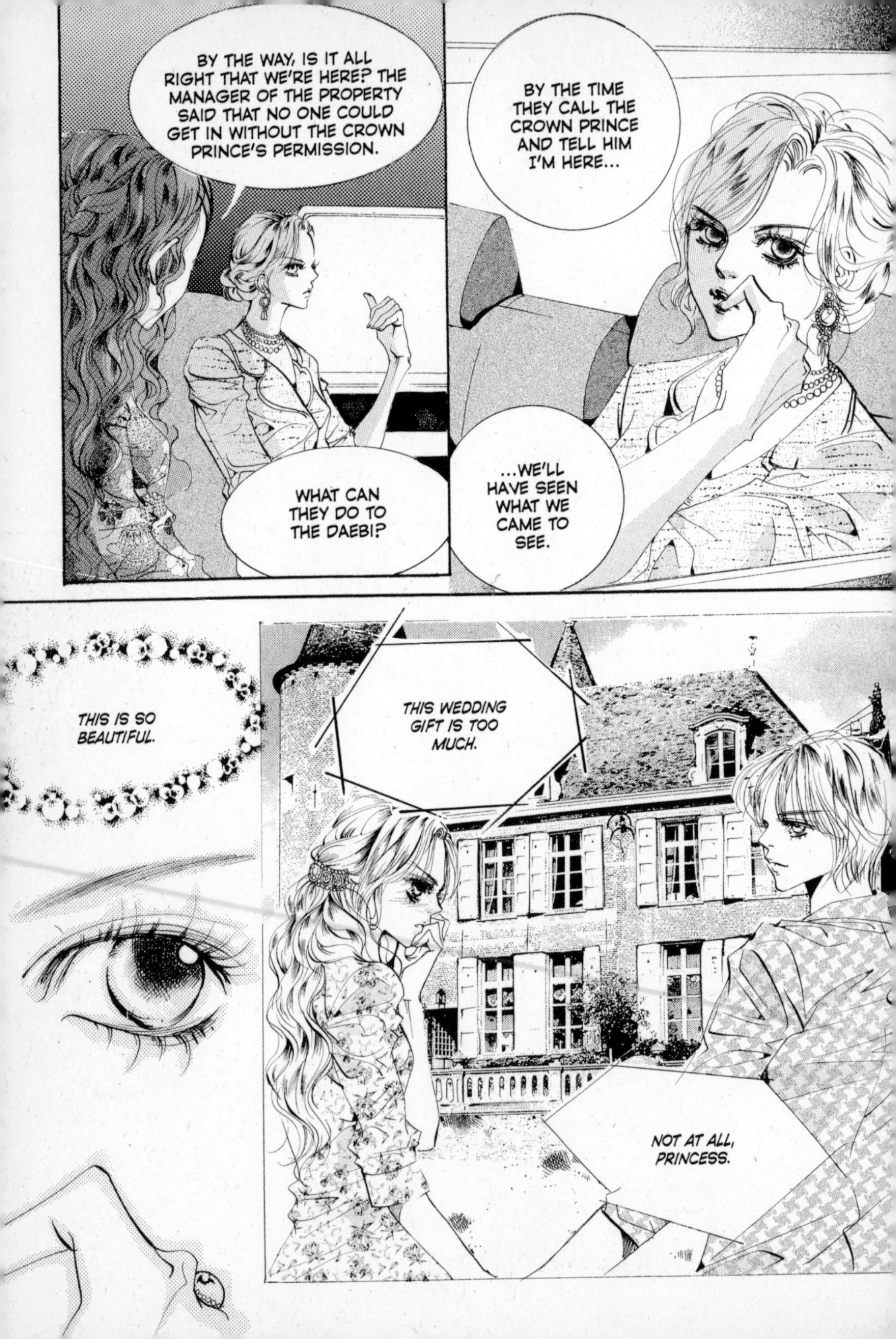
BY THE WAY, IS IT ALL RIGHT THAT WE'RE HERE? THE MANAGER OF THE PROPERTY SAID THAT NO ONE COULD GET IN WITHOUT THE CROWN PRINCE'S PERMISSION.
WHAT CAN THEY DO TO THE DAEBI?
BY THE TIME THEY CALL THE CROWN PRINCE AND TELL HIM I'M HERE...
...WE'LL HAVE SEEN WHAT WE CAME TO SEE.
THIS IS SO BEAUTIFUL.
THIS WEDDING GIFT IS TOO MUCH.
NOT AT ALL, PRINCESS.

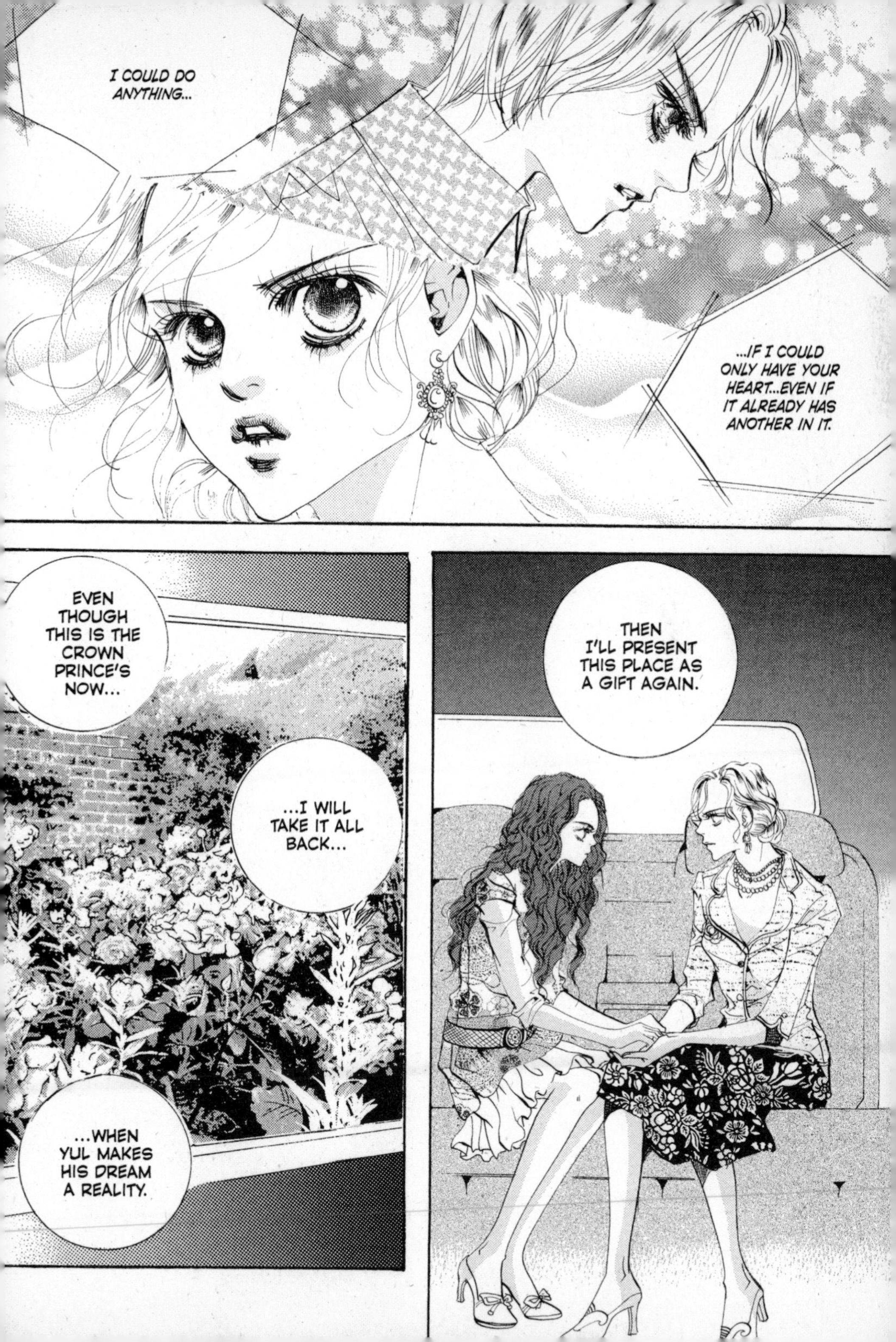
I COULD DO ANYTHING...
...IF I COULD ONLY HAVE YOUR HEART...EVEN IF IT ALREADY HAS ANOTHER IN IT.
EVEN THOUGH THIS IS THE CROWN PRINCE'S NOW...
...I WILL TAKE IT ALL BACK...
...WHEN YUL MAKES HIS DREAM A REALITY.
THEN I'LL PRESENT THIS PLACE AS A GIFT AGAIN.

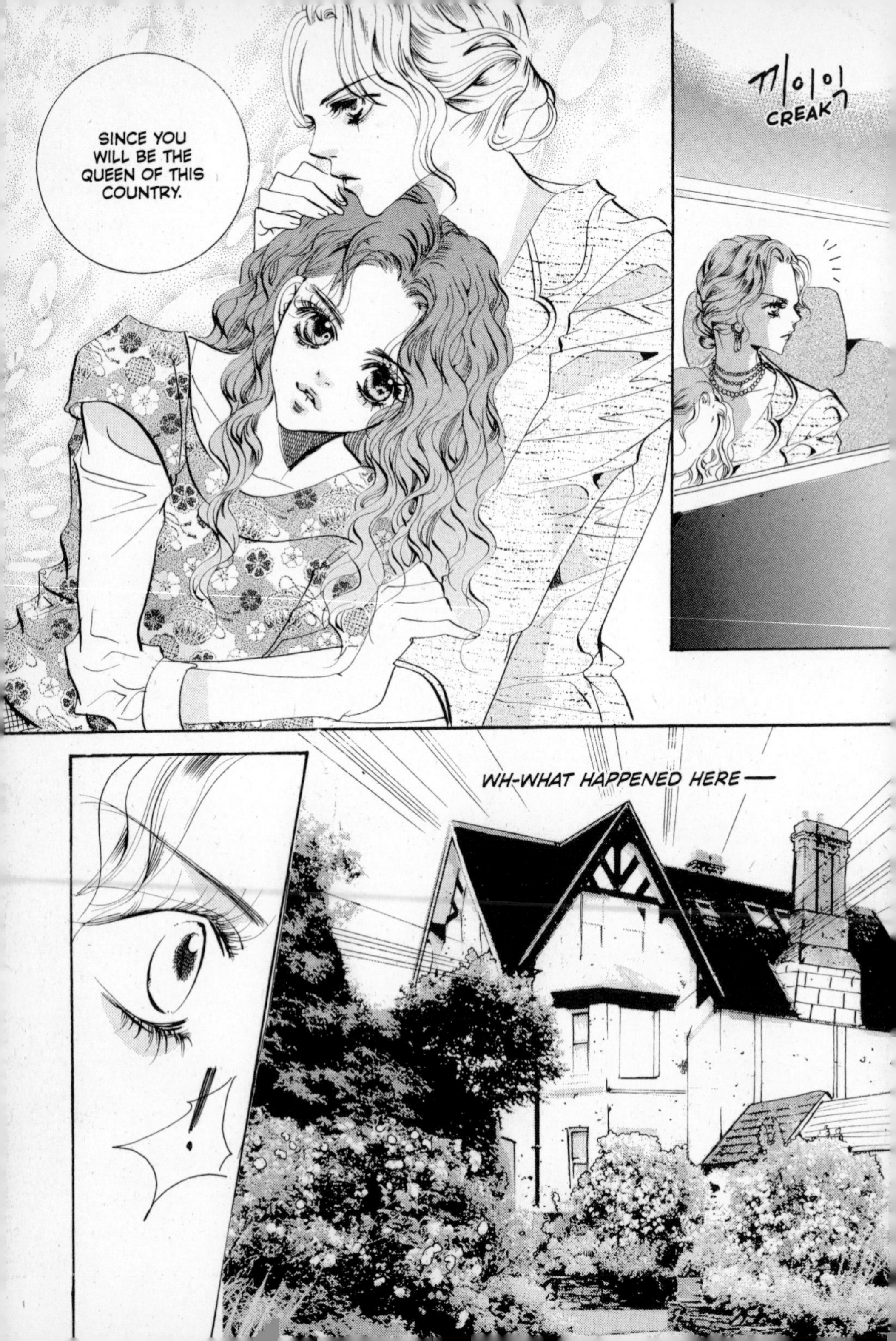
SINCE YOU WILL BE THE QUEEN OF THIS COUNTRY.
끼이익
CREAK
WH-WHAT HAPPENED HERE—

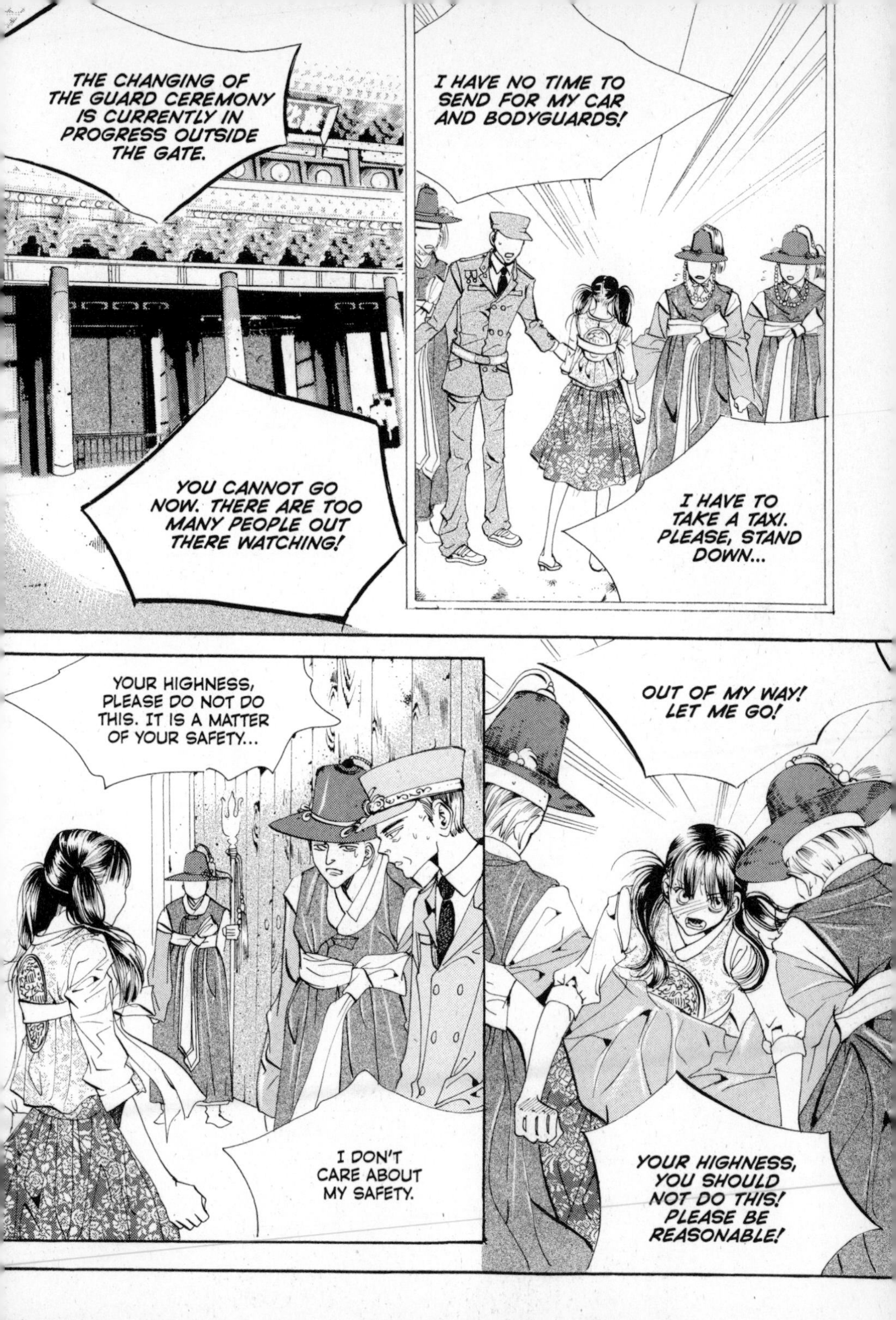
THE CHANGING OF THE GUARD CEREMONY IS CURRENTLY IN PROGRESS OUTSIDE THE GATE.
YOU CANNOT GO NOW. THERE ARE TOO MANY PEOPLE OUT THERE WATCHING!
I HAVE NO TIME TO SEND FOR MY CAR AND BODYGUARDS!
I HAVE TO TAKE A TAXI. PLEASE, STAND DOWN...
YOUR HIGHNESS, PLEASE DO NOT DO THIS. IT IS A MATTER OF YOUR SAFETY...
I DON'T CARE ABOUT MY SAFETY.
OUT OF MY WAY! LET ME GO!
YOUR HIGHNESS, YOU SHOULD NOT DO THIS! PLEASE BE REASONABLE!

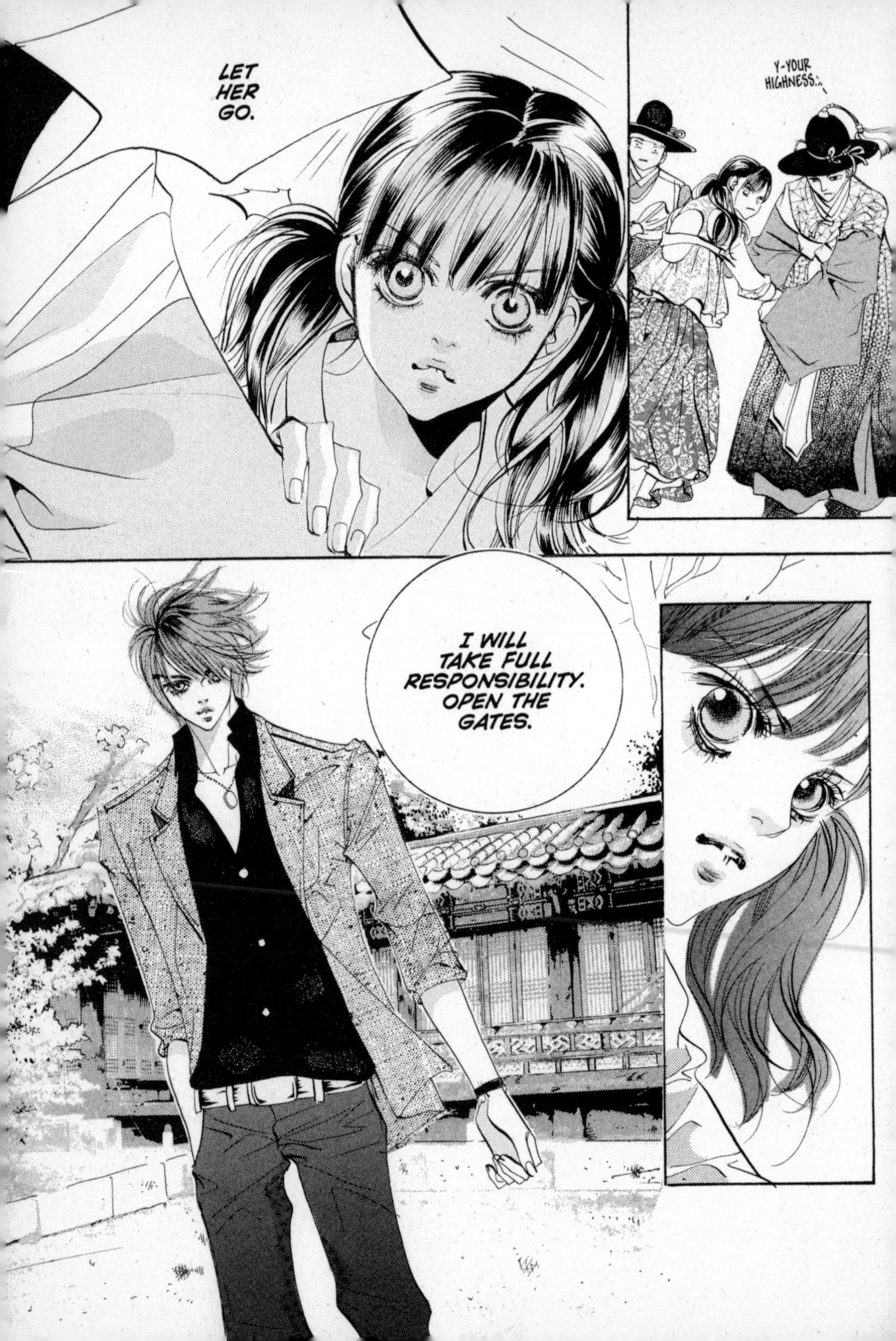
LET HER GO.
Y-YOUR HIGHNESS...
I WILL TAKE FULL RESPONSIBILITY. OPEN THE GATES.

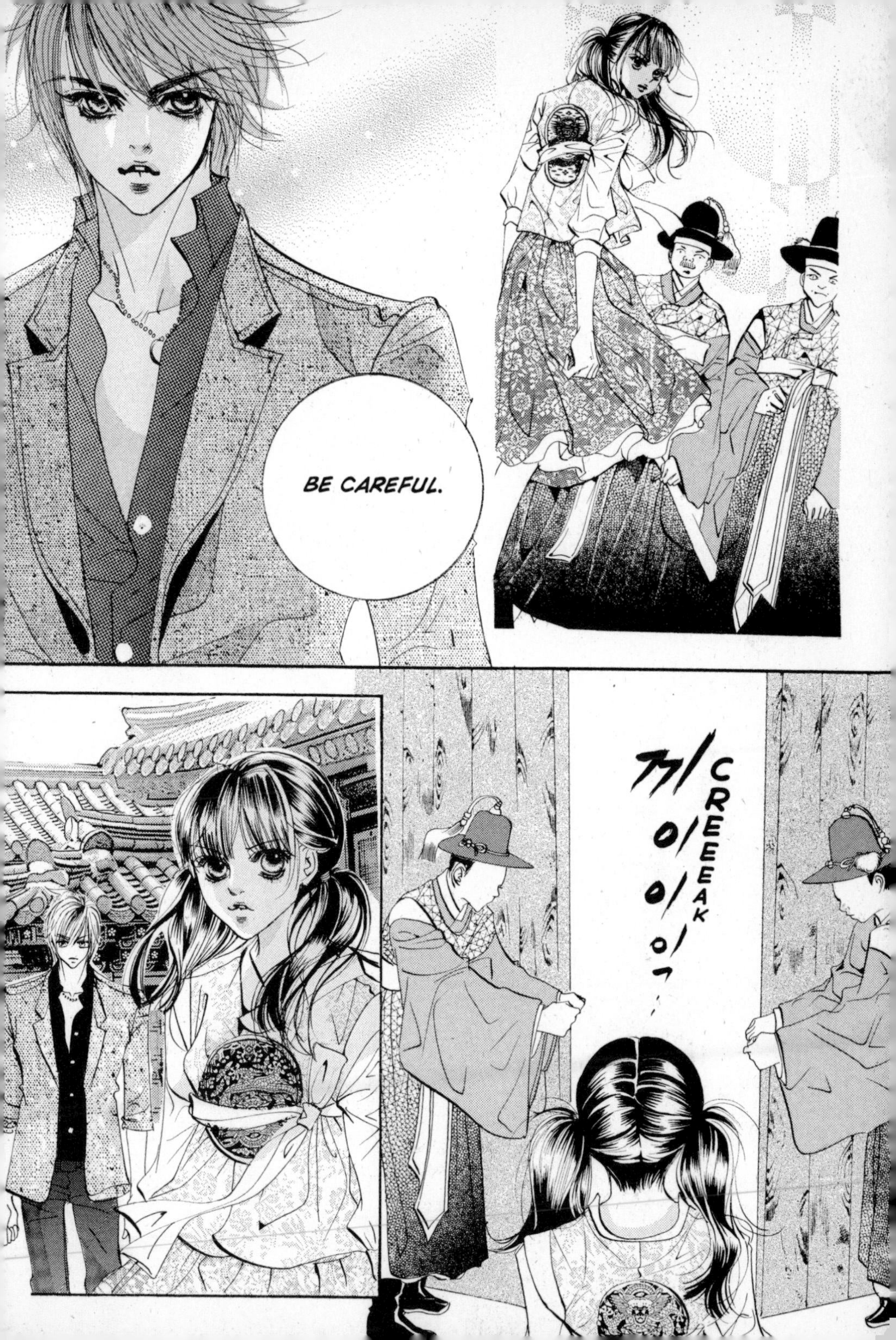
BE CAREFUL.
끼이이익
CREEEAK

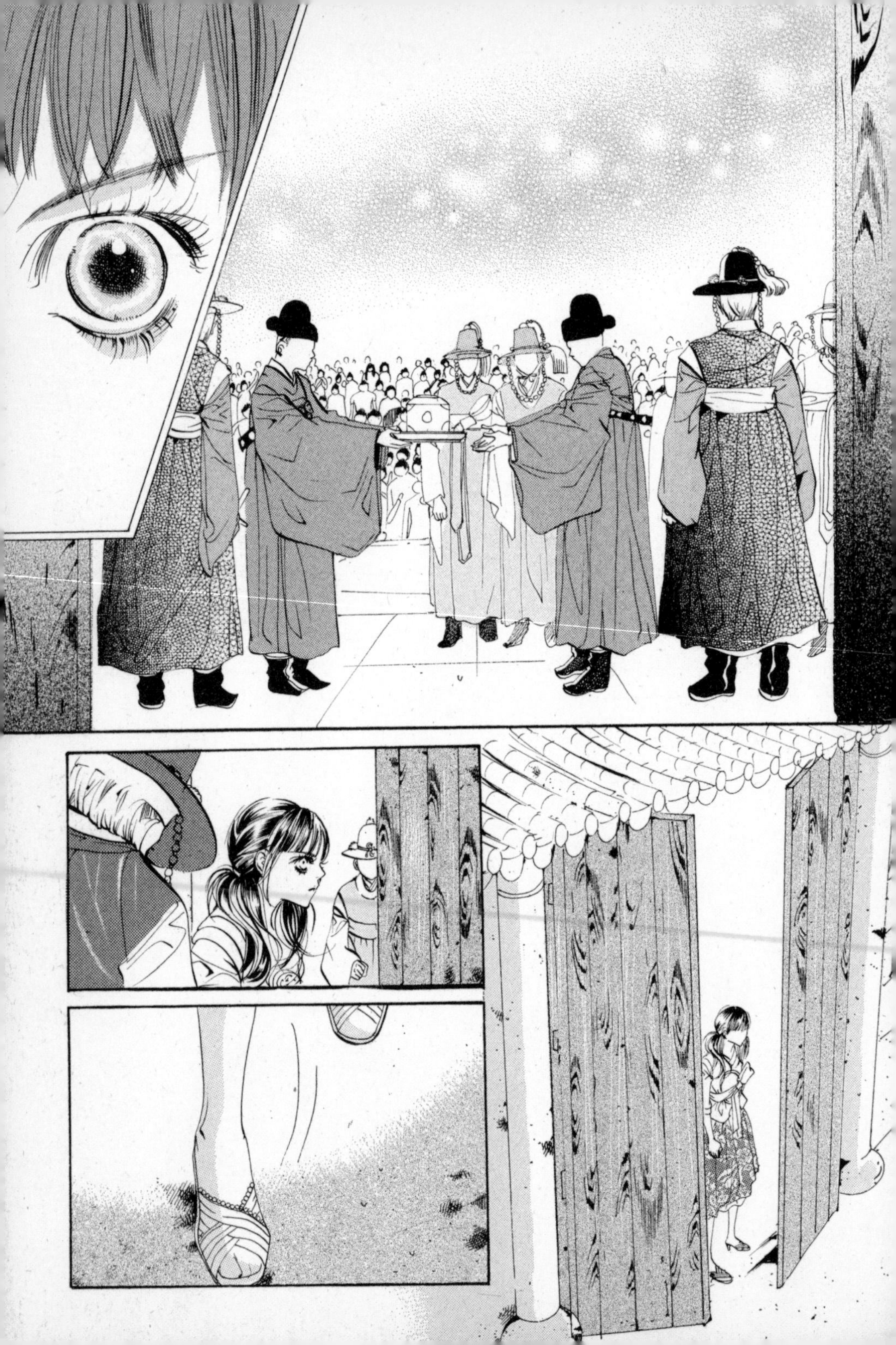

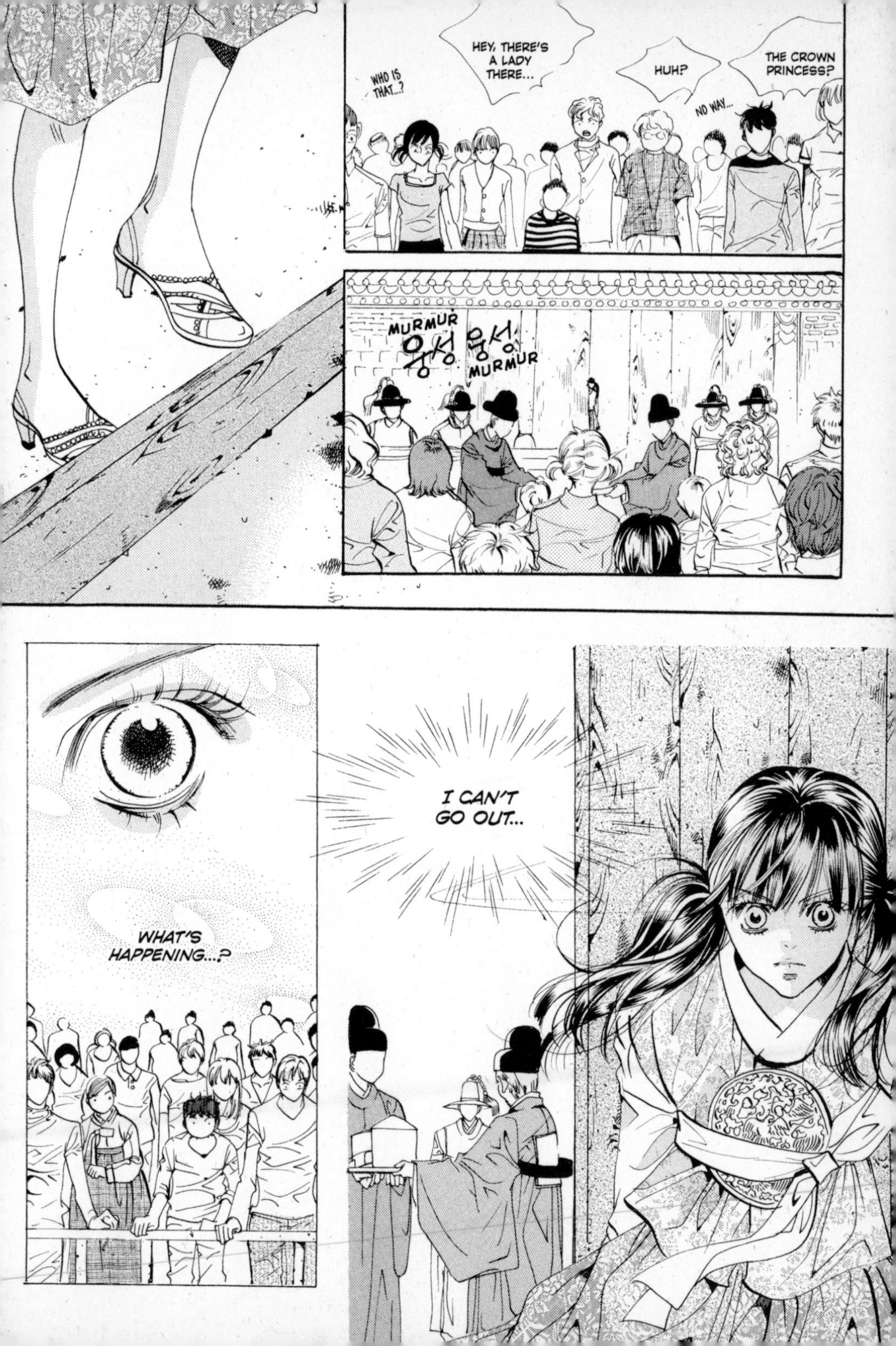

WHO IS THAT...?
HEY, THERE'S A LADY THERE...
HUH?
NO WAY...
THE CROWN PRINCESS?
MURMUR
웅성 웅성
MURMUR
WHAT'S HAPPENING...?
I CAN'T GO OUT...

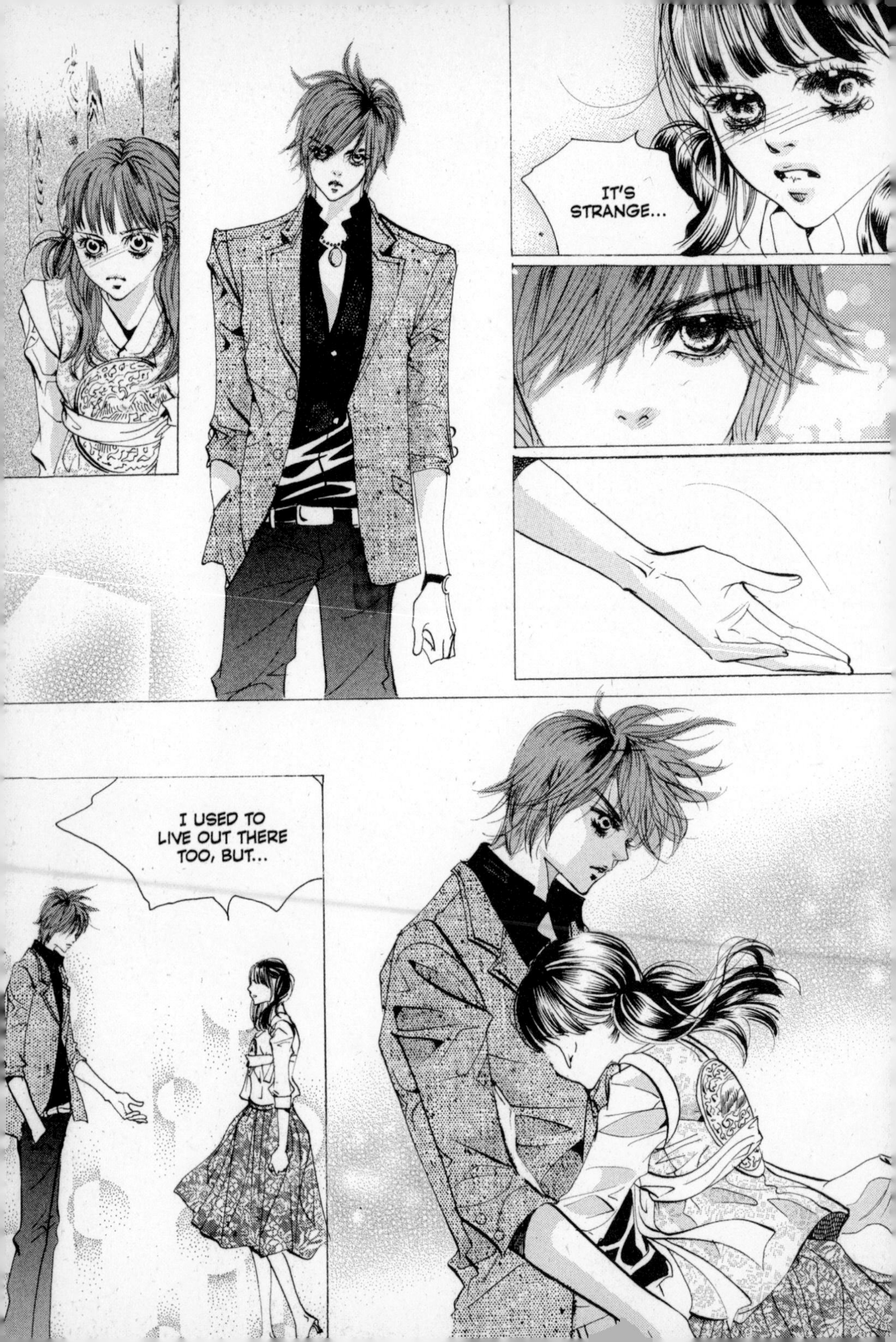
IT'S STRANGE...
I USED TO LIVE OUT THERE TOO, BUT...

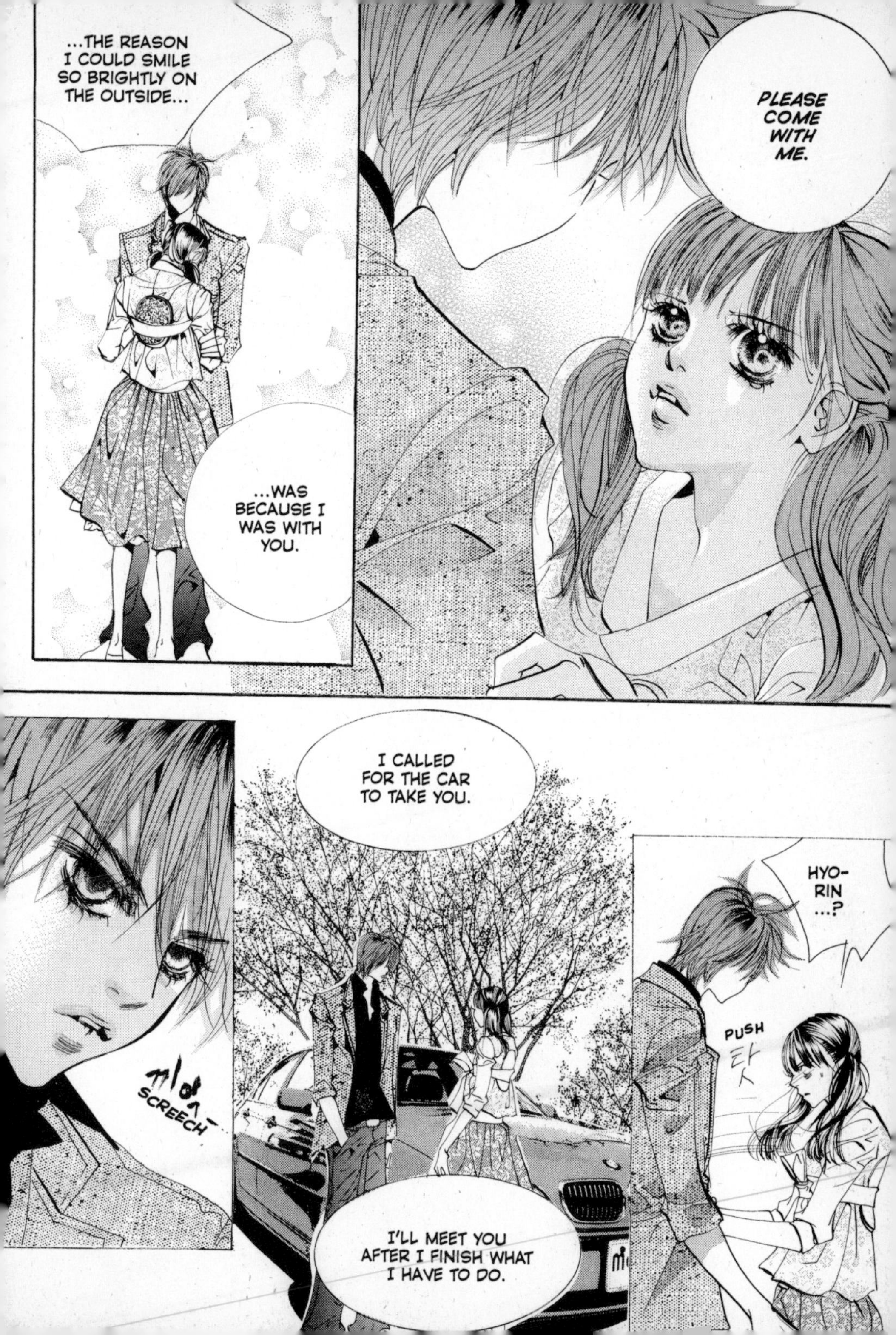
...THE REASON I COULD SMILE SO BRIGHTLY ON THE OUTSIDE...
...WAS BECAUSE I WAS WITH YOU.
PLEASE COME WITH ME.
SCREECH
I CALLED FOR THE CAR TO TAKE YOU.
I'LL MEET YOU AFTER I FINISH WHAT I HAVE TO DO.
HYO-RIN ...?
PUSH

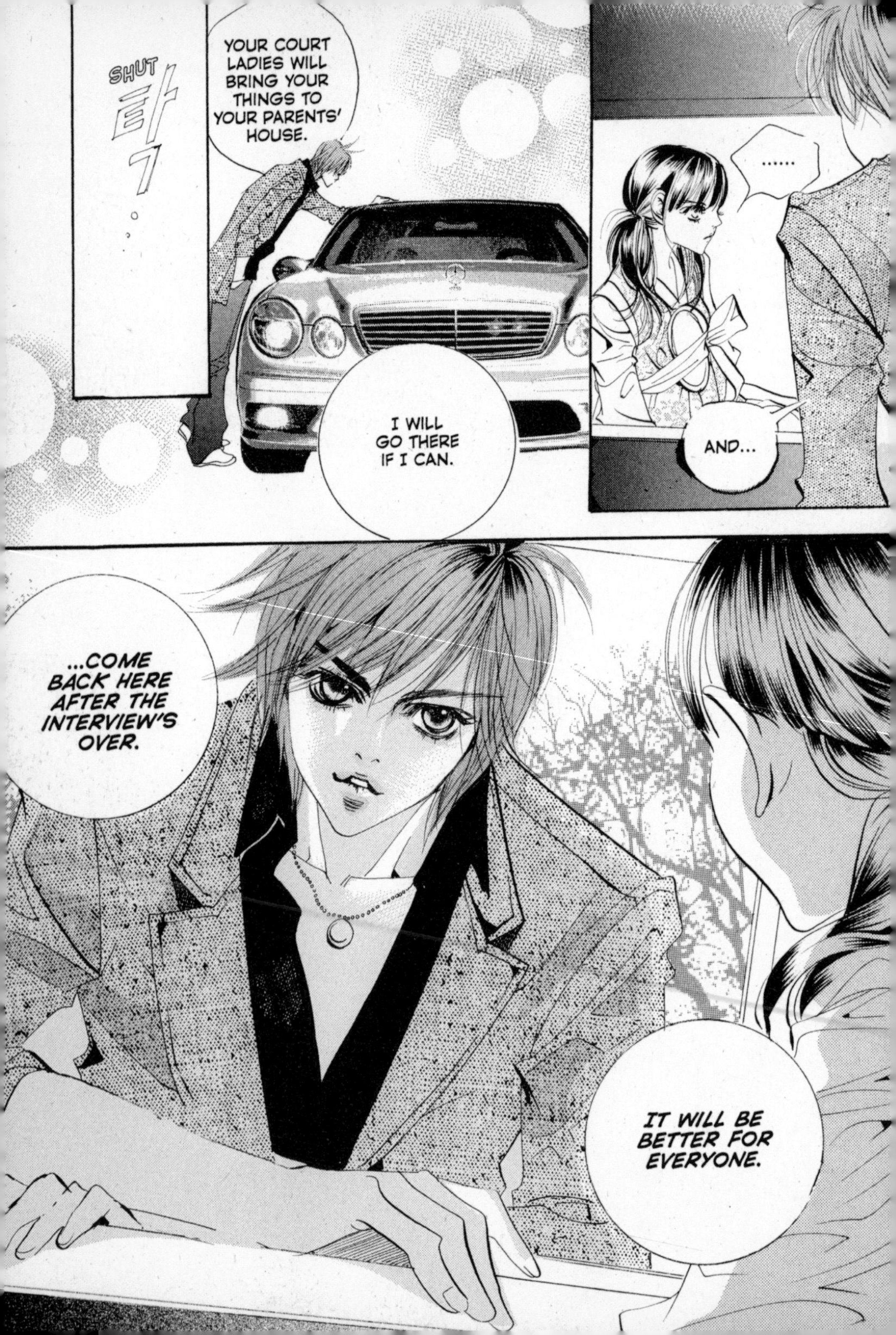
SHUT
탁
YOUR COURT LADIES WILL BRING YOUR THINGS TO YOUR PARENTS' HOUSE.
I WILL GO THERE IF I CAN.
......
AND...
...COME BACK HERE AFTER THE INTERVIEW'S OVER.
IT WILL BE BETTER FOR EVERYONE.

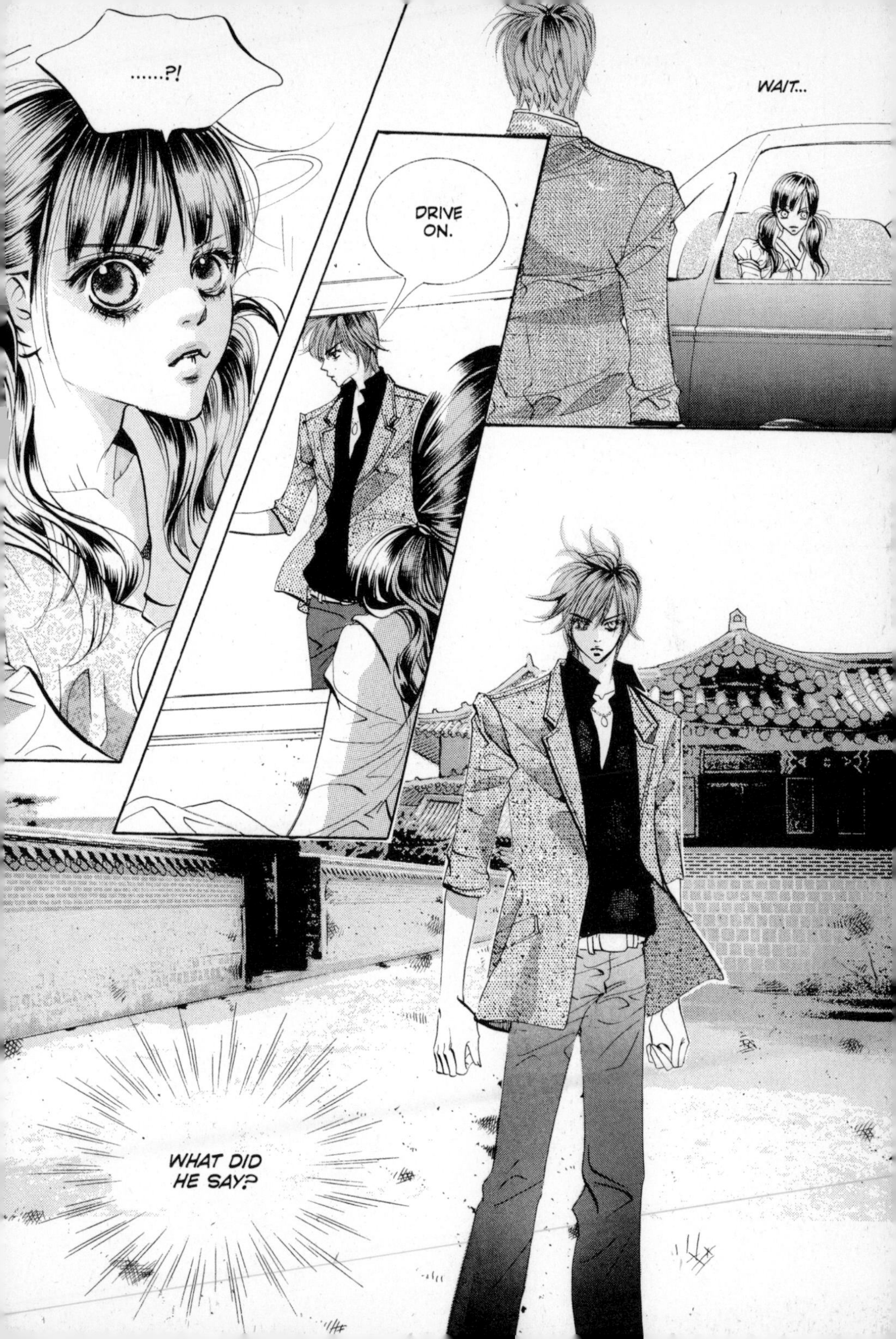
......?!
DRIVE ON.
WAIT...
WHAT DID HE SAY?

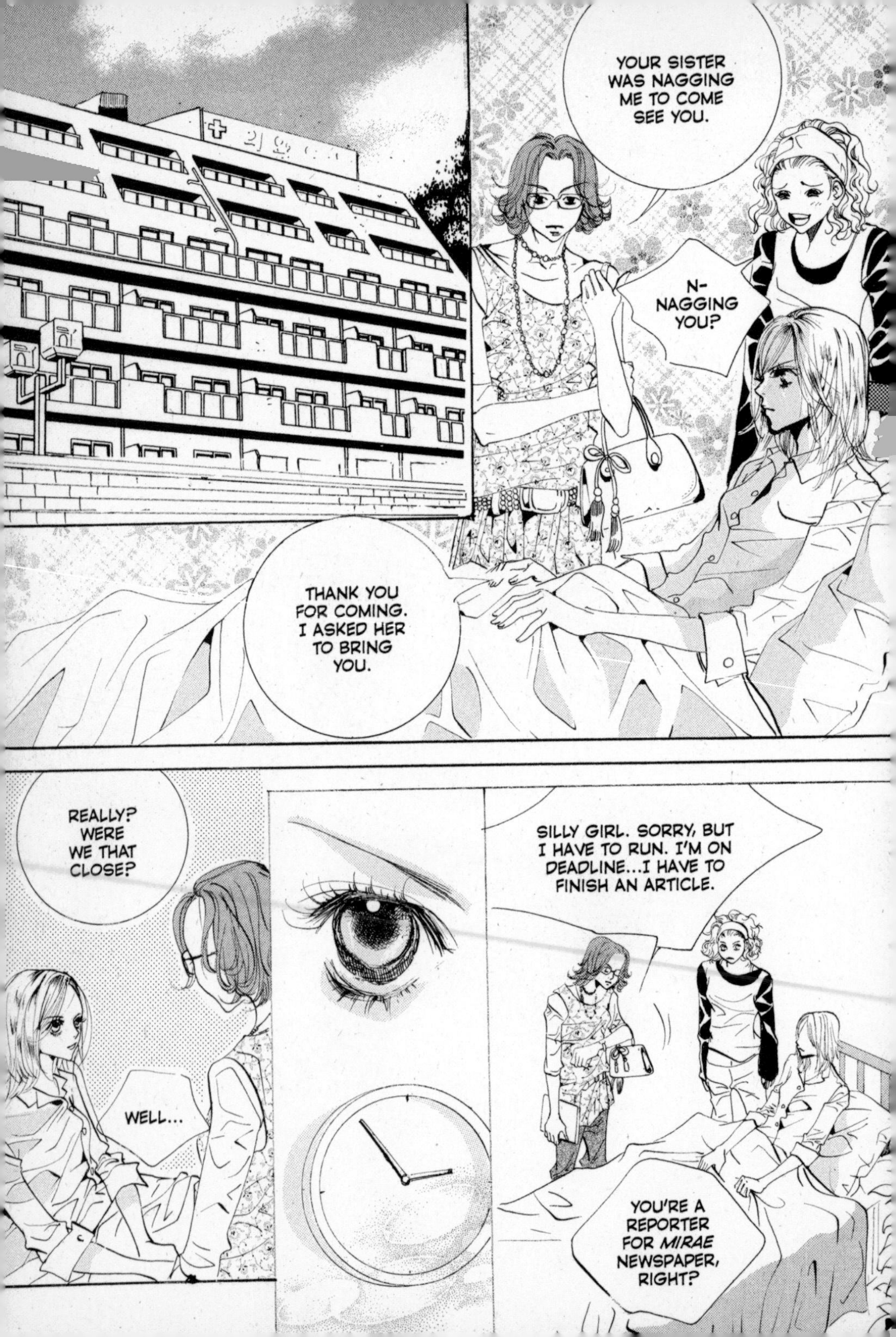
YOUR SISTER WAS NAGGING ME TO COME SEE YOU.
N-NAGGING YOU?
THANK YOU FOR COMING. I ASKED HER TO BRING YOU.
REALLY? WERE WE THAT CLOSE?
WELL...
SILLY GIRL. SORRY, BUT I HAVE TO RUN. I'M ON DEADLINE...I HAVE TO FINISH AN ARTICLE.
YOU'RE A REPORTER FOR *MIRAE* NEWSPAPER, RIGHT?

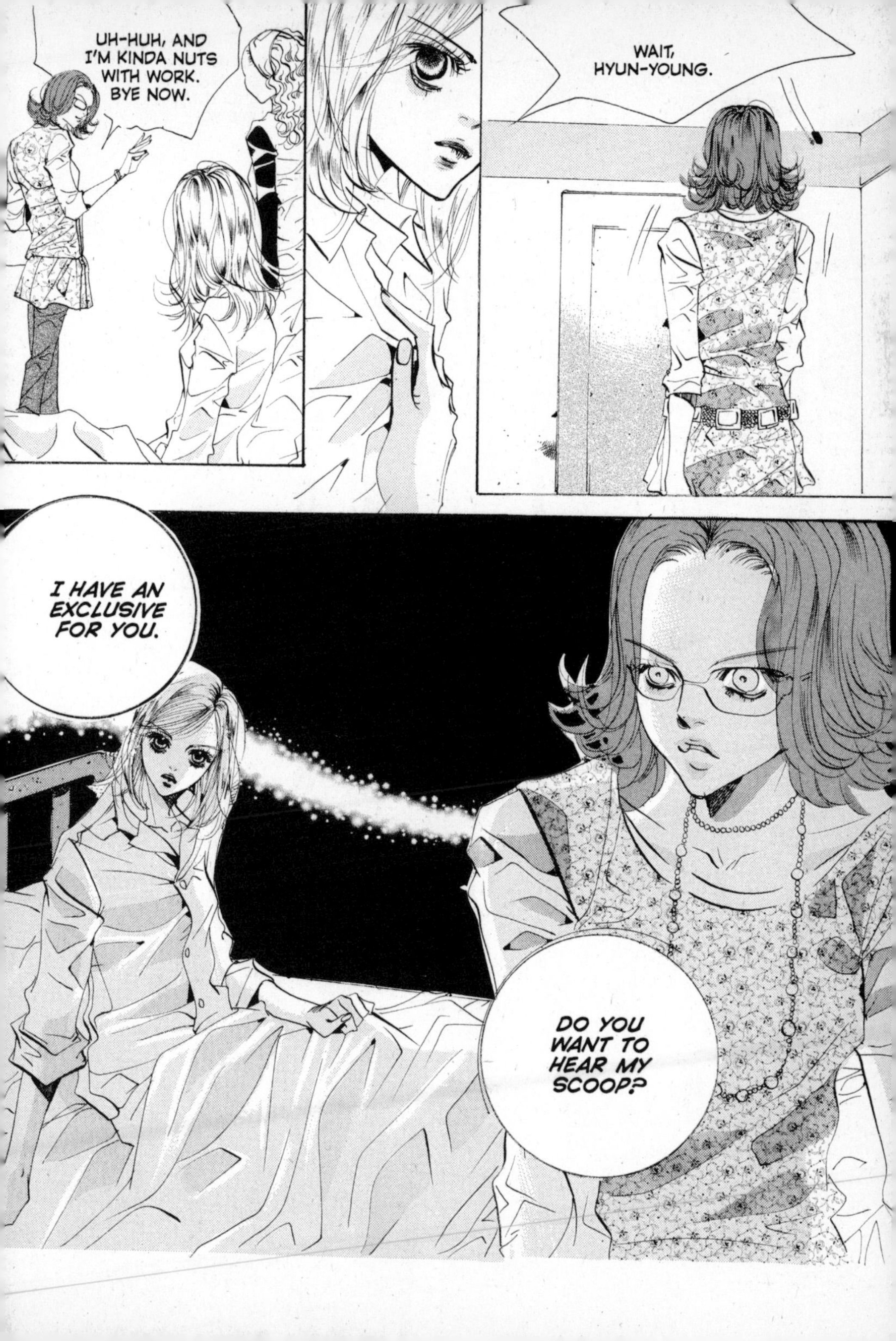
UH-HUH, AND I'M KINDA NUTS WITH WORK. BYE NOW.
WAIT, HYUN-YOUNG.
I HAVE AN EXCLUSIVE FOR YOU.
DO YOU WANT TO HEAR MY SCOOP?

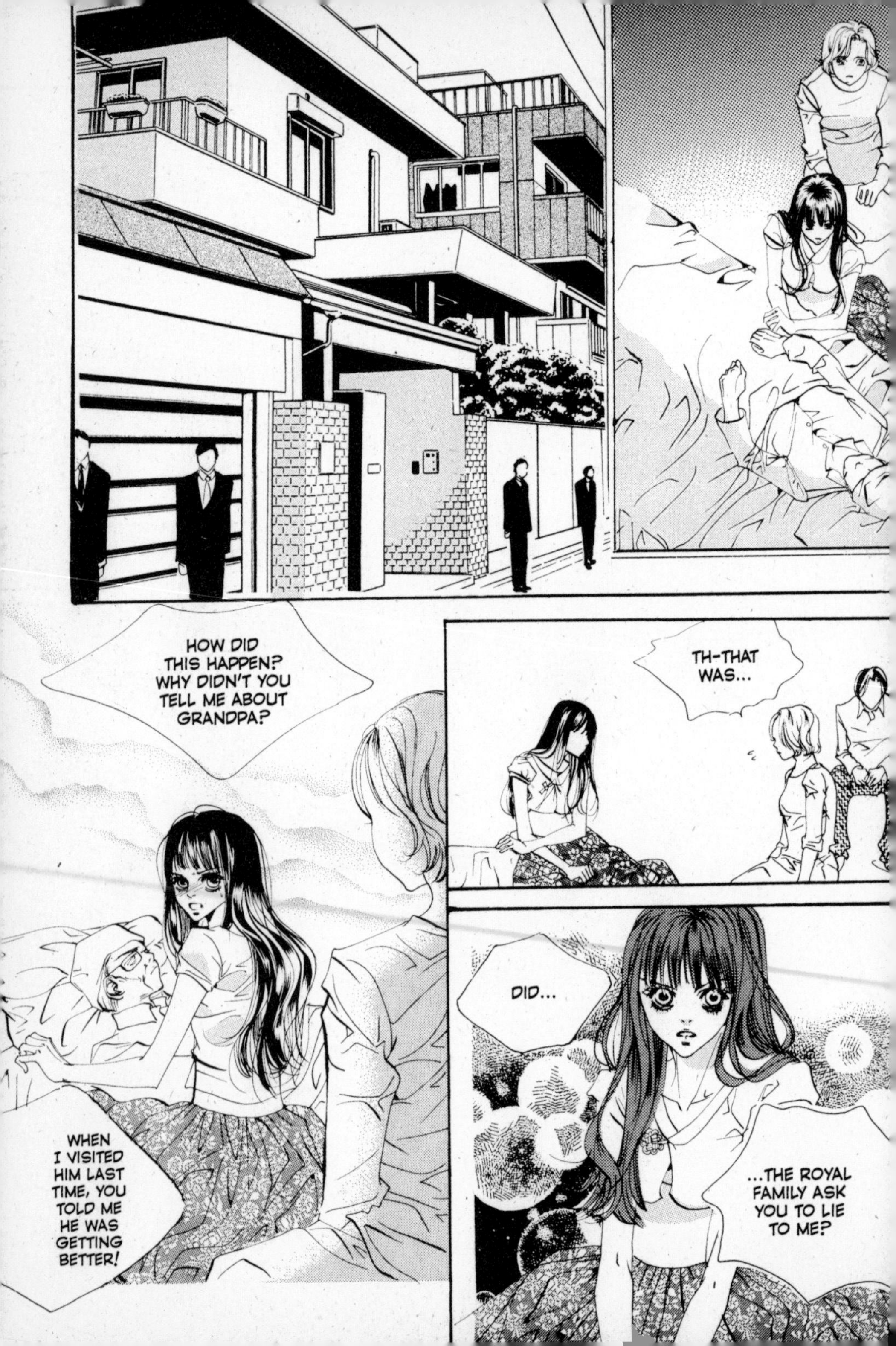
HOW DID THIS HAPPEN? WHY DIDN'T YOU TELL ME ABOUT GRANDPA?
WHEN I VISITED HIM LAST TIME, YOU TOLD ME HE WAS GETTING BETTER!
TH-THAT WAS...
DID...
...THE ROYAL FAMILY ASK YOU TO LIE TO ME?

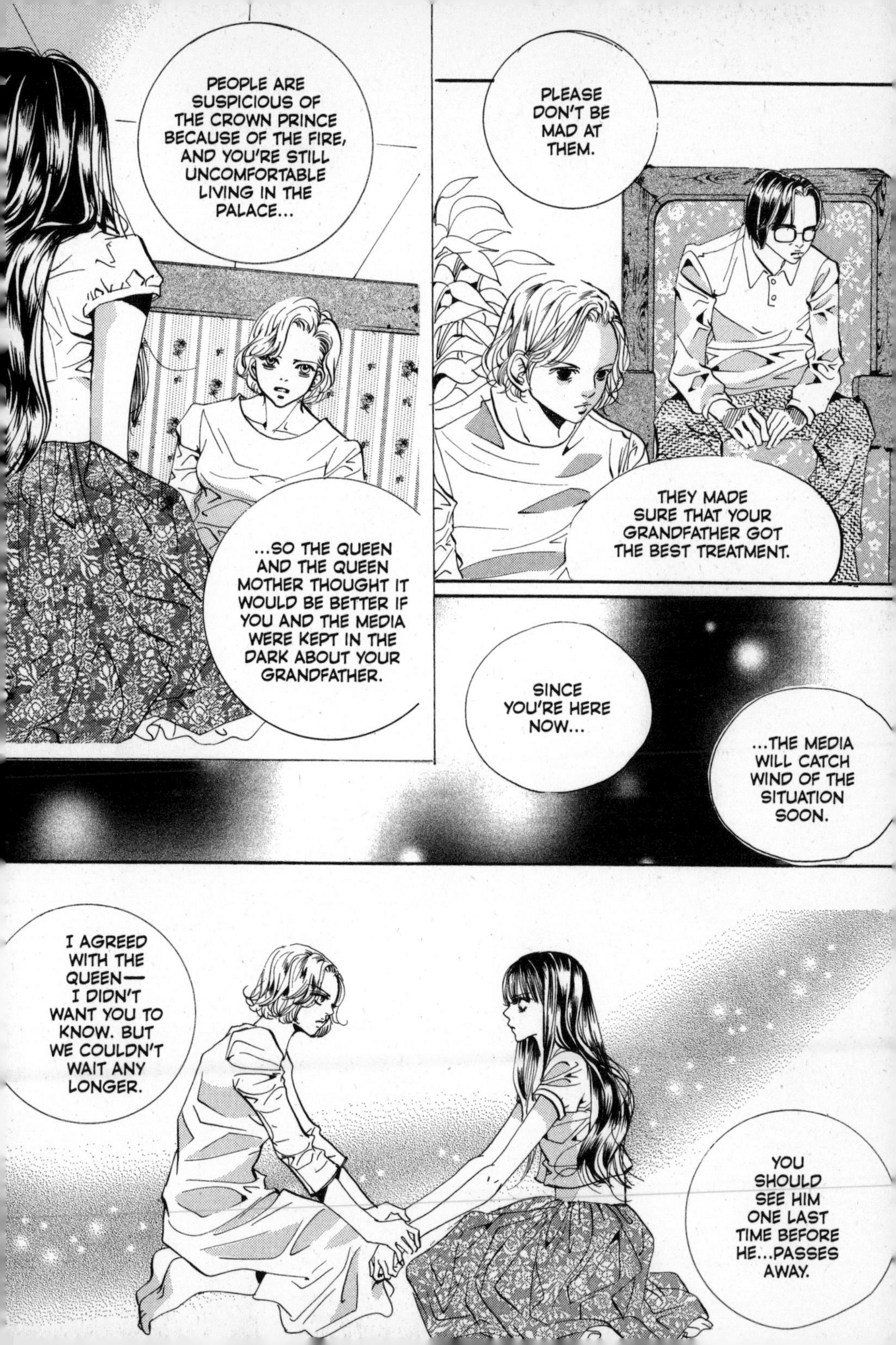
PEOPLE ARE SUSPICIOUS OF THE CROWN PRINCE BECAUSE OF THE FIRE, AND YOU'RE STILL UNCOMFORTABLE LIVING IN THE PALACE...
...SO THE QUEEN AND THE QUEEN MOTHER THOUGHT IT WOULD BE BETTER IF YOU AND THE MEDIA WERE KEPT IN THE DARK ABOUT YOUR GRANDFATHER.
PLEASE DON'T BE MAD AT THEM.
THEY MADE SURE THAT YOUR GRANDFATHER GOT THE BEST TREATMENT.
SINCE YOU'RE HERE NOW...
...THE MEDIA WILL CATCH WIND OF THE SITUATION SOON.
I AGREED WITH THE QUEEN— I DIDN'T WANT YOU TO KNOW. BUT WE COULDN'T WAIT ANY LONGER.
YOU SHOULD SEE HIM ONE LAST TIME BEFORE HE...PASSES AWAY.

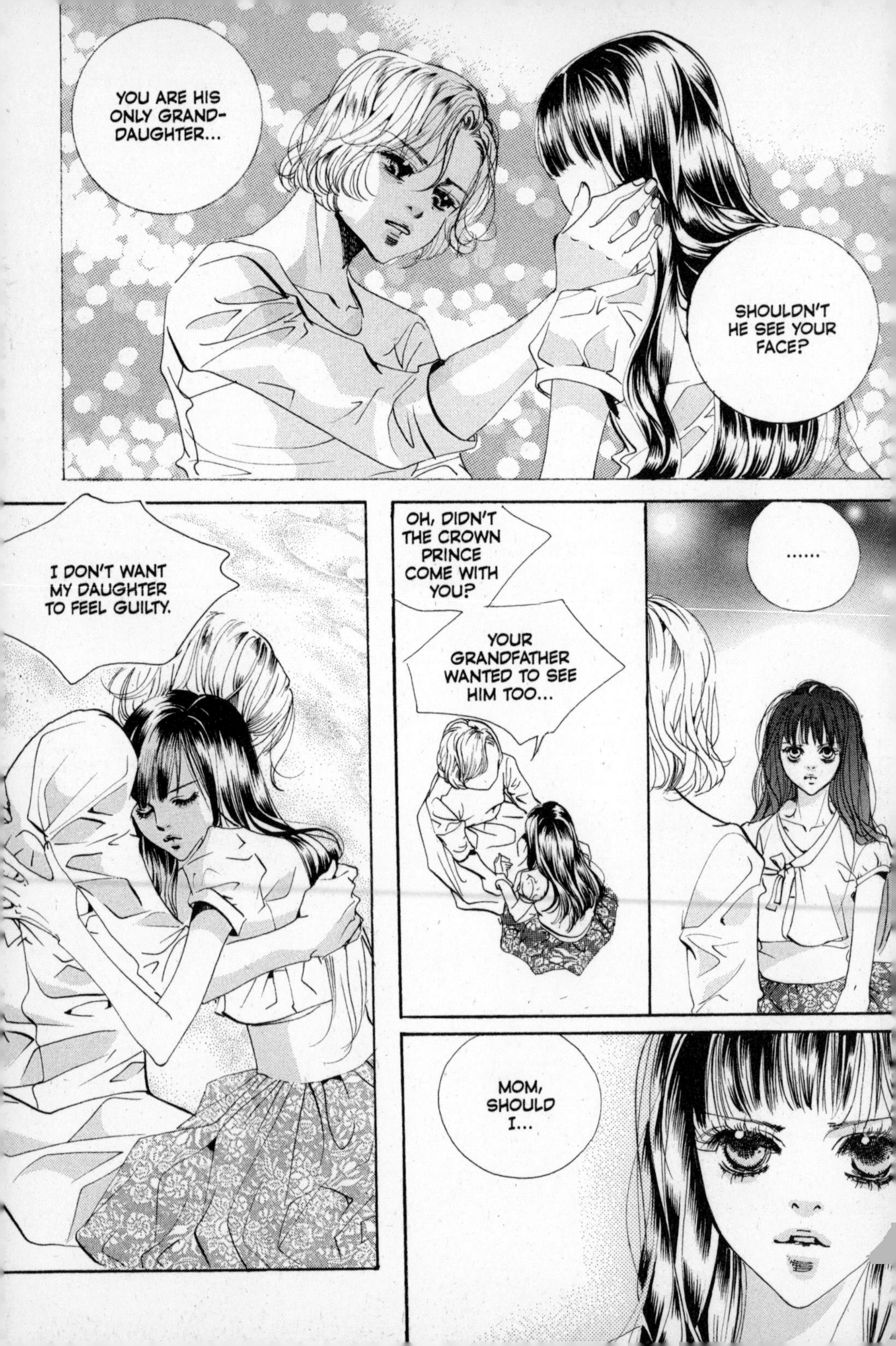
YOU ARE HIS ONLY GRAND-DAUGHTER...
SHOULDN'T HE SEE YOUR FACE?
I DON'T WANT MY DAUGHTER TO FEEL GUILTY.
OH, DIDN'T THE CROWN PRINCE COME WITH YOU?
YOUR GRANDFATHER WANTED TO SEE HIM TOO...
......
MOM, SHOULD I...

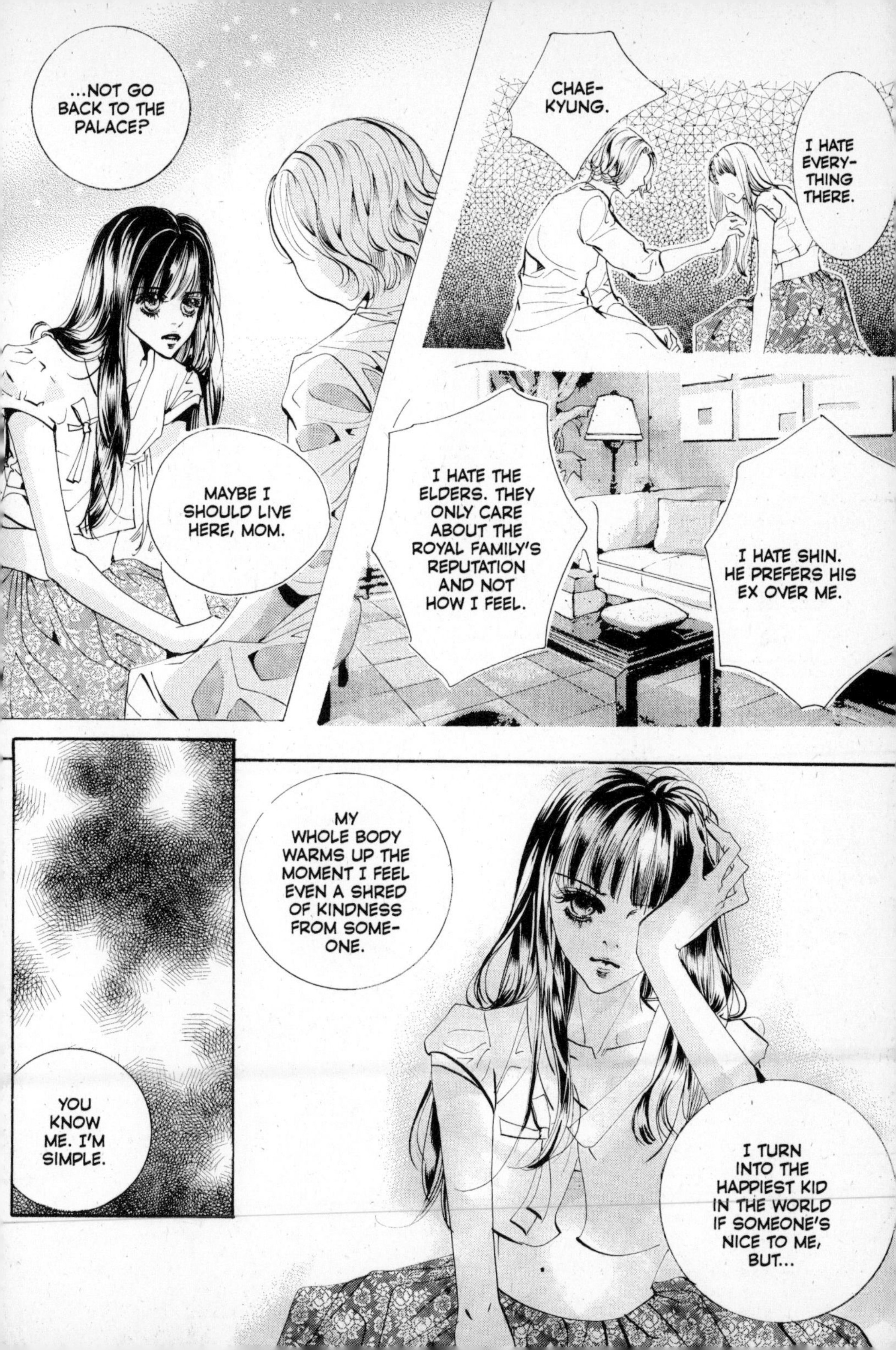
...NOT GO BACK TO THE PALACE?
MAYBE I SHOULD LIVE HERE, MOM.
CHAE-KYUNG.
I HATE EVERY-THING THERE.
I HATE THE ELDERS. THEY ONLY CARE ABOUT THE ROYAL FAMILY'S REPUTATION AND NOT HOW I FEEL.
I HATE SHIN. HE PREFERS HIS EX OVER ME.
YOU KNOW ME. I'M SIMPLE.
MY WHOLE BODY WARMS UP THE MOMENT I FEEL EVEN A SHRED OF KINDNESS FROM SOME-ONE.
I TURN INTO THE HAPPIEST KID IN THE WORLD IF SOMEONE'S NICE TO ME, BUT...

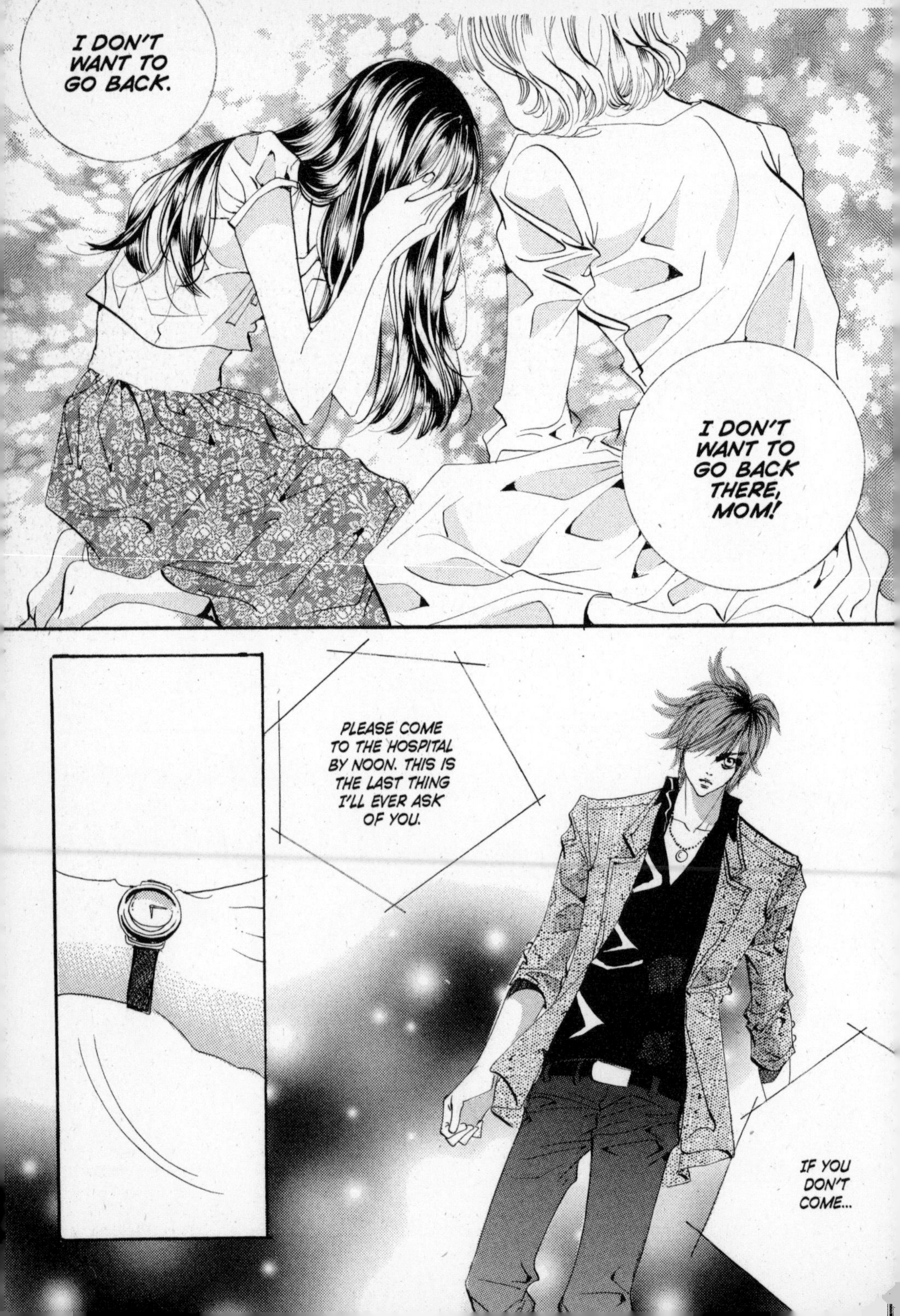
I DON'T WANT TO GO BACK.
I DON'T WANT TO GO BACK THERE, MOM!
PLEASE COME TO THE HOSPITAL BY NOON. THIS IS THE LAST THING I'LL EVER ASK OF YOU.
IF YOU DON'T COME...

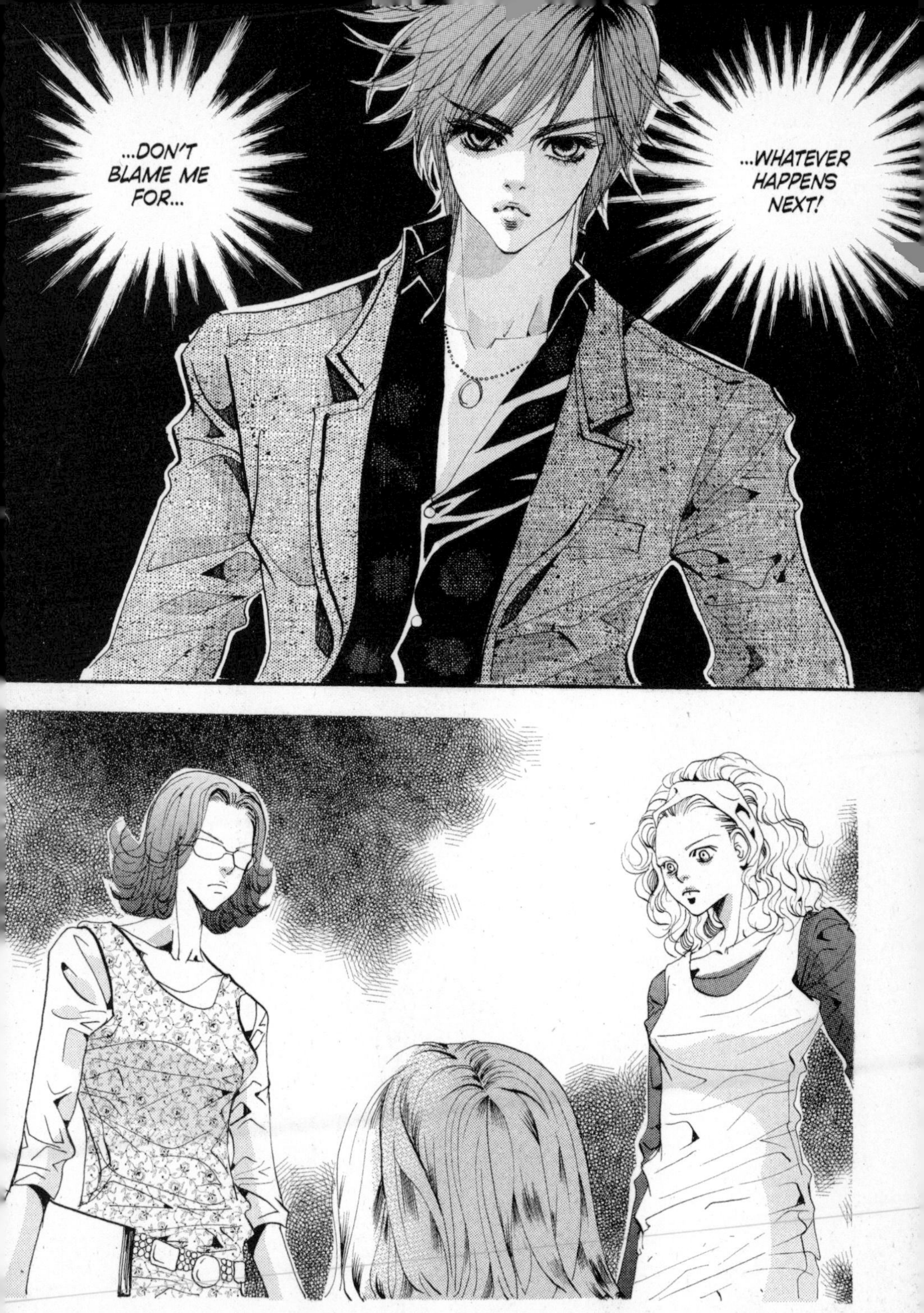
...DON'T BLAME ME FOR...
...WHATEVER HAPPENS NEXT!

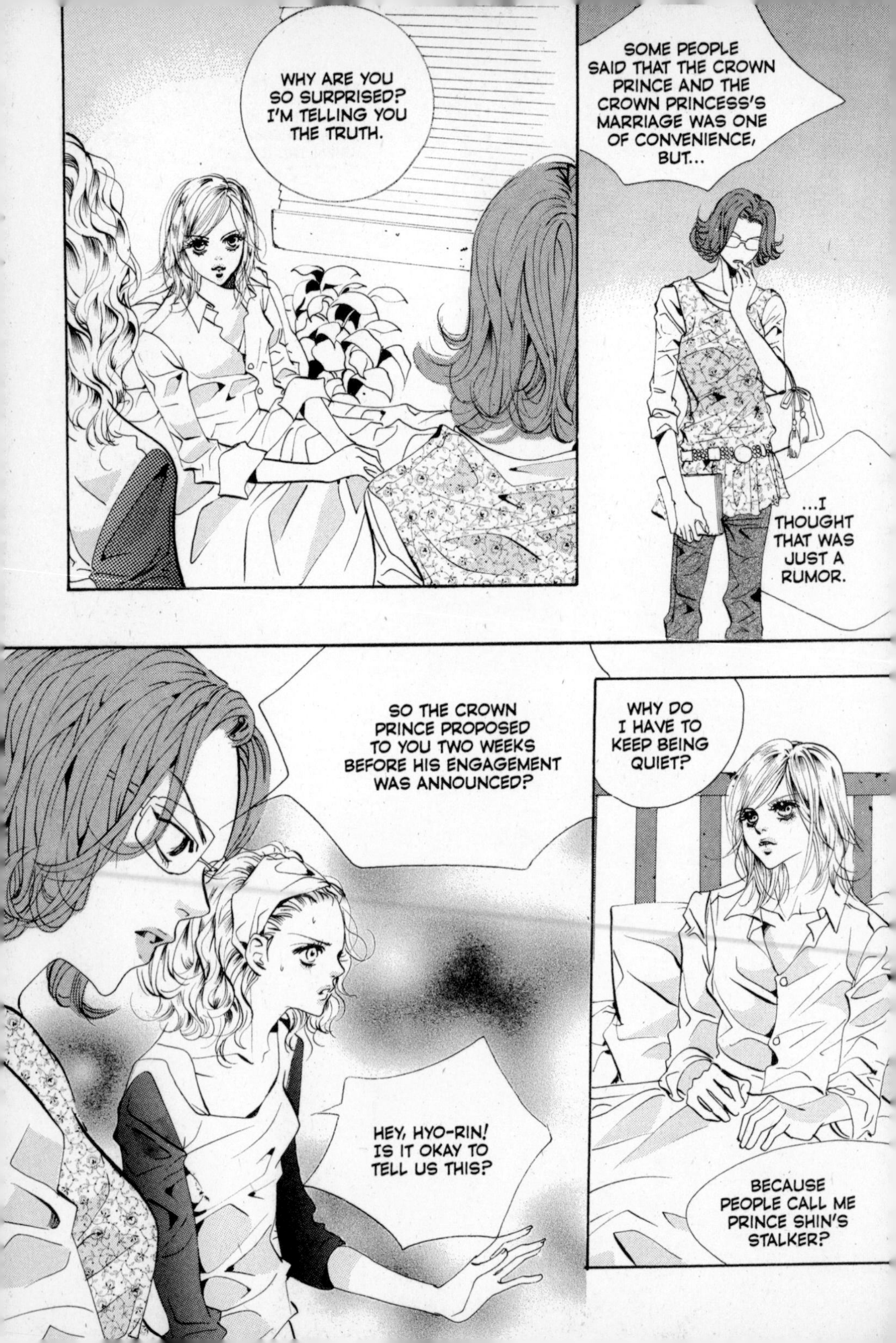
WHY ARE YOU SO SURPRISED? I'M TELLING YOU THE TRUTH.
SOME PEOPLE SAID THAT THE CROWN PRINCE AND THE CROWN PRINCESS'S MARRIAGE WAS ONE OF CONVENIENCE, BUT...
...I THOUGHT THAT WAS JUST A RUMOR.
SO THE CROWN PRINCE PROPOSED TO YOU TWO WEEKS BEFORE HIS ENGAGEMENT WAS ANNOUNCED?
HEY, HYO-RIN! IS IT OKAY TO TELL US THIS?
WHY DO I HAVE TO KEEP BEING QUIET?
BECAUSE PEOPLE CALL ME PRINCE SHIN'S STALKER?

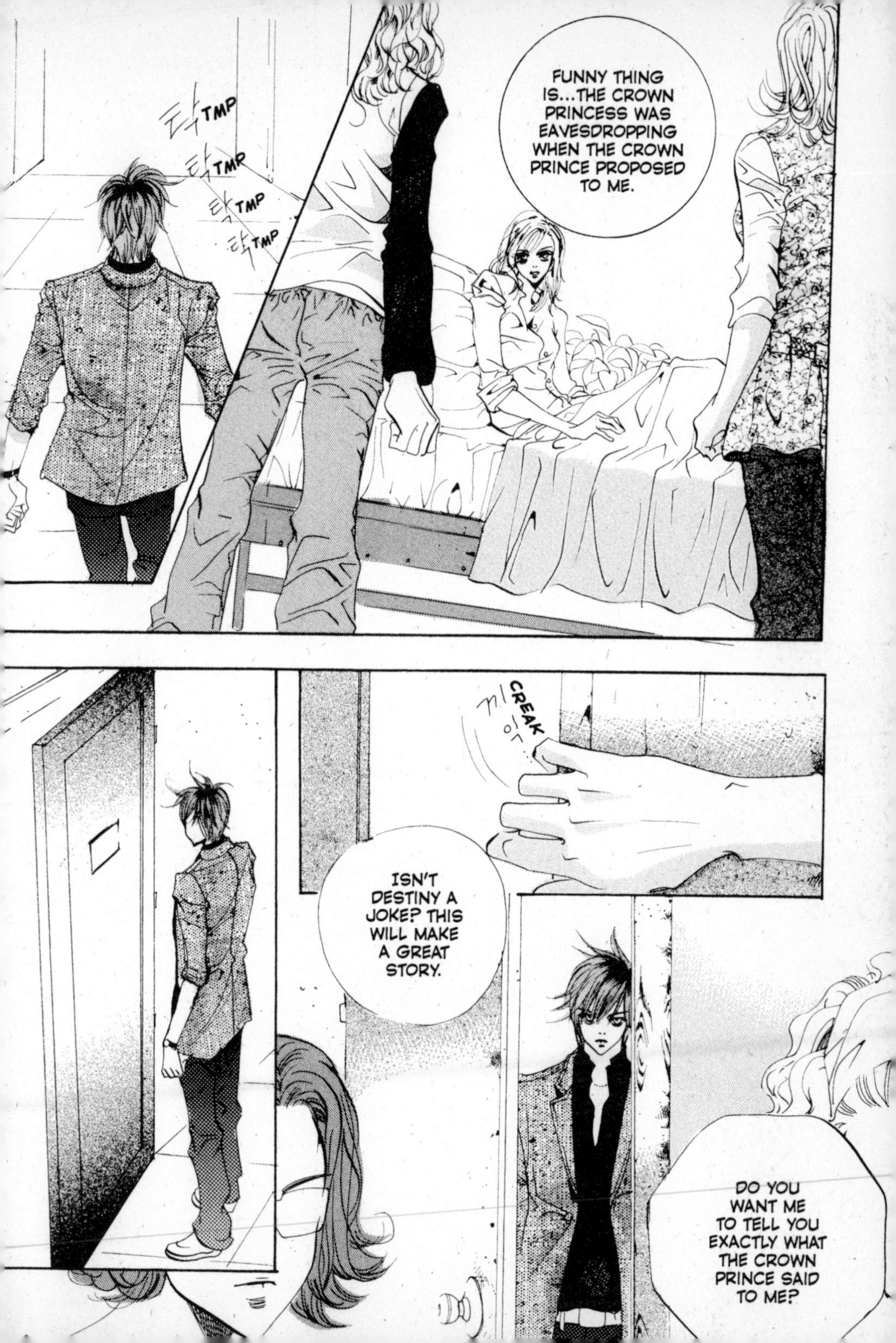
탁 TMP
탁 TMP
탁 TMP
탁 TMP
FUNNY THING IS...THE CROWN PRINCESS WAS EAVESDROPPING WHEN THE CROWN PRINCE PROPOSED TO ME.
CREAK
ISN'T DESTINY A JOKE? THIS WILL MAKE A GREAT STORY.
DO YOU WANT ME TO TELL YOU EXACTLY WHAT THE CROWN PRINCE SAID TO ME?

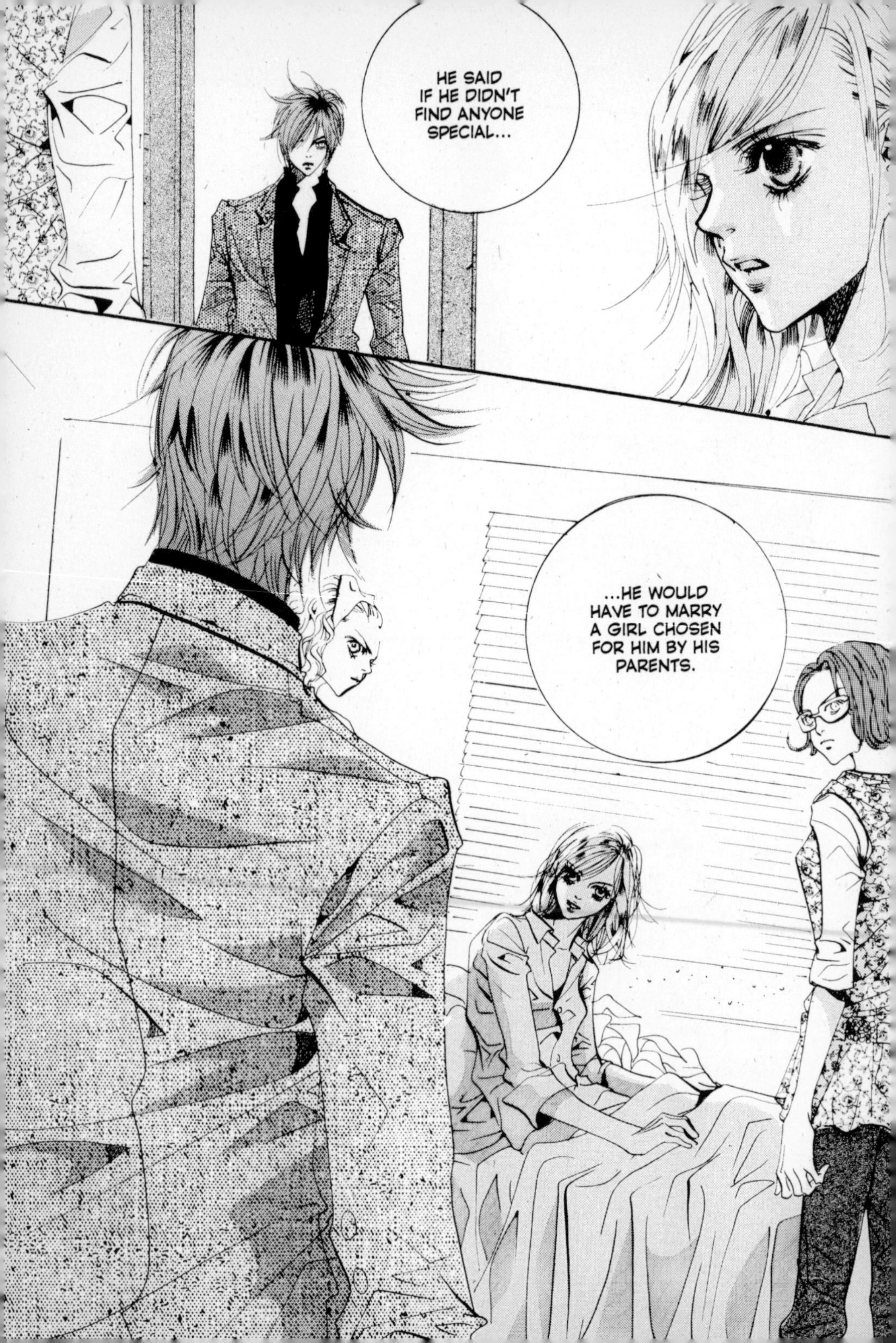
HE SAID IF HE DIDN'T FIND ANYONE SPECIAL...
...HE WOULD HAVE TO MARRY A GIRL CHOSEN FOR HIM BY HIS PARENTS.

THE ROYAL PALACE
Goong

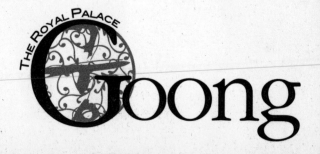

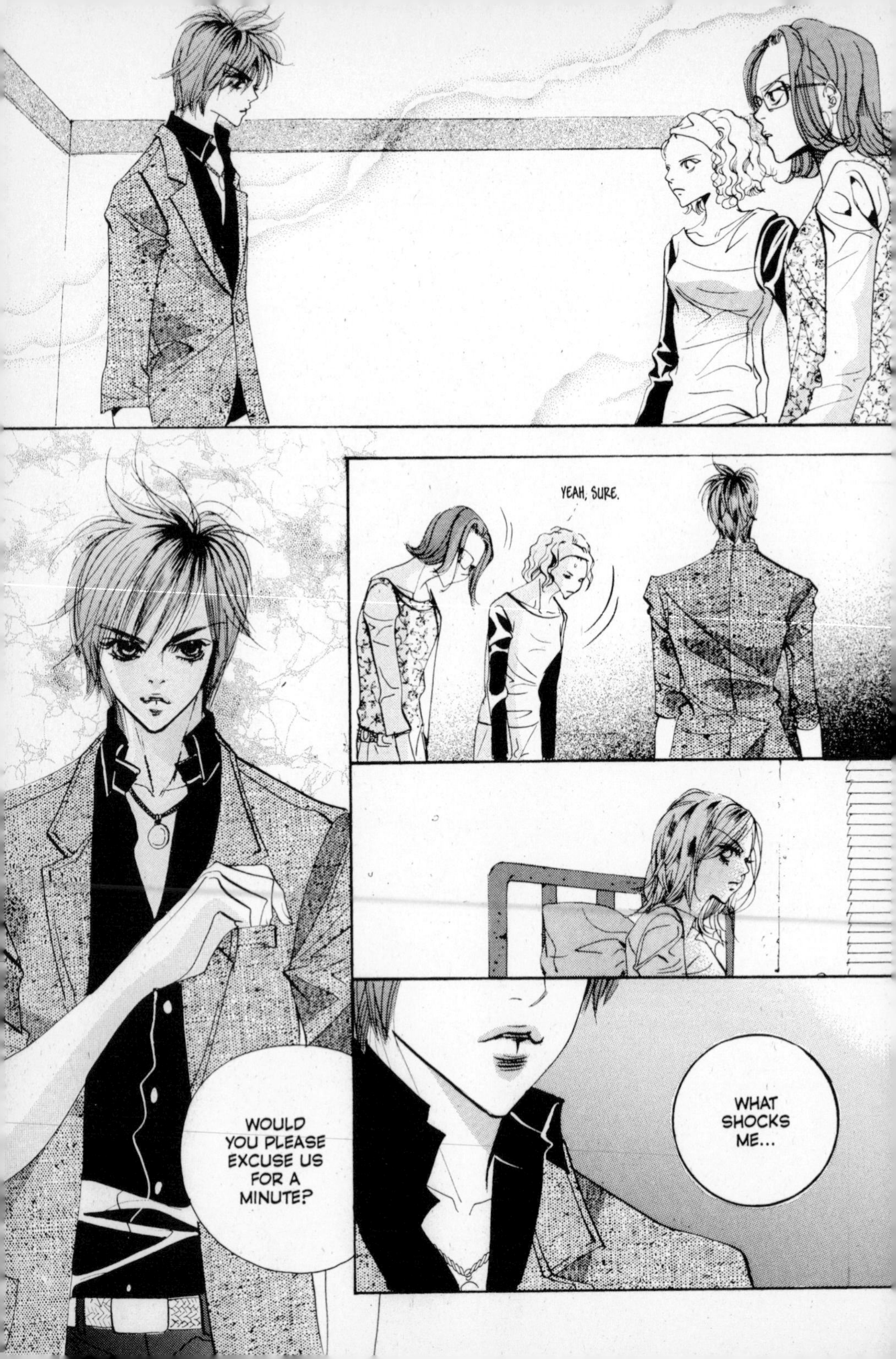
WOULD YOU PLEASE EXCUSE US FOR A MINUTE?
YEAH, SURE.
WHAT SHOCKS ME...

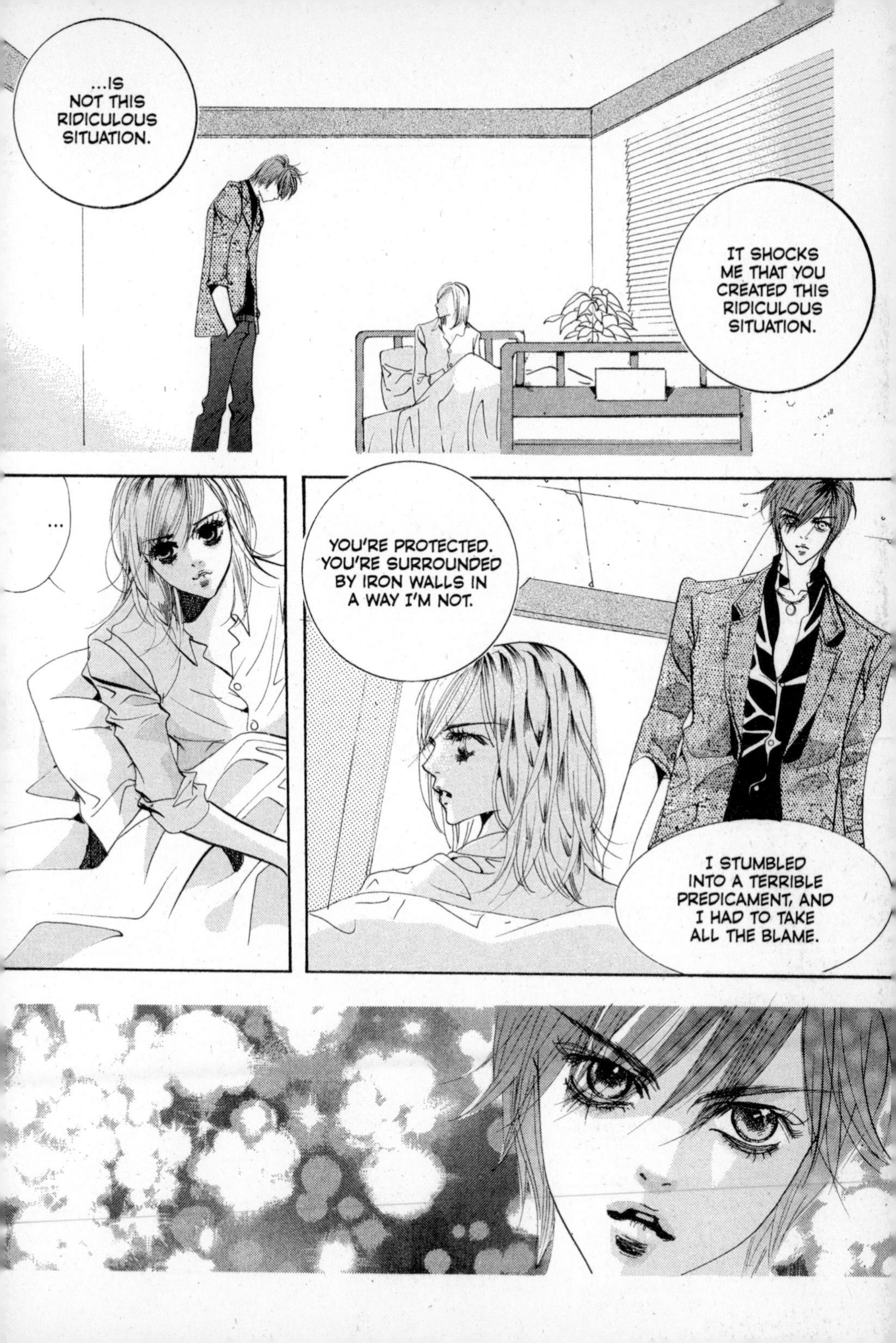
...IS NOT THIS RIDICULOUS SITUATION.
IT SHOCKS ME THAT YOU CREATED THIS RIDICULOUS SITUATION.
...
YOU'RE PROTECTED. YOU'RE SURROUNDED BY IRON WALLS IN A WAY I'M NOT.
I STUMBLED INTO A TERRIBLE PREDICAMENT, AND I HAD TO TAKE ALL THE BLAME.

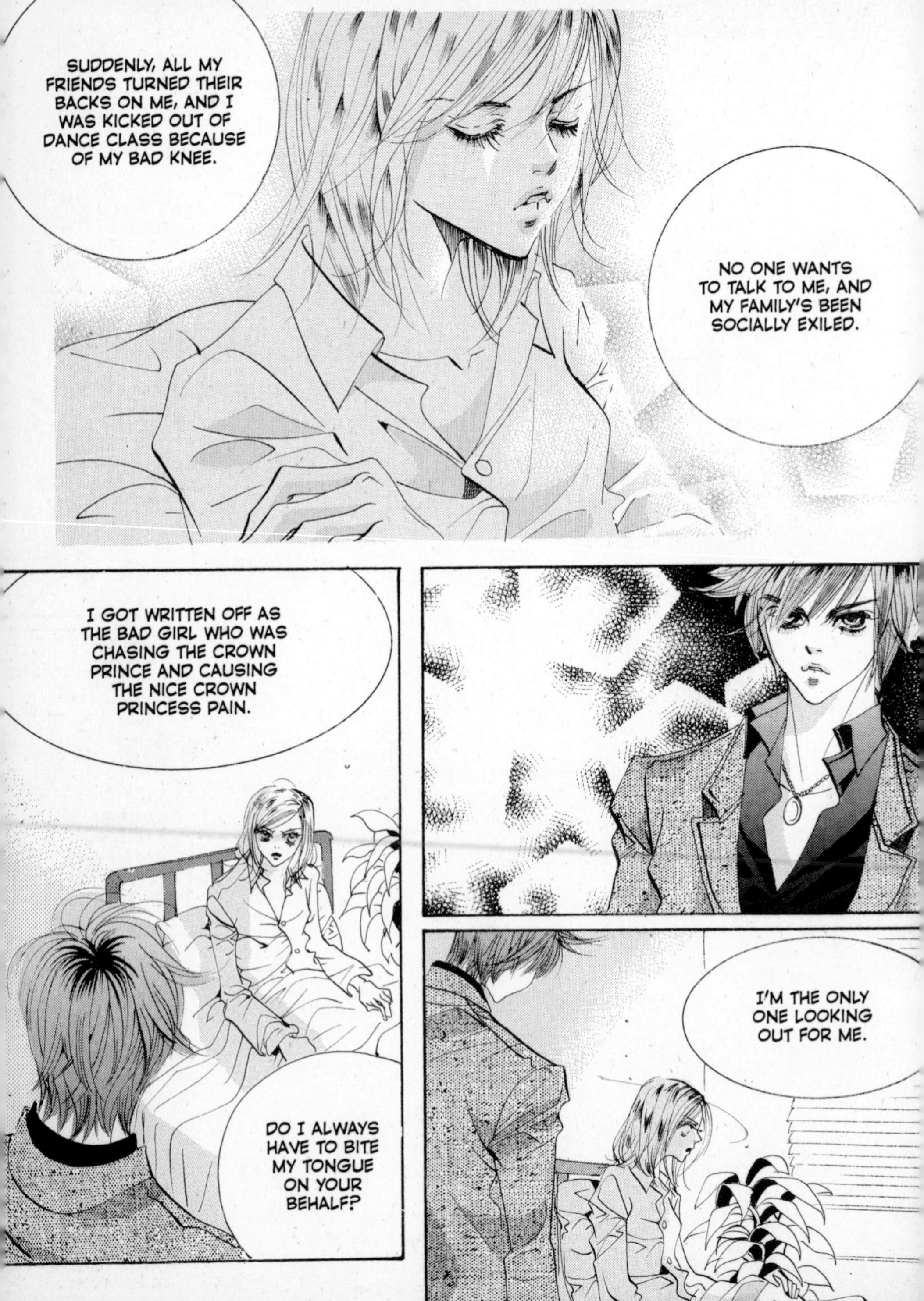
SUDDENLY, ALL MY FRIENDS TURNED THEIR BACKS ON ME, AND I WAS KICKED OUT OF DANCE CLASS BECAUSE OF MY BAD KNEE.
NO ONE WANTS TO TALK TO ME, AND MY FAMILY'S BEEN SOCIALLY EXILED.
I GOT WRITTEN OFF AS THE BAD GIRL WHO WAS CHASING THE CROWN PRINCE AND CAUSING THE NICE CROWN PRINCESS PAIN.
DO I ALWAYS HAVE TO BITE MY TONGUE ON YOUR BEHALF?
I'M THE ONLY ONE LOOKING OUT FOR ME.

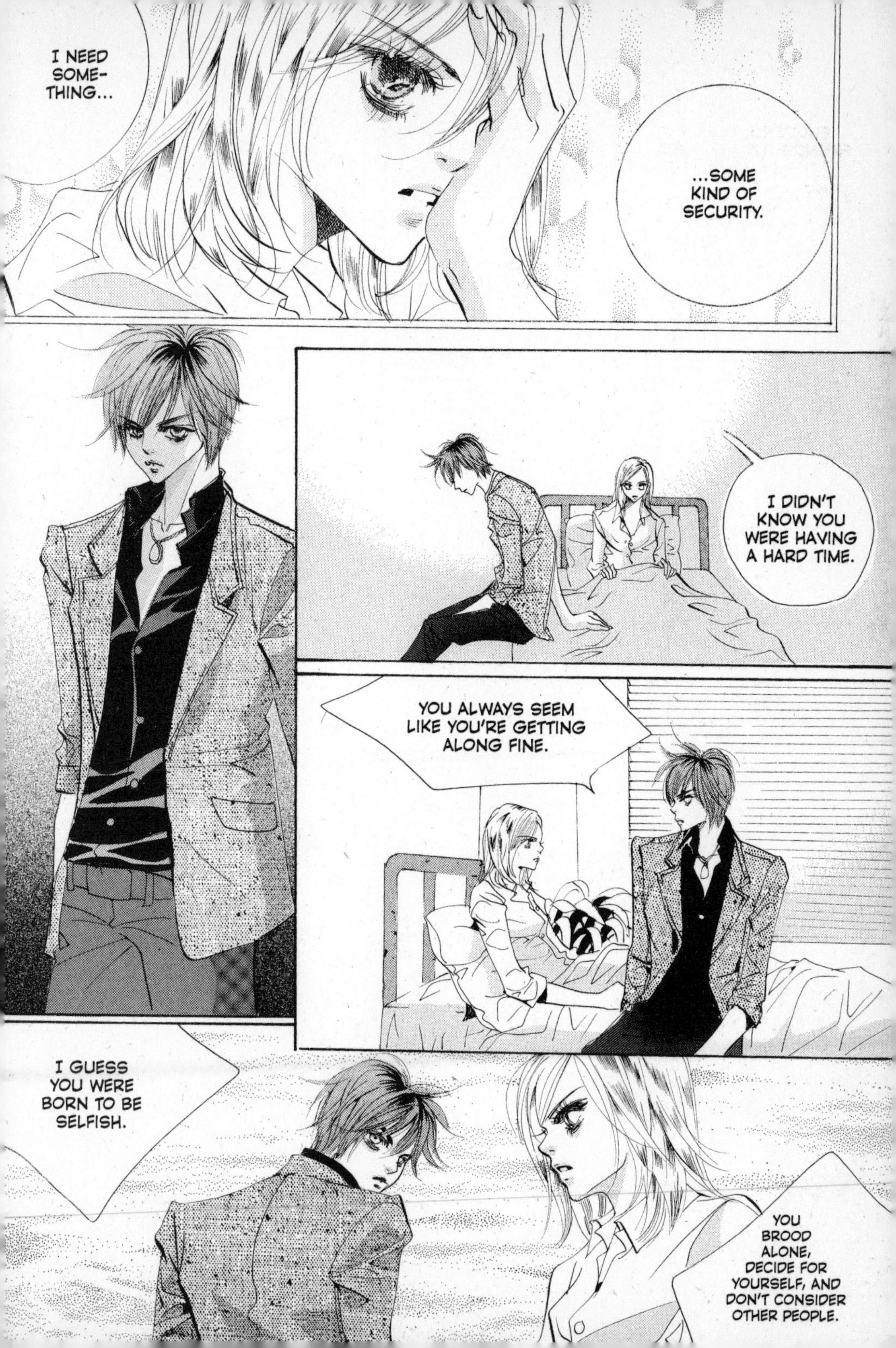
I NEED SOME-THING...
...SOME KIND OF SECURITY.
I DIDN'T KNOW YOU WERE HAVING A HARD TIME.
YOU ALWAYS SEEM LIKE YOU'RE GETTING ALONG FINE.
I GUESS YOU WERE BORN TO BE SELFISH.
YOU BROOD ALONE, DECIDE FOR YOURSELF, AND DON'T CONSIDER OTHER PEOPLE.

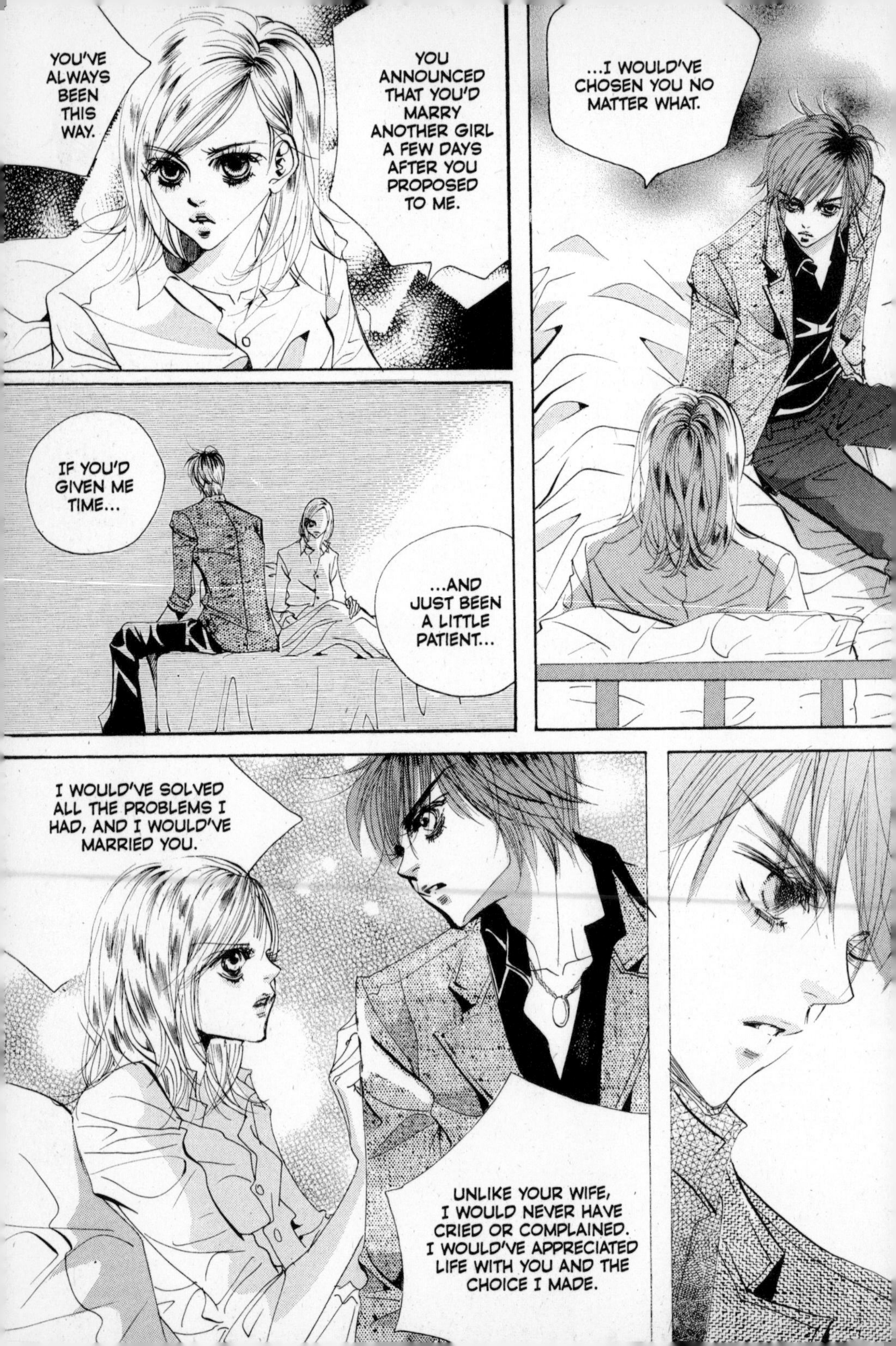
YOU'VE ALWAYS BEEN THIS WAY.
YOU ANNOUNCED THAT YOU'D MARRY ANOTHER GIRL A FEW DAYS AFTER YOU PROPOSED TO ME.
IF YOU'D GIVEN ME TIME...
...AND JUST BEEN A LITTLE PATIENT...
...I WOULD'VE CHOSEN YOU NO MATTER WHAT.
I WOULD'VE SOLVED ALL THE PROBLEMS I HAD, AND I WOULD'VE MARRIED YOU.
UNLIKE YOUR WIFE, I WOULD NEVER HAVE CRIED OR COMPLAINED. I WOULD'VE APPRECIATED LIFE WITH YOU AND THE CHOICE I MADE.

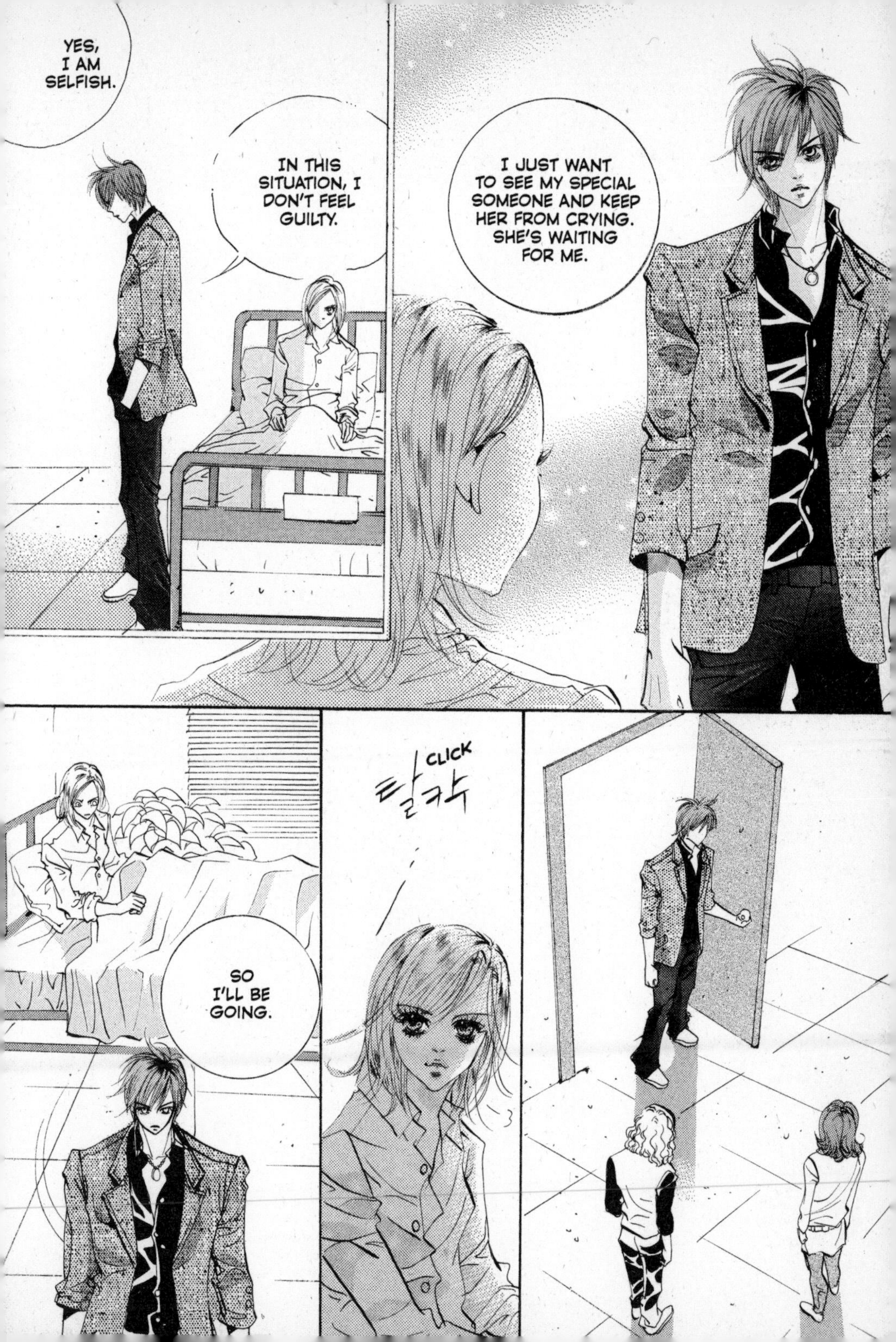
YES, I AM SELFISH.
IN THIS SITUATION, I DON'T FEEL GUILTY.
I JUST WANT TO SEE MY SPECIAL SOMEONE AND KEEP HER FROM CRYING. SHE'S WAITING FOR ME.
SO I'LL BE GOING.
CLICK
탈칵

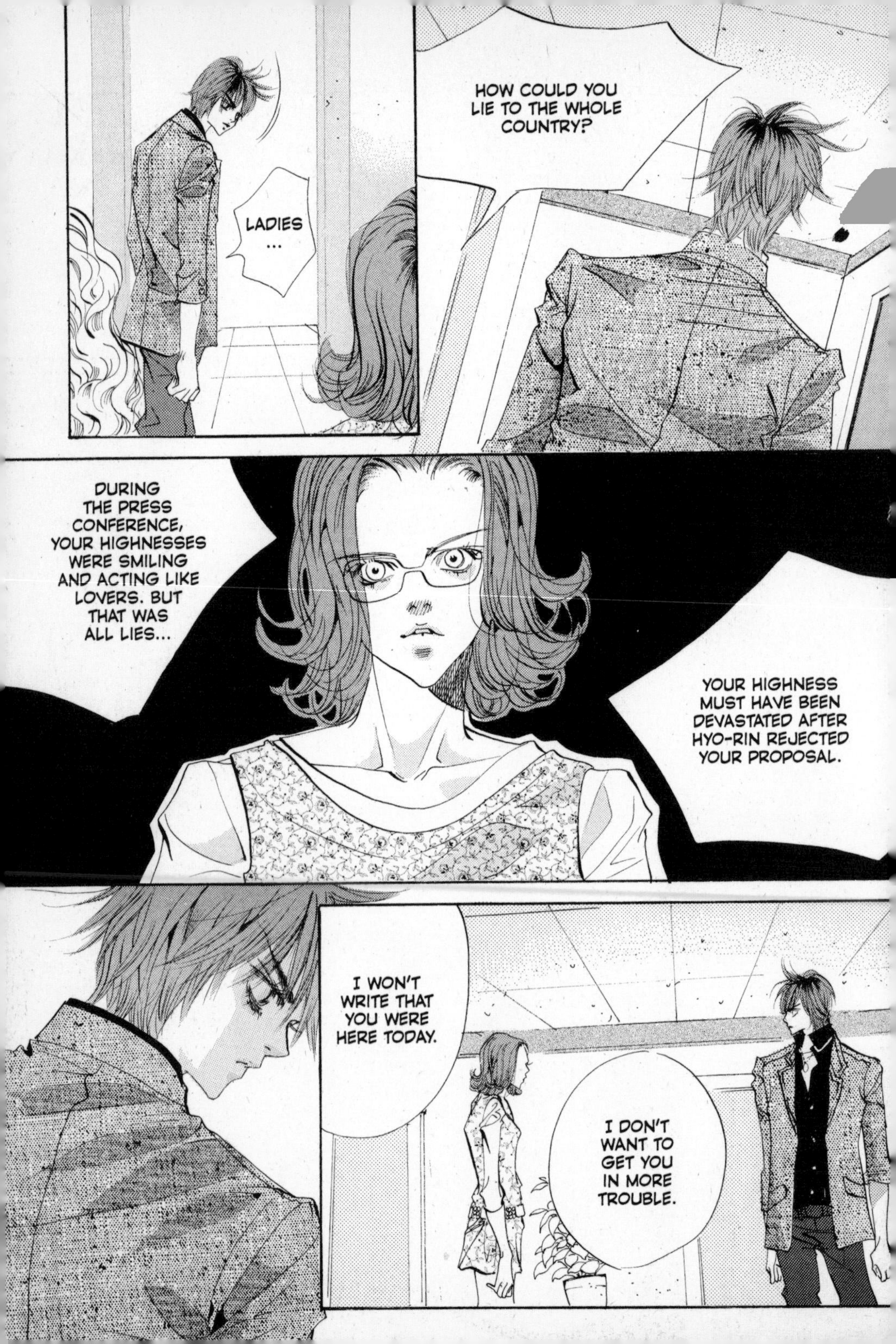
LADIES ...
HOW COULD YOU LIE TO THE WHOLE COUNTRY?
DURING THE PRESS CONFERENCE, YOUR HIGHNESSES WERE SMILING AND ACTING LIKE LOVERS. BUT THAT WAS ALL LIES...
YOUR HIGHNESS MUST HAVE BEEN DEVASTATED AFTER HYO-RIN REJECTED YOUR PROPOSAL.
I WON'T WRITE THAT YOU WERE HERE TODAY.
I DON'T WANT TO GET YOU IN MORE TROUBLE.

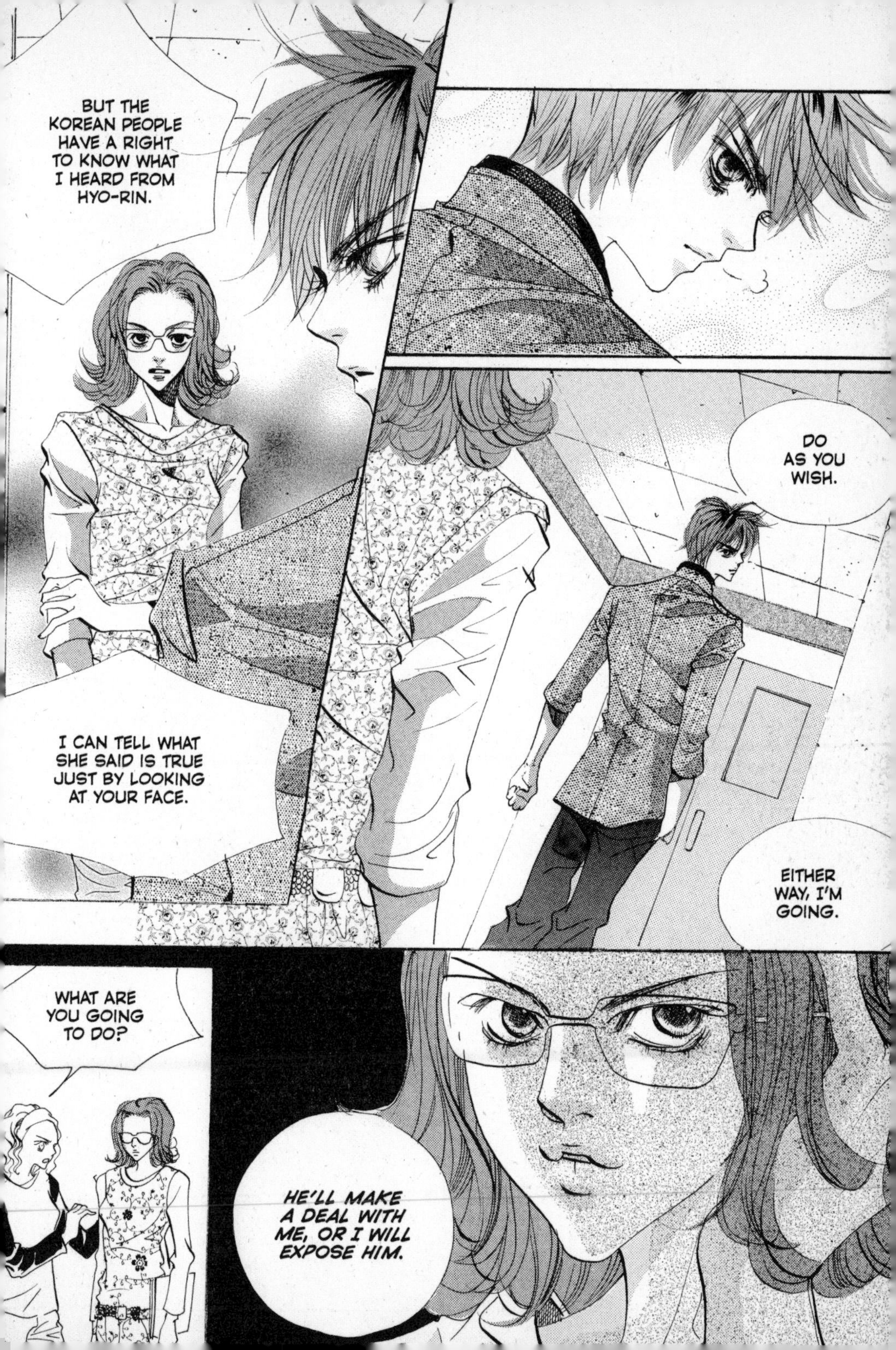
BUT THE KOREAN PEOPLE HAVE A RIGHT TO KNOW WHAT I HEARD FROM HYO-RIN.
I CAN TELL WHAT SHE SAID IS TRUE JUST BY LOOKING AT YOUR FACE.
DO AS YOU WISH.
EITHER WAY, I'M GOING.
WHAT ARE YOU GOING TO DO?
HE'LL MAKE A DEAL WITH ME, OR I WILL EXPOSE HIM.

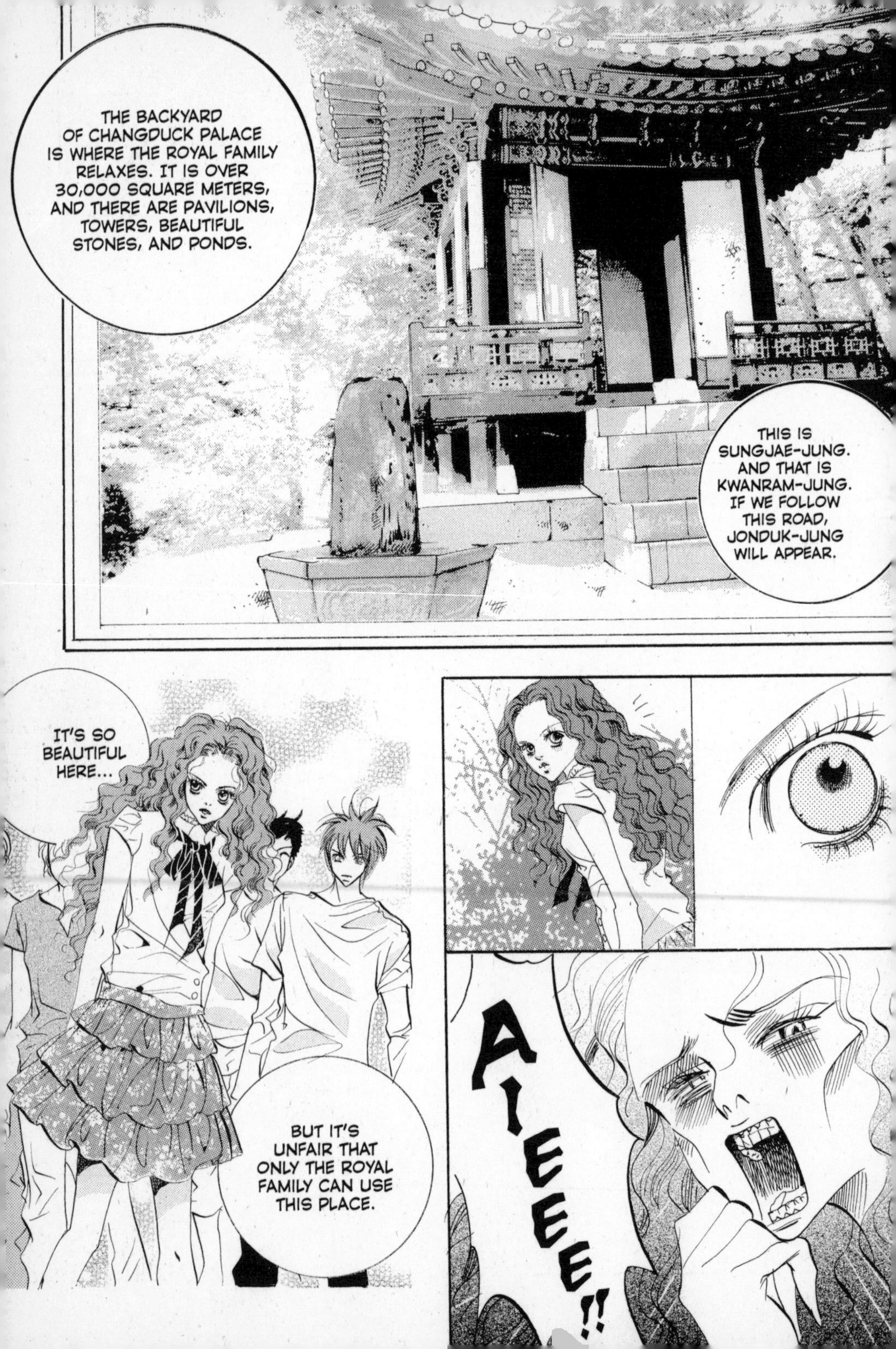
THE BACKYARD OF CHANGDUCK PALACE IS WHERE THE ROYAL FAMILY RELAXES. IT IS OVER 30,000 SQUARE METERS, AND THERE ARE PAVILIONS, TOWERS, BEAUTIFUL STONES, AND PONDS.
THIS IS SUNGJAE-JUNG. AND THAT IS KWANRAM-JUNG. IF WE FOLLOW THIS ROAD, JONDUK-JUNG WILL APPEAR.
IT'S SO BEAUTIFUL HERE...
BUT IT'S UNFAIR THAT ONLY THE ROYAL FAMILY CAN USE THIS PLACE.
AIEEE!!

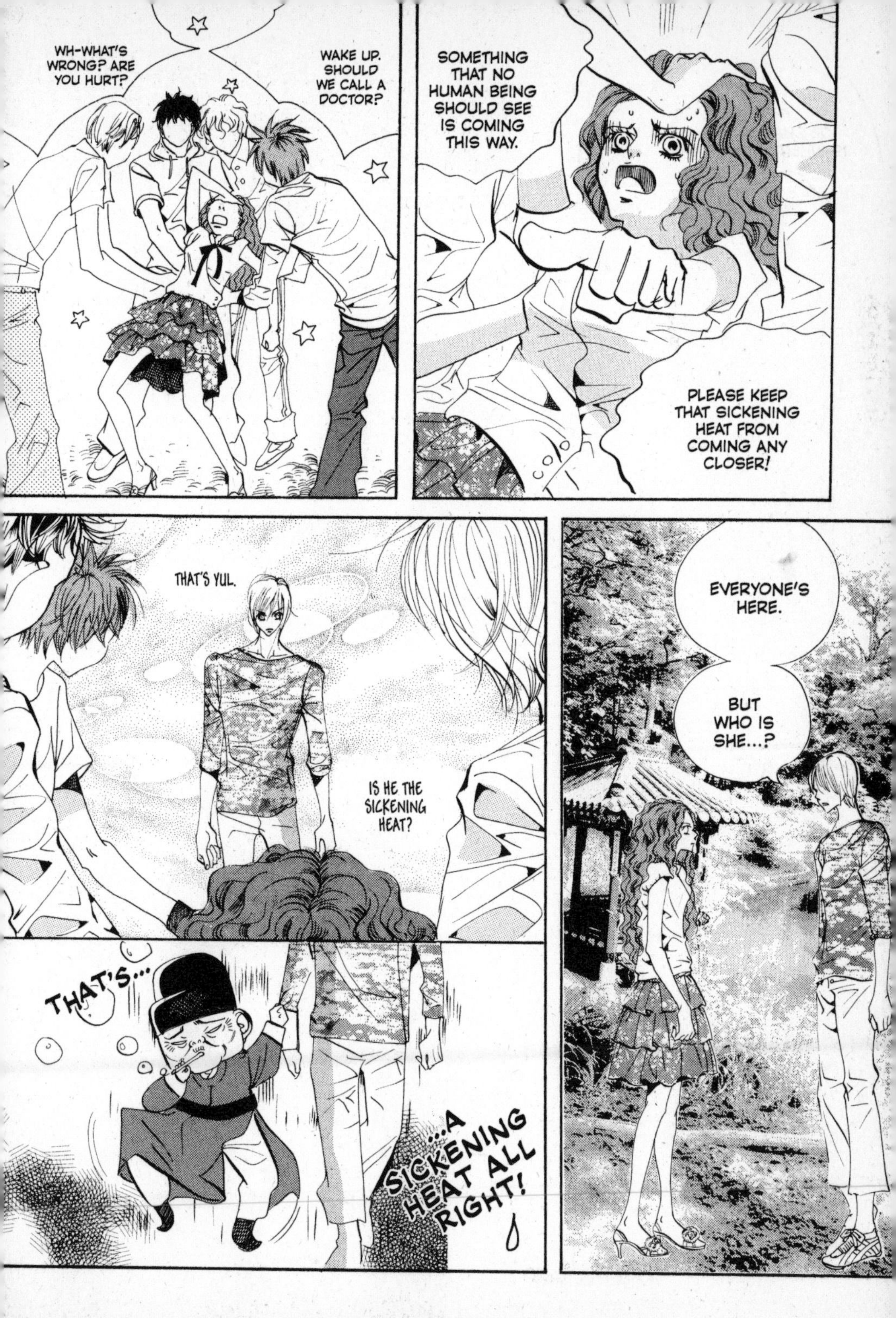
WH-WHAT'S WRONG? ARE YOU HURT?
WAKE UP. SHOULD WE CALL A DOCTOR?
SOMETHING THAT NO HUMAN BEING SHOULD SEE IS COMING THIS WAY.
PLEASE KEEP THAT SICKENING HEAT FROM COMING ANY CLOSER!
THAT'S YUL.
IS HE THE SICKENING HEAT?
THAT'S...
...A SICKENING HEAT ALL RIGHT!
EVERYONE'S HERE.
BUT WHO IS SHE...?

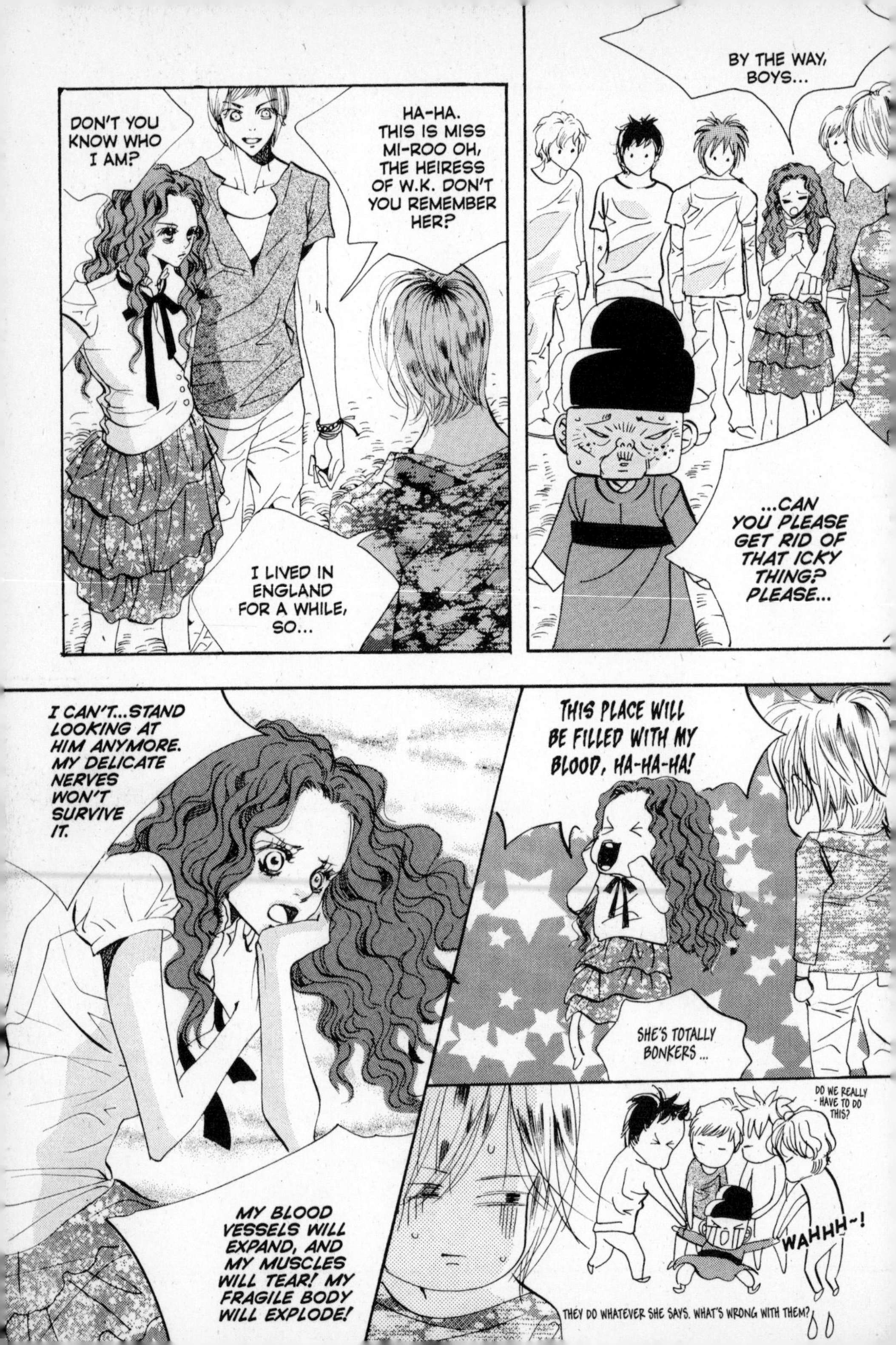
DON'T YOU KNOW WHO I AM?
HA-HA. THIS IS MISS MI-ROO OH, THE HEIRESS OF W.K. DON'T YOU REMEMBER HER?
I LIVED IN ENGLAND FOR A WHILE, SO...
BY THE WAY, BOYS...
...CAN YOU PLEASE GET RID OF THAT ICKY THING? PLEASE...
I CAN'T...STAND LOOKING AT HIM ANYMORE. MY DELICATE NERVES WON'T SURVIVE IT.
MY BLOOD VESSELS WILL EXPAND, AND MY MUSCLES WILL TEAR! MY FRAGILE BODY WILL EXPLODE!
THIS PLACE WILL BE FILLED WITH MY BLOOD, HA-HA-HA!
SHE'S TOTALLY BONKERS ...
DO WE REALLY HAVE TO DO THIS?
WAHHH~!
THEY DO WHATEVER SHE SAYS. WHAT'S WRONG WITH THEM?

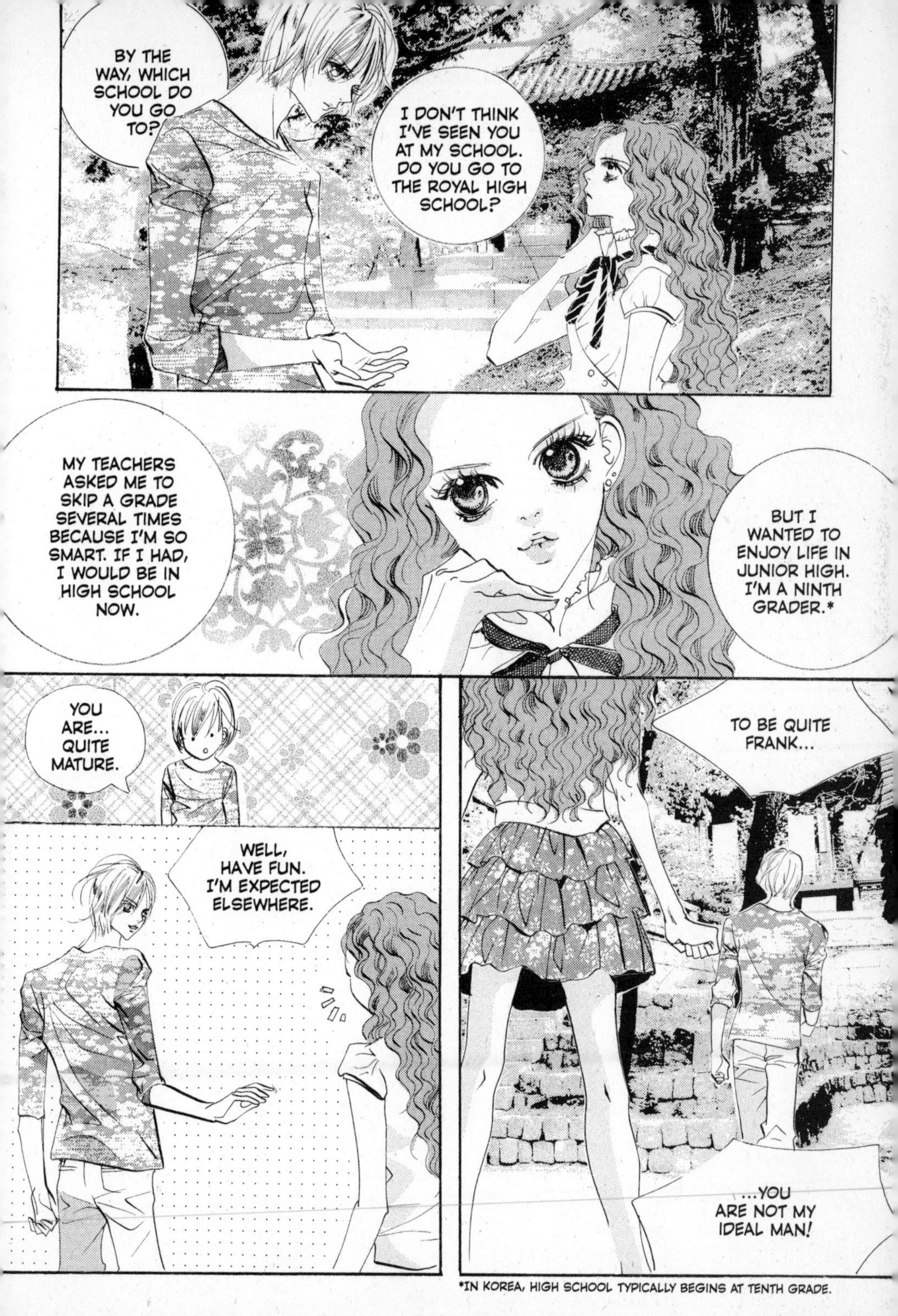
BY THE WAY, WHICH SCHOOL DO YOU GO TO?
I DON'T THINK I'VE SEEN YOU AT MY SCHOOL. DO YOU GO TO THE ROYAL HIGH SCHOOL?
MY TEACHERS ASKED ME TO SKIP A GRADE SEVERAL TIMES BECAUSE I'M SO SMART. IF I HAD, I WOULD BE IN HIGH SCHOOL NOW.
BUT I WANTED TO ENJOY LIFE IN JUNIOR HIGH. I'M A NINTH GRADER.*
YOU ARE... QUITE MATURE.
WELL, HAVE FUN. I'M EXPECTED ELSEWHERE.
TO BE QUITE FRANK...
...YOU ARE NOT MY IDEAL MAN!

*IN KOREA, HIGH SCHOOL TYPICALLY BEGINS AT TENTH GRADE.

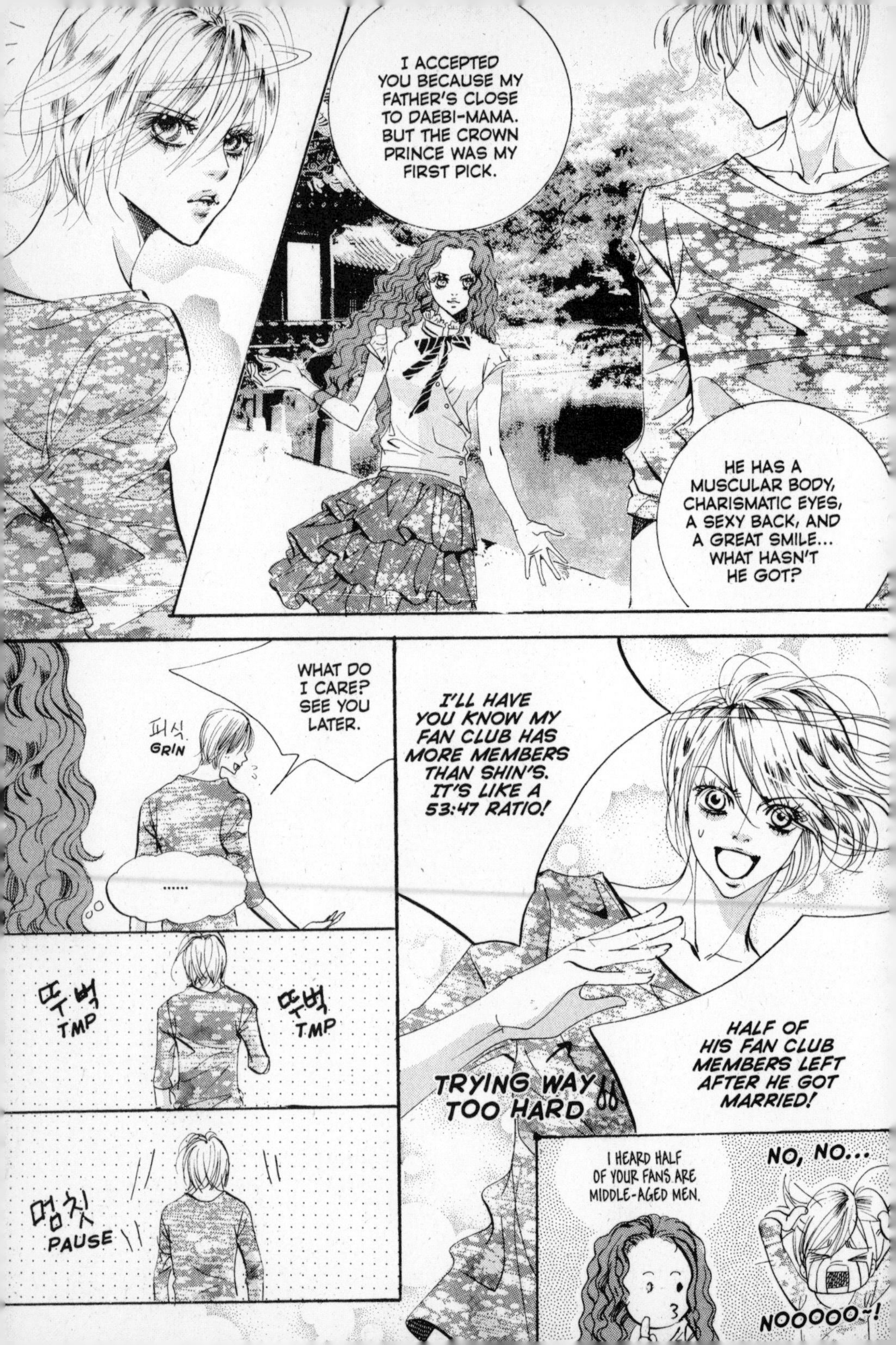

I ACCEPTED YOU BECAUSE MY FATHER'S CLOSE TO DAEBI-MAMA. BUT THE CROWN PRINCE WAS MY FIRST PICK.
HE HAS A MUSCULAR BODY, CHARISMATIC EYES, A SEXY BACK, AND A GREAT SMILE... WHAT HASN'T HE GOT?
WHAT DO I CARE? SEE YOU LATER.
피식
GRIN
......
뚜벅
TMP
뚜벅
TMP
멈칫
PAUSE
I'LL HAVE YOU KNOW MY FAN CLUB HAS MORE MEMBERS THAN SHIN'S. IT'S LIKE A 53:47 RATIO!
HALF OF HIS FAN CLUB MEMBERS LEFT AFTER HE GOT MARRIED!
TRYING WAY TOO HARD
I HEARD HALF OF YOUR FANS ARE MIDDLE-AGED MEN.
NO, NO...
NOOOOO~!

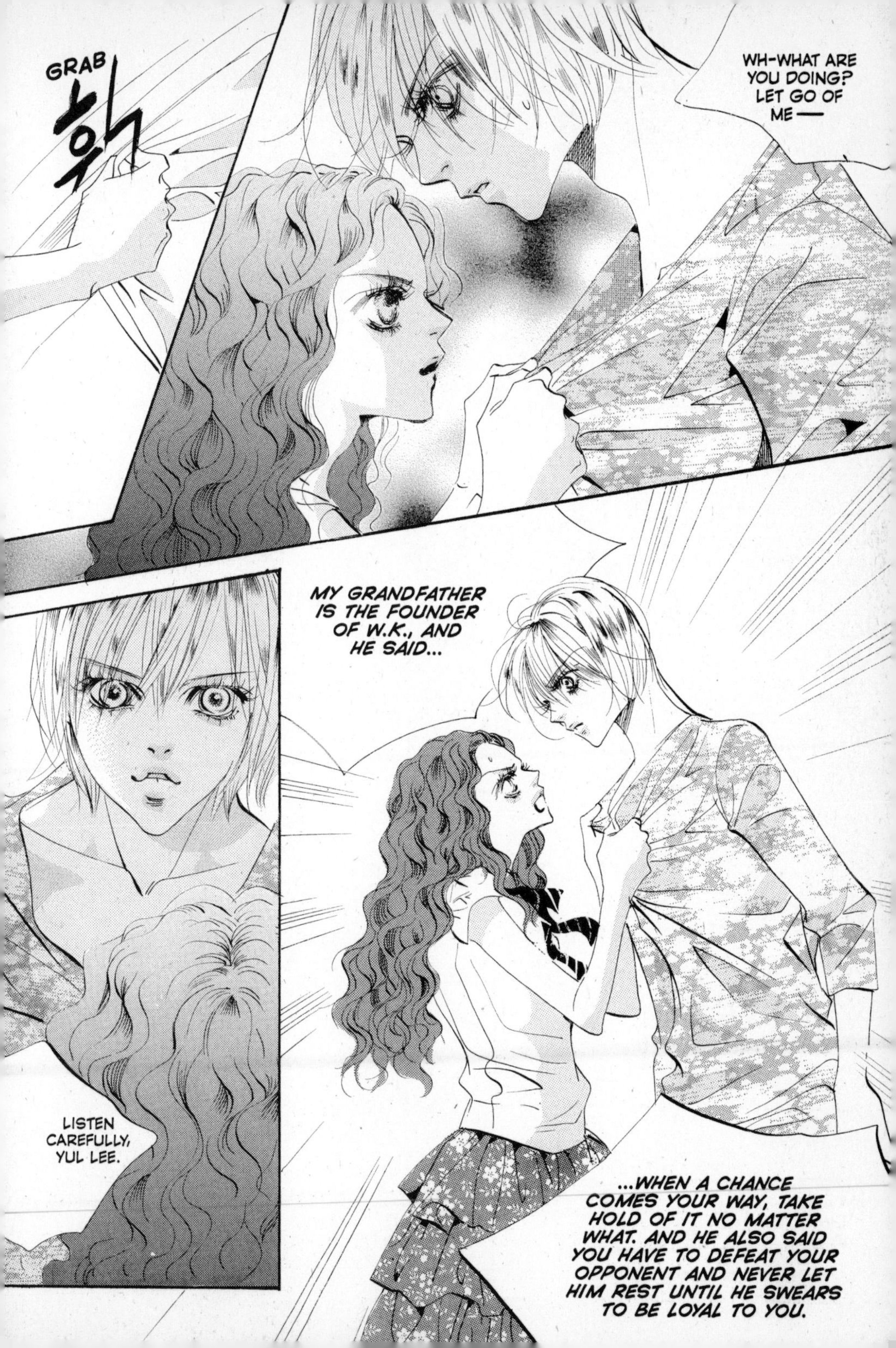
GRAB
WH-WHAT ARE YOU DOING? LET GO OF ME—
LISTEN CAREFULLY, YUL LEE.
MY GRANDFATHER IS THE FOUNDER OF W.K., AND HE SAID...
...WHEN A CHANCE COMES YOUR WAY, TAKE HOLD OF IT NO MATTER WHAT. AND HE ALSO SAID YOU HAVE TO DEFEAT YOUR OPPONENT AND NEVER LET HIM REST UNTIL HE SWEARS TO BE LOYAL TO YOU.

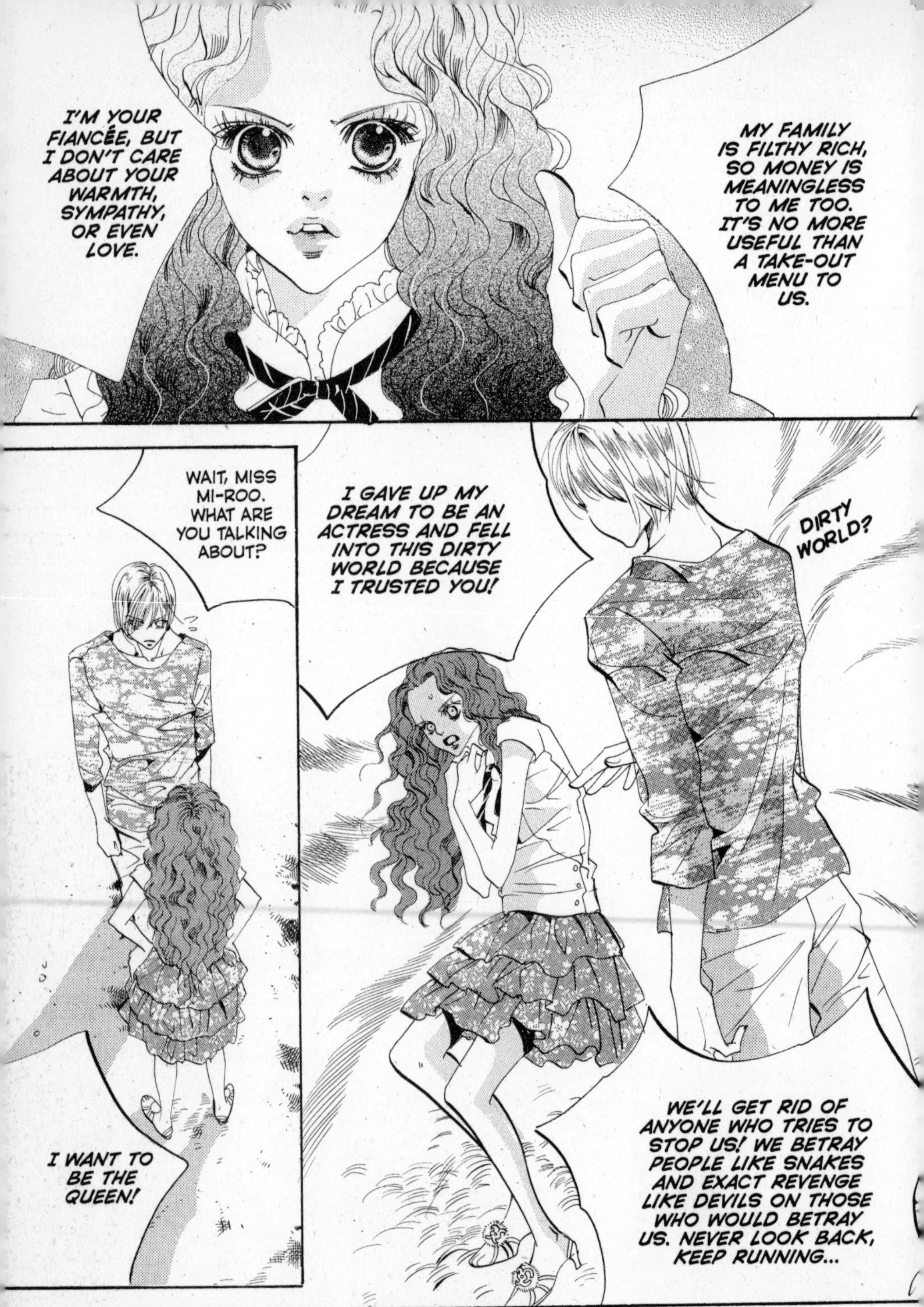
I'M YOUR FIANCÉE, BUT I DON'T CARE ABOUT YOUR WARMTH, SYMPATHY, OR EVEN LOVE.
MY FAMILY IS FILTHY RICH, SO MONEY IS MEANINGLESS TO ME TOO. IT'S NO MORE USEFUL THAN A TAKE-OUT MENU TO US.
WAIT, MISS MI-ROO. WHAT ARE YOU TALKING ABOUT?
I WANT TO BE THE QUEEN!
I GAVE UP MY DREAM TO BE AN ACTRESS AND FELL INTO THIS DIRTY WORLD BECAUSE I TRUSTED YOU!
DIRTY WORLD?
WE'LL GET RID OF ANYONE WHO TRIES TO STOP US! WE BETRAY PEOPLE LIKE SNAKES AND EXACT REVENGE LIKE DEVILS ON THOSE WHO WOULD BETRAY US. NEVER LOOK BACK, KEEP RUNNING...

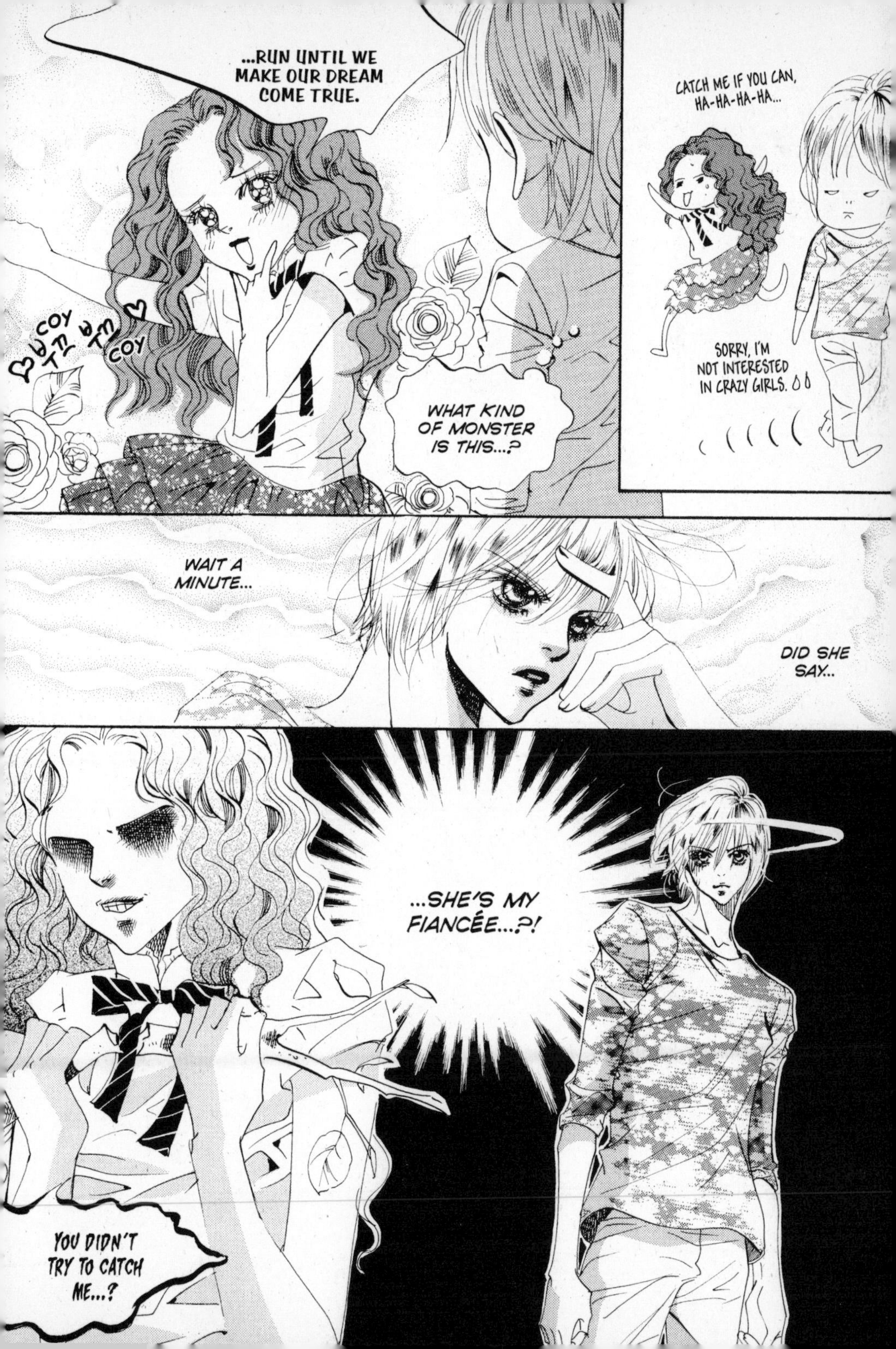
...RUN UNTIL WE MAKE OUR DREAM COME TRUE.
COY
COY
WHAT KIND OF MONSTER IS THIS...?
CATCH ME IF YOU CAN, HA-HA-HA-HA...
SORRY, I'M NOT INTERESTED IN CRAZY GIRLS.
WAIT A MINUTE...
DID SHE SAY...
...SHE'S MY FIANCÉE...?!
YOU DIDN'T TRY TO CATCH ME...?

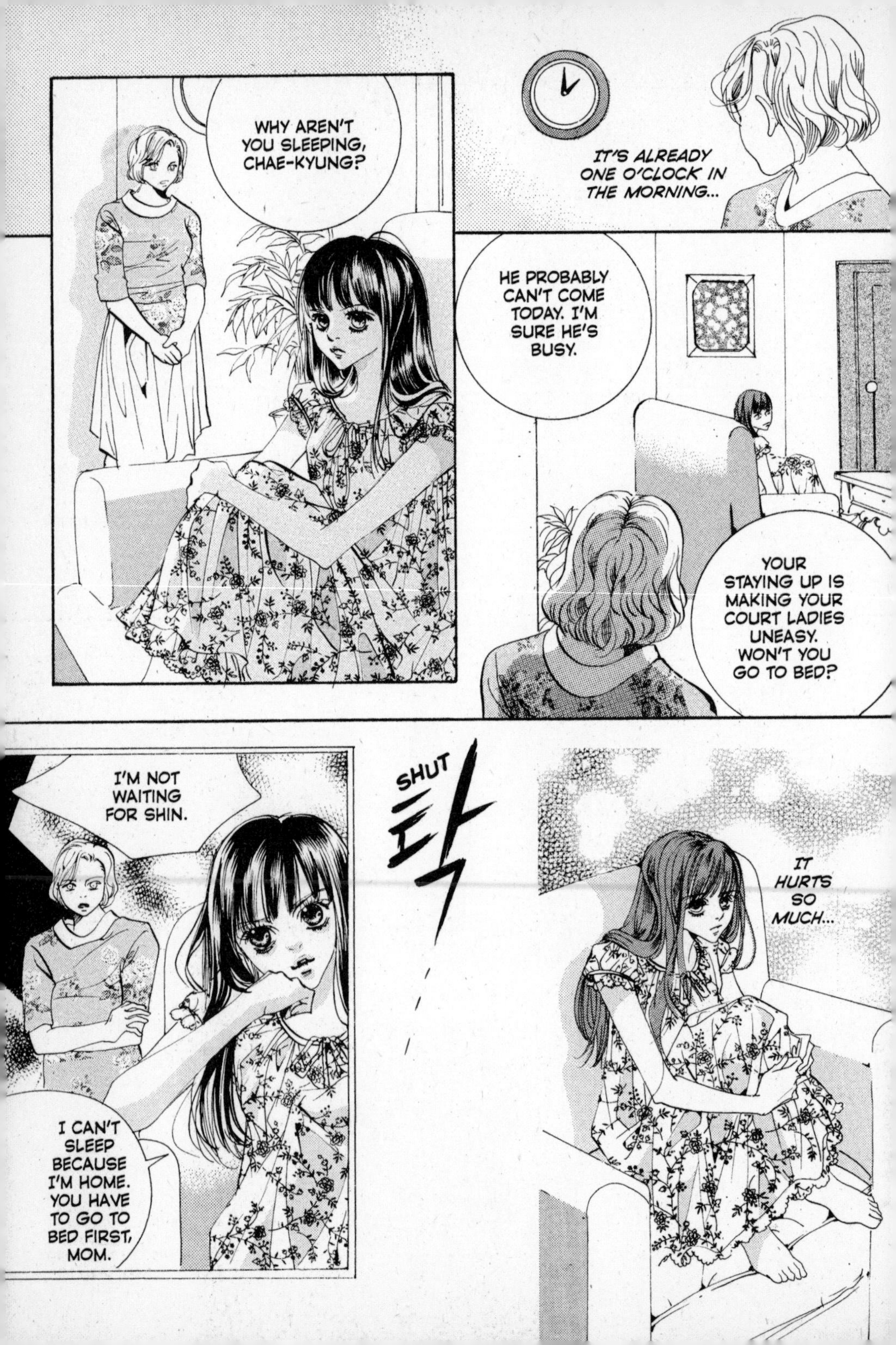
WHY AREN'T YOU SLEEPING, CHAE-KYUNG?
IT'S ALREADY ONE O'CLOCK IN THE MORNING...
HE PROBABLY CAN'T COME TODAY. I'M SURE HE'S BUSY.
YOUR STAYING UP IS MAKING YOUR COURT LADIES UNEASY. WON'T YOU GO TO BED?
I'M NOT WAITING FOR SHIN.
I CAN'T SLEEP BECAUSE I'M HOME. YOU HAVE TO GO TO BED FIRST, MOM.
SHUT
탁
IT HURTS SO MUCH...

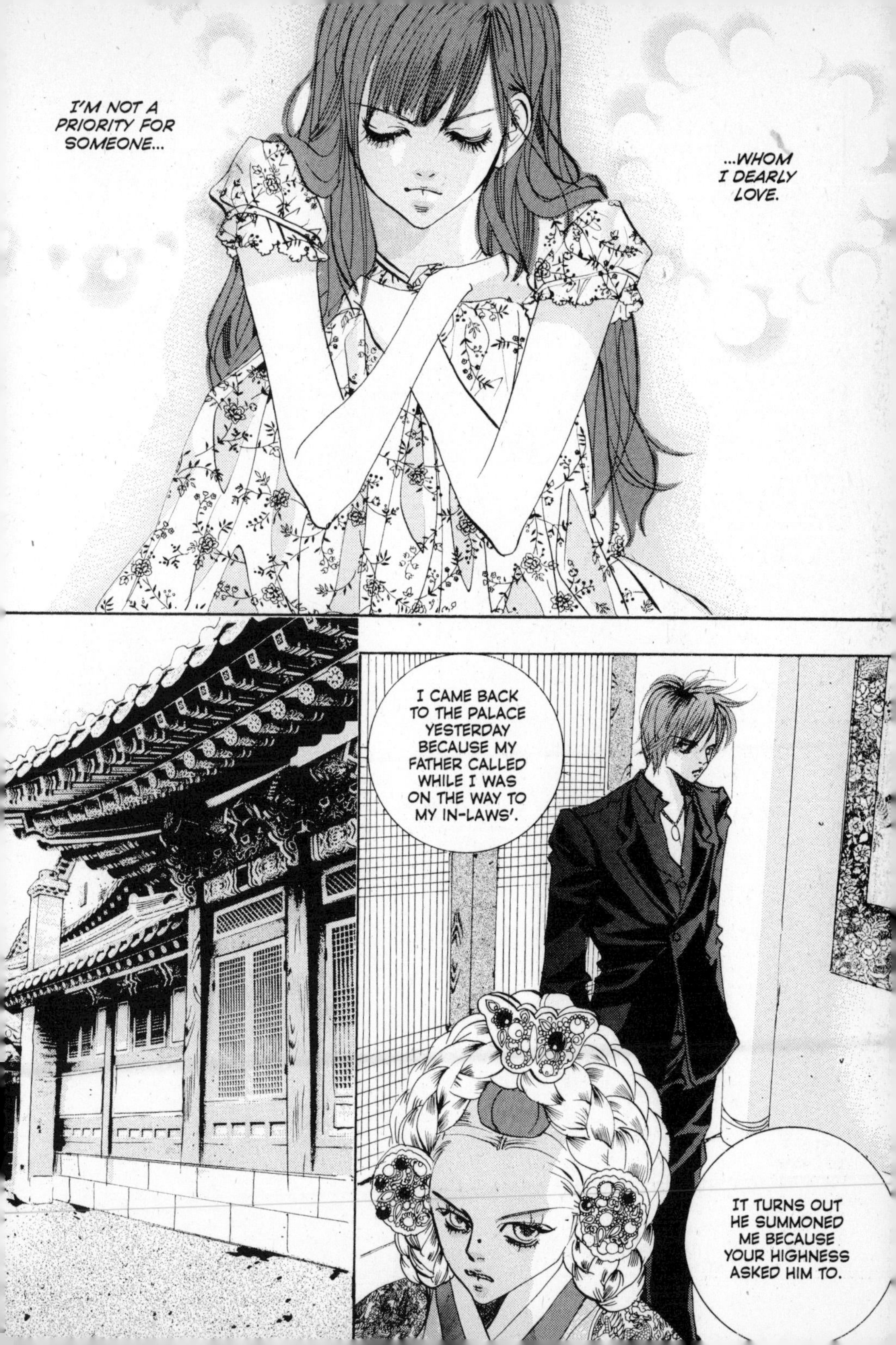
I'M NOT A PRIORITY FOR SOMEONE...
...WHOM I DEARLY LOVE.
I CAME BACK TO THE PALACE YESTERDAY BECAUSE MY FATHER CALLED WHILE I WAS ON THE WAY TO MY IN-LAWS'.
IT TURNS OUT HE SUMMONED ME BECAUSE YOUR HIGHNESS ASKED HIM TO.

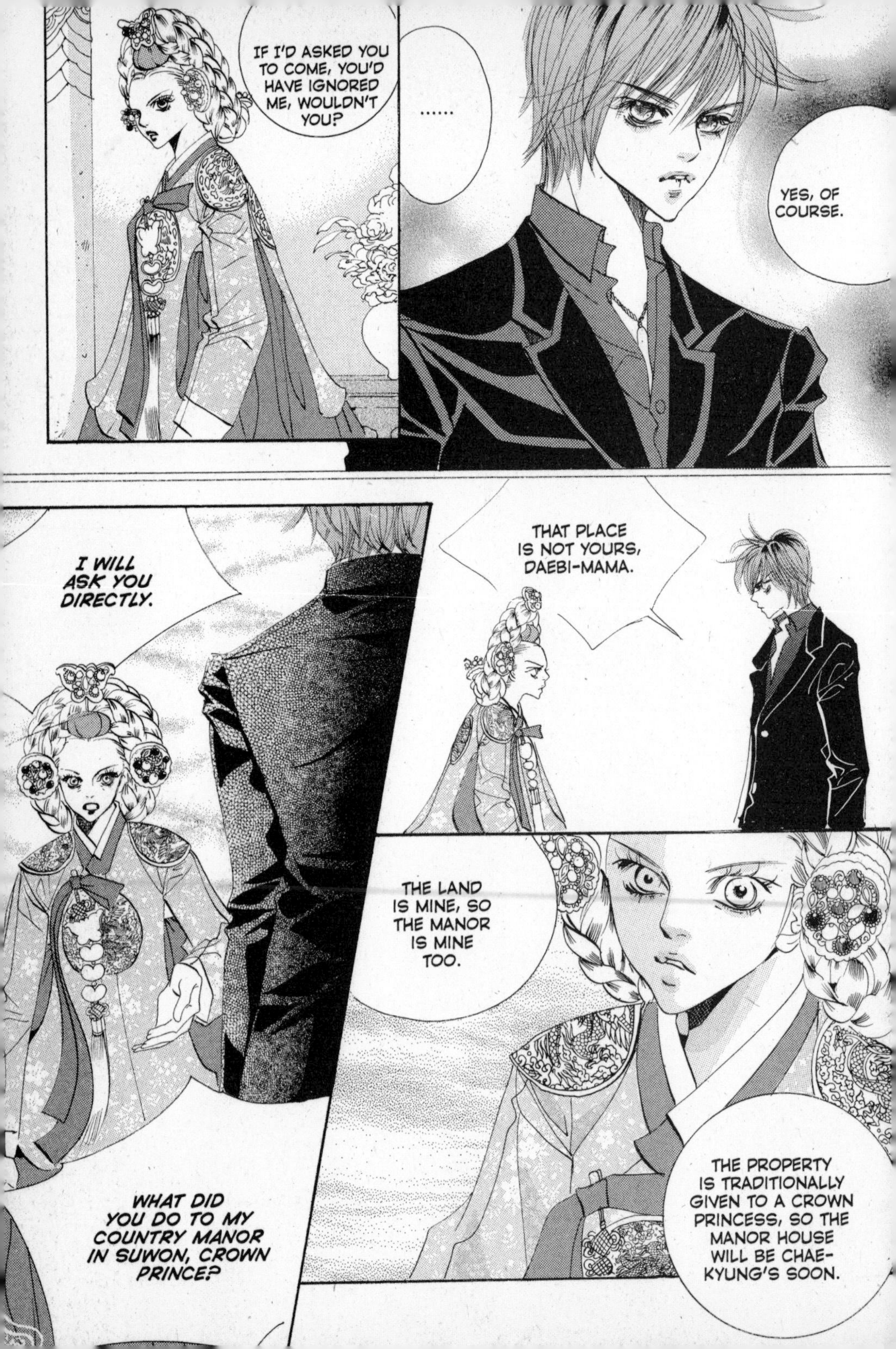
IF I'D ASKED YOU TO COME, YOU'D HAVE IGNORED ME, WOULDN'T YOU?
......
YES, OF COURSE.
I WILL ASK YOU DIRECTLY.
WHAT DID YOU DO TO MY COUNTRY MANOR IN SUWON, CROWN PRINCE?
THAT PLACE IS NOT YOURS, DAEBI-MAMA.
THE LAND IS MINE, SO THE MANOR IS MINE TOO.
THE PROPERTY IS TRADITIONALLY GIVEN TO A CROWN PRINCESS, SO THE MANOR HOUSE WILL BE CHAE-KYUNG'S SOON.

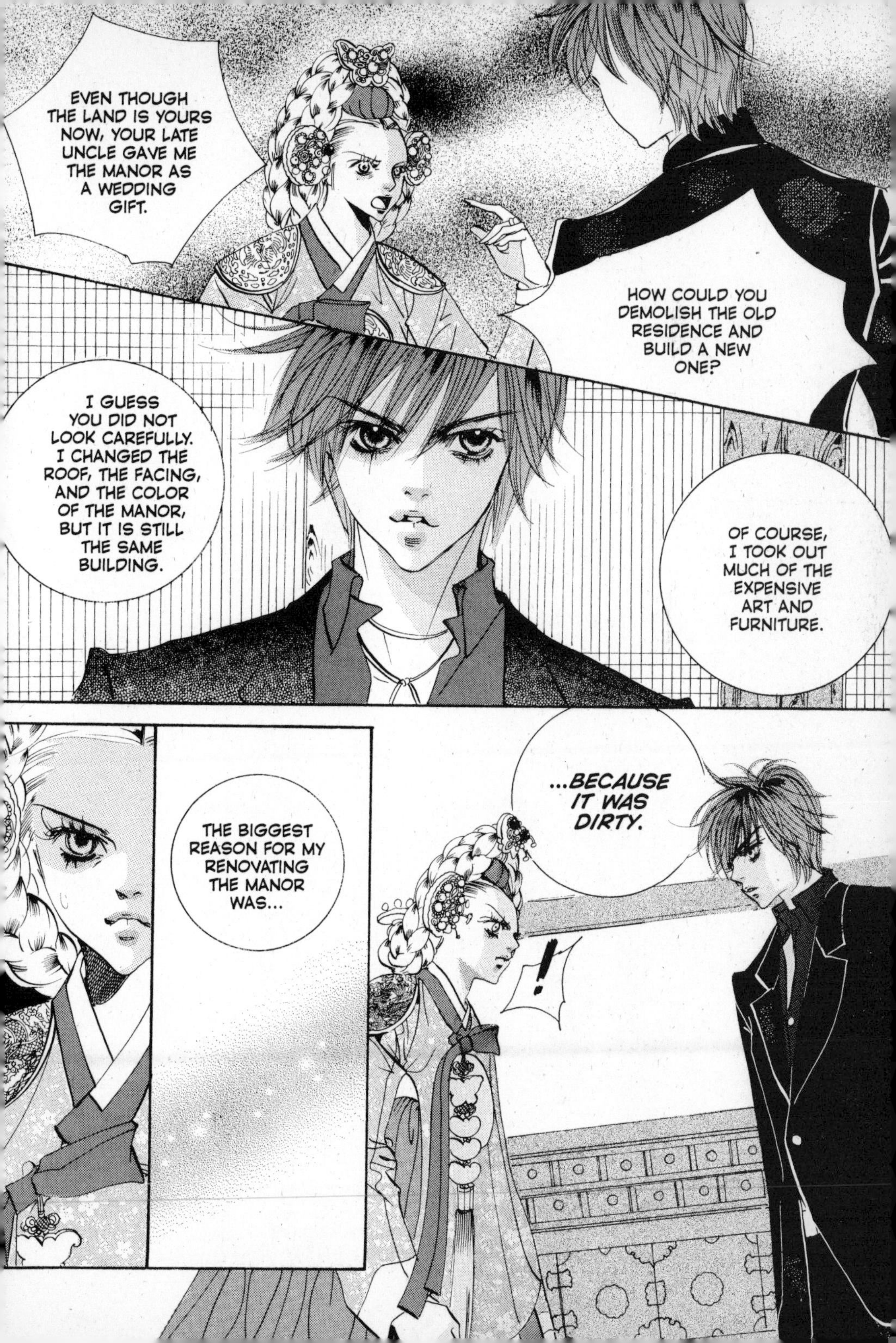
EVEN THOUGH THE LAND IS YOURS NOW, YOUR LATE UNCLE GAVE ME THE MANOR AS A WEDDING GIFT.
HOW COULD YOU DEMOLISH THE OLD RESIDENCE AND BUILD A NEW ONE?
I GUESS YOU DID NOT LOOK CAREFULLY. I CHANGED THE ROOF, THE FACING, AND THE COLOR OF THE MANOR, BUT IT IS STILL THE SAME BUILDING.
OF COURSE, I TOOK OUT MUCH OF THE EXPENSIVE ART AND FURNITURE.
THE BIGGEST REASON FOR MY RENOVATING THE MANOR WAS...
...*BECAUSE IT WAS DIRTY.*
!

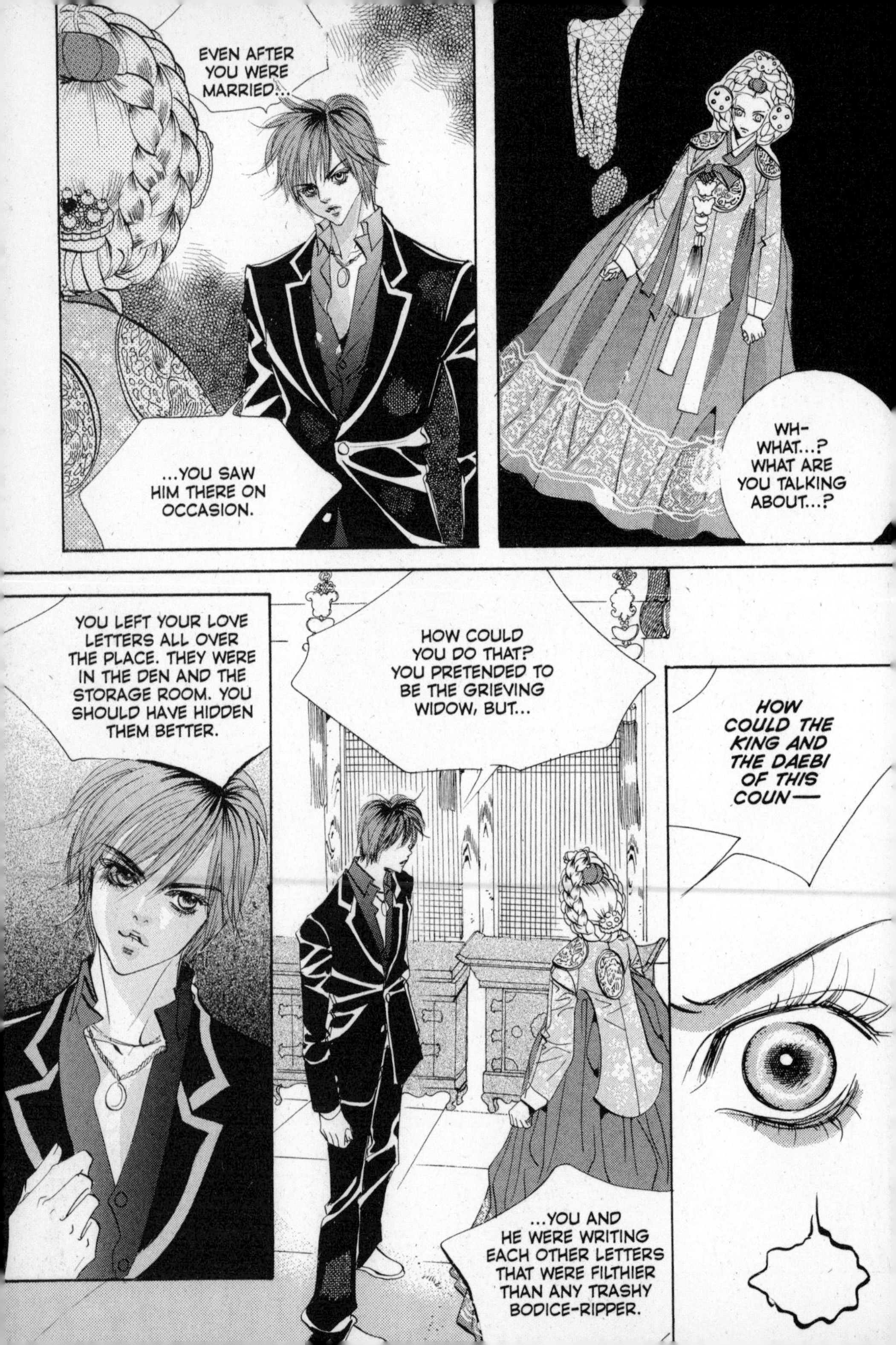
EVEN AFTER YOU WERE MARRIED...
...YOU SAW HIM THERE ON OCCASION.
WH- WHAT...? WHAT ARE YOU TALKING ABOUT...?
YOU LEFT YOUR LOVE LETTERS ALL OVER THE PLACE. THEY WERE IN THE DEN AND THE STORAGE ROOM. YOU SHOULD HAVE HIDDEN THEM BETTER.
HOW COULD YOU DO THAT? YOU PRETENDED TO BE THE GRIEVING WIDOW, BUT...
...YOU AND HE WERE WRITING EACH OTHER LETTERS THAT WERE FILTHIER THAN ANY TRASHY BODICE-RIPPER.
HOW COULD THE KING AND THE DAEBI OF THIS COUN—

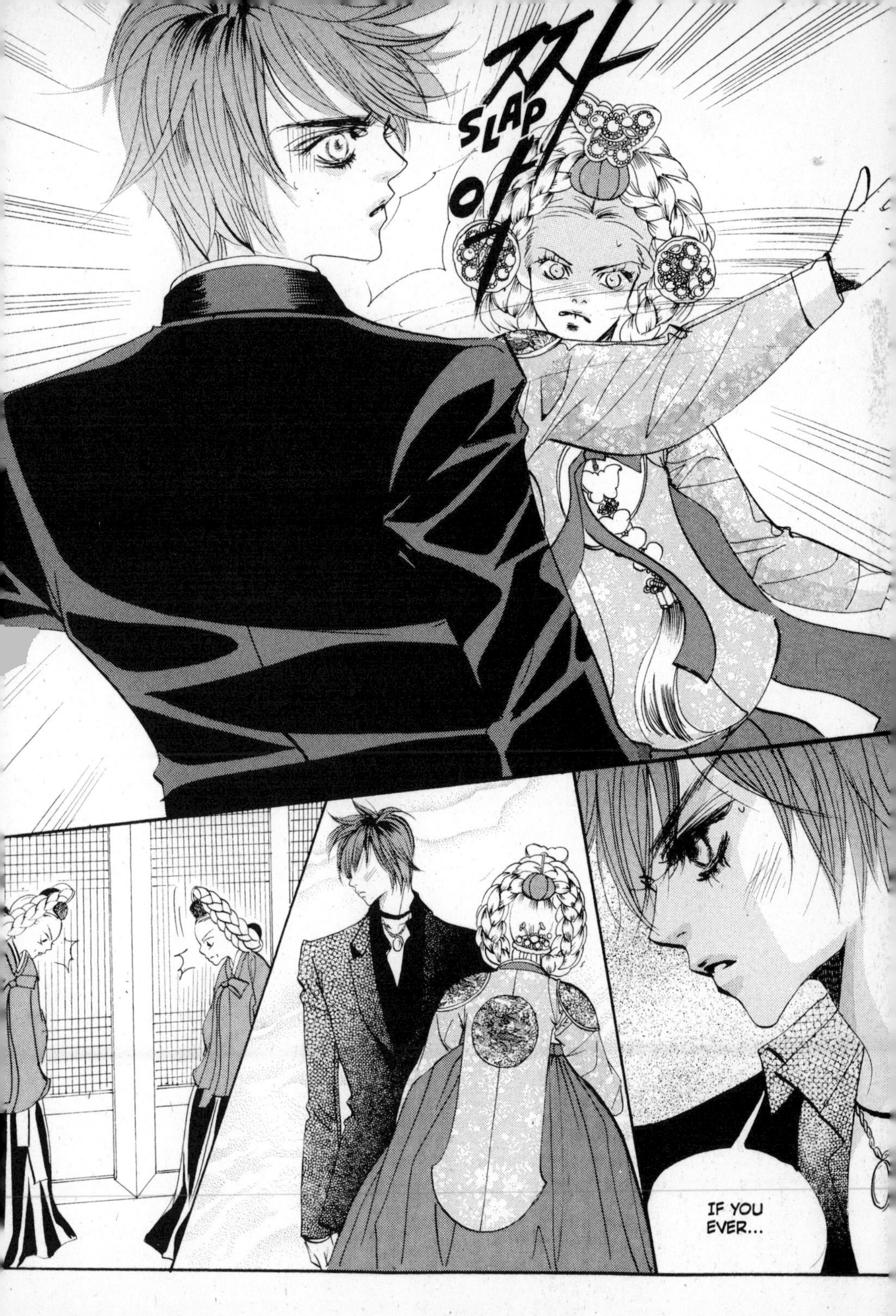

짝
SLAP
IF YOU EVER...

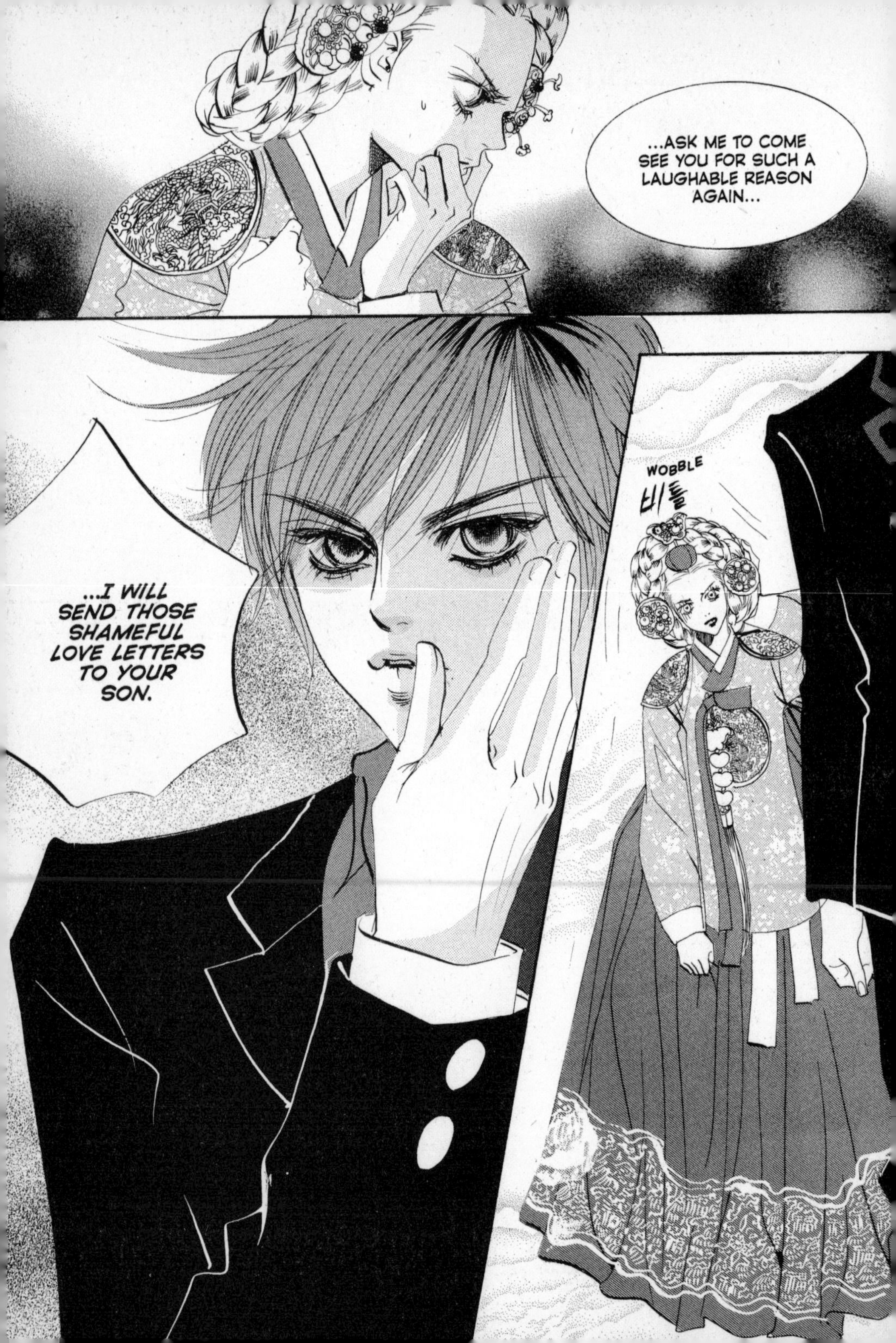
...ASK ME TO COME SEE YOU FOR SUCH A LAUGHABLE REASON AGAIN...
...I WILL SEND THOSE SHAMEFUL LOVE LETTERS TO YOUR SON.
WOBBLE
비틀

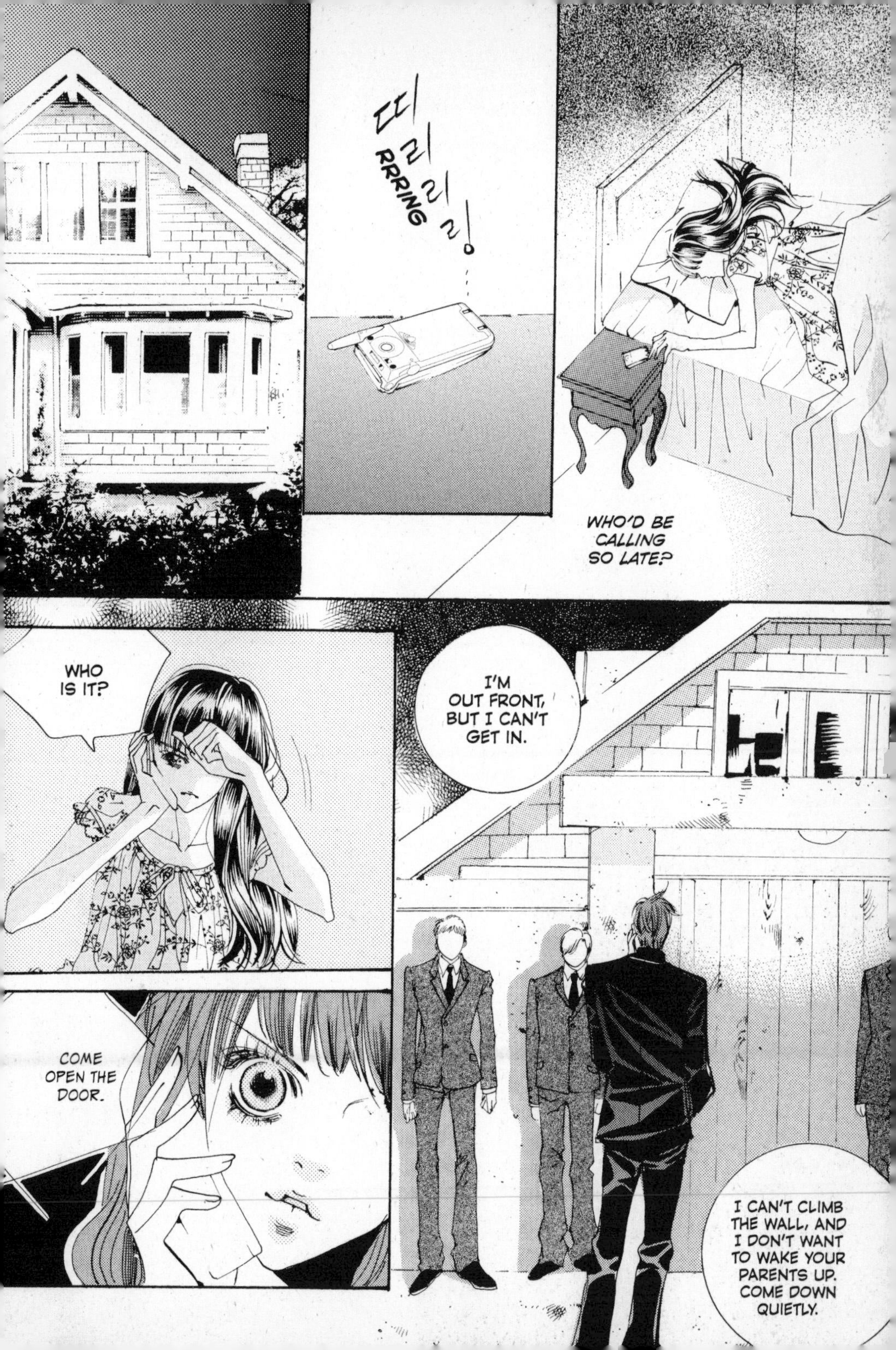

띠리리리!
RRRING
WHO'D BE CALLING SO LATE?
WHO IS IT?
COME OPEN THE DOOR.
I'M OUT FRONT, BUT I CAN'T GET IN.
I CAN'T CLIMB THE WALL, AND I DON'T WANT TO WAKE YOUR PARENTS UP. COME DOWN QUIETLY.

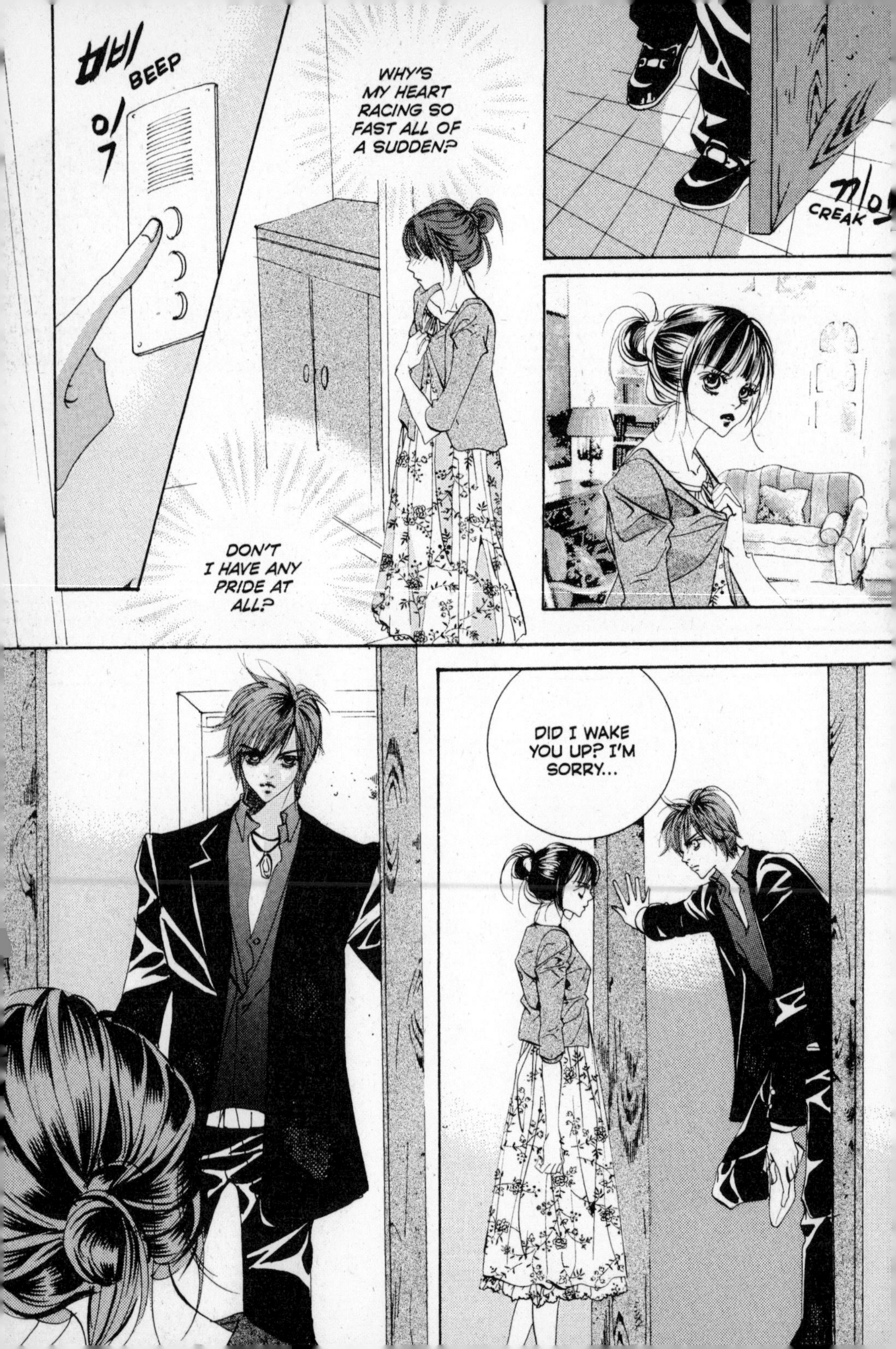
삐비
BEEP
익
WHY'S MY HEART RACING SO FAST ALL OF A SUDDEN?
DON'T I HAVE ANY PRIDE AT ALL?
끼이
CREAK
DID I WAKE YOU UP? I'M SORRY...

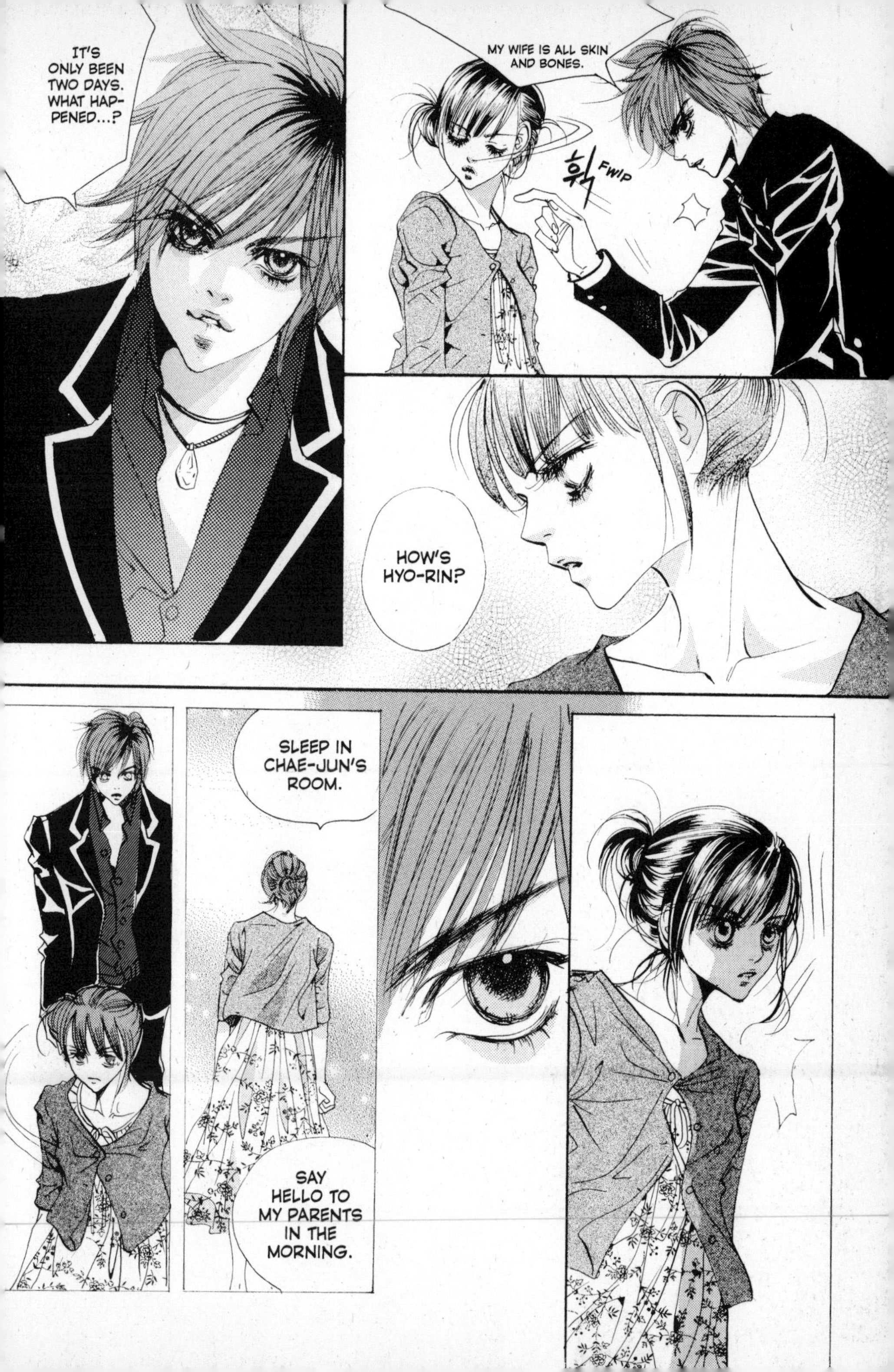
IT'S ONLY BEEN TWO DAYS. WHAT HAP-PENED...?
MY WIFE IS ALL SKIN AND BONES.
휙
FWIP
HOW'S HYO-RIN?
SLEEP IN CHAE-JUN'S ROOM.
SAY HELLO TO MY PARENTS IN THE MORNING.

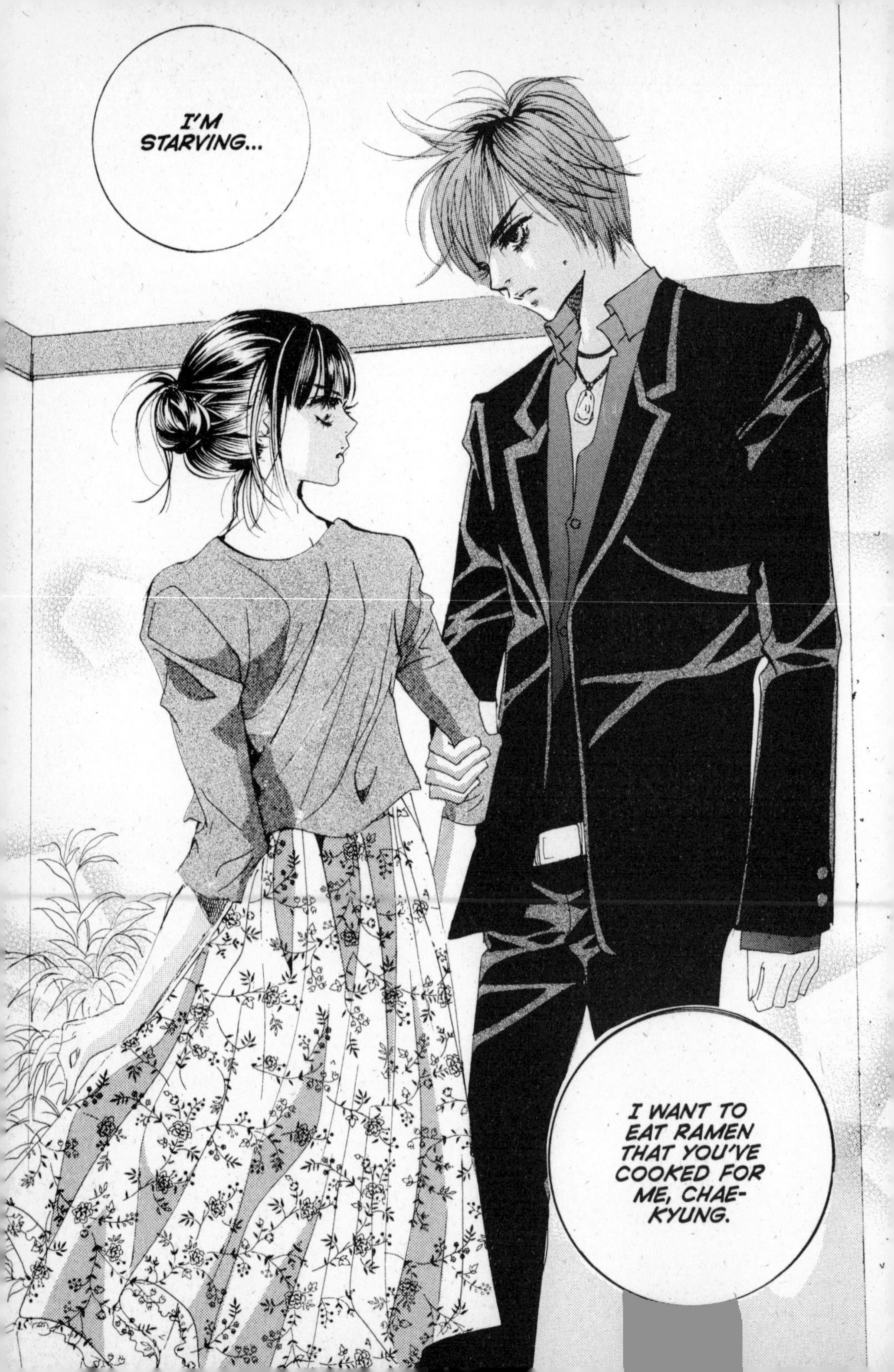
I'M STARVING...
I WANT TO EAT RAMEN THAT YOU'VE COOKED FOR ME, CHAE-KYUNG.

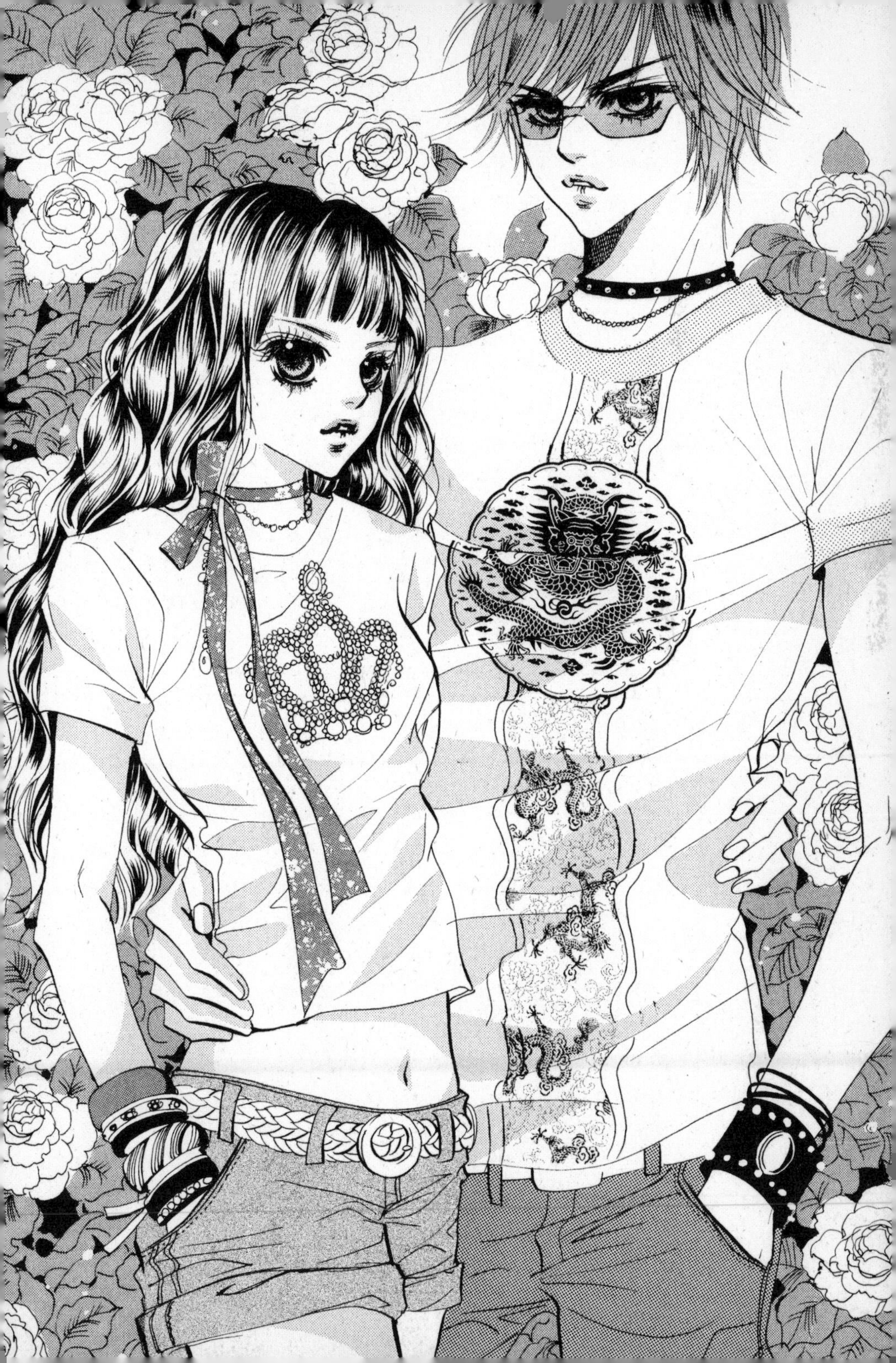

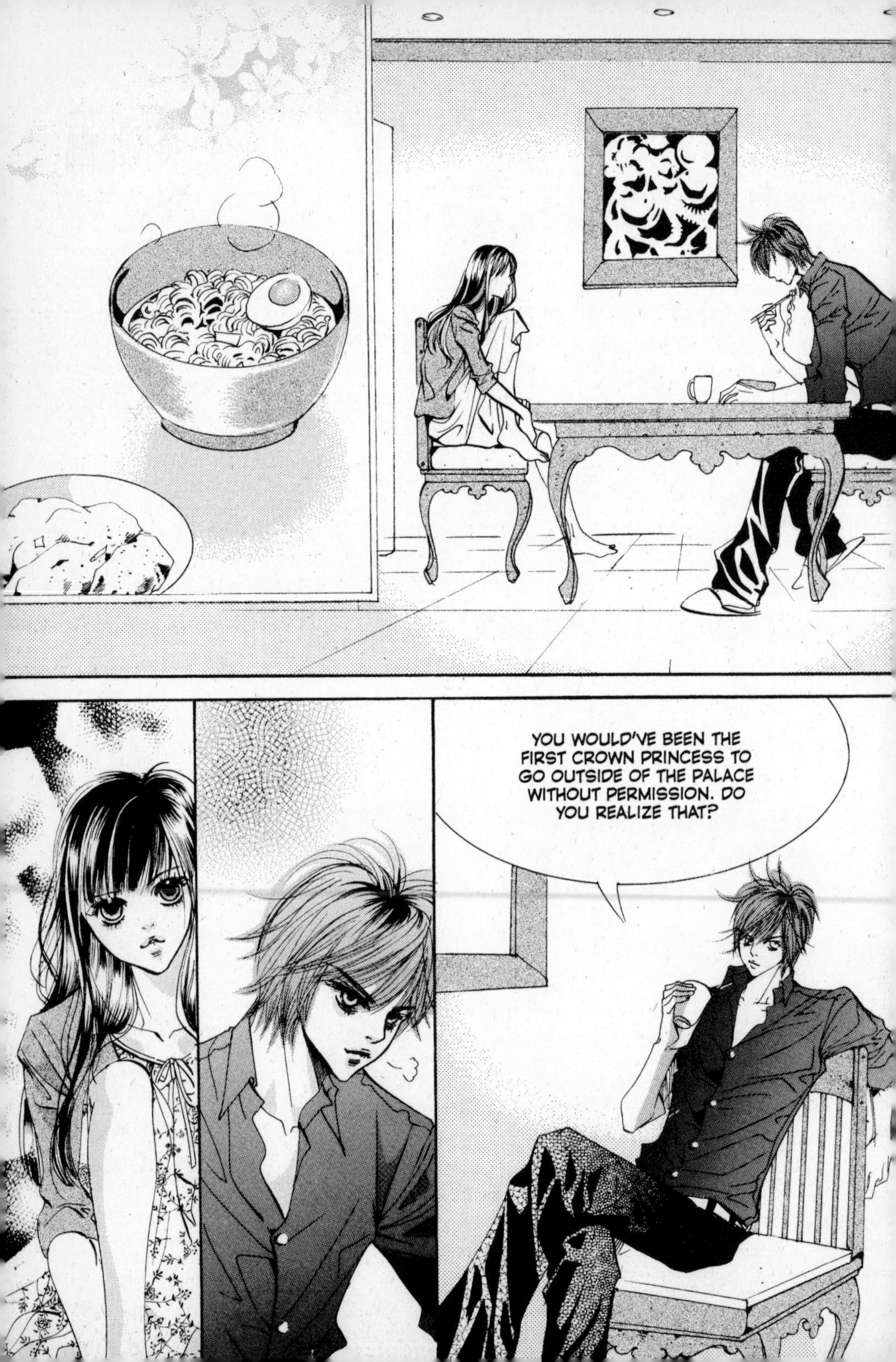
YOU WOULD'VE BEEN THE FIRST CROWN PRINCESS TO GO OUTSIDE OF THE PALACE WITHOUT PERMISSION. DO YOU REALIZE THAT?

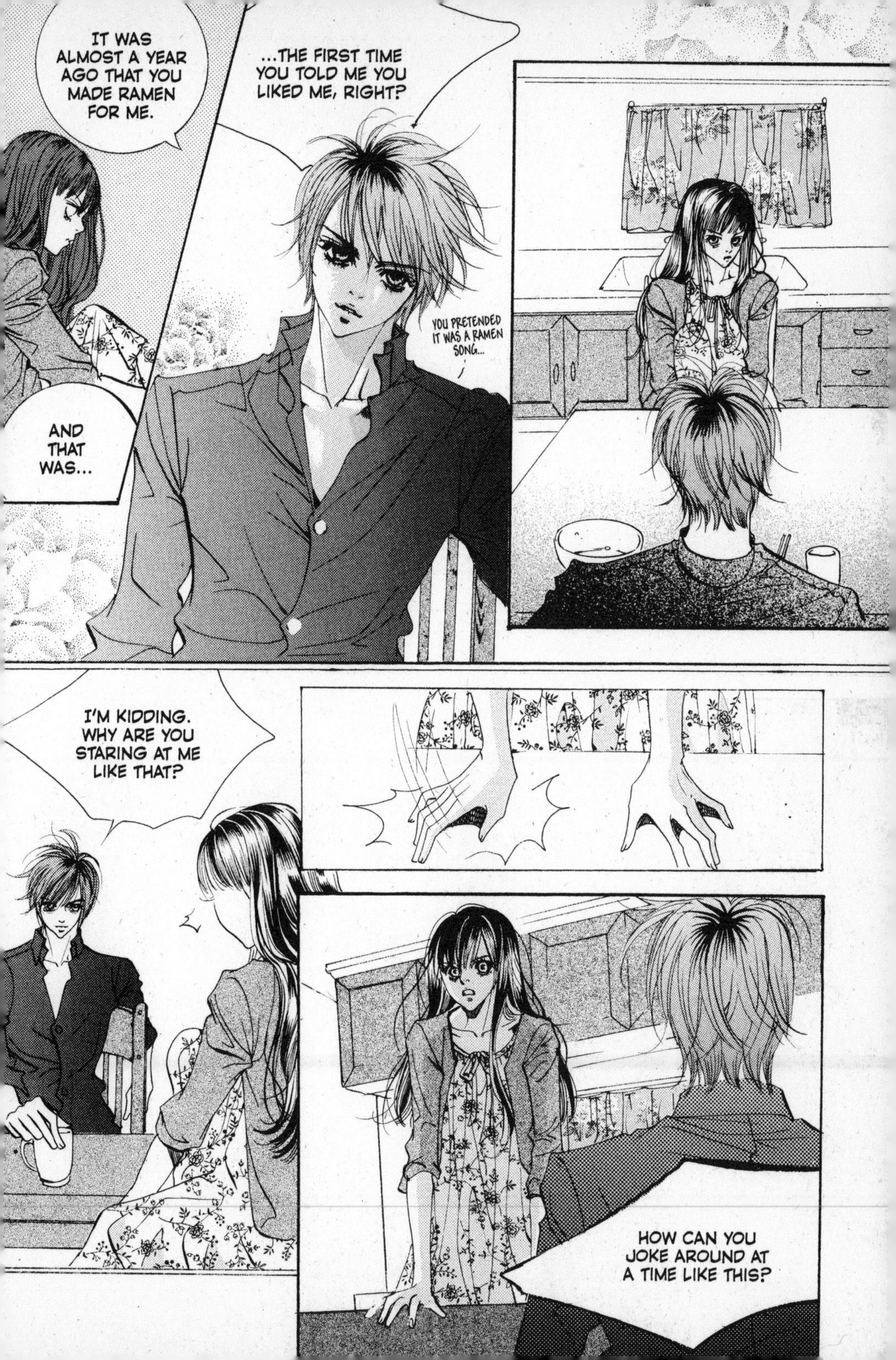
IT WAS ALMOST A YEAR AGO THAT YOU MADE RAMEN FOR ME.
AND THAT WAS...
...THE FIRST TIME YOU TOLD ME YOU LIKED ME, RIGHT?
YOU PRETENDED IT WAS A RAMEN SONG...
I'M KIDDING. WHY ARE YOU STARING AT ME LIKE THAT?
HOW CAN YOU JOKE AROUND AT A TIME LIKE THIS?

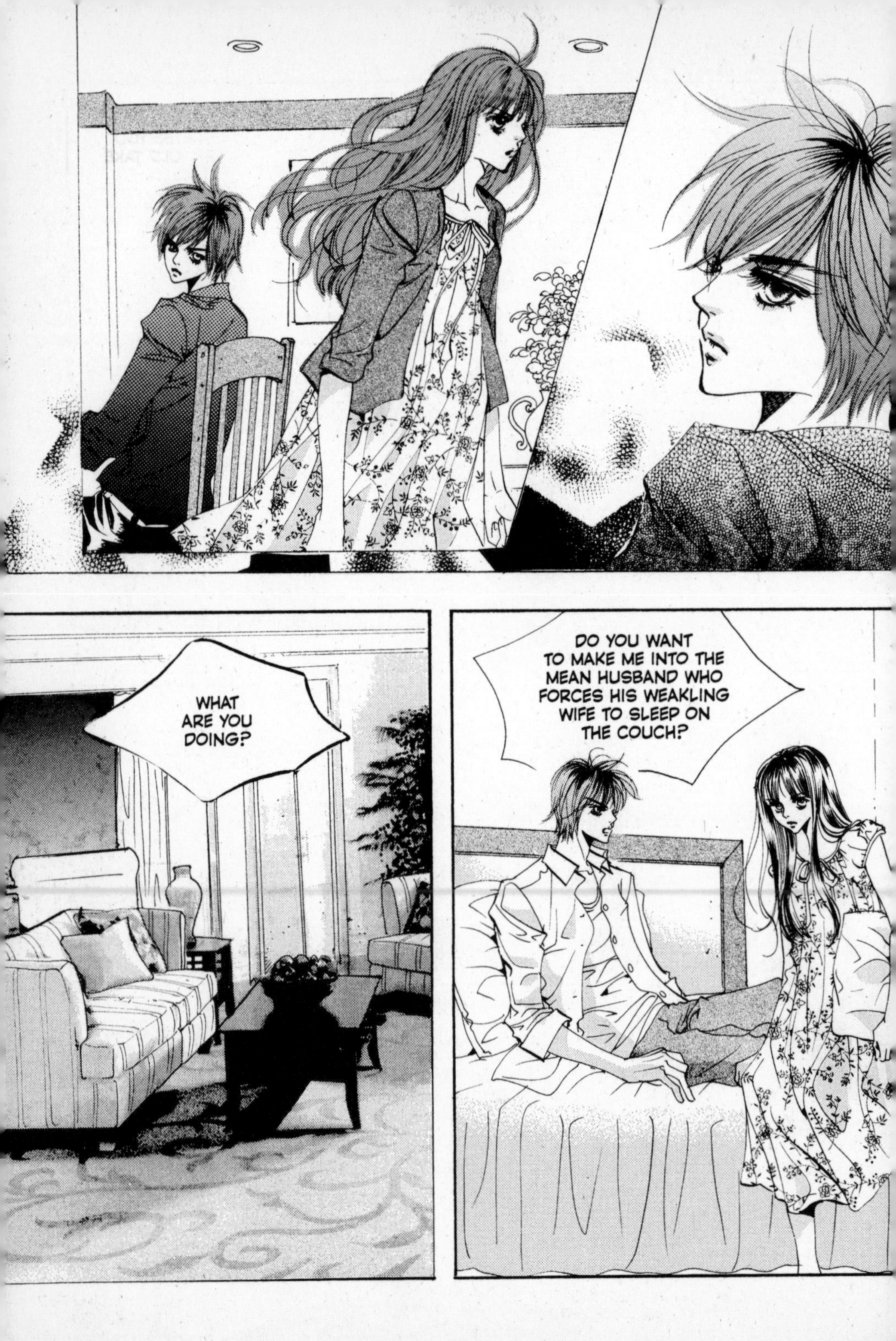
WHAT ARE YOU DOING?
DO YOU WANT TO MAKE ME INTO THE MEAN HUSBAND WHO FORCES HIS WEAKLING WIFE TO SLEEP ON THE COUCH?

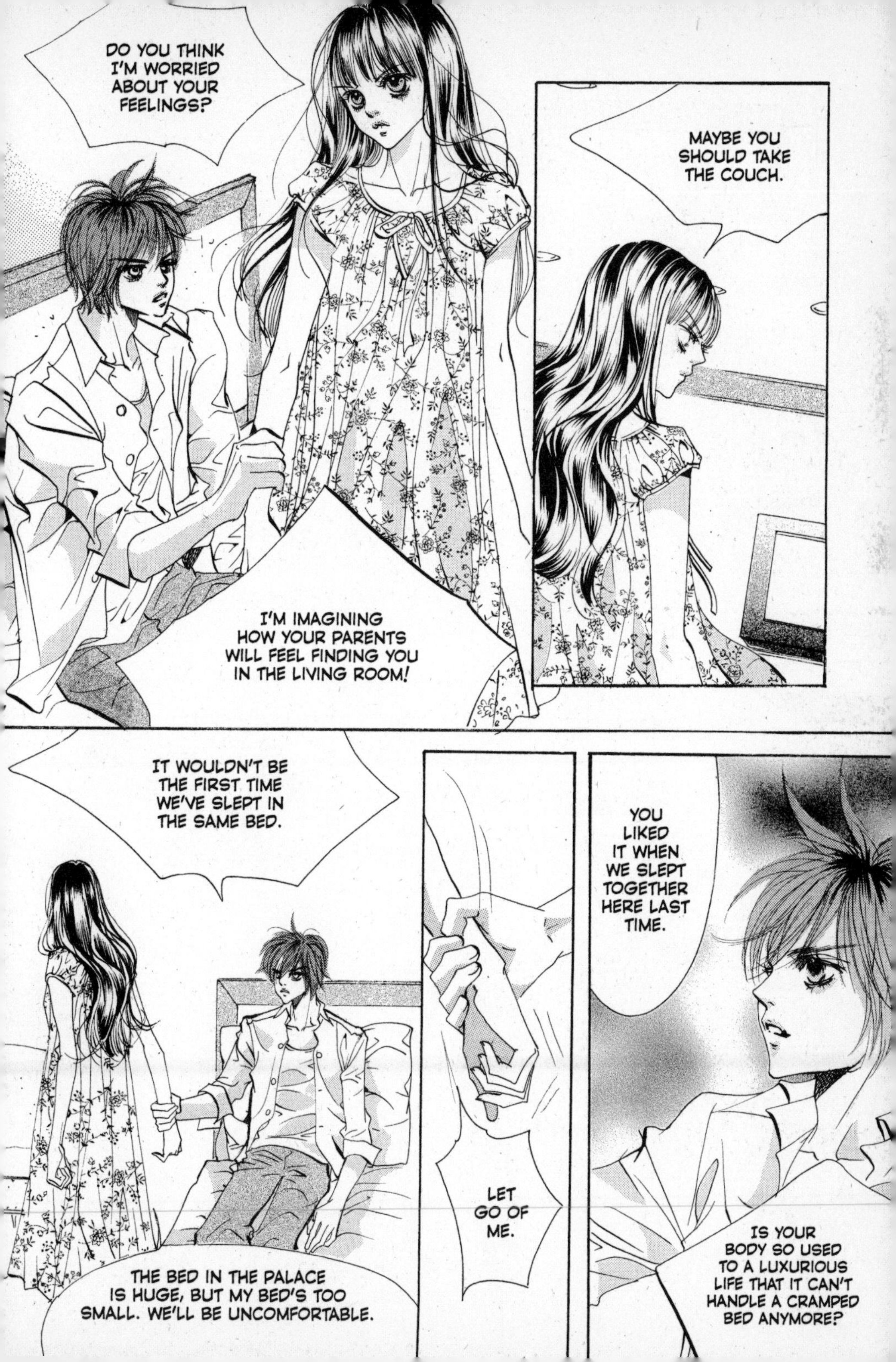
DO YOU THINK I'M WORRIED ABOUT YOUR FEELINGS?
I'M IMAGINING HOW YOUR PARENTS WILL FEEL FINDING YOU IN THE LIVING ROOM!
MAYBE YOU SHOULD TAKE THE COUCH.
IT WOULDN'T BE THE FIRST TIME WE'VE SLEPT IN THE SAME BED.
THE BED IN THE PALACE IS HUGE, BUT MY BED'S TOO SMALL. WE'LL BE UNCOMFORTABLE.
LET GO OF ME.
YOU LIKED IT WHEN WE SLEPT TOGETHER HERE LAST TIME.
IS YOUR BODY SO USED TO A LUXURIOUS LIFE THAT IT CAN'T HANDLE A CRAMPED BED ANYMORE?

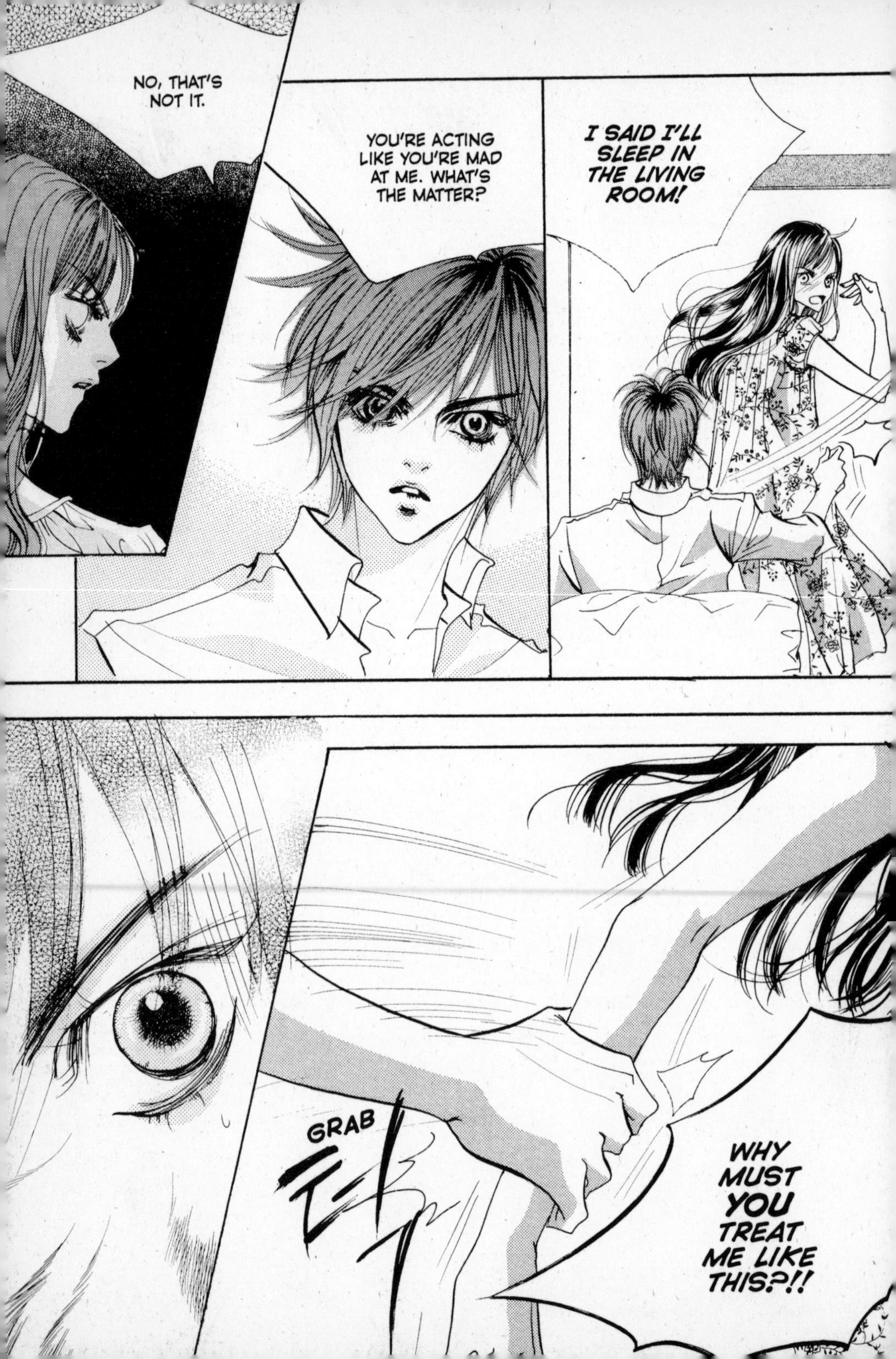
NO, THAT'S NOT IT.
YOU'RE ACTING LIKE YOU'RE MAD AT ME. WHAT'S THE MATTER?
I SAID I'LL SLEEP IN THE LIVING ROOM!
GRAB
WHY MUST YOU TREAT ME LIKE THIS?!!

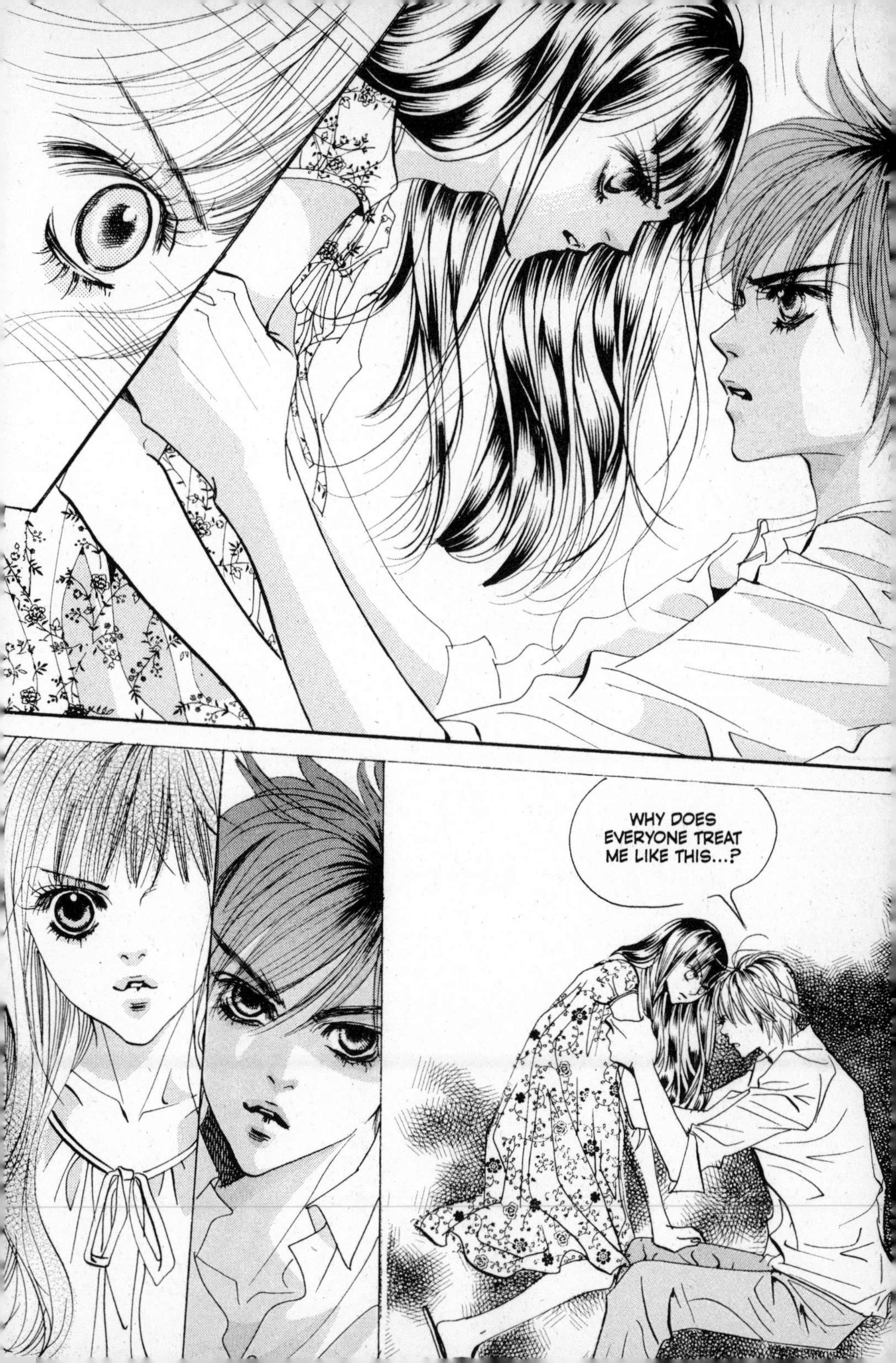
WHY DOES EVERYONE TREAT ME LIKE THIS...?

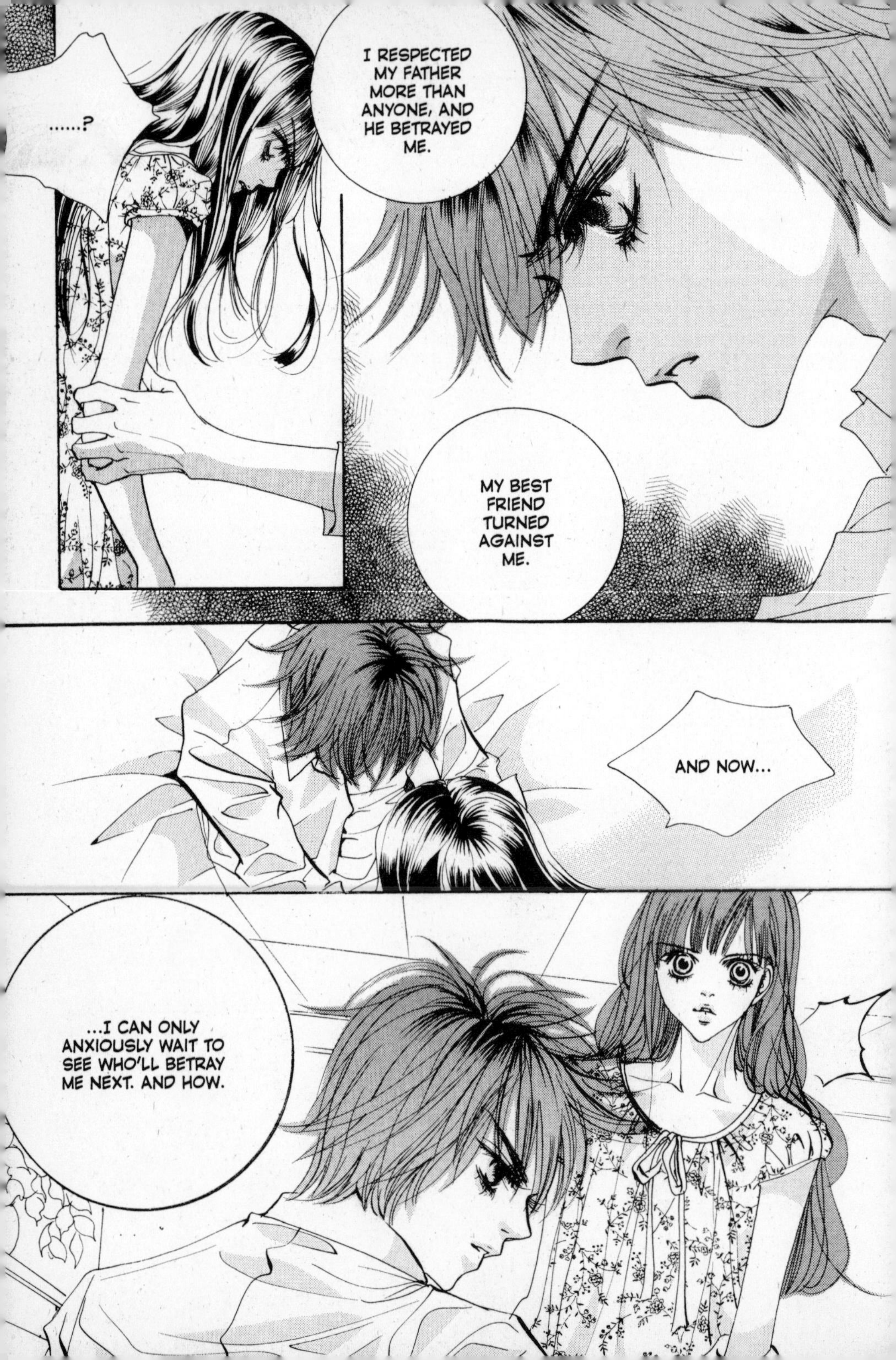
......?
I RESPECTED MY FATHER MORE THAN ANYONE, AND HE BETRAYED ME.
MY BEST FRIEND TURNED AGAINST ME.
AND NOW...
...I CAN ONLY ANXIOUSLY WAIT TO SEE WHO'LL BETRAY ME NEXT. AND HOW.

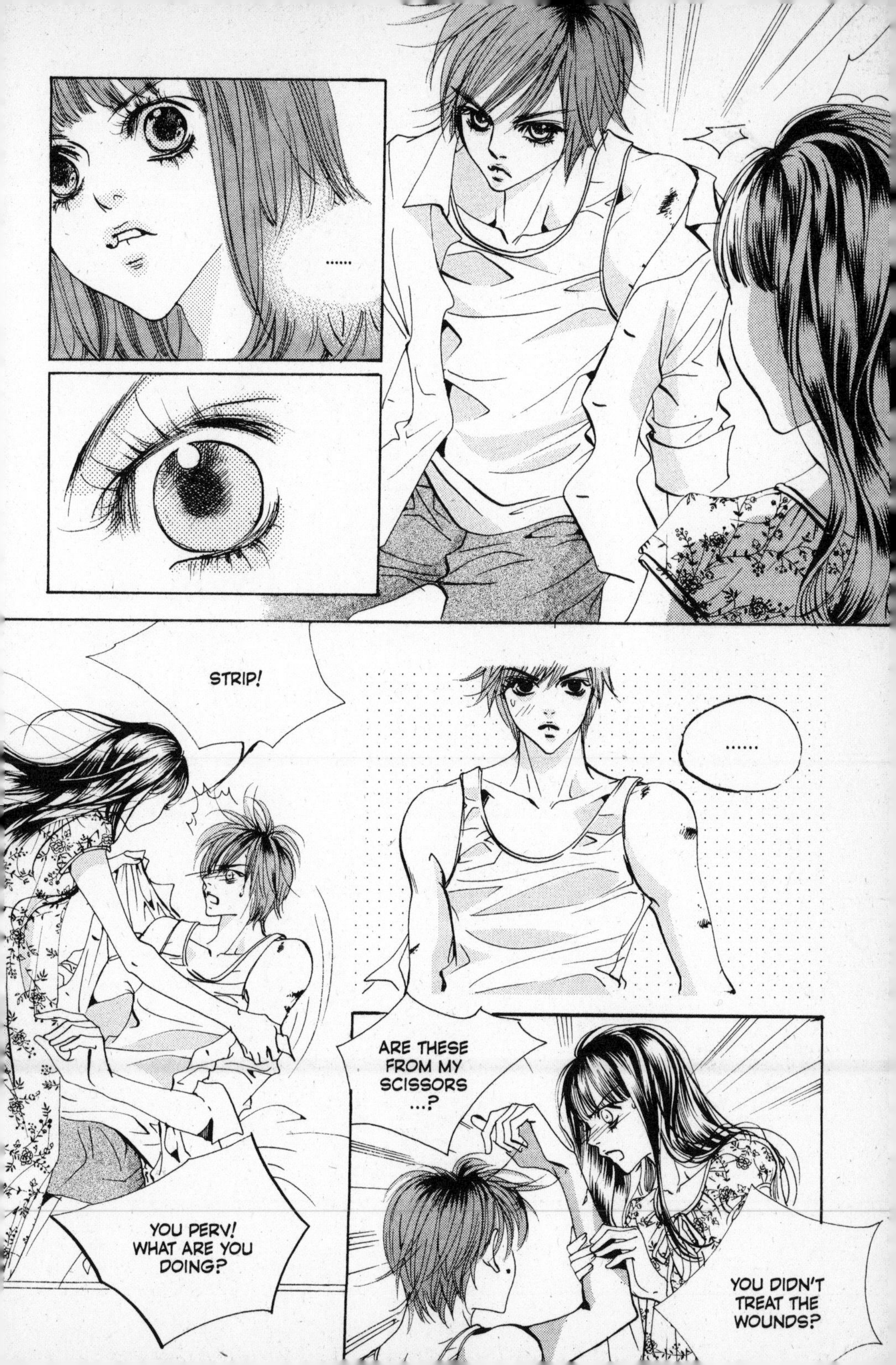
......
STRIP!
YOU PERV! WHAT ARE YOU DOING?
......
ARE THESE FROM MY SCISSORS ...?
YOU DIDN'T TREAT THE WOUNDS?

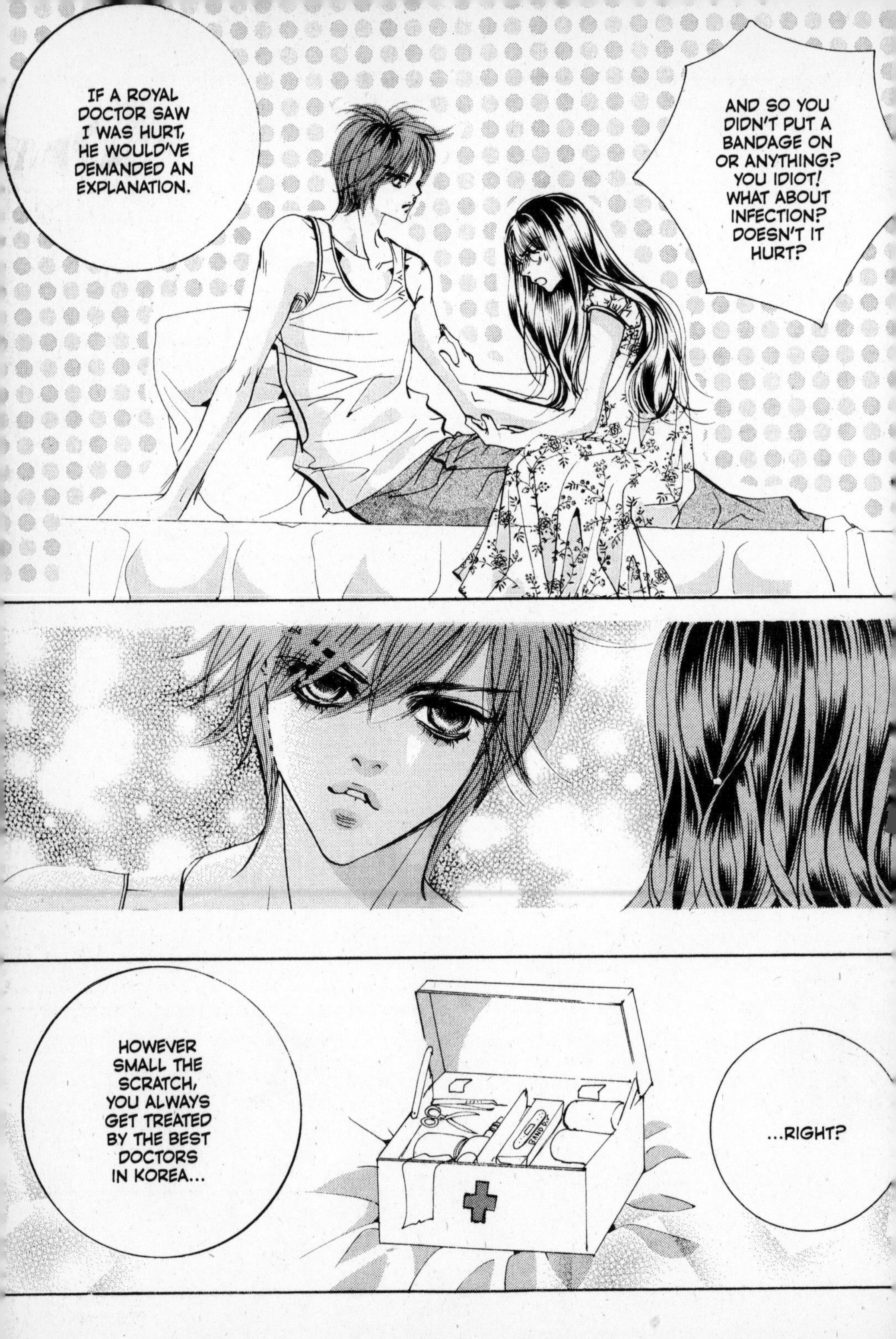
IF A ROYAL DOCTOR SAW I WAS HURT, HE WOULD'VE DEMANDED AN EXPLANATION.
AND SO YOU DIDN'T PUT A BANDAGE ON OR ANYTHING? YOU IDIOT! WHAT ABOUT INFECTION? DOESN'T IT HURT?
HOWEVER SMALL THE SCRATCH, YOU ALWAYS GET TREATED BY THE BEST DOCTORS IN KOREA...
...RIGHT?

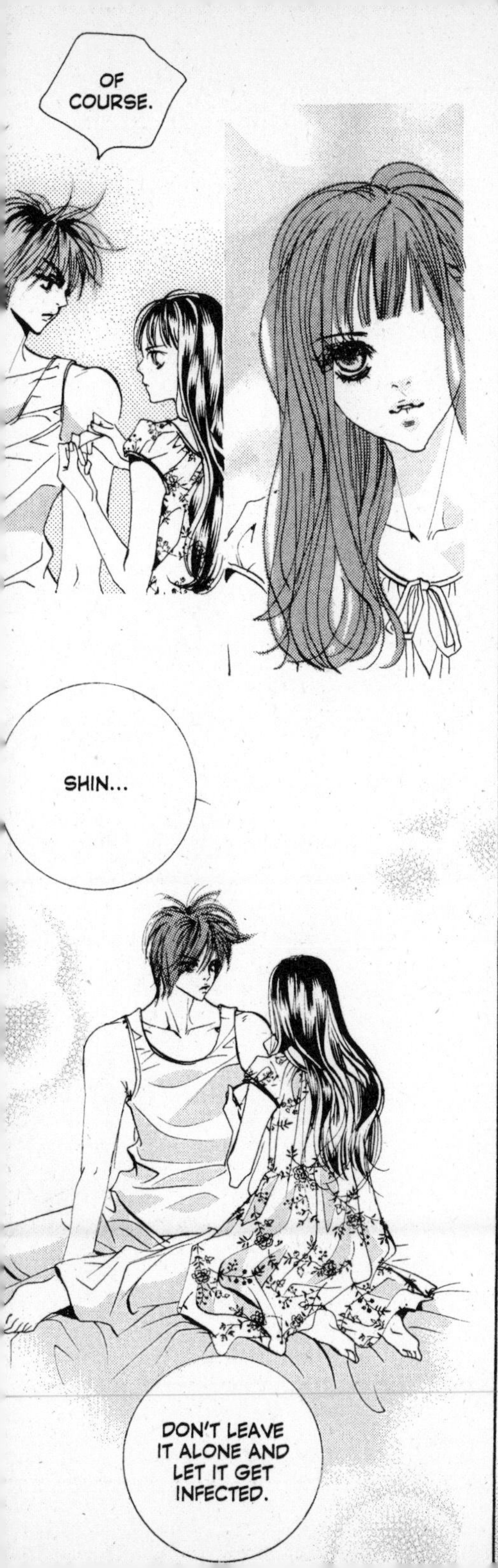
OF COURSE.
SHIN...
DON'T LEAVE IT ALONE AND LET IT GET INFECTED.

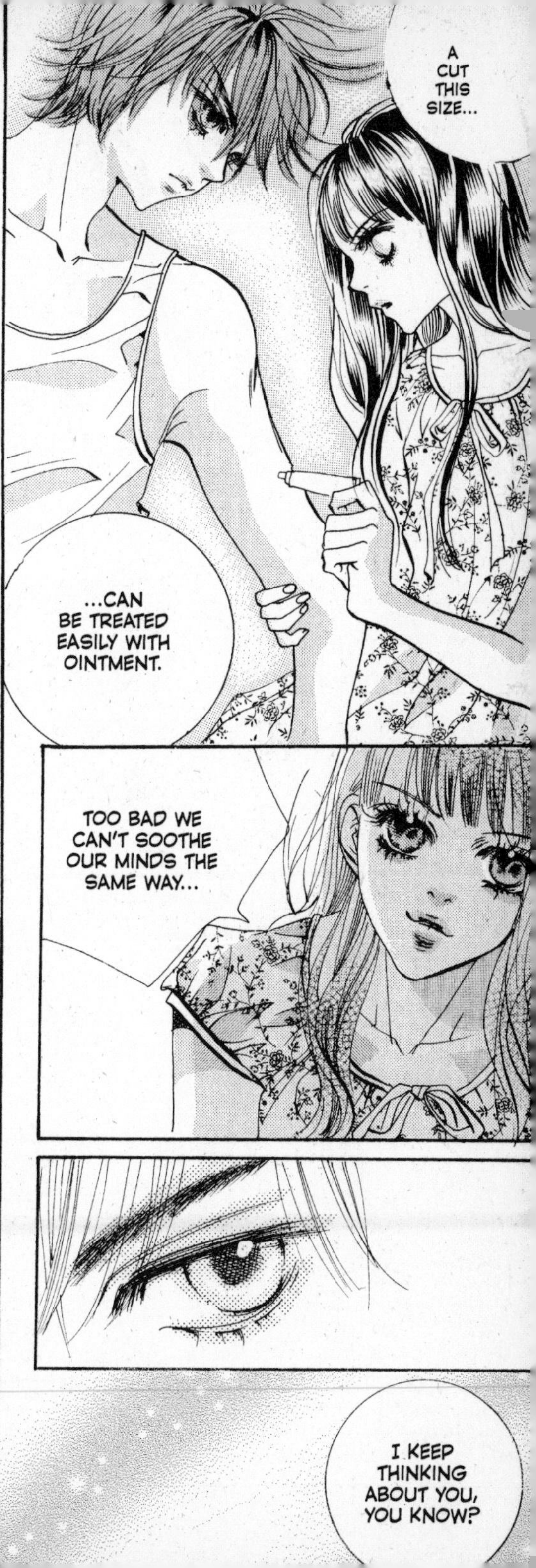
A CUT THIS SIZE...
...CAN BE TREATED EASILY WITH OINTMENT.
TOO BAD WE CAN'T SOOTHE OUR MINDS THE SAME WAY...
I KEEP THINKING ABOUT YOU, YOU KNOW?

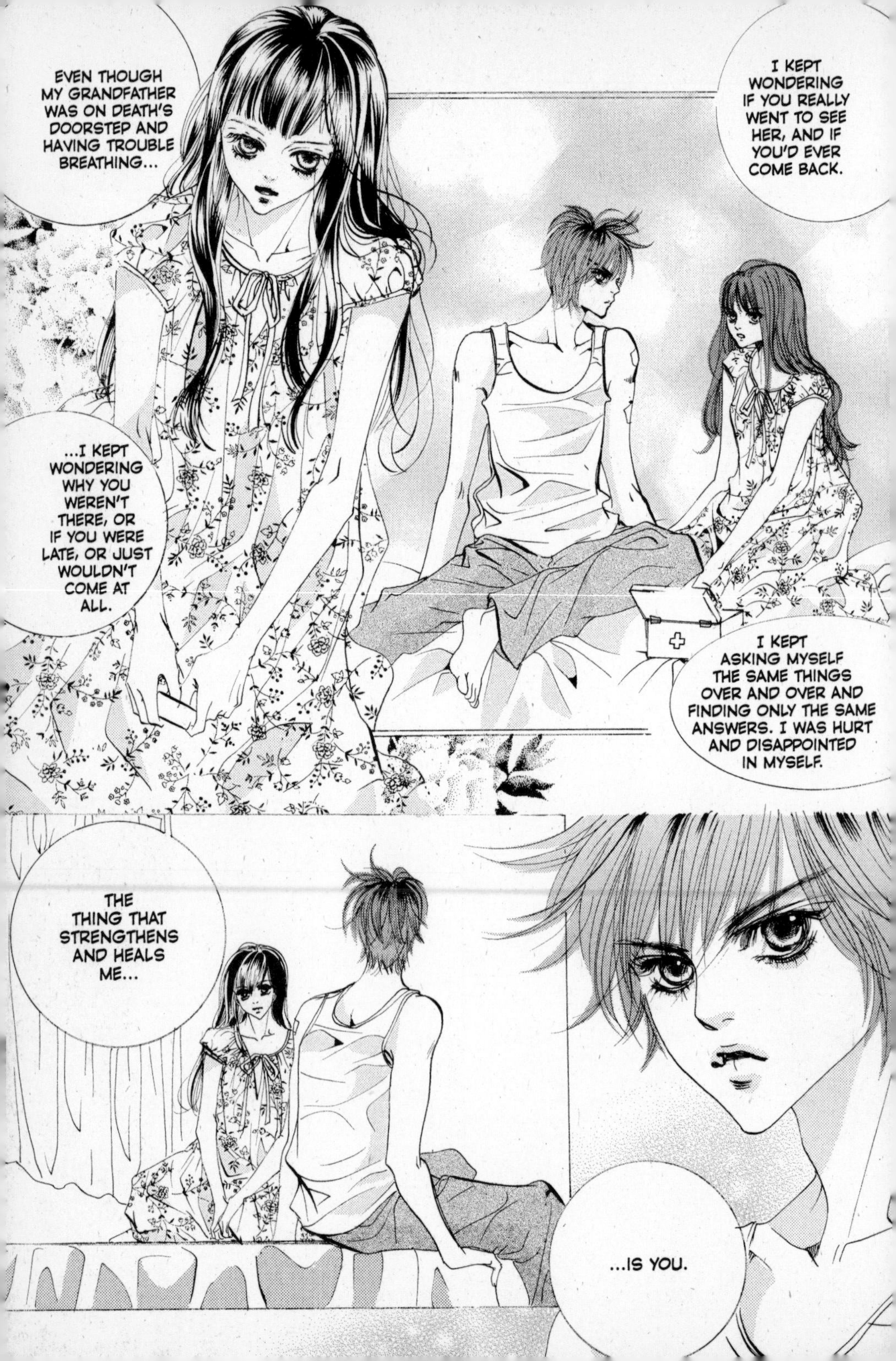
EVEN THOUGH MY GRANDFATHER WAS ON DEATH'S DOORSTEP AND HAVING TROUBLE BREATHING...
I KEPT WONDERING IF YOU REALLY WENT TO SEE HER, AND IF YOU'D EVER COME BACK.
...I KEPT WONDERING WHY YOU WEREN'T THERE, OR IF YOU WERE LATE, OR JUST WOULDN'T COME AT ALL.
I KEPT ASKING MYSELF THE SAME THINGS OVER AND OVER AND FINDING ONLY THE SAME ANSWERS. I WAS HURT AND DISAPPOINTED IN MYSELF.
THE THING THAT STRENGTHENS AND HEALS ME...
...IS YOU.

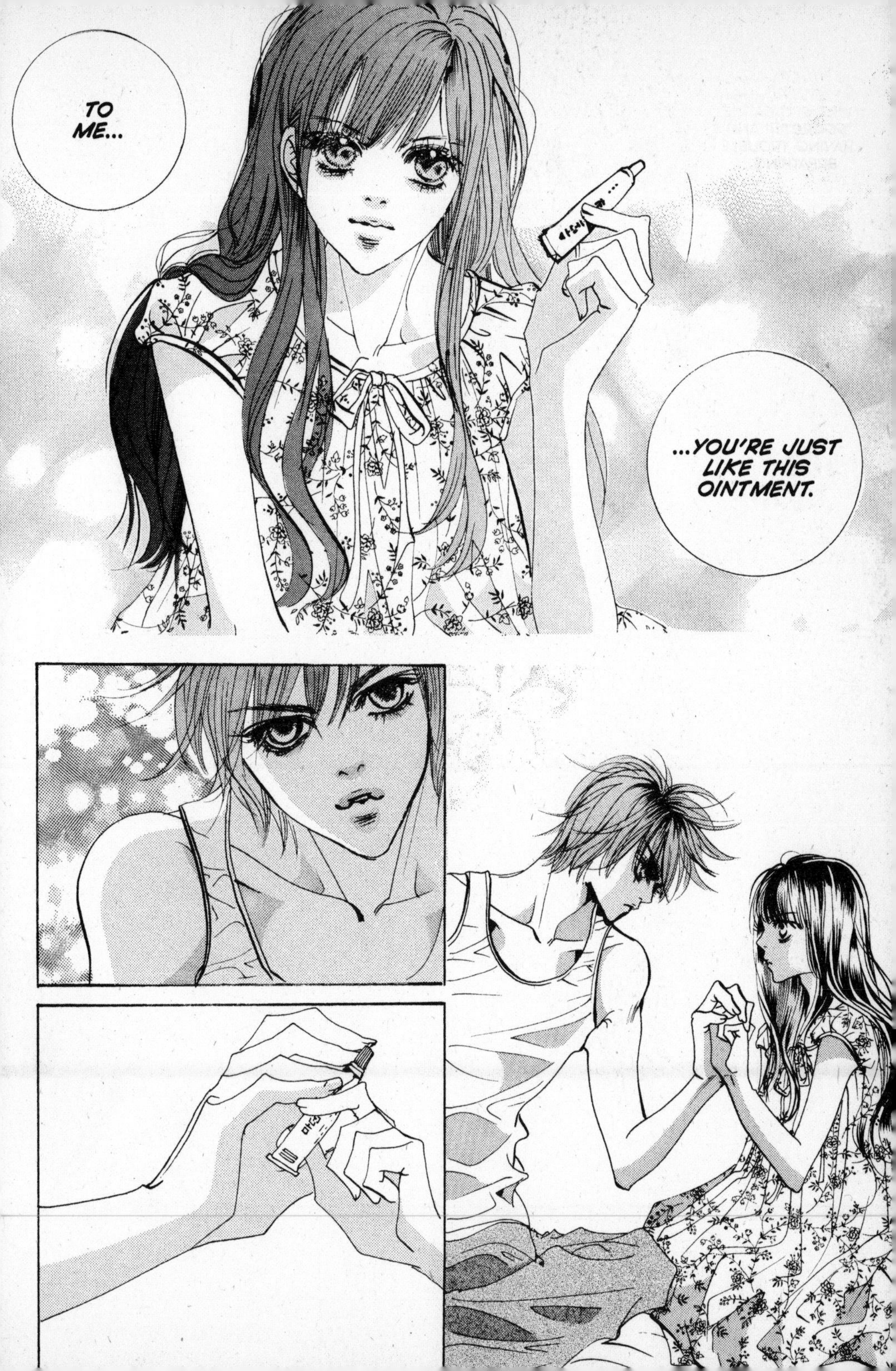
TO ME...
...YOU'RE JUST LIKE THIS OINTMENT.

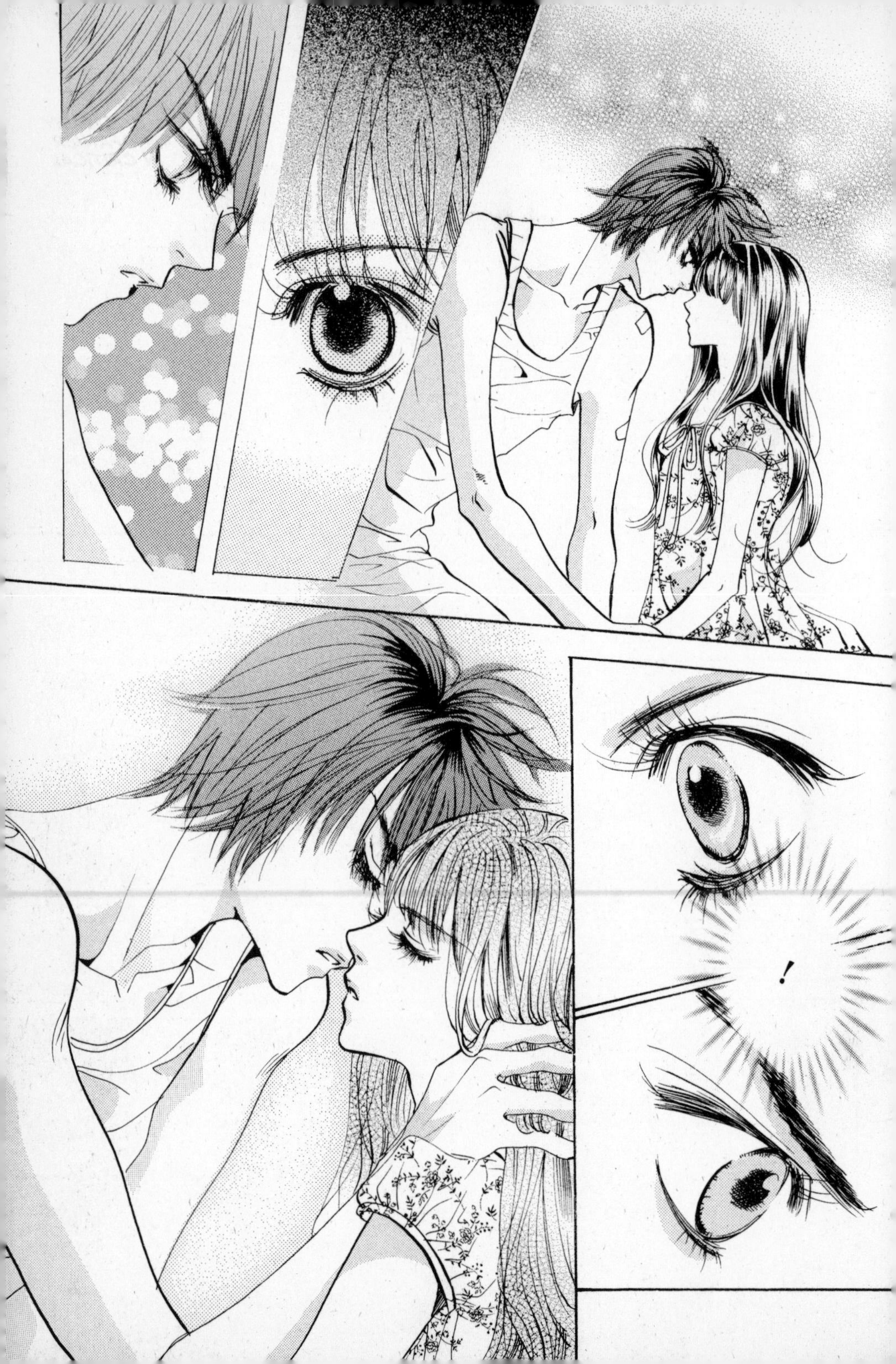
!

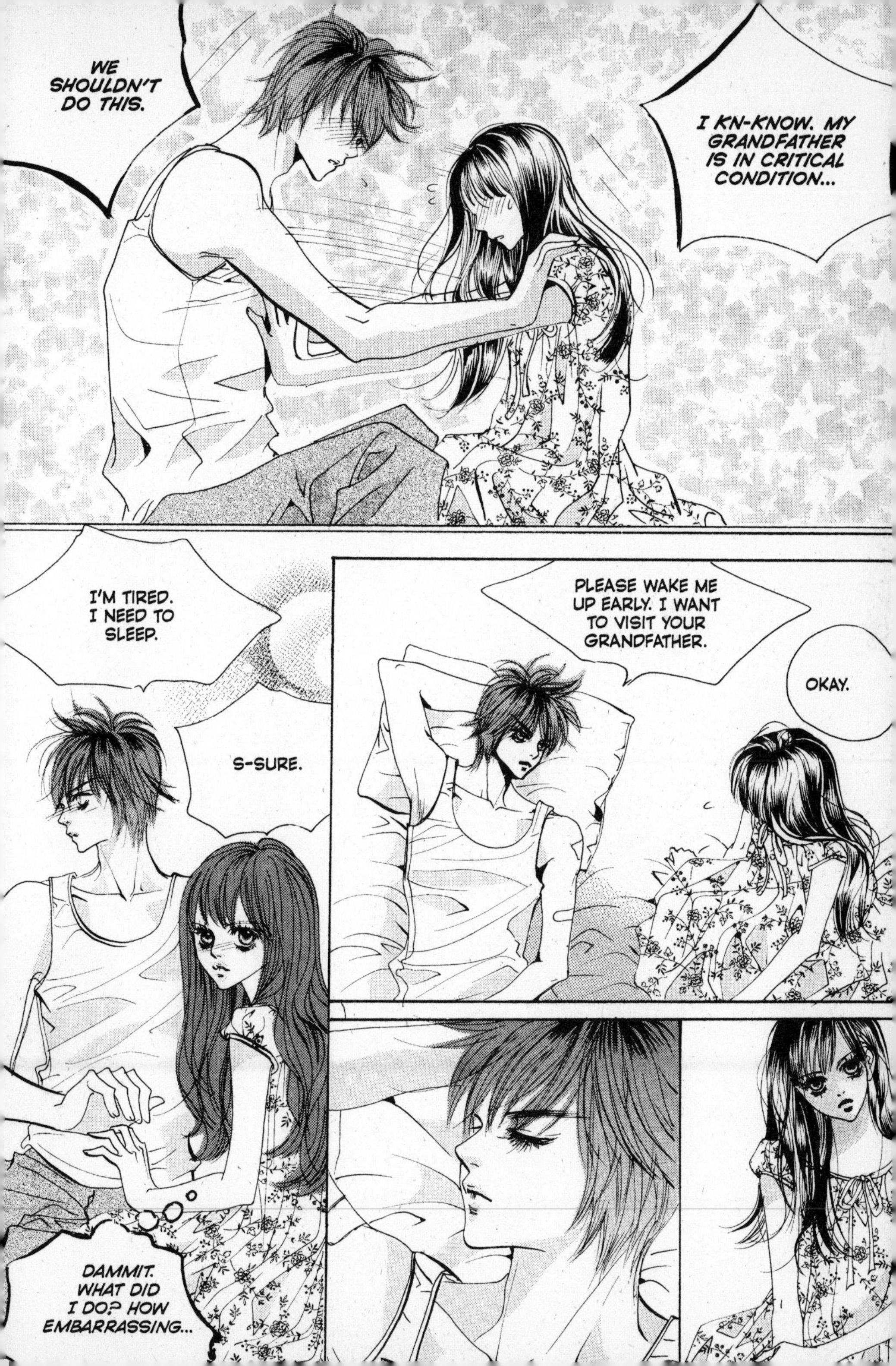
WE SHOULDN'T DO THIS.
I KN-KNOW. MY GRANDFATHER IS IN CRITICAL CONDITION...
I'M TIRED. I NEED TO SLEEP.
S-SURE.
DAMMIT. WHAT DID I DO? HOW EMBARRASSING...
PLEASE WAKE ME UP EARLY. I WANT TO VISIT YOUR GRANDFATHER.
OKAY.

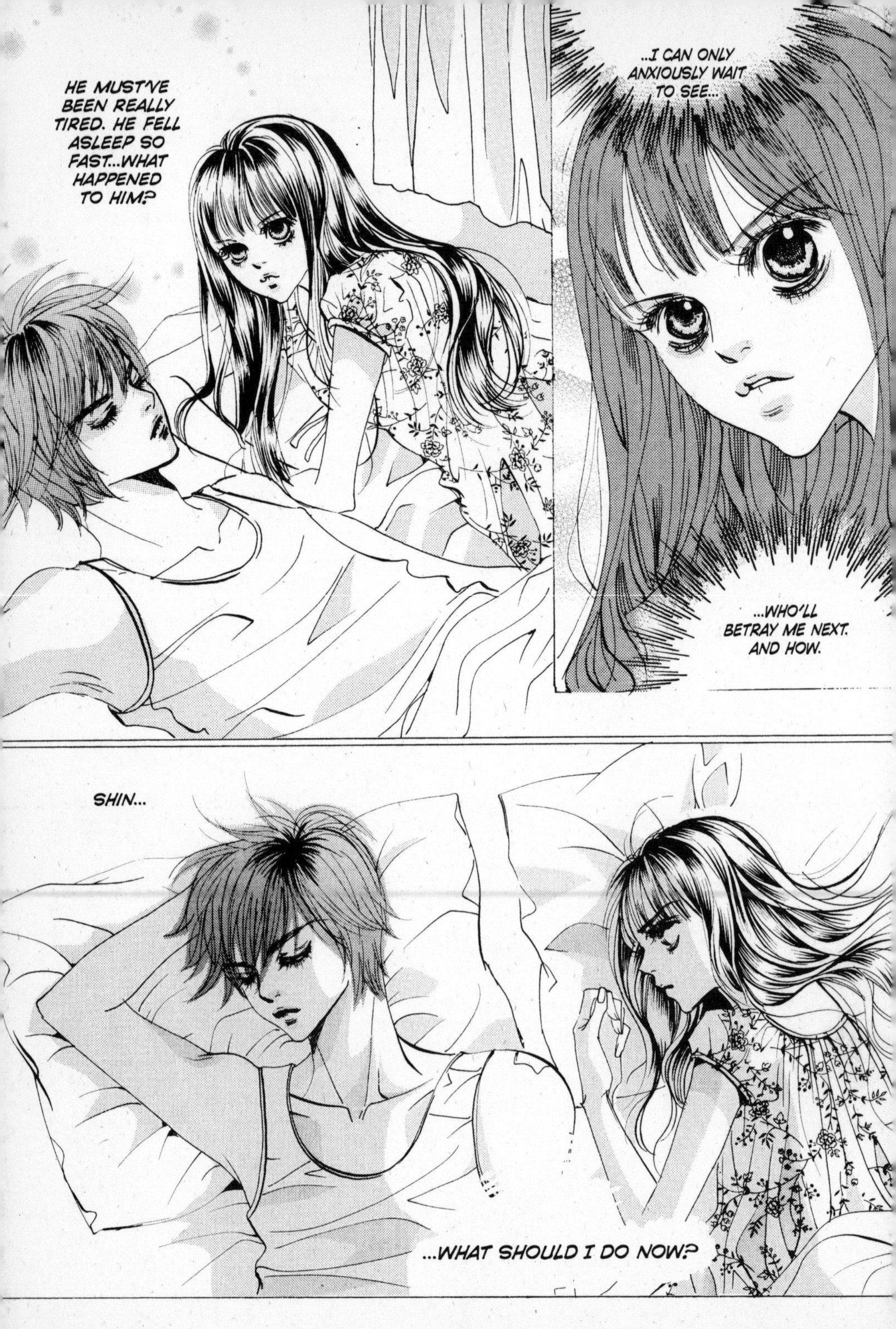
HE MUST'VE BEEN REALLY TIRED. HE FELL ASLEEP SO FAST...WHAT HAPPENED TO HIM?
...I CAN ONLY ANXIOUSLY WAIT TO SEE...
...WHO'LL BETRAY ME NEXT. AND HOW.
SHIN...
...WHAT SHOULD I DO NOW?

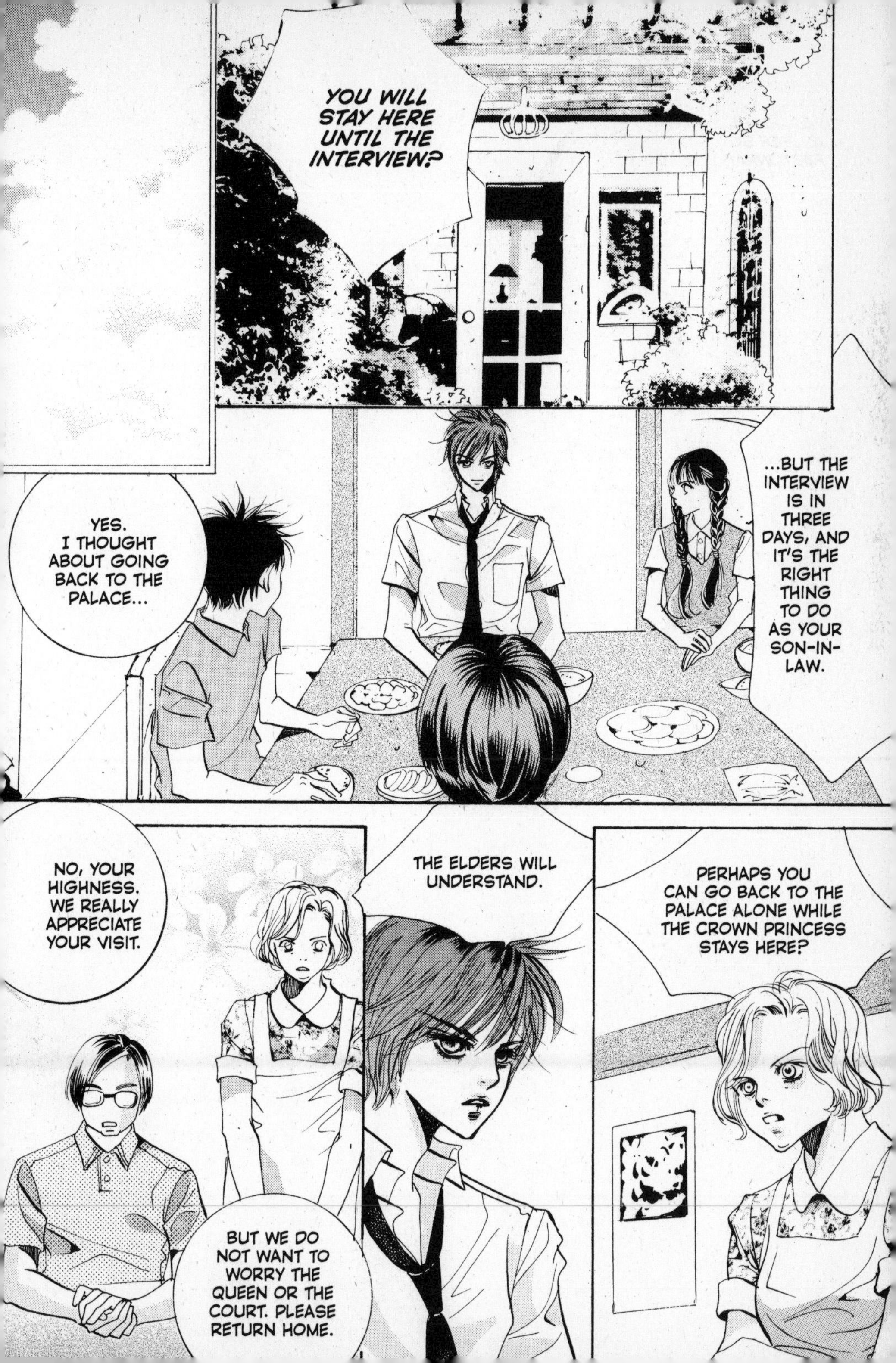
YOU WILL STAY HERE UNTIL THE INTERVIEW?
YES. I THOUGHT ABOUT GOING BACK TO THE PALACE...
...BUT THE INTERVIEW IS IN THREE DAYS, AND IT'S THE RIGHT THING TO DO AS YOUR SON-IN-LAW.
NO, YOUR HIGHNESS. WE REALLY APPRECIATE YOUR VISIT.
BUT WE DO NOT WANT TO WORRY THE QUEEN OR THE COURT. PLEASE RETURN HOME.
THE ELDERS WILL UNDERSTAND.
PERHAPS YOU CAN GO BACK TO THE PALACE ALONE WHILE THE CROWN PRINCESS STAYS HERE?

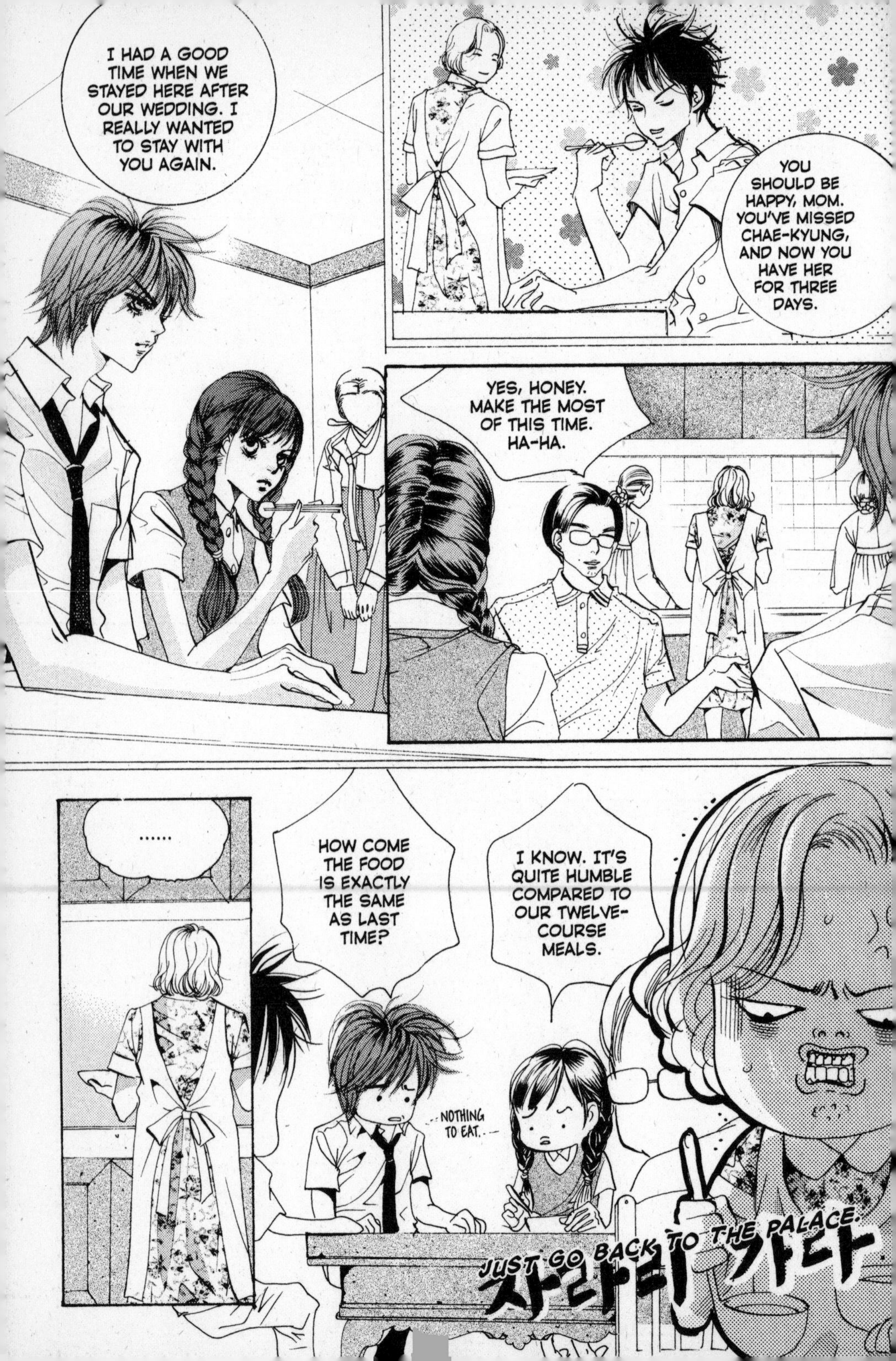
I HAD A GOOD TIME WHEN WE STAYED HERE AFTER OUR WEDDING. I REALLY WANTED TO STAY WITH YOU AGAIN.
YOU SHOULD BE HAPPY, MOM. YOU'VE MISSED CHAE-KYUNG, AND NOW YOU HAVE HER FOR THREE DAYS.
YES, HONEY. MAKE THE MOST OF THIS TIME. HA-HA.
......
HOW COME THE FOOD IS EXACTLY THE SAME AS LAST TIME?
I KNOW. IT'S QUITE HUMBLE COMPARED TO OUR TWELVE-COURSE MEALS.
NOTHING TO EAT.
JUST GO BACK TO THE PALACE.

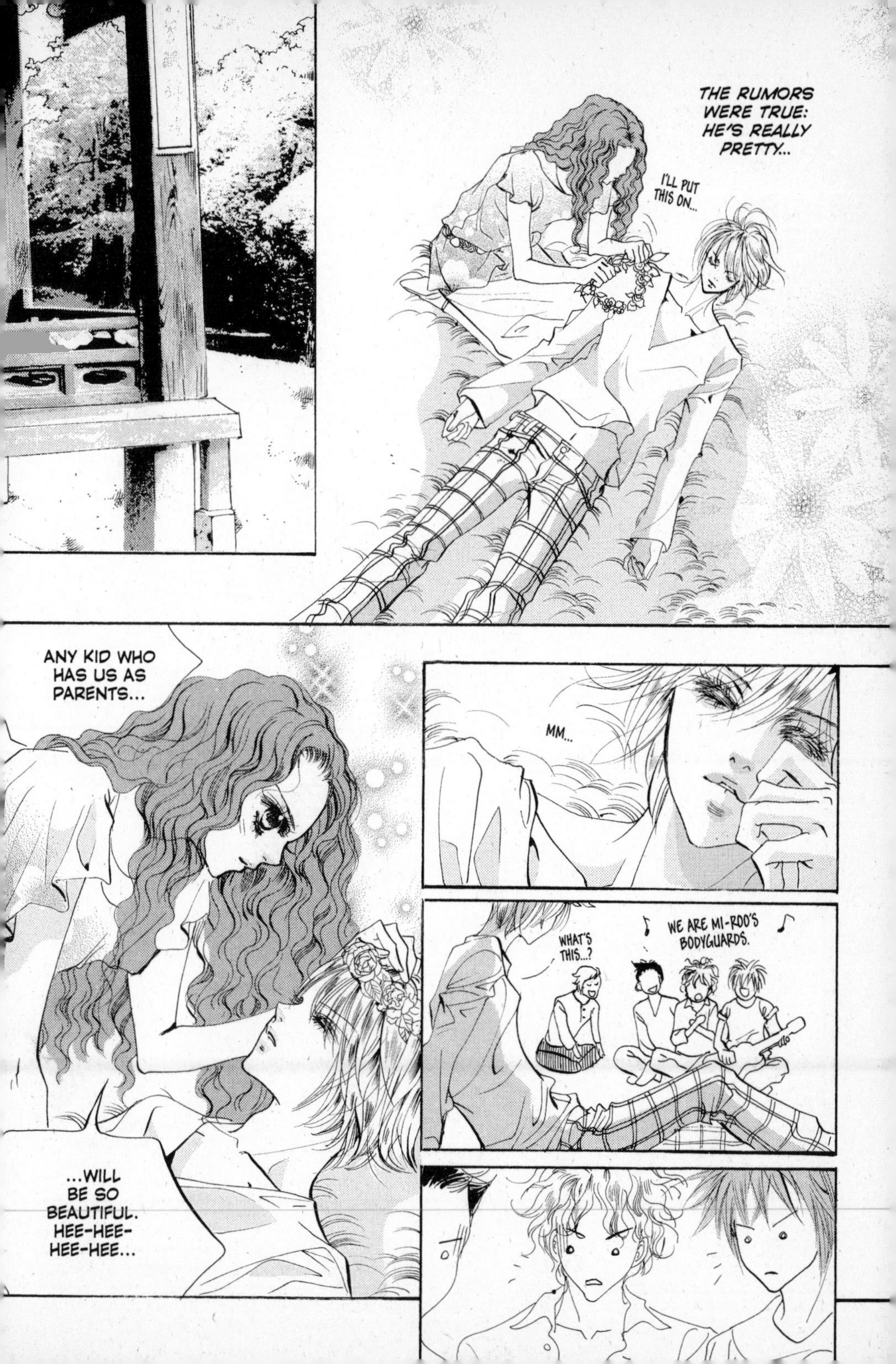
THE RUMORS WERE TRUE: HE'S REALLY PRETTY...
I'LL PUT THIS ON...
ANY KID WHO HAS US AS PARENTS...
...WILL BE SO BEAUTIFUL. HEE-HEE-HEE-HEE...
MM...
WHAT'S THIS...?
♪ WE ARE MI-ROO'S BODYGUARDS. ♪

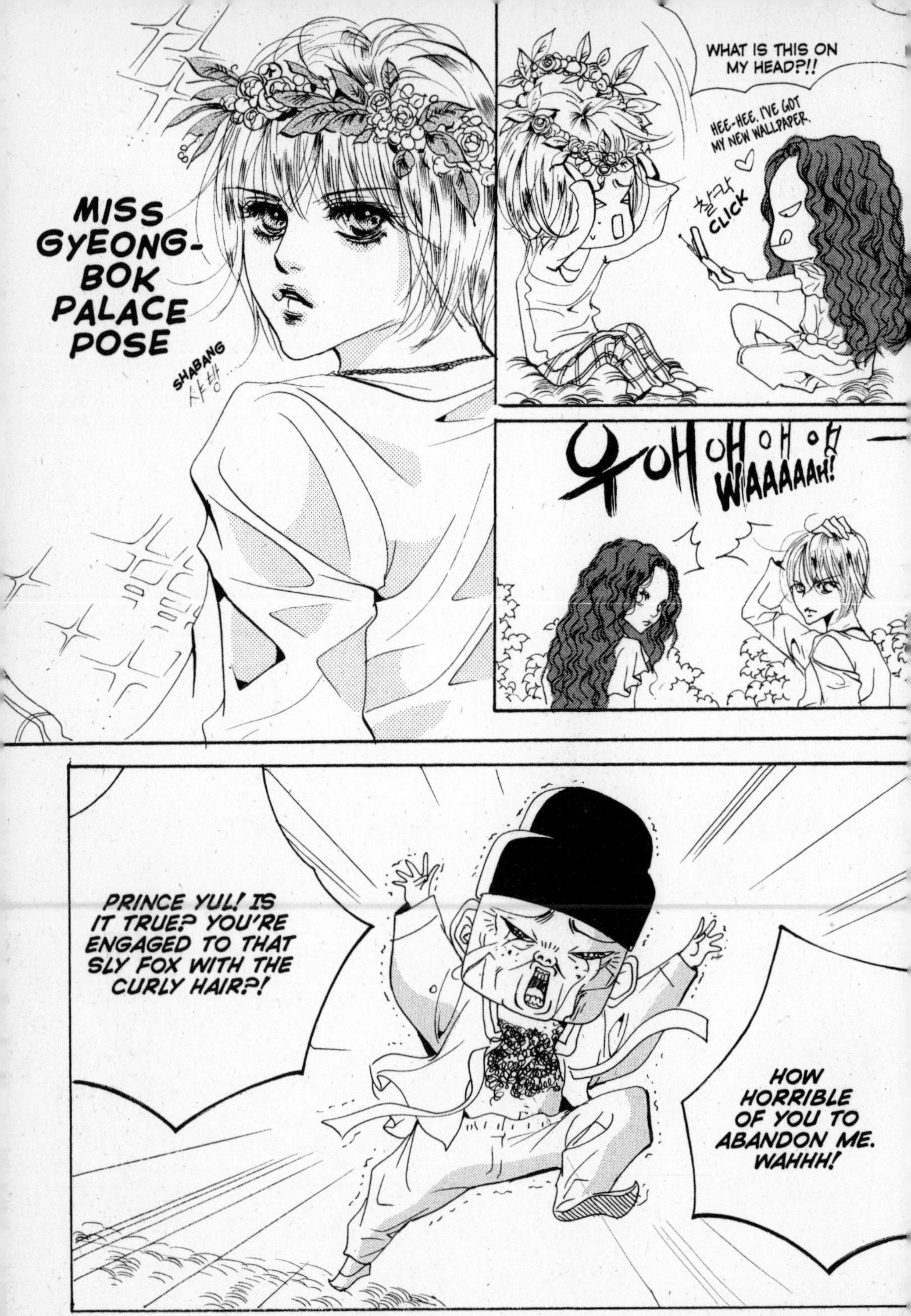
MISS GYEONG-BOK PALACE POSE
SHABANG
샤방
WHAT IS THIS ON MY HEAD?!!
HEE-HEE. I'VE GOT MY NEW WALLPAPER.
찰칵
CLICK
WAAAAAH!
PRINCE YUL! IS IT TRUE? YOU'RE ENGAGED TO THAT SLY FOX WITH THE CURLY HAIR?!
HOW HORRIBLE OF YOU TO ABANDON ME. WAHHH!

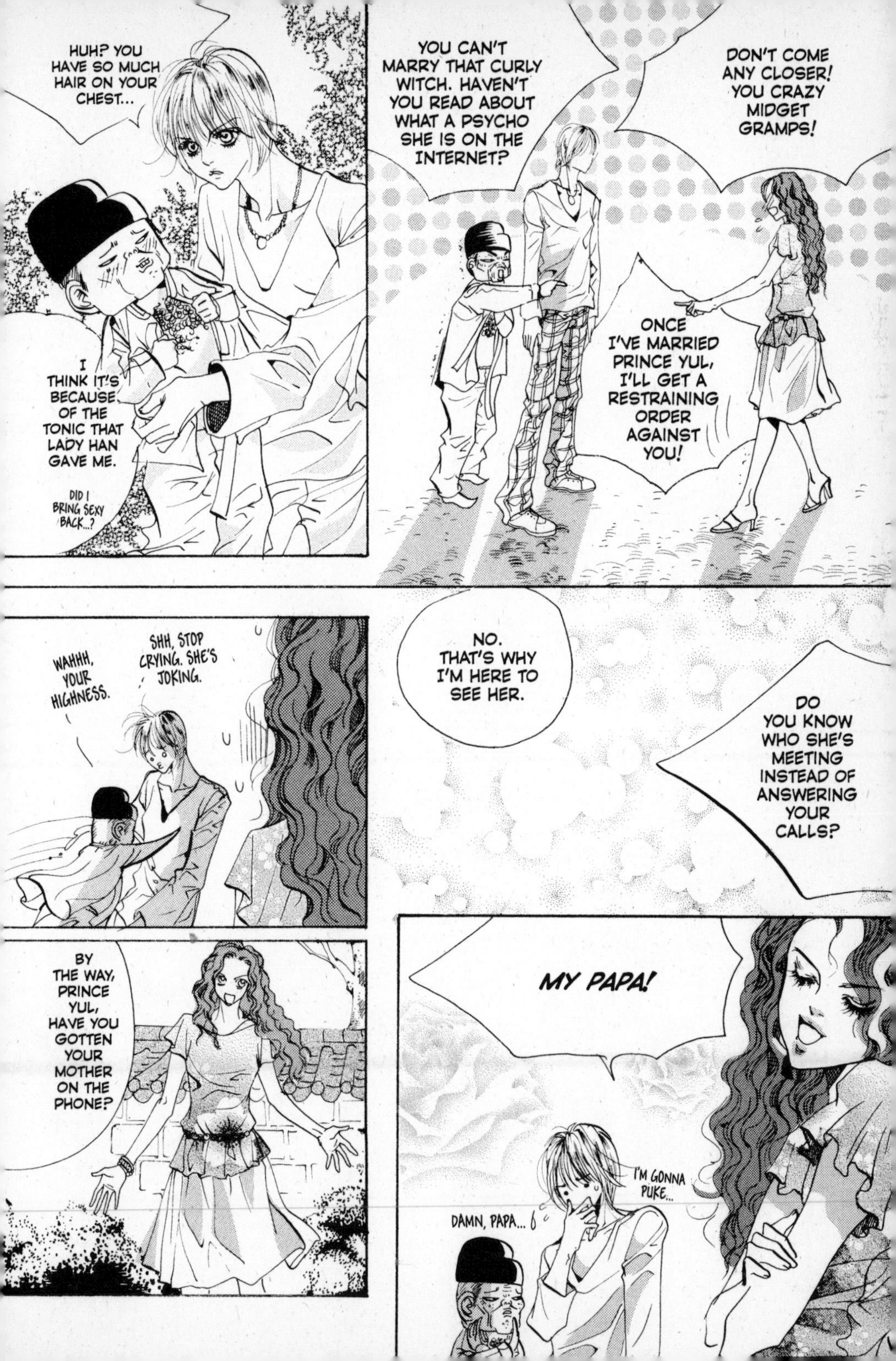
HUH? YOU HAVE SO MUCH HAIR ON YOUR CHEST...
I THINK IT'S BECAUSE OF THE TONIC THAT LADY HAN GAVE ME.
DID I BRING SEXY BACK...?
YOU CAN'T MARRY THAT CURLY WITCH. HAVEN'T YOU READ ABOUT WHAT A PSYCHO SHE IS ON THE INTERNET?
DON'T COME ANY CLOSER! YOU CRAZY MIDGET GRAMPS!
ONCE I'VE MARRIED PRINCE YUL, I'LL GET A RESTRAINING ORDER AGAINST YOU!
WAHHH, YOUR HIGHNESS.
SHH, STOP CRYING. SHE'S JOKING.
NO. THAT'S WHY I'M HERE TO SEE HER.
DO YOU KNOW WHO SHE'S MEETING INSTEAD OF ANSWERING YOUR CALLS?
BY THE WAY, PRINCE YUL, HAVE YOU GOTTEN YOUR MOTHER ON THE PHONE?
MY PAPA!
I'M GONNA PUKE...
DAMN, PAPA...

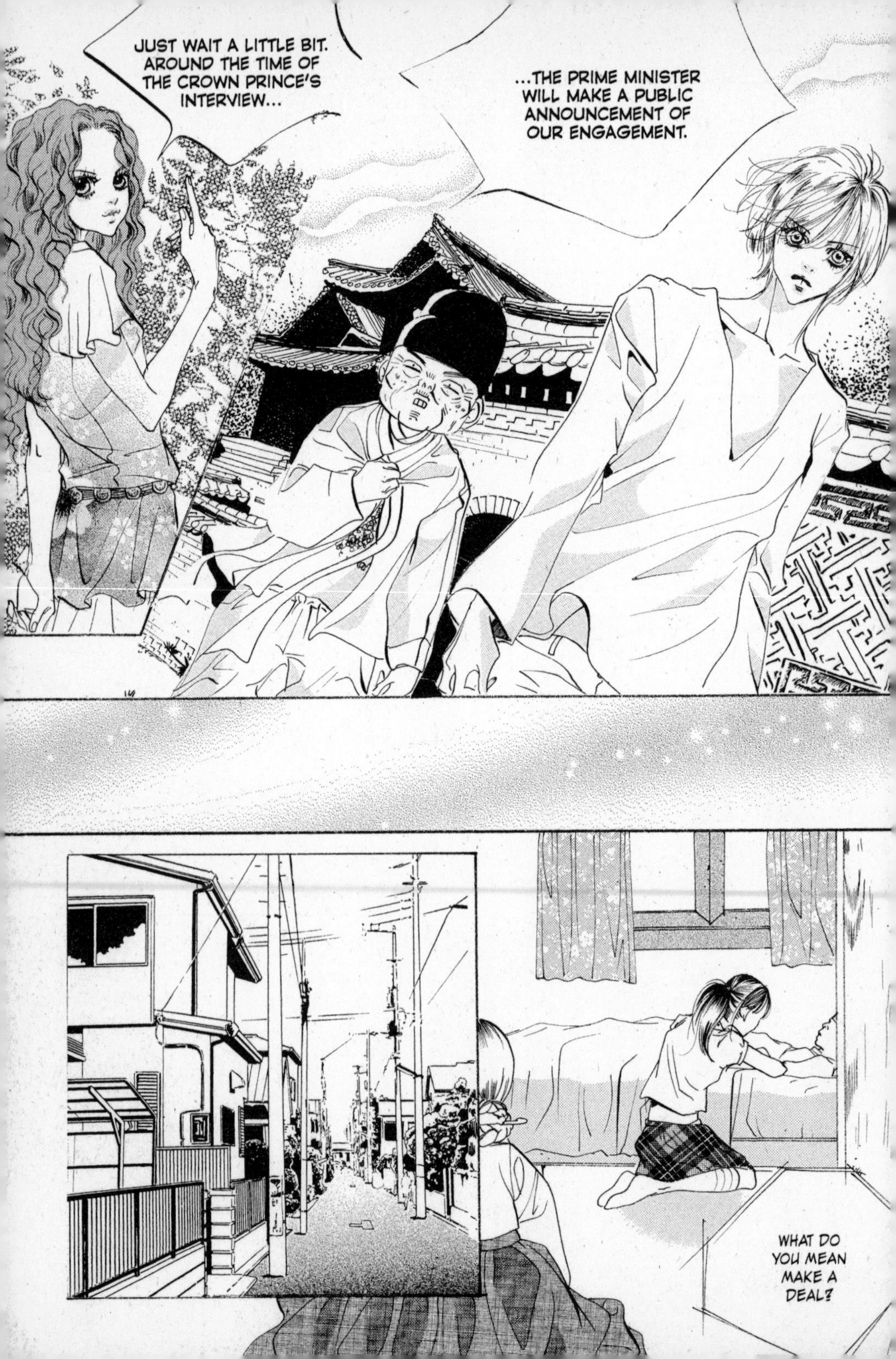
JUST WAIT A LITTLE BIT. AROUND THE TIME OF THE CROWN PRINCE'S INTERVIEW...
...THE PRIME MINISTER WILL MAKE A PUBLIC ANNOUNCEMENT OF OUR ENGAGEMENT.
WHAT DO YOU MEAN MAKE A DEAL?

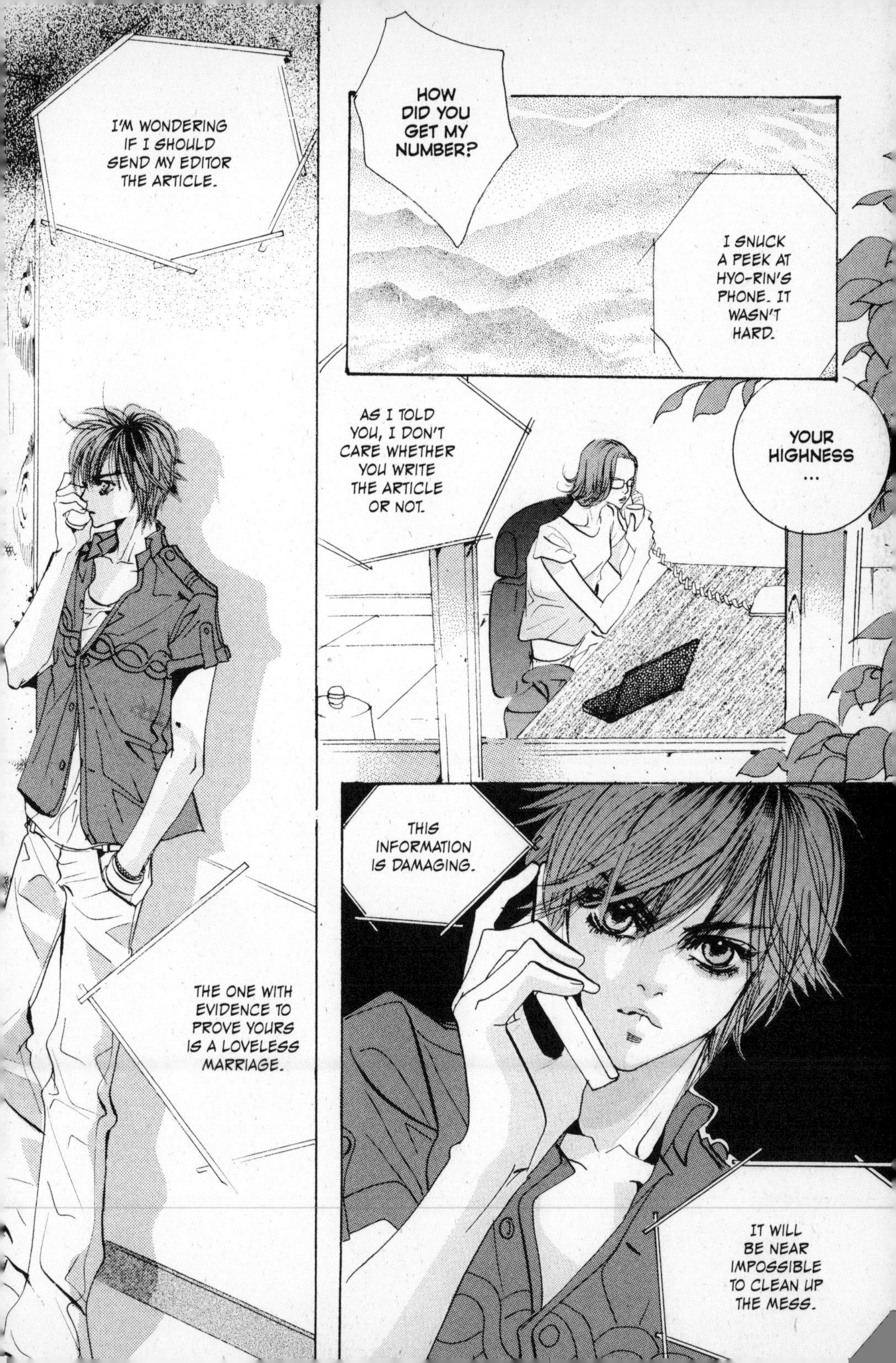
I'M WONDERING IF I SHOULD SEND MY EDITOR THE ARTICLE.
THE ONE WITH EVIDENCE TO PROVE YOURS IS A LOVELESS MARRIAGE.
HOW DID YOU GET MY NUMBER?
I SNUCK A PEEK AT HYO-RIN'S PHONE. IT WASN'T HARD.
AS I TOLD YOU, I DON'T CARE WHETHER YOU WRITE THE ARTICLE OR NOT.
YOUR HIGHNESS ...
THIS INFORMATION IS DAMAGING.
IT WILL BE NEAR IMPOSSIBLE TO CLEAN UP THE MESS.

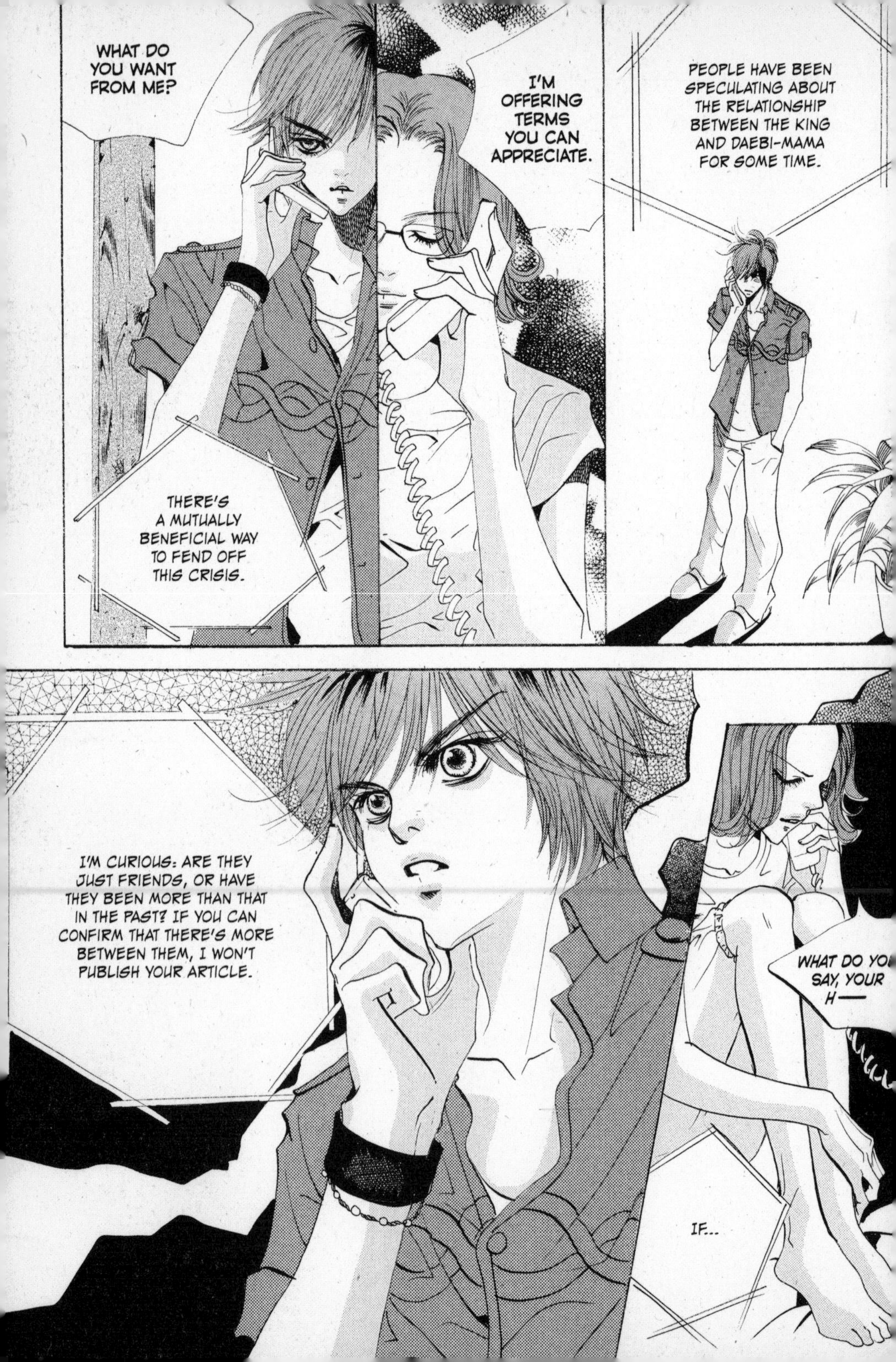
WHAT DO YOU WANT FROM ME?
THERE'S A MUTUALLY BENEFICIAL WAY TO FEND OFF THIS CRISIS.
I'M OFFERING TERMS YOU CAN APPRECIATE.
PEOPLE HAVE BEEN SPECULATING ABOUT THE RELATIONSHIP BETWEEN THE KING AND DAEBI-MAMA FOR SOME TIME.
I'M CURIOUS: ARE THEY JUST FRIENDS, OR HAVE THEY BEEN MORE THAN THAT IN THE PAST? IF YOU CAN CONFIRM THAT THERE'S MORE BETWEEN THEM, I WON'T PUBLISH YOUR ARTICLE.
WHAT DO YO SAY, YOUR H—
IF...

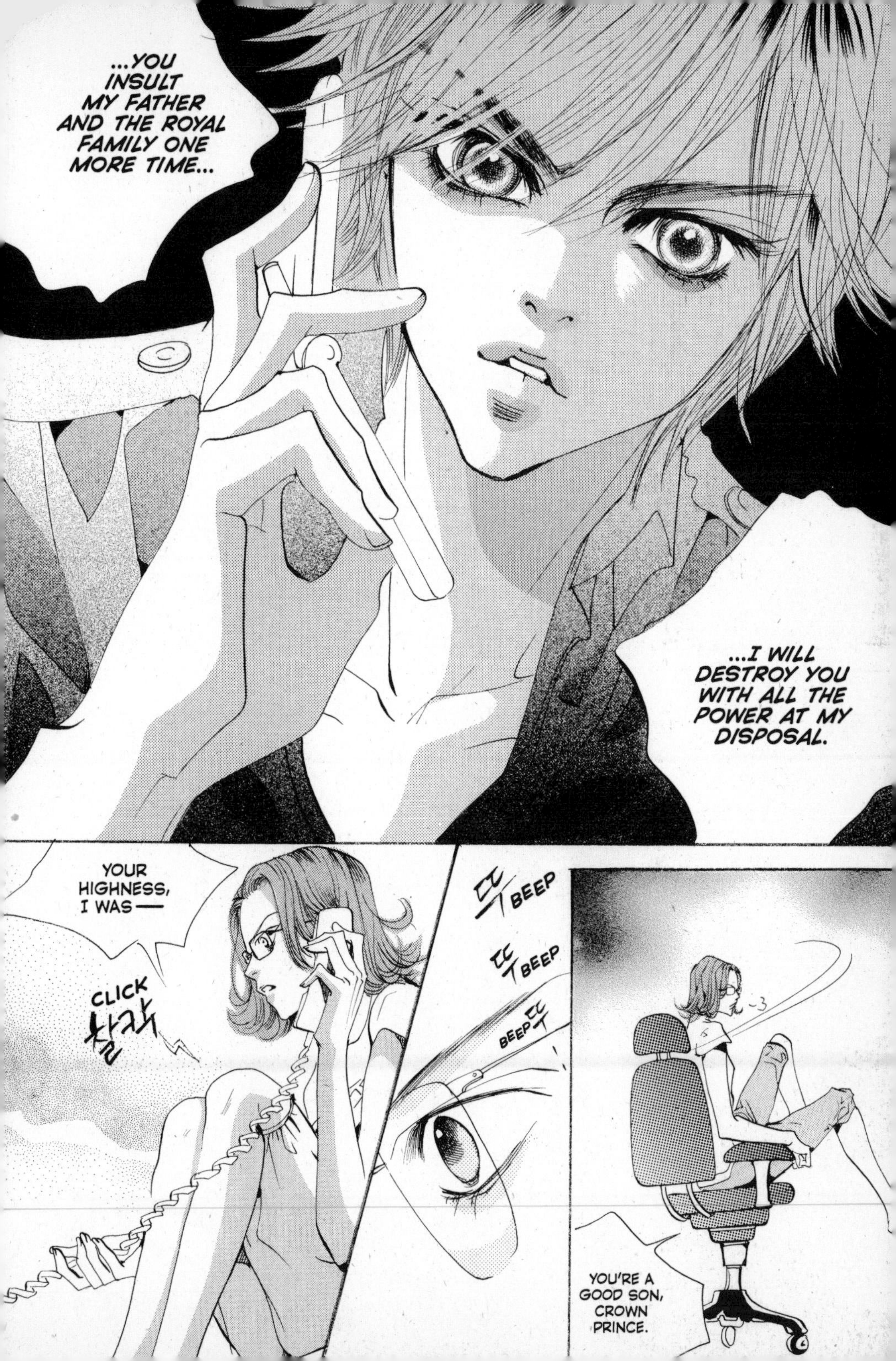
...YOU INSULT MY FATHER AND THE ROYAL FAMILY ONE MORE TIME...
...I WILL DESTROY YOU WITH ALL THE POWER AT MY DISPOSAL.
YOUR HIGHNESS, I WAS—
CLICK
찰칵
뚝 BEEP
뚝 BEEP
BEEP 뚝
YOU'RE A GOOD SON, CROWN PRINCE.

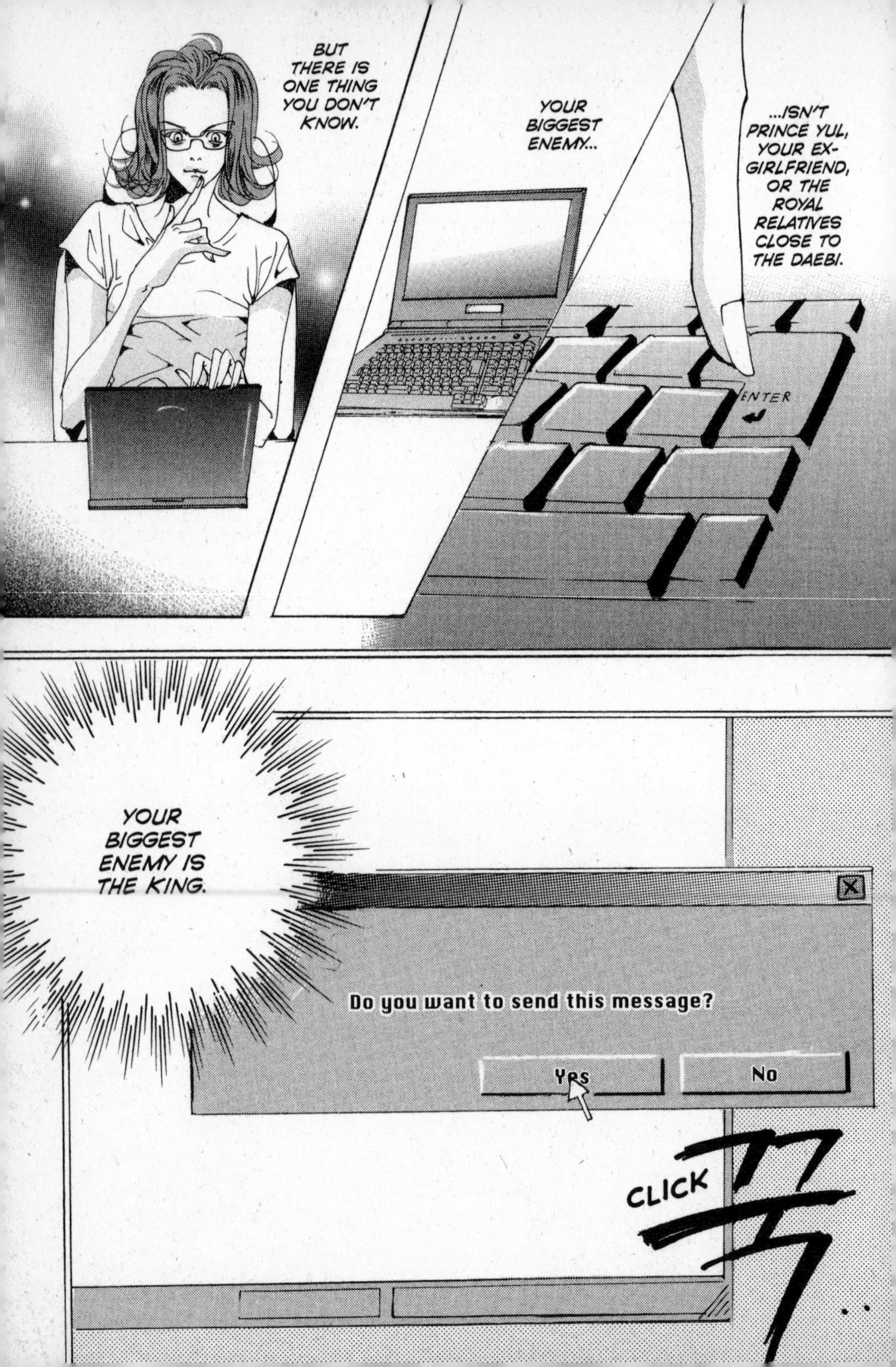
BUT THERE IS ONE THING YOU DON'T KNOW.
YOUR BIGGEST ENEMY...
...ISN'T PRINCE YUL, YOUR EX-GIRLFRIEND, OR THE ROYAL RELATIVES CLOSE TO THE DAEBI.
ENTER
YOUR BIGGEST ENEMY IS THE KING.
Do you want to send this message?
Yes
No
CLICK

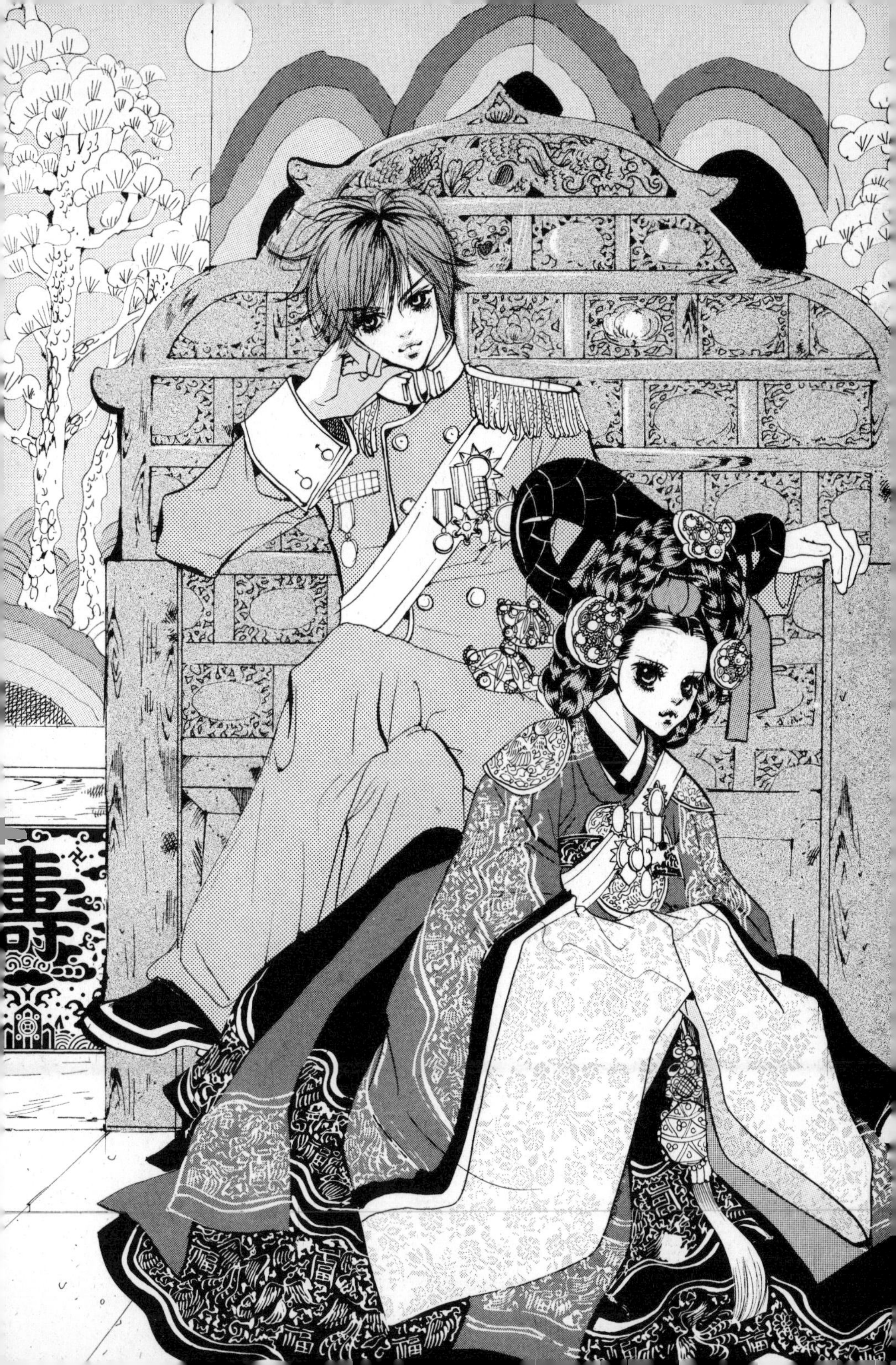

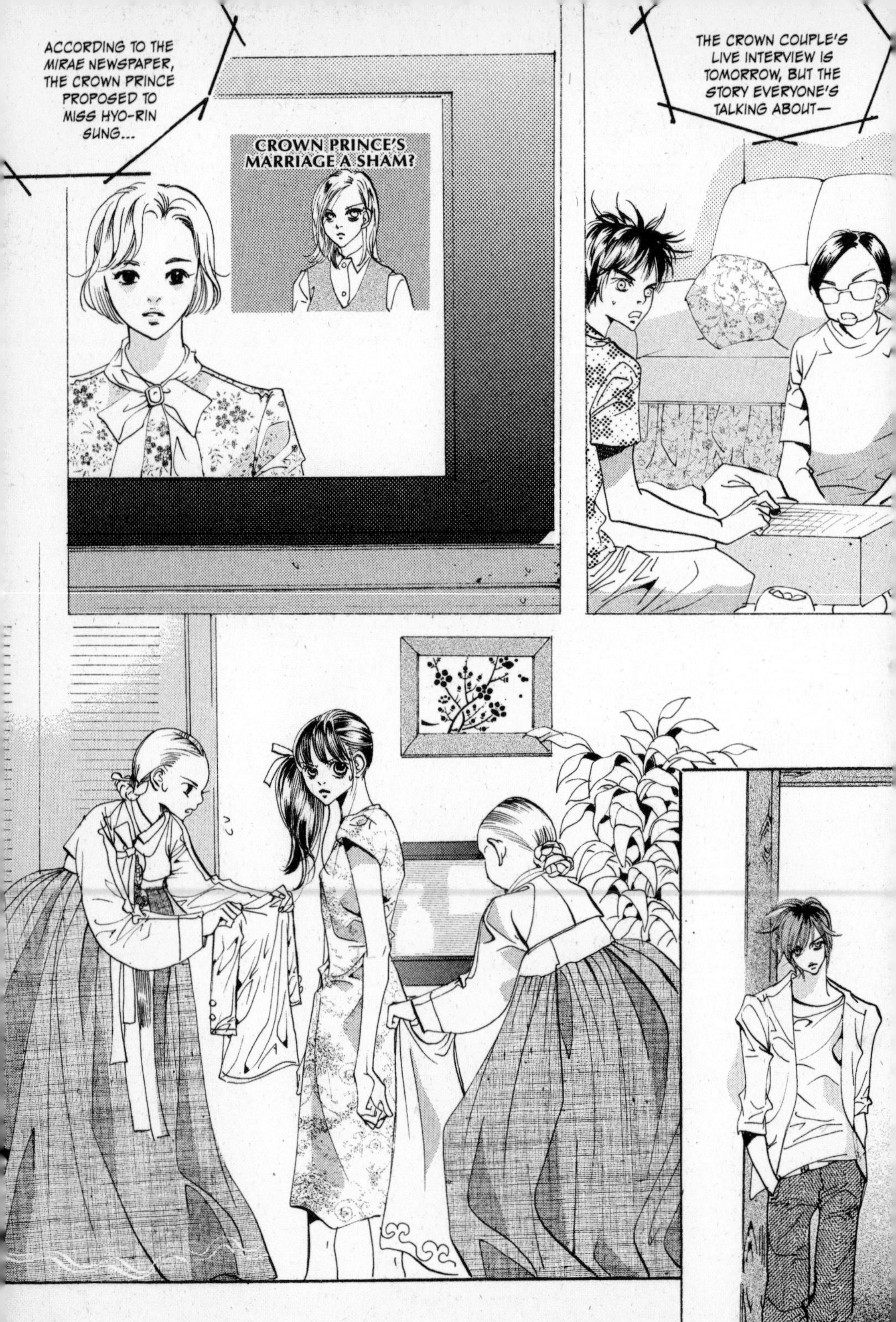
ACCORDING TO THE MIRAE NEWSPAPER, THE CROWN PRINCE PROPOSED TO MISS HYO-RIN SUNG...
CROWN PRINCE'S MARRIAGE A SHAM?
THE CROWN COUPLE'S LIVE INTERVIEW IS TOMORROW, BUT THE STORY EVERYONE'S TALKING ABOUT—

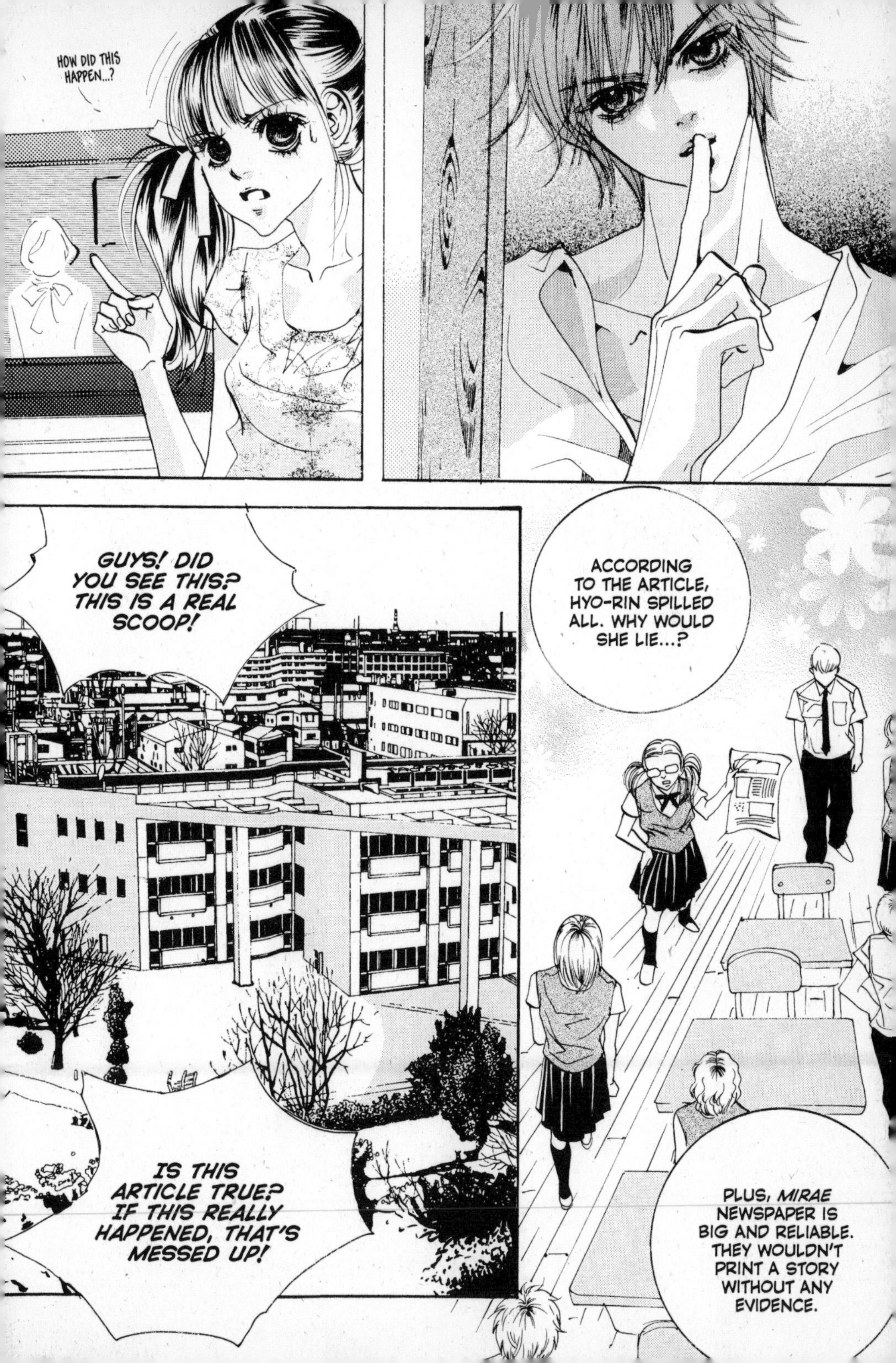
HOW DID THIS HAPPEN...?
GUYS! DID YOU SEE THIS? THIS IS A REAL SCOOP!
IS THIS ARTICLE TRUE? IF THIS REALLY HAPPENED, THAT'S MESSED UP!
ACCORDING TO THE ARTICLE, HYO-RIN SPILLED ALL. WHY WOULD SHE LIE...?
PLUS, *MIRAE* NEWSPAPER IS BIG AND RELIABLE. THEY WOULDN'T PRINT A STORY WITHOUT ANY EVIDENCE.

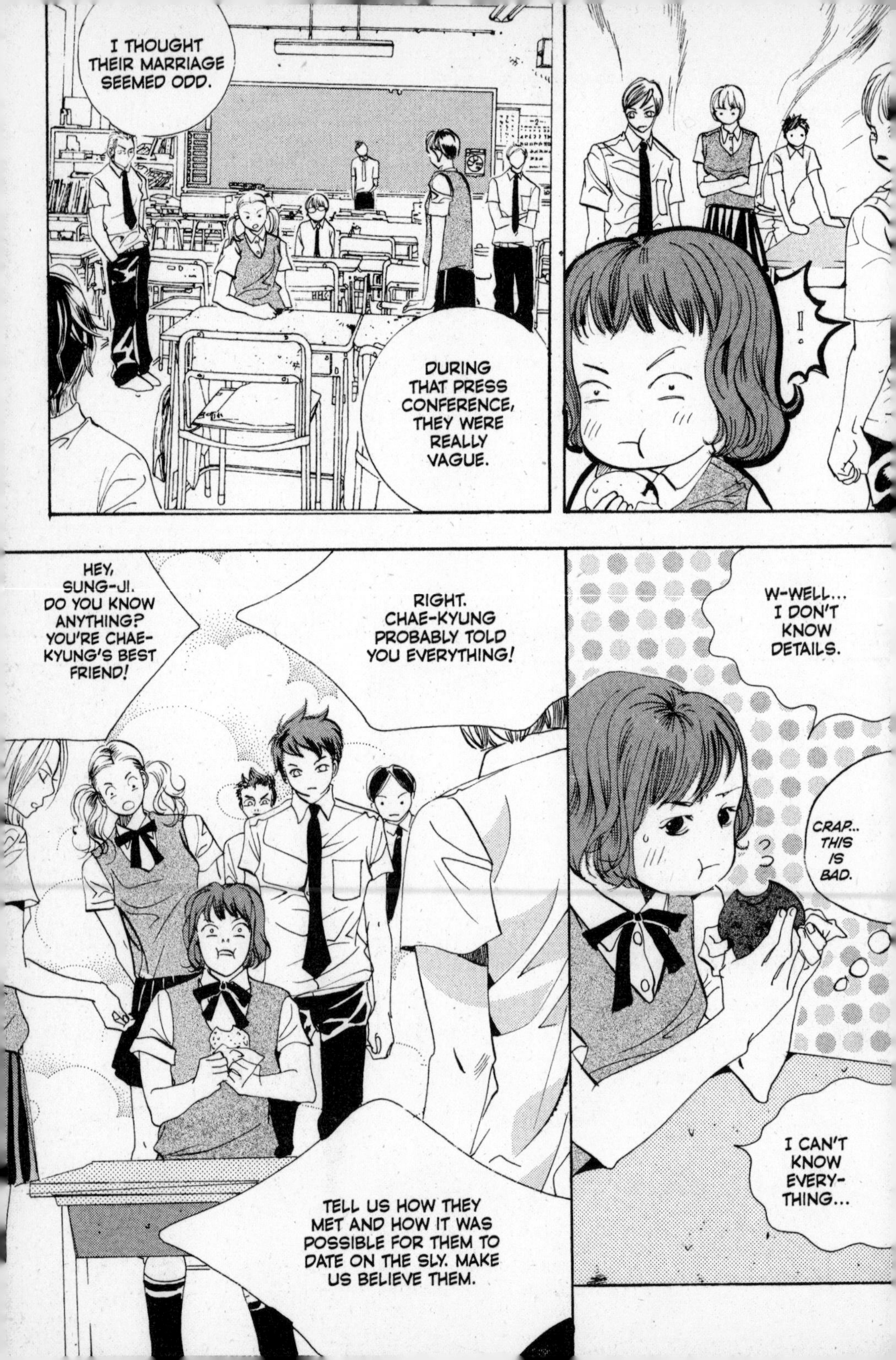
I THOUGHT THEIR MARRIAGE SEEMED ODD.
DURING THAT PRESS CONFERENCE, THEY WERE REALLY VAGUE.
!
HEY, SUNG-JI. DO YOU KNOW ANYTHING? YOU'RE CHAE-KYUNG'S BEST FRIEND!
RIGHT. CHAE-KYUNG PROBABLY TOLD YOU EVERYTHING!
TELL US HOW THEY MET AND HOW IT WAS POSSIBLE FOR THEM TO DATE ON THE SLY. MAKE US BELIEVE THEM.
W-WELL... I DON'T KNOW DETAILS.
CRAP... THIS IS BAD.
I CAN'T KNOW EVERY-THING...

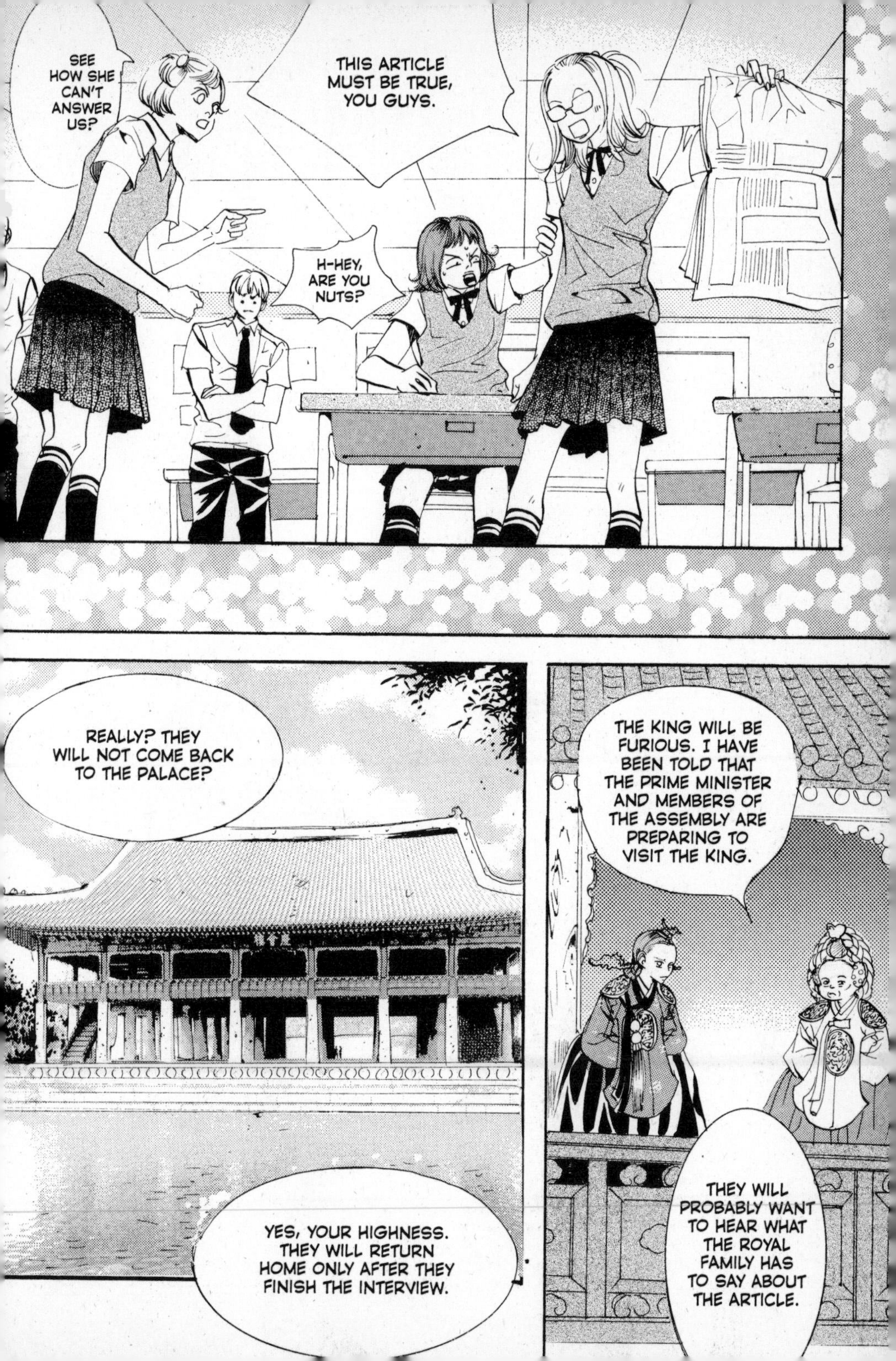
SEE HOW SHE CAN'T ANSWER US?
THIS ARTICLE MUST BE TRUE, YOU GUYS.
H-HEY, ARE YOU NUTS?
REALLY? THEY WILL NOT COME BACK TO THE PALACE?
YES, YOUR HIGHNESS. THEY WILL RETURN HOME ONLY AFTER THEY FINISH THE INTERVIEW.
THE KING WILL BE FURIOUS. I HAVE BEEN TOLD THAT THE PRIME MINISTER AND MEMBERS OF THE ASSEMBLY ARE PREPARING TO VISIT THE KING.
THEY WILL PROBABLY WANT TO HEAR WHAT THE ROYAL FAMILY HAS TO SAY ABOUT THE ARTICLE.

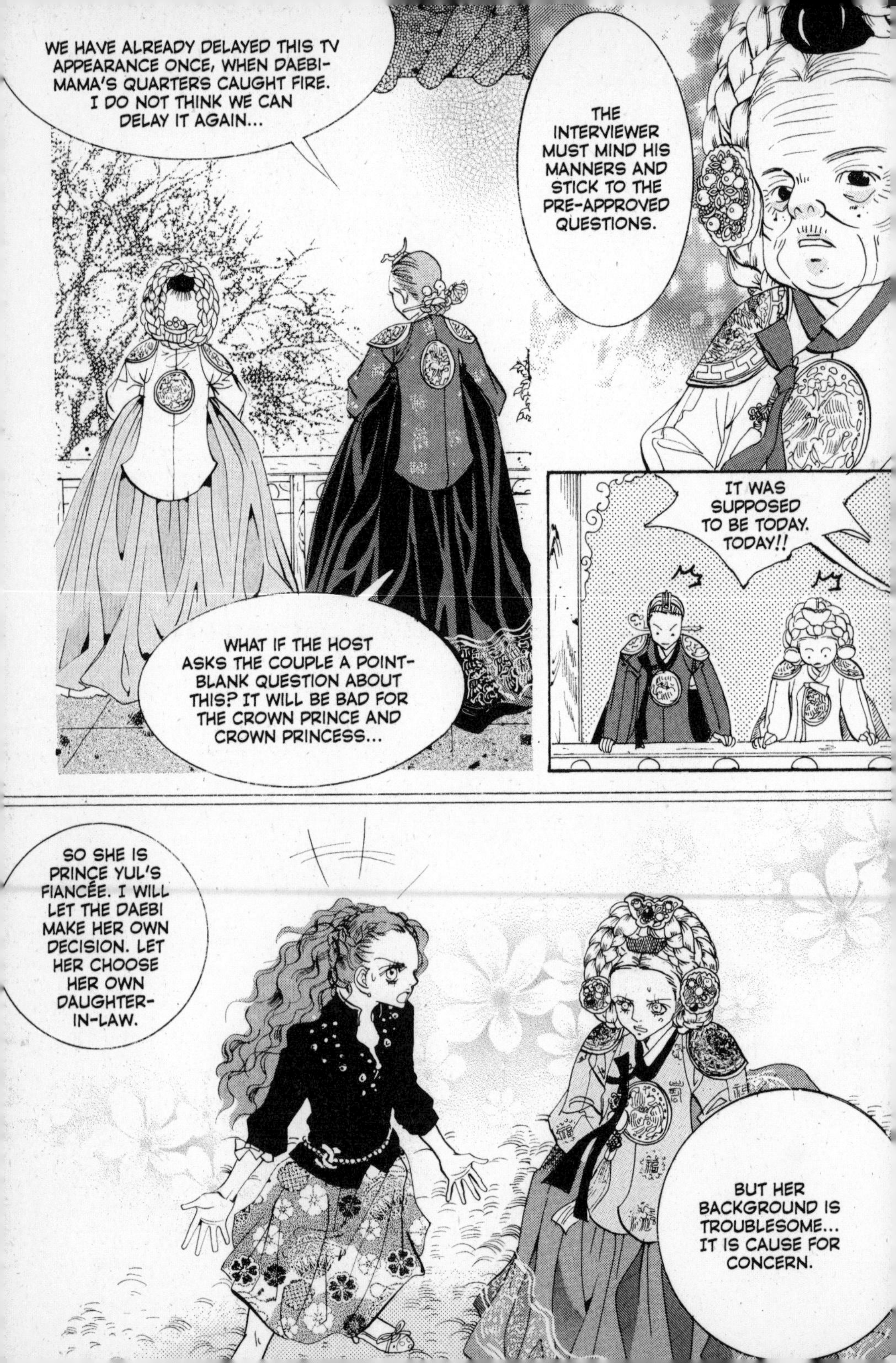
WE HAVE ALREADY DELAYED THIS TV APPEARANCE ONCE, WHEN DAEBI-MAMA'S QUARTERS CAUGHT FIRE. I DO NOT THINK WE CAN DELAY IT AGAIN...
WHAT IF THE HOST ASKS THE COUPLE A POINT-BLANK QUESTION ABOUT THIS? IT WILL BE BAD FOR THE CROWN PRINCE AND CROWN PRINCESS...
THE INTERVIEWER MUST MIND HIS MANNERS AND STICK TO THE PRE-APPROVED QUESTIONS.
IT WAS SUPPOSED TO BE TODAY. TODAY!!
SO SHE IS PRINCE YUL'S FIANCÉE. I WILL LET THE DAEBI MAKE HER OWN DECISION. LET HER CHOOSE HER OWN DAUGHTER-IN-LAW.
BUT HER BACKGROUND IS TROUBLESOME... IT IS CAUSE FOR CONCERN.

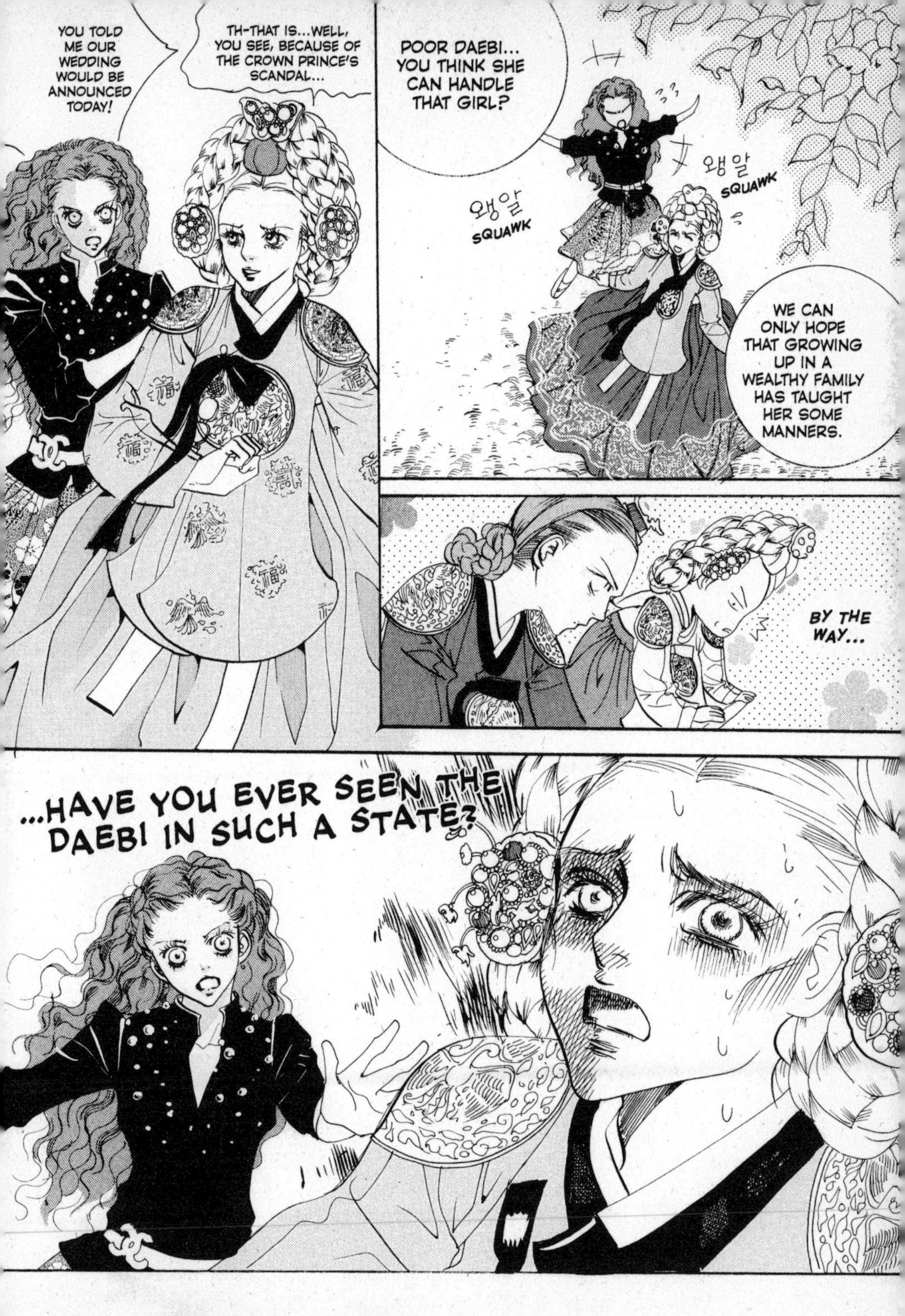
YOU TOLD ME OUR WEDDING WOULD BE ANNOUNCED TODAY!
TH-THAT IS...WELL, YOU SEE, BECAUSE OF THE CROWN PRINCE'S SCANDAL...
POOR DAEBI... YOU THINK SHE CAN HANDLE THAT GIRL?
왱알
SQUAWK
왱알
SQUAWK
WE CAN ONLY HOPE THAT GROWING UP IN A WEALTHY FAMILY HAS TAUGHT HER SOME MANNERS.
BY THE WAY...
...HAVE YOU EVER SEEN THE DAEBI IN SUCH A STATE?

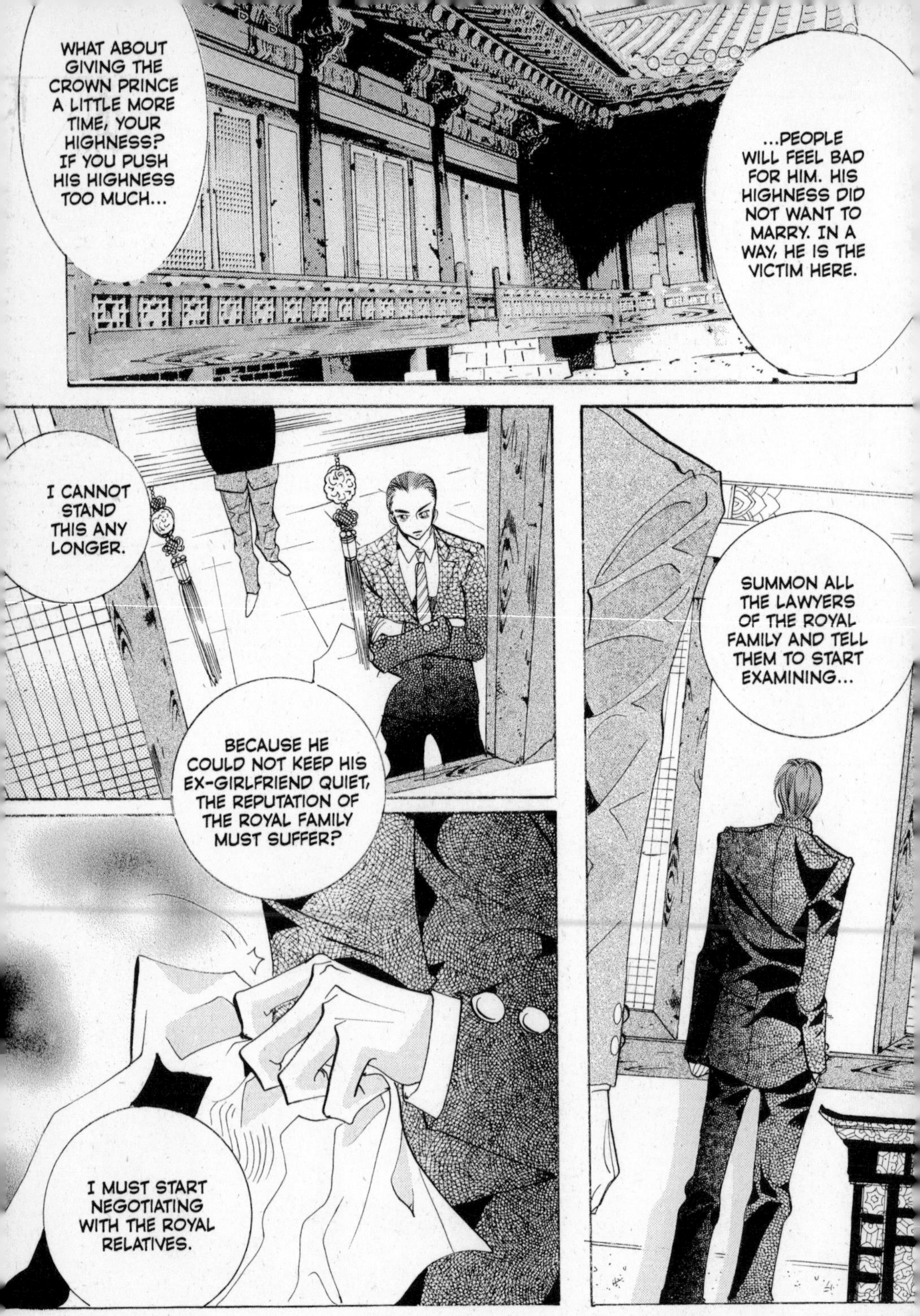
WHAT ABOUT GIVING THE CROWN PRINCE A LITTLE MORE TIME, YOUR HIGHNESS? IF YOU PUSH HIS HIGHNESS TOO MUCH...
...PEOPLE WILL FEEL BAD FOR HIM. HIS HIGHNESS DID NOT WANT TO MARRY. IN A WAY, HE IS THE VICTIM HERE.
I CANNOT STAND THIS ANY LONGER.
BECAUSE HE COULD NOT KEEP HIS EX-GIRLFRIEND QUIET, THE REPUTATION OF THE ROYAL FAMILY MUST SUFFER?
I MUST START NEGOTIATING WITH THE ROYAL RELATIVES.
SUMMON ALL THE LAWYERS OF THE ROYAL FAMILY AND TELL THEM TO START EXAMINING...

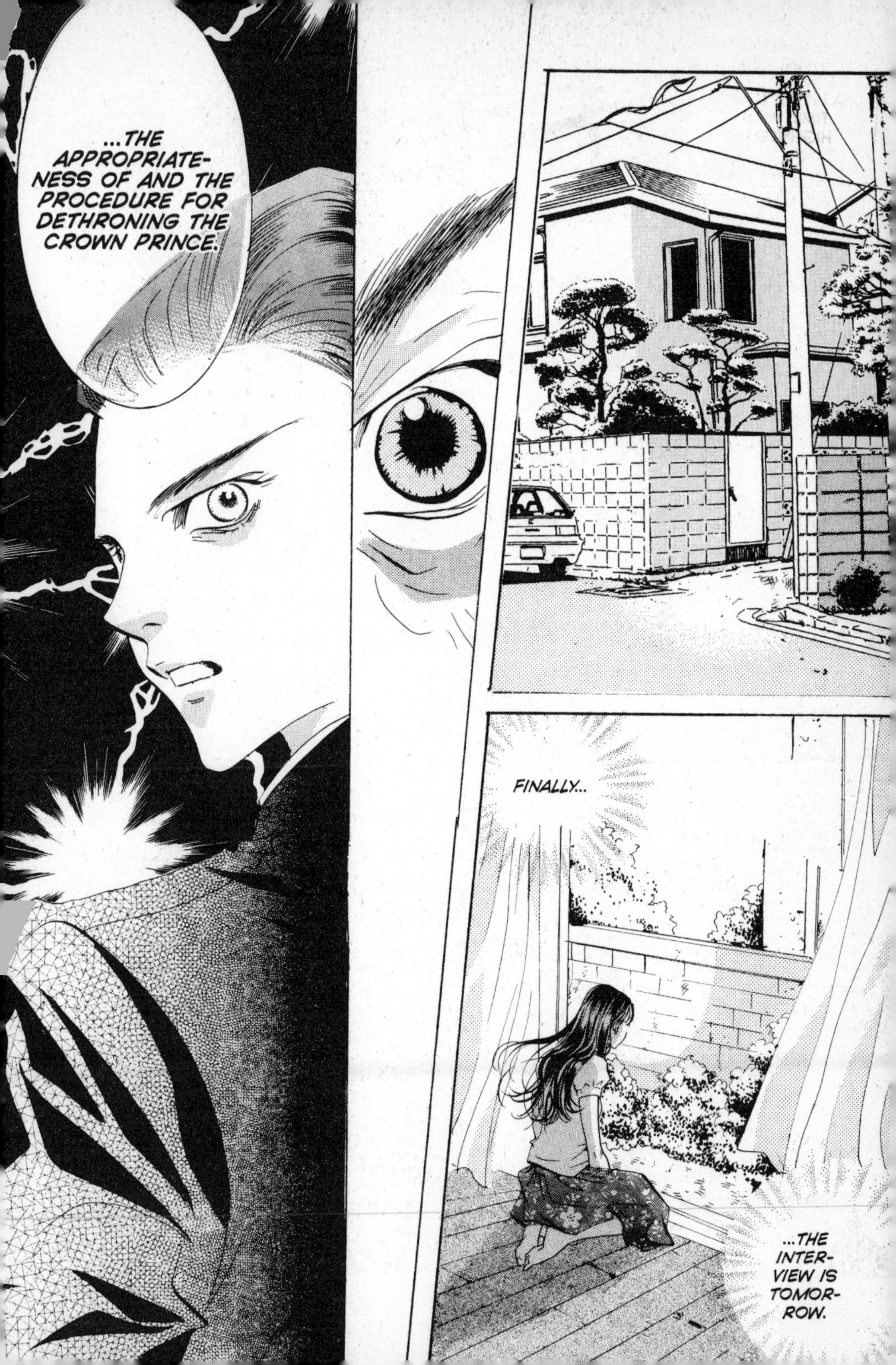
...THE APPROPRIATENESS OF AND THE PROCEDURE FOR DETHRONING THE CROWN PRINCE.
FINALLY...
...THE INTERVIEW IS TOMORROW.

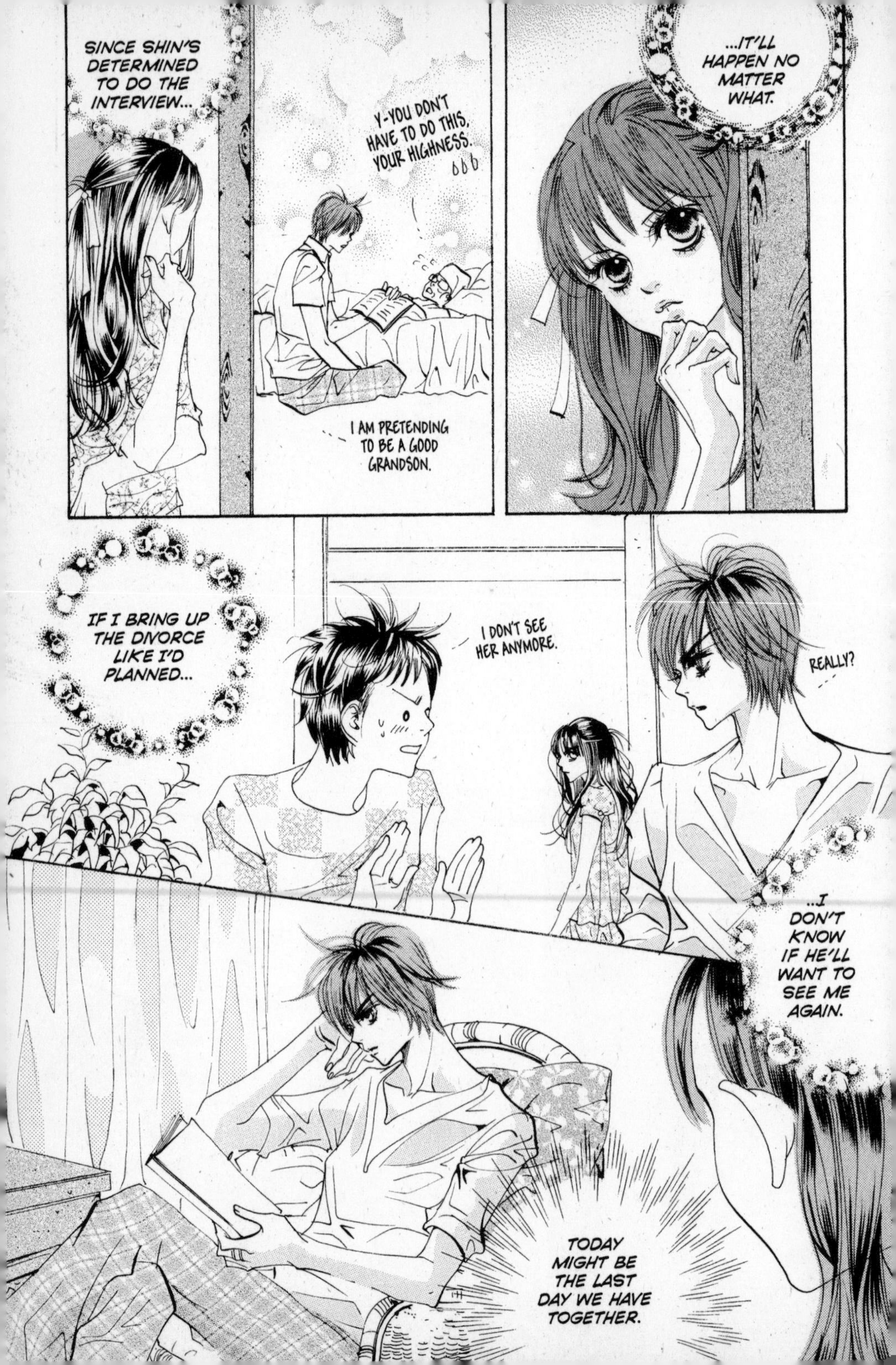
SINCE SHIN'S DETERMINED TO DO THE INTERVIEW...
Y-YOU DON'T HAVE TO DO THIS, YOUR HIGHNESS.
I AM PRETENDING TO BE A GOOD GRANDSON.
...IT'LL HAPPEN NO MATTER WHAT.
IF I BRING UP THE DIVORCE LIKE I'D PLANNED...
I DON'T SEE HER ANYMORE.
REALLY?
...I DON'T KNOW IF HE'LL WANT TO SEE ME AGAIN.
TODAY MIGHT BE THE LAST DAY WE HAVE TOGETHER.

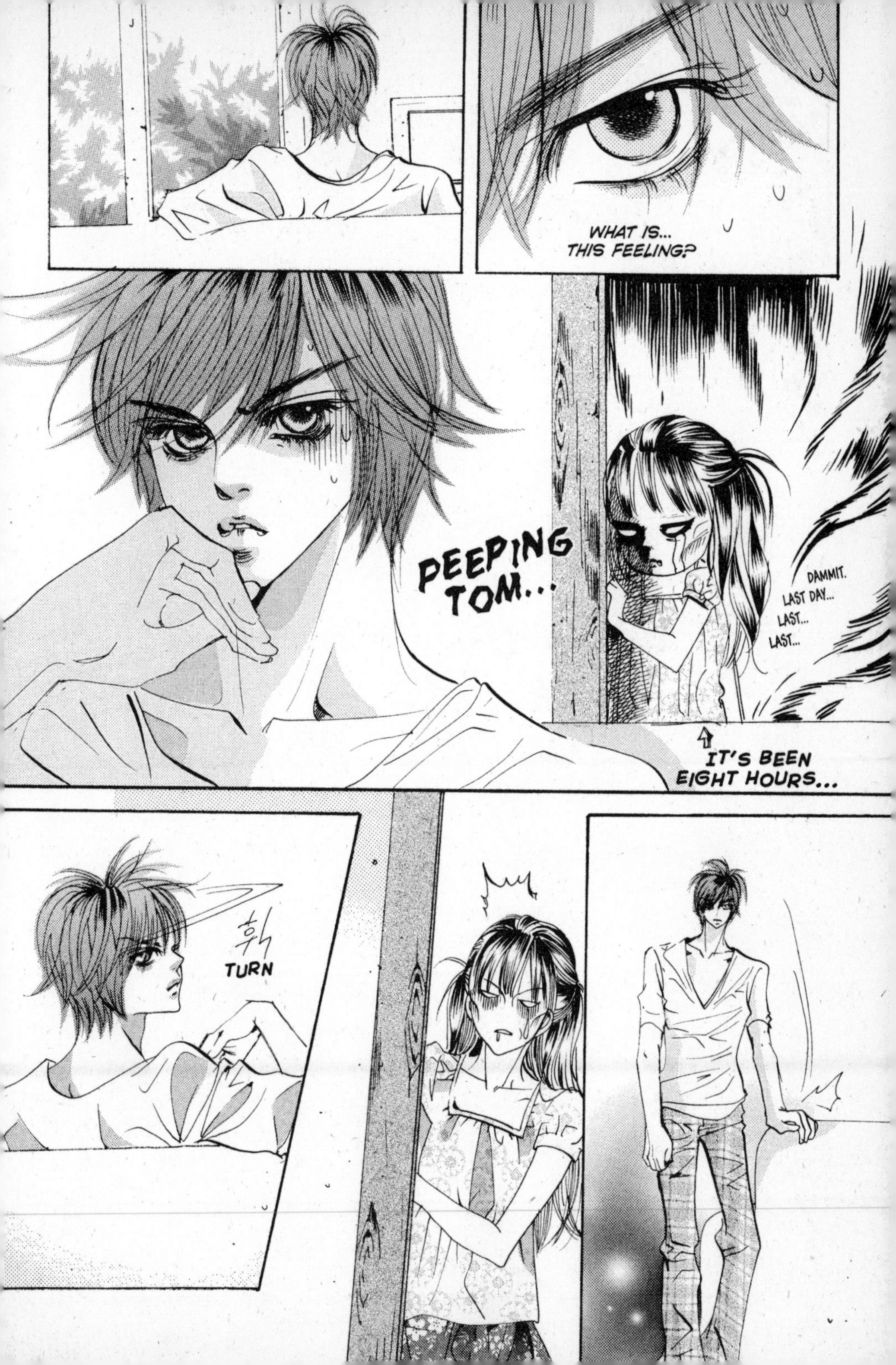
WHAT IS...
THIS FEELING?
PEEPING TOM...
DAMMIT.
LAST DAY...
LAST...
LAST...
IT'S BEEN EIGHT HOURS...
훽
TURN

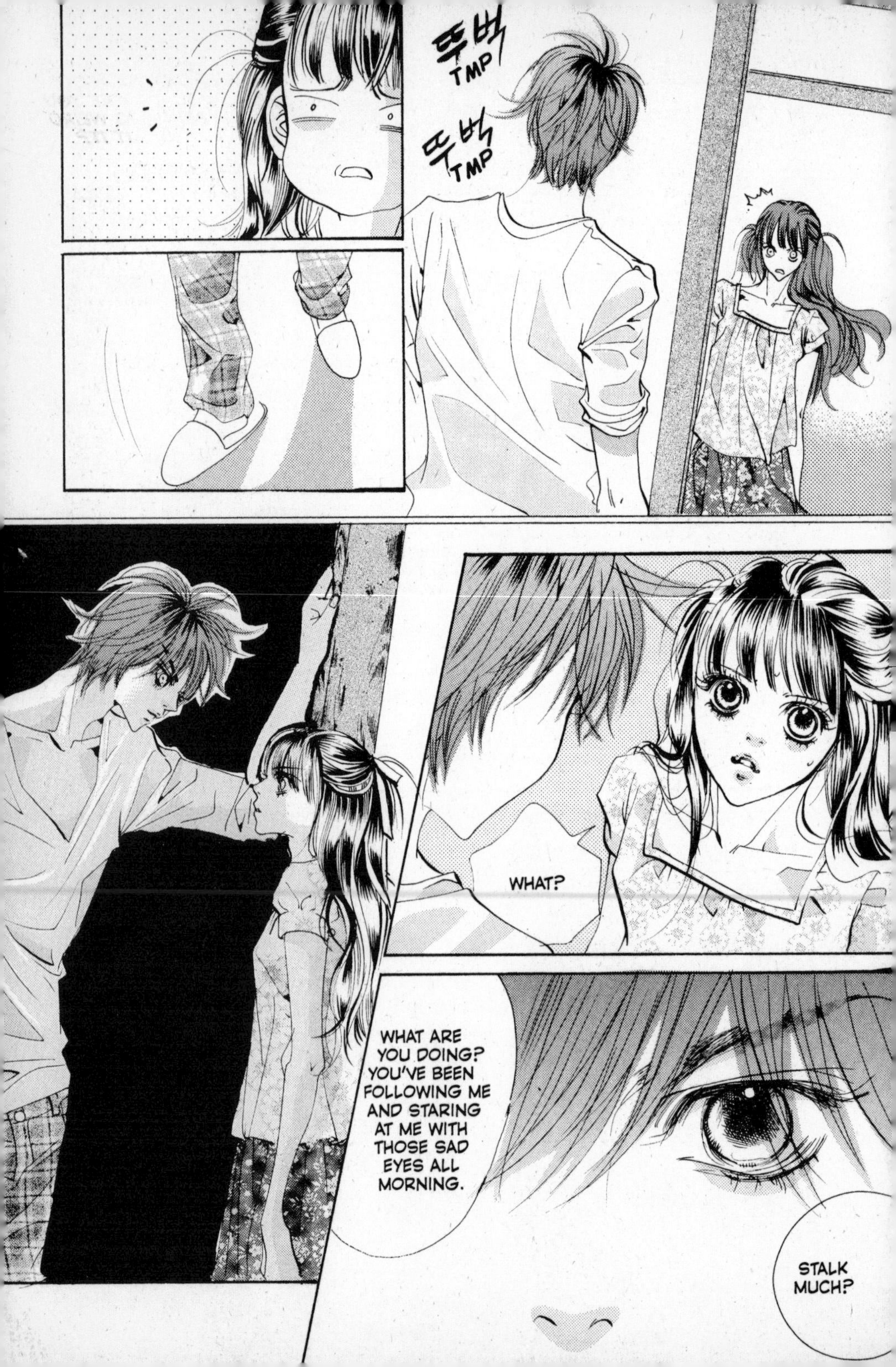
뚜벅
TMP
뚜벅
TMP
WHAT?
WHAT ARE YOU DOING? YOU'VE BEEN FOLLOWING ME AND STARING AT ME WITH THOSE SAD EYES ALL MORNING.
STALK MUCH?

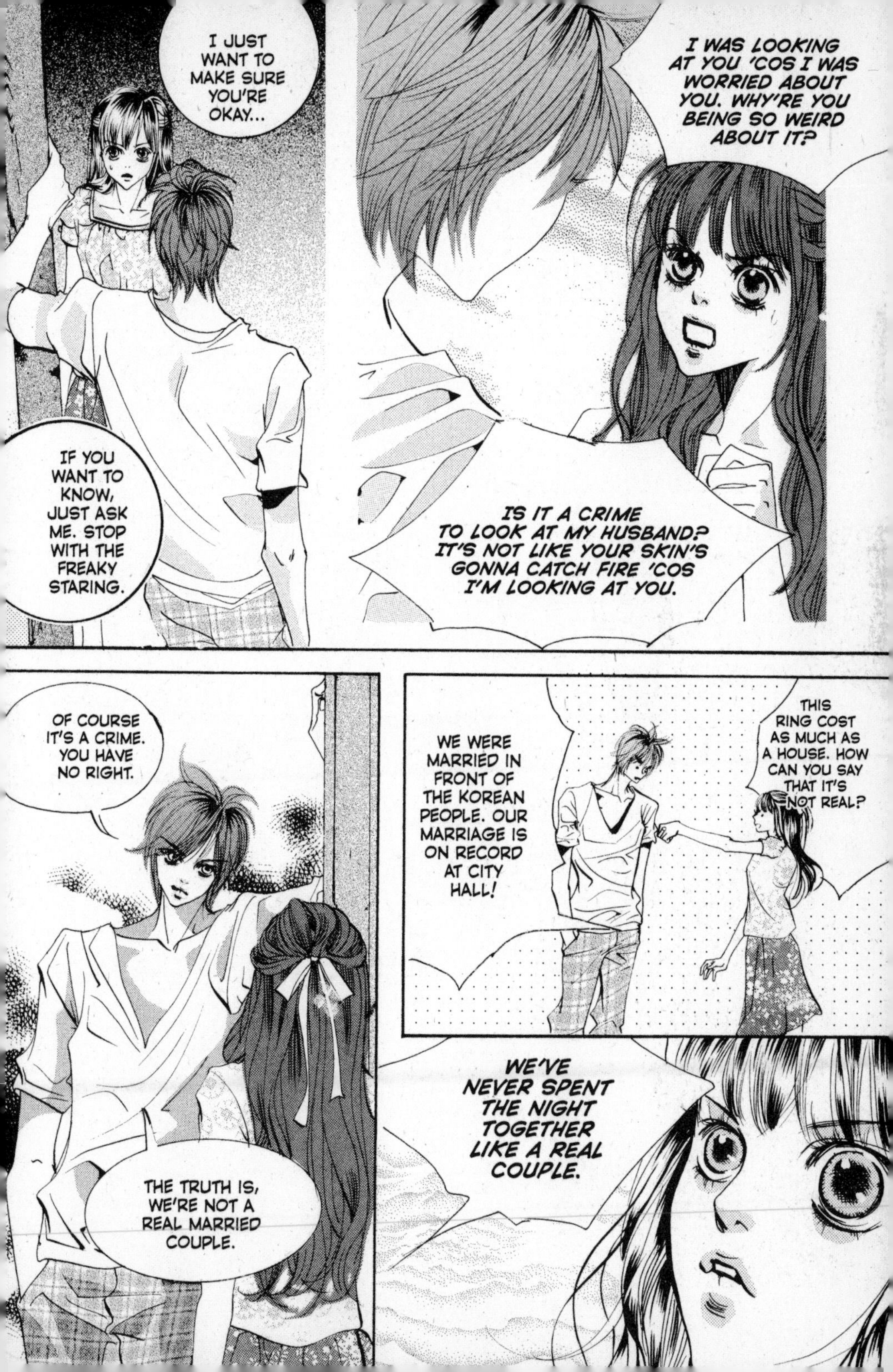
I JUST WANT TO MAKE SURE YOU'RE OKAY...
IF YOU WANT TO KNOW, JUST ASK ME. STOP WITH THE FREAKY STARING.
I WAS LOOKING AT YOU 'COS I WAS WORRIED ABOUT YOU. WHY'RE YOU BEING SO WEIRD ABOUT IT?
IS IT A CRIME TO LOOK AT MY HUSBAND? IT'S NOT LIKE YOUR SKIN'S GONNA CATCH FIRE 'COS I'M LOOKING AT YOU.
OF COURSE IT'S A CRIME. YOU HAVE NO RIGHT.
THE TRUTH IS, WE'RE NOT A REAL MARRIED COUPLE.
WE WERE MARRIED IN FRONT OF THE KOREAN PEOPLE. OUR MARRIAGE IS ON RECORD AT CITY HALL!
THIS RING COST AS MUCH AS A HOUSE. HOW CAN YOU SAY THAT IT'S NOT REAL?
WE'VE NEVER SPENT THE NIGHT TOGETHER LIKE A REAL COUPLE.

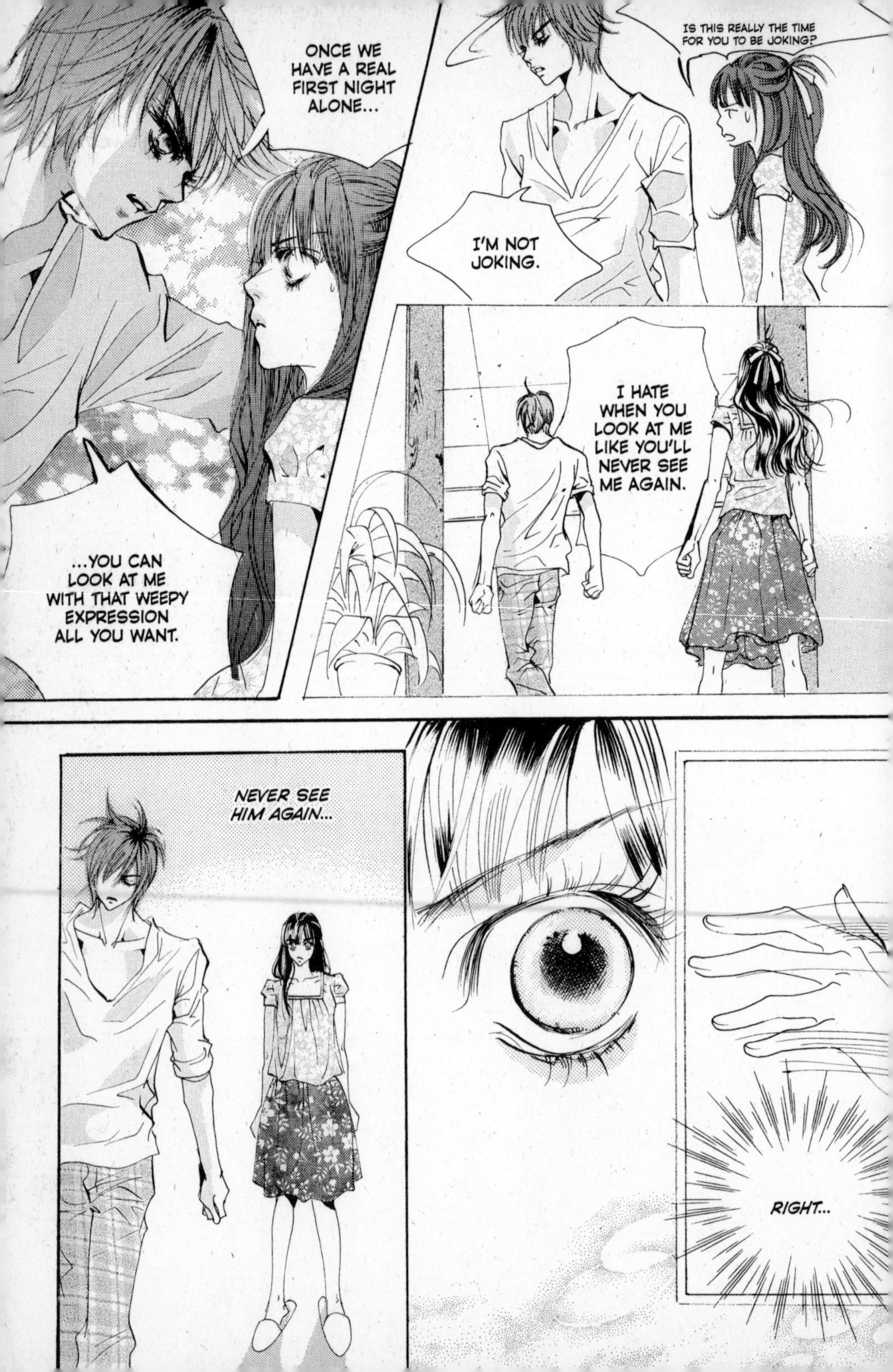
ONCE WE HAVE A REAL FIRST NIGHT ALONE...
...YOU CAN LOOK AT ME WITH THAT WEEPY EXPRESSION ALL YOU WANT.
IS THIS REALLY THE TIME FOR YOU TO BE JOKING?
I'M NOT JOKING.
I HATE WHEN YOU LOOK AT ME LIKE YOU'LL NEVER SEE ME AGAIN.
NEVER SEE HIM AGAIN...
RIGHT...

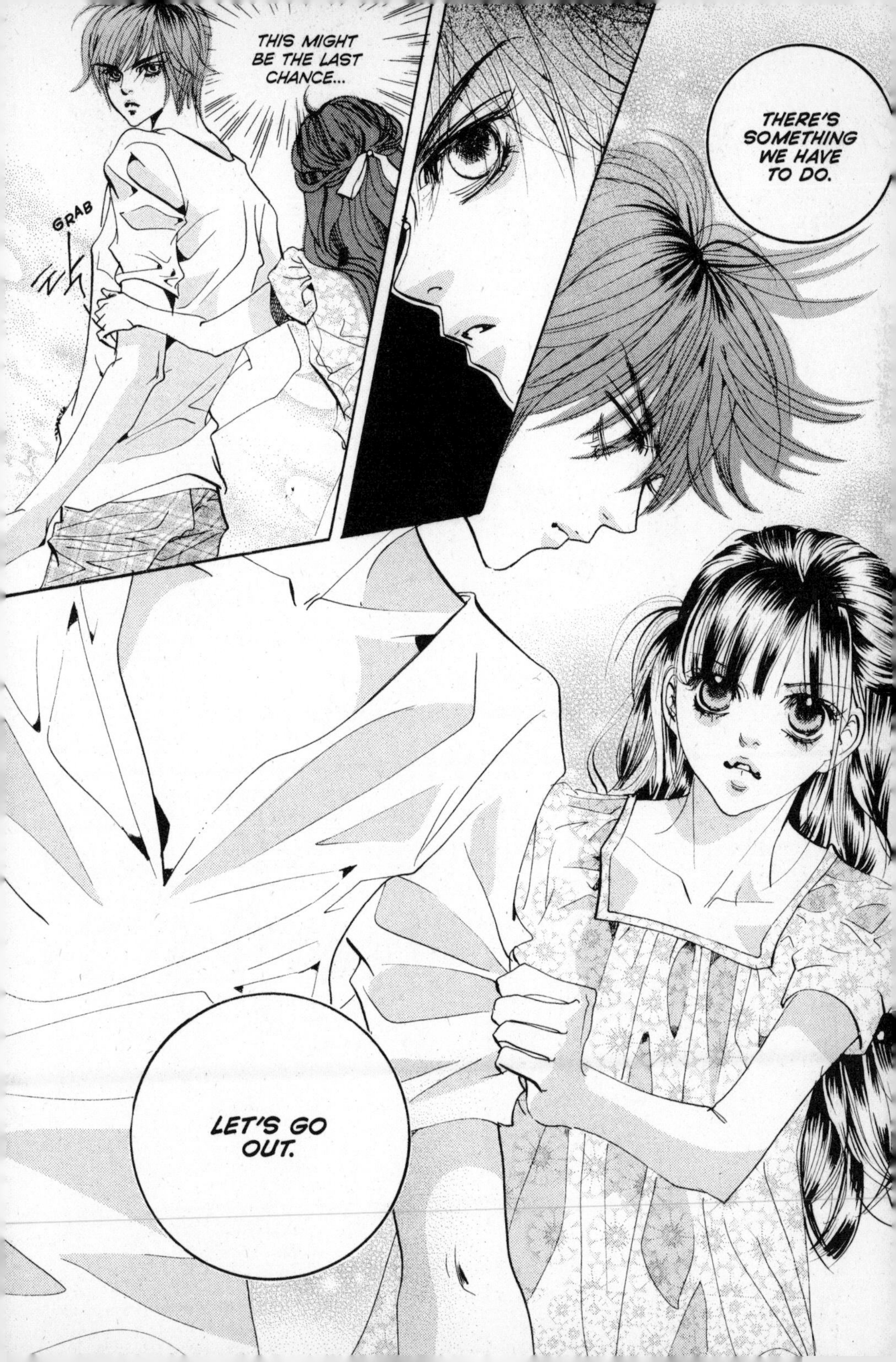
THIS MIGHT BE THE LAST CHANCE...
GRAB
THERE'S SOMETHING WE HAVE TO DO.
LET'S GO OUT.

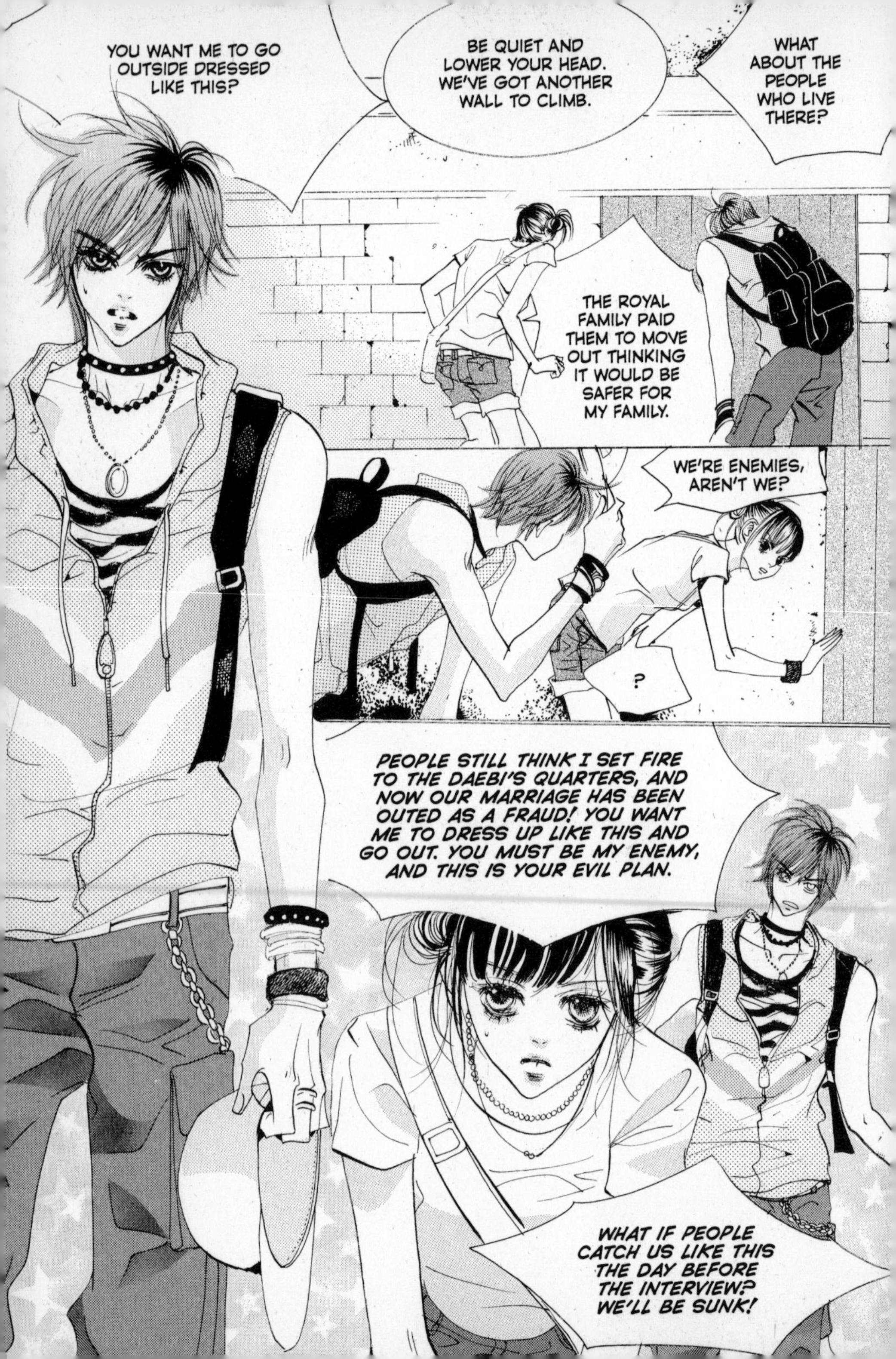
YOU WANT ME TO GO OUTSIDE DRESSED LIKE THIS?
BE QUIET AND LOWER YOUR HEAD. WE'VE GOT ANOTHER WALL TO CLIMB.
WHAT ABOUT THE PEOPLE WHO LIVE THERE?
THE ROYAL FAMILY PAID THEM TO MOVE OUT THINKING IT WOULD BE SAFER FOR MY FAMILY.
WE'RE ENEMIES, AREN'T WE?
?
PEOPLE STILL THINK I SET FIRE TO THE DAEBI'S QUARTERS, AND NOW OUR MARRIAGE HAS BEEN OUTED AS A FRAUD! YOU WANT ME TO DRESS UP LIKE THIS AND GO OUT. YOU MUST BE MY ENEMY, AND THIS IS YOUR EVIL PLAN.
WHAT IF PEOPLE CATCH US LIKE THIS THE DAY BEFORE THE INTERVIEW? WE'LL BE SUNK!

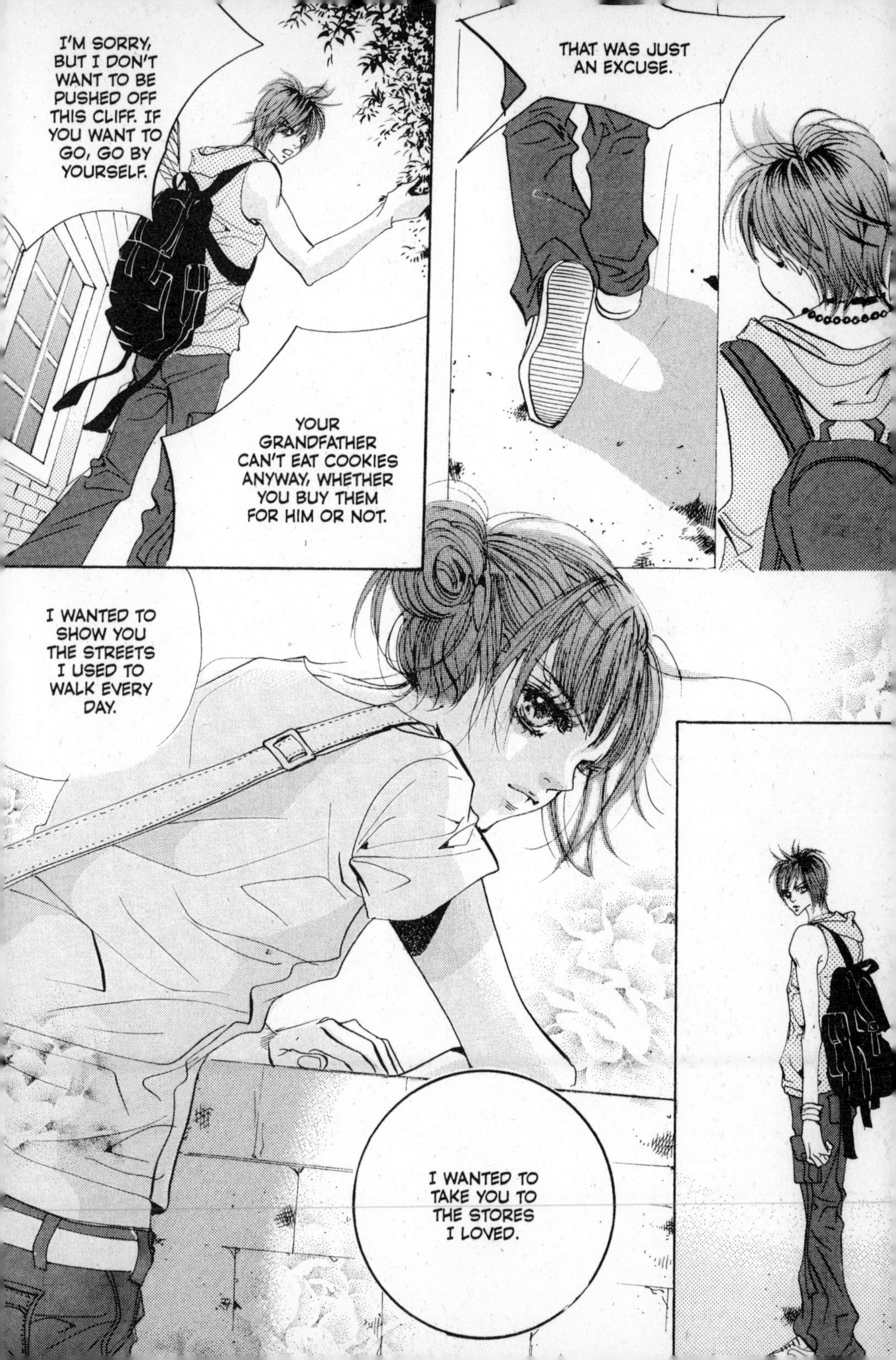
I'M SORRY, BUT I DON'T WANT TO BE PUSHED OFF THIS CLIFF. IF YOU WANT TO GO, GO BY YOURSELF.
YOUR GRANDFATHER CAN'T EAT COOKIES ANYWAY, WHETHER YOU BUY THEM FOR HIM OR NOT.
THAT WAS JUST AN EXCUSE.
I WANTED TO SHOW YOU THE STREETS I USED TO WALK EVERY DAY.
I WANTED TO TAKE YOU TO THE STORES I LOVED.

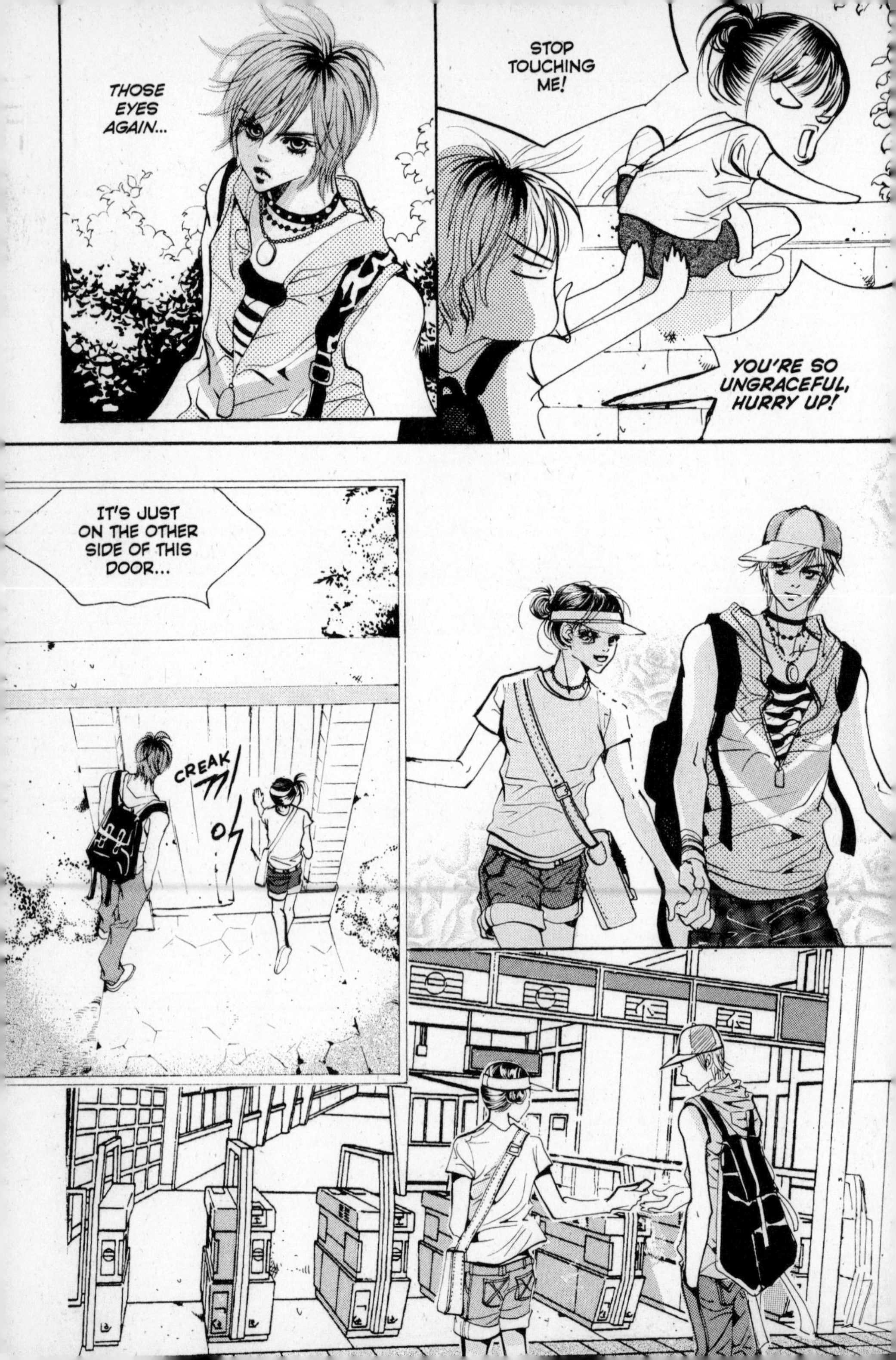
THOSE EYES AGAIN...
STOP TOUCHING ME!
YOU'RE SO UNGRACEFUL, HURRY UP!
IT'S JUST ON THE OTHER SIDE OF THIS DOOR...
CREAK

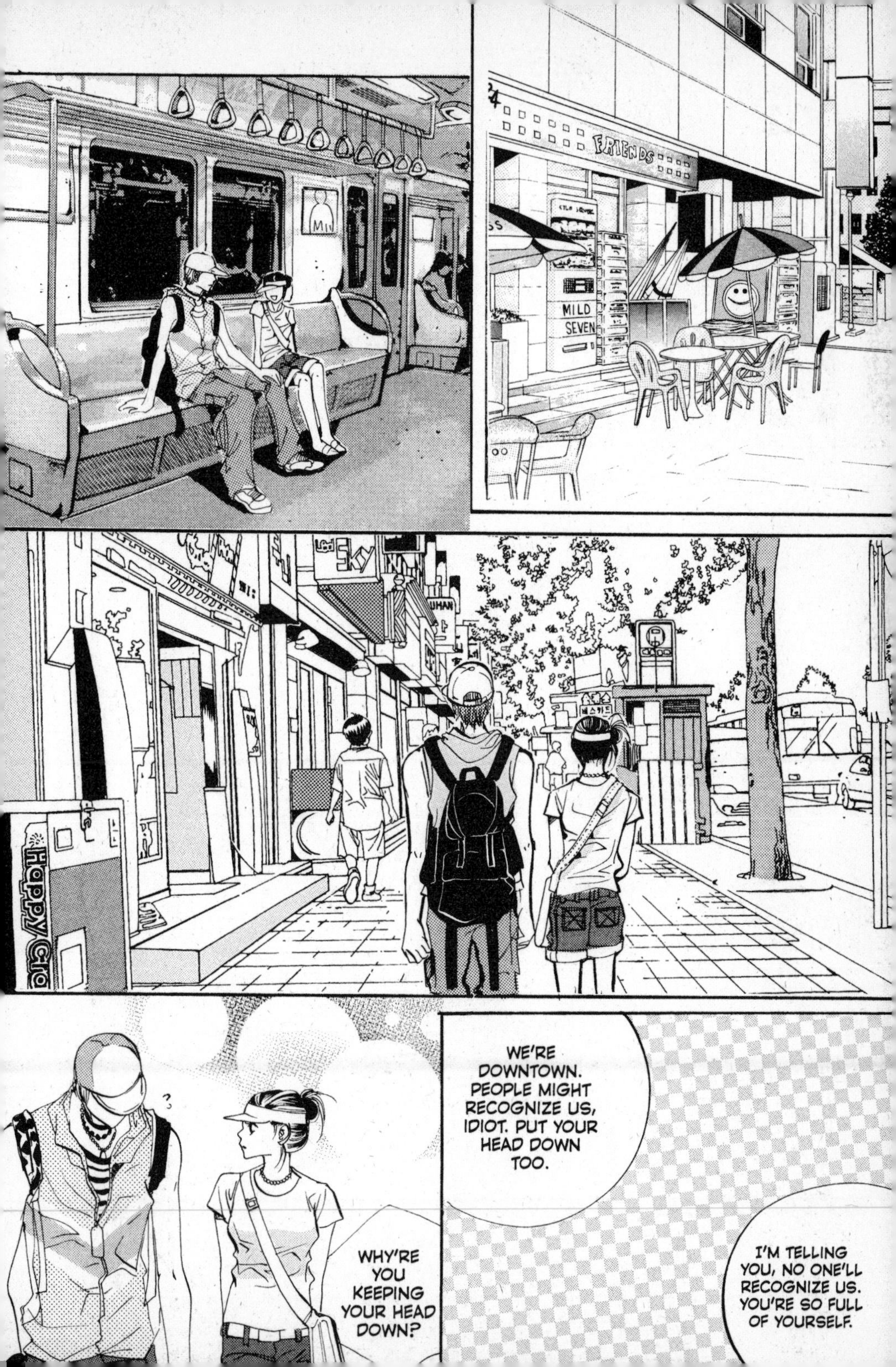
FRIENDS
MILD SEVEN
Sky
WHY'RE YOU KEEPING YOUR HEAD DOWN?
WE'RE DOWNTOWN. PEOPLE MIGHT RECOGNIZE US, IDIOT. PUT YOUR HEAD DOWN TOO.
I'M TELLING YOU, NO ONE'LL RECOGNIZE US. YOU'RE SO FULL OF YOURSELF.

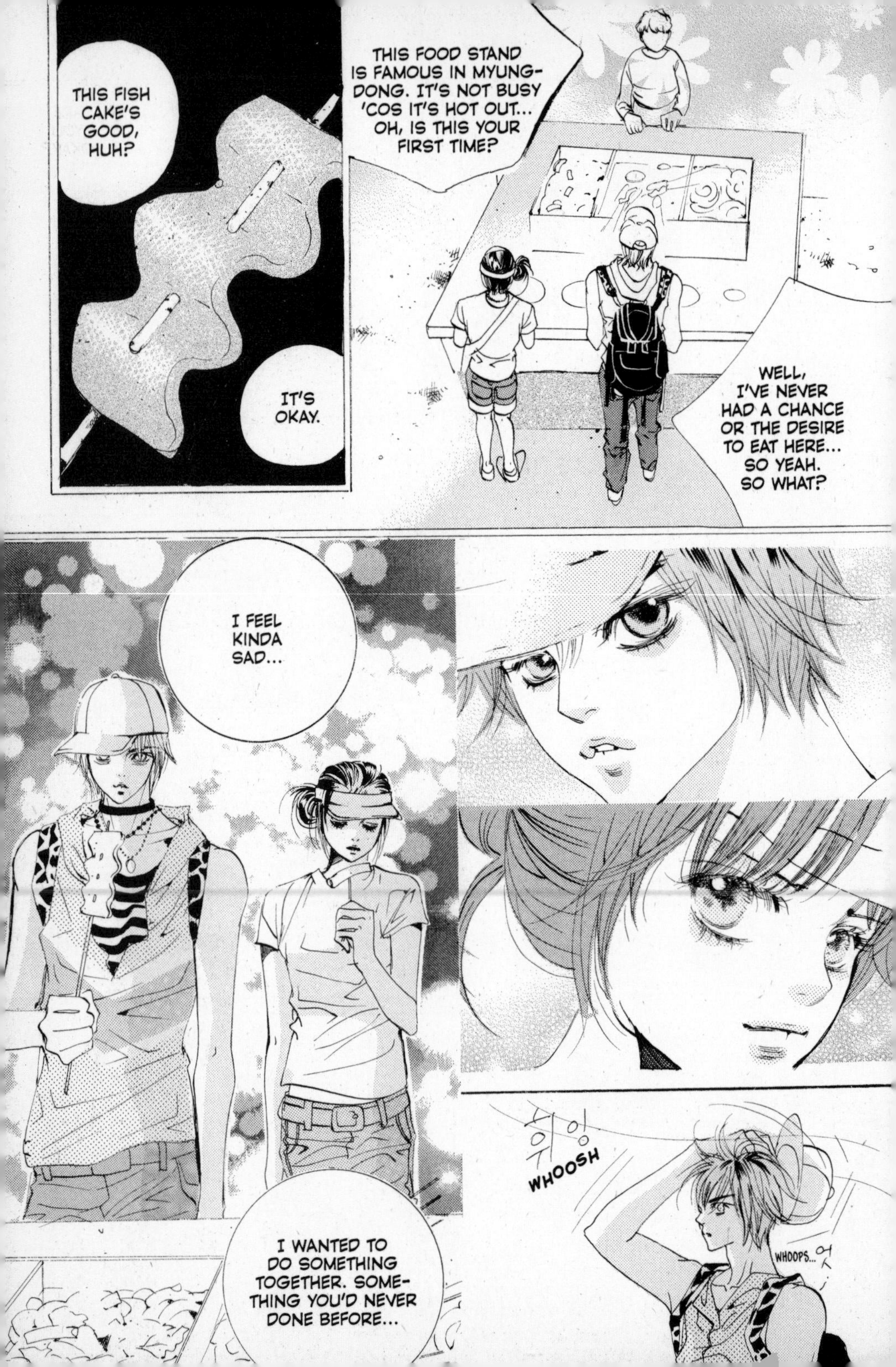
THIS FISH CAKE'S GOOD, HUH?
IT'S OKAY.
THIS FOOD STAND IS FAMOUS IN MYUNG-DONG. IT'S NOT BUSY 'COS IT'S HOT OUT... OH, IS THIS YOUR FIRST TIME?
WELL, I'VE NEVER HAD A CHANCE OR THE DESIRE TO EAT HERE... SO YEAH. SO WHAT?
I FEEL KINDA SAD...
I WANTED TO DO SOMETHING TOGETHER. SOME-THING YOU'D NEVER DONE BEFORE...
쉬잉
WHOOSH
WHOOPS...
앗

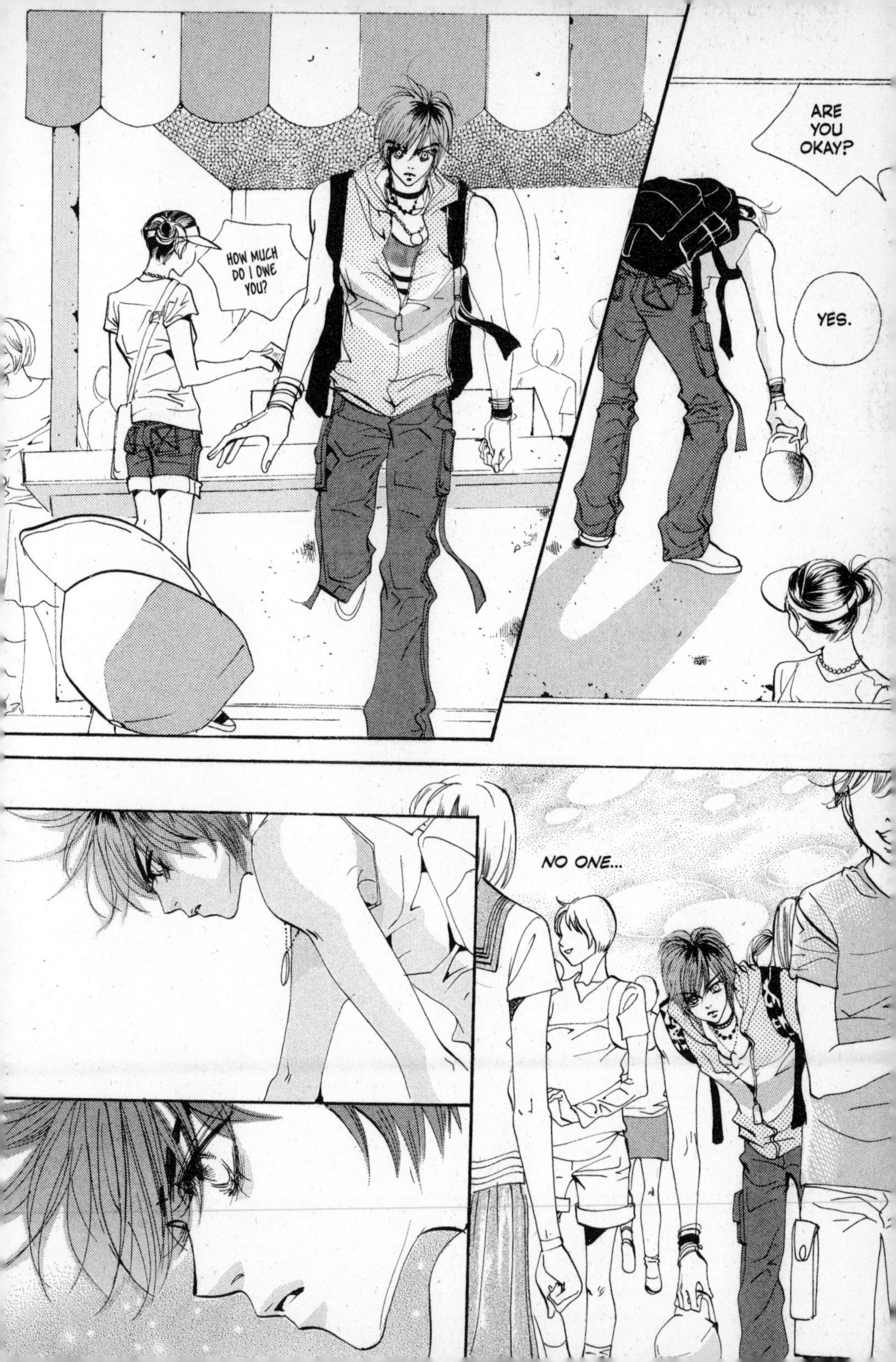
HOW MUCH DO I OWE YOU?
ARE YOU OKAY?
YES.
NO ONE...

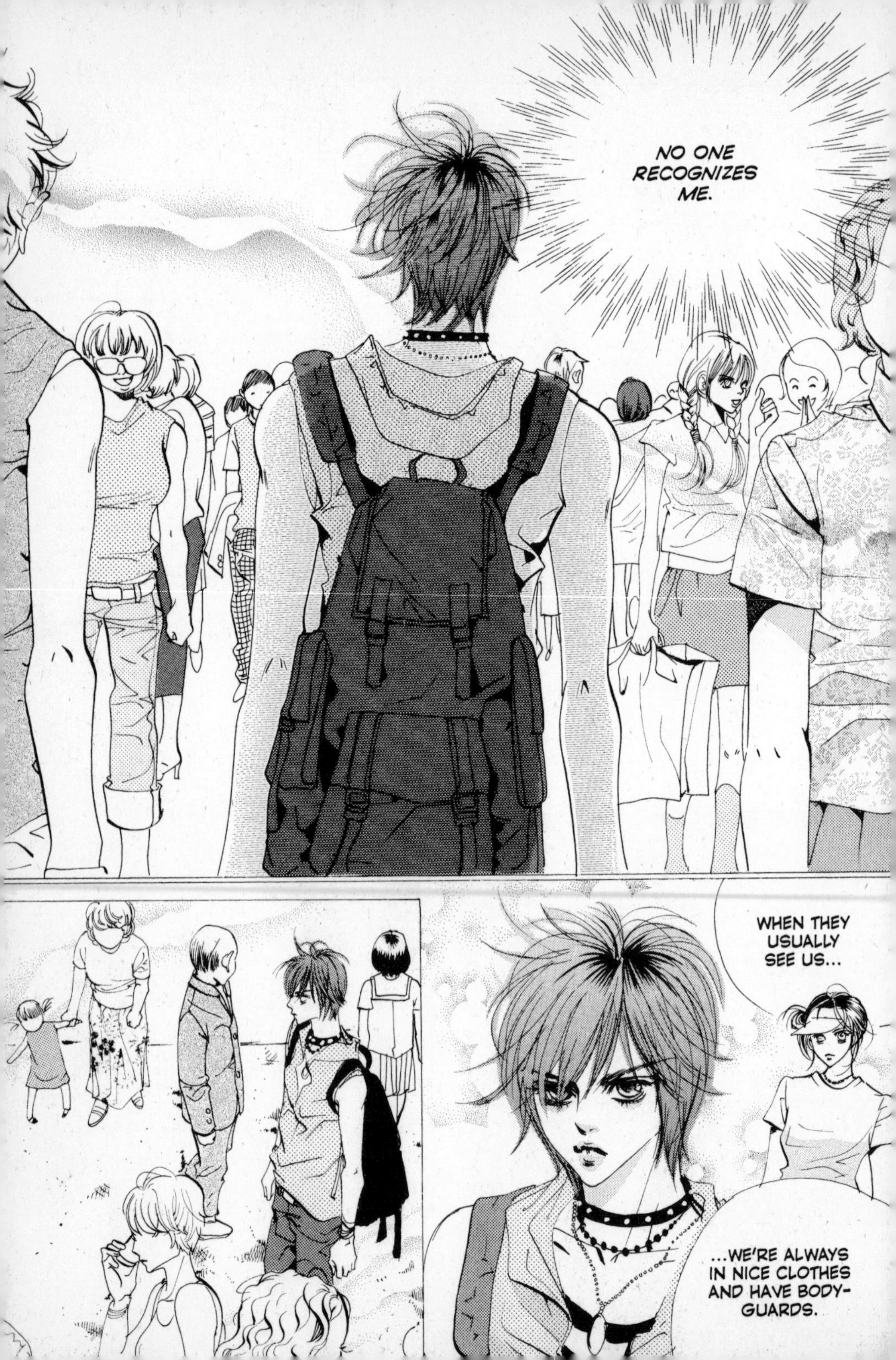
NO ONE RECOGNIZES ME.
WHEN THEY USUALLY SEE US...
...WE'RE ALWAYS IN NICE CLOTHES AND HAVE BODY-GUARDS.

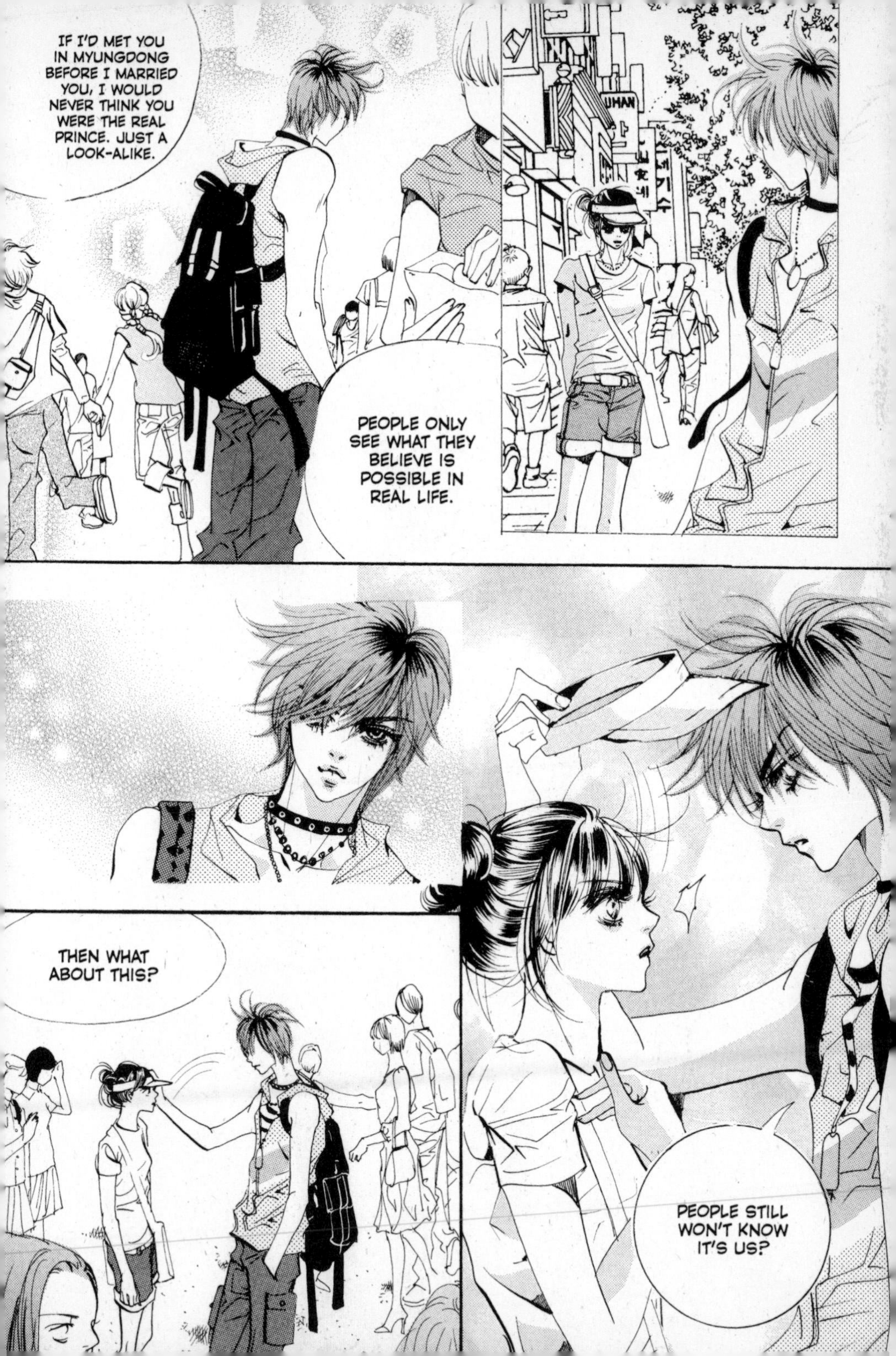
IF I'D MET YOU IN MYUNGDONG BEFORE I MARRIED YOU, I WOULD NEVER THINK YOU WERE THE REAL PRINCE. JUST A LOOK-ALIKE.
PEOPLE ONLY SEE WHAT THEY BELIEVE IS POSSIBLE IN REAL LIFE.
THEN WHAT ABOUT THIS?
PEOPLE STILL WON'T KNOW IT'S US?

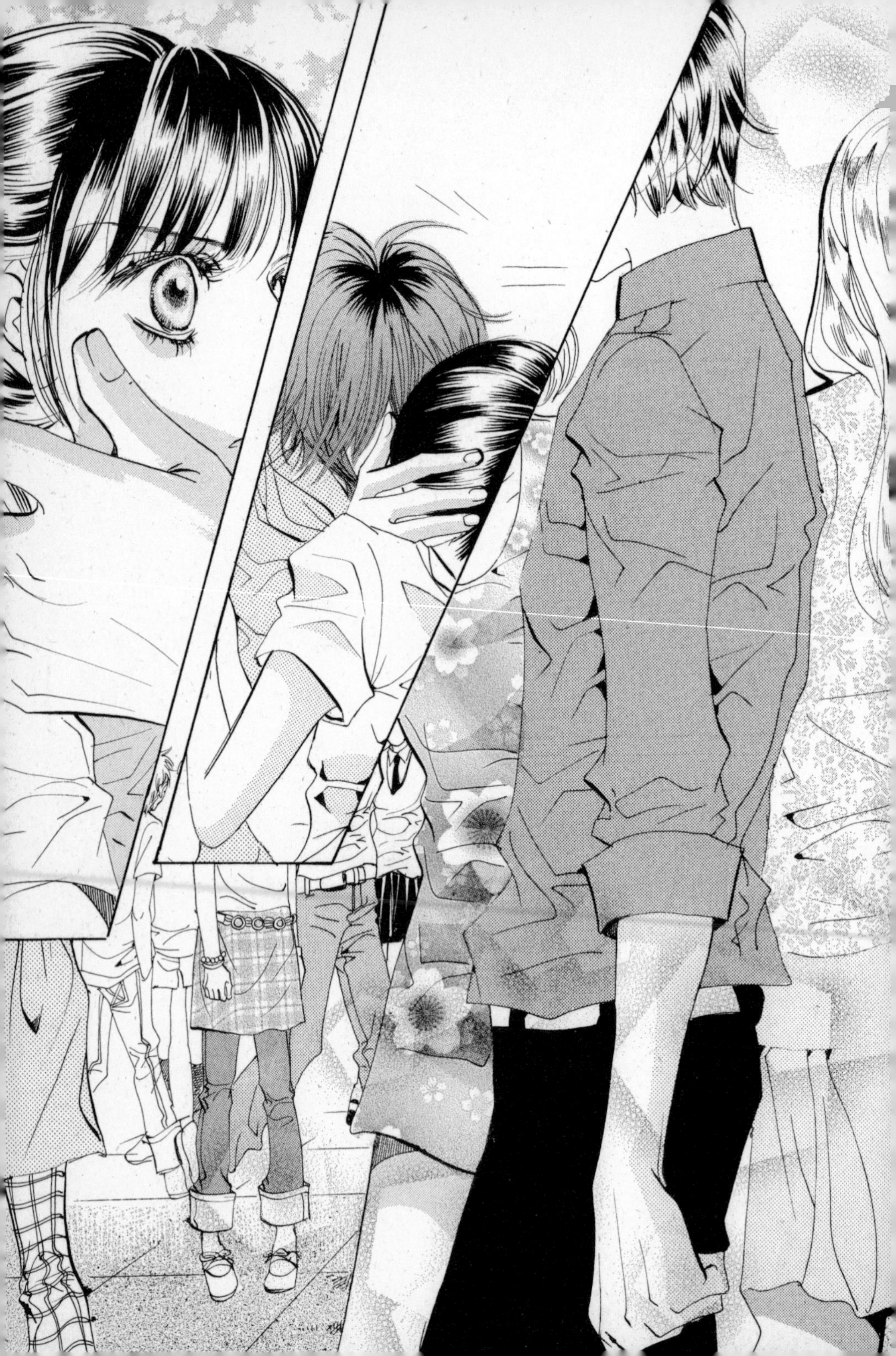

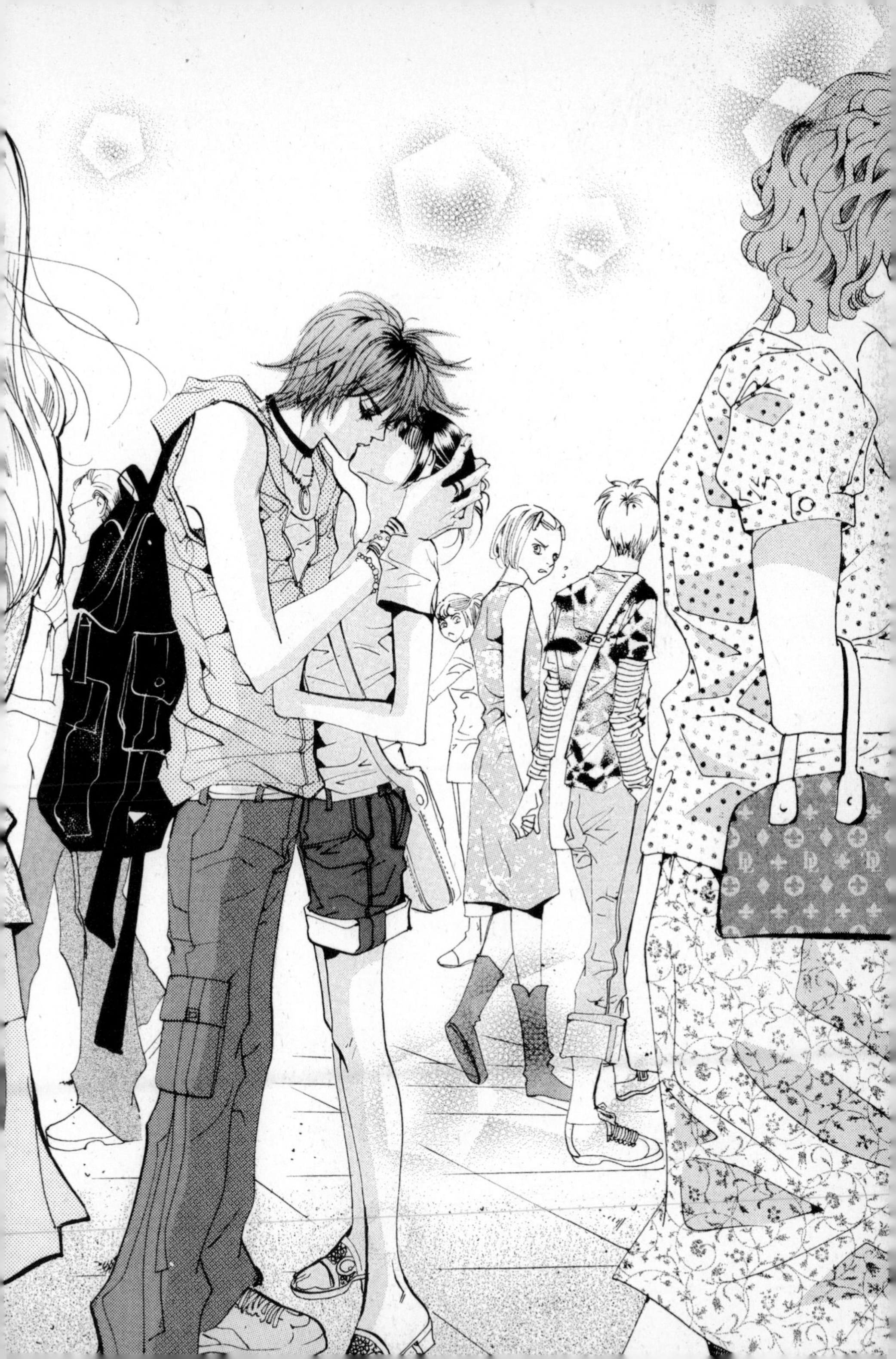

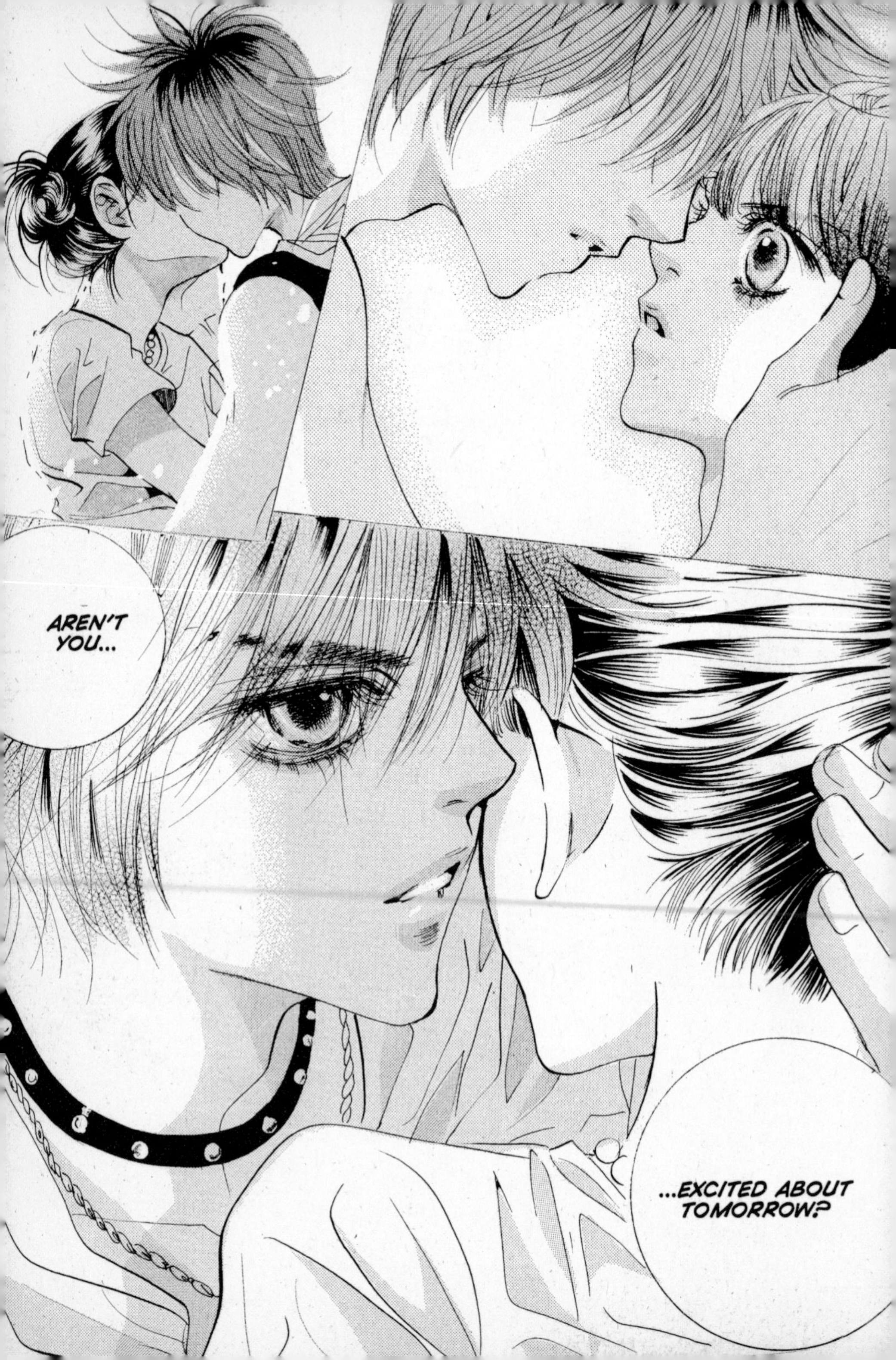
AREN'T YOU...
...EXCITED ABOUT TOMORROW?

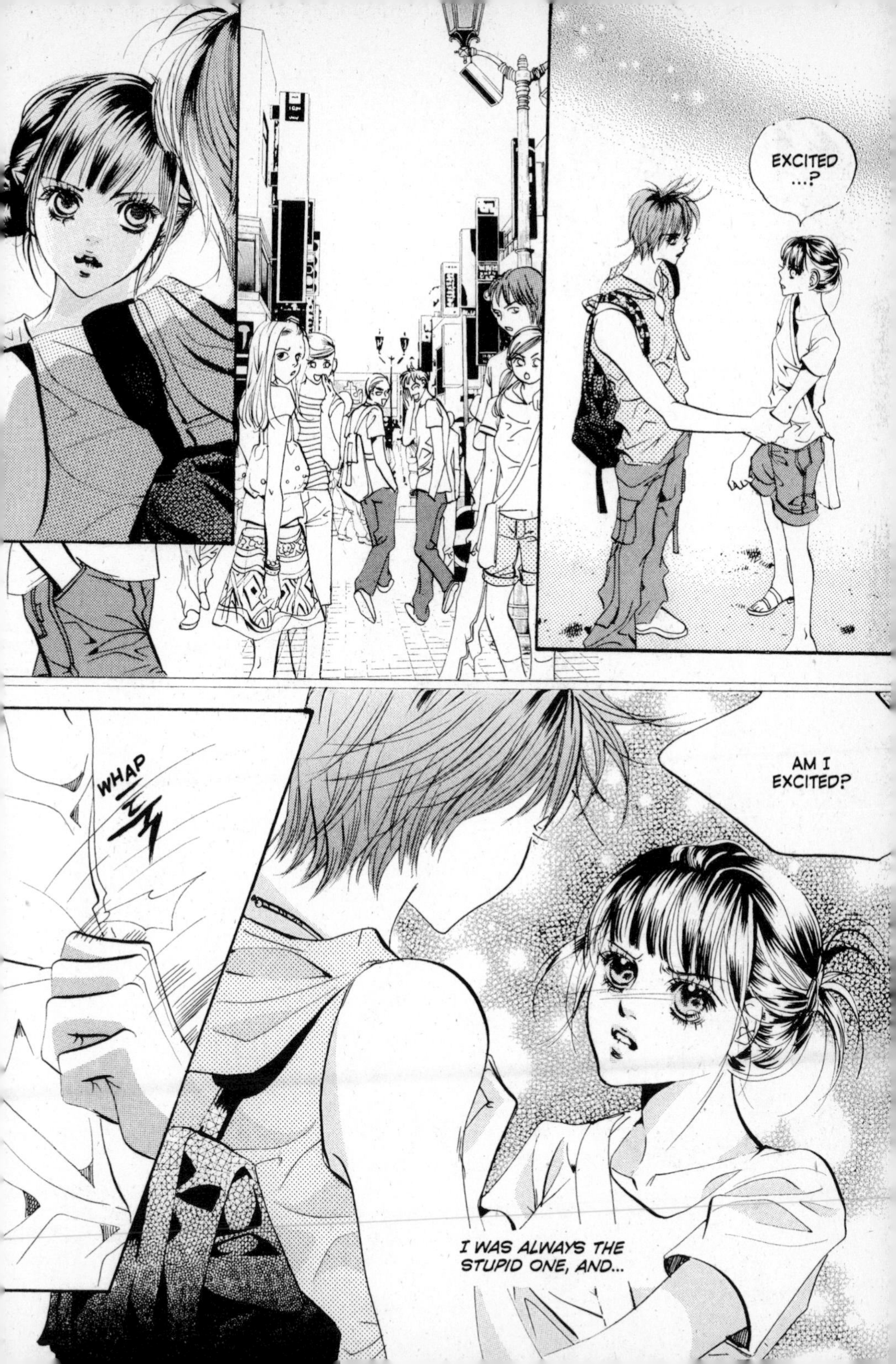
EXCITED ...?
WHAP
AM I EXCITED?
I WAS ALWAYS THE STUPID ONE, AND...

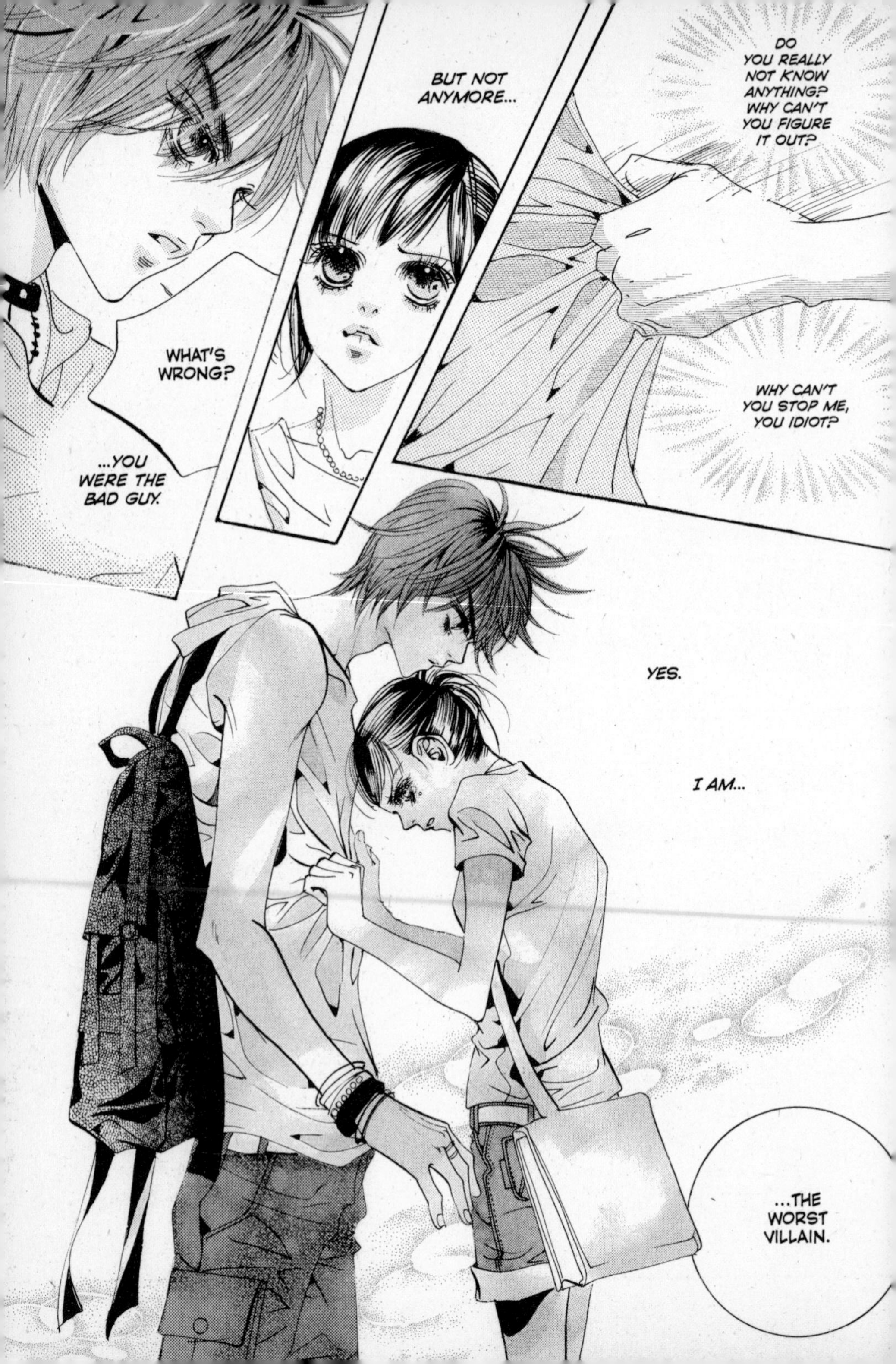
WHAT'S WRONG?
...YOU WERE THE BAD GUY.
BUT NOT ANYMORE...
DO YOU REALLY NOT KNOW ANYTHING? WHY CAN'T YOU FIGURE IT OUT?
WHY CAN'T YOU STOP ME, YOU IDIOT?
YES.
I AM...
...THE WORST VILLAIN.

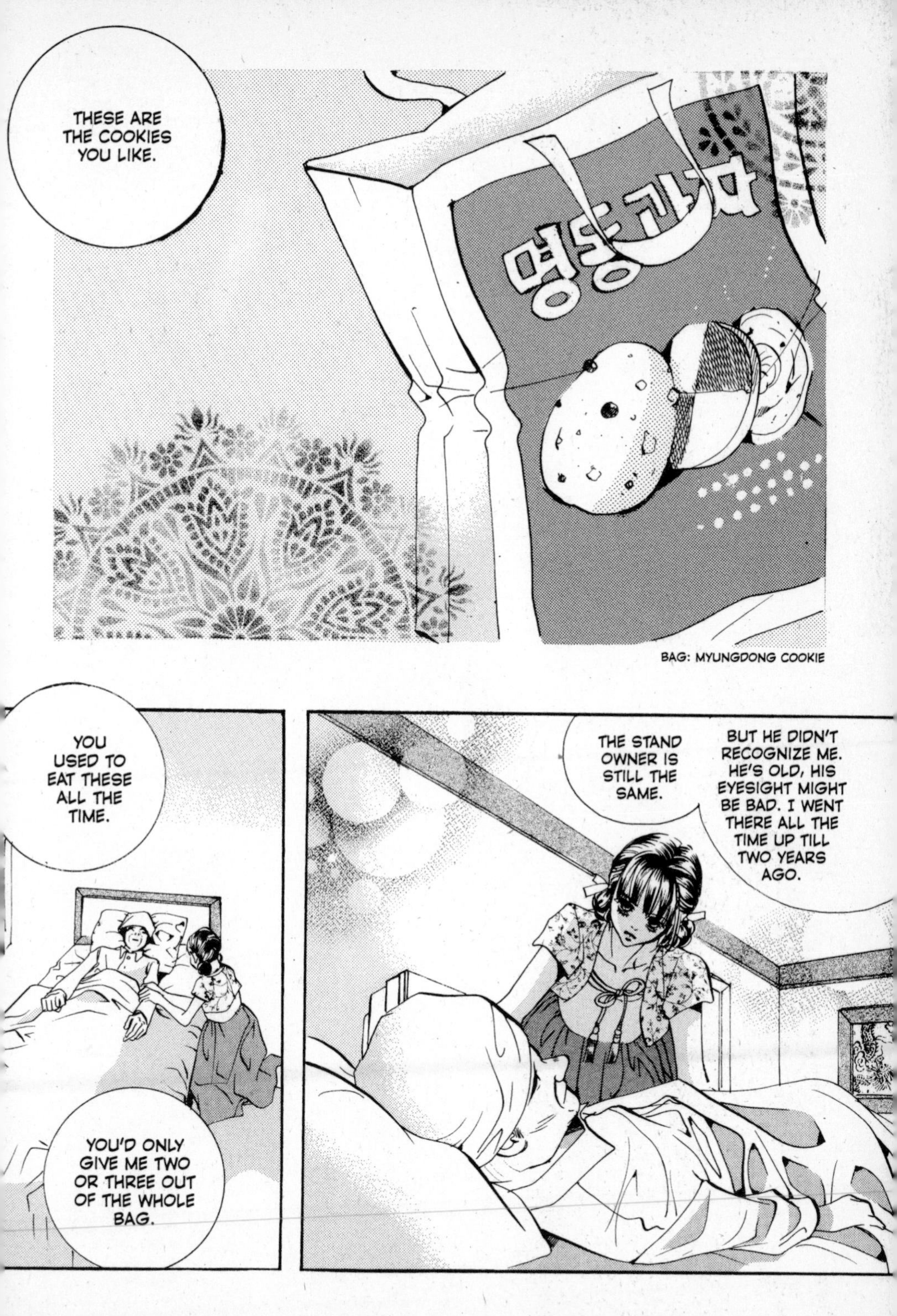
THESE ARE THE COOKIES YOU LIKE.
명동과자
BAG: MYUNGDONG COOKIE
YOU USED TO EAT THESE ALL THE TIME.
YOU'D ONLY GIVE ME TWO OR THREE OUT OF THE WHOLE BAG.
THE STAND OWNER IS STILL THE SAME.
BUT HE DIDN'T RECOGNIZE ME. HE'S OLD, HIS EYESIGHT MIGHT BE BAD. I WENT THERE ALL THE TIME UP TILL TWO YEARS AGO.

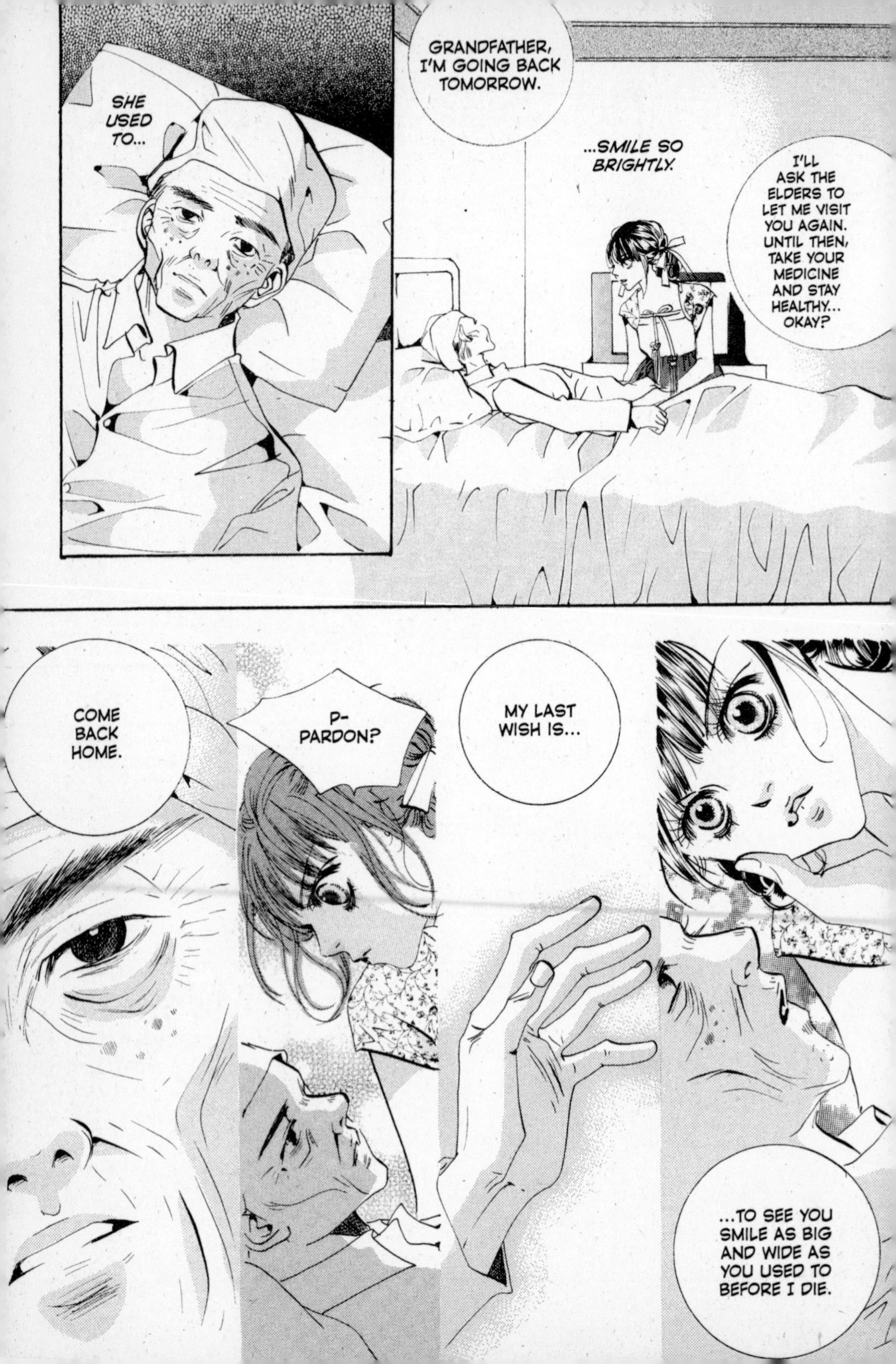
SHE USED TO...
GRANDFATHER, I'M GOING BACK TOMORROW.
...SMILE SO BRIGHTLY.
I'LL ASK THE ELDERS TO LET ME VISIT YOU AGAIN. UNTIL THEN, TAKE YOUR MEDICINE AND STAY HEALTHY... OKAY?
COME BACK HOME.
P- PARDON?
MY LAST WISH IS...
...TO SEE YOU SMILE AS BIG AND WIDE AS YOU USED TO BEFORE I DIE.

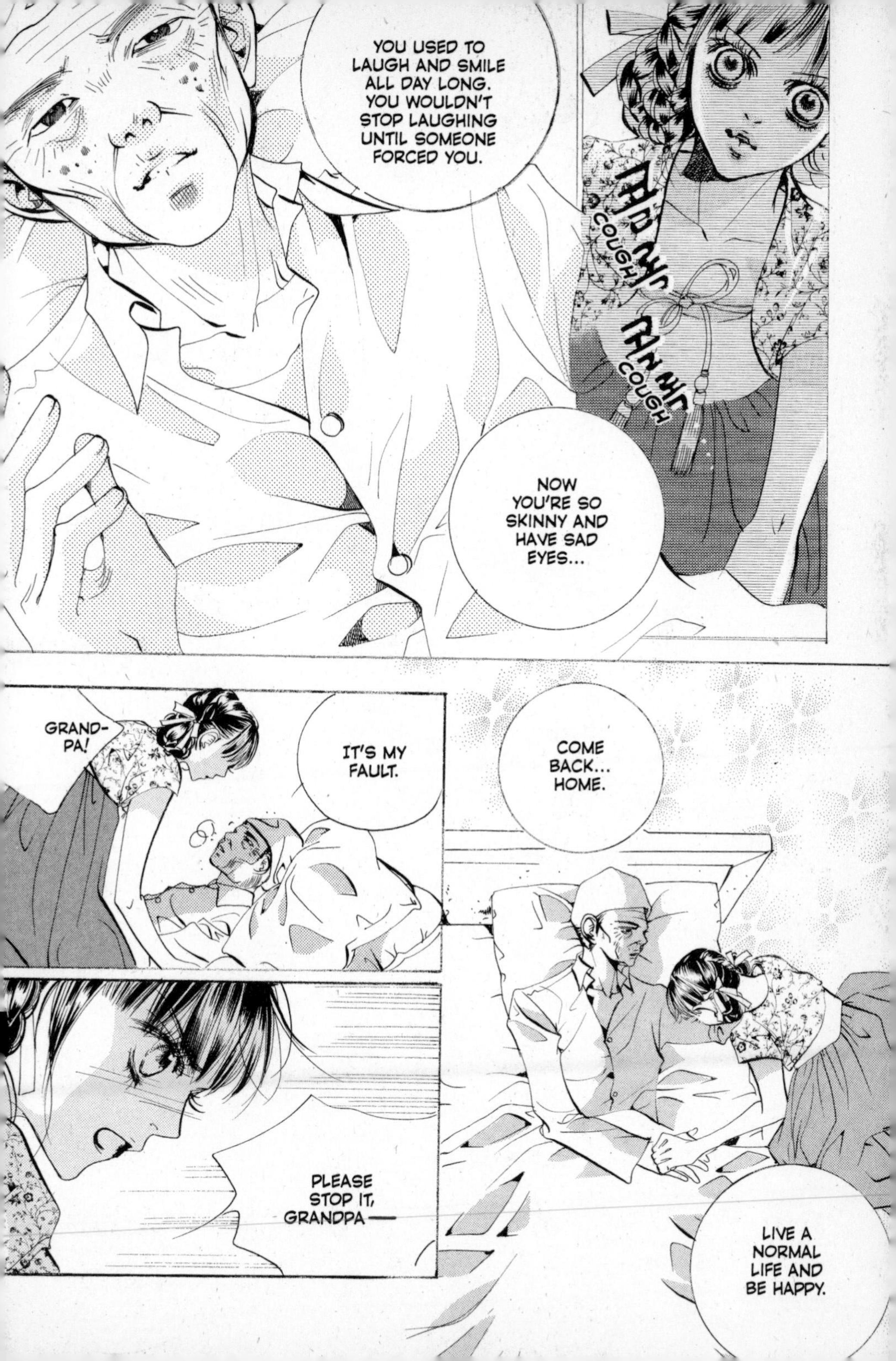
YOU USED TO LAUGH AND SMILE ALL DAY LONG. YOU WOULDN'T STOP LAUGHING UNTIL SOMEONE FORCED YOU.
COUGH
COUGH
NOW YOU'RE SO SKINNY AND HAVE SAD EYES...
GRAND-PA!
IT'S MY FAULT.
PLEASE STOP IT, GRANDPA—
COME BACK... HOME.
LIVE A NORMAL LIFE AND BE HAPPY.

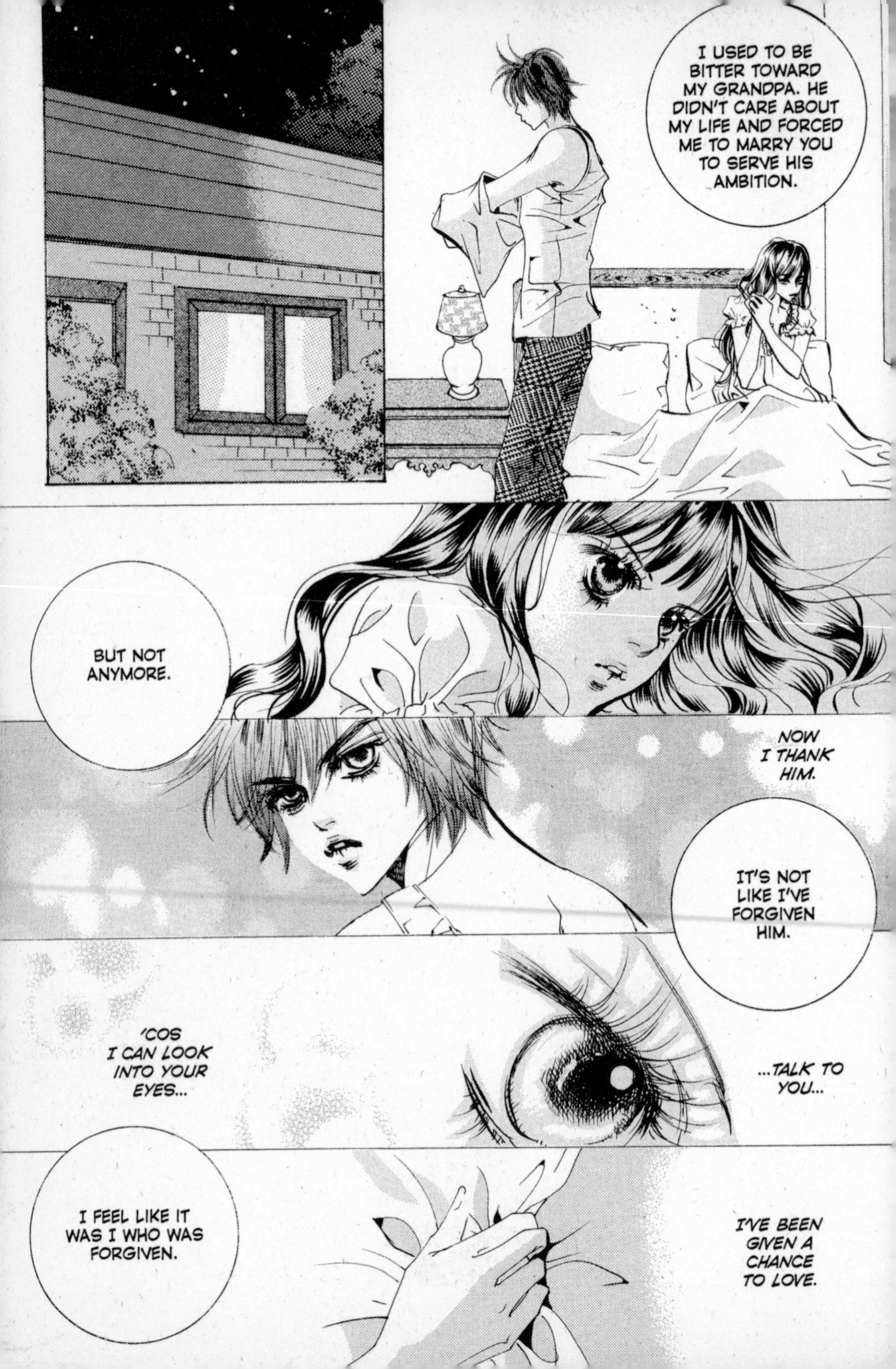
I USED TO BE BITTER TOWARD MY GRANDPA. HE DIDN'T CARE ABOUT MY LIFE AND FORCED ME TO MARRY YOU TO SERVE HIS AMBITION.
BUT NOT ANYMORE.
NOW I THANK HIM.
IT'S NOT LIKE I'VE FORGIVEN HIM.
'COS I CAN LOOK INTO YOUR EYES...
...TALK TO YOU...
I FEEL LIKE IT WAS I WHO WAS FORGIVEN.
I'VE BEEN GIVEN A CHANCE TO LOVE.

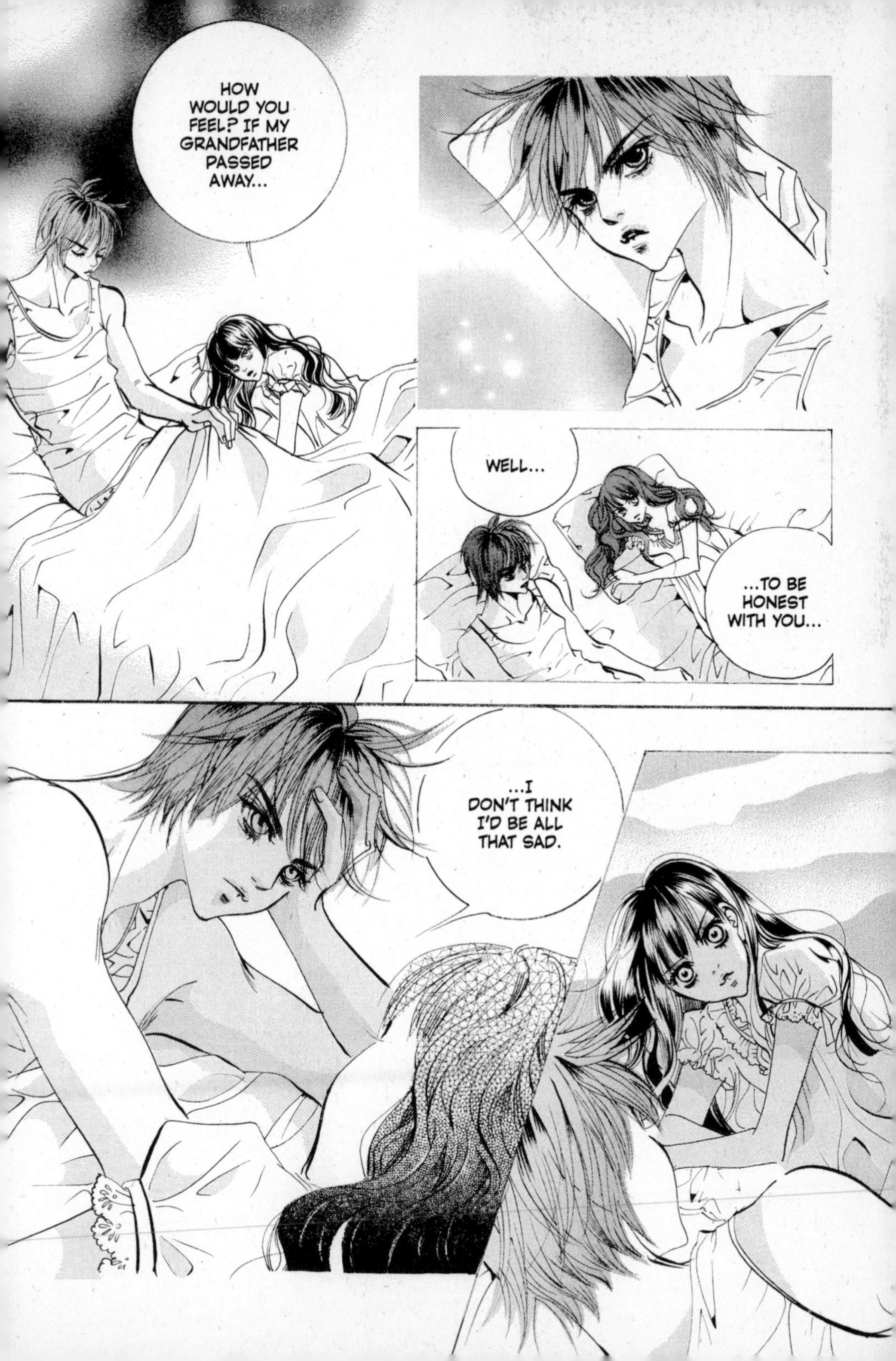
HOW WOULD YOU FEEL? IF MY GRANDFATHER PASSED AWAY...
WELL...
...TO BE HONEST WITH YOU...
...I DON'T THINK I'D BE ALL THAT SAD.

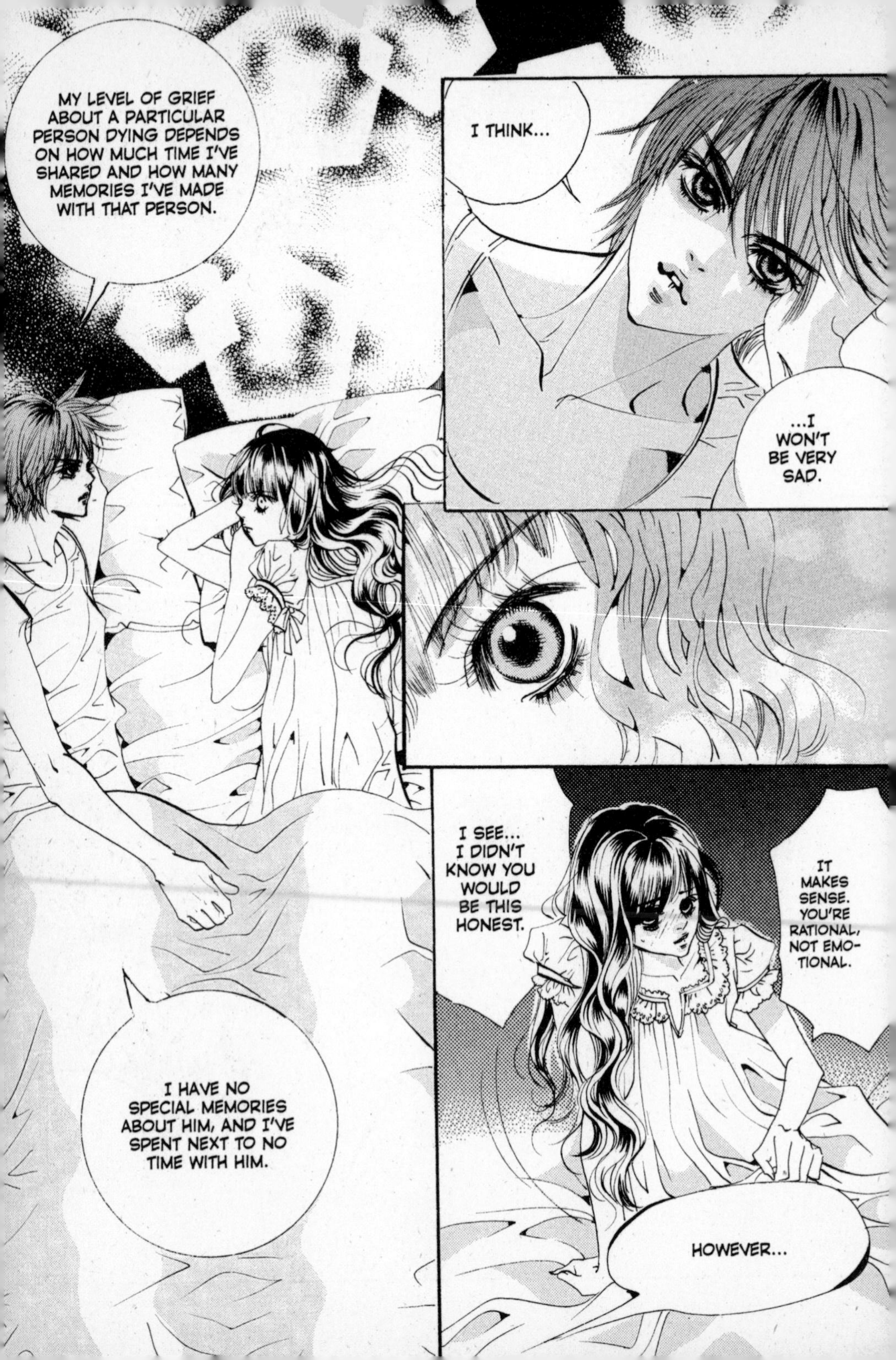
MY LEVEL OF GRIEF ABOUT A PARTICULAR PERSON DYING DEPENDS ON HOW MUCH TIME I'VE SHARED AND HOW MANY MEMORIES I'VE MADE WITH THAT PERSON.
I HAVE NO SPECIAL MEMORIES ABOUT HIM, AND I'VE SPENT NEXT TO NO TIME WITH HIM.
I THINK...
...I WON'T BE VERY SAD.
I SEE... I DIDN'T KNOW YOU WOULD BE THIS HONEST.
IT MAKES SENSE. YOU'RE RATIONAL, NOT EMOTIONAL.
HOWEVER...

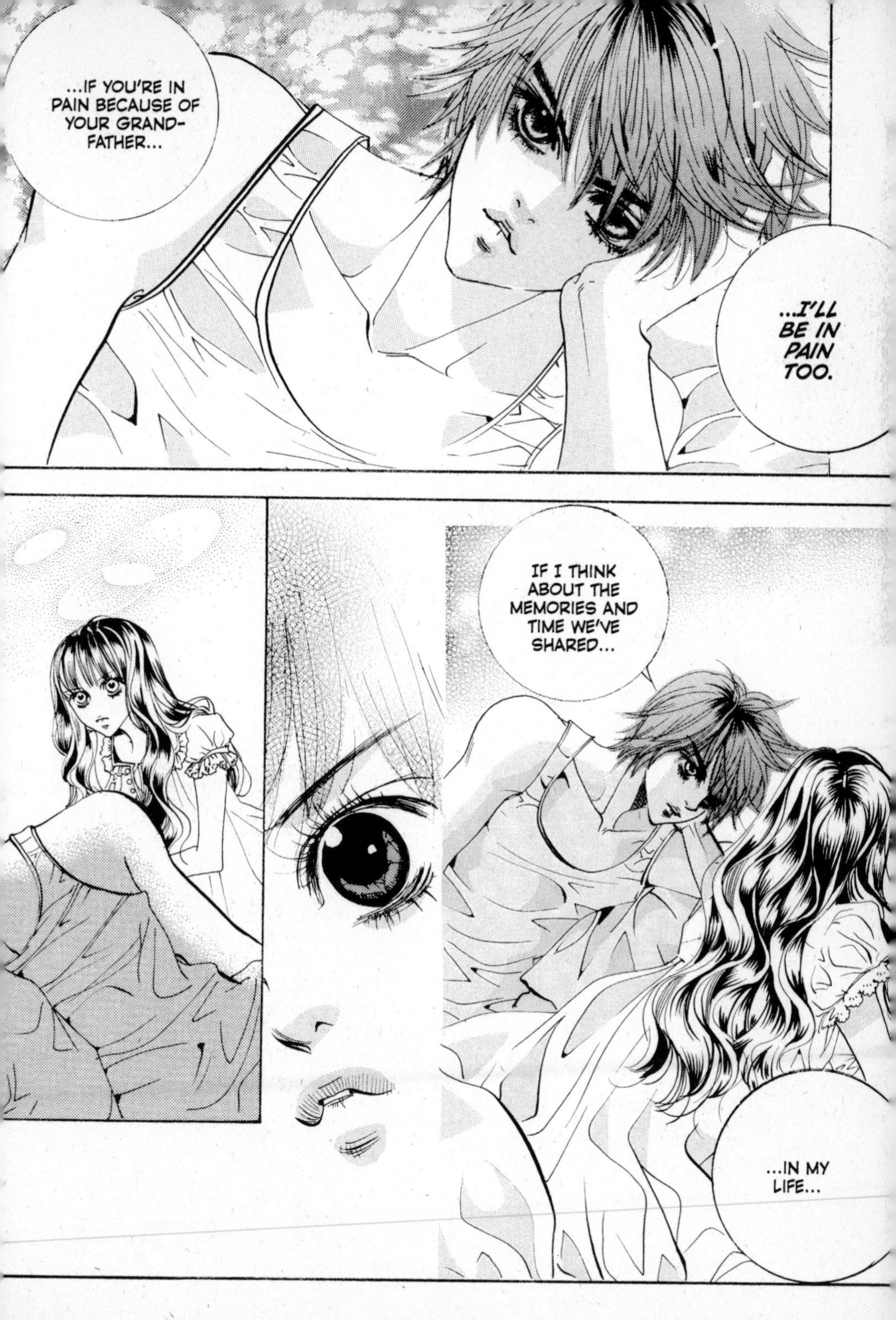
...IF YOU'RE IN PAIN BECAUSE OF YOUR GRAND-FATHER...
...I'LL BE IN PAIN TOO.
IF I THINK ABOUT THE MEMORIES AND TIME WE'VE SHARED...
...IN MY LIFE...

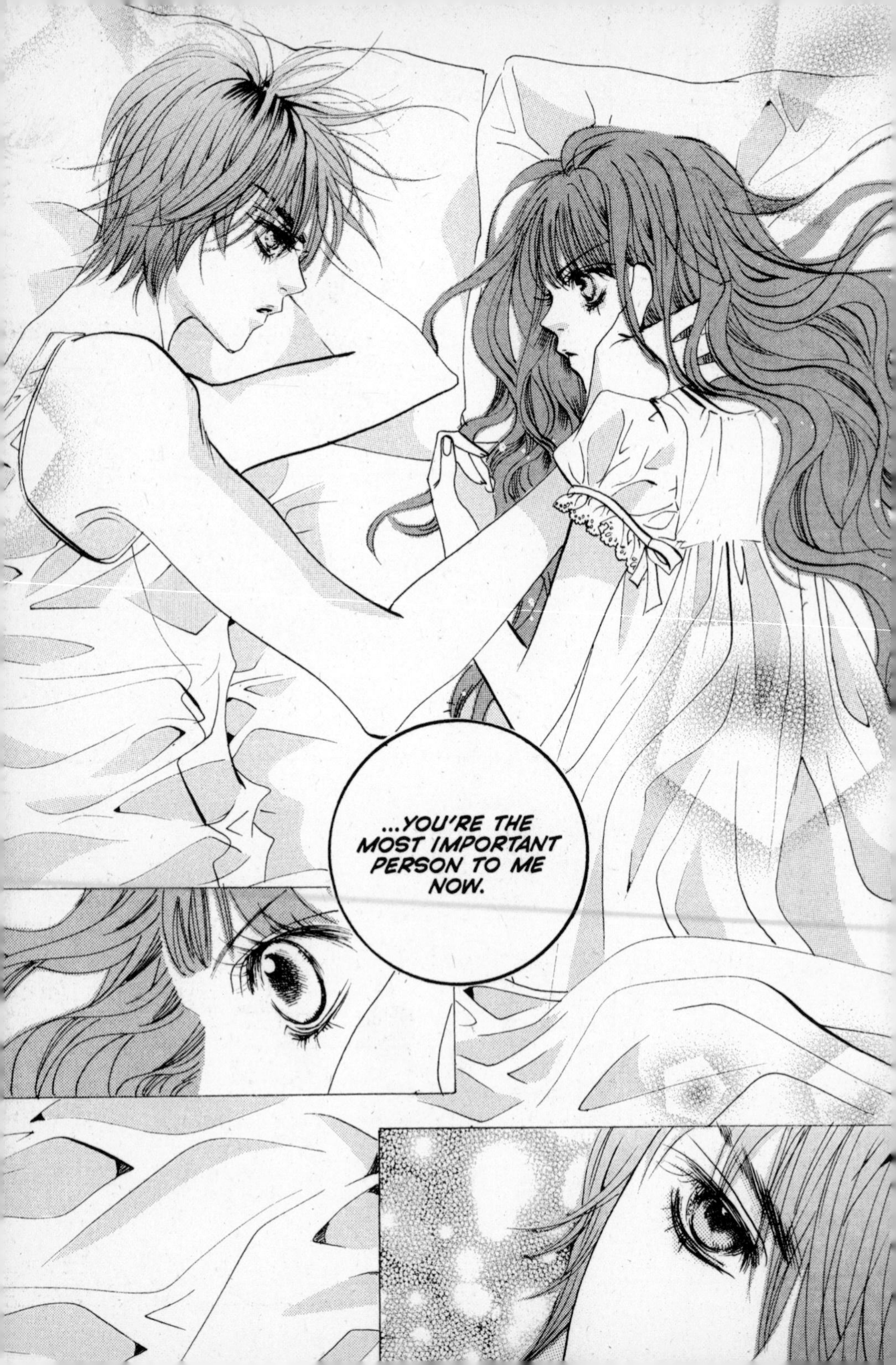
...YOU'RE THE MOST IMPORTANT PERSON TO ME NOW.

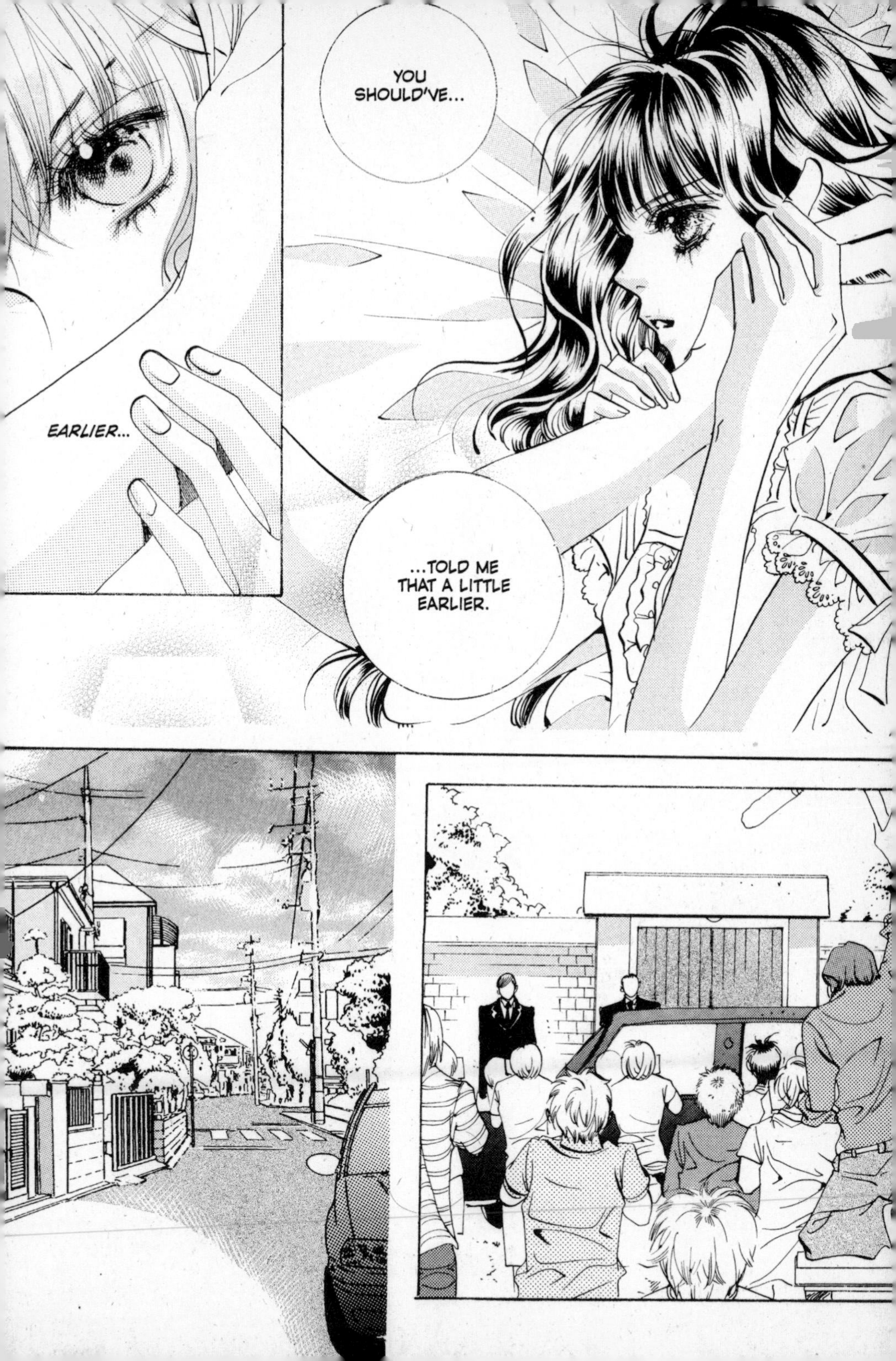
EARLIER...
YOU SHOULD'VE...
...TOLD ME THAT A LITTLE EARLIER.

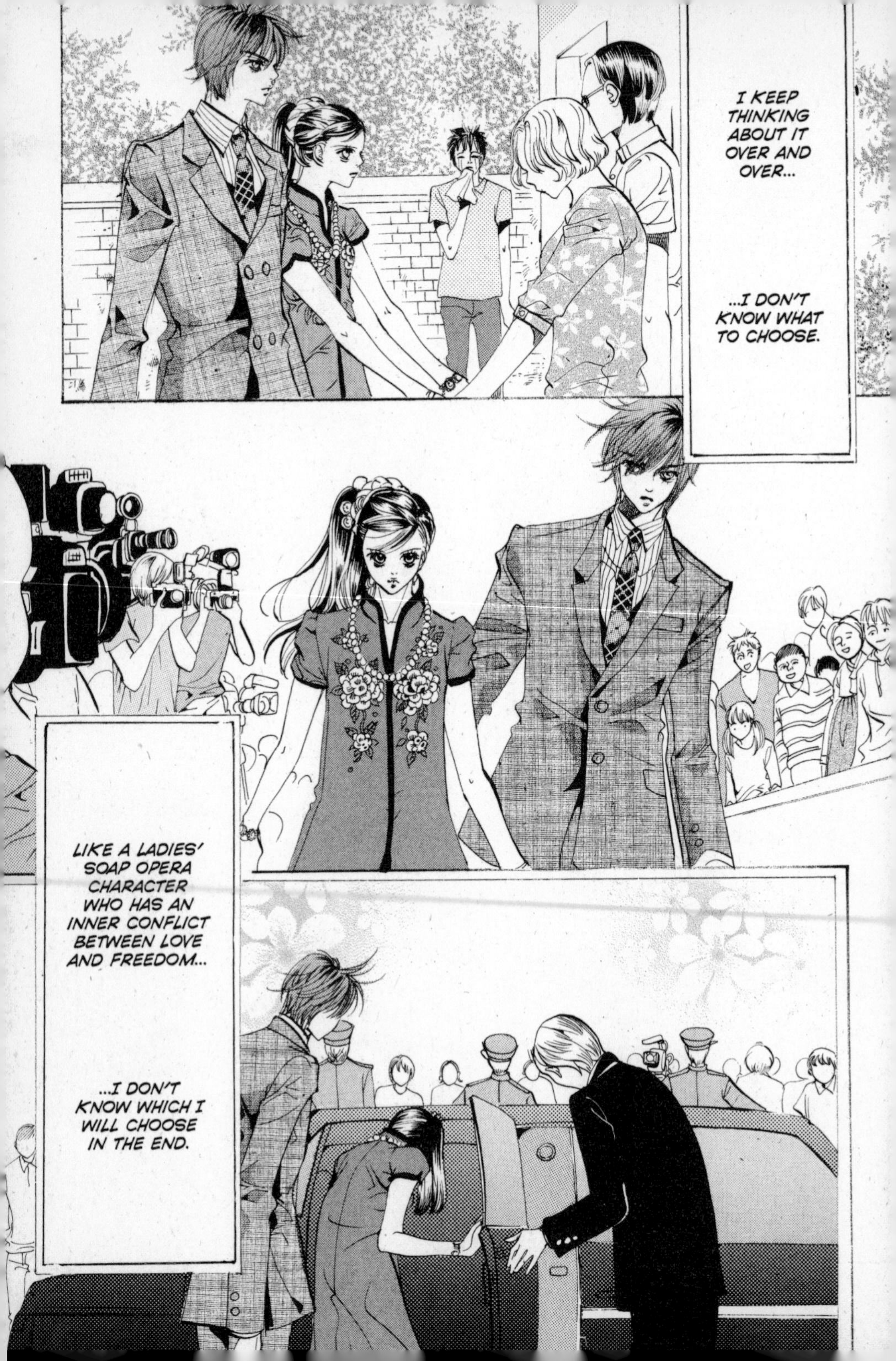
I KEEP THINKING ABOUT IT OVER AND OVER...
...I DON'T KNOW WHAT TO CHOOSE.
LIKE A LADIES' SOAP OPERA CHARACTER WHO HAS AN INNER CONFLICT BETWEEN LOVE AND FREEDOM...
...I DON'T KNOW WHICH I WILL CHOOSE IN THE END.

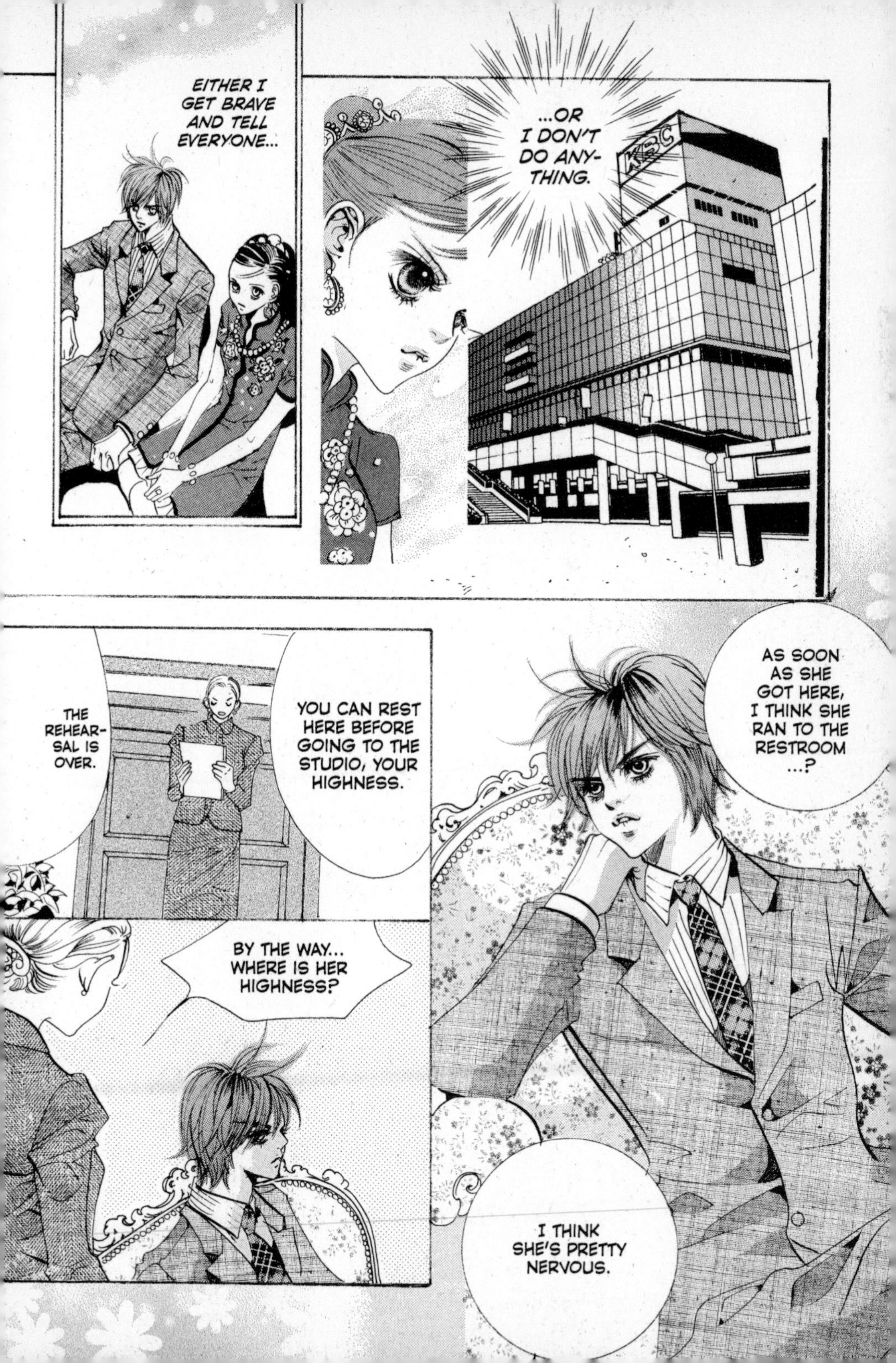
EITHER I GET BRAVE AND TELL EVERYONE...
...OR I DON'T DO ANY-THING.
KBC
THE REHEARSAL IS OVER.
YOU CAN REST HERE BEFORE GOING TO THE STUDIO, YOUR HIGHNESS.
AS SOON AS SHE GOT HERE, I THINK SHE RAN TO THE RESTROOM ...?
BY THE WAY... WHERE IS HER HIGHNESS?
I THINK SHE'S PRETTY NERVOUS.

CAN I TELL EVERYONE THAT I WANT TO DIVORCE SHIN?

I'VE TRIED TO BE REAL ABOUT THIS.

DO I REALLY NEED TO DIVORCE HIM?

WHO CARES IF I'M LOCKED AWAY IN THE PALACE FOREVER?

I COULD LIVE NEXT TO THE MAN I LOVE WITHOUT WORRYING ABOUT MONEY OR GETTING A JOB.

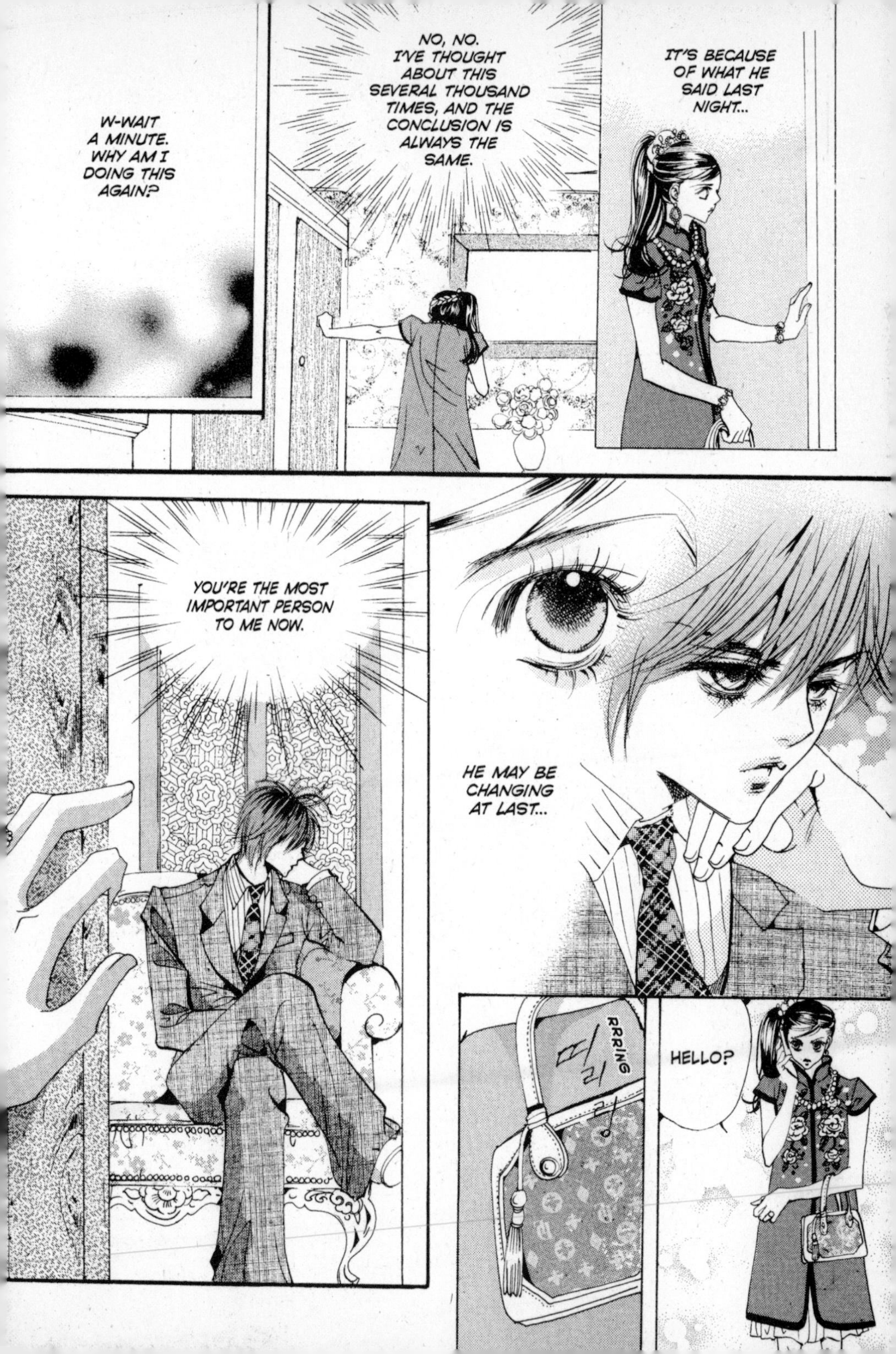
W-WAIT A MINUTE. WHY AM I DOING THIS AGAIN?
NO, NO. I'VE THOUGHT ABOUT THIS SEVERAL THOUSAND TIMES, AND THE CONCLUSION IS ALWAYS THE SAME.
IT'S BECAUSE OF WHAT HE SAID LAST NIGHT...
YOU'RE THE MOST IMPORTANT PERSON TO ME NOW.
HE MAY BE CHANGING AT LAST...
RRRING
HELLO?

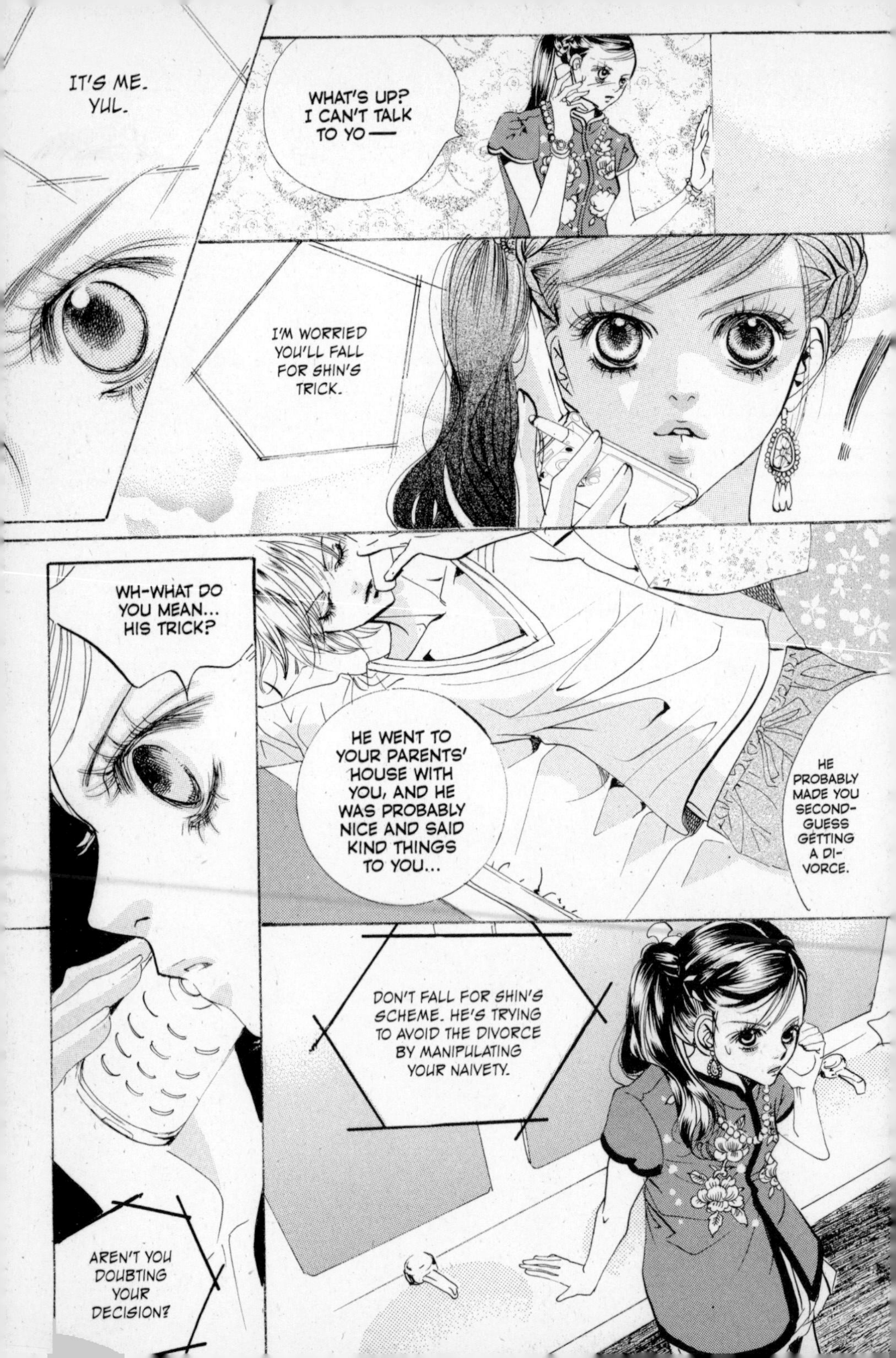
IT'S ME. YUL.
WHAT'S UP? I CAN'T TALK TO YO—
I'M WORRIED YOU'LL FALL FOR SHIN'S TRICK.
WH-WHAT DO YOU MEAN... HIS TRICK?
HE WENT TO YOUR PARENTS' HOUSE WITH YOU, AND HE WAS PROBABLY NICE AND SAID KIND THINGS TO YOU...
HE PROBABLY MADE YOU SECOND-GUESS GETTING A DI-VORCE.
ARE'N'T YOU DOUBTING YOUR DECISION?
DON'T FALL FOR SHIN'S SCHEME. HE'S TRYING TO AVOID THE DIVORCE BY MANIPULATING YOUR NAIVETY.

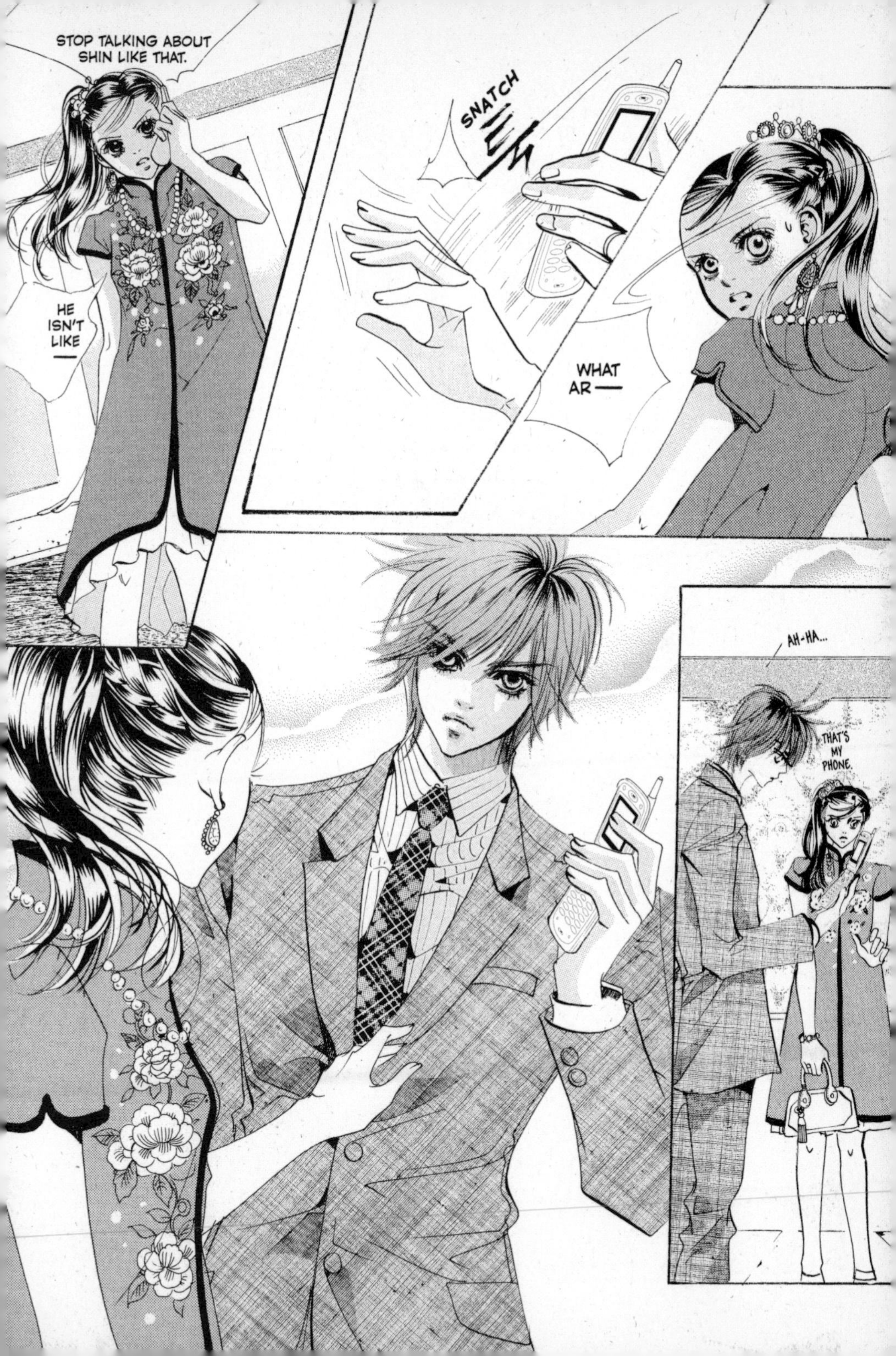
STOP TALKING ABOUT SHIN LIKE THAT.
HE ISN'T LIKE —
SNATCH
WHAT AR—
AH-HA...
THAT'S MY PHONE.

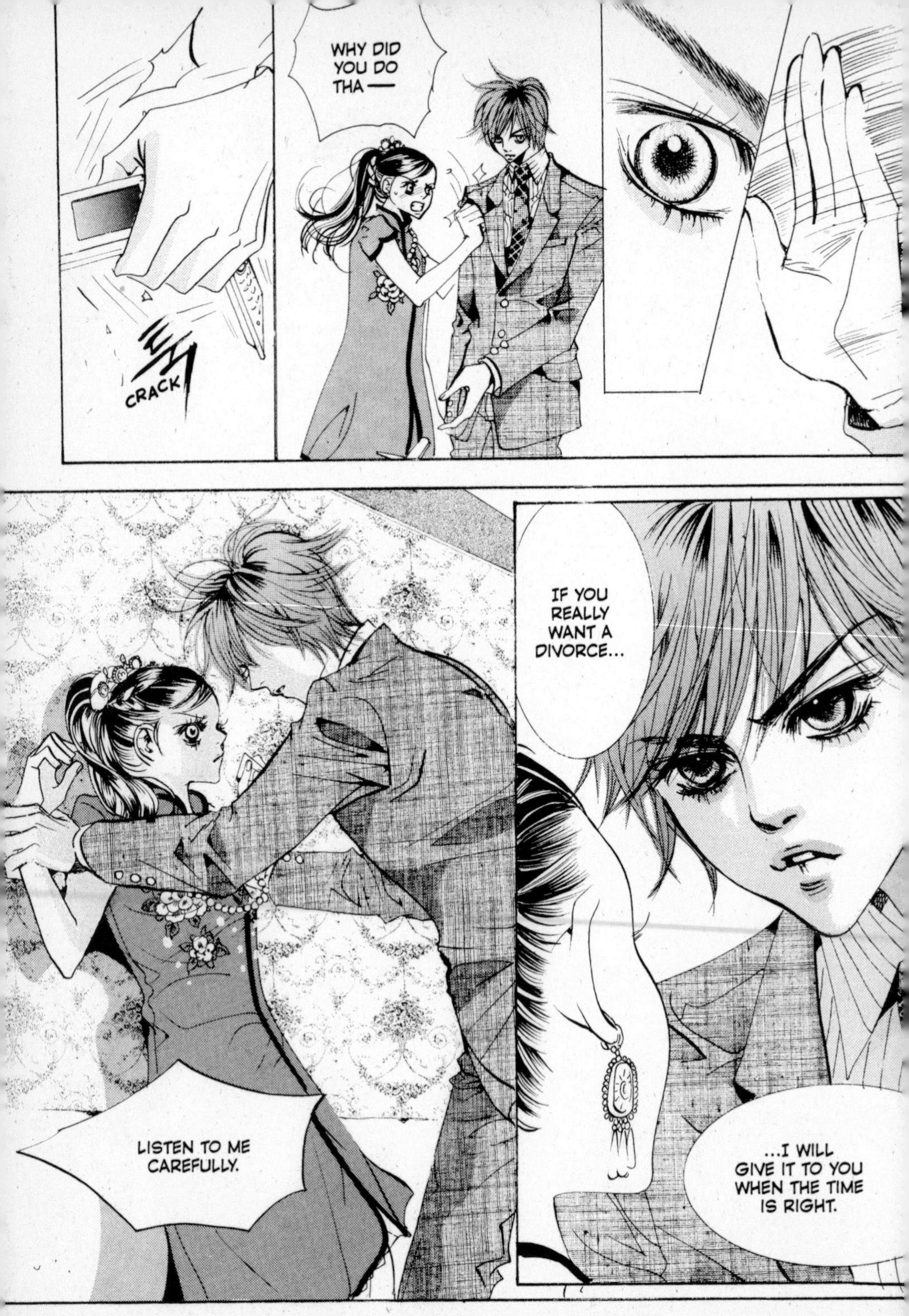
CRACK
WHY DID YOU DO THA—
LISTEN TO ME CAREFULLY.
IF YOU REALLY WANT A DIVORCE...
...I WILL GIVE IT TO YOU WHEN THE TIME IS RIGHT.

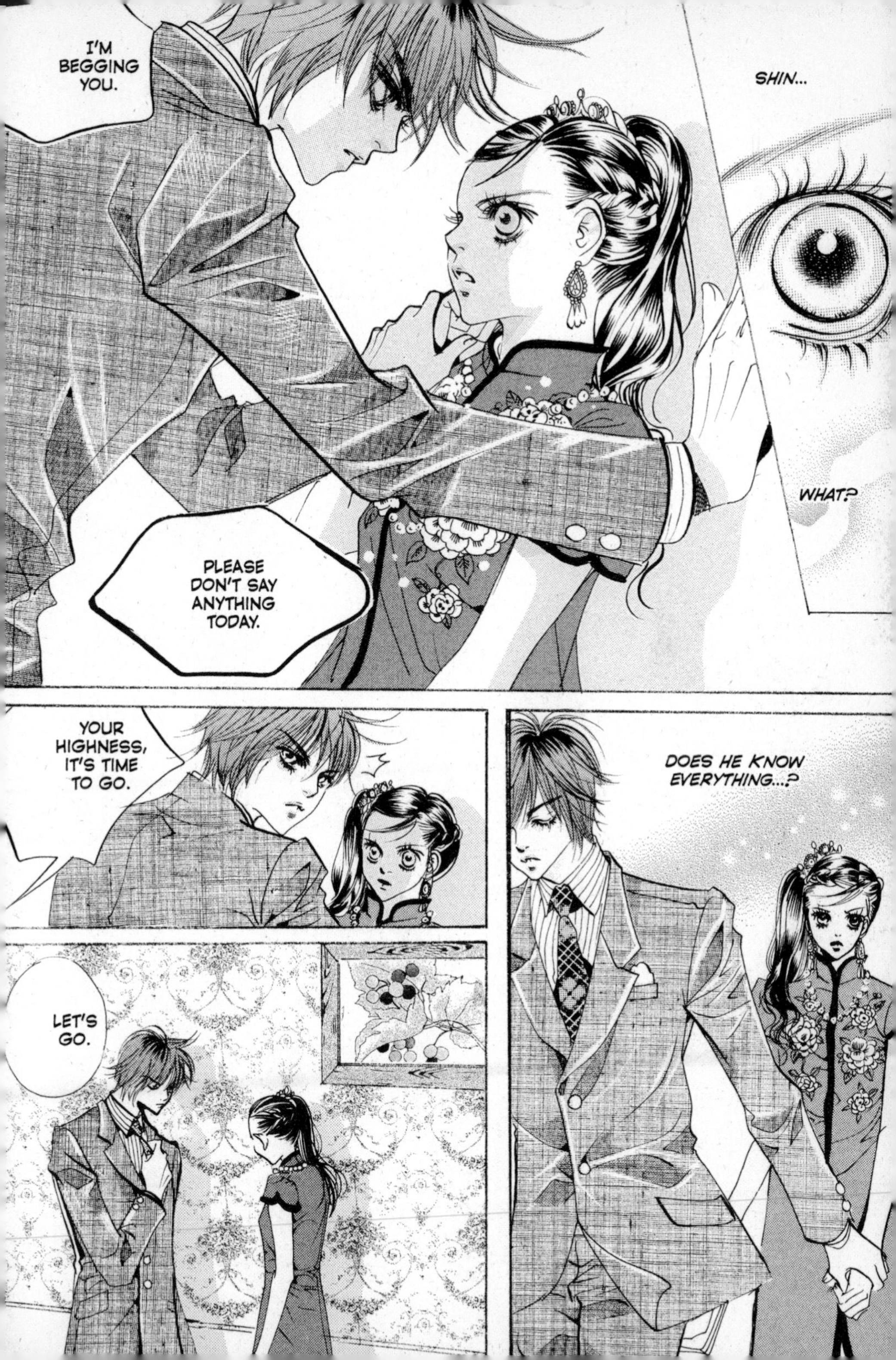
I'M BEGGING YOU.
PLEASE DON'T SAY ANYTHING TODAY.
SHIN...
WHAT?
YOUR HIGHNESS, IT'S TIME TO GO.
LET'S GO.
DOES HE KNOW EVERYTHING...?

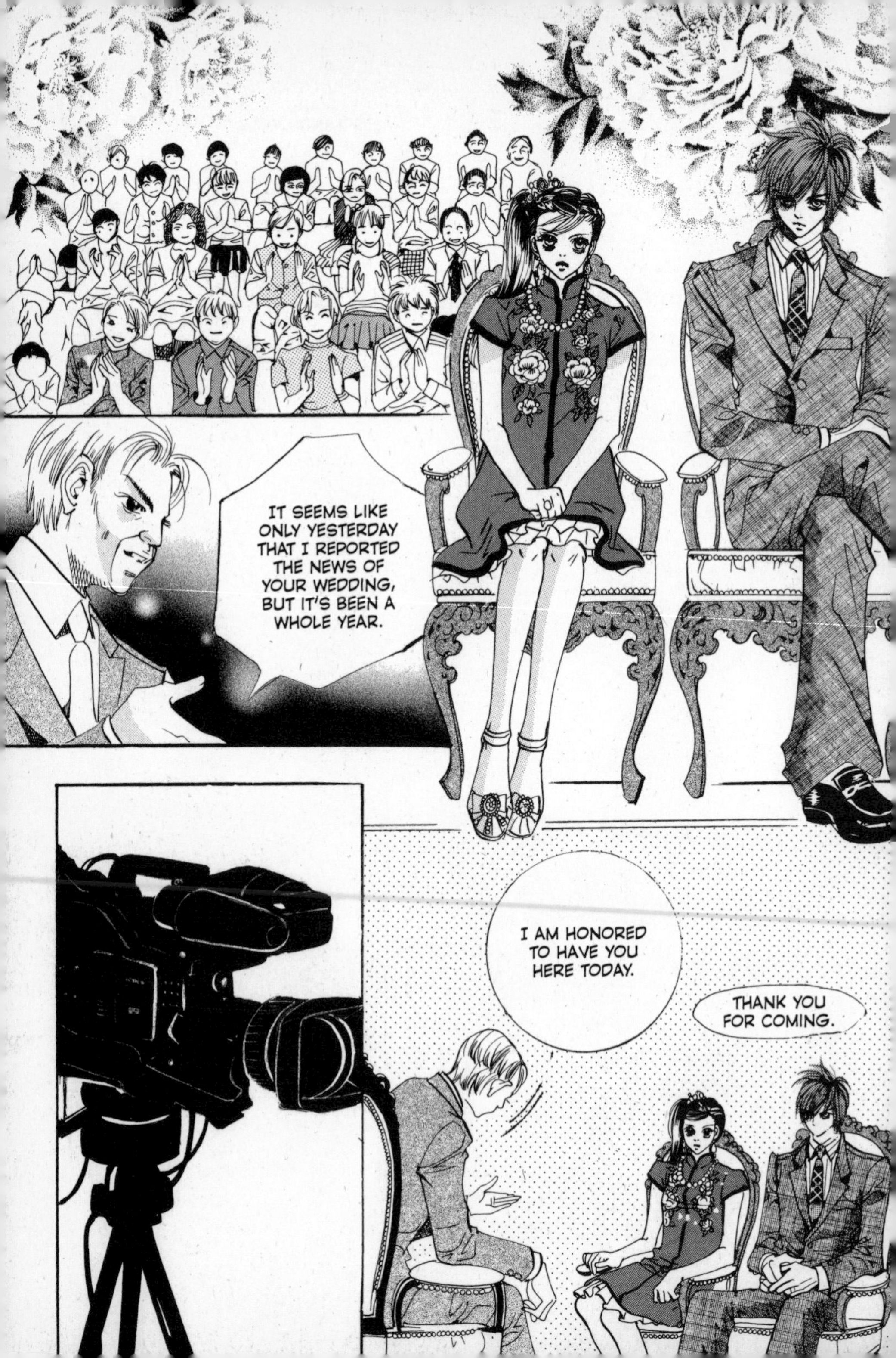
IT SEEMS LIKE ONLY YESTERDAY THAT I REPORTED THE NEWS OF YOUR WEDDING, BUT IT'S BEEN A WHOLE YEAR.
I AM HONORED TO HAVE YOU HERE TODAY.
THANK YOU FOR COMING.

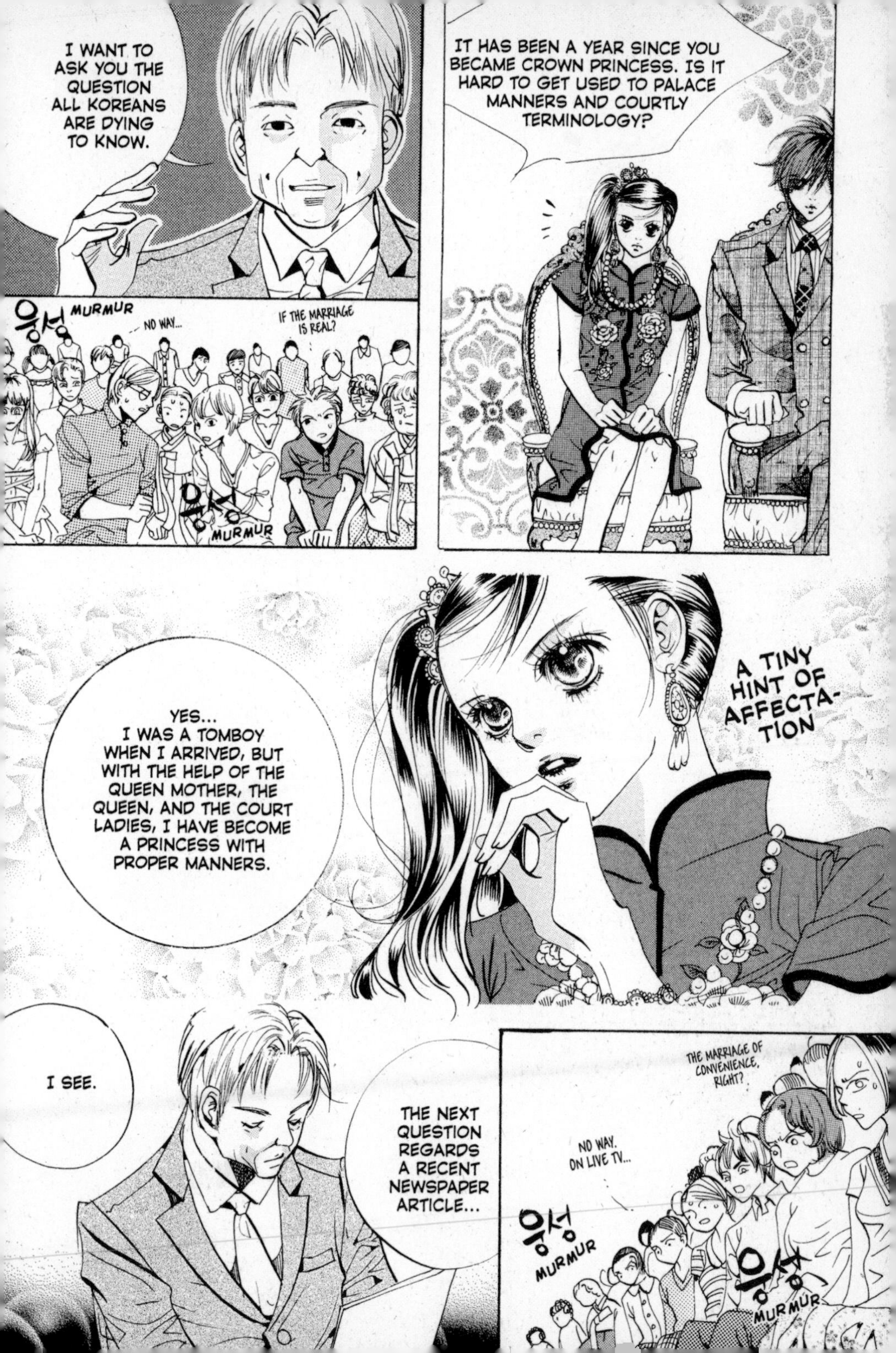
I WANT TO ASK YOU THE QUESTION ALL KOREANS ARE DYING TO KNOW.
웅성
MURMUR
... NO WAY...
IF THE MARRIAGE IS REAL?
웅성
MURMUR
IT HAS BEEN A YEAR SINCE YOU BECAME CROWN PRINCESS. IS IT HARD TO GET USED TO PALACE MANNERS AND COURTLY TERMINOLOGY?
YES... I WAS A TOMBOY WHEN I ARRIVED, BUT WITH THE HELP OF THE QUEEN MOTHER, THE QUEEN, AND THE COURT LADIES, I HAVE BECOME A PRINCESS WITH PROPER MANNERS.
A TINY HINT OF AFFECTA-TION
I SEE.
THE NEXT QUESTION REGARDS A RECENT NEWSPAPER ARTICLE...
THE MARRIAGE OF CONVENIENCE, RIGHT?
NO WAY. ON LIVE TV...
웅성
MURMUR
웅성
MURMUR

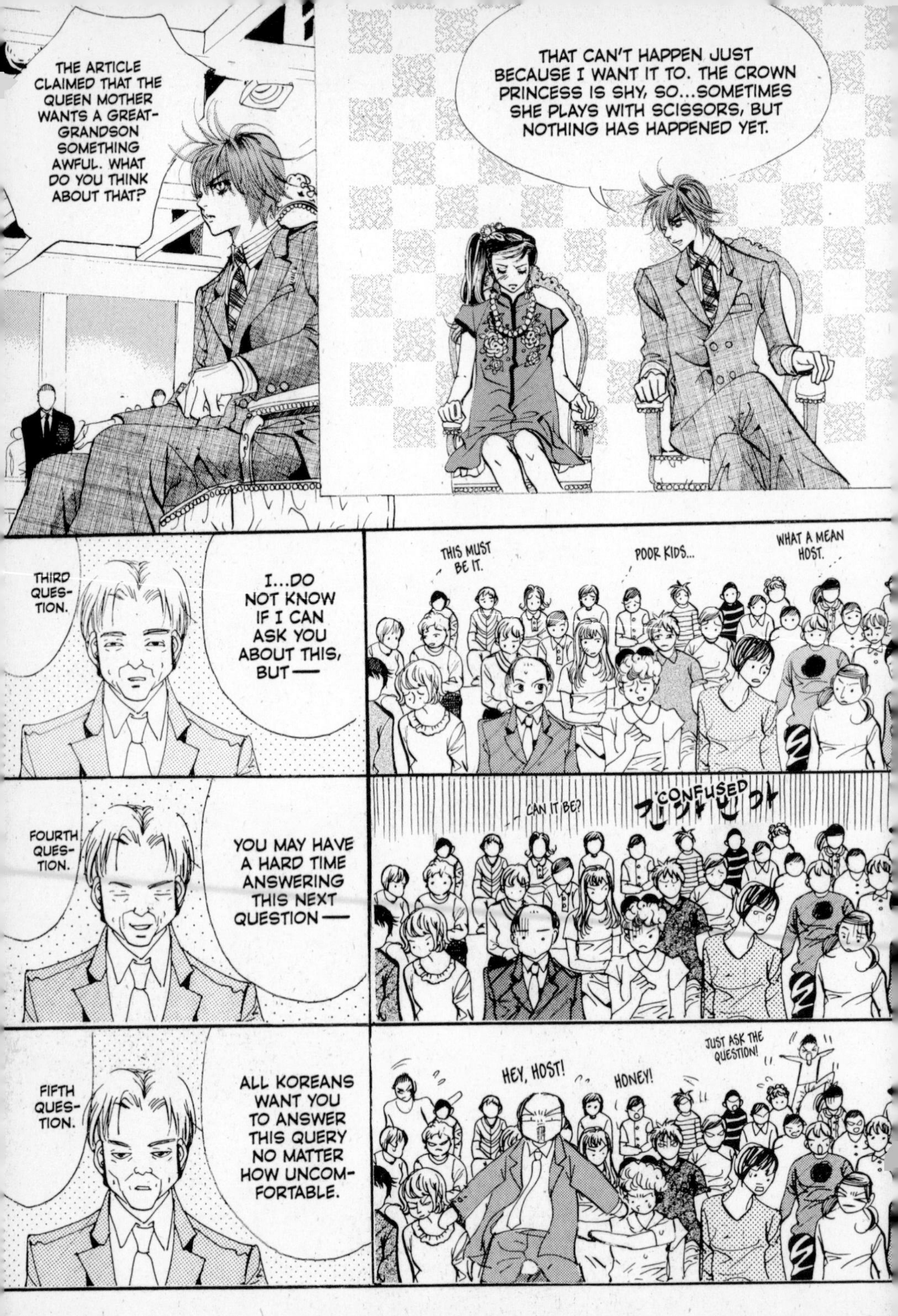
THE ARTICLE CLAIMED THAT THE QUEEN MOTHER WANTS A GREAT-GRANDSON SOMETHING AWFUL. WHAT DO YOU THINK ABOUT THAT?
THAT CAN'T HAPPEN JUST BECAUSE I WANT IT TO. THE CROWN PRINCESS IS SHY, SO...SOMETIMES SHE PLAYS WITH SCISSORS, BUT NOTHING HAS HAPPENED YET.
THIRD QUES-TION.
I...DO NOT KNOW IF I CAN ASK YOU ABOUT THIS, BUT—
THIS MUST BE IT.
POOR KIDS...
WHAT A MEAN HOST.
FOURTH QUES-TION.
YOU MAY HAVE A HARD TIME ANSWERING THIS NEXT QUESTION—
CAN IT BE?
CONFUSED
FIFTH QUES-TION.
ALL KOREANS WANT YOU TO ANSWER THIS QUERY NO MATTER HOW UNCOM-FORTABLE.
HEY, HOST!
HONEY!
JUST ASK THE QUESTION!

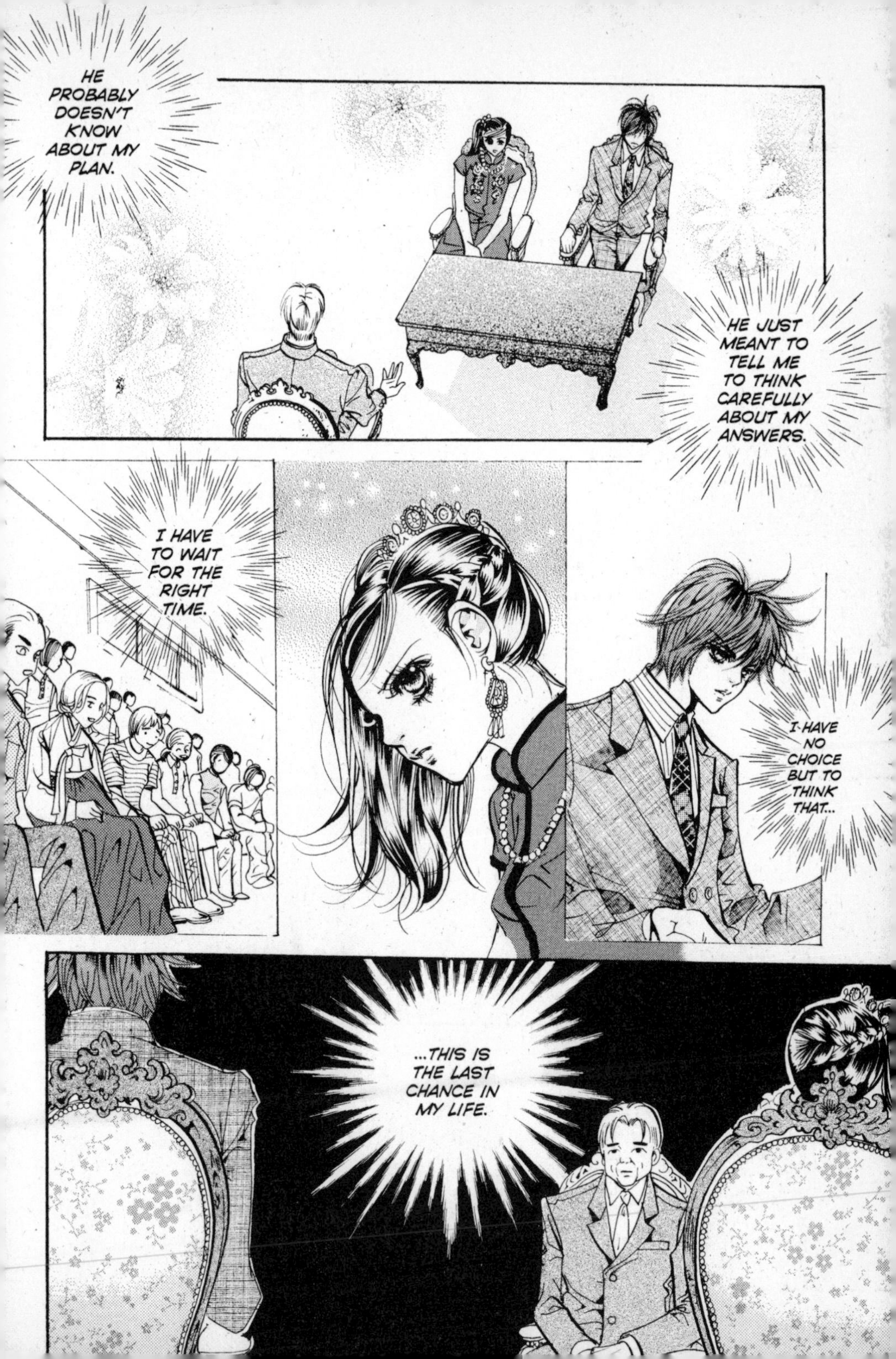
HE PROBABLY DOESN'T KNOW ABOUT MY PLAN.
HE JUST MEANT TO TELL ME TO THINK CAREFULLY ABOUT MY ANSWERS.
I HAVE TO WAIT FOR THE RIGHT TIME.
I HAVE NO CHOICE BUT TO THINK THAT...
...THIS IS THE LAST CHANCE IN MY LIFE.

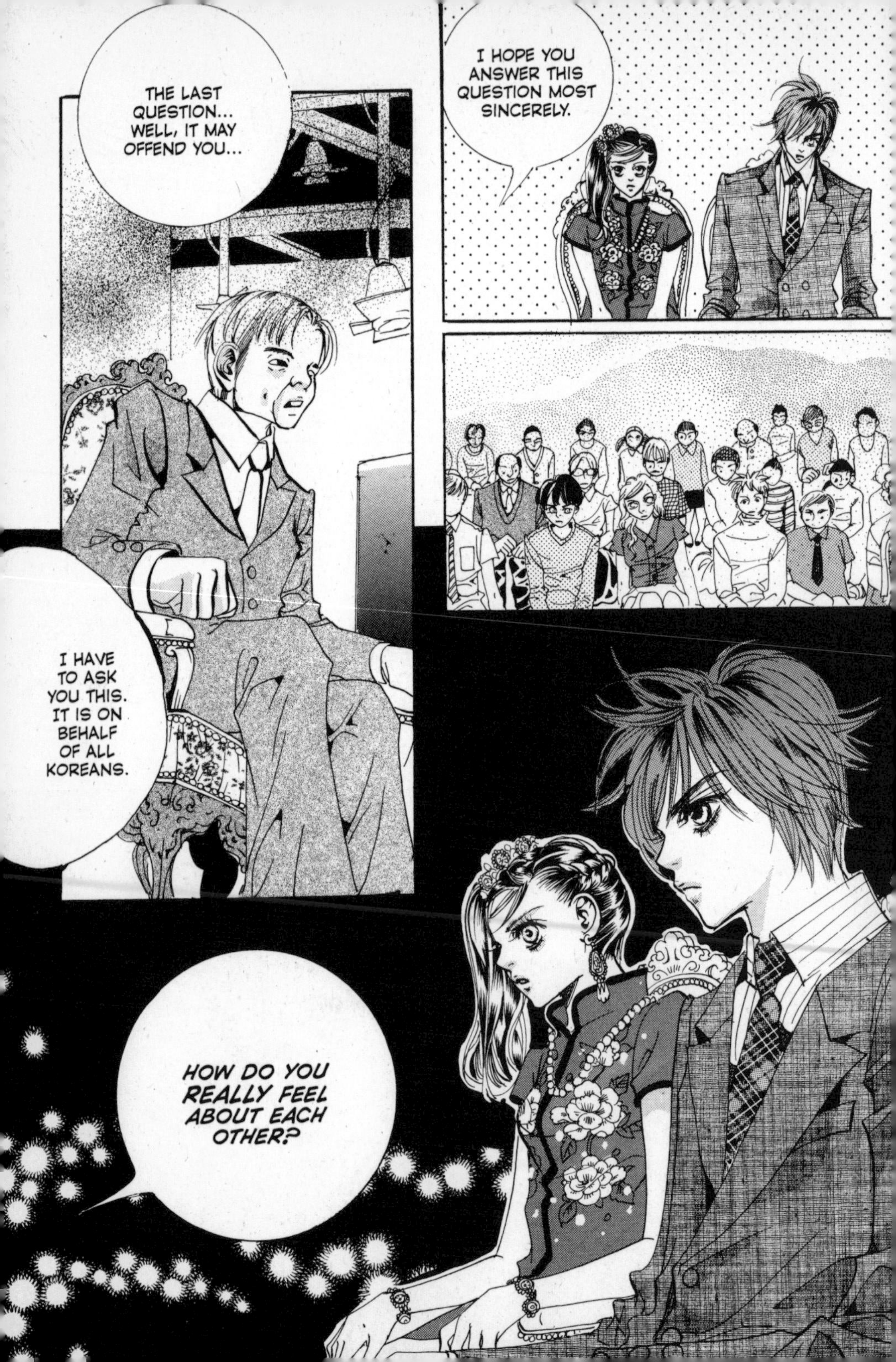
THE LAST QUESTION... WELL, IT MAY OFFEND YOU...
I HAVE TO ASK YOU THIS. IT IS ON BEHALF OF ALL KOREANS.
I HOPE YOU ANSWER THIS QUESTION MOST SINCERELY.
HOW DO YOU REALLY FEEL ABOUT EACH OTHER?

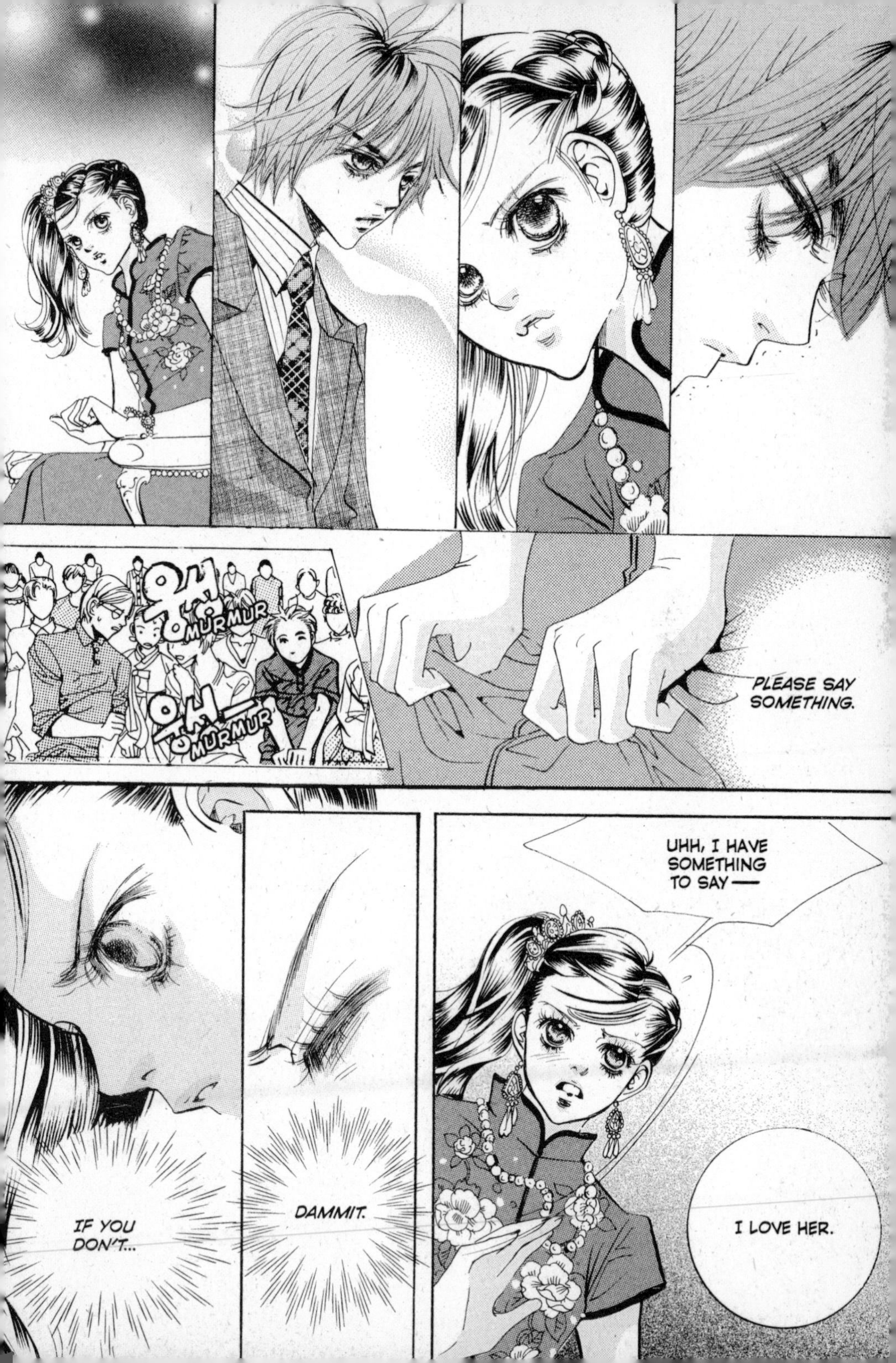
웅성
MURMUR
웅성—
MURMUR
PLEASE SAY SOMETHING.
IF YOU DON'T...
DAMMIT.
UHH, I HAVE SOMETHING TO SAY—
I LOVE HER.

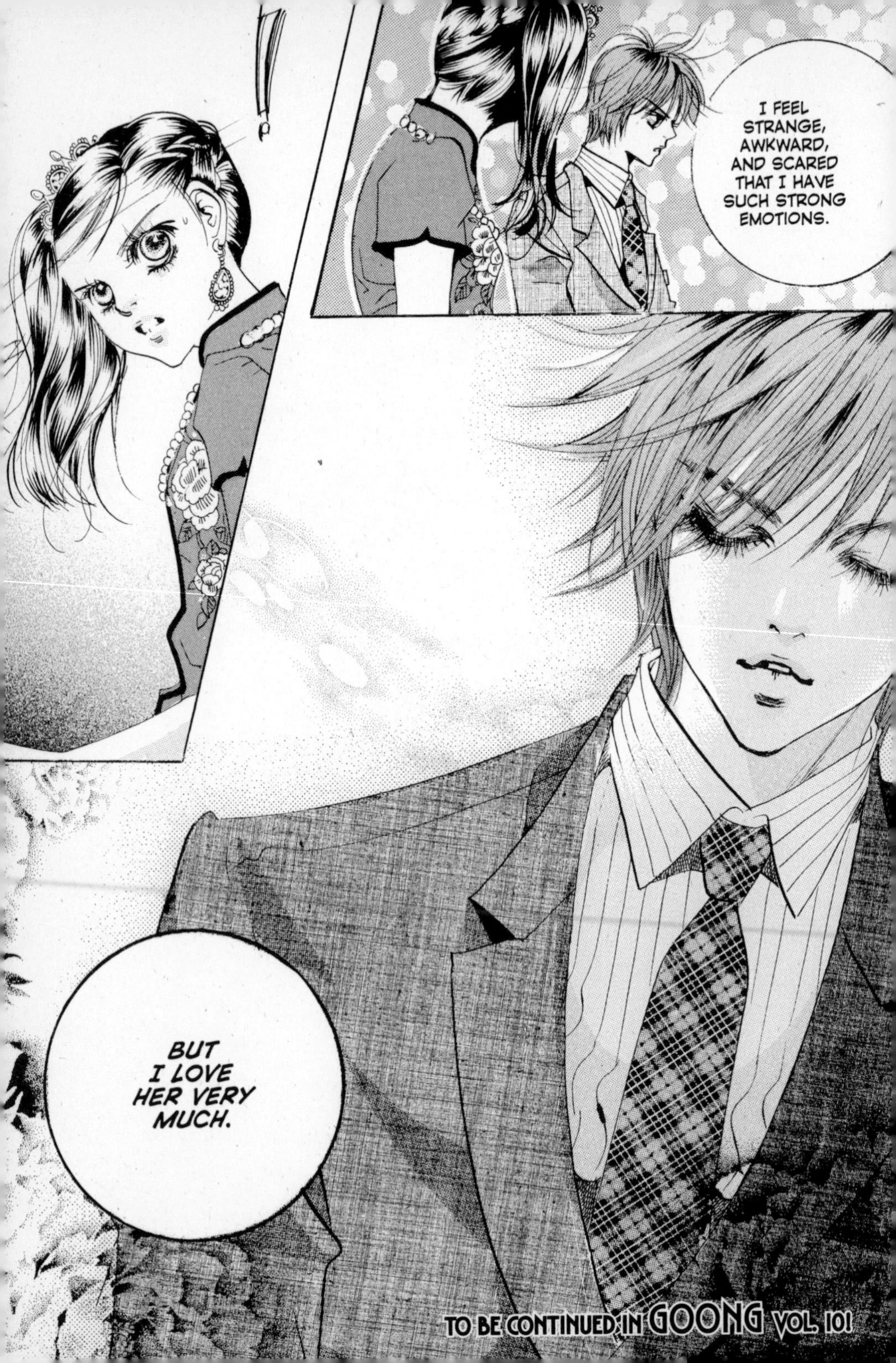
!
I FEEL STRANGE, AWKWARD, AND SCARED THAT I HAVE SUCH STRONG EMOTIONS.
BUT I LOVE HER VERY MUCH.
TO BE CONTINUED IN GOONG VOL. 10!

THE ROYAL PALACE

Goong

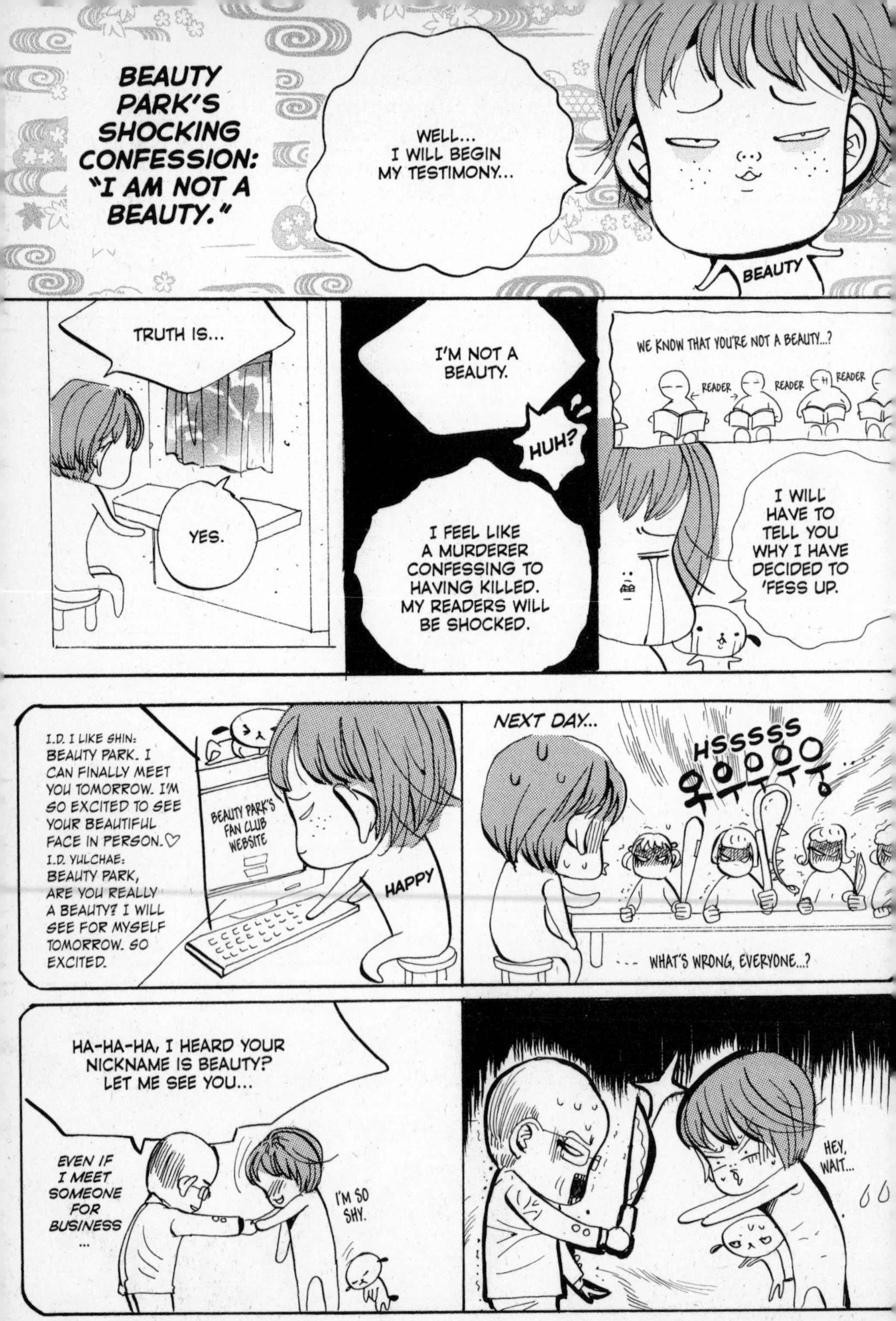
BEAUTY PARK'S SHOCKING CONFESSION: "I AM NOT A BEAUTY."
WELL... I WILL BEGIN MY TESTIMONY...
BEAUTY
TRUTH IS...
YES.
I'M NOT A BEAUTY.
HUH?
I FEEL LIKE A MURDERER CONFESSING TO HAVING KILLED. MY READERS WILL BE SHOCKED.
WE KNOW THAT YOU'RE NOT A BEAUTY...?
READER
READER
READER
I WILL HAVE TO TELL YOU WHY I HAVE DECIDED TO 'FESS UP.
I.D. I LIKE SHIN: BEAUTY PARK. I CAN FINALLY MEET YOU TOMORROW. I'M SO EXCITED TO SEE YOUR BEAUTIFUL FACE IN PERSON.♡
I.D. YULCHAE: BEAUTY PARK, ARE YOU REALLY A BEAUTY? I WILL SEE FOR MYSELF TOMORROW. SO EXCITED.
BEAUTY PARK'S FAN CLUB WEBSITE
HAPPY
NEXT DAY...
HSSSSS
WHAT'S WRONG, EVERYONE...?
HA-HA-HA, I HEARD YOUR NICKNAME IS BEAUTY? LET ME SEE YOU...
EVEN IF I MEET SOMEONE FOR BUSINESS ...
I'M SO SHY.
HEY, WAIT...

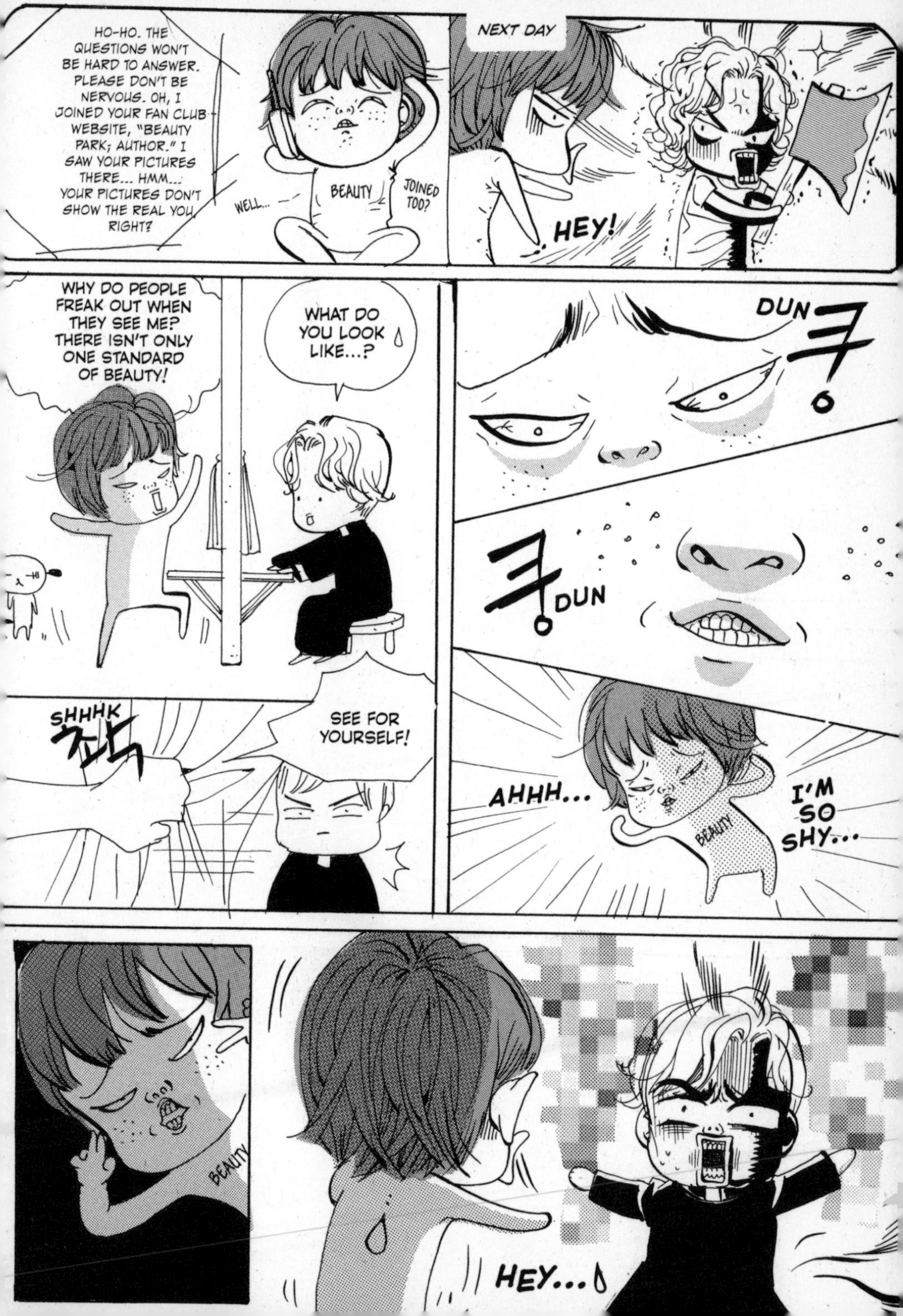

HO-HO. THE QUESTIONS WON'T BE HARD TO ANSWER. PLEASE DON'T BE NERVOUS. OH, I JOINED YOUR FAN CLUB WEBSITE, "BEAUTY PARK; AUTHOR." I SAW YOUR PICTURES THERE... HMM... YOUR PICTURES DON'T SHOW THE REAL YOU, RIGHT?
WELL...
BEAUTY
JOINED TOO?
NEXT DAY
HEY!
WHY DO PEOPLE FREAK OUT WHEN THEY SEE ME? THERE ISN'T ONLY ONE STANDARD OF BEAUTY!
WHAT DO YOU LOOK LIKE...?
SHHHK
SEE FOR YOURSELF!
DUN 쿵
쿵 DUN
AHHH...
BEAUTY
I'M SO SHY...
BEAUTY
HEY...

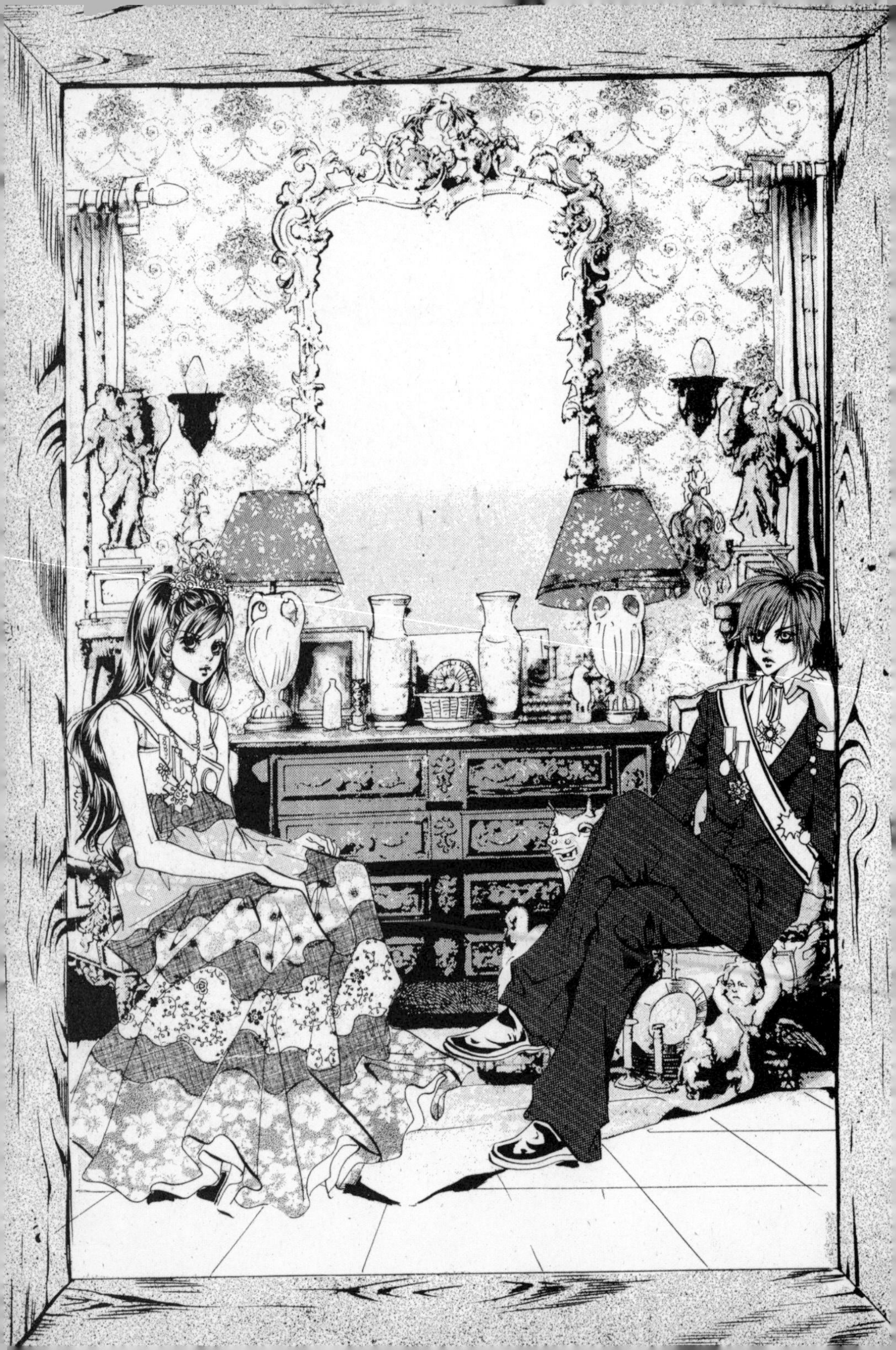

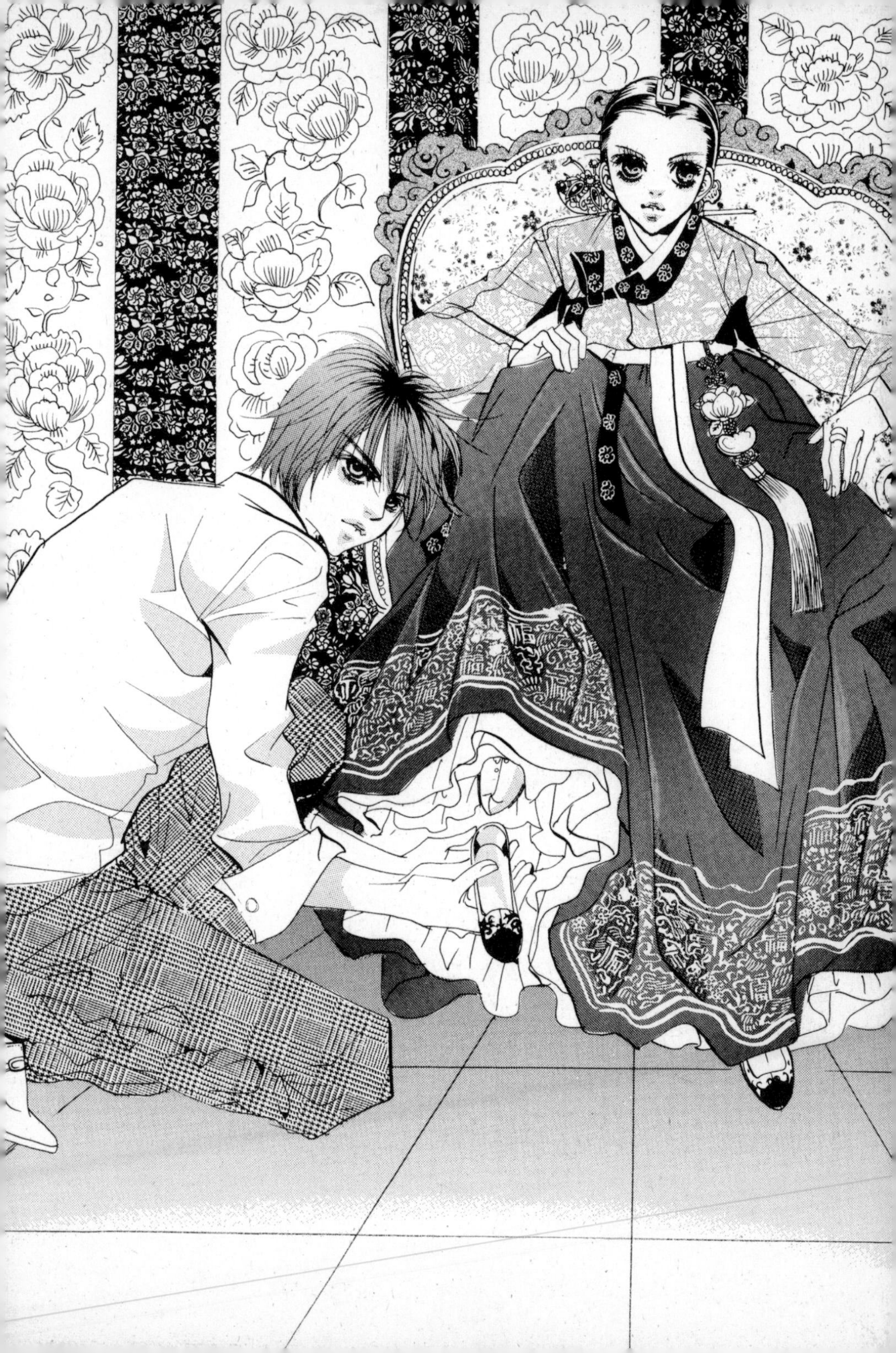

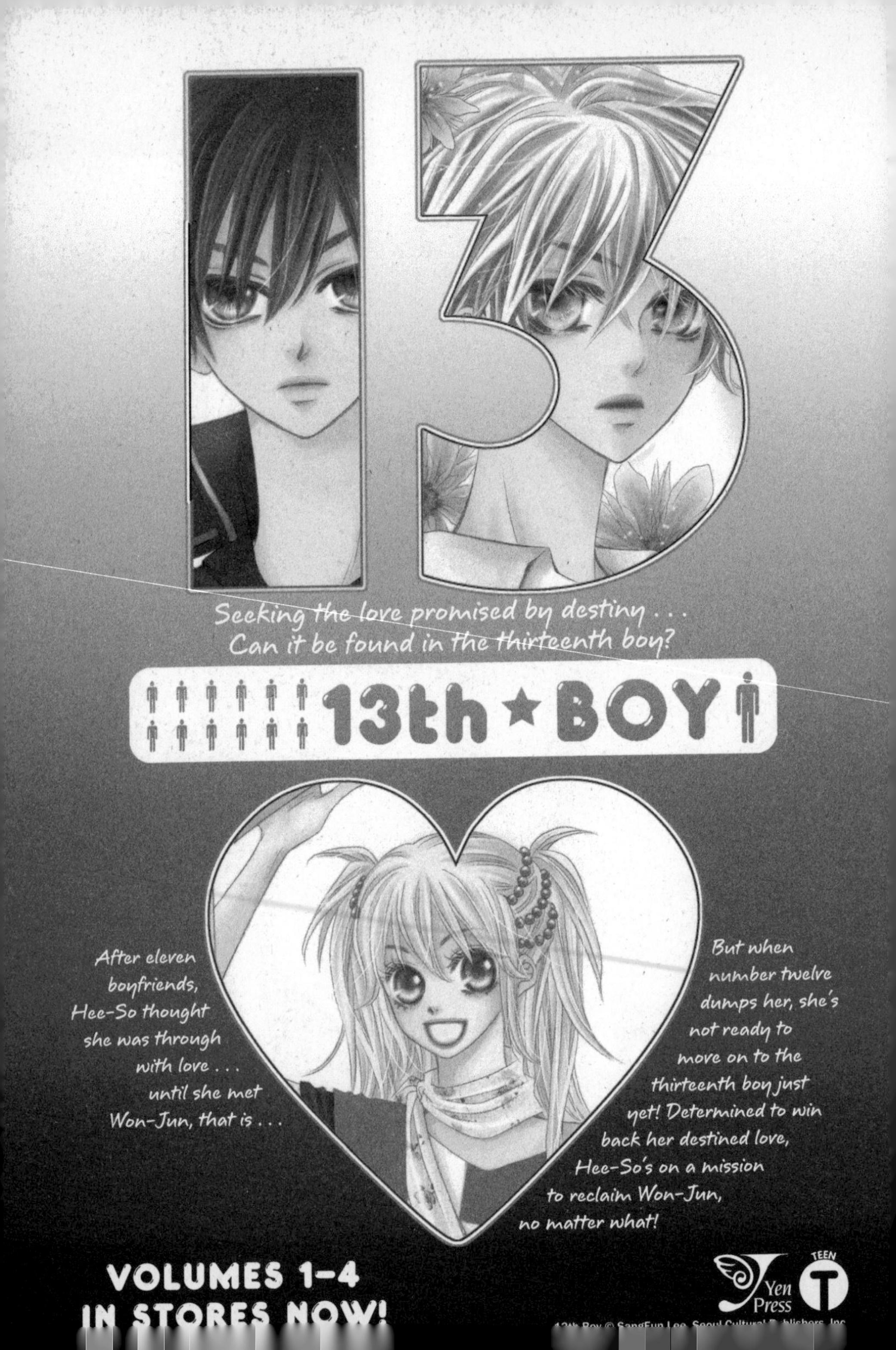
Seeking the love promised by destiny . . .
Can it be found in the thirteenth boy?
13th ★ BOY
After eleven boyfriends, Hee-So thought she was through with love . . . until she met Won-Jun, that is . . .
But when number twelve dumps her, she's not ready to move on to the thirteenth boy just yet! Determined to win back her destined love, Hee-So's on a mission to reclaim Won-Jun, no matter what!
VOLUMES 1–4
IN STORES NOW!
Yen Press
TEEN
T
12th Boy © SangEun Lee, Seoul Cultural Publishers, Inc.

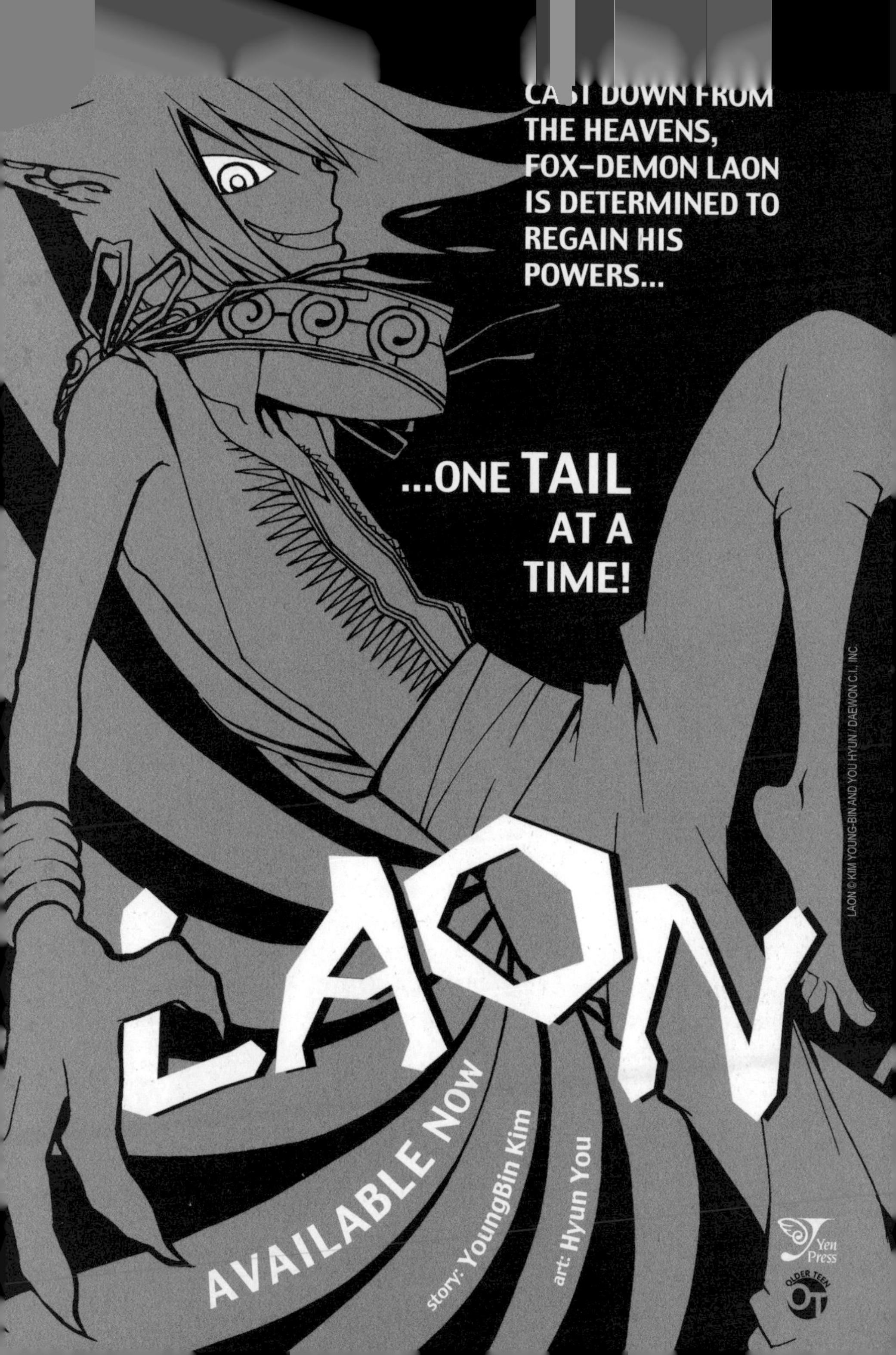

CAST DOWN FROM
THE HEAVENS,
FOX-DEMON LAON
IS DETERMINED TO
REGAIN HIS
POWERS...
...ONE TAIL
AT A
TIME!
LAON © KIM YOUNG-BIN AND YOU HYUN / DAEWON C.I., INC.
LAON
AVAILABLE NOW
story: YoungBin Kim
art: Hyun You
Yen Press
OLDER TEEN
OT

Yen Press

www.yenpress.com

THE MOST BEAUTIFUL FACE, THE PERFECT BODY,
AND A SINCERE PERSONALITY... THAT'S WHAT HYE-MIN HWANG HAS.
NATURALLY, SHE'S THE CENTER OF EVERYONE'S ATTENTION.
EVERY BOY IN SCHOOL LOVES HER, WHILE EVERY GIRL HATES HER OUT OF JEALOUSY.
EVERY SINGLE DAY, SHE HAS TO ENDURE TORTURES AND HARDSHIPS FROM THE GIRLS.

A PRETTY FACE COMES WITH A PRICE.

THERE IS NOTHING MORE SATISFYING THAN GETTING THEM BACK.
WELL, EXCEPT FOR ONE PROBLEM... HER SECRET CRUSH, JUNG-YUN.
BECAUSE OF HIM, SHE HAS TO HIDE HER CYNICAL AND DARK SIDE
AND DAILY PUT ON AN INNOCENT FACE. THEN ONE DAY, SHE FINDS OUT
THAT HE DISLIKES HER ANYWAY!! WHAT?! THAT'S IT! NO MORE NICE GIRL!
AND THE FIRST VICTIM OF HER RAGE IS A PLAYBOY SHE JUST MET, MA-HA.

vol.1~9

Cynical Orange

Yun JiUn

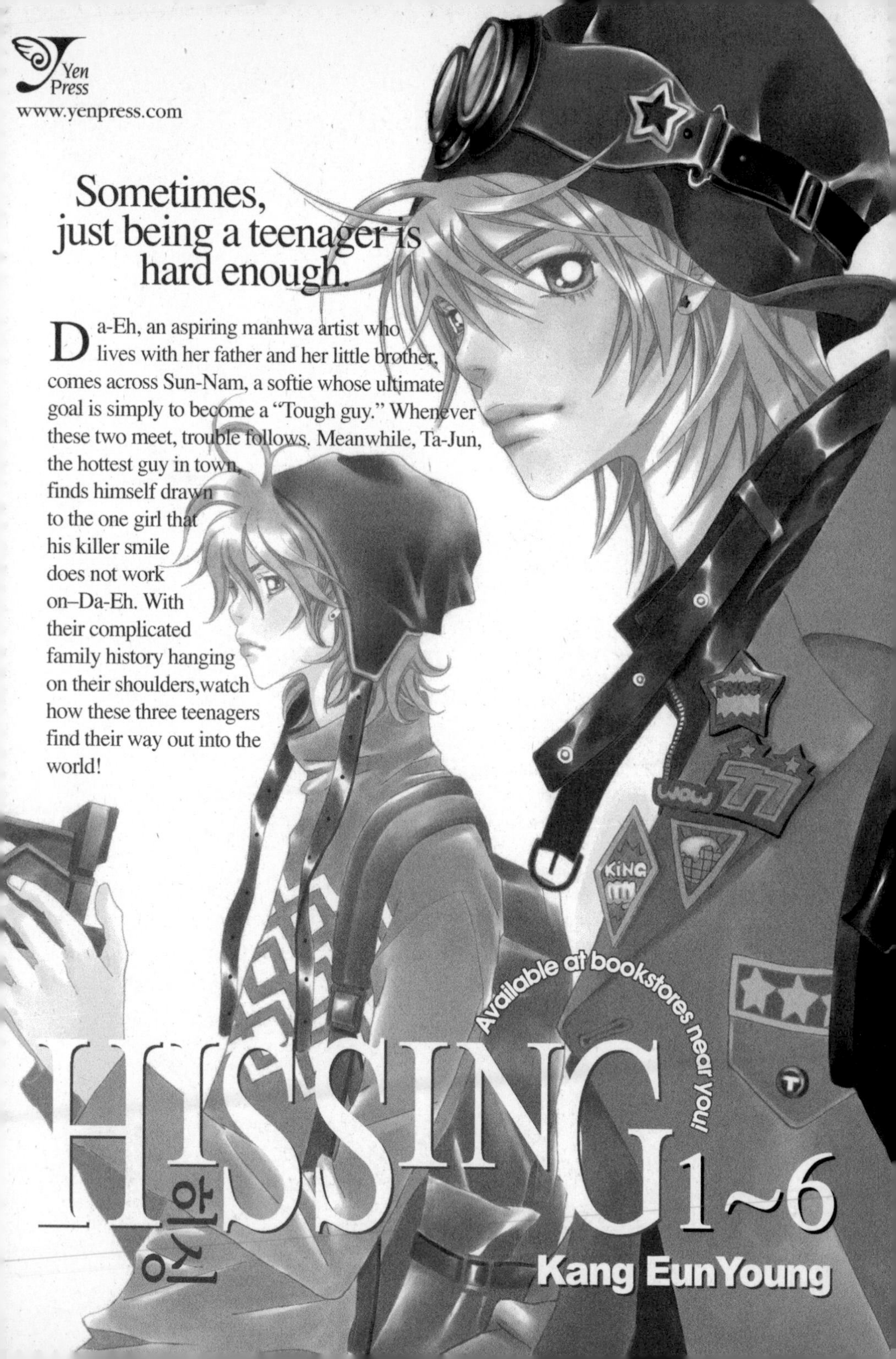
Yen Press
www.yenpress.com
Sometimes, just being a teenager is hard enough.
Da-Eh, an aspiring manhwa artist who lives with her father and her little brother, comes across Sun-Nam, a softie whose ultimate goal is simply to become a "Tough guy." Whenever these two meet, trouble follows. Meanwhile, Ta-Jun, the hottest guy in town, finds himself drawn to the one girl that his killer smile does not work on–Da-Eh. With their complicated family history hanging on their shoulders,watch how these three teenagers find their way out into the world!
Available at bookstores near you!
HISSING 1~6
히싱
Kang EunYoung

The newest title from the creators of \<Demon Diary\> and \<Angel Diary\>!

Once upon a time, a selfish king summoned the monstrous Bulkirin into the real world. The monster killed half of all human beings, leaving the rest helpless as to what to do. That is, until one day when a hero appeared and defeated the Bulkirin with the legendary "Seven Blade Sword." But...what does all this have to do with 8th grader Eun-Gyo Sung?! First, she gets suspended from school for fighting. Then, she runs away from home. The last thing she needed was to be kidnapped—and whisked into the past by a mysterious stranger named No-Ah!

Available at bookstores near you!

Legend

1-8

Kara · Woo SooJung

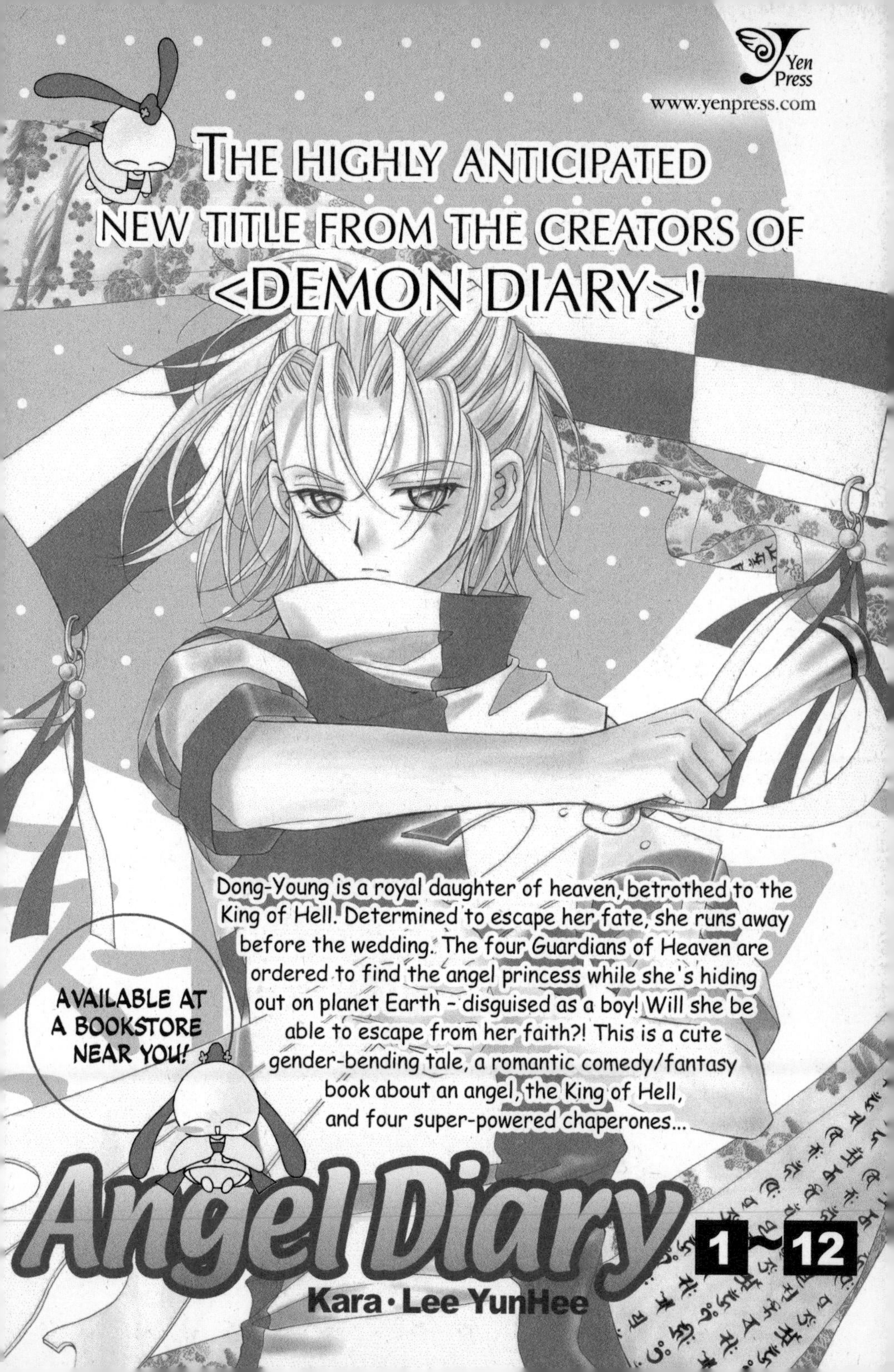
Yen Press
www.yenpress.com
THE HIGHLY ANTICIPATED
NEW TITLE FROM THE CREATORS OF
<DEMON DIARY>!
Dong-Young is a royal daughter of heaven, betrothed to the King of Hell. Determined to escape her fate, she runs away before the wedding. The four Guardians of Heaven are ordered to find the angel princess while she's hiding out on planet Earth – disguised as a boy! Will she be able to escape from her faith?! This is a cute gender-bending tale, a romantic comedy/fantasy book about an angel, the King of Hell, and four super-powered chaperones...
AVAILABLE AT A BOOKSTORE NEAR YOU!
Angel Diary
1~12
Kara · Lee YunHee

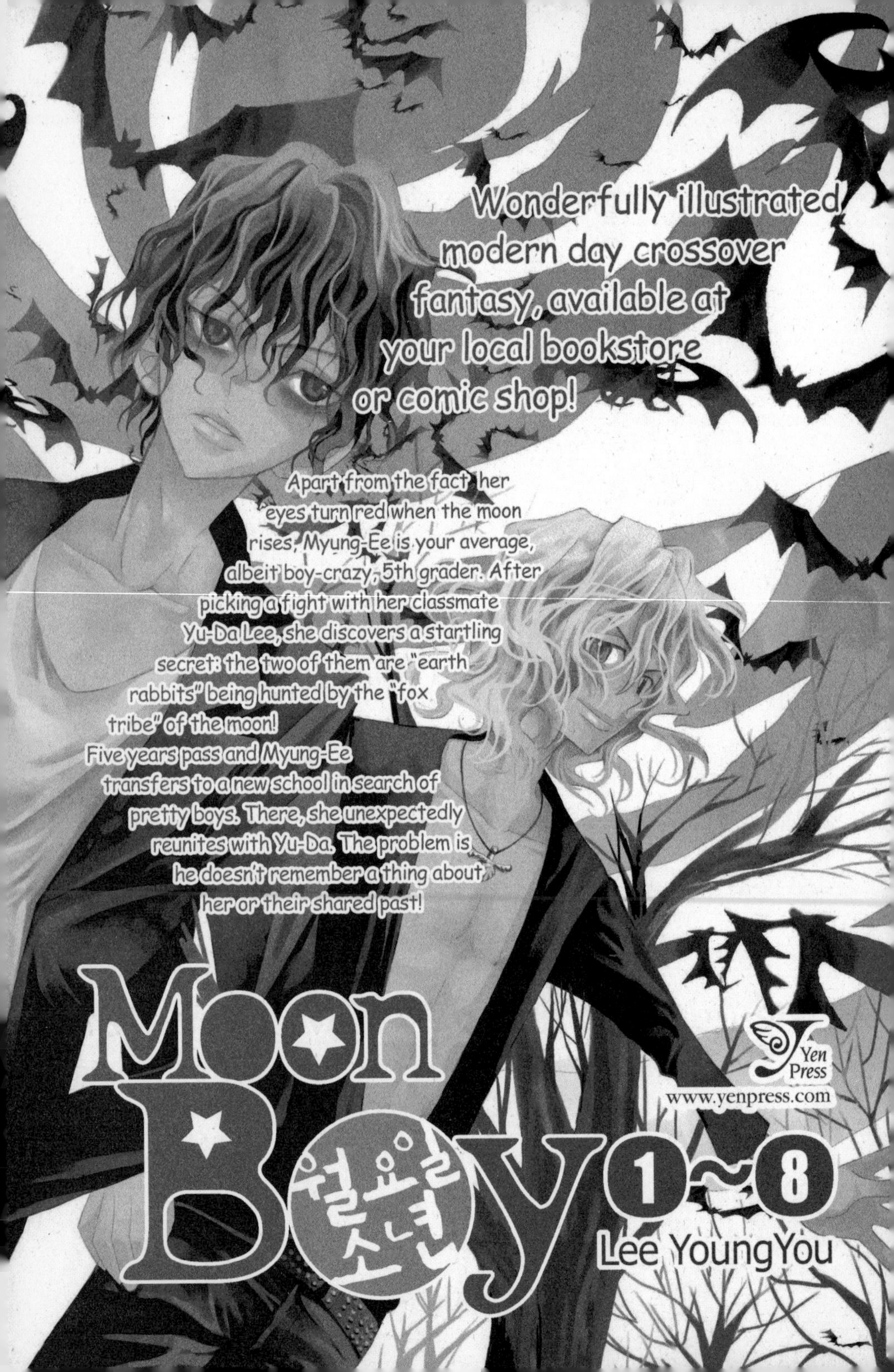
Wonderfully illustrated modern day crossover fantasy, available at your local bookstore or comic shop!
Apart from the fact her eyes turn red when the moon rises, Myung-Ee is your average, albeit boy-crazy, 5th grader. After picking a fight with her classmate Yu-Da Lee, she discovers a startling secret: the two of them are "earth rabbits" being hunted by the "fox tribe" of the moon! Five years pass and Myung-Ee transfers to a new school in search of pretty boys. There, she unexpectedly reunites with Yu-Da. The problem is he doesn't remember a thing about her or their shared past!
Moon Boy
월요일 소년
1~8
Lee YoungYou
Yen Press
www.yenpress.com

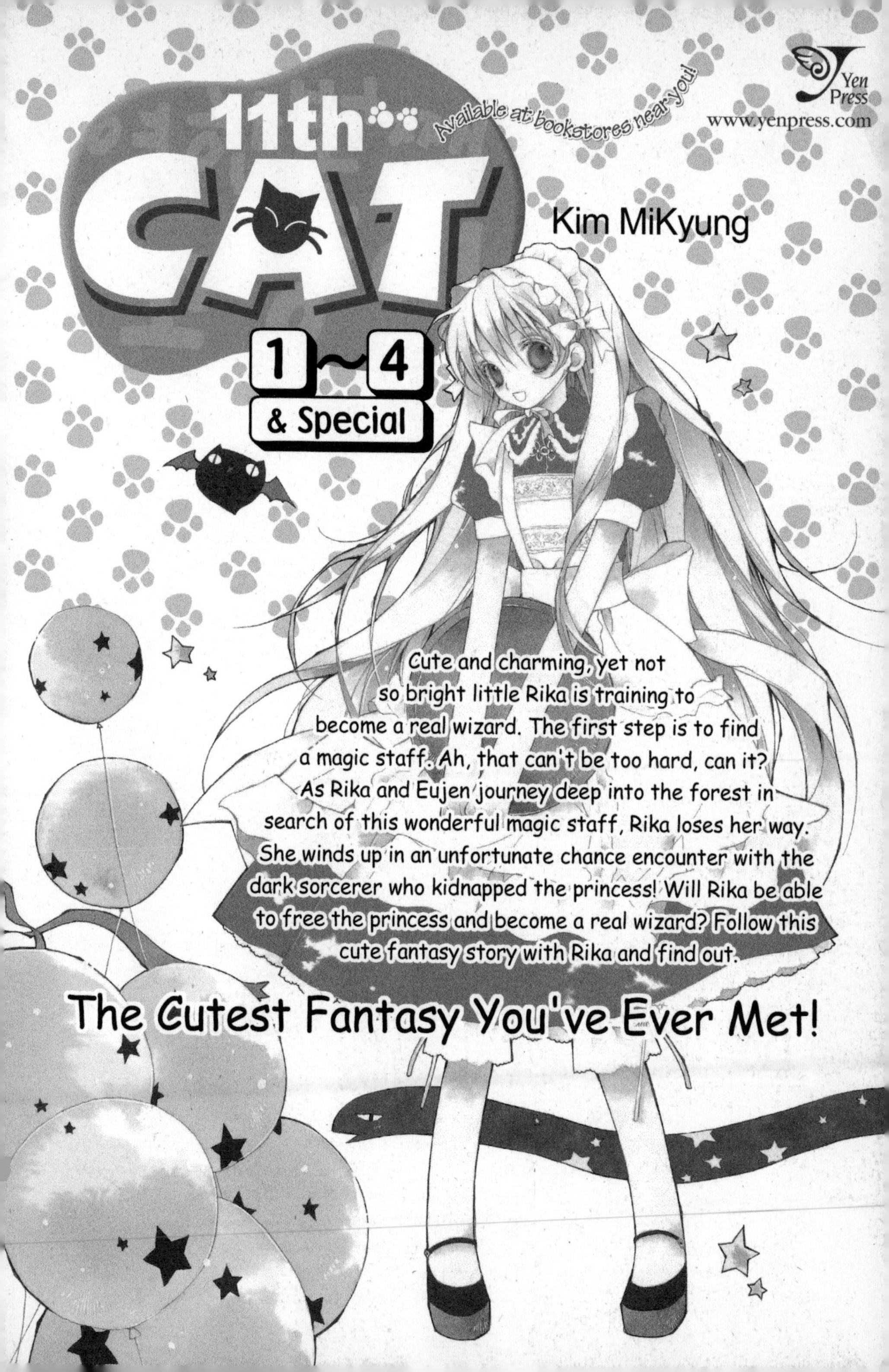
11th CAT
Available at bookstores near you!
Yen Press
www.yenpress.com
Kim MiKyung
1~4
& Special
Cute and charming, yet not so bright little Rika is training to become a real wizard. The first step is to find a magic staff. Ah, that can't be too hard, can it? As Rika and Eujen journey deep into the forest in search of this wonderful magic staff, Rika loses her way. She winds up in an unfortunate chance encounter with the dark sorcerer who kidnapped the princess! Will Rika be able to free the princess and become a real wizard? Follow this cute fantasy story with Rika and find out.
The Cutest Fantasy You've Ever Met!

A totally new Arabian nights, where Scheherazade is a guy!

Everyone knows the story of Scheherazade and her wonderful tales from the Arabian Nights. For one thousand and one nights, the stories that she created entertained the mad Sultan and eventually saved her life. In this version, Scheherazade is a guy who disguises himself as a woman to save his sister from the mad Sultan. When he puts his life on the line, what kind of strange and unique stories will he tell? This new twist on one of the greatest classical tales might just keep you awake for another ONE THOUSAND AND ONE NIGHTS!

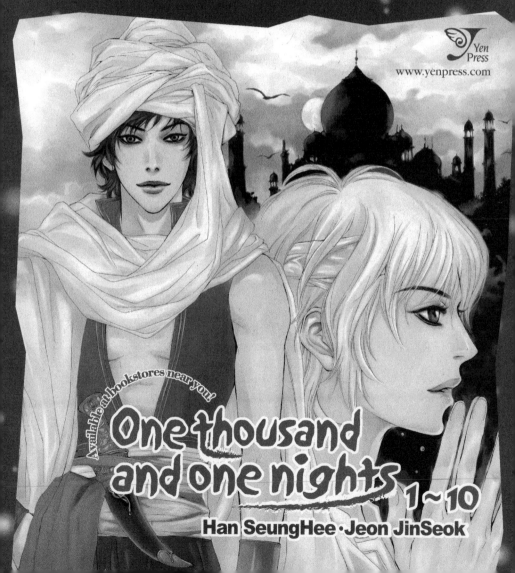

Yen Press

www.yenpress.com

Available at bookstores near you!

One thousand and one nights

1~10

Han SeungHee · Jeon JinSeok

Available at bookstores near you!

CHOCOLAT
1~7
Shin JiSang · Geo

Kum-ji was a little late getting under the spell of the chart-topping band, DDL. Unable to join the DDL fan club, she almost gives up on meeting her idols, until she develops a cunning plan–to become a member of a rival fan club for the brand-new boy band Yo-I. This way she can act as Yo-I's fan club member and also be near Yo-I,

How far would you go to meet your favorite boy band?

who always seem to be in the same shows as DDL. Perfect plan...except being a fanatic is a lot more complicated than she expects. Especially when you're actually a fan of someone else. This full-blown love comedy about a fan club will make you laugh, cry, and laugh some more.

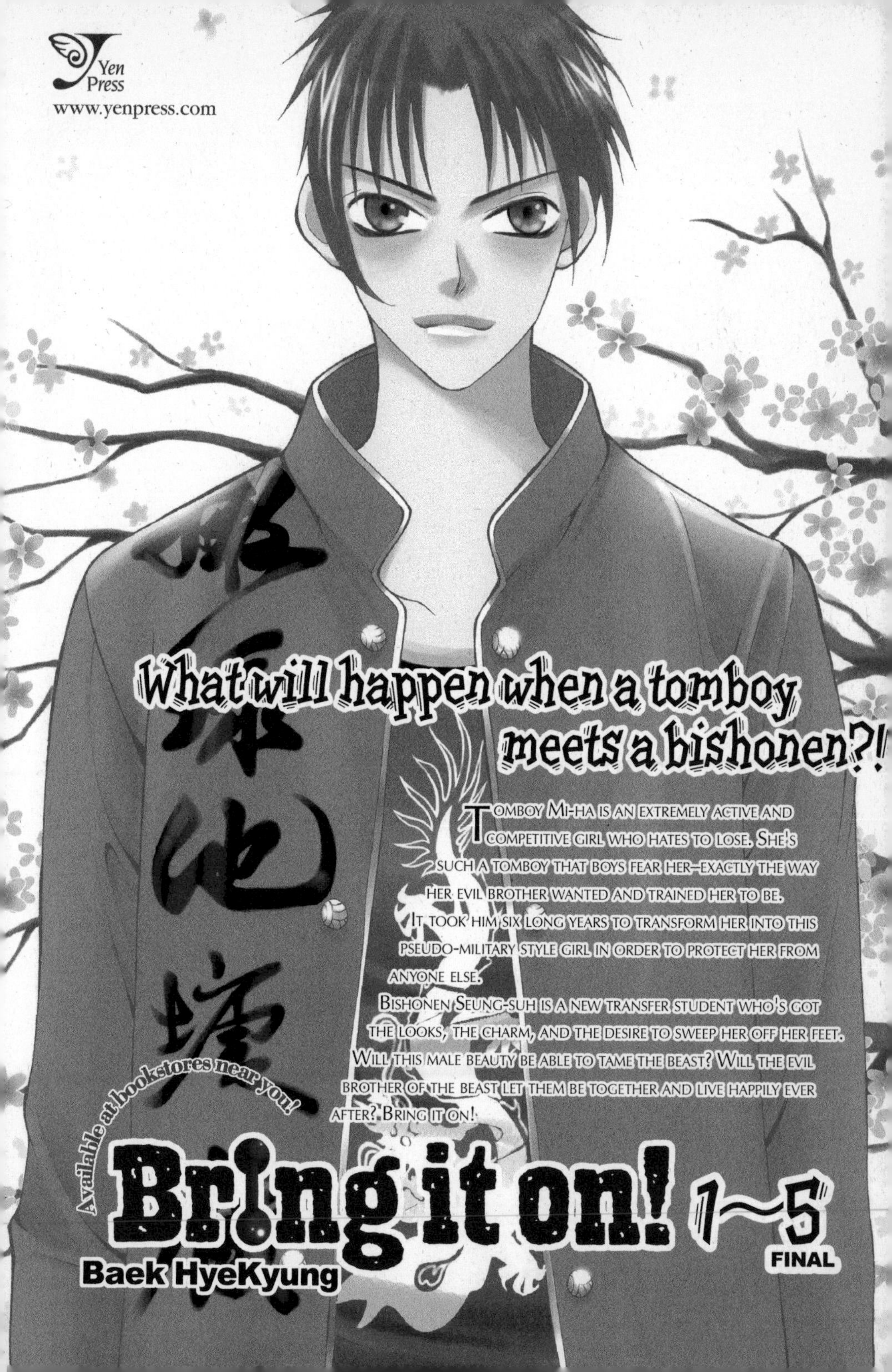

Yen Press
www.yenpress.com
What will happen when a tomboy meets a bishonen?!
Tomboy Mi-ha is an extremely active and competitive girl who hates to lose. She's such a tomboy that boys fear her–exactly the way her evil brother wanted and trained her to be.
It took him six long years to transform her into this pseudo-military style girl in order to protect her from anyone else.
Bishonen Seung-suh is a new transfer student who's got the looks, the charm, and the desire to sweep her off her feet. Will this male beauty be able to tame the beast? Will the evil brother of the beast let them be together and live happily ever after? Bring it on!
Available at bookstores near you!
Bring it on! 1~5
FINAL
Baek HyeKyung

Goong vol. 9

Story and art by SoHee Park

Translation HyeYoung Im
English Adaptation Jamie S. Rich
Lettering Alexis Eckerman

Goong, Vol. 9 & 10 © 2005, 2005 SoHee Park. All rights reserved. First published in Korea in 2005, 2005 by SEOUL CULTURAL PUBLISHERS, Inc. English translation rights arranged by SEOUL CULTURAL PUBLISHERS, Inc.

English edition copyright © 2010 Hachette Book Group, Inc.

Yen Press
Hachette Book Group
237 Park Avenue, New York, NY 10017

www.HachetteBookGroup.com
www.YenPress.com

Yen Press is an imprint of Hachette Book Group, Inc.
The Yen Press name and logo are trademarks of Hachette Book Group, Inc.

First Yen Press Edition: August 2010

ISBN: 978-0-7595-3153-6

10 9 8 7 6 5 4 3 2 1

BVG

Printed in the United States of America